The Information Retrieval Series   Volume 37

More information about this series at http://www.springer.com/series/6128

Mihai Lupu • Katja Mayer • Noriko Kando •
Anthony J. Trippe

Editors

Current Challenges in Patent Information Retrieval

Second Edition

 Springer

Editors
Mihai Lupu
Institute for Software Engineering &
   Interactive Systems
Vienna University of Technology
Vienna, Austria

Katja Mayer
Research Platform Responsible Research
   and Innovation in Academic Practice
University of Vienna
Vienna, Austria

Noriko Kando
Information & Society Research Division
National Institute of Informatics
Tokyo, Japan

Anthony J. Trippe
Patinformatics, LLC
Dublin, OH
USA

ISSN 1387-5264
The Information Retrieval Series
ISBN 978-3-662-57164-4   ISBN 978-3-662-53817-3   (eBook)
DOI 10.1007/978-3-662-53817-3

This Springer imprint is published by Springer Nature
The registered company is Springer-Verlag GmbH Germany
The registered company address is: Heidelberger Platz 3, 14197 Berlin, Germany

Preface

Patent information retrieval is an economically important activity. Today's economy is becoming increasingly knowledge based and intellectual property in the form of patents plays a vital role in this growth. According to the WIPO IP Statistics Data Center, between 2004 and 2014, the number of patent applications filed worldwide grew by more than 70 %. With the exception of 2009, the year immediately after the economic collapse, every year has shown an increase in the number of filed applications. The number of granted patents worldwide continues to increase, even in 2009, reaching in 2014 1,176,600 grants versus only 625,100 grants in 2004 (an 88 % increase). The substantial increase in patents granted is due, in part, to efforts by patent offices to reduce backlogs as well as the significant growth in the number of patents granted by China and, to a lesser extent in more recent years, by the Republic of Korea. According to these statistics, the total number of patents in force worldwide at the end of 2014 was approximately 10.2 million (WIPO Report 2015). A prior art search might have to cover as many as 100 million patents. By combining data from Ocean Tomo's Intangible Asset Market Value Survey and Standard and Poor's 1200 Index, we can estimate that the global value of patents exceeds US$12 trillion in 2015. In the United States alone, a 2012 study by the Commerce Department found that 'intellectual property intensive industries support at least 40 million jobs and contribute more than US$5 trillion to, or 34.8 percent of, US gross domestic product'.

A patent is a contract between inventors and the state. The inventors must teach the community how to perform the invention and use the techniques they have invented in return for a limited monopoly that gives them a predefined time to exploit the invention and realise its value. Patents are used for many reasons, e.g. to protect inventions, to create value and to monitor competitive activities in a field. Much knowledge is distilled through patents, which is never published elsewhere. Thus patents form an important knowledge resource—e.g. much technical information represented in patents is not represented in scientific literature—and are at the same time important legal documents. In fact, a study done by one of the editors of this volume found that in the chemical domain 95 % of patented substances did not appear in non-patent literature references. In the context of today's drive towards open innovation, particularly in the European Union and its framework programmes, it seems that patent search should take a more visible role, speeding up knowledge discovery for tackling societal changes.

In the past 15 or 20 years, search technology in general and Web search engines in particular have made tremendous advances. Yet still, we see a considerable gap between the technologies emerging from research labs and in use by major Internet search engines and the systems in day-to-day use by the patent search communities. This gap is unlikely to ever completely disappear, simply for the reasons of corporate practice, whereby only proven systems make their way, through a relatively complicated adoption procedure, to the regular processes of professional searchers. Nevertheless, we have observed in the last 5 years an increasingly active drive towards adoption of the search technology state of the art in several major players in the field.

In 2010, just before the publication of the first edition of this book, a study commissioned by the US Federal National Institute of Standards and Technology (NIST) estimated that since 1991, when the Text Retrieval Conference (TREC) evaluation campaign began, the available information retrieval and search systems have improved 40 % or more in their ability to find relevant documents. And yet the technologies underlying the patent search system were largely unaffected by these changes. Patent searchers generally used the same technology as in the 1980s. Boolean specification of searches and set-based retrieval are still common. Nevertheless, tools have improved over the years, as have the requirements and expectations of the users. Semantic search (under its various interpretations) is now on practically every provider's table. And yet there had not been the kind of revolution in patent search which Google had represented for Web search. Perhaps there will never be a revolution, and we should indeed expect gradual transition to systems that are first well tested in other domains.

This first edition of this book, which appeared in 2011, was part of the development of a joint understanding between IR researchers and IP specialists, understanding that resulted from a series of symposia organised by the Information Retrieval Facility (IRF) in Vienna, Austria, between 2007 and 2011. Its origins lie in the idea of producing post-proceedings for the first IRF symposium. That idea was not fully followed up, in part because of pressure to produce more practical, action-oriented work, and in part because many of the participants felt their approaches were at too early a stage for formal publication. In the course of the following years, it became apparent there really was a demand to produce a volume which was accessible to both the patent search community and the information retrieval research community, to provide a collected and organised introduction to the work and views of the two sides of the emerging patent search research and innovation community and to provide a coherent and organised view of what has been achieved and, perhaps even more significantly, of what remains to be achieved.

A secondary result of the efforts invested by the IRF was an uptake in the academic community of the patent search problem. While the IRF stopped operating in 2011, research continued across the world, with the term 'patent search' being indelibly added to the Call for Papers of major conferences in the field. Since that time, a number of PhD theses have been written on the topic by outstanding young researchers. We found that a second edition of the book was indeed needed to showcase these as well as the other research advances of the past half-decade.

At the same time, this second edition revisits some of the original chapters from the first edition, as it maintains the original objective to allow the IR researchers to better understand why the patent domain has different needs and what it means in practice. Furthermore, it is our hope that these two books will also be a valuable resource for IP professionals in learning about current approaches of IR in the patent domain. It has often been difficult to reconcile the focus on useful technological innovation from the IP community, with the demands for scientific rigour, and to proceed on the basis of sound empirical evidence, which is such an important feature of IR (in contrast to some other areas of computer science).

Moreover, patent search is an inherently multilingual and multinational topic: the novelty of a patent may be dismissed by finding a document describing the same idea in any language anywhere in the world. Patents are complex legal documents, even less accessible than the scientific literature. These are just some of the characteristics of the patent system which make it an important challenge for the search, information retrieval and information access communities.

Even more than the first edition, the second edition of the book has had a lengthy and difficult gestation: the list of authors has been revised many times as a result of changes in institutional, occupational and private circumstances. Although we, the editors, do feel we have succeeded in producing a volume which will provide important perspectives of the issues affecting patent search research and innovation at the time of writing, as well as a useful, brief introduction to the outlook and literature of the community accessible to its members, regardless of their background, there will always be some areas that are not covered, mostly because there is, at this time, insufficient research on the topic. Most importantly here are the applications of new statistical semantics methods on the patent domain. While these are extremely popular methods in current research, there exist only inconclusive studies on their application in the patent field.

On the other hand, we are very happy to have managed to include in this edition something we had missed in the previous one: a chapter on NTCIR, the first of the evaluation campaigns to focus seriously on patents.

Several of the chapters have been written jointly by intellectual property and information retrieval experts. Members of both communities with a background opposite to the primary author have reviewed the chapters. It has not always been easy to reconcile their differing viewpoints: we must thank them for taking the time to resolve their differences and for taking the opportunity to exchange their knowledge across fields and disciplinary mindsets and to engage in a mutual discourse that will hopefully foster understanding in the future.

Finally, we would like to thank the IRF for making the first edition possible and triggering much research in the area; the publisher, Springer, and in particular Ralf Gerstner, for the patience with which he accepted the numerous delays; as well as the external reviewers who read each chapter and provided the authors with valuable advice.

The editors are very grateful to the following persons, who agreed to review the manuscripts of the two editions of this book:

Stephen Adams, Linda Andersson, Leif Azzopardi, Geetha Basappa, John M. Barnard, Shariq Bashir, Helmut Berger, Katrien Beuls, Ted Briscoe, Ben Carterette, Suleyman Cetintas, Chen Chaomei, Paul Clough, Bruce Croft, Szabolcs Csepregi, Barrou Diallo, Ramona Enache, Nicola Ferro, Árpád Figyelmesi, Karl A. Froeschl, Norbert Fuhr, Eric Gaussier, Julio Gonzalo, Jacques Guyot, Allan Hanbury, Christopher G. Harris, Ilkka Havukkala, Bruce Hedin, Peter Johnson, Cornelis H.A. Koster, Mounia Lalmas, Aldo Lipani, Patrice Lopez, Teresa Loughbrough, Ilya Markov, Marie-Francine Moens, Anastasia Moumtzidou, Roland Mörzinger, Henning Müller, Masaaki Nagata, Iadh Ounis, Doug Oard, Florina Piroi, Keith van Rijsbergen, Patrick Ruch, Georg Thallinger, Philip Tetlow, Henk Thomas, Ingo Thon, Steve Tomlinson, Suzan Verberne, Ellen M. Voorhees, Jianqiang Wang, Peter Willett and Christa Womser-Hacker

Vienna, Austria	Mihai Lupu
Vienna, Austria	Katja Mayer
Tokyo, Japan	Noriko Kando
Dublin, OH, USA	Anthony J. Trippe
August 2016	

Contents

Contributors

Doreen Alberts Theravance, Inc., South San Francisco, CA, USA

Linda Andersson TU Wien, Vienna, Austria

Cynthia Barcelon Yang Bristol Myers Squibb, Princeton, NJ, USA

Shariq Bashir Department of Computer Science, Mohammad Ali Jinnah University, Islamabad, Pakistan

Lou Boves Radboud University Nijmegen, Nijmegen, The Netherlands

Gabriela Csurka Xerox Research Centre Europe, Meylan, France

Eva D'hondt LIMSI-CNRS UPR 3251, Orsay, France

Dominic DeMarco DeMarco Intellectual Property, LLC, South Arlington, VA, USA

Barrou Diallo European Patent Office, Rijswijk, The Netherlands

Geoff M. Downs Digital Chemistry Ltd., Sheffield, UK

Igor V. Filippov VIF Innovations, LLC, Rockville, MD, USA

Denise Fobare-DePonio Amgen, Thousand Oaks, CA, USA

Atsushi Fujii Department of Computer Science, Tokyo Institute of Technology, Tokyo, Japan

Allan Hanbury TU Wien, Vienna, Austria

Bruce Hedin San Francisco, CA, USA

John D. Holliday Information School, The University of Sheffield, Sheffield, UK

Makoto Iwayama Hitachi, Ltd., Tokyo, Japan

Noriko Kando National Institute of Informatics, Tokyo, Japan

Luciano Kay Center for Nanotechnology in Society, University of California, Santa Barbara, CA, USA

Ken Koubek Koubek Information Consulting Services, Wilmington, DE, USA

Josep Lladós Dept. Ciències de la Computació, Computer Vision Center, Bellaterra, Spain

Mihai Lupu TU Wien, Vienna, Austria

Nils Newman Intelligent Information Services Corporation, Atlanta, GA, USA

Douglas W. Oard University of Maryland, College Park, MD, USA

Nelleke Oostdijk Radboud University Nijmegen, Nijmegen, The Netherlands

Florina Piroi TU Wien, Vienna, Austria

Alan L. Porter School of Public Policy, Georgia Institute of Technology, Norcross, GA, USA

Ismael Ràfols Ingenio (CSIC-UPV), Universitat Politècnica de València, Valencia, Spain

SPRU, University of Sussex, Brighton, UK

Andreas Rauber TU Wien, Vienna, Austria

Suzanne Robins Patent Information Services, Inc., Westborough, MA, USA

Matthew Rodgers CPA Global, Alexandria, VA, USA

Marçal Rusiñol Dept. Ciències de la Computació, Computer Vision Center, Bellaterra, Spain

Ian Ruthven Department of Computer and Information Sciences, University of Strathclyde, Glasgow, UK

Michail Salampasis Alexander Technology Educational Institute (ATEI), Thessaloniki, Greece

Alan P. Sexton University of Birmingham, Birmingham, UK

Edlyn Simmons Simmons Patent Information Service, Fort Mill, SC, USA

Veronika Stefanov TU Wien, Vienna, Austria

John Tinsley Iconic Translation Machines, Ltd., Dublin, Ireland

Stephen Tomlinson Open Text Corporation, Ottawa, ON, Canada

Anthony Trippe Patinformatics, LLC, Dublin, OH, USA

Suzan Verberne Radboud University Nijmegen, Nijmegen, The Netherlands

Peter Willett Information School, The University of Sheffield, Sheffield, UK

Jan Youtie Enterprise Innovation Institute & School of Public Policy, Atlanta, GA, USA

Part I
Introduction to Patent Searching

Chapter 1
Introduction to Patent Searching

Practical Experience and Requirements for Searching the Patent Space

Doreen Alberts, Cynthia Barcelon Yang, Denise Fobare-DePonio, Ken Koubek, Suzanne Robins, Matthew Rodgers, Edlyn Simmons, and Dominic DeMarco

Abstract This chapter introduces patent search in a way that should be accessible and useful to both researchers in information retrieval and other areas of computer science and professionals seeking to broaden their knowledge of patent search. It gives an overview of the process of patent search, including the different forms of patent search. It goes on to describe the differences among different domains of patent search (engineering, chemicals, gene sequences and so on) and the tools currently used by searchers in each domain. It concludes with an overview of open issues.

D. Alberts (✉)
Theravance Biopharma US, Inc., 901 Gateway Blvd., South San Francisco, CA 94080, USA
e-mail: doalberts@theravance.com

C.B. Yang
Bristol-Myers Squibb, 311 Pennington Rocky Hill Rd., Pennington, NJ 08534, USA

D. Fobare-DePonio
Amgen, Thousand Oaks, CA, USA

K. Koubek
Koubek Information Consulting Services, Wilmington, DE, USA

S. Robins
Patent Information Services, Inc., 18 Longmeadow Rd., Westborough, MA, USA

M. Rodgers
CPA Global, Alexandria, VA, USA

E. Simmons
Simmons Patent Information Service, Fort Mill, SC, USA

D. DeMarco
DeMarco Intellectual Property LLC, 2433 Fort Scott Drive, Arlington, VA, USA

© Springer-Verlag GmbH Germany 2017
M. Lupu et al. (eds.), *Current Challenges in Patent Information Retrieval*,
The Information Retrieval Series 37, DOI 10.1007/978-3-662-53817-3_1

1.1 Introduction

Patents are legal documents issued by a government that grants a set of rights of exclusivity and protection to the owner of an invention. The right of exclusivity allows the patent owner to exclude others from making, using, selling, offering for sale or importing the patented invention during the patent term, typically 20 years from the earliest filing date, and in the country or countries where patent protection exists. This temporary 'monopoly' provides the patentee with a competitive advantage. Patent owners can also derive value from their inventions by licensing them to others who have the entrepreneurial capacity and innovative ability to develop, manufacture and market their inventions. In exchange for this right of exclusivity, the patentee is obligated to disclose to the public details of the invention and related technical or scientific background information and state-of-the-art basis for the invention. Thus, patents typically contain more details and are more exhaustive than scientific papers. According to a United States Patent and Trademark Office (USPTO) study [1] published in the 'Eighth Technology Assessment and Forecast Report', patents provide a significant amount of unique and valuable technological information that is largely not available elsewhere.

First, it is important to consider the typical patent life cycle and become familiar with a few terms. Patents are granted by patenting authorities or central offices that are usually part of the national governments in hundreds of countries around the world. The process by which patenting authorities and inventors negotiate towards the terms of a patent is called **patent examination** and is also referred to as **patent prosecution**. Patent examiners, who are employed by a national or regional patenting authority, conduct patent examination. During examination, the patent examiner will search for prior art, or public disclosures of the features of the invention, that were available prior to the filing of the patent application. The examiner may also initially reject the patent application based on the similarity of the prior art uncovered during the search or provided by the inventor. An inventor may represent himself or herself to prosecute the patent application. Alternatively, the inventor may hire a patent attorney or patent agent, generically referred to as patent practitioners, to prosecute the application on the inventor's behalf.

After a patent application undergoes examination and is deemed to satisfy the requirements for a patent set forth by the governing laws of the patenting authority, once it is granted by the patenting authority and is valid, the patent may be used to enforce the right to exclude others from making, using, selling and distributing the patented invention. After a patent is granted, the patent owner is usually required to pay maintenance fees to the granting patenting authority at certain intervals for the patent to remain enforceable. At this stage, and provided that all maintenance fees are paid, the patent is considered 'in force', 'active' or 'live'. The patent may be asserted in a lawsuit against parties who are allegedly making, using, selling or distributing the invention within the jurisdiction or country of the patenting authority that granted the patent, or the patent may be licensed for use by another party in exchange for a licensing fee. The patent may be enforced for the duration of its patent term—the limited period of time granted for the patent. Once the patent expires, the invention then belongs to the public or is 'in the public domain' and can be made, used, sold or distributed by anyone. A company that is aggressive in enforcing their patents may frequently seek licensing agreements or file suit against others who are allegedly practicing the invention protected by their patents and likewise may frequently engage in patent litigation.

There are many business and legal decisions that may need to be made throughout the patent life cycle. Even prior to having an invention, a company or individual may have the need to evaluate what has already been patented in their industry in order to know what areas of their industry to focus their innovating energy and resources on. A company may already be involved in research and development for a technology or product and may need to know how they should design around the boundaries already protected by other in-force patents. When approaching a large product rollout, a company may need to conduct one last check to be sure the features of the product can be made, used, sold or distributed without infringing upon other in-force patents. Business decisions relating to product rollouts or product designs can have major financial implications. Prior to filing or even drafting a patent application, an inventor and their patent practitioner may want to gauge the success which the hypothetical patent application may have when it is sent to be examined by a patenting authority. In the preceding stages of either protecting a company's patent portfolio or in seeking licensing agreements, the company may seek evidence of the company's already patented technology being made, used, sold or distributed by others. In the event that a company is sued by another for patent infringement, the defendant may attempt to find prior art that precedes the plaintiff's patents to demonstrate that the patents are invalid and unenforceable.

All of these business and legal needs bring us to the focus of this chapter and this book—they all require patent searching. While the term 'patent searching' can mean 'the act of searching patent information' or 'searching for patents', the phrase is more commonly used to describe **searching and filtering a body of information in light of and guided by an intellectual property-related determination**. This is the definition you should carry forward with you as you read this book. The business and legal needs above represent a variety of intellectual property determinations, or drivers that render the need for patent searching.

The body of information invoked in our definition of patent searching can comprise any collection of published information, whether patents, peer-reviewed papers, press releases, conference proceedings, industry standards definitions, product literature, product packaging, textbooks, drawings, diagrams or anything that can adequately describe the subject matter at hand. The body of literature to be searched may change in scope and volume depending on the need for the patent search.

With more than one million patents applied for worldwide each year, the amount of information available to researchers and the opportunity to derive business value and market innovative new products from detailed inventions is huge. However, patent documents present several peculiarities and challenges to effective searching, analysis and management:

- They are written by patentees, who typically use their own lexicon in describing their inventive details.
- They often include different data types, typically drawings, mathematical formulas, biosequence listings or chemical structures which require specific techniques for effective search and analysis.
- In addition to the standard metadata (e.g. title, abstract, publication date, applicants, inventors), patent offices typically assign some classification coding to assist in managing their examination workload and in searching patents, but these classification codes are not consistently applied or harmonised across different patenting offices.

This chapter describes the practical experiences in and requirements for effective searching, analysis, monitoring and overall management of patent information, from the perspective of professional patent information users. It is not meant to be exhaustive, but rather to provide an overview of the key aspects and requirements for effective patent information search and analysis. The subject matter is subdivided into three general areas:

- Overview and requirements of different types and sources of information and types of searches, depending on the purpose of the retrieval, such as patentability or potential infringement
- Description and requirements based on information management approaches, such as metadata or bibliographic data indexing, taxonomy, controlled vocabulary, value-added indexing and classification schemes
- Considerations in and requirements for searching specialised invention technologies, such as chemical structures, biosequences or device/engineering drawings

The ultimate purpose is that this practical view along with the description of key requirements for effective retrieval of patent information would contribute towards advancement of emerging retrieval technologies to support the user in patent search, analysis and information management processes.

1.2   Information Types

For the purposes of patent searching and our discussions in this book, searchable information can be thought of in a few major buckets. Bear in mind that 'searchable' more accurately means 'accessible', whether by actually searching an electronic database or by manually retrieving and reviewing technical journals in a library. We can group the basic buckets of searchable information by the extent to which each one is readily searchable. For convenience, we can call this 'searchability'. The basic buckets are:

- Patent literature
- Technical journal-grade literature
- Everything else (press releases, conference proceedings, industry standards definitions, product literature, product packaging, textbooks, drawings, diagrams, etc.)

Table 1.1 Searchability governed by the level of organisation of the literature

Overall level of organisation	Level of format uniformity	Accessibility	Level of consolidation	Searchability
Patent literature	High	High	High	High
Technical journal-grade literature	–	–	–	–
Academic journal-grade literature/dissertations	Medium	Medium	Medium	Low
Industry journal-grade literature	Low	Low	Low	Low
Everything else	–	–	–	–
Market information	Medium	Medium	Medium	Medium
Financial information	Medium	Medium	Medium	Medium
Legal	Medium	Medium	Medium	Medium
Press releases/news	Medium low	Low	Medium	Low
Product literature/ manuals	Low	Very low	Very low	Very low

Patent literature refers to both granted patents and published patent applications. Both are available for searching at many of the world's patenting authorities. Technical journal-grade literature refers to organised papers written with a focus on a specific topic and usually published by a well-known periodic industry journal. Everything else refers to the catchall bucket of any other type of disclosure of technical information that could exist. The types of searchable information have been broken down into these categories simply due to the distinct levels of organisation that can be seen in each one.

The 'searchability' of each bucket is governed by the level of organisation of the literature in each bucket, the level of format uniformity between individual documents, the accessibility of the literature in each bucket and how consolidated the various avenues to search the literature in each bucket have become (Table 1.1).

Patent literature is one of the most highly concentrated collections of technical information available in the world. It enjoys a high level of organisation due to the various patent classification systems used globally. In addition, many patents are marked as being member of patent families linking patents for the same invention but accepted in different jurisdictions or countries.[1] The level of format uniformity between individual documents is extremely consistent compared to other types of literature. Even comparing two patent documents that originated from two different patenting authorities, the format and arrangement is highly similar

---

[1] See http://www.epo.org/patents/patent-information/about/families.html (Accessed 15 Dec 2010).

between documents. For example, patents always contain extensive bibliographic information, a title and abstract, a set of claims specifying the claimed scope of the invention and background information. This enables electronic patent data to be arranged in quite a number of discrete data fields that can be searched individually or strategically together. Patent data is both very accessible and consolidated since much of it is either freely available via portals provided by patenting authorities or by commercially available search engines that serve as 'meta-' search engines enabling the user to search globally through one interface. Commercial search engines have brought a high level of consolidation to patent data and much of it can be accessed using very few separate channels.

Technical journal-grade literature has benefited from some organisation and some uniformity. Some very common value-added collections like EI Compendex by Elsevier leverage classification and theme-based organisational schemes. The level of uniformity between documents is mostly consistent; however the data fields that journal-grade literature documents have in common are significantly fewer than patent documents. This yields fewer and less sophisticated options to search the data. Journal-grade literature is graded as moderately accessible since, while a large amount of literature has been aggregated in collections like Compendex, a world of un-digitised and un-abstracted literature still exists in manual, paper collections. Journal-grade literature suffers significantly from the fact that literature aggregators like Elsevier and Dialog that supply journal title collections in 'files' limit the transparency the user has in knowing what is actually being searched and what the overlap is between data files and collections from other providers. **A searcher's efficiency drops significantly when the exact scope of the information being searched is unknown.** For this reason, the level of consolidation of journal-grade literature is low since an effective search requires a far greater number of unique access points than patent literature to be effective.

All other forms of literature are scattered across all reaches of resources and locations. Collections such as press releases and conference proceedings are consolidated individually, but under most circumstances need to be searched separately from all other sources. Product literature and product catalogs are perhaps the least searchable of all valuable literature resources.

1.3 Information Sources

What sources to search is dictated by what type of search is required, the legal and financial implications of the search, how much time to complete it in and how much one is willing to pay to get the information needed. The sayings 'You get what you pay for' and 'Buyer beware' are important to keep in mind when choosing sources. Fee-based sources are not always complete just as free sources are not always erroneous and incomplete. It depends on the searcher's comfort level. Searching both types of sources would give a sense of how complete the search is. But how does one know if he/she has done as thorough a search as one can? One criterion is when the same answers are retrieved from different sources, regardless of the cost.

The following are issues patent searchers generally consider when reviewing whether to use services that are fee-based, or services that are free at the point of use:

- Patenting authorities offer free searching; however coverage is limited to the authority's specific country or jurisdiction only. When looking for legal and prosecution history, these sites are invaluable.
- Fee-based search services tend to cover multiple databases and are more comprehensive.
- Customisations, such as linking to other sources, are available from fee-based services.
- Precision searching and advanced search and analysis features tend to be available more often from fee-based sources.
- Fee-based sources tend to have reliable servers.
- Users of fee-based sources have input in the product updates and development with respect to timeliness, comprehensiveness and user interface.

Also note that sources differ in:

- Quality, comprehensiveness and types of content
- Time coverage
- Indexing
- Timeliness
- Ability to search a number of databases at the same time and remove duplicates to get unique answers
- Cost
- Post-search analysis features

Finding relevant information has been compared to finding a needle in the haystack. No one can argue that there is not enough information out there. It is important to be able to search the whole document in addition to indexed fields, which is an issue in some services. Further, the freshness and coverage of the data need to be considered.

1.4 Patent Search Types

This section discusses the attributes of state of the art, patentability, validity, freedom to operate and due diligence searches. Common elements that need to be identified for all of these searches are: the purpose, time coverage and the most relevant sources to search.

Before proceeding further, it is important to state upfront the basic assumptions and principles of the patent searching process: no search is 100 % complete. For patentability type of searches (see Table 1.2), the goal is to conduct a better search

Table 1.2 Types of patent searches

Search type	Purpose	Applicable information
State-of-the-art search	To sample each major facet of a broad technology within a recent period. To gain a comprehensive overview of a product or technology before any R&D investment is made or when looking for a technology to license	All information published prior to today. Includes broad coverage of information and time frame. Both patent and non-patent literature sources are included
Evidence of use search	To identify literature supporting evidence that a product encompassed by the claims of an active subject patent is being made, used, sold or distributed within the jurisdiction or country of origin of the patent	Any literature published prior to the appropriate date associated with the subject patent
Prefiling patentability search	To identify prior art pertaining to both the core inventive concept and all sub-features for the purposes of drafting a patent application in light of the identified prior art	Anything published prior to today
Patentability or novelty search	To identify prior art pertaining to the core inventive concept of an invention that may preclude the invention from being patentable	All information published prior to today
Clearance or freedom-to-operate search	To identify any enforceable, granted patents claiming the subject matter of a product that is intended to be made, used or sold, in a target jurisdiction or country	Enforceable patents and published patent applications originating from only the target jurisdiction or country
Validity or invalidity search	To identify prior art that describes the technology recited by the claims of a granted, target patent that would render the patent unpatentable as of the date it was applied for	All information published prior to the appropriate date associated with the target patent
Patent portfolio search, patent landscape search	The needs for landscape searches vary wildly and are typically business driven, to assess gaps of patent protection in an industry or comparing patent portfolios between two or more competitors	Depends on purpose and extent of search: typically global patents and published patent applications and business data

than the patent examiner. For other patent search types, the goal is to be as complete as the resources and time allow.

When conducting a patent search, three factors will affect the results—cost, quality and time:

Cost
- Fee-based sources vs. free sources
- Complexity of the search
- Technical expertise and proficiency of the searcher

Quality
- Technical expertise and proficiency of the searcher (whether employed in-house or outsourced)
- Database content and integrity, indexing quality

Time
- Searching is an iterative process; allocating enough time to discuss the search request with the requestor is important.
- Exhaustive search and analysis—the chance of missing a relevant publication is less for a 20 h search vs. a 2 h search.

A brief introduction to the major search types is worthwhile to understand generally when the major collections of information should be searched. The table below summarises the main search types, their purposes and literature collections that are appropriate (but not always practical to search) for each one. As you gain exposure to the field, you will see that the names associated with some search types can be either interchangeable or distinctly different depending on whom you consult. For example, state-of-the-art searches and evidence-of-use searches are closely related, as are prefiling patentability and patentability or novelty searches. Sometimes these terms are used interchangeably. Also bear in mind that the table below is a summary. There are many caveats associated with the criteria of applicable information for each search type that depend upon the governing laws of each patenting authority. There are also arguably many additional search types. These are only the most common.

1.4.1 State-of-the-Art Patent Search (Evidence of Use Search)

The purpose of the state-of-the-art search is to gain a comprehensive overview of a product or technology. Ideally, this search is done before any R&D investment is made. In some companies, results from this search impact the selection and funding of a new project. This search is also useful when looking for a technology to license. This comprehensive search typically includes patent and non-patent literature sources. The interview process is critical in order to develop the appropriate search strategy, which tends to be broad. The data set retrieved can be large. The searcher needs to have a good understanding of what the requestor is looking for to enable a quick review of the answers for relevancy. Another way to digest the result is to sort references using 'patent' as a document type. It is fairly easy to rank by assignees, inventors and patent classification codes. From the tabular list, one will be able to identify competitors, technology experts and technology fields. When the patent search results are analysed using graphics and charts to visualise results, this type of report is called a patent landscape analysis [2]. It is a graphical representation of how patent publications are related. There are a number of products [3] that specialise in patent landscape analysis, each with its own strengths and weaknesses. Using these tools, a more elegant analysis is possible. For example, by looking at the level of patenting activity by classification codes over time, one may get an insight into the maturity of the field as well as patenting trends identifying technology decay and rise. Just like any type of data analysis, the conclusion is only as good as the data set used. It is advisable to be cautious when drawing conclusions derived from patent landscape analysis. To be comprehensive, multiple sources should be searched. This introduces additional issues to consider in merging the results: (1) standardisation of data fields to integrate the appropriate values from similar data fields, (2) duplicate removal and (3) one record per patent family representation to avoid skewing the analysis results.

1.4.2   Patentability (Novelty)

The purpose of a patentability search is to find all relevant prior art that may impact the likelihood of getting a patent granted. Issues such as novelty, non-obviousness and utility criteria need to be addressed. This type of search is typically conducted before writing the patent application, as the search results may change the scope of the claim or if needed lead to a 'draft around'. Since the coverage should include 'everything made available to the public, in writing, by public use, or otherwise' [4], it is not enough just to rely on patent publications, books and refereed journal articles. Other atypical sources need to be searched as well: press releases, brochures, white paper, websites, conference materials, theses and dissertations, technical disclosures and defensive filings. For a typical patentability search, the searcher uses the following techniques:

- Keyword search
- Classification code (IPC, ECLA, F-terms) search
- Forward and backward citation of relevant documents
- Inventor or author search of relevant documents
- Patent assignee search
- Chemical structure, sequence or mechanical drawing search, depending on the nature of the request. Detailed descriptions of these specialised data types can be found in Sect. 1.7 and in Chap. 15 by Downs, Holliday, and Willett in this book.

1.4.3   Freedom to Operate (Infringement, Right to Use, Clearance)

The purpose of a freedom-to-operate search is to make sure that one does not infringe upon anyone else's patent that is still in force. The focus of this search is on any granted patent that covers the invention and patent applications that may be granted on the same invention. For patent applications, the search should include data from file wrapper and prosecution history. This type of search is country specific, so local agencies should be consulted to confirm the status of the patent. In addition, close attention to the patent claims is prudent since they may change from country to country. Although results may technically be limited to the last 20 years, it is wiser to limit results to the last 25 years [5]. When conducting a freedom-to-operate search, the scope of the claim is the key. It is best not to limit the search to patents on the product itself but also look at the processes needed to manufacture it, including everything from raw materials to packaging designs. For a typical freedom-to-operate search, the following attributes are also searched:

- Ownership/patent assignee
- Patent family
- File history
- Legal status (e.g. patent term extension)
- Maintenance fee payments

1.4.4   Validity (Invalidity, Enforcement Readiness)

The purpose of a validity search is to determine if a patent already granted for an invention is valid. It is also a measure of the strength of a patent. All sources mentioned in the patentability search (Sect. 1.4.2) are searched. However, the time frame of the search can be limited to those results published before the filing date and a number of years after the filing date. As a rule of thumb, 5 years after the filing date is a good start; however this is subjective, so it would be wise to seek a legal counsel. The immediate availability of information can be troublesome when identifying publication dates. Publishers like ACS and Springer offer ASAP and Online First articles, respectively. These are edited submissions that are published online ahead of print. Another potential problem is tracking Internet page changes and the time stamp for any modification on the Web page. A bigger issue is if the Web page has been removed altogether.

For patent publications, the focus is on the validity of each claim and not necessarily on the general purpose of the patent. Keep in mind that if the search is based on a patent application, the claims may change from the time the application is submitted to the time the patent is granted. If the search covers patents in more than one country, the claims may be different from country to country. When starting with a specific patent, in addition to the sources mentioned in the patentability search, the searcher also needs to consider:

- Non-Latin language publications
- File history (found in, e.g. US Patent Application Information Retrieval (PAIR), European Patent Office (EPO) register, and non-published patent office files)
- Examiner search history
- Documents cited by examiner and inventors
- Examiner's reason for allowance

1.4.5 Patent Portfolio Analysis (Due Diligence, Patent Landscape Search)

The purpose of a due diligence search is to assess if a company's patents are robust enough to exclude competitors and market the invention with the least probability of an infringement lawsuit. A due diligence search can be useful for companies looking to buy or partner with a company and for companies who are looking to sell patents. A thorough due diligence search is expensive and will require a lot of time searching for and analysing data. The question is not how much it will cost to do a due diligence search, but 'What is the cost of not doing a complete due diligence search?'. A due diligence search is a validity search plus freedom-to-operate search plus an analysis of the company's patent portfolio. The purpose of the deal and the results/findings from the due diligence search may guide investors in assigning a fair price to the desired product or technology. The buyer should not be the only party conducting a due diligence search. It is a good strategic move for the seller to conduct due diligence on its product or technology to ensure that the asking price is competitive.

1.5 Practical Considerations in the Searching Process

No matter what type of search is requested, it is important for the patent searcher to really understand why the search is being requested. As mentioned earlier, searching is an iterative process [6]. Sometimes the requestor is not asking the correct question, so the interview process is critical. The searcher's knowledge of information resources that are available and past searches can be useful in defining the scope of the search. A searcher needs to be proficient in searching different information sources [7, 8] as well as possess technical or scientific background specific to the subject matter at hand. For example, having a degree in science is an advantage in the pharmaceutical industry, but even with that, some level of specialisation may be required. 'You can teach a chemist how to conduct a structure search in less time than it takes to teach a non-chemist' [9].

The remainder of this introductory chapter will focus on the nuances and searching strategies associated with patent literature. As discussed, patent literature is highly organised and highly consolidated and has very high consistency between documents. The major benefits that these characteristics bring to the 'searchability' of patent literature are that a highly systematic methodology can be used. Searchers of patent literature have a number of valuable tools at their disposal: citation searching, bibliographic data searching, classification searching and full-text searching.

Before the influx of Web-based applications and search tools, a searcher only needed to be proficient in using command lines to search STN, Dialog and Questel Orbit databases. This is not the case anymore. Stand-alone products are getting more and more popular and a searcher has to learn how to search each product well. Internet searching opens a whole new world of information. Occasional users and accidental searchers prefer the Internet. When they are asked why, the most popular answer is 'I always get an answer when I search the Internet'. The answer set might be full of false hits, but they prefer that to getting no answers. But then, how many of us have found an important document serendipitously on the Internet? Since it is free, the Internet should be searched first to gauge how much information is out there. Some results may be full-text documents, which may provide the searcher with better keywords to use.

Selection of search tools will depend on:

- Types of subject matter inventions

  - Chemical structures
  - Biosequence data
  - Device/mechanical/electrical drawings
    Section 1.7 describes in more detail these subject matter inventions and requirements for searching these specialised invention technologies.

- Search techniques desired or most appropriate

  - Boolean logic
  - Natural language processing or semantic technologies
  - Similarity
  - Proximity
  - Linking to full-text documents, external and internal depositories
  - Left and right word truncation
  - Case sensitivity when searching for acronyms
  - Keyword and synonym selection
  - Search term weighing
  - Search guidance on the fly
  - Controlled vocabulary or value-added indexing
  - Chemical structure based on textual description
  - Foreign words and characters such as Greek alphabet and mathematical symbols
  - Search limits by sentence, section, etc.

- – Multilanguage search query or translation to English from non-Latin languages (e.g. Japanese, Chinese, Korean)
- • Post-search analysis features
  - – Relevancy ranking
  - – Sorting features
  - – Subject relatedness
  - – Citation mapping (citing and cited)
  - – Concept mapping
- • Alerting features by:
  - – Keywords
  - – Structures (biologics and small molecules)
  - – Legal status
  - – Classification codes

1.6 Information Retrieval Approaches to Patent Searching

This section describes the various methods for patent information retrieval that have traditionally been employed to achieve high recall and precision: full-text searching, bibliographic data indexing, use of taxonomy/controlled vocabulary and classification schemes and value-added indexing.

1.6.1 Classification Searching

Classification codes [10, 11] are created and maintained by each patenting authority for the purposes of organising patent and applications according to their technical application, structural features, intended use or the resulting product produced by a process. The major classification systems in use worldwide include the International Patent Classification (IPC) system, the European Classification (ECLA) system, the United States Patent Classification (USPC) system, and the Japanese File Index and F-Term (FI/F-Term) classification system. Many other patenting authorities maintain their own classification systems; however these four are the systems predominantly used when publishing and classifying patent data. The USA and Japan are singled out because the patent examiners in these countries rely heavily on their own classification codes to classify patents. Examiners in these countries classify their patent documents in IPC and sometimes ECLA classification areas as a secondary measure and not as precise as their native classification areas. Due to the staggering volume of patent data produced by these countries, a global classification search is not complete without a search specifically within the US and Japanese classification systems in addition to IPC and ECLA.

1.6.1.1   International Patent Classification

The International Patent Classification (IPC) [12] system was established under the 1971 treaty and has replaced national classifications or supplements them over the years since. The schedule of classes under the IPC is a true taxonomy, dividing all areas of technology into eight sections (A–H), the sections subdivided by notations for class, subclass, group and subgroup. The classification system was originally updated at 5-year intervals, retaining the existing hierarchy. With the eighth edition of the IPC, a reclassification system was established so that all patents in a database use the same version. One of the IPC codes assigned to the athletic shoe in Fig. 1.1 has the following definition:

SECTION A — HUMAN NECESSITIES

A43   FOOTWEAR
A43B   characteristic features of footwear; parts of footwear
A43B 13/00   Soles; Sole and heel units
A43B 13/14   · characterized by the constructive form

1.6.1.2   United States National Classification

The USA has continued to use its national system as the primary classification for patents [13]. The system consists of three-digit class definitions, arranged numerically without any attempt to relate the numerical class code to its place in the sequence, creating new classes as new technologies emerge. Each class code is followed by a hierarchy of numerical subclasses, for example, class 36/129 for the athletic shoe in Fig. 1.1:

US007594345B2

(12) **United States Patent**　　　　　　(10) **Patent No.:**　　**US 7,594,345 B2**
Fusco　　　　　　　　　　　　　　　　(45) **Date of Patent:**　　　**Sep. 29, 2009**

(54) **ARTICLE OF FOOTWEAR HAVING SOLE WITH RIBBED STRUCTURE**

(75) Inventor: **Ciro Fusco**, Portland, OR (US)

(73) Assignee: **NIKE, Inc.**, Beaverton, OR (US)

(*) Notice: Subject to any disclaimer, the term of this patent is extended or adjusted under 35 U.S.C. 154(b) by 200 days.

(21) Appl. No.: **11/247,591**

(22) Filed: **Oct. 12, 2005**

(65) **Prior Publication Data**

US 2007/0079530 A1　　Apr. 12, 2007

(51) **Int. Cl.**
A43C 15/02　　(2006.01)
A43B 13/14　　(2006.01)
(52) **U.S. Cl.** .... **36/59 R**; 36/59 C; 36/103
(58) **Field of Classification Search** .... 36/59 R, 36/59 C, 129, 25 R, 103; D2/953, 960
See application file for complete search history.

(56) **References Cited**

U.S. PATENT DOCUMENTS

D172,787 S　　8/1954　Frary

4,546,559 A	*	10/1985	Dassler 36/129
4,578,883 A		4/1986	Dassler
4,615,126 A	*	10/1986	Mathews 36/102
D292,443 S		10/1987	Ihlenburg
D302,900 S		8/1989	Kolman et al.
4,972,613 A	*	11/1990	Loveder 36/105
D395,743 S	*	7/1998	Ryan D2/960
D399,342 S		10/1998	Carlson
5,829,172 A	*	11/1998	Kaneko 36/108
D405,597 S		2/1999	Carlson
D471,347 S	*	3/2003	Haas et al. D2/953
D487,331 S	*	3/2004	Rogers et al. D2/952
6,793,996 B1		9/2004	Umezawa
6,857,205 B1	*	2/2005	Fusco et al. 36/114
D512,553 S	*	12/2005	Robbins et al. D2/954
2003/0131499 A1	*	7/2003	Silverman 36/88
2004/0111922 A1	*	6/2004	Fusco .... 36/59 R
2005/0155254 A1	*	7/2005	Smith et al. 36/28

* cited by examiner

Primary Examiner—Ted Kavanaugh
(74) *Attorney, Agent, or Firm*—Banner & Witcoff, Ltd

(57)　　　　　　　　　**ABSTRACT**

An article of athletic footwear comprising an upper for receiving the foot of a wearer and a sole structure attached to the upper, the sole structure having a heel portion including a rigid or semi-rigid ground contacting surface having a plurality of ribs located in the heel portion.

34 Claims, 3 Drawing Sheets

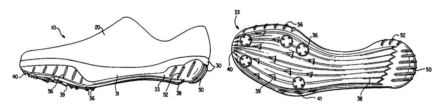

Fig. 1.1　First page of US 7,594,345 B2, assigned to Nike, Inc., published 29 September 2009

CLASS 36 BOOTS, SHOES, AND LEGGINS

83 BOOTS AND SHOES
113　　· Occupational or athletic shoe (e.g., roof climbing, gardening, etc.)
114　　·· Athletic shoe or attachment therefore
129　　··· For track

1.6.1.3 European Patent Classification (ECLA)

The European Patent Office created a more precise variant of the IPC, assigning it to all of the patents in the examiner search files [14]. ECLA codes do not appear on printed patents, but they are added to some databases. The ECLA code assigned to the athletic shoe in Fig. 1.1 has the definition shown below, a narrower definition than the IPC code shown above:

SECTION A—HUMAN NECESSITIES

A43	FOOTWEAR
A43B	characteristic features of footwear; parts of footwear
A43B 13/00	Soles; Sole and heel units
A43B 13/22	· soles made slip-preventing or wear-resisting, e.g., by impregnation or spreading a wear-resisting layer
A43B 13/22B	·· Profiled soles
A43B 13/22B2	··· the profile being made in the foot facing surface

1.6.1.4 Japanese File Index Classification

FI terms are a system of refinements to the IPC, applied by the Japanese Patent Office (JPO) to Japanese patent documents [15]. The JPO also applies supplementary indexing terms, called F-terms, in addition to IPC and FI classifications, to assist in searching Japanese patent documents.

1.6.2 Full-Text Searching

Another significant benefit of patent data, in contrast to journal-grade literature, is the wide availability of full document text among the major patenting authorities [16, 17]. Other forms of organised literature are often only abstracted. While for a number of years the bulk of full-text patent data was confined to the major seven patenting authorities (Europe, World Intellectual Property Organization, Germany, France, Great Britain, the USA and Japan), many more patenting authorities are beginning to make their full-text patent data available. As well, several of the commercial data aggregators are translating the patent information from dozens of less conventional patenting authorities and making the data available within their search systems alongside the major seven.

The text of patents differs in significant ways from the text of other forms of scholarly publications. The objective of patents is to obtain the patent owner's right to exclude others from practicing an invention described in the claims section of the patent specification, and the patent laws and regulations of the country or patenting authority in which the patent application is filed largely control the language and formatting of the text. Customary phrases and sentence structure known as 'patentese' are used in patent documents and are seldom used in other types of documents. There is no editorial process comparable to peer review before patent documents are published. The specification of a patent application is usually published 18 months after the first filing of an application covering the claimed invention, without any changes from the document filed by the applicant. The patent application undergoes examination to determine whether the claims define a patentable invention. Deficiencies in meeting the legal requirements for a patentable invention will prevent grant of patent rights and the publication of a granted patent, but pre-grant publication occurs whether the specification is well written or not.

The technical disclosure of a patent specification is provided in an abstract, claims and the main body of the specification, which is often divided into sections:

- *The background of the invention:* a summary of the problem to be solved, ways it has been handled in the past and relevant prior publications.
- *A brief summary of the invention:* a short description of the invention being claimed, often a restatement of the claims.
- *A detailed description of the invention:* a full description of all aspects of the invention, with definitions of the terms used and specific examples of ways in which the invention may be carried out. The description may be a few paragraphs or thousands of pages long. It may refer to defined terms and images in drawing pages or to chemical structures.

Because the patent claims define the owner's right to exclude others from practicing an invention, patentees attempt to define their inventions in the broadest language possible. To expand the scope of a patent, the claims and accompanying disclosure often use generic language in place of simple terms. Shoes will be described as 'footwear', house paint as 'exterior finish', pills as 'unitary dosage forms' and computer as 'a system having a storage for storing data, an output device to display information, a terminal for entering information and a component that modifies the input data and controls flow of data between different parts'. Any terminology that defines the invention unambiguously is acceptable, and new technologies often require new terminology. Patent attorneys and agents often create new terminology to describe their clients' inventions under the rule that 'the patentee is his own lexicographer'. A full-text search must include any and all terms and phrases that may have been used to describe the technology of interest.

Patent claims are listed in the form of single sentences, with the leading phrase, 'I claim', implied or preceding the numbered list of claims. The precise wording and punctuation of the claims are essential to the understanding of the scope of legal protection, as is the meaning of each term defined in the specification. Claims may be 'independent', where all limitations of the claim are stated, or 'dependent', where limitations are carried over from an earlier claim. The entire text of independent claims is implied, but not stated in their dependent claims, so attempting to search the claim text using proximity operators often misses important references. An example of an independent claim and one of its dependent claims of the exemplary patent shown in Fig. 1.1 is presented below. Note that claim 3 must be read as including the entire description given in claim 1, with the added feature that the sole of the shoe is comprised of a polyamide. The word 'comprising' is understood as meaning 'including, but not limited to'.

I claim:

1. An article of athletic footwear comprising an upper for receiving the foot of a wearer and a sole structure attached to the upper, the sole structure having a heel portion, the sole structure including a rigid or semi-rigid ground contacting surface, wherein a plurality of distinct ribs is located longitudinally in the heel portion and each of the distinct ribs extends in a substantially parallel direction, wherein the heel portion is cup-shaped so that the back portion of the heel portion extends upwards from a bottom portion of the ground contacting surface and wraps around the backside of the heel, wherein at least a portion of the plurality of ribs curve around the back portion of the heel portion; wherein the plurality of ribs comprises a slippery material.
3. The article of footwear of claim 1 wherein the ground-contacting surface comprises a polyamide.

(Sample independent and dependent claim language: US 7,594,345 B2, assigned to Nike, Inc., published 29 September 2009. Article of footwear having sole with ribbed structure.)

Patent documents are written in the language of the patent issuing authority, and a multinational database will contain documents written in many languages and alphabets. In addition to countries that specify a single language, for example, English in the USA and Japanese in Japan, there are some countries and international patenting authorities that allow the applicant to file a patent specification in one of several languages: the Patent Cooperation Treaty (PCT) allows applicants to file applications in any of ten languages as of 2010, including Japanese, Chinese, Korean, Russian and Arabic, as well as languages written in the Latin alphabet. Databases of PCT applications provide English language abstracts, and many other databases also add English language abstracts to the native language text records or substitute an English language abstract for the patent text, but a search in English misses potentially relevant documents in other languages. The growing availability of machine translations helps to overcome the language barrier in databases that provide them, but the grammar and choice of words given by a machine translation engine often differ from those intended by the patentee.

Patents cover all technologies and even methods of doing business, and each area of technology has its own terminology in every language, often giving words a different meaning from their ordinary dictionary definition. The English word 'furnish', for example, is used in the papermaking industry to indicate the materials of which paper is made. Unless a search is limited to the technological context of the subject matter being searched, the results will not be sufficiently precise. Better precision can be achieved by searching text terms in combination with patent classification codes or other indications of context.

Searching full-text patent data requires a careful strategy and being constantly mindful of how a technology can be described from a scientist's or engineer's perspective versus how a technology can be described in the language of patent practitioners. The following key measures must be taken when leveraging the full-text data available in patent literature:

- Exhaustive usage of synonyms
- Effective use of Boolean operators, proximity operators and truncation operators
- Appropriate clustering of concepts into discrete search queries
- Combining saved search queries appropriately
- Appropriate usage of broad-to-narrow and narrow-to-broad search query progression
- Iterative modification of previously stored search queries in light of newly acquired phrases and terminology

What are the pros and cons of full-text searching?

- Pros:
    - Easy to perform, no search training required
    - Allows for serendipity in searching
- Cons:
    - Optical character resolution (OCR) errors for those patents from countries/time ranges that aren't created from original digital records
    - High recall, therefore relevancy ranking is needed
    - When searching for numbers—numeric versus text
    - Less precision: no control on which portion of the document the keyword appears as long as it is present in any part of the document

1.6.3 Citation Searching

Patents originating from the vast majority of patenting authorities are issued with a list of other documents that were cited during the prosecution of the patent application either by the patent examiner or the patent practitioner or inventor.

Since the migration of patent information into electronic form, a patent searcher not only has immediate access to documents cited by patents but also immediate access to documents that cite each patent. The processes of searching both of these sets of documents are referred to as 'backward citation searching' and 'forward citation searching': backward referring to the documents a patent cites and forward referring to the documents citing the patent under review. Citation searching is a patent searcher's most powerful tool in quickly generating a highly concentrated collection of relevant search results at the beginning of a search. Search engine providers are making citation searching easier and easier. A common search strategy in beginning a search is to conduct a highly targeted search of only very relevant patent documents and then citation searching the most closely related documents for others of interest. Searchers can 'follow their nose' through multiple generations of patent citations, both forward and backward, to rapidly collect highly relevant documents [18].

1.6.4 Bibliographic Data Indexing and Searching

The first page of a patent document includes bibliographic data relating to the filing details and ownership of the patent and includes additional data fields relating to the handling of the application within the patent office. References cited by the patent examiner may appear either on the cover page of the patent or in a search report appended to the patent publication. Databases index these metadata fields to facilitate searching. Bibliographic information is the focus of due diligence searching and some technical and competitive intelligence studies. Even in full-text searches, combining keywords with bibliographic data, especially patent classification codes, can increase precision and limit search results to a desired range of filing or publication dates.

- **Title**

    Patent documents are required to have a descriptive title. Although patent regulations state that the title should reflect the claims, most original titles are relatively short and only hint at the novel features of the patent. Commercial databases may provide enhanced titles; in the case of the Derwent World Patents Index (DWPI), the title is an English language mini-abstract of the patent.

- **Patentee (applicant, assignee)**

    The patentee is the owner of the patent rights, either the company or institution that sponsored the research leading to the patent or the individual inventor or inventors. Patent databases normally index the patent owner or assignee named on the patent document at the time of publication. Some databases apply standardised or normalised versions of the patentee name as an aid to searching or apply company coding that attempts to track corporate divisions and ownership changes over time. Some databases supplement records with the name of organisations to which patent rights were reassigned after publication, obtaining the data from other patent office databases.

- **Inventor**

  The inventor or joint inventors are named on a patent document. Unlike the authors of journal articles, only individuals who contributed to the conception of the invention should be included.
- **Patent publication number**

  The serial number assigned by a patent office to the patent publication.
- **Publication date**

  The date on which the patent issuing authority published either the patent document or an announcement of the patent document in an official gazette. The publication date of most granted patents is the date when exclusive rights begin.
- **Application number**

  The serial number assigned to a patent application when it is filed at the patent office.
- **Application date**

  The date on which the patent application corresponding to the published document was filed at the patent office.
- **Designated states**

  Patent Cooperation Treaty applications and regional patenting authorities list the names or ISO country codes of the states for which the patent application is effective.
- **Priority applications**

  The Paris Convention for the Protection of Industrial Property, the World Trade Organization and other treaties allow patent applicants to file applications on a single invention in member countries within a year of a first patent filing by claiming priority based on the application filed in the first country. The application numbers of the applications claimed for priority are shown as priority application numbers in the records on the later patent applications.
- **Patent family members**

  Patents based on the same priority applications form a patent family of patent publications from multiple countries covering aspects of the same invention. Some databases combine all family members in a single record and apply indexing to a single patent document, known as 'the basic patent'.
- **Priority dates**

  The filing dates of the applications claimed for priority.
- **Patent classification codes**

  The national and/or international classification codes assigned to the patent at the time of publication are printed on the patent specification at the time of publication. Some patent databases enhance the classification data by adding classification codes assigned by patent offices during post-publication reclassification procedures.
- **Cited references**

  Patent examiners perform a search of the prior art to determine whether patent claims are new and inventive as defined by the patent law. Prior publications that teach or suggest aspects of the claimed invention are provided to the applicant for discussion and possible amendment of the application and are listed on the patent document if it is eventually published. In addition to the cited references, some patent databases obtain information about later citations of the patent and add the citing patents to the record.

- **Additional search fields**

  Patent offices print the names of the patent applicant's legal representative and the patent examiner on the patent document, and these are included in the records of some, but not all, patent databases. Changes in the legal status of a patent or published application are included in some databases, in many cases obtaining the data from the European Patent Office's INPADOC legal status file.

1.6.4.1   Important Preliminary Considerations of Searching Bibliographic Data

Searching bibliographic data includes the ability to research prolific corporate entities and inventors who are known to have patented frequently in a given technology. However, searching for companies and inventors is not quite as simple as typing in the company or inventor name into a field. A number of precautions need to be taken into account when searching for specific names:

- Patent ownership can change frequently. A search for a company name may yield only older patents originally assigned to the company and not newer patents reassigned to them after issuance.
- Company subsidiaries change frequently. Individual business units are bought and sold regularly. Further, searching only for a parent company name may not necessarily capture all company subsidiaries.
- Company suffixes (e.g. Co., Inc.) vary wildly and must be accounted for.
- Inventor names are commonly spelled in a wide variety of fashions, with and without suffixes, with or without initials, or completely misspelt altogether.
- Patents are very often not printed with assignment data upon issuance such that the owner files assignment data after printing.
- Correspondence address information can sometimes be used to approximate the ownership of patents.

What are the pros and cons of bibliometric data and abstract searching?

- Pros:

  - Errors in documents can be detected during database creation.
  - Keyword synonyms and thesaurus available.
  - Specific data fields like classification codes can be searched.

- Cons:

  - Indexing errors can be introduced during database creation.
  - Keywords that appear in non-indexed fields will not be searchable.
  - Time lag from published date to database entry.

1.6.5 Taxonomy, Controlled Vocabulary and Other Value-Added Indexing

In the days before full-text searching was available, patent searchers were forced to rely on patent classification and controlled indexing systems for both manual and online searches. The codes or terms were normally arranged hierarchically, permitting the searcher to use the narrowest appropriate term or the term at the latest position of a taxonomy, allowing the searcher to assemble a collection of documents, which would be reviewed for relevance, fully expecting that the limited number of indexing concepts would yield a great many irrelevant documents.

Patent classification systems were created for manual searching of printed patent collections. Patent offices designed numeric or alphanumeric schemes that assigned codes to all known technologies and marked each patent with one or more of the appropriate class codes. Class codes were updated periodically, creating a taxonomy by subdividing the classes to create collections of patents that were small enough that a searcher could review them. The schedules of class definitions formed a controlled vocabulary of generic terminology for each category of technology, and knowledgeable indexers and patent search specialists were able to select the nearest class definition for an invention of interest. Using the proper class code, one would be able to limit a search for a shoe sole such as the one in Fig. 1.1 without knowing whether the patentee called it a shoe sole, a ground-contacting surface, *une semelle* or *eine Schuhsohle*, and without retrieving patents on fishing gear.

Subject-based databases, such as Chemical Abstracts, and commercial patent databases, such as IFI CLAIMS, created systems of controlled indexing terms, applying the terms to indexing records in place of the actual terminology used by the patentee. The controlled indexing terms are collected in thesauri or vocabulary listings, which may be organised into a taxonomy in which broader, narrower or related terms are listed for each of the controlled indexing terms. A searcher can use the controlled terms from the thesaurus without having to create an exhaustive list of synonyms.

Chemical formulae lend themselves particularly well to controlled indexing, as there are a finite number of elements, and the empirical formulae of molecules disclosed in a document can be organised in a standardised alphanumeric fashion, for example, the Hill system created for the Chemical Abstracts Formula Index. The molecular structures of chemical substances can also be indexed into systematic hierarchical systems, substituting a controlled indexing name or registry number for whatever name is used by the author or patentee in a document.

1.6.5.1 Chemical Substance Registries

A more precise system for retrieving information about chemical substances than a molecular formula or substance name is a registry system that gives a unique identifier to each indexed substance. An indexer reads a patent or other publications, recognises each substance from a name or chemical structure drawing and assigns an existing registry number or creates a new one, allowing searchers to find all references to that substance in the database by searching for the chemical structure or name in a registry database and then using the registry numbers to search in the corresponding bibliographic database.

The largest chemical substance registry is the Chemical Abstracts Service (CAS) Registry [19], which covers both patents and non-patent literature from around the world. It assigns a registry number to each unique substance exemplified in a publication or claimed in a patent. The Derwent Chemistry Resource (DCR) covers compounds claimed or exemplified in international patents indexed in the Derwent World Patents Index (DWPI) [20]. The IFI CLAIMS Compound Vocabulary [21] has compounds mentioned in five or more US patent publications. Because their indexing policies and database coverage differ, the number of compounds listed in the various registries and the number of patents associated with them are very different.

For example, the non-steroidal anti-inflammatory drug diclofenac, and its salts, has 299 registry numbers in the CAS Registry file, 24 registry numbers in the Derwent Chemistry Resource and 3 registry numbers in the IFI Compound Vocabulary. Figure 1.2 illustrates the CAS Registry record for the acid form of diclofenac with its chemical structure diagram, a list of names that have appeared in the literature and the number of bibliographic records in the database indexed to this registry number. Searching the registry number 15307-86-5 in the Chemical Abstracts databases on STN (see Fig. 1.3) will retrieve all documents that disclose the acid form of diclofenac, regardless of the name used by the author of the original document, but it will not retrieve documents that disclose only the sodium salt of diclofenac, the active ingredient in Voltaren Gel.

1.6.5.2 Derwent Multipunch and Manual Codes

The Derwent World Patents Index was designed during the 1960s to facilitate in-house searches for English language abstracts of chemical patents. The abstracts were printed on two types of cards: IBM cards for sorting by use of a code

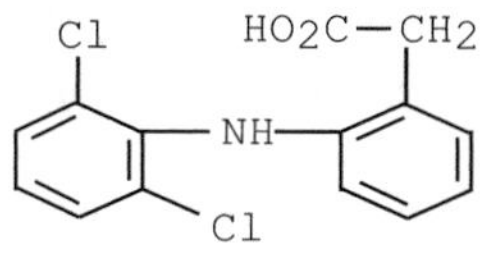

6291 REFERENCES IN FILE CA (1907 TO DATE)
212 REFERENCES TO NON-SPECIFIC DERIVATIVES IN FILE CA
6325 REFERENCES IN FILE CAPLUS (1907 TO DATE)

Fig. 1.2 Chemical Abstracts Service Registry database (CAS): structure record for diclofenac

Chemical Abstracts Service Registry Database
Structure Record for Diclofenac

L1   ANSWER 1 OF 1 REGISTRY COPYRIGHT 2010 ACS on STN
RN   15307-86-5 REGISTRY
CN   Benzeneacetic acid, 2-[(2,6-dichlorophenyl)amino]- (CA INDEX NAME)
OTHER CA INDEX NAMES:
CN   Acetic acid, [o-(2,6-dichloroanilino)phenyl]- (8CI)
OTHER NAMES:
CN   2-(2,6-Dichloroanilino)phenylacetic acid
CN   2-(2,6-Dichlorophenylamino)phenylacetic acid
CN   2-[(2,6-Dichlorophenyl)amino]benzeneacetic acid
CN   2-[2-(2,6-Dichlorophenylamino)phenyl]acetic acid
CN   Dichlofenac
CN   Diclac
CN   Diclofenac
CN   Diclofenac acid
CN   Diclofenamic acid
CN   Diclomelan
CN   Dicloreuma
CN   N-(2,6-Dichlorophenyl)-o-aminophenylacetic acid
CN   Pennsaid
CN   Transfenac
CN   Voltaflan
CN   [o-(2,6-Dichloroanilino)phenyl]acetic acid
DR   76595-40-9, 87180-41-4
MF   C14 H11 Cl2 N O2

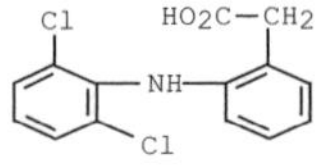

6291 REFERENCES IN FILE CA (1907 TO DATE)
212 REFERENCES TO NON-SPECIFIC DERIVATIVES IN FILE CA
6325 REFERENCES IN FILE CAPLUS (1907 TO DATE)

Fig. 1.3 15307-86-5 in the Chemical Abstracts databases on STN

represented by the positions of holes punched in the card and Manual Code cards for searching by hand in filing cabinets.

The multipunch code was originally represented by 720 card positions, each position dedicated to a specific type of bibliographic data, chemical structure fragment or other technical features of an indexed patent. All of the codes relating to inventive features of the indexed patent were punched, and the searcher reviewed the abstracts of patents with all of the appropriate codes directly on the cards after they had passed through the sorter. After digital computers replaced card sorters, the code was reformatted into alphanumeric symbols, and the code continues to be used. The chemical fragmentation section of the code is discussed in Sect. 1.7.

The Manual Code is a patent classification system, organising technologies into a hierarchy that takes both structure and function into account. When it was used as a manual search tool, a searcher would identify a single code that best matched the inventive feature he or she wished to search and would visually scan through all of the abstracts in that section of the file drawer. Since the transition to computerised searching, Manual Codes have become a valuable tool for limiting retrieval in searches based on full-text and keyword searches, specifying a required feature and eliminating all records covering features occurring higher in the hierarchy.

1.7 Specialised Invention Technologies: Considerations and Requirements

While keywords and text terms are commonly employed in searching patents, certain subject matter inventions claimed in patents warrant specialised techniques for precise and high recall retrieval of relevant art. These include:

- Chemical structures
- Biosequences and biotechnology topics
- Device/engineering drawings

This section describes considerations and requirements for effective retrieval of these specialised invention technologies.

1.7.1 Chemical Structure Searching

Searching for chemical compounds poses many challenges. There is a wide variability in nomenclature; the search may be directed to a species or a genus that encompasses many possible species, and the chemical compound(s) of interest may be disclosed in a Markush structure.

Even exact compounds can be difficult to search, and a professional searcher does not rely on chemical nomenclature for comprehensive retrieval. For example, something as simple as ethanol can be described as: ethanol, ethyl alcohol, grain alcohol, pure alcohol, hydroxyethane, drinking alcohol, ethyl hydrate and absolute alcohol.

Ethanol could be also depicted structurally, instead of mentioned by name, as shown in Fig. 1.4.

Exact compounds can also be described generically. For example, ethanol is a 'hydroxy alkane'. Structurally, ethanol is also one of the compounds encompassed by either of the following two generics.

A search request may be a generic query, as shown in Fig. 1.5, that defines many possible compounds, in which case the goal is to retrieve records that relate to any of the compounds defined by the genus. This is called a Markush search [22]. The term 'Markush' originated from the generic claims filed by Dr. Eugene A. Markush, which was granted as US 1,506,316 in 1924. A Markush is essentially a way to claim many compounds in a single patent claim and the term is used to describe

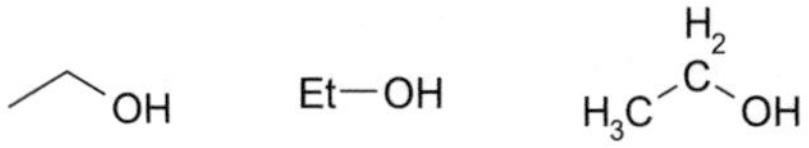

Fig. 1.4 Different chemical structural representations of ethanol

G_1-OH

Wherein: G1 = C1-C6 alkyl, aryl, or heteroaryl.

Ak-R

Wherein: Ak = any C1-C3 alkyl chain; and
                  R = OH, halogen, alkyoxy.

Fig. 1.5 Examples of genus representations of ethanol

An Example of a Markush Claim from US 7,659,407

The invention claimed is:

1. A Pyrazole derivative of formula (I), having affinity for the cannabinoidergic CB1 and/or CB2 receptors:

(I)

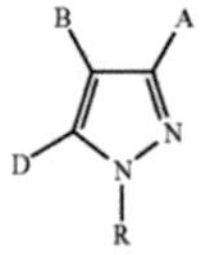

R is

aryl, not substituted or having from one to five substituents, equal to or different from each other, selected from halogen, C_1-C_7 alkyl, C_1-C_7 alkylthio, C_1-C_7 alkoxy, C_1-C_7 haloalkyl, C_1-C_7 haloalkoxy, cyano, nitro, amino, N-alkylamino, N,N-dialkylamino, saturated or unsaturated heterocycle, and phenyl;

A is

an amidic substituent of formula —C(O)—NH-T', wherein T' is

a group NR_1R_2, wherein R_1 and R_2 are equal or different and have the following meanings:

C_1-C_7 alkyl;

aryl, arylalkyl or arylalkenyl not substituted or optionally having on the aromatic rings from one to four substituents, equal to or different from each other, selected from halogen, C_1-C_7 alkyl, C_1-C_7 haloalkyl, C_1-C_7 haloalkoxy, C_1-C_7 alkylthio, C_1-C_7 alkoxy, wherein in the previous substituents comprising C_1-C_7 aliphatic chains, C_1-C_3 chains are preferably used; wherein R_1 may additionally be hydrogen;

or R_1 and R_2 together with the nitrogen atom to which they are linked form a, saturated or unsaturated, heterocycle from 5 to 10 atoms comprising carbon atoms and including the nitrogen of NR_1R_2, and optionally an additional S, O or N atom, not substituted or optionally having from one to four substituents, equal to or different from each other, selected from C_1-C_7 alkyl, phenyl, and benzyl, said phenyl or benzyl optionally substituted with one or more groups, equal to or different from each other, selected from: halogen, C_1-C_7 alkyl, C_1-C_7 haloalkyl, C_1-C_7 haloalkoxy, C_1-C_7 alkylthio and C_1-C_7 alkoxy;

B is a group selected from: hydrogen and C_1-C_4 alkyl; and

D is an heteroaryl with a ring size of from 5 to 6 atoms, selected from the group consisting of thiophene, pyridine, furan, oxazole, thiazole, imidazole, pyrazole, isoxazole, isothiazole, triazole, pyridazine, pyrimidine, pyrazine, triazine and pyrrole; wherein the heteroaryl is optionally substituted with one, two, three or four substituents, equal to or different from each other, selected from the following: halogen, C_1-C_3 alkyl, C_1-C_3 alkylthio, C_1-C_3 alkoxy, C_1-C_3 haloalkyl, and C_1-C_3 haloalkoxy.

Fig. 1.6 An example of a Markush Claim from US 7,659,407

any generic structure that encompasses multiple species. An example of a Markush claim is shown in Fig. 1.6.

A typical patentability search request might be 'find patents, patent applications, and literature references that claim or disclose compounds defined by the following generic' (as shown in Fig. 1.7), in which case the patent (US 7,659,407) above should be retrieved with the correct search query and appropriately indexed retrieval system.

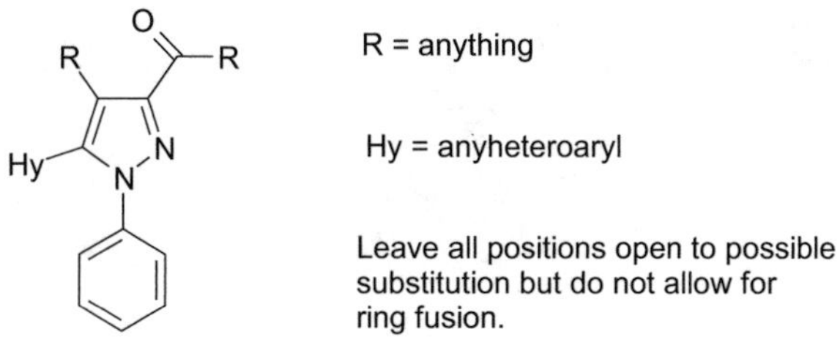

Fig. 1.7 A typical chemical structure query

Chemical structures represent molecules composed of atoms linked together by chemical bonds. There are groupings that occur in many molecules—rings of atoms, patterns of atoms and bonds that chemists refer to as 'functional groups'. Database producers created indexing systems that fragment the molecules into their component rings and functional groups and assign an alphanumeric code to each of the resulting substructures. Indexers evaluate each chemical structure in a patent and add all of the applicable codes to the database record. Some systems have been able to partially automate this process. These fragmentation codes allow a searcher to look for either specific molecules or Markush structures with alternative substructures, using Boolean logic rather than resource-intensive structure searching algorithms. Because Markush structures often contain a great many alternative fragments, the systems include codes for fragments that are either required or optional in embodiments of the structure and a set of negation codes for fragments that can never be present in an embodiment.

There are different types of systems [23] available for searching chemical structures in the patent and non-patent published literature. Topological search systems are used to match graphical structures created by a searcher with specific compounds or Markush structures contained in a database. An indexer adds chemical structure indexing to the search system based on the indexer's understanding of the patent or literature document. Special software is used by the searcher to create the structure query. Chemical fragmentation code search systems, such as Derwent fragmentation codes and IFI CLAIMS chemical vocabulary codes, match alphanumeric codes from strategies created by a searcher with codes added to a database record by indexers.

As computing systems advanced, connection tables were created that index how these atoms and groups of atoms are interlinked together to allow more precise retrieval. For example, graphical searches in several structure searchable databases hosted by STN can be an exact search (EXA), which is used to retrieve substances that exactly match the query; a family search (FAM), which is used to retrieve substances that exactly match the query plus multicomponent substances such as salts; a closed substructure search (CSS), which will retrieve substances that match the query without substitution allowed; or a substructure search (SSS), which will retrieve substances that match the query with any substitution allowed. To conduct a search using a structure query, a searcher first creates the chemical structure query using software, such as STN Express.

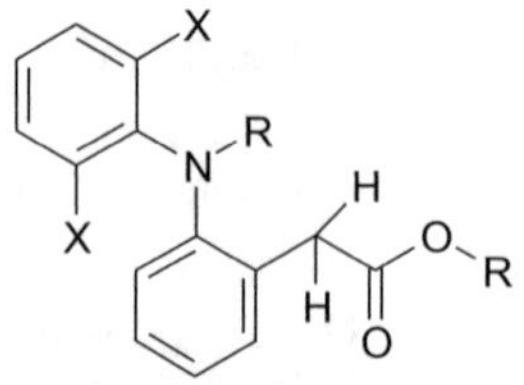

Fig. 1.8 Generic chemical
structure search query for
diclofenac

X = any halogen
R = anything
The two phenyl rings may be further substituted but not fused.

1.7.1.1 Diclofenac Chemical Structure Search Strategy

An example is described here for conducting a chemical structure-based search of
diclofenac as a gel formulation in a freedom-to-operate assessment. There are two
concepts to consider: the compound diclofenac and gel formulation. Figure 1.8
exemplifies the chemical structure search strategy on how one might conduct a
freedom-to-operate search for diclofenac. The second concept, gel formulations,
could be searched using full-text searching, classification schemes and other value-
added indexing described earlier in Sect. 1.6.

The compound diclofenac (2-[2-[(2,6-dichlorophenyl)amino]phenyl]acetic acid)
is marketed under several trade names, such as Voltaren and Cataflam. Trade names,
chemical names and synonyms would need to be identified and incorporated into the
search. There are many ways to identify these names, such as reading the compound
records found in Chemical Abstracts Registry File, Derwent World Patent Index, IFI
CLAIMS, Medline, Embase, and other free Internet sources. The compound registry
numbers of diclofenac applied by the database indexers would also be searched. An
initial keyword search for diclofenac in various databases could help identify some
of the value-added indexing and classifications available.

Searching for the exact compound alone is not sufficient for a freedom-to-operate
search since the search must also retrieve patents with broad claims that encompass
diclofenac, so a generic search query is needed. An example of a generic query that
encompasses diclofenac is shown in Fig. 1.8.

This generic query can be executed using the STN International system as
depicted in Fig. 1.9.

This query could be searched in any of the structure searchable databases [24]
hosted on STN such as registry, Derwent DCR, Beilstein and Marpat. Care must
be taken when creating a search query since designations of bond types, match
level, element count and connectivity can greatly alter the results. The above query
searched as a substructure search (SSS) on STN would allow for substitution
everywhere except at node 16, require the two rings to be isolated and allow for
retrieval of records in the Marpat database with broad claim language such as 'aryl'
for the phenyl rings and 'electron withdrawing group' for the halogens.

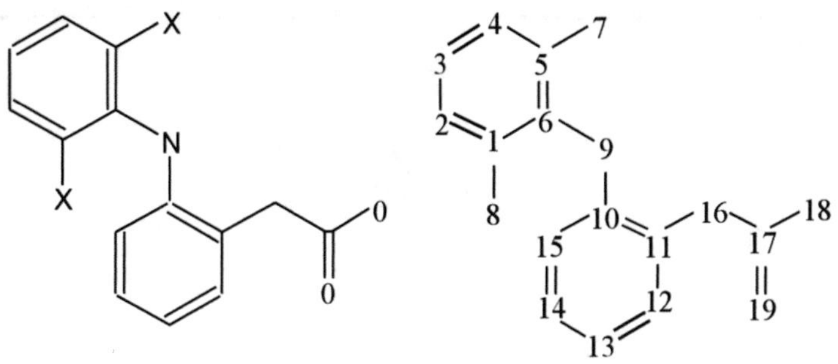

chain nodes :
7 8 9 16 17 18 19
ring nodes :
1 2 3 4 5 6 10 11 12 13 14 15
chain bonds :
1-8 5-7 6-9 9-10 11-16 16-17 17-18 17-19
ring bonds :
1-2 1-6 2-3 3-4 4-5 5-6 10-11 10-15 11-12 12-13 13-14 14-15
exact/norm bonds :
6-9 9-10 17-18 17-19
exact bonds :
1-8 5-7 11-16 16-17
normalized bonds :
1-2 1-6 2-3 3-4 4-5 5-6 10-11 10-15 11-12 12-13 13-14 14-15
isolated ring systems :
containing 1 : 10 :

Connectivity :
16:2 E exact RC ring/chain
Match level :
1:CLASS 2:CLASS 3:CLASS 4:CLASS 5:CLASS 6:CLASS 7:Any 8:Any 9:CLASS 10:CLASS
11:CLASS 12:CLASS 13:CLASS 14:CLASS 15:CLASS 16:CLASS 17:CLASS 18:CLASS
19:CLASS

Fig. 1.9 STN Express generic (genus) structure query for diclofenac

A searchable query for the above genus can also be executed using the Markush DARC system, as shown in Fig. 1.10.

The above query searched in Questel's Merged Markush System (MMS) [25] would allow for substitution everywhere except at node 14, require the two rings to be isolated and allow for retrieval of records that relate to compounds defined by the above generic either specifically or generically.

Chemical fragmentation code strategies should encompass the specific compound, as well as a generic representation. Figure 1.11 outlines a Derwent chemical fragmentation code strategy for diclofenac to be searched in the World Patent Index (DWPI) database [20]. Figure 1.12 illustrates the IFICDB [26] chemical fragmentation code search for diclofenac. The list of negation codes has been shortened due to space limitation.

Results from each of the above structure and chemical fragmentation code searches would be combined with the strategy for gel formulations, limited to patents or published patent applications, limited by country as requested and then limited by date to capture patents that are still in force.

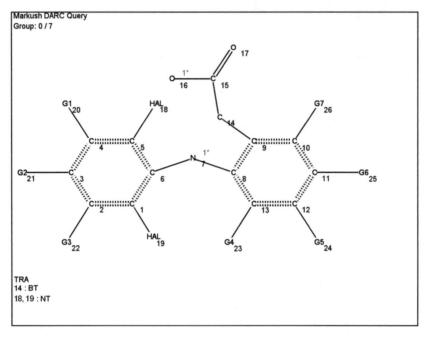

G1-G7:

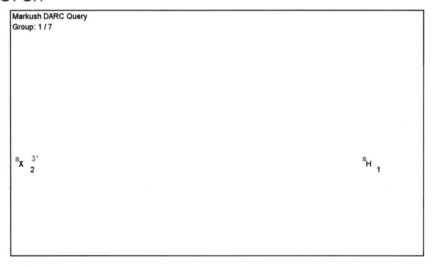

Fig. 1.10 Questel's MMS Markush Darc structure query for diclofenac

The above sample search strategy is not meant to be exhaustive, but rather to illustrate some of the common approaches taken when conducting a freedom-to-operate search that includes a chemical compound. Each type of search and each type of search system provides value. It is up to the searcher to determine which

```
=>S (G100(P)H141(P)H602(P)H608(P)J171(P)M414(P)M532)/M0,M2,M3 \>_line1
=>S _line1(P)(M121(P)M143)/M2,M3 \>_line2
=>S _line2(P)(M280(P)M311(P)M321(P)M342(P)M391(P)(M370 OR M372))/M2,M3 \>_line3
=>S _line3(P)(G011(P)G014(P)H102(P)H642(P)J011)/M2,M3 \>_line4
=>S (_line1(P)M900/M0) OR (_line2(P)M901/M2,M3) OR (_line3(P)M902/M2,M3) \>_line5
=>S _line5 OR _line4 \>_line6
=>S _line6(NOTP)(H2 OR H3 OR H4 OR H5 OR H7 OR H8 OR H9 OR J2 OR J3 OR J4)/M2,M3
\>_line7
=>S _line7(NOTP)(J5 OR J6 OR J9 OR K0)/M2,M3 \>_line8
```

Fig. 1.11 Derwent chemical fragmentation code strategy in WPI for diclofenac

```
S 30035/FG (L) 30047/FG (L) 30295/FG (L) 32742/FG (L) 34194/FG (L) 34701/FG (L) (10 or 20 or
30)/RL
S L1 (NOTL) 30037/FG (NOTL) 30040/FG (NOTL) 30039/FG (NOTL) 30038/FG
S L2 (NOTL) 34205/FG (NOTL) 30027/FG (NOTL) 34246/FG (NOTL) 31080/FG
[ 26 more lines of negation codes]
```

Fig. 1.12 IFICDB chemical fragmentation code strategy for diclofenac

type of searches and which search systems to use for any given search. Whenever possible, multiple databases and systems should be used since each system provides unique features, different coverage and different indexing policies. It is also not uncommon for a chemical search to retrieve a wide range of records depending on the databases and systems used. For example, 50 patent family and literature records might be retrieved from searching a structure query in various databases, while 1000 or more patent family records might be retrieved using fragmentation codes. The professional searcher must understand the details of how each of the systems works in order to explain and analyse these results properly.

In spite of recent advances in chemical structure searching, there are still many areas that could be improved. For example, it would be useful for analysis purposes to be able to search and retrieve records with compounds of interest that are specifically claimed versus compounds that are only disclosed in the specifications, or to search and retrieve records with compounds of interest that are only claimed generically. It should be noted also that the indexing conducted by database producers is applied to the basic member of a family and not to each subsequent family member added to a database record. Claim coverage can change from one document to another, so it would be helpful to have every family member indexed. And finally, chemical concentrations or percentages are currently not indexed, and often the novelty of an invention is not a particular compound but rather its concentration in a formulation.

In conclusion, some minimum requirements for an effective chemical structure retrieval system are nomenclature searching that includes generic descriptions, the ability to search by chemical structure and Markush searching. To be effective, the database must also provide details of its indexing policies and any changes over time.

1.7.2   Biosequences/Biotechnology Searching

As with other domain searches for patent and scientific literature, a professional patent searcher in biotechnology must be able to perform comprehensive text word searches and utilise controlled vocabulary terminology, classification schemes, sequence code match (SCM) techniques and algorithms for finding biosequence homology (similarity attributed to descent from a common ancestor [27]).

One of the difficulties for a biotechnology patent searcher is locating and compiling comprehensive data from many sources. Such information can be provided in different (non-) textual formats (articles, biological sequences, patent documents, tables summarising and comparing biological data, images of biological samples, graphics representing experiments, etc.) and scattered among many types of publications and databases or published directly through the Internet [28].

1.7.2.1   Nomenclature Challenge

Similar to chemical substance nomenclature, locating a gene or a protein name is a challenge due to various nomenclature systems, aliases and sources needed to be consulted. Genes can have several names, synonyms and redundant gene symbols. As an example, the human gene GBJ2 has several names and aliases/synonyms:

> Gene symbol: GBJ2
> Gene name: gap junction protein, beta 2, 26 kDa
> Previous gene symbols: DFNB1, DFNA3
> Previous gene names: gap junction protein, beta 2, 26 kD; connexin 26, gap
>   junction protein, beta 2, 26 kDa
> Gene aliases: CX26, NSRD1

Professional searchers must consider if they need to include genetic alleles (phenotypic gene variation, e.g. green vs. blue eyes), if the request is for a specific species' gene (mouse vs. human gene) and mutated gene names. The names of protein and peptides have similar nomenclature issues. Protein receptors and their ligands can have similar names that can result in false hit retrieval. Recombinant proteins will also have different names and designated abbreviations. Determining a comprehensive search hedge (a collection of search terms) of nucleic or protein names is important for intellectual property searches necessary to compliment a comprehensive biosequence search.

1.7.2.2 Biosequence Searching Considerations

Patent sequence information found in both commercial and public databases is not comprehensive [29]. A sequence of interest may or may not be disclosed in patent documents, necessitating the need for additional text word searches in combination with a biosequence search. Database inclusion of the sequences from a patent document is determined by the producer's indexing policies. A professional searcher will need to be aware of each system's indexing policies and limitations:

- Does the search system have a biosequence length limitation? Nucleic sequences are often long.
- Are all the sequences found in a patent publication indexed or are only the claimed sequences included in the database?
- What year did the publisher start including biosequences in their database?
- How are short biosequences indexed? Are the short sequences (<9 nucleic or amino acid units) included in the database as a sequence or is it necessary to search the biomolecule as a chemical structure?
- Mega sequence (containing many different sequences or a single extremely long sequence) patent documents may or may not be indexed in databases.

Biosequences are searched as either sequence code match (SCM) or as a homology search. In code match searches, the search system aligns the query search sequence codes against a database of sequences by the code of each nucleic/amino acid unit (e.g. see Fig. 1.13).

On the STN system, biosequences can be searched as an exact sequence search, matching the same code motifs and length. However, deoxyribonucleic acid (DNA) and proteins can tolerate changes in molecular structure without necessarily manifesting any biological significant consequences [30]. Other sequence search options should be utilised for both nucleic and amino acid molecules in order to introduce variability and retrieve biological functionally similar molecules. SCM allows subsequence search for the query sequence embedded in a larger nucleic or amino acid sequence. Amino acid sequences can also be searched as sequence family search. A family exact or family subsequence search will match the exact amino acid code or a functionally similar amino acid code. An example of a family group is the hydrophilic basic amino acids: arginine, histidine and lysine. Additional variability is introduced in the search query by utilising additional characters in the search string to represent uncommon or ambiguous amino acids or nucleic acids. Pattern search variability includes a defined set of nucleic/amino

```
Q:    1 MALWMRLLPLLALLALWGPDPAAAFVNQHLCGSHLVEALYLVCGERGFFYTPKTRREAED 60
        ||||||||||||||||||||||||||||||||||||||||||||||||||||||||||||
S:    1 MALWMRLLPLLALLALWGPDPAAAFVNQHLCGSHLVEALYLVCGERGFFYTPKTRREAED 60

Q:   61 LQVGQVELGGGPGAGSLQPLALEGSLQKRGIVEQCCTSICSLYQLENYCN 110
        |||||||||||||||||||||||||||||||||||||||||||||||||
S:   61 LQVGQVELGGGPGAGSLQPLALEGSLQKRGIVEQCCTSICSLYQLENYCN 110
```

Fig. 1.13 Code match search

Table 1.3 Types of biosequence searches

Search type	Nucleic sequence	Amino acid sequence
Exact sequence	X	X
Subsequence	X	X
Family exact or family subsequence	–	X
Motif or pattern sequence	X	X

acids that can replace a select motif, allow a range of nucleic/amino acid residues in unknown region (gaps), cause negation of defined nucleic/amino acids or allow the professional searcher to designate a number or a range of nucleic/amino acids or gaps to repeat within the larger sequence [31]. Biosequence search types are listed in Table 1.3.

Homology biosequence searches are utilised to discover nucleic and amino acid sequences that are biologically related or have a similar sequence composition. Several algorithms exist with different sensitivity levels and processing speed, and the two that professional searchers use are FASTA and Basic Local Alignment Search Tool (BLAST) available in both commercial and publically available Web databases. Both algorithms work based upon the calculation of homology between a query sequence and retrieved sequences; hence, both tools retrieve homologous sequences, which might be biologically related to the query sequence [32]. However, sequence patent claims are often written as fragments of specific sequences, which are based on % identity and/or length of certain amino acid regions [32]. GenomeQuest's GenePAST/Fragment search is based on GenomeQuest proprietary algorithm, which is defined as 'The GenePAST percent identity' that finds the best fit between the query sequence and the subject sequence and expresses the alignment as an exact percentage [33].

1.7.2.3   GBJ2 Biosequence Search Strategy

An example is described here on a sequence freedom-to-operate assessment based upon the genetic sequence of gap juncture protein beta 2 (GBJ2) and the protein for therapeutic use. GBJ2 may have a genetic component in hereditary deafness. The search can be accomplished by utilising nucleotide sequence and amino acid homologous sequence searches. The professional searcher should consider additional search types, such as full-text, classification and value-added indexing searches for comprehension. There are publically available gene and protein database to assist the searcher in locating the gene and protein biosequences, names and synonyms, if necessary. Databases on National Center of Biotechnology Information, European Bioinformatics Institute, DNA Data Bank of Japan, The Jackson Laboratory and other Web-based sites are helpful in locating data and information on genes and proteins for search preparation.

Execution of biosequence homology searches would ideally be completed on publically available Web sites and commercial databases. However, in many industrial companies, transmitting sequence data over the Internet is prohibited, so commercial databases are searched. Prior to the search, the professional will need to determine the relevant percent identity of similarity and the sequence length that is appropriate. BLAST and FASTA algorithms were designed for biological researchers and their needs, not for patent searchers, and should be considered when analysing the retrieval. If the biosequence is less than 30 residues in length, BLAST options need to be adjusted to retrieve the best hits, along with other sequence search strategies.

Homology sequence search is not comprehensive for a freedom-to-operate request. The search may need to cover genetic variants, chemically modified sequences, mutations and claims that discuss similar biological function but without a disclosed sequence. As with other patent searching, the biosequence search should include keyword or text-based, enhanced indexing, full-text and classification strategies. The above strategy is not meant to represent a comprehensive search but rather to illustrate factors to consider in constructing a search strategy.

Biosequence searching has improved in comprehensiveness of available data. However, there is a demand to include more sequence data from the whole patent document. It is not unusual to find the sequence of interest in a patent diagram. Comprehensive sequence data from every patent family member, not just the basic patent, is desirable from all database producers. USGENE includes sequence information from all the US patent family members and has increased patent biosequence data availability generated from the US Patent Office. Finally, searchers and patent analysts require additional similarity algorithms, which have the capability to search biosequences and deliver similarity scores in alignment with how claims are crafted.

In conclusion, biosequence databases contain incomplete information and necessitate searching biosequences found in patent and scientific literature in both commercial and, if allowed, publicly available sources and systems. Complementing biosequence search with text-based search strategies is important for comprehensive retrieval and intellectual property analysis. In addition, a professional searcher needs to have an understanding and working knowledge of the indexing policies and limitations of each database.

1.7.3   Searching Device/Engineering Drawings

The retrieval of patent information within the disciplines of engineering, and more specifically the mechanical/electrical fields of engineering, is a case study in the application of the 'No Free Lunch' theory [34]. The application of this premise to patent information retrieval is very clearly visible in the methodologies a professional patent searcher uses in locating art of relevance. From an initial keyword-based search limited to abstracts to full classification searches to multigenerational citation analysis to combining focused keywords with classification ranges, all of the algorithms used by a searcher are performed to search and retrieve more efficiently.

What is most overwhelming to an outsider used to the relative ease of locating information based upon words is the volume of references that are traditionally reviewed by a patent searcher within the engineering disciplines. For a single, relatively simple project, a mechanical patent searcher may manually review upwards of 5000 patent documents to locate a mere ten of particular relevance (manual review denotes a physical eyeballing of all figures, not a title-based review of the document). And why is this? Because traditional search engines and the algorithms employed are very inefficient in the engineering arts, which are heavily dependent upon drawings to clearly convey a concept.

While a physical picture may clearly show a car bumper, the text of a patent may describe a safety device for the protection of people or objects, said safety device utilising multiple materials, said multiple materials comprising a rigid material and one or more less rigid materials, said rigid material selected from plastics and foam and said less rigid materials selected from plastics and foam. The picture may be recognised by a patent searcher in less than 3/10 of a second as external to motor vehicle, while the text could be parsed dozens of times for some hint as to whether they intended a bumper, an internal padded vehicle component, a helmet or even shin guards for a soccer player.

The single biggest issue that causes this inefficiency and must always be noted with regard to search and retrieval of engineering drawings is that while 'a picture may speak a thousand words', it also does so in such a direct and succinct manner. In contrast, the mundane and simple can easily be transformed into the obtuse and unclear by a quality wordsmith or lexicographer (typically the patent attorney/agent). Therefore, to avoid the dependency upon words, a searcher of patent information in the mechanical/electrical engineering disciplines learns to rely upon additional tools or algorithms for the location of relevant documents combined with rapid vetting via image analysis. These other algorithms are classification schemes described in Sect. 1.6.1, classification limited by keywords and citation analysis. Then, using a circular flow path to emphasise the iterative process of searching, multiple iterations will be performed to locate the documents of relevance.

An additional important means for removing the dependency upon words within the mechanical and electrical engineering disciplines is the formulation of specific search strategies. Most inventions or improvements lend themselves to a formulaic combination of features: (A) specific field of technology, (B) problem to be solved and (C) solution to be applied.

An ideal reference will encompass A, B and C. Of almost equal relevance will be the subcombinations of A, B and C (A and B, A and C, B and C). This is particularly true when setting up a search strategy or field of search. For example, when C (solution to be applied) is best represented by a picture or figure, a search strategy must be set up to search for all documents with A (technology field) and B (problem to be solved). Those with C will inherently be included and only by manual review will C be recognised and identified.

Going further down the thought pattern, often multiple features (e.g. B and C) are poorly defined by anything other than a picture. Then a professional searcher must manually review all references within A (the field of technology) and examine the figures to identify those of interest to B and/or C. This is also the ideal time to apply our first mentioned means (classification, classification limited by keywords and citations) to avoid the dependency upon words, and these are further detailed below.

How Is Classification Used: Using the example above regarding a car bumper, the US classification schedule has a class (293) labelled 'vehicle fenders'. With this class 293, a range of subclasses in an outline format running from 102 to 155 is labelled 'buffer or bumper type'. What this means is that all patents classified in class 293/subclass 102 to class 293/subclass 155 are primarily focused upon vehicle fenders and specifically on buffer or bumpers (approximately 7000 documents). And more specifically, subclass 120 depends on the broad subclass 102 and is titled 'composite bumper' which very closely reads upon the plastic and foam combination of rigid and less rigid materials. Thus, a review of the documents in class 293/subclass 120 will put over 700 documents of high relevance in front of a professional patent searcher without using a single keyword limitation.

How Is Classification Limited by Keywords Used: Again using the bumper sample, the International Patent Classification (IPC) for bumpers, which corresponds to the abovementioned US Classification Range 293/102–155, is B60R19/02–19/50. More specifically, subclasses 19/03 reads on composite bumpers, 19/18 reads on impact absorbing and 19/22 expressly reads upon a 'bumper containing cellular material, e.g. solid foam'. While subclass 19/22 should probably be reviewed in its entirety, the other two subclasses (19/03 and 19/18) will not be as relevant to the inventive concept. Instead, those two subclasses are searched using the Boolean operator 'AND' along with the term 'foam' to garner a higher precision search [e.g. (B60R19/03 OR B60R19/18) AND 'foam']. This allows the classification scheme to weed out the soccer shin guards and helmets, which may use the same terms as this bumper invention.

How Is Citation Analysis Used: When a patent of relevance is located, it does not stand on an island by itself. Like the vast majority of advances in science and development, a patent is a baby step forward. By reviewing the art cited within the prosecution history of the patent (back citing), one can see the baby steps that preceded a particular improvement. Likewise, by reviewing all patents prosecuted after the patent of relevance (forward citing), one can see the baby steps that proceeded from a particular improvement. Performing this operation in a sideways manner (a forward cite followed by a back cite or a backward cite followed by a forward cite), one can locate parallel art to the patent of relevance.

How Are Iterations Used: An initial keyword-based search should be performed to learn about proper classification areas. Classification areas must be reviewed to learn new terms within the art. Forward and backward citation must be performed to learn both new terms within the art and new classification areas. Broad

Table 1.4 An example of the search process for device/engineering drawings

Step	Action	References manually reviewed
1	Simple keyword search limited to titles or abstracts	300
2	Class/subclasses combined with focused keywords	700
3	Forward and backward citation searches	500
4	Medium complexity keyword search	1000
5	Class/subclasses combined with looser keywords	300
6	Class/subclasses in their entirety	500
7	Highly complex keyword search	500
8	Additional forward and backward citation searches	500
9	Class/subclass ranges combined with focused keywords	500
10	Final forward and backward citation searches	200
	Total	5000

classifications combined with keywords must be performed to locate art that may not have been properly placed in a subclass. Further keyword searching should be performed to locate art outside the proper classification areas entirely.

It is important to note that all algorithms must be tried. Only after doing so will the most efficient algorithm be identified (similar to the identification of mathematical benchmarks by Wolpert and Macready [34]). At that point, additional resources may be assigned to the more efficient algorithms. Additionally, algorithms outside the basics identified above may be pursued depending upon the technology and nature of the information to be retrieved. These could encompass inventor searches, assignee searches (owner of the patent) and geographic searches (e.g. looking for pachinko machines should probably focus on Japan).

With these basic algorithms for identifying relevant documents summarised, it must be noted with large and bold letters that image retrieval is the key. While one may start with general algorithms and carefully make algorithms more efficient through iterations, one can only identify the information of relevance through the use of rapid image retrieval.

A simplified example of the search process that would take a professional patent searcher 6–8 h (this is using an engine with no image retrieval delays—e.g. a patent office in-house system) is shown in Table 1.4.

1.8 Conclusion

Patent search, analysis and monitoring are business critical, yet very time-consuming tasks that are performed primarily by manual means. A proper search methodology will include usage of the major search mechanisms outlined above, will be well planned in advance, will exhaustively leverage the information collections appropriate for the search and will use a constantly iterative approach. In this chapter, we have attempted to describe the practical experiences in and requirements for effective searching, analysis, monitoring and overall management of patent information, from the perspective of patent information professionals. While databases and tools have long been supporting this process, advanced technologies are emerging to address age-old issues such as database quality as well as tackle new challenges [35]. These new challenges include:

- Traditionally neglected issue of multilingualism and increasing volume of patent applications
- Wider variety of users from different backgrounds with various interests ranging from scientific and legal to business
- Expansion of patent information use to explore new technical and business opportunities in addition to the traditional IP protection approaches

We hope that this chapter has contributed towards an understanding of the current searching practices, systems and tools that would help in the further development of emerging retrieval technologies to assist the user in patent search, analysis and information management processes.

While new technology tools may greatly advance the patent search, analysis and monitoring processes, it is important to be reminded that tools simply assist and cannot replace the human mind. A good patent searcher is knowledgeable not only about the intricacies of different types of patent searching but also the changing requirements of international patent laws, technical innovations and current developments in the different types of information sources available. The central role of the patent searcher continues to be essential in balancing the search requirements for recall and precision and for insightful analysis of the results.

The following chapters will investigate many of the topics addressed in this introduction in addition to many more to provide a comprehensive cross section of the many challenges patent information retrieval faces today.

References

1. United States Patent & Trademark Office. (1977). Eighth Technology Assessment and Forecast Report. Section II: 37. http://www.ntis.gov. Accessed 10 July 2010. NTIS Order Number PB 276375
2. Yang Y et al (2010) Enhancing patent landscape analysis with visualization output. World Patent Inf. doi:10.1016/j.wpi
3. Yang Y et al (2008) Text mining and visualization tools – Impressions of emerging technologies. World Patent Inf 30:280–293
4. van Staveren M (2009) Prior art searching on the internet: further insights. World Patent Inf 31:54–56
5. Hantos S (2010) Helping others acquire, license, or invest in patents with confidence – A guide for patent searchers to patent due diligence. World Patent Inf 32:188–197
6. Simmons E (2001) Patents. In: Armstrong CJ, Large JA (eds) Manual of online search strategies, 3rd edn. Gower, Aldershot

7. Adams S (2006) Information sources in patents. In: McIlwaine IC et al (eds) Guides to information sources. De Gruyter Saur, Munich
8. Simmons E (2006) Patents (literature). Kirk-Othmer encyclopedia of chemical technology, 5th edn. 18:197–276
9. Alberts D (2008) The ever-changing role of information professionals in pharmaceutical R&D. World Patent Inf 30:233–237
10. Adams S (2000) Using the International Patent Classification in an online environment. World Patent Inf 22(4):291–300
11. Adams S (2001) Comparing the IPC and the US classification systems for the patent searcher. World Patent Inf 23(1):15–23
12. World Intellectual Property Office. http://www.wipo.int/classifications/ipc/en. Accessed 10 July 2010
13. US Patent & Trademark Office. http://www.uspto.gov/web/patents/classification/selecttnumwithtitle.htm. Accessed 10 July 2010
14. European Patent Office. http://v3.espacenet.com/eclasrch?.&locale=en_ep&classification=ecla. Accessed 10 July 2010
15. Schellner I (2002) Japanese file index classification and F-terms. World Patent Inf 23:197–201
16. Adams S (2010) The text, the full text and nothing but the text: Part 1 – Standards for creating textual information in patent documents and general search implications. World Patent Inf 32:22–29
17. Adams S (2010) The text, the full text and nothing but the text: Part 2 – The main specification, searching challenges and survey of availability. World Patent Inf 32:120–128
18. Hunt D, Nguyen L, Rodgers M (2007) Patent searching. Tools and techniques. Wiley, Hoboken, NJ, pp 72–74
19. Chemical Abstracts Service (CAS) Registry. http://www.cas.org/expertise/cascontent/registry/index.html. Accessed 10 July 2010
20. Derwent World Patent Index. http://thomsonreuters.com/products_services/legal/legal_products/intellectual_property/DWPI?parentKey=442831. Accessed 10 July 2010
21. IFI Claims Patent Services. http://www.ificlaims.com/searchaids_chemterms.html. Accessed 10 July 2010
22. Austin R (2001) The complete Markush structure search: mission impossible? PIUG Northeast Workshop. http://www.stn-international.com/uploads/tx_ptgsarelatedfiles/piug1.pdf. Accessed 10 July 2010
23. Simmons E (1991) The grammar of Markush structure searching: vocabulary vs. syntax. J Chem Inf Comput Sci 31:45–53
24. STN Structure Searching Cluster Databases. http://www.cas.org/support/stngen/clusters/structure.html. Accessed 10 July 2010
25. Questel Merged Markush Service. http://www.questel.com/Prodsandservices/mms_chemistry.htm. Accessed 10 July 2010
26. IFI Comprehensive Database. http://stneasy.cas.org/dbss/help.IFICDB.html. Accessed 10 July 2010
27. National Center for Biotechnology Information BLAST Glossary. http://www.ncbi.nlm.nih.gov/Education/BLASTinfo/glossary2.html. Accessed 20 July 2010
28. Falciola L (2009) Searching biotechnology information: a case study. World Patent Inf 31:36–47
29. Andree PJ (2008) A comparative study of patent sequence databases. World Patent Inf 30:300–308
30. Sheiness D (1996) Patenting gene sequences. J Patent Trademark Off Soc 78:121–137
31. Brown J (2010) STN international presentations on databases and products. http://www.stn-international.com/fileadmin/be_user/STN/pdf/presentations/res_IPsearching_0806.pdf. Accessed 17 July 2010
32. Yoo H (2005) Intellectual property management of biosequence information from a patent searching perspective. World Patent Inf 27:203–211
33. GenomeQuest Search Strategies (2009) In: GenomeQuest user manual. 5.2 edn

34. Wolpert DH, Macready WG (1995) No free lunch theorems for search. Technical Report SFI-TR-95-02-010. Santa Fe Institute
35. Bonino D, Ciaramella A, Corno F (2010) Review of the state-of-the-art in patent information and forthcoming evolutions in intelligent patent informatics. World Patent Inf 32:30–38

Chapter 2
An Introduction to Contemporary Search Technology

Mihai Lupu, Florina Piroi, and Veronika Stefanov

Abstract This chapter is the counterpart of the preceding chapter. It gives an overview of some of the most important terms and concepts used in search technology and information retrieval (IR) today. We hope it can be useful to readers who are not researchers in these areas. After a short dip into the history of the field, we start with a high level overview of the different types of search, then move on to the gap between user requirements and how search systems can be evaluated and finally narrow it down to the main evaluation methodology used today. This is followed by a step-by-step guide to the architectural components of a generic fulltext document search system and its design implications. We then describe how the underlying models define to a large extent what the system can and cannot do. This chapter concludes with a short introduction to semantic search and an outlook to the challenges in patent IR, the main subject of this book.

2.1 Search Technologies and Information Retrieval

We have called this chapter 'Introduction to Contemporary Search Technology' rather than, for example, 'Introduction to Information Retrieval' because the subject of information retrieval as a whole is very broad and some of it is of little or no interest to those involved with practical patent search.

Information retrieval might be defined as the science *and* technology of searching for and accessing information in documents, or in parts of documents. This

---

M. Lupu • F. Piroi (✉)
TU Wien, Vienna, Austria
e-mail: mihai.lupu@tuwien.ac.at; lupu@ifs.tuwien.ac.at; florina.piroi@tuwien.ac.at

V. Stefanov
TU Wien, Wien, Austria
e-mail: veronika.stefanov@tuwien.ac.at

© Springer-Verlag GmbH Germany 2017   47
M. Lupu et al. (eds.), *Current Challenges in Patent Information Retrieval*,
The Information Retrieval Series 37, DOI 10.1007/978-3-662-53817-3_2

definition by Manning et al. [32] can be useful to see the core as well as the whole area:

> Information Retrieval is finding material (usually documents) of an unstructured nature (usually text) that satisfies an information need from within large collections (usually stored on computers).

It is a classic scientific endeavour, with both theoretical and experimental (or perhaps better empirical) branches, and a well-established scientific paradigm subscribed to by many in the field, whether in the universities or the industry. The scientific aspect has always (since the 1940s or 1950s) been closely related to (or perhaps even generated by) a practical engineering aspect which seeks to deliver operational systems, and of course these operational systems have very wide use and implications through, for example, well-known Internet search engines like Google and Microsoft's Bing.

In other areas, there is a well-recognised terminological distinction between the scientific and technological aspects: for example, between physics (science) and mechanical or electrical engineering (technology). As is all too often the case in computing, information retrieval is unfortunately a portmanteau term for both the scientific and engineering aspects.

This is not to say that the practical patent searcher might not find the science of information retrieval useful. Over the years, theoretical considerations, supported by many empirical studies in IR, have led to surprising results about which technologies are the most effective for search, and these of course should help practitioners reflect on and improve their practice. Information retrieval owes its origins to nineteenth-century library science (e.g. see Schrettinger [49]), but was inspired and transformed by the development of computerised 'mechanised' information systems after World War II, and perhaps especially by Vannevar Bush's prescient Memex article [9]. The first use we can find of the name information retrieval is by Mooers in 1950 [34] who was, incidentally, an early and vocal critic of the use of Boolean Logic (as opposed to ranking) in search technology systems [35]. Boolean retrieval, of course, despite this, remains the mainstay of practical patent search. In fact, the early systems would invariably be described today as searching metadata: typically the data they searched was author, title, some index terms or keywords, and perhaps an abstract: it was only in the 1960s or even 1970s that it became commonplace to analyse and index (and therefore make searchable) the fulltext of the document. As a consequence, in practice the field is principally driven by experimental work. Prime amongst this was the work by Cleverdon and others at the Cranfield Institute of Technology in England in the 1960s [12, 13], which continues to be influential (see also Chaps. 3 and 4 in this volume, on CLEF-IP and NTCIR, respectively, or Carterette in the previous edition of this volume [11]).

It is worth noting that patent search has been an application of interest from the earliest days of information retrieval, although in the early literature it is sometimes difficult to distinguish between computerised information retrieval and the use of older mechanical sorting and selection devices, like card sorters.

A complete survey of search technology, let alone information retrieval as a whole, goes beyond the scope of this chapter (or the whole volume). There are now a wide range of textbook introductions to the subject ([10, 32], etc.), although generally they focus on Web search.

By way of introduction to the rest of the chapter, a couple of points are worth making, which might surprise patent searchers.

First, it is the accepted wisdom of the information retrieval research community, based on a significant body of experimental evidence accumulated over many years, that ranked retrieval systems are more effective than Boolean or other structured query systems. That is, systems experiments almost always show that familiar set-based Boolean retrieval systems are less effective than systems, which present the searcher with a list of potentially relevant documents ordered, with the most likely to be relevant first, then the next most likely to be relevant and so on towards progressively less relevant documents. We will return to this later in the chapter. This has been extensively documented in an independent study on the economic effects of retrieval evaluation benchmarks performed by the National Institute of Standards and Technology [44].

Second, a recent insight has been that retrieval from very large (Web scale, petabyte scale) collections of documents may be different in kind from retrieval from smaller-scale collections. The reasons for this remain unknown at the present time, but may be the result of the pervasive nature of phenomena matching Zipf's law (see [4] for more).

At the same time, the IR academic community has also in recent years put more distinct emphasis on domain-specific search [31] and on 'slow search' [51, 52] as a counterweight to the millisecond, high-precision retrieval characteristic of Web search.

As noted above, experimental work is the hallmark of IR research. Therefore, rather than diving into the technology, in the next section we give a brief introduction to IR evaluation, as a central element in any experimental procedure.

2.2 Finding a Search Technology that Works for You

There are many ways of looking at the variety of IR systems: from an information theory perspective, a historical perspective, a systems engineering perspective and an IR researcher's or a librarian's perspective. We begin with the final purpose for which such systems are designed: searching and finding what you are looking for.

Which techniques and tools are useful greatly varies with the type of search task. In fact, searching can take many different forms. One way of structuring them could be according to the following types [36, 45]:

Known-item search: The user is searching for an information object which is already known to them. Also known as direct search.

Exploratory search: The user is seeking to learn about a topic but does not know in advance what may be important.

Browsing: The goal is unclear; the user is not sure whether or how the requirements can be met.

Exhaustive search: The user is trying to learn everything about a particular topic.

Only the first type, known-item search, is fully supported by classic search systems. The information need is well defined and can be expressed by the user (subject terms are known, maybe also the author, document type, creation date, etc.), and the correct answer may be found with no or very few iterations.

In an exploratory search, the user cannot provide an exact query at the beginning and so will be confronted with a large amount of potentially interesting results. The approach will be very iterative, with the user needing to review the results of every step to refine the query, gradually learning about the topic. Supporting functionality such as aggregation and visualisation of search results as well as automated query rewriting can support the user.

Browsing can take advantage of links inherent to the document collection, such as weblinks or citations. If users have a fairly good idea of what they are looking for, following link pathways allows them to refine their perception of their information need.

Exhaustive search enjoys only very limited support from any existing IR system. The requirements on both the users (in terms of background knowledge) and the system performance are high. Nevertheless, exhaustive searching is an everyday requirement in many domains (law, patents, medicine, intelligence).

2.2.1 Can You Choose the Best IR System?

How can you choose an IR system for your tasks? How do you test and compare? The first thing most people probably do is to give a system some test queries and look at the results. But how can you judge whether these documents are the best matches in the whole collection? The sad answer is that the only way to really know would be to look at all documents in the whole collection and check. For any meaningful IR situation, this is not feasible (if the collection is small and you know all the documents in it, you don't need a retrieval system...).

One way of looking at it could be to assume that if many people use many systems over a long time, certain trends might become apparent. They might stop using less useful systems and switch to the systems that save them time and effort, meaning that users actually vote with their feet (or computer mice).[1] But is the most widely used system also the best *for you*? How do users choose?

Professional users have to choose from tools they might buy, and this can be done with trial licences or calls for bids to system vendors. They also often don't have a real choice (lack of information, prohibitive switching costs from vendor lock-in, licensing, knowledge/training investment, etc.). As criteria for selecting patent

---

[1]This seems to have happened in the late 1990s between Web search engines. Those that viewed Web sites as plain text documents were replaced by search engines that used the links between sites to choose those that were most likely more useful to more people. The quality of the search results using link analysis was so much better that people switched.

search tools, for example, the data coverage, document delivery, import and export functions and the company behind the tool are equally important if not more than the pure retrieval effectiveness [19].

For some systems, it is possible to infer user satisfaction metrics from secondary values. Ad revenues, e-commerce deals or measures of returning users can be meaningful for Web-based applications, whereas enterprise search solutions try to measure productivity gains.

Professional users know their use cases intimately. They can focus on just their own needs and ignore all other issues, which in turn allows them to select tools for their work.

2.2.2 User Knows Best: User-Centred Evaluation

The final overall test of a system is the usefulness to its users. User-centred evaluations can be and are being done, but they are expensive and difficult to do correctly for a number of reasons [22, 24]:

1. A large, representative sample of actual users is needed.
2. Each system must be equally well developed and must have a user interface.
3. Each participant must be equally well trained on each system.
4. The learning effect must be controlled for (the fact that a user that tests a system learns about that system and adapts to it).

Because of these issues, real user-centred evaluation is rare, which has led to a certain unfortunate lack of communication and feedback between IR researchers and those who might potentially use their search systems. Some specific ways forward for patent search are explored in Trippe and Ruthven's chapter in this volume (Chap. 5).

In a more general context, the usability of a system is a compound of three aspects: its effectiveness, its efficiency and user satisfaction [23]. The last element is the one that attempts to quantify user preferences and perspectives on the system and therefore the one that cannot be scaled up or generalised. The efficiency is on the other hand the most easily quantifiable: it is primarily about how fast the system is, how many (computational) resources it uses and how many requests it is able to handle in any given unit of time. Finally, effectiveness—the ability of the system to provide documents according to a specified relevance criteria—is the component most commonly evaluated (because it can be done in a 'laboratory' environment) and the one we will focus on now.

2.2.3   Laboratory Tests: The Cranfield Model

Already in the early days of computer-based IR, researchers devised testing methods that can be likened to laboratory tests in other scientific areas. They ignore a large amount of the 'noise' and ambiguities of the real use cases and allow for empirical, reproducible tests that yield quantitative results on large amounts of data. The so-called Cranfield tests, named after the place where they were conducted in the 1960s, led to the main evaluation methodology still used today. The remainder of this section discusses evaluation methodologies within the Cranfield paradigm in more detail.

For such an evaluation, the following items are needed:

- A suitable collection of documents
- Some (representative) queries on this collection
- For every query, a list of documents from the collection (ideally a complete list) that are relevant (the relevance judgements)

Given this information, automated tests can be run to compare the actual results with the target results and quantify the differences.

For the particular case of IR in the patent domain, the first requirement, a suitable collection of documents, is the easiest to fulfil. In the last 5 years the amount of patent documents freely available has increased dramatically, thanks to either direct distribution (e.g. USPTO via Google) or public APIs (e.g. Open Patent Service at the EPO). While access to other national publications is still problematic, there exist sufficient documents in most languages to make testing meaningful. However, the second and especially the third requirement are the real hurdles to large-scale testing.

How are the relevance judgements produced? The gold standard is manually judged results, for which a large number of highly skilled and motivated judges are needed. Ideally, all relevant documents are collected beforehand for all test queries. Apart from the fact that for many queries there simply is no 'right' answer, research has also shown that human judges tend to disagree in what they find relevant [48].

Additionally, new test queries have to be found for every laboratory comparison of two or more systems to ensure fair conditions as well as to avoid over-optimisation of the systems to the training set. It is not surprising that many approaches have been developed over the last decades that are able to create relevance judgements automatically from the collection and the queries. These values are tainted with uncertainty, but are still useful for many types of evaluation, which otherwise could not be performed at all. Chapters 3 and 4 describe how in the area of patent information retrieval evaluation, the citations contained in the documents can be used to obtain usable relevance judgements. While it is well known that the citations do not represent a complete list of relevant documents to any particular document, studies of the evaluation procedures have shown that, even in the presence of such incomplete judgements, the results are reliable when deciding which of two or more systems is likely to perform best in the future [14].

2.2.3.1   Evaluation Conferences

The Cranfield paradigm forms the basis for a number of long-standing evaluation conferences, where the organisers provide the data, queries and relevance judgements. The efforts of TREC,[2] CLEF,[3] NTCIR,[4] and FIRE[5] have improved the situation of IR evaluation greatly by providing researchers not only with urgently needed data and frameworks but also with a community of comparable research [40]. Within this volume one can read more about activities focused on patent search in Chaps. 3 and 4, describing relevant evaluation campaigns at CLEF and NTCIR, while in the first edition of this book, readers learn about TREC [30] and the general aspects of IR evaluation [11]. Attempts to foster the direct interaction between creators of retrieval systems and patent information professionals, such as the PatOlympics[6] organised in 2010 and 2011, are interesting events for both parties, but are difficult to organise at either scientific conferences or commercial gatherings.

2.2.4   Quantifying the Difference: IR Measures

Assuming that the three requirements have been taken care of and the experiments have been conducted, how should the difference between the actual results and the target results then be analysed? It helps to know the goals of the system to be able to select substantive values. The Cranfield tests established desirable characteristics of an IR system—precision and recall—which are at the heart of every IR evaluation.

2.2.4.1   Precision and Recall

Precision looks at how many 'wrong' documents were caught together with the right ones, while recall looks at how many 'right' documents were missed. Both are numbers between 0 and 1 (often expressed as percentages), where 1 is best.

$$Precision = \frac{\text{number of relevant items retrieved}}{\text{number of items retrieved}} \tag{2.1}$$

$$Recall = \frac{\text{number of relevant items retrieved}}{\text{number of relevant items}} \tag{2.2}$$

---

[2]Text REtrieval Conference (TREC), http://trec.nist.gov/.
[3]Conference and Labs of the Evaluation Forum (CLEF), http://www.clef-initiative.eu/.
[4]NII Test Collection for IR Systems (NTCIR) Project, http://research.nii.ac.jp/ntcir/index-en.html.
[5]Forum for Information Retrieval Evaluation (FIRE), http://www.isical.ac.in/~clia/.
[6]PatOlympics Interactive Patent Retrieval Competition, http://www.ir-facility.org/events/irf-symposium/irf-symposium-2011/patolympics.

Table 2.1 Precision is 0.67; recall is 0.5

Relevant documents	Retrieved documents
A	A
B	B
C	E
D	

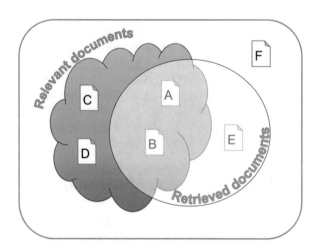

Fig. 2.1 Illustrating Table 2.1: Recall compares the overlap (A, B) to the *whole dark area* (A,B,C,D), precision compares the overlap to the *whole white area* (A, B, E)

A precision of 0.8 means that for every four correct documents in the result list there is a mistaken one that is not relevant to the query. A recall of 0.8 on the other hand tells you that the result list contains only 80 % of all the documents that should have been retrieved (see also Table 2.1 and Fig. 2.1 for another example).

You can view them as measures of false positives (also known as type I error or α error) and false negatives (also known as type II error or β error). They only make sense together, as it is trivial to increase just one of them,[7] and they are usually contradictory in the sense that tools that increase precision tend to negatively affect recall and vice versa. This is best observed if we plot a so-called precision–recall curve as in Fig. 2.2. As the size of the retrieved set of documents increases, recall tends to increase and precision to decrease.

For most systems, it is generally unknown which levels of recall and precision they can achieve. For commercial search tools, no published evaluations exist. For the academic systems that are submitted to evaluation conferences, the results must be taken with caution. It lies in the nature of the Cranfield paradigm that the absolute values of the evaluation measures are not meaningful by themselves. They can only

[7]How do you reach a 'perfect' recall of 1.0? Put the whole collection in the result set.
How do you achieve a very high precision? Limit the result set to just a few documents.

Fig. 2.2 Synthetic example
of a precision–recall curve

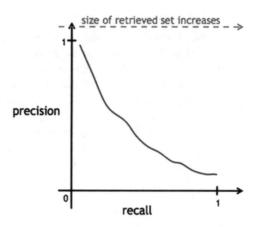

be used to compare different runs on the same test setup. Unfortunately this also means that the results obtained at an evaluation conference in a year cannot be directly compared to the previous year, although all the major evaluation campaigns have maximising reproducibility as a goal [7, 8].

2.2.4.2   Beyond Precision and Recall

Recall and precision work on sets and have no notion of ranking [50]. Since ranked result lists are a common feature of search systems and the quality of the ranking greatly influences the quality of the result for the users, derived measures had to be found. The precision–recall curve was one of the first to address this, as the ranking is in fact implicit behind the two axes of the plot. How to best calculate this curve was a matter of significant discussion since the 1960s and a well-documented report of these earlier efforts can be found in Chap. 7 of Van Rijsbergen's seminal book on information retrieval [54].

The precision–recall curve, while it is still being used every now and then, does not meet one of the initial desiderata for IR evaluation metrics: to be a single number (in order to make comparisons between systems univocal). However, if one has two curves and desires a single value to meaningfully compare them, one can use the area under each curve as a measure.

Nowadays, a commonly used measure is the *mean average precision* (MAP). The precision value is different depending on how far down the result list you look. Average precision (AP) is the average of all precision values at the point where each relevant document is found in the ranked list. MAP is the mean of the average precisions for a group of queries, since the values can depend heavily on the queries. MAP is an approximation of the area under the precision–recall curve [32].

Additionally, since many use cases favour recall over precision or vice versa, metrics matching these requirements can be used. For a stronger focus on precision, metrics that only look at a smaller amount of documents at the top of the list are useful, whereas for recall-oriented cases, it can help to measure the precision at a given level of recall, which would indicate how many wrong documents the user will encounter before the desired recall is reached. Chapter 3 of the first edition of this book contains examples of more advanced measures.

Interested readers taking a look at the proceedings of IR conferences and evaluation workshops will find advanced charts and tables comparing these measures [29, 43]. It is usually not intuitively understandable what the results 'mean' for every day search tasks. Compared to the types of tasks outlined above, the Cranfield type evaluations do not represent iterative or complex searches. It is possible to evaluate individual supporting methodologies such as query rewriting methods by comparing the results of the original query to the modified one, but anything that resembles users extracting information from one result and applying it to the next query while using information from a third source cannot be represented in this model, although there have been recent attempts to overcome this problem [6]. In fact, new evaluation metrics are constantly proposed and a valid question is then *what makes a good metric?* The answer is threefold:

1. Appropriateness to the task: as stated before, some tasks require focus on precision, while others on recall; the new metric must strike the right balance for the task.
2. Metric stability: the decisions to prefer a system versus another made on two similar test collections must, with high likelihood, coincide.
3. Ability to distinguish: the metric must be able to quantify all the differences in two ranked lists. A (negative) example of this is indeed precision and recall: they are not able to distinguish different rankings of the same set of documents.

2.2.5 System Characteristics

Apart from the result list, other characteristics of an IR system can be measured in a straightforward way [32], as for example:

- Latency of showing results (as function of index size) in seconds
- Collection size (and how it is distributed over topics in megabytes or documents)
- Timeliness of the data in the collection: what is the latest date at which the index is guaranteed to match the current version of a document

For users, the query interface and query languages are very important, but their features cannot be captured so easily:

- Expressiveness of the query language (languages can only be 'measured' in terms of feature checklists).
- Performance (speed) when using complex queries (as opposed to retrieval latency due to index size).

2.3 System Components and Architecture

If you wanted to build your own IR system, how would you do it? As different as they might appear on the outside, most systems follow a similar overall architecture.

Contrary to how it is displayed in movies and on TV, or how simple desktop file search tools work, IR systems do not start to scan all documents when you submit a query. Instead, most of the work is performed before, at index time ('offline'), and only some tasks are performed live at query time ('online'). Depending on the use case, it makes sense to do more or less offline. Such design decisions make or break a successful IR system.

In general, a system will have the following components:

1. Indexing
2. Querying
3. Result presentation

This section gives an overview of the main steps, the purpose and the challenges of each part, as summarised in Fig. 2.3.

Before starting indexing, it is necessary to identify the documents that shall be retrievable through the systems (either now or in the future), obtain them and prepare them for indexing. This process in itself may be considerably complex, as evidenced, for example, by the current competitive landscape in patent data provision services. Instead, we shall briefly focus now on the final step, the 'preparation' for indexing.

Indexing based on the terms in a document collection requires a working definition of 'term'. *Tokenisation* is the process of splitting text into individual words or terms. The straightforward approach of splitting at spaces and punctuation marks can lead to problems with numbers, URLs, acronyms and the like, so more advanced rules with exceptions, word lists and thesauri can greatly improve the performance of the final system. Tokenisation is language specific and benefits from linguistic knowledge: in many Asian languages, no spaces are used to separate words, which requires advanced methods of word segmentation; German or Dutch compound nouns also require a compound splitter.

For languages with inflection, *stemming* or *lemmatisation* is often the next step. Stemming removes suffixes from the terms, reducing them to their core or stem in a mechanical way (e.g. in English, removing the *-ing* suffix from all words). Lemmatisation performs a similar function but taking into account even more details about the language. Unlike stemming, which often results in simply truncated words, lemmatisation results in the dictionary form of the term (i.e. the lemma). Both of these processes are language specific, and while they lose a significant amount of information that is contained in the endings (distinctions between plural and singular, verb and noun, past and present), it makes querying easier, as the user does not have to enumerate all possibly matching variations in the query string.

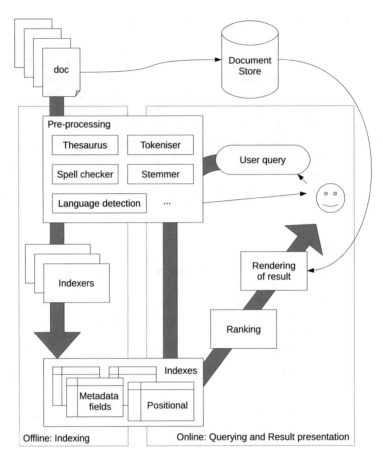

Fig. 2.3 Overview of the components of a search system, cf. [3, 32]

When the size of the index is an issue, terms that occur in practically all documents and many sentences, such as most non-content-bearing parts of speech (prepositions, articles, conjunctions, etc.), called stop words, can be removed from the index, as on their own they do not add any discriminative information that could improve the results, while making up a large portion of the size of the index. However, it should be noted that in modern IR systems, where storage is no longer an issue, stop words are often maintained because they play an essential role when searching for phrases, or, as we will see later in this chapter, in defining the proper context for semantic search.

Further processing of the word list might include checking and treating spelling, OCR or transcription errors [25].

Finally, individual words may be compounded back together in situations where their meaning together significantly diverges from the sum of their individual meanings. As explained at length in Chap. 9 later in this book, patent texts often use so-called multi-word units or multi-word terms (e.g. central processing unit). Nevertheless, the extent to which this phase helps or damages index performance is still debated.

2.3.1 Indexing

The process of indexing means preparing a second, separate representation of the documents that is optimised for retrieval. If we assume that the user will be searching with terms as queries and will want to get all the documents that contain these terms, it would be useful to have a list of the terms and for each term a list of the documents where it occurs. This simple list is the so-called inverted index, also known as *postings list*. It is the most basic index and at the same time the fundamental component for every modern search engine. A conceptual, bidirectional mapping between terms and documents is known as *term-document matrix*, but in practice it is never the case that a full term-document matrix is ever stored or used directly. The term-document matrix, as the simplest inverted index, loses the order of the terms in the document, so if the users are to be able to search for multi-words or phrases, or use positions of the terms with wildcards, the index will have to store this information also [3].

The basic index can only give the information that is stored in it, so if the result presentation should contain a snippet of the document with a highlighted search term, this has to be taken into account and the necessary data stored in the index. For ranked result lists, the information that is needed for the weighting of terms and documents also has to be included in the index. See Sect. 2.4.2.1 for examples.

2.3.1.1 Fulltext, Metadata, and Other Information

Considerable amounts of content are actually of a semi-structured nature. It contains unstructured parts such as text or images, which have to be prepared to become searchable, as well as structured content such as dates and other document metadata which lend themselves much easier to searching (e.g. retrieve all PDF documents created between February 7 and 10). Should these values be searchable together, also be prepared at the indexing step. The same is true for any additional enhanced search methods, for example, semantic information extraction of events and relationships. Whenever fulltext and metadata are used together, they share between themselves the functions of filtering and ranking. For instance, we may retrieve all documents published between certain dates and rank them on their fulltext similarity to the query. Or, we may rank on publication date and filter on the fulltext similarity being above a certain threshold. Rarely is it the case that a ranking function is combining fulltext and metadata, and there are good reasons for this absence: first, it is semantically ambiguous how the two should be combined in a meaningful way; and second, it removes control options from the user.

2.3.1.2   System Characteristics and Engineering Decisions

Other important distinguishing features of indexers are the indexing speed (in documents or kilobyte per second), the resulting index size (compared to the original documents) and whether the index can be updated when there are changes in the collection or whether it has to be completely recreated from scratch. Querying speed depends on how easily the index can be accessed. The index can be a single large file, a collection of files or a database, and stored on one machine or distributed. Complete books have been written on the engineering aspects of IR, and the topic is vastly beyond of the scope of this chapter, but we refer the interested reader to the slightly old but still very relevant book by Croft, Metzler and Strohman, *Search Engines: Information Retrieval in Practice* [15].

2.3.2   Querying

The querying component of an IR system consists of a query parser and whatever tools necessary to match the user's query to what is contained in the index. A free text query is treated similarly to the documents in the indexing step: it goes through the same preprocessing steps as the documents to be indexed, as described at the beginning of this section. 'Did you mean ...' suggestions can be created by performing a spellcheck on the query or by comparing it to a list of frequent queries.

Users are generally not able to construct perfect queries. They might get close for known-item searches, but for all other types of search, they simply cannot know beforehand. The search system can support them with automated query rewriting. Users often come across concepts that can be expressed in many different ways, where they cannot know which one will lead them to the desired results. On the other hand, many words have more than one meaning, which is clarified based on the context of a sentence or paragraph, but remains ambiguous when used in a query.

A thesaurus can be used to improve the situation by automatically adding synonyms to the query. But since the terms in the original query often lack context, this will typically lead to much less precise queries, as terms from unrelated domains are added to the query.

Since not even the most advanced algorithm will know more about the domain context of the query than the user, another method is to perform an initial search and then ask the user directly for feedback to the retrieved documents. The user marks a few of the top retrieved documents as (non-)relevant, which makes it possible to automatically modify the query in a way that finds more relevant documents, much the same way that users would modify their queries to include and exclude items after seeing the first results. This type of relevance feedback has been used since the 1960s and is known to be effective [42, 50].

Sometimes user feedback is not available, so in the 1990s, pseudo-feedback was invented. It assumes that the top documents retrieved initially are close enough to the intended result, so that related terms can be taken from these documents to create a second, improved query. The modified query contains related terms and synonyms to the original query terms. The result of the second query is presented to the user. This approach fundamentally depends on the quality of the initial query. As it automatically learns from the top results, it intensifies the effects of the query: a good one will be followed by more good results, and a terrible one will be followed by even worse results. Pseudo relevance feedback is therefore to be used when there is a fair expectation that the system will respond with a high precision, and this is not shown to be the case for patent search.

After the documents have been retrieved, they have to be scored by whichever model the IR system uses (see Sect. 2.4.2 for ranking models). If the result list is constructed from different sources, they may have to be merged into one uniform result with one overall ranking before being presented to the user (see Chap. 8 on federated search for additional details in this situation).

2.3.3   Result Presentation

The most common presentation mode is still the linear result list. It can be sorted and filtered (by the available metadata of the documents, such as date, size, file type). If the underlying model does not support ranking, sorting the documents, for example, chronologically can be useful.

The requirements for the presentation of results depend heavily on the domain. Web search engines have evolved to provide snippets from the pages as well as summaries, direct links to parts of the pages found, maps or images, as this saves searcher's time. Patent or legal searches value depth of knowledge more than time and will not be satisfied with snippets or summaries alone and need easy access to the full document, with highlighting of query terms or other indications of why this document is in the result list.

Result snippets and summaries can be static (independent of the query) or dynamic. The static ones can be created and stored at indexing time, whereas creating dynamic summaries at query time may require access to the full document or elaborate calculations and can be a costly operation. They can help to explain why the document was retrieved for the particular query.

There are many quite sophisticated summarisation approaches in the area of natural language processing. A simpler method is to show the search term surrounded by the words that precede and follow it in the text, which is called keyword in context or KWIC. The context can be a fixed window or adjusted to sentence boundaries with linguistic methods [32, Chap. 8.7].

For document collections with metadata that can be seen as a network, such as academic publications, a visualisation of the network graph can be useful (e.g. MS academic search uses people who have published together), whereas geographic metadata can be visualised on maps.[8]

Other options include word clouds that show words that occur together (in a document, in a group of documents, in the search results) and words that occur more often larger.[9]

For browsing or explorative searches, faceted search can be very useful to get an overview over a large result set. Facets are attributes of the documents, either given as metadata or computed on the fly with clustering or classification algorithms. They are well known from the user interfaces of online stores (where you can filter the thousands of available shoes by colour, size, manufacturer, material, etc.) and act as a kind of drill down into 'regions' of the result set. They are a convenient alternative to complex search forms with multiple fields because they can be used on demand after the query returns and only until the result set is small enough for browsing.

2.4 IR Models

So far, we spoke about the way documents are transformed from their original state (potentially paper) into data structures which allow us to identify, with extreme efficiency, which documents contain which words. We have also summarily presented how users' information need, equally expressed through words, is matched against those structures. Finally, we dedicated a few words to how the results are presented. Throughout this exposition, there was an implied assumption about what we want to do: we want to match terms from the query to the documents. It seems beyond discussion that this is in fact what we are supposed to be doing. Yet the science of IR is about questioning the obvious and, in the process, creating models for relevance. Ultimately, we will still rely on words—there is simply nothing else to rely on. Even in the case of images, the state of the art on patent images fundamentally has to rely on the words describing them. This section is therefore a compendiary view on the science behind IR.

2.4.1 Boolean IR

The simplest way to consider relevance is to assume that if a document contains a word, then it is relevant to the concept denoted by that word. Otherwise, it is not relevant. The Boolean model is therefore clear and precise: a document either

---

[8]For example, Freepatentsonline shows inventors' addresses on a map at http://www.freepatentsonline.com/maps.

[9]http://www.wordle.net.

matches or it does not match the query. The user is in control and has transparency over what is retrieved. The search terms are linked with Boolean operators: AND, OR and NOT. Using AND greatly increases precision and lowers recall, whereas OR quickly lowers precision and increases recall.

Boolean systems are generally good for expert users with a clear understanding of their needs and the collection, as it requires a lot of skills to come up with a manageable number of hits. In this model, all terms are weighted equally, so it can be quite challenging to find the sweet spot between a huge result set with too many documents and an (almost) empty result set.

In extended versions, term proximity operators and wildcards can be used. Boolean operations are set operations on a set of documents, which implies that the results cannot be ranked. In practice, using some of the document metadata to display the documents in an order (e.g., chronologically) can work very well for many applications.

Boolean systems have dominated commercial tools for decades. In the 1990s, Turtle [53] first showed that free text queries performed better than expert Boolean queries on a legal document collection.

2.4.2   Ranked IR

Boolean retrieval is arguably an extremely coarse model of the user's information need. While it is indeed desirable to have a set of relevant documents distinct from all other non-relevant documents, user studies have shown beyond doubt that no such set exists: different users consider different sets. As early as the late 1960s, Rees and Schultz [38] had reported that users agreed more with each other when asked questions of the form 'Which of these two documents is more relevant to the query?' than when asked to provide absolute judgements (e.g., 'Is this document relevant to the query?'). So, while for practical purposes it may be desirable to have clear-cut sets, this is simply not how the world is. Consequently, almost all contemporary search technologies are based on ranked retrieval, and it is the accepted wisdom amongst the IR community that ranked retrieval is almost always more effective than Boolean retrieval.

Ranked retrieval needs a scoring formula that can provide a numeric value of how likely a document is useful to the searcher, of how well it matches the query. This property makes it possible to 'narrow' or 'broaden' a search.

Before diving in into the specifics of some of the 'classic' IR models, let us note that the problem of IR is related to machine learning: based on a set of features (i.e. words in documents and query), classify a document as being of the class 'relevant' or 'not relevant'. Yet the field of IR has developed in parallel to that of machine learning, and the science of IR combines statistics with linguistics and rarely uses generic machine learning techniques. But rarely does not mean never, and in fact there is a sub-branch of IR called 'learning to rank' that has obtained very good results in the last decade [27]. Nowadays, with the resurgence in neural networks research, it is generally expected that we shall see accelerated progress in information retrieval as well [28].

Models in which word order is fundamentally disregarded are known as 'bag of words' models. Most of the models we consider now are such models. However, this does not entirely exclude the usage of word order in queries: it is more an issue of efficiency.

2.4.2.1 Vector Space Model

A vector is a geometric object representing a direction and a length. In a two-dimensional space, it is an arrow drawn on a sheet of paper. In a three-dimensional space, you can visualise it as a ruler pointed at any direction around you. To describe this ruler mathematically, we must fix a coordinate system (perhaps along the walls and floor of the room, if we are in a rectangular room) and consider the end we are holding to be the origin—the centre of the room. Then, our ruler is completely described by three values, denoting the displacement of its other end with respect to the end we are holding, along the three directions. The result is a list of numeric values, one per dimension. The three-dimensional vector $(2, 3, -1)$ represents the direction 'two steps to the right along the x-axis, three steps ahead along the y-axis, and 1 step down along the z-axis' (Fig. 2.4). Any list of numbers, no matter how

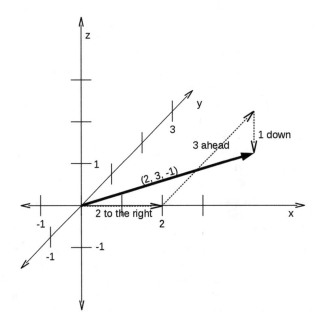

Fig. 2.4 A vector in three-dimensional space: $(2, 3, -1)$

long, can be viewed as a vector. The corresponding space has as many dimensions as there are values in the vector, which might be unimaginable to humans, but mathematically it works just the same.

The vector space model uses vectors to represent documents and queries. The dimensions of the vectors correspond to the distinguishing features of the documents, so if terms are what will be used for querying, then the vectors will have as many dimensions as there are unique terms in the collection. A document's vector will contain a non-zero value at the slot of a term if the term occurs in the document and zero if not [47]. These very large vectors are also very sparse, meaning that most of their values are zero, a property which can be exploited in the implementation to improve the data model.

In order to use such a system to score a document's relevance to a query, the query is treated as a small document, and a vector is created for it at query time. The similarity between the query and a document is then assumed to correspond to some property of the angle—typically the cosine—between their vectors. This approach is very useful for ranking the search results because it can represent a continuous degree of similarity. The cosine, for example, is 1 for equal documents and 0 for documents that have nothing in common.

This technique works for all kinds of data that can be represented as vectors (images, music, network graphs, molecule structures) and is useful also for classification and clustering.

Term Weighting: tf.idf

For this model to work, some numbers have to be inserted. Which values should be used for the non-zero values in the term vectors? Zeros and ones, or how often the term occurs in the document? Should they be normalised in any way?

Typically, tf.idf or one of the many values derived from it is used. Tf.idf, the ratio of *term frequency* to *document frequency*, reflects the searcher trying to find terms that are rare overall (discriminative) but frequent in the requested document.

$$\frac{\text{term frequency}}{\text{document frequency}} = \frac{\text{tf}}{\text{df}} = \text{tf.idf} \qquad (2.3)$$

The document frequency (df) of a term is the number of documents in the collection in which the term occurs. Each term has one df for the whole collection. The term frequency (tf) of a term is given the number of times a term occurs in a document. A term therefore has one tf per document in the collection. The formula above is just an exemplification. In reality, the formulas tend to be slightly more complex, but the idea remains the same: directly proportional to the tf (importance of term in the document) and inversely proportional with df (commonality of term in collection): if a term is rare throughout the whole collection, its df and tf are small and the tf.idf for all documents is similar. If it is rare overall but frequent in a single document, its df is still small, but the tf for that document is large, making the tf.idf larger.

All similarity depends on the keywords, so this approach is sensitive to vocabulary differences and the preprocessing of the documents (see Sects. 2.3.1 and 2.3.2). It assumes that the frequencies are independent and disregards the order of the terms in the documents. It can be extended with phrase search, wildcards and (quasi-) Boolean operators though.

Other Vector Operations

As mentioned in the section about querying above, using the terms that occur in the documents directly for searching means a lot of noise and ambiguities caused by synonyms,[10] and polysems[11] are introduced. Latent semantic indexing [17] is a strategy that uses matrix computation methods to resolve some of the problems caused by synonyms. A (computationally expensive) multistep process on the term-document matrix (i.e. the set of document vectors) finds a much smaller approximation to the original matrix that replaces the terms with 'concepts', grouping terms with similar semantics [18]. The method was patented in 1988 (US Patent 4,839,853, [16]). Latent semantic indexing is a statistical approach to detecting semantic information in unstructured text. Section 2.5 contains more on semantic methods in general.

2.4.2.2   Probabilistic Models

Probabilistic methods are based on the idea that it is possible to estimate the probability of a term appearing in a relevant document if you have some known relevant and non-relevant documents. Probabilistic IR is somewhat similar to the approach taken with the vector space model, in that they are generally based on the bag of words approach, but based on the sound foundation of probability theory. The documents can be ranked by their probability of being relevant to the query:

Probability(document is relevant to the query|document, query)

Probabilistic Relevance Framework

One of the fundamental ways of thinking probabilistically about information retrieval is the Probabilistic Relevance Framework [41]. It is the so-called *classical* probabilistic model because it has its roots Maron and Kuhns [33] in the early 1960s and later in that of Van Rijsbergen [54] and Spark Jones [21]. Its most conspicuous advocate is however Robertson [39].

---

[10]Several words for one meaning.

[11]One word with several meanings.

As discussed above in this chapter, documents and queries are transformed to some common representation and then compared. This comparison, while it may, mathematically, be very precise (e.g. comparing two vectors is well defined and for any distance function we will have a deterministic output), is in reality unavoidably subjected to the uncertainty of language. Mathematically, the only way we can quantify and work with uncertainty are probabilities.

The Probabilistic Relevance Framework (PRF) ranks the documents by the estimated probability that a hidden random variable R takes one of the two values (some authors use 1/0, others $r/\bar{r}$ or even $l/\bar{l}$ to denote *relevance* and *not relevance*). Estimating this probability for information retrieval consists of fundamentally two steps:

1. Finding measurable statistics that we consider indicative of relevance (e.g. term frequency, collection frequency)
2. Combining these statistics to estimate the probability of a document's relevance to the query

The affability of the PRF derives from the probability ranking principle, first publicly formulated by Robertson [39], but credited by him to private communication with W. Cooper of the University of California at Berkeley, and first hinted at by Maron and Kuhns:

> If a reference retrieval system's response to each request is a ranking of the documents in the collections in order of decreasing probability of usefulness to the user who submitted the request, where the probabilities are estimated as accurately as possible on the basis of whatever data has been made available to the system for this purpose, then overall effectiveness of the system to its users will be the best that is obtained on the basis of this data.

The methods developed as a consequence of this principle, while often restricted to statistics that come out of the text, are not bound to this limitation. As the principle states, we can base this calculation on 'whatever data has been made available to the system'. In the Web domain this freedom has been used to combine, for instance, Roberston's BM25 Relevance Status Value with PageRank [41], thereby defining relevance as a combination of topical relevance and importance in a network.

The Probabilistic Relevance Framework, as extensively described most recently by Robertson and Zaragoza [41], assumes that the term frequency of individual words is generated by the composition of two Poisson distributions: one for the occurrence of the term and one of the term being *elite* or not (where by *elite*, Roberston denotes those terms that bear the meaning of documents). However, as the two Poisson distributions are in practice impossible to estimate accurately, the weight of each term t in a document d is approximated by

$$w_t = \log \frac{|D| - \mathrm{df}_t + 0.5}{\mathrm{df}_t + 0.5} \cdot \frac{\mathrm{tf}_{t,d}}{k_1 + \mathrm{tf}_{t,d}}$$

Since BM25 does not use the cosine similarity (there are no vectors), a length normalisation is directly applied on the term frequency component. Thus, a score is computed for each document d and query q as follows:

$$S(q,d) = \sum_{t \in T_d \cap T_q} \frac{(k_3 + 1)\text{tf}_{t,q}}{k_3 + \text{tf}_{t,q}} \frac{(k_1 + 1)\overline{\text{tf}_{t,d}}}{k_1 + \overline{\text{tf}_{t,d}}} \log \frac{|D| + 0.5}{\text{df}_t + 0.5} \qquad (2.4)$$

where

$$\overline{\text{tf}_{t,d}} = \frac{\text{tf}_{t,d}}{B} \qquad B = (1 - b) + b \frac{L_d}{avgdl}$$

where $\text{tf}_{t,q}$ and $\text{tf}_{t,d}$ are the term frequency of a term in the query and the document, T_q and T_d are the set of unique terms in the query and the document, $|D|$ is the total number of documents in the collection, L_d is the length of document d (i.e. number of tokens) and $avgdl$ is the average length of a document in the collection. This scoring method is widely known as *BM25*.

Language Modelling

In addition to the Probabilistic Relevance Framework mentioned above, language modelling [37] and divergence from randomness [1] are also part of the probabilistic category of models. Amongst them, language modelling has received most of the attention of the community.

The original model introduced by Ponte and Croft in 1998 [37] (although similar ideas were developed in parallel by other researchers) is commonly known as the *document likelihood* model because it calculates the likelihood that the document before us is generated from a model constructed based on the query. Conceptually, the idea is that the user has a knowledge model in mind, from which it randomly outputs a set of keywords (the query), and the task of the system is to calculate the probability that the same knowledge model would have resulted in the set of words that the document consists of. We can then rank the documents in decreasing order of this likelihood. Subsequent iterations of this have turned it around (i.e. computing a query likelihood based on a document of the model) or otherwise extended the probabilistic reasoning.

While they are conceptually different (most notably with respect to the probability spaces in which they operate), there is a strong relationship between the PRF and language modelling [26]. Language modelling methods are very sensitive to parameter tuning. As Zhai [56] pointed out:

> This may be the reason why language models have not yet been able to outperform well-tuned full-fledged traditional methods consistently and convincingly in TREC evaluation.

This is probably why, when Lucene,[12] in its 6th version released in 2015, changed its scoring function, it went for PRF's BM25 rather than language modelling as the default scoring method. Nevertheless, it has been repeatedly shown that, under careful optimisation, language modelling is the current state of the art.

2.5   Semantic Search

Semantic technology is the subject of many hopes, as it can allow search systems to take (some of) the meaning of the words into account, as opposed to 'just counting' them. If applicable to the domain and done successfully, it can be expected to improve recall while keeping precision at least constant if not also increasing precision [32]. The requirements are a suitable information representation and the ability to perform natural language processing.

There are two interpretations of 'semantic' that are confusingly used in search technologies:

- **Statistical**: considering the context of occurrence of terms in documents, grounded in Wittgenstein's Philosophical Investigations [55] about the meaning of words.
- **Explicit**: taking advantage of manually created knowledge resources

In terms of statistical semantics, we have already mentioned latent semantic analysis. Later we have random indexing [46] and, most recently, a variety of neural network approaches. All of them are essentially grounded in Wittgenstein's observation that the meaning is defined by usage. For instance, the following three sentences *'He drives a car'*, *'He drives a truck'* and *'He drives a bus'* should lead us to believe that *car*, *truck* and *bus* are semantically related. As humans we would acknowledge that yes these are things that can be driven, but that is irrelevant for the computer: the simple fact that they appear in similar contexts is important.

In the other category, knowledge bases (ontologies, thesauri and taxonomies) represent concepts and relationships—usually within a subject area—that a community can agree on. They are used to classify, structure, define or represent, and have the additional value of aiding cross-language interoperability and are often created for company-specific data. They can be used in semantic search for query expansion, searching by concepts instead of terms, as well as broadening or narrowing a search.

Controlled vocabulary/glossary: A list of terms and definitions. Used to reduce the variability of terminology use.

Taxonomy: A knowledge hierarchy where items are connected to each other by parent–child, part-of or instance-of relationships. Classification hierarchies like the International Patent Classification (IPC) are a kind of taxonomy.

---

[12]http://lucene.apache.org.

Thesaurus: A network of terms connected by hierarchical, equivalence or associative relationships. Synonym dictionaries used by patent searchers are a kind
of thesaurus.

Ontology: A taxonomy with multiple, precisely defined links between the items
that represents knowledge as a set of concepts and their relationships. Different
kinds of ontologies are suitable for different purposes (reasoning on the data,
fuzzy search, etc.)

Information extraction is the identification of facts from unstructured text, so
that knowledge bases can be built with little or no human effort. It depends
in part on named entity recognition which uses lists of known multi-words (as
found in dictionaries, thesauri, ontologies, taxonomies) to recognise entities such as
places, organisations, persons and events in text documents [50]. Relation extraction
finds the relationships between entities (person [works at] organisation). These
feats can be accomplished with pattern-based, with statistical (as described in
Sect. 2.4.2.1 above for latent semantic indexing), or with hybrid methods. State-of-
the-art systems have some ability to deal with previously unseen terms, and named
entity recognition has proved itself ready for deployment in industrial settings,
like business intelligence. Given the prevalence in patents of complex and newly
coined and variant technical terminology, company names and so on, named entity
recognition is likely to have an important place in future patent search systems.

2.6   Outlook

To summarise the preceding sections, the key characteristics of information retrieval
are:

- Unstructured information, mostly semi-structured data
- No right answers (except for known-item search)
- Separation of indexing and query time processing: offline (crawl/index time) vs
  online (query time) processing
- Strong empirical method, reproducibility and evaluation required

What this means for applications such as patent search is the subject of the rest
of this book. As outlined in [5], there are indications that iterative search is coming
into focus, as newer methodologies such as faceted search or clustering features
are becoming more common. However, while progress has been made in the past 5
years, iterative search and its effectiveness evaluation remain on the TODO list of
the research community as well as on that of the industry.

A survey conducted in 2010 [2, 20] compared the features offered by open-
source IR systems (from the more academic to industry-strength systems) to the
features that are important to patent searchers. While options of the query languages
(which depend on the underlying IR models and their extensions) such as wildcards,
field operators or proximity search are well covered, requirements related to the

iterative and explorative nature of the search process (which would require greater changes to the whole system) were found to be not covered at all. Functionalities such as combining multiple queries or results, keyword highlighting in the results or grouping the documents by non-explicit metadata like patent families are missing and have to be implemented outside of the core applications.

References

1. Amati G, Van Rijsbergen CJ (2002) Probabilistic models of information retrieval based on measuring the divergence from randomness. ACM Trans Inf Syst 20(4):357–389
2. Azzopardi L, Vanderbauwhede W, Joho H (2010) Search system requirements of patent analysts. In: Proceeding of the 33rd international ACM SIGIR conference on research and development in information retrieval (SIGIR '10). ACM, New York, NY, pp 775–776
3. Baeza-Yates RA, Ribeiro-Neto B (1999) Modern information retrieval. Addison-Wesley Longman, Boston, MA
4. Belew RK (2000) Finding out about: a cognitive perspective on search engine technology and the WWW. Cambridge University Press, Cambridge
5. Bonino D, Ciaramella A, Corno F (2010) Review of the state-of-the-art in patent information and forthcoming evolutions in intelligent patent informatics. World Patent Inf 32(1):30–38
6. Buckley C, Robertson S (2008) Relevance feedback track overview. In: Proceedings of The seventeenth text REtrieval Conference, TREC 2008, Gaithersburg, Maryland, USA, 18–21 November 2008. Volume Special Publication 500–277. National Institute of Standards and Technology (NIST)
7. Buckley C, Dimmick D, Soboroff I, Voorhees E (2006) Bias and the limits of pooling. In: Proceedings of the 29th annual international ACM SIGIR conference on research and development in information retrieval (SIGIR '06). ACM, New York, NY, pp 619–620
8. Buckley C, Dimmick D, Soboroff I, Voorhees E (2007) Bias and the limits of pooling for large collections. Inf Retr 10(6):491–508
9. Bush V (1945) As we may think. The Atlantic Monthly. Reprinted in Life magazine, 10 Sept 1945
10. Büttcher S, Clarke C, Cormack G (2010) Information retrieval: implementing and evaluating search engines. MIT Press, Cambridge, MA
11. Carterette B, Voorhees EM (2011) Overview of information retrieval evaluation. In: Current challenges in patent information retrieval, Chap. 3. Springer, Berlin, Heidelberg
12. Cleverdon CW (1991) The significance of the Cranfield tests on index languages. In: Proceedings of the SIGIR. ACM Press, New York, pp 3–12
13. Cleverdon C, Mills J (1963) The testing of index language devices. Aslib Proc 15:106–130
14. Clough P, Sanderson M (2013) Evaluating the performance of information retrieval systems using test collections. Inf Res 18(2):1–10
15. Croft B, Metzler D, Strohman T (2011) Search engines: information retrieval in practice. Pearson Education, Newmarket, ON
16. Deerwester SC, Dumais ST, Furnas GW, Harshman RA, Landauer TK, Lochbaum KE, Streeter LA (1988) Computer information retrieval using latent semantic structure, US Patent US4839853 A
17. Deerwester SC, Dumais ST, Landauer TK, Furnas GW, Harshman RA (1990) Indexing by latent semantic analysis. J Am Soc Inf Sci (6):391–407
18. Grossman DA, Frieder O (2004) Information retrieval: algorithms and heuristics, 2nd edn. Springer, Berlin
19. Hunt D, Nguyen L, Rodgers M (2007) Patent searching: tools & techniques. Wiley, New York

20. Joho H, Azzopardi LA, Vanderbauwhede W (2010) A survey of patent users: an analysis of tasks, behavior, search functionality and system requirements. In: Proceeding of the third symposium on Information interaction in context, IIiX '10. ACM, New York, NY, pp 13–24
21. Jones KS (1981) Information retrieval experiment. Butterworths, London
22. Jones KS, Willett P (1997) Evaluation. In: Readings in information retrieval, Chap 4. Morgan Kaufmann, San Francisco, CA, pp 167–174
23. Kelly D (2009) Methods for evaluating interactive information retrieval systems with users. Found Trends Inf Retr 3(1–2):1–224
24. Kelly D, Sugimoto CR (2013) A systematic review of interactive information retrieval evaluation studies, 1967–2006. J Am Soc Inf Sci Technol 64(4):745–770
25. Korfhage RR (1997) Information storage and retrieval. Wiley, New York
26. Lafferty JD, Zhai C (2003) Probabilistic relevance models based on document and query generation. In: Language modeling and information retrieval. Springer, Berlin
27. Liu T-Y (2009) Learning to rank for information retrieval. Found Trends Inf Retr 3(3):225–331
28. Liu X, Gao J, He X, Deng L, Duh K, Wang Y-Y (2015) Representation learning using multi-task deep neural networks for semantic classification and information retrieval. In: Proceedings of NAACL
29. Lupu M, Huang J, Zhu J, Tait J (2009) Trec-chem: large scale chemical information retrieval evaluation at trec. SIGIR Forum 43:63–70
30. Lupu M, Huang J, Zhu J (2011) Evaluation of chemical information retrieval tools. In: Current challenges in patent information retrieval, Chap 5. Springer, Berlin, Heidelberg
31. Lupu M, Salampasis M, Hanbury A (2014) Domain specific search. In: Professional search in the modern world. http://link.springer.com/chapter/10.1007%2F978-3-319-12511-4_6
32. Manning CD, Raghavan P, Schütze H (2008) Introduction to information retrieval. Cambridge University Press, New York, NY
33. Maron ME, Kuhns JL (1960) On relevance, probabilistic indexing and information retrieval. J ACM 7(3):216–244
34. Mooers CE (1950) Coding, information retrieval and the rapid selector. Am Doc 1(4):225–229
35. Mooers CE (1961) From the point of view of mathematical etc. techniques. In: Towards information retrieval. Butterworths, London, pp xvii–xxiii
36. Morville P, Rosenfeld L (2006) Information architecture for the world wide web. O'Reilly, Sebastopol, CA
37. Ponte JM, Croft WB (1998) A language modeling approach to information retrieval. In: Proceedings of the 21st annual international ACM SIGIR conference on research and development in information retrieval, SIGIR '98. ACM, New York, NY, pp 275–281
38. Rees AM, Schultz DG (1967) A field experimental approach to the study of relevance assessments in relation to document searching. Final report to the national science foundation, vol i
39. Robertson SE (1977) The probability ranking principle in IR. J Doc 33(4):294–304
40. Robertson SE, Jones KS (1994) Simple, proven approaches to text retrieval. Technical report UCAM-CL-TR-356, Computer Laboratory, University of Cambridge
41. Robertson S, Zaragoza H (2009) The probabilistic relevance framework: Bm25 and beyond. Found Trends Inf Retr 3(4):333–389
42. Rocchio JJ (1971) Relevance feedback in information retrieval. In: Salton G (ed) The Smart retrieval system - experiments in automatic document processing. Prentice-Hall, Englewood Cliffs, NJ, pp 313–323
43. Roda G, Tait J, Piroi F, Zenz V (2010) Clef-ip 2009: Retrieval experiments in the intellectual property domain. In: Peters C, Di Nunzio GM, Kurimo M, Mostefa D, Penas A, Roda G (eds) Multilingual information access evaluation I. Text retrieval experiments 10th workshop of the cross-language evaluation forum. Lecture notes in computer science, vol 6241. Springer, Berlin, pp 385–409
44. Rowe B, Wood D, Link A, Simoni D (2010) Economic impact assessment of NIST's Text REtrieval Conference (TREC) program. Technical report, National Institute of Standards and Technology

45. Rowley J, Farrow J (2000) Organizing knowledge: an introduction to managing access to information, 3rd edn. Ashgate Publishing, Guildford
46. Sahlgren M (2005) An introduction to random indexing. Technical report, SICS, Swedish Institute of Computer Science
47. Salton G, Wong A, Yang CS (1975) A vector space model for automatic indexing. Commun ACM 18:613–620
48. Schamber L (1994) Relevance and information behavior. Annu Rev Inf Sci Technol 29:3–48
49. Schrettinger M (1803) Versuch eines vollständigen Lehrbuches der Bibliothek-Wissenschaft. Munich
50. Singhal A (2001) Modern information retrieval: a brief overview. IEEE Data Eng Bull 24(4):35–43
51. Teevan J, Collins-Thompson K, White RW, Dumais S, Kim Y (2013) Slow search: information retrieval without time constraints. In: Proceedings of the symposium on human-computer interaction and information retrieval, HCIR '13. ACM, New York, NY, pp 1:1–1:10
52. Teevan J, Collins-Thompson K, White RW, Dumais S (2014) Slow search. Commun ACM 57(8):36–38
53. Turtle HR (1994) Natural language vs. Boolean query evaluation: a comparison of retrieval performance. In: Proceedings of the 17th annual international ACM-SIGIR conference on research and development in information retrieval. Dublin, Ireland, 3–6 July 1994 (special issue of the SIGIR Forum). ACM, New York, pp 212–220
54. Van Rijsbergen CJ (1979) Information retrieval, 2nd edn. Butterworths, London
55. Wittgenstein L (1963) Philosophical investigations, 3rd edn. Basil Blackwell, Oxford
56. Zhai CX (2008) Statistical language models for information retrieval a critical review. Found Trends Inf Retr 2(3):137–213

Part II
Evaluating Patent Retrieval

As was noted in the previous chapter, information retrieval (IR) as a scientific subject is characterised by a strongly empirical approach, backed up by a rigorous approach to experimental methodology.

A key question for anyone selecting systems to search patents is whether one system or another is better for their purpose. A core value of information retrieval as an academic subject is that "improvements" in systems must be rigorously tested, to determine whether they actually deliver better results than previous systems. This has led to the development of thorough empirical methods in information retrieval, which have influenced commercial practice of well-known search companies, like Google, as well as academic practice in formal international evaluation campaigns, like NTCIR, TREC and CLEF.

Compared to the first edition of the book, this part contains one completely new chapter, two significantly updated chapters and one reproduced chapter. It will begin with two chapters dedicated to patent evaluation campaigns, followed by two chapters discussing complementary issues from the perspective of patent searchers and from the perspective of related domains, notably legal search.

The first, contributed by a wide set of authors spanning three continents, gives an overview of the patent-related evaluation campaigns organised in the context of NTCIR in Japan. It will cover not only the retrieval part but also the other issues that NTCIR addressed over the years, such as translation, classification and text mining. The reader will find here the most up-to-date information about academic work in the area of East Asian languages for the patent domain.

The next chapter describes the CLEF-IP evaluation campaign, which took place in Europe until 2013, focusing specifically on the evaluation efforts of the last 3 years, after the publication of the first edition of this book. During those 3 years, the CLEF-IP team expanded significantly into other tasks than prior art: passage retrieval, chemical structure identification and flow chart retrieval.

An important assumption in IR evaluation is that we are trying to measure the effectiveness of the search system (indexer, query processor etc.) *Independently* of the data being searched. In practice, for most operational trials (as Trippe and Ruthven call them) of commercial patent search services, one cannot distinguish the issues in the quality of the search system from issues in the quality of the underlying data feeds. This issue, which goes beyond the scope of this volume, perhaps deserves more thought in the patent search community. On one hand, the IR scientists need to adapt their evaluation measures and methods, or to create new ones, for the issues specific to this domain. On the other, professional patent searchers, as well as commercial vendors, must make their processes more easily subjected to an objective, scientific evaluation.

Finally, this part concludes with a revised chapter by Tomlinson and Hedin taking a look at efforts done to understand search in a similar domain: e-Discovery. Based on the TREC Legal Track, we see that contemporary search technologies can outperform Boolean models, but also learn of the many pitfalls of evaluating systems expected to return a large number of documents. The authors discuss ways to estimate recall, precision and the F1 measure based on a manageable amount of human evaluation and point out the extreme effects that human assessment error can have on these estimations.

Chapter 3
Patent-Related Tasks at NTCIR

Mihai Lupu, Atsushi Fujii, Douglas W. Oard, Makoto Iwayama, and Noriko Kando

Abstract The NII Testbeds and Community for Information access Research (NTCIR) has been the first benchmarking campaign that created a test collection specifically for patent retrieval, in 2001/2002. Over the course of just over a decade, organisers and participants at NTCIR patent-related challenges have addressed the problem of mono- and multilingual patent search and automated translation. In doing so, the only available East Asian language patent test collections have been created and made publicly available for research purposes. This chapter provides a reference summary of the efforts undertaken in NTCIR, helping the reader understand the challenges addressed, the datasets created and the solutions observed.

3.1 Introduction

The current NTCIR Conference, an event occurring every 18 months attracting researchers interested in the evaluation of information access technologies from Japan, Asia and the world, started as the NTCIR Workshop in 1999, co-sponsored by the National Center for Science Information Systems (NACSIS), the former

M. Lupu
TU Wien, Vienna, Austria
e-mail: mihai.lupu@tuwien.ac.at; lupu@ifs.tuwien.ac.at

A. Fujii (✉)
Department of Computer Science, Tokyo Institute of Technology, Tokyo 152-8550, Japan
e-mail: fujii@cs.titech.ac.jp

D.W. Oard
University of Maryland, College Park, MD, USA
e-mail: oard@umd.edu

M. Iwayama
Hitachi, Ltd., Tokyo 185-8601, Japan
e-mail: makoto.iwayama.nw@hitachi.com

N. Kando
National Institute of Informatics, Tokyo 101-8430, Japan
e-mail: kando@nii.ac.jp

© Springer-Verlag GmbH Germany 2017
M. Lupu et al. (eds.), *Current Challenges in Patent Information Retrieval*,
The Information Retrieval Series 37, DOI 10.1007/978-3-662-53817-3_3

organisation of the National Institute of Informatics (NII) and the Japan Society for the Promotion of Science. Its goals, as stated in the first edition, are:

- To encourage research in information retrieval (IR), cross-lingual information retrieval and related areas by providing a large-scale Japanese test collection and a common evaluation setting that allows cross-system comparison
- To provide a forum for research groups interested in comparing results and exchanging research ideas and opinions in an informal atmosphere
- To improve the quality of the test collections based on feedback from participants
- To investigate methods for constructing a large-scale test collection and corpus including Japanese text and evaluation methods

Hereafter, the notation NTCIR-X is used to refer to the Xth running of NTCIR workshop.

In NTCIR-1 and NTCIR-2, academic research abstracts and newspaper articles were used to produce test collections. In NTCIR-3, the use of Web pages and patents was introduced. The use of patents in information retrieval research dates back to at least the 1970s, with 76 US patents [3] being used to evaluate the effectiveness of local feedback techniques.

Since then, a number of research papers on the processing of patents have been published, but they have been relatively infrequent in the field of information processing. In spite of its importance to science, engineering and industry, it was not until the NTCIR initiated a patent retrieval task that patent processing became a focus of interest for the information retrieval (IR) and natural language processing (NLP) research communities. The problem was partially that, unlike Web searching, for which researchers are also users, researchers had difficulty formulating problems and requirements related to the business of real-world patents (see Chap. 1 for details of the patent business).

In pursuing their research interests, researchers are often tempted to propose a fully automated system that does not allow for user involvement. Conversely, in practical situations, a user might wish to adapt the system to a particular working environment. To maintain a reasonable balance between these objectives, the organisers of the patent-related tasks have had occasional round-table conferences with patent attorneys, examiners and searchers, as well as researchers and engineers. This chapter is devoted to these pioneering efforts of the NTCIR to define new models for the use of patents in academic research fields.

The remainder of this chapter is organised as follows. Section 3.2 is a brief history of the patent-related tasks at the NTCIR. Section 3.3 describes the available test collections, while Sect. 3.4 provides details of experiments and subsequent observations. Each of these latter two sections is subdivided into four subsections: retrieval, classification, text mining and machine translation. Finally, Sect. 3.5 provides a short summary.

3.2 History of the Patent-Related Tasks at the NTCIR

3.2.1 Preliminaries

In 2000, the Workshop on Patent Retrieval was colocated with the ACM SIGIR conference on Research and Development in Information Retrieval [30]. The purpose of this workshop was to provide a forum for researchers and practitioners associated with patent retrieval to exchange their knowledge and experiences from different perspectives, which included operational systems, research issues and evaluation methodologies. The outcome of this workshop motivated researchers involved in the NTCIR to foster research and development in patent retrieval by means of a large, practical test collection.

3.2.2 NTCIR-3 (2001–2002)

As the first trial for patent retrieval, a technology survey task was performed, in which patents related to a specific technology, such as 'blue light-emitting diode', could be searched for [26]. Because patent retrieval was a new research area for the NTCIR community at that time, developing a completely new task was too ambitious. Instead, the target collection was changed to a manageable number of patent documents while maintaining the retrieval task itself. Each search topic was a newspaper clipping related to a specific technology, and the document collection comprised unexamined Japanese patent applications over a 2-year period.

3.2.3 NTCIR-4 (2003–2004)

NTCIR-3 demonstrated the feasibility of using existing IR techniques via its technology survey task. In NTCIR-4, therefore, a patent-specific task was performed, namely, invalidity search, in which prior art related to a patent application was searched for [11]. Apart from academic research, invalidity searches are performed by examiners in government patent offices and investigators in the intellectual property divisions of private companies. Each search topic was a claim in a patent application that had been rejected by the Japan Patent Office (JPO). The document collection was extended to unexamined patent applications over 5 years because, compared with the technology survey task, an invalidity search usually requires a larger number of documents for investigative purposes. For each topic, the citations provided by JPO examiners and prior art patents found by human experts were used as relevant documents. In preparation for NTCIR-4, the organisers arranged a tutorial on patent retrieval by an ex-patent examiner and searcher to guide participants in the new task.

In addition, a patent map generation task was performed. This called for inter-patent analysis to organise patent documents in specific technology fields. However, because systematic evaluation is inherently difficult, and although human experts subjectively assessed the patent maps generated by automatic methods, a reusable test collection and a systematic evaluation method for patent map generation have yet to be established.

3.2.4   NTCIR-5 (2004–2005)

In NTCIR-5, three patent-related tasks were performed [13]. First, as in NTCIR-4, an invalidity search was performed, but using only citations provided by JPO examiners as the relevant documents. The size of the document collection was increased to comprise unexamined Japanese patent applications over 10 years. By this stage, the size of the document collection was no longer problematic for most of the active participants in the NTCIR.

Second, because patent documents are lengthy, it is useful to point out significant fragments ('passages') in a relevant patent. Therefore, passage retrieval was also performed. Each search topic involved a relevant patent for the accompanying invalidity search, and the target for each topic was the set of all passages in the topic patent. The relevant passages were those that provided grounds for judging whether the patent was relevant.

Finally, patent classification was also performed [27]. The target documents were patent applications submitted to the JPO over 2 years, and the correct classification codes were determined according to a multidimensional classification system called 'F-term' [45]. The patents, already classified into technological fields, were further classified in terms of one or more viewpoints, such as 'purpose', 'function' and 'effect'.

3.2.5   NTCIR-6 (2006–2007)

In NTCIR-6, both invalidity search [15] and F-term classification [29] were again performed. In the invalidity search, patent documents published over a 10-year period by the JPO and the US Patent and Trademark Office (USPTO) were independently used as target document collections. Having explored patent retrieval issues for 7 years, the organisers determined that the patent retrieval task could be concluded. Figure 3.1 shows a summary of the patent retrieval tasks from NTCIR-3 to NTCIR-6. In Fig. 3.1, only the major datasets are shown. In addition to the 10 years' worth of data in the JPO and USPTO collections being a representative dataset for the patent retrieval task, it appeared to have great potential for the exploration of other patent-related research fields.

	NTCIR-3	NTCIR-4	NTCIR-5	NTCIR-6
Task	Technology survey	Invalidity search		
Documents	JPO unexamined application			USPTO grant
	2 years	5 years	10 years	
Relevance judgment	By expert searcher			Cited patent
		Citation		
Related task	Cross-lingual patent retrieval			
		Patent map generation	Passage retrieval	
			F-term classification	

Fig. 3.1 Overview of the patent retrieval tasks at NTCIR

3.2.6 NTCIR-7 and NTCIR-8 (2007–2010)

In NTCIR-7, the organisers for the patent retrieval task determined to address other issues in patent processing, namely, machine translation (MT) and text mining. For each of these tasks, a number of researchers related to the topic were invited to join the organising team.

For the patent MT task in NTCIR-7 [16], the 10 years of data in the JPO and USPTO patent collections, which had progressively been enhanced from NTCIR-3 to NTCIR-6, were used to produce a Japanese–English (J–E) parallel corpus for training purposes. After extracting patent families, each of which is a set of patent documents for the same inventions usually in more than one language, pairs of sentences in J–E were identified automatically. Whereas NTCIR-7 involved approximately 1.8 million J–E sentence pairs, the number expanded to approximately 3.2 million in NTCIR-8 [17], with an additional 5 years of JPO and USPTO patent documents. This is one of the largest bilingual sentence-aligned corpora available to the public. In preparation for NTCIR-7, the organisers invited prospective participants to a hands-on MT tutorial aimed at guiding them in the new task.

The patent mining tasks in NTCIR-7 [38] and NTCIR-8 [40] were aimed at summarising and visualising patents and research papers in multidimensional technical trend maps, which resembled the patent map generation task in NTCIR-4. However, here, the evaluation and analysis were more systematic and thorough. The tasks involved categorising research abstracts based on the International Patent Classification (IPC) so that they could be associated with patents. The 10 years of data in the JPO and USPTO patent collections were used to train a classifier that could assign one or more IPC codes to a given document.

3.2.7   NTCIR-9 and NTCIR-10 (2010–2013)

In NTCIR-9 [20] and NTCIR-10 [21], the patent MT task was the only patent-related task. Although the J–E bilingual corpus was the same as in NTCIR-8, patent documents in Chinese were also used for training and testing purposes. These comprised approximately one million English–Chinese sentence pairs. The participation of world-leading research groups made possible exhaustive comparisons of different systems under different conditions. One remarkable finding was that the evaluation results for statistical MT were comparable with or even better than that for commercial rule-based MT systems, under particular conditions.

3.2.8   Summary

Although the patent-related activity at the NTCIR has ended after 13 years, the large collection of patent documents in Japanese and English has been made available to the public. Currently, the Chinese–English sentence pairs are also available, but for a fee. Figure 3.2 shows a summary of the MT and text mining tasks from NTCIR-7 to NTCIR-10. As in Fig. 3.1, Fig. 3.2 shows only the major datasets. Details of all the datasets and evaluations are presented in subsequent sections.

The organisers of the patent retrieval tasks also organised the ACL 2003 Workshop on Patent Corpus Processing and edited a special issue on patent processing in *Information Processing & Management* [14]. All of these activities have contributed to establishing research trends in the IR and NLP communities and increasing the number of publications related to patent processing (including this chapter). A list of publications related to patent information processing is maintained, with occasional updating, at the following URL: http://www.cl.cs.titech.ac.jp/~fujii/pat_proc_pub.html.

Fig. 3.2 Overview of the machine translation and text mining tasks at NTCIR

	NTCIR-7	NTCIR-8	NTCIR-9	NTCIR-10
Task	Machine translation			
Document	JPO application & USPTO grant			
				Chinese
Sentence				1M E-C
pair	1.8M J-E		3.2M J-E	

	NTCIR-7	NTCIR-8
Task	Text mining	
Purpose	IPC-based classification	
Document	Scientific abstract	Technical trend map creation
	JPO application & USPTO grant	

3.3 Data Collections and Tools

3.3.1 Retrieval

The patent retrieval task was executed between NTCIR-3 (2001) and NTCIR-6 (2007), thus spanning four editions of NTCIR.

The first test collection consists of approximately 700,000 full-text unexamined (at that time) patent applications from the Japan Patent Office (JPO) as well as approximately 1.7 mil. Japanese patent abstracts and their translations in English. Thirty-one topics have been created for this first evaluation exercise, based on newspaper articles. Each topic was available in traditional and simplified Chinese, Korean, Japanese and English.

The following year, a new collection was released, complementing the existing dataset with more full-text Japanese patent applications as well as more English abstracts, but removing the Japanese version of the abstract subset [12]. The set of topics was also increased to 101 and selected in a different way. The 2001 topics were taken from newspaper articles, but for 2003 each topic is a claim extracted from Japanese patent applications. For 34 of the 101 (the so-called main topics), manual assessments are available. They were created by a total of 12 experts, members of the Japan Intellectual Property Association (JIPA). For the remaining 67 topics (the so-called additional topics), only the citations recorded in the search reports from the Japan Patent Office are used.

For NTCIR-5 the collection was further increased to 3.5 mil English abstracts of Japanese patents and the corresponding 3.5 million Japanese full-text patent applications, covering 10 years of patent data from the JPO (Japan Patent Office). The full-text Japanese subset includes the entire text provided by the JPO except diagrams. In addition to the 34 main topics from NTCIR-4, that year's test collection includes 1189 new topics, of a similar nature (i.e. a claim from an existing application), and is evaluated based on the existing search reports (i.e. the same as the 67 *additional topics* from the previous year). All topics were originally in Japanese, but manual translations to English are provided by the organisers.

In addition to document retrieval, NTCIR-5 introduced a passage retrieval task, where the participants are asked to identify relevant paragraphs in 356 of the 378 documents relevant to the 34 main topics mentioned above. The 22 documents excluded passages consisting of images or diagrams—not retrievable by text search engines. The task benefits from a clear determination of passages in documents, given by the nature of their format, as well as from the exhaustive relevance evaluation at passage level done in the previous year by the 12 human assessors. The design of the task models an invalidity search [13]. The organisers provided 41 topics, of which 7 were used for training (dry-run) and the remaining 34 for testing.

Finally, NTCIR-6, the last year when a patent retrieval collection was made available, maintained the set from the previous iteration and added 1.3 million English full-text granted patents from the USPTO (United States Patent and Trademark Office). NTCIR-6 adds 1685 new Japanese topics to the already existing set of 1243 topics, all consisting of the first claim of a Japanese patent application. Additionally, it adds a completely new set of 3221 English topics, each consisting of one claim from a USPTO patent.

For all topics in these test collections, NTCIR provides graded relevance judgements, with three or four levels of relevance.

3.3.2   Classification

In two of its editions (2005, 2007), NTCIR also organised a patent classification task in parallel to the retrieval task mentioned above. The data collection is of course the same, and only the task definition changes, as well as the topics.

As a Japanese-led evaluation effort, NTCIR created patent classification tasks against the classifications used at the Japan Patent Office (JPO), namely, the F-terms (file forming terms). The reader may of course be aware that JPO also uses a file index (FI) classification, which is an extension of the IPC (International Patent Classification). Efforts on classifying against the IPC have been reported as early as 2003 [6] and have been evaluated extensively in the CLEF-IP track discussed in Chap. 4. Unlike the FI, F-terms are less dependent on the IPC. As indicated on the JPO website, 'F-terms re-classify or further segment each specific technical field of IPC from a variety of viewpoints (i.e. objective, application, structure, material, manufacturing process, processing and operation method, control method, etc.). Combining F-terms with IPC effectively narrows down relevant documents in prior art search'. The essential difference compared to the IPC is that F-terms, in addition to a five-digit theme code which could essentially be compared to the IPC subclasses or groups (there are about 1800 theme codes), add a four-character term code which is composed of a two-character *viewpoint symbol* and a two-digit numerical code. Optionally, an additional one-character extension code can be added to the F-term. Table 3.1 shows a small subset of the F-term information for Theme 2H050 (optical fibre cores).

In NTCIR-5 there are 2008 patent applications to be classified according to theme and 500 to be classified according to the F-term. The task follows closely the behaviour of patent experts in performing their classification according to the JPO practice: first a theme classification, assigning the application in one of the technology themes defined by the JPO (e.g. 2H050 in Table 3.1), and then a more refined classification within each theme, indicated by a term code (e.g. AB02, BB22 in Table 3.1).

NTCIR-6 continued the experiments on classification by asking participants to classify 21,606 patent applications, but only against the F-terms (i.e. provided the themes for each application).

Table 3.1 F-terms (extract)

Theme	Theme title				
2H050	Optical fibre cores				
Viewpoint	Description	Term codes			Additional codes
AB	Optical fibre strand materials	AB01 .Optical fibre core or cladding materials	AB02 ..Glass core or cladding materials	AB03 ...Quartz core or cladding materials AB23 ...Containing Ge AB33 ...Containing fluorides	X: Those for core only Y: Those for clad only Z: Those for core and clad
BB	Coating materials for the optical fibre core	BB01 .Materials for coating optical fibre core	BB02 ..Resin materials BB22 ..Glass materials	BB03 ...Polyamide (i.e. nylon) materials BB13 ...Polyester materials	Q: Those used as the innermost layer R: Those used for intermediate layers S: Those used as the outermost layer W: Those not limited to specific layer

3.3.3 Text Mining

After the initial classification tasks of NTCIR-5 and NTCIR-6, NTCIR-7 and NTCIR-8 expanded the scope from classification alone to classification plus (in NTCIR-8) extraction, and the combination was referred to collectively as the 'patent mining' task. In contrast to the original classification task in which the objective was to assign theme and F-term codes to patents, the classification task in patent mining is to classify a set of abstracts from research papers according to the IPC. The abstracts to be classified are English and Japanese abstracts of papers presented at conferences in Japan between 1988 and 1999. These abstracts had been originally used for retrieval experiments in the first two editions of NTCIR: NTCIR-1 provided about 300,000 abstracts published between 1988 and 1997, of which over 150,000 are in both languages, while NTCIR-2 provided about 530,000 abstracts from 1997 to 1999 and extended summaries of grant reports for the entire period (1988–1999). In this second collection, about 400,000 of the abstracts and extended summaries are in Japanese and the rest in English.

NTCIR-7 provides 1956 topics chosen from among the research articles (divided evenly between English and Japanese). For each of them, a set of IPCs is used as ground truth. For 1050 topics, the IPCs are highly relevant, while for the rest they are relevant but not highly relevant. Expertise in patent laws was used to identify potentially correct IPC codes for each topic in an efficient manner. In Japanese patent law, an applicant is not granted a patent for an invention available to the public. However, Article 30 permits a 6-month grace period during which an invention will not lose its novelty if the disclosure was made by an inventor through publication for a designated association. Patent applications filed by means of this exception must indicate the name of the publication and when the invention claimed was disclosed.

From the 10 years' worth of JPO documents, more than 9000 applications via Article 30 were collected automatically and then associated manually with the corresponding research abstract. The manual verification step was necessary because details of the disclosure contain only the name of the journal or proceedings and the date of publication, but the authors and titles of the paper are not available. In summary, for each topic, the IPC codes assigned with the corresponding research abstract were used as the correct answers, with the average number of correct IPC codes per topic being 2.3.

The same patent mining classification task as NTCIR-7 was repeated at NTCIR-8 using the same test collection. In addition, the NTCIR-8 patent mining task also added an extraction subtask called technical map creation. This is a very ambitious task, as it requires the participants to extract 'technology', 'effect', 'attribute' and 'value' entities from the plain text of the patents and research articles in Japanese and English. A total of 2000 documents were manually analysed and annotated (500 for each of the four types of documents). Half are provided as training data, 10 % for the 'dry run' and the remaining 40 % for the test itself.

3.3.4 Machine Translation

Starting from 2008, NTCIR introduced a machine translation benchmark, based on the existing sets of patent data. For NTCIR-7 the training data consists of 1.8 million Japanese–English sentence pairs, while the test set consists of 1381. The gold standard for intrinsic measurement of translation accuracy is inherent in the paired sentences, and participants could use either language as the source language and the other as the target language. Additionally, a set of 124 search topics from the previous year (i.e. claims from Japanese patent applications) were provided to participants, together with manual translations of those topics into English. Cross-lingual retrieval results obtained with English queries are then used as a basis for extrinsic evaluation by assessing the effect of different automated translation techniques on the mean average precision (MAP) for the retrieval of Japanese patents.

For NTCIR-8 the collection was expanded with patent applications from JPO and granted patents from USPTO up to and including 2007, reaching over five million Japanese and over two million English documents. Consequently, the training set increased to 3.2 million Japanese–English sentence pairs extracted from the 1993 to 2005 subcollections of JPO and USPTO patent documents. The test data is different compared to the previous year: 1251 Japanese–English and 1119 English–Japanese aligned sentence pairs are provided to participants, to make sure that the analysis can identify any difference in performance due to the original language of the sentences. As in the previous year, evaluation is done both intrinsically based on the BLUE score and extrinsically using 91 of the NTCIR-6 topics.

Chinese was added to the machine translation collection of NTCIR-9, though the training data was initially only available to registered participants. Currently, the Chinese–English sentence pairs are also available, but for a fee. About one million Chinese–English sentence pairs were made available for training, and participants had to provide translations for 2000 Chinese sentences. For the English–Japanese and Japanese–English subtasks, the training data for NTCIR-9 remained the same as in the previous edition, and for each of the direction, the test data consisted of 2000 sentences to be translated.

3.4 Experiments and Observations

Now that we have an overview of all the available patent-related data generated and made available in the context of NTCIR events between 2000 and 2014, we can look at some of the results obtained over the years. In each of the following sections, we first review the ground truth creation and then summarise the results. This is intended to put into context those results and to allow the reader a critical perspective on the observations.

3.4.1 Retrieval

For retrieval experiments, we further need to subdivide the analysis in three categories: monolingual document retrieval, monolingual passage retrieval and cross-lingual document retrieval.

3.4.1.1 Monolingual

When discussing the results of the retrieval tasks, it is worth making a distinction between the experiments of NTCIR-3 and those that came afterwards. Such a distinction is necessary because of the different nature of the retrieval tasks. NTCIR-3 considered patent retrieval from the perspective of a technically savvy user who is not necessarily a patent examiner. To model that, the trigger for the request for information is a newspaper article, and the expected results are related patents that may provide additional information about the item described in the article. For NTCIR-4, NTCIR-5 and NTCIR-6, the user modelled is a patent examiner tasked with identifying other patents that may invalidate a specific claim of a given patent application.

News Article-Based Task

This particular task and its corresponding topics are quite different from everything else that happened afterwards in evaluation campaigns that focused on patent documents, with the exception perhaps of the TREC Chemical Retrieval track [35], which also had a 'technology survey' task focusing on the type of information requests specific to a technical user who is not necessarily a patent examiner.

An example topic can be found in the final report of the NTCIR-3 patent retrieval task [26], but it essentially contains a title, the headline and the text of the article that triggered the request for information; a description and narrative in their traditional TREC meaning, as well as a set of concepts pertinent to the topic; and a 'supplement' with more information about what should be considered relevant.

The top performing system focused on reweighting the terms based on their statistics in the different collections (patents vs newspaper articles). The insight is based on the observation that the nature of the texts is significantly different and therefore the weighting of the terms should take into account the frequency of terms in the two collections. The authors called this *'term distillation'* [25], but essentially it is the explicit combination of a weight based on the domain of the query (i.e. articles) and that of the target document (i.e. patents). The issue of terminology has been later revisited and confirmed by Nanba et al. [39], Mahdabi et al. [36] and Andersson et al. [1], so it appears to be a reasonable conclusion to draw from the first benchmark on patent retrieval.

At the other end of the spectrum, the lowest results were obtained by a method based on random indexing [44]. This low performance of statistical semantics on patent retrieval had been also reproduced for latent semantic indexing by Moldovan et al. in 2005 [37], by Aono in NTCIR-6 in 2007 [2] and by a more recent revisiting of random indexing [34], albeit each using different collections. This is not to say that statistical semantics do not have a word to say in the problem of patent retrieval, but rather that perhaps their direct application to the problem needs to be more nuanced.

For the rest of the spectrum, the relatively small set of topics, and the large variance in the intermediary steps taken by each participant (tokenisers, stemmers, filters of various kinds), makes it risky to draw any conclusions. The organisers of NTCIR-3 observed this and made their own study, keeping everything fixed except the retrieval model [28]. The conclusion they draw is that the methods which are known to perform best on other tasks also perform best on this particular test case (e.g. BM25, among all the probabilistic models tried in the study). In particular, the methods that perform best are those that control for document length. This is of course reminiscent of the discussions in the early years of TREC [22], when it was observed that different methods would perform significantly differently on subcollections that differed in their average document length or in their document length distribution.

For the patent data, the length aspect was revisited in more detail by one of the participants, Fujita [18], who reapplied the analysis performed in the early TREC test collections. The study complemented the one done 2 years before by the task organisers [28] by also considering language modelling in addition to the different variants of the TF*IDF. After having observed no correlation between relevance and document length in terms of words, Fujita also considered document length in terms of claims—a very patent-specific approach—under the assumption that it is actually the number of claims that models the multiple topicality present in longer newspaper articles, but this showed similar results: no correlation with relevance, a tendency of TF*IDF methods to retrieve longer documents and a tendency of LM methods to retrieve shorter documents. In the end the author concludes that simply using a higher document length penalty in the TF*IDF model (i.e. a higher b parameter in BM25) is enough to obtain good performance, but reasonably stops short of claiming that language modelling will not perform better if more efforts are directed towards it.

Patent Application Claim-Based Tasks

Starting with NTCIR-4, the patent retrieval tasks moved away from the general, technology survey model of information need, towards the specific model of a patent examiner [11]. This is referred to here as *invalidity* search and corresponds to the *prior art* task organised later in CLEF-IP [42] or TREC-CHEM [35].

It is particularly instructional to look at participants' systems over the three evaluation campaigns. Among them, the teams from Hitachi (HTC) and the one from the Graduate School of Library at the University of Tsukuba (AFLAB) submitted runs in all 3 years.

HTC observed that the number of stop words did not have a significant effect in 2004 and therefore that number reduced significantly (from approximately 3000 to only 30) in later years. Their experiments also show that using only the claim as input to the search system is not recommended because it does not contain sufficient information. Not only are the claims in general rather information sparse, but the use of only the first claim may, in hindsight, also be problematic.

The best method from the HTC group was the one that used all of their filters: stop words, special weights for measurement terms, TF calculated based on the entire query document, addition of terms from abstract and the entire document to the query, co-occurrence-based term weighting and, finally, filtering or score adjustment using theme codes. These observations are consistent across the different query sets.

The group at NTT DATA (RDNDC runs in Table 3.2) also obtained consistently good results in the 2 years it participated in the track. The characteristic feature of their system was query expansion with keywords from the *'detailed description of the invention'*. They show that this provides more useful keywords compared to a standard query term expansion based on Local Context Analysis (LCA) [49]. In both NTCIR-4 and NTCIR-5, the team put an impressive amount of effort into manual morphosyntactic rules to both extract the components of the invention from the claim (241 patterns) and identify the sentences in the detailed description of the invention that correspond to the previously identified components of the invention (104 patterns). While the first appear to be reasonably feasible due to the nature of the genre in the patent claims, the second are, as the authors point out, a 'challenging problem'. They therefore provide an alternative which removes the general rules and replaces them with a greedy approach: find those sentences which contain the most terms of the component of the invention, in the same order.

RDNDC runs also use IPC information. In NTCIR-4 this was used to reweight terms based on their frequency in different IPC classes, while in NTCIR-5 the RDNDC team used the IPC information as a basis for re-ranking: after their ranking systems provided initial results, the retrieved patents having at least one IPC class in common with the query patent application received a multiplicative boost. According to their experiments, this added 2.5–5 % to the mean average precision for all their runs.

The team at the University of Tsukuba (runs denoted by IFLAB or AFLAB in NTCIR reports) also used a module to split the claim into its constituent components as a first step. In 2004, they compared a simple punctuation-based method with a more complex set of morphosyntactic patterns based on rhetorical structure theory initially introduced by Shinmori and colleagues [46, 47] the year before in NTCIR-3. They found that the simpler method worked just as well, thanks to the regularity of the rules of proper patent claim editing, and in subsequent years they continued only with this simpler method.

Perhaps the most interesting thing to observe in the experiments performed at the University of Tsukuba is that the effect of the IPC differed across the years.

Table 3.2 Ranking and MAP scores of systems across years and test collections according to the 'relaxed' relevance criteria

Evaluation reported	May 2004	Dec 2005		May 2007		
Document set	NTCIR-4	NTCIR-5		NTCIR-6		
Topics	NTCIR-4	NTCIR-4	NTCIR-5	NTCIR-4	NTCIR-5	NTCIR-6
# topics	34	34	1189	34	1189	1685
1	RDNDC9 .27	HTC10[a] .25	AFLAB5[b] .17	HTC10 .26	HTC10 .20	HTC10 .12
2	RDNDC2 .25	RDNDC501.24	RDNDC517.17	HTC06 .23	HTC05 .17	HTC06 .10
3	HTC20[c] .25	fj002-02 .22	HTC12 .16	AFLAB1.16	AFLAB1.15	HTC04 .08
4	ricoh[d]3 .22	ricoh2 .20	fj002-07 .16	hcu1 .16	JSPAT3 .09	AFLAB1 .08
5	AFLAB11[b].20	AFLAB3[b] .18	ricoh3 .15	JSPAT3 .12	hcu1 .08	hcu1 .05
6	fj002-10 .19	kle-patent1 .16	BOLA2 .14	JSPAT1 .11	BETA6-1.06	JSPAT0 .04
7	PLLS6 .17	BOLA3 .15	kle-patent1 .08	BETA6-1.11		BETA6-1 .04
8	TRL8 .13	TRL12 .11	TRL1 .07			
9	NUT1 .08	TUT-K2 .09	JSPAT1 .05			
10		JSPAT2 .08	TUT-K2 .04			

Consecutive runs of the same group with difference less than 10 % are omitted

[a]HTC10 in NTCIR-5 is different from HTC10 in NTCIR-6

[b]In the NTCIR-4, and -5 proceedings, the system was referred to as 'IFLAB'. We rename it here to make it consistent with its latest version in NTCIR-6

[c]In the NTCIR-4 proceedings, the system was referred to as 'JAPIO'. We rename it here to make it consistent with NTCIR-5 and NTCIR-6

[d]In the NTCIR-4 the system was referred to as 'LAPIN'. We rename it here to make it consistent with its latest version in NTCIR-5

In NTCIR-4 the use of the IPC (as a hard filter) was apparently detrimental to the precision of the results (5.9 % and 3.5 % reduction in the rigid 'highly relevant' and the relaxed 'relevant' evaluation, respectively); in NTCIR-5 the same approach to the use of IPC codes showed an apparent improvement (8 % and 7.5 % on the rigid and relaxed evaluations, respectively). This difference might be explained by the nature of the ground truth in the 2 years: in NTCIR-4 it was (partially) manually created, while in NTCIR-5 it was completely automatic (based on citations). If we further imagine that search patterns at a patent office often rely on metadata (IPC or related classifications), we could reasonably hypothesise that there is a bias towards patents in the same class in the ground truth. This is not a problem of NTCIR (nor is it certain to be a problem at all), but rather an issue that has to be considered in all evaluation campaigns using the citations.

Finally another system that was consistently among the top performers in terms of MAP was the one created at RICOH Ltd [24]. In their first year of participation, they considered whether it is sufficient to index only the abstract and claims of the patent collection. Their experiments showed that in fact the information present in the entire patent is needed for better relevance estimation. This confirms the findings of the other systems presented above and complements them because if the others had considered this additional information on the query side, RICOH experiments consider it on the target document side.

In the following year, RICOH experiments also confirmed that the use of IPC codes as filters, either on the query side (as usual filters on the retrieved documents) or on the target documents side (as a form of pseudo-relevance feedback), improves the precision of the results. Echoing the University of Tsukuba results, they observe that this improvement is clearly visible for NTCIR-5, but arguable for NTCIR-4. Additionally, RICOH conducted experiments with the use of synonyms for query expansion. Synonyms were generated based on an English–Japanese dictionary (by collecting all terms which appeared in the definition of English terms containing one of the query terms to collect 'term siblings' from the dictionary). This yielded only marginal improvements, in marked contrast to all of the methods discussed above, which had also considered query expansion and had observed more marked improvements. The difference here is probably in the fact that the others had selected query expansion terms on a query-by-query basis (or just reweighted them), while in this case the synonym set was created a priori and used consistently for all queries. It is easy to imagine why this might be less effective: if we were to take an example in English, consider the synonyms on the term 'bank': 'depository', 'exchequer', or 'beach', 'shore', or 'chair', 'seat'.

All the experiments mentioned so far were Japanese monolingual. While topics were always available in Japanese and English, and some documents existed in English as well (i.e. for the PAJ subcollection), the focus of NTCIR-4 and NTCIR-5 had been on Japanese monolingual retrieval. In NTCIR-6 the organisers introduced a separate task for English monolingual patent retrieval, with its own set of topics and its own target document collection (from the USPTO). Five teams participated in this English retrieval subtask at NTCIR-6. Table 3.3 shows the top results for each participant.

Table 3.3 Best performing
results for each of the
participants in the NTCIR-6
English retrieval subtask

Run ID	Strict	Run ID	Relaxed
AFLAB2	0.04	AFLAB2	0.08
hcu1	0.03	NTNU	0.07
KLE1	0.03	KLE1	0.07
NTNU	0.02	JSPAT2	0.06
JSPAT0	0.01	hcu1	0.02

The best performing system integrated content and citation information in scoring. Fujii compares no citation information with PageRank and with a domain-specific method and observes the most improvement with the domain-specific method. This is the first system that explicitly uses patent citations in ranking, and the use of this kind of information has been proven beneficial both at CLEF-IP in the system built by Lopez and Romary [33] and in TREC-CHEM in the system built by the group at Geneva University Hospitals [19].

Overall, the results from the English retrieval subtask are hard to qualify. The values are certainly lower, but they are a different task, so a direct comparison cannot be made. Based on the participants' report, it seems that there was some unfamiliarity with the nature of the USPTO documents. For instance, if, as we have seen, most of the systems had used IPC codes to improve their precision when searching JPO patents, this was no longer as useful because the USPTO, at the time, primarily used a very different classification scheme and only assigned one IPC code to each patent. Another example is the APP-DATE field, which does not necessarily have the same meaning as the FDATE field of the Japanese applications. The experiments done at Pohang University of Science and Technology (POSTECH) [31] had shown that the use of the APP-DATE field actually reduced precision, and this, in principle, should never happen if it had the meaning that the team had expected it to have.

3.4.1.2 Passage Retrieval

In NTCIR-3 it was observed that patents are significantly longer documents than newspaper articles, and, apart from the implications of this in the document scoring methods, it was also decided to have a subtask on retrieving passages as opposed to full documents. NTCIR-4 first defined such a subtask, but it was not evaluated that year, so NTCIR-5 considered it again. This time, participants were given both topics and relevant documents, and the passage retrieval task consisted of retrieving relevant passages from the known relevant documents. Therefore, there were 41 topics (7 for the dry-run and 34 for the formal run of NTCIR-4) and 378 relevant documents. For each of the relevant documents, participants had to rank its paragraphs in order of their expected utility as a basis for judging the relevance of the document. A new evaluation metric was defined—the Combinational Relevance Score (CRS)—proportional to the rank at which the list of paragraphs contains at least one relevant paragraph (or set of paragraphs, if the evaluators considered a set

Table 3.4 Passage retrieval evaluation results in NTCIR-5

Document relevance: strict				Document relevance: relaxed			
174 documents				356 documents			
		MAP, passage relevance				MAP, passage relevance	
Run	CRS	Strict	Relaxed	Run	CRS	Strict	Relaxed
IFLAB4	12.34	0.47	0.45	IFLAB4	10.91	0.49	0.46
IFLAB5	13.06	0.51	0.47	IFLAB5	11.23	0.49	0.46
RDNDCP503	13.07	0.47	0.45	JSPAT1	11.67	0.49	0.46
RDNDCP507	13.07	0.47	0.46	HTC1	11.70	0.50	0.47
HTC1	13.24	0.50	0.47	RDNDCP503	12.10	0.43	0.42
JSPAT1	13.25	0.52	0.48	RDNDCP505	12.13	0.44	0.44
HTC2	14.41	0.48	0.46	HTC5	12.14	0.51	0.48
BASE	16.32	0.34	0.35	BASE	16.23	0.37	0.37

instead of just one). Table 3.4 shows the results of the runs, for each document and paragraph relevance category (strict or relaxed). Here, the mean average precision (MAP) is calculated on the ranking of the paragraphs within a target document.

Most participants' runs were essentially the same as for document retrieval, with the difference that instead of indexed documents, they indexed passages as documents. IPC codes were no longer used because they were irrelevant given that the re-ranking was taking place inside a target document known to be relevant to the query. Only HTC substantially changed their indexing scheme and moved from a term-based index to a character n-gram index. The motivation for this was the relatively small amount of text in a passage and the resulting desire to have a more flexible matching scheme. Unfortunately, a direct comparison with a term-based index was not made, and it is consequently difficult to estimate the benefit of this approach.

3.4.1.3 Cross-Lingual

NTCIR had organised cross-lingual evaluation tracks before and continued to organise one in parallel to the patent retrieval track [32]. The organisers of the early patent retrieval tracks had encouraged participants to use the multilingual collections that were provided in their experiments. Some did use those collections to enhance system performance on a monolingual retrieval task [9, 10], and others did provide a few cross-lingual runs for the sole purpose of exploring and evaluating cross-lingual systems. Nevertheless, the number of cross-lingual runs was considerably smaller than that of monolingual runs: NTCIR-3 had some cross-lingual runs (3 of 8 participants submitted such runs), NTCIR-4 had only one cross-lingual run of the 111 runs submitted, and NTCIR-5 had none.

In NTCIR-3 IFLAB [8] created a query translation engine based on both a commercial dictionary and language and translation models built on the available corpora. In particular, their translation engine kept the word order of the source language because it had been previously observed [7] that between English and Japanese technical terms use the same word order about 95 % of the time.

The groups at the University of California, Berkeley [4], and the Swedish Institute of Computer Science (SICS) [44], while not having Japanese-speaking members, attempted the task of cross-lingual retrieval. Berkeley used external dictionaries (Babelfish) to translate the queries for both English-to-Chinese and English-to-Japanese retrieval. The innovative part was that when the dictionary did not find a translation, the team submitted the query to a Chinese or Japanese search engine and took, from the top 200 documents, the Chinese or Japanese terms surrounding the English terms, weighting them by the distance to the English terms. This amounts to a cross-lingual pseudo-relevance feedback.

The SICS team used random indexing [43] to construct a bilingual thesaurus, which they then used to generate cross-lingual queries. The approach was purely statistical and, in the absence of a manual check on the results of the bilingual thesaurus generation process, the results were significantly poorer than those using existing dictionaries.

In NTCIR-4, RICOH [24] performed English-to-Japanese cross-lingual retrieval. They did query translations and search on a multilingual database. Their officially submitted English-to-Japanese run (LATIN5) obtained a P@10 score comparable to their English-to-English run (0.16 and 0.17, respectively), but P@10 scores on different collections cannot be directly compared and their English-to-Japanese results were significantly lower than those of their Japanese-to-Japanese run (0.20). Given that queries were available in both English and Japanese, they were able to compare the performance of the query translator with the results obtained in retrieval. They showed that these two elements do not necessarily correlate: the query translation (from English to Japanese) closest to the original Japanese query did not obtain the best result in terms of P@10.

3.4.2 Classification

As mentioned in Sect. 3.3.2, the initial patent classification tasks at NTCIR addressed two classification problems: first, a classification of patents against the set of themes (technology areas) present in the F-terms; and second, a classification against the set of term codes (i.e. viewpoint + 2-digit code) known as F-terms. The first one can be seen as a coarse classification based exclusively on topicality, while the second one a refinement of the first, aiming to identify different aspects within the same technical domain. Theme classification was only evaluated in 2005 at NTCIR-5 (Table 3.5); in the following NTCIR, the focus was exclusively on the more challenging F-term classification (Table 3.6).

From Tables 3.5 and 3.6, we can see that the simplest vector similarity methods (vector space model, χ^2) are not up to par with typical machine learning methods (K-nearest neighbour, Naive Bayes, support vector machine). We should note that

Table 3.5 Results of theme classification tasks

NTCIR-5				
Runid	Model	MAP	R-Precision	F-measure
BOLA1	K-NN	0.69	0.59	0.27
JSPAT2	Naive Bayes	0.66	0.56	0.53
WGLAB9	K-NN	0.62	0.53	0.07
FXDM3	VSM	0.49	0.39	0.38

what is denoted here by χ^2 (run NUT05 [23] in NTCIR-6) is actually similar to a typical vector space model (VSM) but with a change in the weighting function, reminiscent of information content studies.

For this study, it is particularly of interest to look at K-nearest neighbour (K-NN) methods, since they have obtained both very good and very poor results in experiments in both years. As usual, it is not straightforward to compare two systems, even if they use the same method, because there are numerous components or steps that can change. Nevertheless, we can see that the differences between BOLA1 and WGLAB9 in NTCIR-5 are: (1) the information sources from the document (i.e. PAJ, 'technological field', 'purpose' or 'method'); and (2) the similarity function (cosine similarity for a vector space based on BM11 versus a similarity function based on structural similarity between documents). More subtle is the difference observed between RDNDC14 and NICT01 in NTCIR-6. Both systems used K-NN on top of a vector space built on BM25, with terms extracted using the same NLP tool (ChaSen) and from the same parts of the document (abstract and claims). Yet their results are significantly different (a drop of 30–40 % in scores). The difference probably lies in the fact that RDNDC14 only used the first claim, as opposed to the entire set of claims used in NICT01, and the latter weighted the score of each F-term by a constant determined using experiments.

3.4.3   Text Mining

The first attempt to do text mining (in the general sense) had actually been at NTCIR-4 with the patent map generation task. Its purpose was to generate a patent map driven by a specific theme (e.g. automobiles), in an automatic or semi-automatic way. The desired map is a two-dimensional plot generated by considering pairs of relevant concepts. For one topic this might mean that on one axis different 'problems to be solved' are to be placed and on the second axis the 'solutions' are expected. For another topic the axes might be 'form of product' and 'date of publication'. The cells were then to indicate patent numbers connecting the two concepts, in the context of that topic. From the outset, this was a difficult task, both for the organisers and the participants. It requires a much deeper understanding of the content of the patent than relevance evaluation and a sufficiently large set of topically relevant documents for each topic.

Table 3.6 Results of term classification tasks

NTCIR-5

RunID	Model	MAP	R-Prec.	F-measure
NICT5	K-NN	0.50	0.46	0.44
JSPAT1	SVM	0.40	0.39	0.28
FXDM10	VSM	0.21	0.20	0.16
	–	–		
	–	–		
	–	–		
	–	–		

NTCIR-6

RunID	Model	Exact match		Relaxed match	
		MAP	F-measure	MAP	F-measure
NCS02	N. Bayes	0.49	0.40	0.58	0.50
GATE03	SVM	0.48	0.41	0.58	0.51
NICT01	K-NN	0.45	0.38	0.55	0.48
JSPAT01	SVM	0.44	0.30	0.54	0.37
NUT05	χ^2	0.41	0.24	0.51	0.38
RDNDC14	K-NN	0.27	0.24	0.36	0.34
Baseline		0.28		0.37	

The organisers selected six topics from NTCIR-3, each having at least 100 relevant documents, and the participants had to define the axes on their own and populate the matrix correspondingly. This required experience in a large number of domains related to information access, which resulted in only two teams participating, each consisting of several institutions.

The task can be treated in two steps: identification of meaningful concepts and population of the cells with patents connecting the two concepts. One team focused on clustering, using, among other methods, latent semantic analysis. The other team focused on claim analysis, using morphosyntactic patterns. In hindsight, we may argue that a combination of the two methods would potentially bring even better results.

The organisers created reference patent maps which were used to guide the assessors in their evaluation, but given the nature of the task, there was only a qualitative assessment of the results, not a quantitative one. Participants received their evaluation as statements of the assessors, for five of the six topics. It was observed that in the absence of an ontology, it becomes extremely difficult to populate the axes meaningfully. Both participants received positive and negative comments on the different topics, and probably the lesson learned is that, while the task is quite challenging, current tools may assist a user who has to create such a map manually.

In NTCIR-7, the long-term goal was the automatic production of technical trend maps. These resemble the patent maps described above but with the source of the maps not being restricted to patents. As a first step in this research, the task was to classify research papers according to their IPCs to enable technical or technological trends in academia and industry to be summarised together in a single map. One challenge was the need for cross-genre classification involving research papers and patents.

Another challenge was cross-lingual classification. To train a classifier that can assign one or more IPC codes to an input document, the JPO and USPTO patent collections were used. Each document was a research abstract in Japanese or English, resulting in four combinations of languages for the training and test documents. Table 3.7 shows the mean average precision for different runs and combinations of languages [38]. In Table 3.7, 'J-to-J' and 'E-to-E' indicate that both the test and training documents were in the same language, while 'J-to-E' indicates a cross-lingual classification for which the training documents were in English. There were no submissions to an 'E-to-J' classification.

Table 3.7 shows that the MAP of the top run for J-to-E closely matched those for E-to-E (and for J-to-J). All of these runs used variations of the K-nearest neighbour method. The MAP for each of the top systems was fairly high compared with that for ad hoc retrieval, which makes sense because the use of multiple training examples made the task more like relevance feedback than ad hoc retrieval.

The MAP of the top J-to-E run, xrce_j2e (0.44), was higher than those of E-to-E runs by the same group, such as xrce_e2j2e (0.42). This system [5] used a language modelling information retrieval approach, calculating the similarity between an input document q_s and a particular training document d_t as the probability $P(q_s|d_t)$

Table 3.7 Evaluation for the IPC-based classification of research abstracts

J-to-J		E-to-E		J-to-E	
RunID	MAP	RunID	MAP	RunID	MAP
HTC13	0.44	NEUN1_S1	0.49	xrce_j2e	0.44
HTC11	0.44	NEUN1_S2	0.47	AINLP05	0.11
HTC12	0.44	NEUN1_S3	0.45	AINLP06	0.10
HTC07	0.44	xrce_e2j2e	0.42	AINLP02	0.09
HTC01	0.43	xrce_en_lm	0.42	AINLP03	0.09
HTC06	0.43	xrce_en_filter	0.42		
HTC05	0.43	xrce_en_pp	0.41		
HTC08	0.43	nttcs2	0.35		
HTC10	0.43	nttcs1	0.34		
HTC03	0.43	KECIR	0.29		
HTC02	0.43	rali2	0.14		
HTC09	0.42	ICL07	0.14		
HTC04	0.42	rali1	0.14		
nttcs4	0.40	ICL07_2	0.13		
HCU1	0.39	BRKLYPM-EN-02	0.13		
HCU2	0.39	AINLP04	0.10		
HTC14	0.39	BRKLYPM-EN-04	0.10		
nttcs3	0.36	AINLP01	0.10		
nttcs2	0.34	BRKLYPM-EN-03	0.09		
nttcs1	0.33	PI-5b	0.04		
KECIR	0.27				
HCU3	0.14				
nut1-1	0.07				
nut2-1	0.04				

that q_s would be generated from d_t. For the cross-lingual runs, the NTCIR-1 bilingual document collection was used to estimate the probability that a source-language word w_s would be translated into a target-language word w_t. The resultant probability $P(w_t|w_s)$ was summed over w_s and w_t to calculate $P(q_s|d_t)$. Therefore, using more than one w_s and w_t led to an effect similar to query expansion, which presumably accounts for xrce_j2e outperforming the corresponding monolingual runs.

To compare the MAP of the paper-to-patent cross-genre runs with that of a patent-to-patent classification, one of the organisers who submitted HCU1 in Table 3.7 performed a classification of JPO patent applications, obtaining a MAP of 0.37, which was comparable to that of HCU1 for J-to-J runs (0.39).

The IPC-based classification was also performed in NTCIR-8, with a variable granularity for the IPC codes (e.g. subclass, main group and subgroup) being used for evaluation purposes. As expected, the MAP was generally higher for the coarse-grained classes. As in NTCIR-7, there were no E-to-J submissions, but three

J-to-E runs were submitted by one participating group, which also submitted E-to-E runs [48]. Although it is not clear how this group matched an input document in Japanese to documents in English, their presentation slide at the NTCIR-8 meeting suggested the use of Google language tools.[1] Comparing the runs for this group, the MAPs for J-to-E runs were slightly higher than those for E-to-E runs, irrespective of the granularity of the IPC codes.

In NTCIR-8, the creation of technical trend maps was also undertaken. The purpose was to extract fundamental technologies and their effects from the research abstracts or patent documents in question. The effect of a technology is represented by an attribute and its value. These were the definitions of the elements to be extracted [40]:

- TECHNOLOGY: algorithms, tools, materials and data used in each study or invention.
- EFFECT: pairs of ATTRIBUTE and VALUE tags.
- ATTRIBUTE and VALUE: effects of a technology that can be expressed by a pair comprising an attribute and a value.

The following is an example sentence annotated with the above tag set:

```
Through <TECHNOLOGY>closed-loop feedback control
</TECHNOLOGY>, the system could<EFFECT><VALUE>
minimize</VALUE> the <ATTRIBUTE>power loss
</ATTRIBUTE></EFFECT>.
```

Although the input documents were not actually organised as a map, the extracted elements could be of help in determining appropriate axes for a map. The submitted runs were evaluated by recall, precision and F-measure on an element-by-element basis for different combinations of document types (research abstract or patent) and languages (Japanese or English).

The general trends presented in the evaluation results were as follows. First, the precision was higher than the recall, irrespective of the document type, language or element type. This suggests that it was difficult to identify exhaustively the various technical terms and expressions used to describe technologies. Moreover, because recall and precision were calculated on an element-by-element basis, the recall becomes zero if even a single word in an element is mislabelled. Second, the evaluation results for the patents were higher than that for the research abstracts, which suggests that technical terms and expressions in patents are more standardised than those in research papers. Finally, the evaluation results for documents in Japanese were higher than those for documents in English. However, this tendency could be caused by differences between participating systems, because no group submitted runs involving both languages.

---

[1] http://research.nii.ac.jp/ntcir/workshop/OnlineProceedings8/NTCIR/03-NTCIR8-PATMN-TeodoroD_slides.pdf

Table 3.8 Evaluation for the technical trend map creation (R, recall; P, precision; and F, F-measure)

	Japanese						English					
	Research			Patent			Research			Patent		
RunID	R	P	F	R	P	F	R	P	F	R	P	F
TRL7	0.18	0.57	0.28	0.41	0.52	0.46	–	–	–	–	–	–
HCU	0.16	0.49	0.24	0.43	0.55	0.48	–	–	–	–	–	–
NUSME-3	–	–	–	–	–	–	0.11	0.38	0.16	0.17	0.37	0.24

Table 3.8 shows the evaluation for the groups that achieved the best F-measure in any configuration. The complete evaluation is available in the overview paper [40]. In Table 3.8, all the groups formulated the extraction task in terms of 'BIO' chunking, which labels each token in a sentence as being the beginning (B), inside (I) or outside (O) of the span of interest. Whereas TRL and NUSME used CRF (conditional random field) models to perform sequential labelling, HCU used an SVM (support vector machine) to classify individual words according to the BIO labels. The general trends described above can also be observed in Table 3.8. In addition, HCU [41] identified typical causes of errors, as follows:

- Specific function words, such as 'by' and 'of', may occur inside or outside an element.
- Technologies can be expressed by a long noun phrase, such as 'a device equipped with functions A, B, … and Z', especially in patents.
- The order of an attribute and its value can vary depending on the grammatical construction, such as in 'high recognition rate' and 'the recognition rate becomes high'.

These individual errors are ultimately caused by the target-element structure not necessarily being a simple sequence of content words.

3.4.4 Machine Translation

While NTCIR started as an evaluation series for information retrieval, it quickly expanded to incorporate other tasks that were also related to the broader topic of information access. Part of this broader information access focus is machine translation (MT), which is both a research topic on its own (and as such is evaluated intrinsically) and a tool for other information access systems (e.g. cross-lingual IR, and as such is evaluated extrinsically). The following two sections cover these two approaches to evaluation.

3.4.4.1 Intrinsic Evaluation

In NTCIR-7, all reference translations used for intrinsic evaluation of machine translation are influenced by rule-based MT systems. This includes both the S600 set of 600 Japanese sentences (three translators, each used rule-based MT systems) and the S300 set of 300 Japanese sentences (three translators, one of whom used a rule-based MT system). Participating systems were compared using BLUE scores. Additionally, human translators evaluated 100 sentences of each participant and assessed them for *adequacy* (essentially, how much of the original information is present in the translation?) and *fluency*, each with a score between 1 (not good) and 5 (good).

In the following year, BLUE was again used as a metric for intrinsic evaluation, and an additional effort was made to invite participants to propose new evaluation metrics. However, this approach resulted in only one participant, and it was not continued in subsequent years. Instead, the following 2 years disposed with the BLUE metric and used only adequacy and *acceptability* (i.e. to what extent can the meaning be understood by a human user?). Table 3.9 shows the BLEU scores from 2008 and 2010, while Table 3.10 shows the adequacy scores from 2008, 2011 and 2013. Comparing the two sets of results, there is one thing that stands out: while statistical machine translation systems (SMTs) clearly outperform the rule-based or example-based systems (RBMTs or EBMTs), in terms of the BLUE scores, the opposite is the case for manual evaluations of adequacy.

Only in NTCIR-9 and NTCIR-10 did one SMT system manage to outperform RBMTs. This system (NTT) also obtained good scores in the automatic evaluation. Nevertheless, we do not go into the details of the machine translation methods here, but rather refer the reader to Chap. 16, which addresses this technology at length. Direct comparison between the numbers obtained in each year is not recommended, because the sets to be translated are different, but the organisers of NTCIR-10 also asked participants to translate the test set of the previous year and in their track report [21] present these results, showing that the vast majority of participants had managed to increase the performance of their systems.

3.4.4.2 Extrinsic Evaluation

All cross-lingual retrieval evaluations are, in essence, extrinsic evaluation of some form of translation technology, but in the NTCIR patent MT tasks, the MT technology was foregrounded and thus the role of cross-lingual IR as extrinsic evaluation of MT was foregrounded.

The NTCIR-7 patent MT task included an extrinsic evaluation of patent translation that the organisers called cross-language patent retrieval (CLPR). The key idea was to view the purpose of machine translation (MT) as being to support ranked retrieval of existing patents to identify previously awarded patents that invalidate some claim in a new patent application. The specific design of the task was:

Table 3.9 BLEU scores for intrinsic evaluation of MT

NTCIR-7						NTCIR-8		
Group	Method	BLEU-SRB	BLEU-MRB300	BLEU-MRB600		Group	Method	BLEU
Japanese to English translation								
NTT	SMT	27.20	35.93	43.72		EIWA-1	RBMT[a]	34.3
Moses[b]	SMT	27.14	36.02	43.40		NICT-1	SMT	30.32
(MIT)	SMT	27.14	36.02	44.69		Moses[b]	SMT	29.08
NAIST-NTT	SMT	25.48	34.66	41.89		KLE-1	SMT	27.75
NiCT-ATR	SMT	24.79	32.29	39.40		DCU-1	SMT	27.61
KLE	SMT	24.49	33.59	40.20		TUTA-2	SMT	26.27
(tsbmt)	RBMT	23.10	37.51	48.02		NICT-4	SMT	25.79
tori	SMT	22.29	27.92	35.02		(TORI-1)	RBMT[a]	25.65
Kyoto-U	EBMT	21.57	29.35	35.49		NICT-3	SMT	24.96
(MIBEL)	SMT	19.93	27.84	32.99		DCU-3	SMT	24.01
HIT2	SMT	19.48	29.33	33.60		TUTA-1	SMT	22.66
JAPIO	RBMT	19.46	32.62	41.77		TORI-2	RBMT[a]	21.56
TH	SMT	15.90	24.20	28.72		KYOTO-1	EBMT	21.23
FDU-MCand	SMT	9.55	19.94	20.27		DCU-4	SMT	20.68
(NTNU)	SMT	1.41	2.48	2.63				

(continued)

Table 3.9 (continued)

NTCIR-7					NTCIR-8		
Group	Method	BLEU-SRB	BLEU-MRB300	BLEU-MRB600	Group	Method	BLEU
English-to-Japanese translation							
Moses[b]	SMT	30.58	–	–	NICT-2	SMT	35.87
HCRL	SMT	20.97	–	–	Moses[b]	SMT	35.27
NiCT-ATR	SMT	29.15	–	–	DCU-1	SMT	33.03
NTT	SMT	28.07	–	–	DCU-7	SMT	30.08
NAIST-NTT	SMT	27.19	–	–	KLE-1	SMT	29.18
KLE	SMT	26.93	–	–	TUTA-2	SMT	28.5
tori	SMT	25.33	–	–	DCU-6	SMT	27.93
(MIBEL)	SMT	23.72	–	–	TUTA-1	SMT	27.82
HIT2	SMT	22.84	–	–	DCU-9	SMT	27.23
(Kyoto-U)	SMT	22.65	–	–	TORI-1	RBMT[a]	26.02
(tsbmt)	RBMT	17.46	–	–	KYOTO-1	EBMT	24.13
FDU-MCand	SMT	10.52	–	–	DCU-14	SMT	1.27
TH	SMT	2.23	–	–			

[a]These RBMT systems also contained a statistical component
[b]This Moses system was not part of the official runs

Table 3.10 Adequacy scores for intrinsic evaluation of MT

NTCIR-7			NTCIR-9			NTCIR-10		
Group	Method	Score	Group	Method	Score	Group	Method	Score
Japanese-to-English translation								
(tsbmt)	RBMT	3.81	JAPIO-1	RBMT	3.67	JAPIO-1	RBMT	3.67
JAPIO	RBMT	3.71	RBMT1-1	RBMT	3.51	RBMT1-1	RBMT	3.57
(MIT)	SMT	3.15	EIWA-1	Hybrid	3.43	EIWA-1	Hybrid	3.53
NTT	SMT	2.96	RBMT3-1	RBMT	3.13	TORI-1	Hybrid	3.48
Kyoto-U	EBMT	2.85	NTT-UT-1	SMT	2.75	NTITI-1	SMT	3.32
Moses[a]	SMT	2.81	TORI-1	Hybrid	2.73	RWTH-1	SMT	3.07
NAIST-NTT	SMT	2.66	RWTF-1	SMT	2.66	HDU-1	SMT	3.01
KLE	SMT	2.59	Baseline1-1	SMT	2.62	ONLINE1-1	SMT	2.94
tori	SMT	2.58	NAIST-1	SMT	2.61	FUN-NRC-1	SMT	2.89
NiCT-ATR	SMT	2.47	FRDC-1	SMT	2.52	NTITI-2	SMT	2.87
HIT2	SMT	2.44	Baseline2-1	SMT	2.43	Baseline1-1	SMT	2.81
(MIBEL)	SMT	2.38	KYOTO-2	SMT	2.41	KYOTO-1	EBMT	2.74
TH	SMT	1.87	KYOTO-1	EBMT	2.38	Baseline2-1	SMT	2.68
FDU-Mcand	SMT	1.75	UOTTS-1	SMT	2.38	OKAPU-1	SMT	2.61
(NTNU)	SMT	1.08	NEU-1	SMT	2.37	TRGTK-1	SMT	2.55
			ONLINE1-1	SMT	2.27	BJTUX-1	SMT	2.25
			ICT-1	SMT	2.27	ISTIC-1	SMT	1.08
			KLE-1	SMT	2.04			

(continued)

Table 3.10 (continued)

English-to-Japanese translation

NTCIR-7			NTCIR-9			NTCIR-10		
(tsbmt)	RBMT	3.53	NTT-UT-1	SMT	3.67	NTITI-2	SMT	3.84
Moses[a]	SMT	2.90	RBMT6-1	RBMT	3.51	JAPIO-1	RBMT	3.53
NTT	SMT	2.74	JAPIO-1	RBMT	3.46	RBMT6-1	RBMT	3.47
NiCT-ATR	SMT	2.59	RBMT4-1	RBMT	3.25	EIWA-1	Hybrid	3.42
(Kyoto-U)	EBMT	2.42	RBMT5-1	RBMT	2.84	ONLINE1-1	SMT	3.38
			ONLINE1-1	SMT	2.67	BJTUX-1	SMT	2.84
			Baselins1-1	SMT	2.69	TSUKU-1	SMT	2.79
			TORI-1	Hybrid	2.60	Baseline1-1	SMT	2.69
			Baseline2-1	SMT	2.48	FUN-NRC-1	SMT	2.67
			KLE-1	SMT	2.35	Baseline2-1	SMT	2.53
			FRDC-1	SMT	2.35	KYOTO-1	EBMT	2.50
			ICT-1	SMT	2.32	TRGTK-1	SMT	2.45
			UOTTS-1	SMT	2.19	ISTIC-1	SMT	2.30
			KYOTO-2	SMT	2.18			
			KYOTO-1	EBMT	2.05			
			BJTUX-1	SMT	1.80			

NTCIR-7	NTCIR-9			NTCIR-10		
Chinese-to-English translation[b]						
	BBN-1	SMT	4.03	BBN-1	SMT	4.15
	NEU-1	SMT	3.51	RWSYS-1	HYBRID	3.52
	RWTH-1	SMT	3.42	SRI-1	SMT	3.51
	LIUM-1	SMT	3.40	HDU-1	SMT	3.5
	IBM-1	SMT	3.39	RWTH-1	SMT	3.49
	FRDC-1	SMT	3.34	ONLINE1-1	SMT	3.45
	KLE-1	SMT	3.34	ISTIC-1	SMT	3.39
	ICT-1	SMT	3.30	SJTU-1	SMT	3.32
	BUAA-1	HYBRID	3.30	TRGTK-1	SMT	3.3
	UOTTS-1	SMT	3.29	BASELINE1-1	SMT	3.23
	BASELINE1-1	SMT	3.29	BJTUX-1	SMT	3.19
	NTT-UT-1	SMT	3.23	MIG-1	SMT	3.05
	ISTIC-1	HYBRID	3.19	BASELINE2-1	SMT	2.82
	NTHU-1	SMT	3.13	EIWA-1	HYBRID	2.8
	BJTUX-1	SMT	3.11	BUAA-1	SMT	2.3
	EIWA-1	HYBRID	3.05	BJTUX-2	EBMT	2.26

[a]This Moses system was not part of the official runs

[b] Only the top 16 systems represented here

- The first claim for each of 124 rejected patent applications was obtained from the Japan Patent Office (JPO) and manually translated into English.
- This English claim was translated by MT into Japanese by each participating team.
- A standard patent retrieval system was used to search the patent collection with the MT-generated Japanese claim as a bag-of-words query.
- Each patent (in Japanese) that was cited in the decision document rejecting the application was treated as a relevant document, and all other documents were treated as not relevant.
- Mean average precision was reported as an evaluation measure.

The NTCIR-8 patent MT task included an extrinsic evaluation of patent translation using the same CLPR design, this time with 91 rather than 124 claims. In NTCIR-7, the claims were selected to be relatively easy (monolingual average precision (AP) between 0.3 and 0.9); in NTCIR-8 the claims were selected to be relatively hard (monolingual AP below 0.4).

The NTCIR-10 patent MT task included an extrinsic evaluation of patent translation that the organisers call the patent examination evaluation (PEE). The key idea is to view the purpose of MT as being to support making a decision on whether to grant a new patent based on an understanding of whether some other (existing) patent invalidates the claims of the new patent application. The specific design of the task is:

- Some number of rejected patent applications to the JPO are selected.
- Bilingual volunteers from the Nippon Intellectual Property Translation Association served as the assessors.
- For each rejected patent, the assessor is given:

  - The decision document (in Japanese) that identifies specific facts found in some specific prior patent that led (perhaps in part) to the rejection of the patent application
  - The translated patent (translated by MT from Japanese to English) in which those specific facts were found

- The assessor is asked to determine (on a graded scale) whether the degree to which those specific facts could have been ascertained from the translated patent.
- A second version of PEE, in which the prior patent is first manually translated by hand from Japanese to Chinese and then by machine from Chinese to English was also run.

It is worth noting that the CLEF-2010 and CLEF-2011 Intellectual Property lab (CLEF-IP, see also Chap. 4) has produced a test collection that could be (but has not yet been) used for extrinsic evaluation of Patent MT. That test collection includes a patent application as a query document and citations from various sources as relevance judgements. The query document is available in a single language (English, French or German), but the EPO granted patents contain two fields (title and claims) in all three languages. These could be suppressed for experimental purposes (although that is not done at CLEF).

3.5 Summary

NTCIR has been a pioneer in creating test collections for patent retrieval. The NTCIR-3 retrieval task, based on information needs extracted from newspaper articles, was not repeated either in NTCIR or in CLEF-IP, primarily due to the cost of assessment. Another common observation with CLEF-IP was the rather reduced interest or ability of teams to provide cross-lingual systems. For monolingual retrieval task, query expansion was one of the features that appears to consistently improve results (see the RDNDC runs in both NTCIR-4 and NTCIR-5, as well as the HTC runs in NTCIR-4, NTCIR-5 and NTCIR-6). For machine translation, intrinsic evaluation based on BLEU shows equal results between rule-based and statistical MT systems (see the NTT run in NTCIR-7 and the EIWA-1 run in NTCIR-8). Classification seems to depend less on the algorithm itself (K-NN, Naive Bayes, SVM, have obtained comparable results in NTCIR-5 and NTCIR-6) but, unsurprisingly, depend more on the features used, though no clear trend can be observed. Finally, text mining is a difficult task to both address and evaluate. A qualitative evaluation performed in NTCIR-4 on six topics from NTCIR-3 provides a starting point, on which further efforts can be built.

References

1. Andersson L, Lupu M, Palotti JRM, Piroi F, Hanbury A, Rauber A (2014) Insight to hyponymy lexical relation extraction in the patent genre versus other text genres. In: Proceedings of IPaMin@KONVENS
2. Aono M (2007) Leveraging category-based LSI for patent retrieval. In: Proceedings of NTCIR-6
3. Attar R, Fraenkel AS (1977) Local feedback in full-text retrieval systems. J Assoc Comput Mach 24:397–417
4. Chen A, Gey F (2002) Experiments on cross-language and patent retrieval at NTCIR-3 workshop. In: Proceedings of NTCIR-3
5. Clinchant S, Renders JM (2008) XRCE's participation to patent mining task at NTCIR-7. In: Proceedings of NTCIR-7
6. Fall C, Torcsvari A, Benzineb K, Karetka G (2003) Automated categorization in the international patent classification. ACM SIGIR Forum 37(1):10–25
7. Ferber G (1989) English-Japanese, Japanese-English dictionary of computer and data-processing terms. MIT Press, Cambridge
8. Fujii A, Ishikawa T (2002) Patent retrieval experiments at ULIS. In: Proceedings of NTCIR-3
9. Fujii A, Ishikawa T (2004) Document structure analysis in associative patent retrieval. In: Proceedings of NTCIR-4
10. Fujii A, Ishikawa T (2005) Document structure analysis for the NTCIR-5 patent retrieval task. In: Proceedings of NTCIR-5
11. Fujii A, Iwayama M, Kando N (2004) Overview of patent retrieval task at NTCIR-4. In: Proceedings of NTCIR-4
12. Fujii A, Iwayama M, Kando N (2004) Test collections for patent-to-patent retrieval and patent map generation in NTCIR-4 workshop. In: Proceedings of the 4th international conference on language resources and evaluation, pp 1643–1646

13. Fujii A, Iwayama M, Kando N (2005) Overview of patent retrieval task at NTCIR-5. In: Proceedings of NTCIR
14. Fujii A, Iwayama M, Kando N (2007) Introduction to the special issue on patent processing. Inf Process Manag 43(5):1149–1153
15. Fujii A, Iwayama M, Kando N (2007) Overview of the patent retrieval task at the NTCIR-6 workshop. In: Proceedings of NTCIR-6
16. Fujii A, Utiyama M, Yamamoto M, Utsuro T (2008) Overview of the patent translation task at the NTCIR-7 workshop. In: Proceedings of NTCIR-7
17. Fujii A, Utiyama M, Yamamoto M, Utsuro T, Ehara T, Echizen-ya H, Shimohata S (2010) Overview of the patent translation task at the NTCIR-8 workshop. In: Proceedings of NTCIR-8
18. Fujita S (2005) Revisiting document length hypotheses: a comparative study of Japanese newspaper and patent retrieval. ACM Trans Asian Lang Inf Process 4(2):207–235
19. Gobeill J, Gaudinat A, Ruch P, Pasche E, Teodoro D, Vishnyakova D (2010) BiTeM site report for TREC Chemistry 2010: impact of citations feedback for patent prior art search and chemical compounds expansion for ad hoc retrieval. In: Proceedings of TREC
20. Goto I, Lu B, Chow KP, Sumita E, Tsou BK (2011) Overview of the patent machine translation task at the NTCIR-9 workshop. In: Proceedings of NTCIR-9
21. Goto I, Chow KP, Lu B, Sumita E, Tsou BK (2013) Overview of the patent machine translation task at the NTCIR-10 workshop. In: Proceedings of NTCIR-10
22. Harman D (1993) Overview of the second text retrieval conference (TREC-2). In: Proceedings of TREC
23. Hashimoto K, Yukawa T (2007) Term weighting classification system using the chi-square statistic for the classification subtask at NTCIR-6 patent retrieval task. In: Proceedings of NTCIR-6
24. Itoh H (2004) NTCIR-4 patent retrieval experiments at RICOH. In: Proceedings of NTCIR-4
25. Itoh H, Mano H, Ogawa Y (2003) Term distillation in patent retrieval. In: Proceedings of the ACL workshop on patent corpus processing
26. Iwayama M, Fujii A, Kando N, Takano A (2003) Overview of patent retrieval task at NTCIR-3. In: Proceedings of ACL workshop on patent process processing
27. Iwayama M, Fujii A, Kando N (2005) Overview of classification subtask at NTCIR-5 patent retrieval task. In: Proceedings of NTCIR-5
28. Iwayama M, Fujii A, Kando N, Marukawa Y (2006) Evaluating patent retrieval in the third NTCIR workshop. Inf Process Manag 42(1):207–221
29. Iwayama M, Fujii A, Kando N (2007) Overview of classification subtask at NTCIR-6 patent retrieval task. In: Proceedings of NTCIR-6
30. Kando N, Leong MK (2000) Workshop on patent retrieval SIGIR 2000 workshop report. ACM SIGIR Forum 34(1):28–30
31. Kim J, Lee Y, Na SH, Lee JH (2007) POSTECH at NTCIR-6 English patent retrieval subtask. In: Proceedings of NTCIR-6
32. Kishida K, Chen KH, Lee S, Chen HH, Kando N, Kuriyama K, Myaeng SH, Eguchi K (2004) Cross-lingual information retrieval (CLIR) task at the NTCIR workshop 3. ACM SIGIR Forum 38(1):17–20
33. Lopez P, Romary L (2010) PATATRAS: retrieval model combination and regression models for prior art search. In: Peters C, Di Nunzio G, Kurimo M, Mandl T, Mostefa D, Peñas A, Roda G (eds) Multilingual information access evaluation I. Text retrieval experiments. Lecture Notes in Computer Science, vol 6241. Springer, Berlin
34. Lupu M (2014) On the usability of random indexing in patent retrieval. In: Proceedings of ICCS
35. Lupu M, Jiashu Z, Huang J, Gurulingappa H, Filipov I, Tait J (2011) Overview of the TREC 2011 chemical IR track. In: Proceedings of TREC
36. Mahdabi P, Andersson L, Keikha M, Crestani F (2012) Automatic refinement of patent queries using concept importance predictors. In: Proceedings of the 35th international ACM SIGIR conference on research and development in information retrieval, pp 505–514

37. Moldovan A, Bot RI, Wanka G (2005) Latent semantic indexing for patent documents. Int J Appl Math Comput Sci 15(4):551–560
38. Nanba H, Fujii A, Iwayama M, Hashimoto T (2008) Overview of the patent mining task at the NTCIR-7 workshop. In: Proceedings of NTCIR-7
39. Nanba H, Kamaya H, Takezawa T, Okumura M, Shinmori A, Tanigawa H (2009) Automatic translation of scholarly terms into patent terms. In: Proceeding of the 2nd international workshop on patent information retrieval, pp 21–24
40. Nanba H, Fujii A, Iwayama M, Hashimoto T (2010) Overview of the patent retrieval task at the NTCIR-8 workshop. In: Proceedings of NTCIR-8
41. Nanba H, Kondo T, Takezawa T (2010) Hiroshima City University at NTCIR-8 patent mining task. In: Proceedings of NTCIR-7
42. Piroi F, Tait J (2010) CLEF-IP 2010: Retrieval experiments in the intellectual property domain. In: Proceedings of CLEF
43. Sahlgren M (2005) An introduction to random indexing. Technical report, SICS, Swedish Institute of Computer Science
44. Sahlgren M, Hansen P, Karlgren J (2002) English-Japanese cross-lingual query expansion using random indexing of aligned bilingual text data. In: Proceedings of NTCIR
45. Schellner I (2002) Japanese File Index classification and F-terms. World Patent Inf 24:197–201
46. Shinmori A, Okumura M, Marukawa Y, Iwayama M (2002) Rhetorical structure analysis of Japanese patent claims using cue phrases. In: Proceedings of NTCIR-3
47. Shinmori A, Okumura M, Marukawa Y, Iwayama M (2003) Patent claim processing for readability - structure analysis and term explanation. In: Proceedings of the ACL workshop on patent corpus processing
48. Teodoro D, Pasche E, Vishnyakova D, Gobeill J, Ruch P, Lovis C (2010) Automatic IPC encoding and novelty tracking for effective patent mining. In: Proceedings of NTCIR-8
49. Xu J, Croft WB (1996) Query expansion using local and global document analysis. In: Proceedings of the 19th annual international ACM SIGIR conference on research and development in information retrieval, pp 4–11

Chapter 4
Evaluating Information Retrieval Systems on European Patent Data: The CLEF-IP Campaign

Florina Piroi and Allan Hanbury

Abstract Although not always evident, patents have an economic and legal impact on our everyday life. The increase of digitally available patent data has triggered a growing interest in the use of information retrieval solutions in the intellectual property (IP) domain. The CLEF-IP benchmarking activity took place from 2009 to 2013 as part of the Conference and Labs of the Evaluation Forum (CLEF). It encouraged and facilitated research in multilingual and multimodal patent retrieval by providing a clean and comprehensive data set for experimentation and realistic retrieval tasks. We describe in this chapter the collection of patents used in the evaluation campaign and the motivation behind the campaign's tasks. We describe each of the seven types of tasks that were organised. We explain how the topics and judgements for each of the tasks were created, as well as the measures involved in assessing the experiments submitted. All the data used in our evaluation activities can be downloaded from the CLEF-IP website under a Creative Commons licence.

4.1 Introduction

The patent system is designed to encourage disclosure of new technologies by granting exclusive rights on the use of inventions to their inventors, for a limited period of time [33]. An important requirement for a patent to be granted is that the described technology should be novel: there is no earlier patent, publication or public communication of a similar idea. To ensure the novelty of an invention, patent offices as well as other intellectual property (IP) service providers perform thorough searches called 'prior art searches' or 'validity searches'. The number of patents in a company's patent portfolio affects the company market value. Therefore, well

F. Piroi (✉) • A. Hanbury
TU Wien, Vienna, Austria
e-mail: florina.piroi@tuwien.ac.at; allan.hanbury@tuwien.ac.at; hanbury@ifs.tuwien.ac.at

© Springer-Verlag GmbH Germany 2017   113
M. Lupu et al. (eds.), *Current Challenges in Patent Information Retrieval*,
The Information Retrieval Series 37, DOI 10.1007/978-3-662-53817-3_4

performed prior art searches that lead to solid, difficult-to-challenge patents are of high importance.

Patent data was of interest for information retrieval (IR) researchers as early as in 1977 when a 'technology survey'-like search was done on a set of 76 US patents [4]. Two decades later, an 'invalidity search' was performed on 60,000 US patents [30]. More recently, research on IR methods for the IP domain has significantly intensified due, not least, to the availability of patent data in digital formats. Workshops, conferences and evaluation tracks were organised in an effort to bring IR and IP communities into discussion (see [13, 17, 22, 42]). The National Institute of Informatics (NII), Japan, initiated a series of workshops and evaluations using patent data as part of the NTCIR (NII Testbeds and Community for Information access Research) Project,[1] focusing on Japanese and Chinese patents and their translations into English. In 2009, two further evaluation activities using patent data were launched, with the purpose of providing large, clean data sets for experimentation: TREC-CHEM and CLEF-IP. TREC-CHEM ran from 2009 to 2011 and was organised as a chemical IR track in TREC (Text Retrieval Conference, [43]), addressing challenges in chemical and patent IR [24, 26]. The collection corpus was restricted to chemical patent documents and chemical journal articles, all in English. The CLEF-IP campaign used European patent data.

In patent search, a novelty breaking document may be published in any language. When an IP expert undertakes a patent search, this search is, therefore, inherently cross-lingual, especially when it should be exhaustive. The CLEF-IP effort encouraged research on multilingual patent retrieval by providing a data set that contains patents in three European languages, patents published by the European Patent Office (EPO). CLEF-IP grew out of the desire to promote research work involving European languages beyond English and to encourage academic use of a large clean collection of patents being made available to researchers.

This chapter continues with a brief description of the patenting process. The purpose of Sect. 4.2 is to spell out in context the patent-related terminology that is used in subsequent sections. Section 4.3 describes the origins of the CLEF-IP collection and how it evolved over the years. It also gives an overview of all the CLEF-IP tasks running in the 5 years that the campaign was organised. Sections 4.4.1–4.4.7 detail the design of each task type in CLEF-IP. They explain how the topics of the tasks were selected, how the relevance judgements were obtained and which metrics were used to assess the efficiency of the runs submitted by task participants. Section 4.5 summarises the methods employed by the participants to solve the posed tasks and shows evaluation results for each of the tasks.

---

[1]NTCIR (NII Testbeds and Community for Information access Research) Project http://research.nii.ac.jp/ntcir/index-en.html.

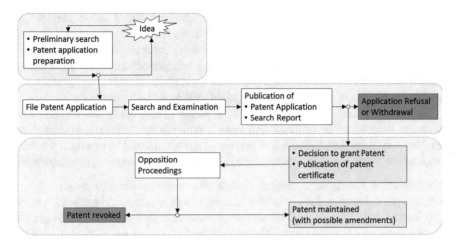

Fig. 4.1 Main steps of the patent granting process

4.2   Patent Background for Information Retrieval

This section aims to define some common terminology used in the patent domain, terminology that helps the IR research community understand the various types of documents that constitute a patent and the relationships between them.[2] We summarise here the patenting process and, with it, explain some patent terminology which is relevant for understanding our choice of tasks, topics and relevance assessments in CLEF-IP.

4.2.1   The Patent Granting Process

The essence of the patent concept can be defined as follows: A patent is an exclusive legal right for the use and exploitation of an invention in exchange for its public disclosure. The holder of a patent may prevent third parties from exploiting their invention in the countries where the patent is deemed valid. The exclusive rights a patent holder has are usually time limited to a period of 20 years. Figure 4.1 shows the main steps in obtaining a patent certificate. We observe in the patenting process three main phases, which we describe in the following:

Pre-application Phase: A person having developed an invention for which exclusive rights are aimed for will first write down a document describing the invention's

---

[2]For extensive introductions to the patent domain and terminology, see previous chapters in this book, or introductory chapters in [2] and [15].

background and a detailed description. He or she also lists a set of claims that specify the extent of the protection sought for the invention. The claims part of this document is a legal text; therefore it is usual to get the help of a patent attorney to draft it. This leads to the document having a mixture of writing styles, with the description of the invention being written in a narrative, technical style, while the claims are written in a legal style (also called 'attornish' or 'patentese').

Before registering this document with a patent office, the inventor (herself or with the help of an IP professional) does a preliminary 'technology survey' on various existing patent databases, in the area of the invention. The results of this pre-application phase search possibly trigger a change in the invention's specifications.

Examination Phase: The document with the invention description and claims prepared in the previous phase is filed at a patent office and becomes thus a 'patent application document.' It receives an alphanumerical code that uniquely identifies it among other patent applications. The date of the filing is known as the 'application date' and is an important attribute of the patent.

When a patent application is filed at a patent office, the application is given to patent professionals for examination. Patent offices follow different patent laws, depending on their jurisdictions, but there is a set of worldwide common criteria that have to be fulfilled by any application before a patent can be granted [11]:

- **Novelty:** the invention should not be previously known.
- **Inventive step:** the invention should not be obvious for experts in the technological area of the invention.
- **Realisable:** the invention can be manufactured by experts in the area.

The novelty check for an invention is done by performing a thorough search on patent and non-patent data collections available to the patent expert examining the application with the aim to find relevant documents. On a regular basis, patent examiners search more than one patent database, and quite often they have to look at documents written in a different language than the language of the patent application. The novelty search is, thus, the most time consuming and expensive part of the application examination. The result of a novelty search (also known as a 'prior art search') is a list of relevant documents stored into a 'search report'; the relevant documents are called patent citations.[3] The citations listed in the search reports have different degrees of relevancy to the application patent, which, in the context of this chapter, we label as follows:

- **Less relevant:** citations that describe prior work but do not destroy the novelty of the application
- **Relevant:** citations that, in combination with other citations in the same report, destroy the novelty of an application
- **Highly relevant:** citations which, taken alone, make a patent application not novel.

---

[3]Note the different meaning of the word 'citation' compared to academic publications.

Granting and Opposition Phases: After the search report is created, a series of official communications between the applicant and the patent office takes place. As an output of these communications, claims are usually modified in order not to infringe on existing patents. Quite often, patent applications are withdrawn.

When the patent office takes the decision to grant a patent, a 'granted patent document' (also known as 'patent certificate') is published. From this point on, for a certain amount of time (9 months at the European Patent Office, EPO), oppositions to a granted patent may be filed to the patent office.

Before the publication of the granted patent, an important procedural step at the EPO—especially for the research on multilingual patent retrieval—is the requirement to provide a translation of the claims in all three official EPO languages (English, German and French) [8].

4.2.2 Patent Administrative Data

During the patenting process, a large number of documents are usually created, both by the patent office and by the applicant or her attorney. The patent application document, the granted patent document, communications to and from the patent office, application document amendments, registration of fee payments and designating the states where the patent is valid are all examples of information that belong to the patent itself.

The general understanding of the patent concept is that, through its claims, it bars other parties from exploiting the invention described in the respective granted patent. However, if we view patents as the complete set of documents generated during the patenting process, we immediately notice that patent data has a substantial administrative side. The administrative data includes, for example, application dates, addresses of the inventors and/or patent assignees, priority references, legal status and so on. Two components of the administrative side of patent documents are of importance to the CLEF-IP tasks, as we will see in the following sections: the patent classification system and the patent families.

Patent Clustering by Technological Areas: Patent classification systems are designed to categorise the patent documents by technological areas and subareas, using the technical features of the disclosed inventions. Several patent classification systems are in use, systems created both by patent offices and by private companies. The most well known are the International Patent Classification System (IPC) [16], the United States Patent Classification (USPC) [44], the F-term Japanese Classification System [40] or the Derwent Classification System [7]. Since January 2013, the EPO and the USPTO (US Patents and Trademarks Office) use a joint classification system: the Cooperative Patent Classification (CPC) System [5].

In the early days of the patent system, patent classification systems were designed as a shelf-location tool for paper files [1]. Even today, these systems are manually maintained by experts and represent a ubiquitous resource for augmenting the query terms of patent retrieval environments.

Patent Clustering by Families: In the current global economy, often enough after filing an initial patent application, inventors will pursue legal protection for their invention in additional countries of interest for them. Following the general patenting process, they will file subsequent applications at each patent office in the countries of interest referring to the original filing as the 'priority claim'. Even though these applications may somewhat differ in content, depending on the patent laws in force at the various patent offices, it is obvious that, worldwide, patent content is often replicated. To assist patent practitioners with minimising the necessary documents they might need to inspect, several methods to group 'parallel' patent documents were devised. The group of patent documents worldwide pertaining to the same invention is called a 'patent family'.

There is no single definition of what a patent family is. Moreover, each provider of patent data constructs the patent families differently. For example, the EPO uses three types of patent family, while the World Intellectual Property Organization (WIPO) additionally defines three further types [14]. Nevertheless, as with the patent classification systems, the patent families are widely used when dealing with patent data.

4.3   A Collection of European Patent Documents

One of our aims when embarking on the CLEF-IP endeavour was to create a test collection to experiment with patent data, a collection that faithfully mirrors the features and challenges of the data used in the daily work of a patent professional. Recall that, in IR, test collections are data sets that are used to measure effectiveness of information retrieval algorithms and systems. They generally contain a set of information needs (topics or queries), a collection of documents where the answers to the information needs are to be found and relevance judgements for the given information needs [37, 39]. In this section, we describe the collection of documents that were used in the CLEF-IP evaluation campaigns. The information needs and relevance judgements are described in the subsequent sections for each of the retrieval tasks that were run.

The CLEF-IP document collection uses actual patent documents from the European Patent Office, EPO, and from the World Intellectual Property Organization, WIPO. These documents contain most of the information that is actively used by patent practitioners in their daily work with patent data.

The bulk of the collection's corpus is made up of patent documents stored as XML files. These are mainly patent application and granted patent documents, additional search report documents and amendments to the patents. Letters of communication between patent offices and applicants, payment of fees, etc., are not part of the CLEF-IP data.

Table 4.1 Number of documents in the CLEF-IP collection

Year	#patents	#XML documents	Source	Application years
2009	~ 1 mil.	~ 1.9 mil.	EPO	1985–2000
2010	~ 1.5 mil.	~ 2.6 mil.	EPO	Up to 2001
2011–2013	~ 1.5 mil.	~ 3.5 mil.	EPO, some WIPO	Up to 2001

Since its first release in 2009, consecutive additions were made to the CLEF-IP test collection, so that it currently contains almost 1.5 million patents stored into approximately 3.5 million XML documents (Table 4.1) and uses about 75GB of hard disk space. These patents are an extract from the larger MAREC[4] collection, which contains documents representing over 19 million patents published at the European Patent Office (EPO), the United States Patent and Trademark Office (USPTO), World Intellectual property Organization (WIPO) and Japan Patent Office (JPO), stored in a common normalised XML format. The XML patent documents in the CLEF-IP collection have XML elements to hold the patent document's abstract, description and claim fields, as well bibliographic information of the administrative data associated with a patent (application and publication dates and references, patent family identifiers, classification symbols, inventors, postal addresses of the inventors, the invention title in three languages, etc.).

The patent documents in the CLEF-IP collection correspond to patent application documents published by the EPO prior to 2002. The patent documents which were published later by the EPO (2002–2009 as available in MAREC) were used to form a *topic pool* out of which we extract subjects for the CLEF-IP tasks [10]. The size of the topic pool was of approximately 800,000 patent documents.

A high percentage of the patent documents published by the EPO (and included in the CLEF-IP collection) refer to applications internationally filed under the Patent Cooperation Treaty [31], also known as 'EuroPCTs'. In these cases, the EPO does not republish the whole patent application, but only bibliographic entries linking to the original application published by the WIPO. Using text-based methods to retrieve such documents is problematic, and therefore for these patent documents we added their WIPO equivalent to the CLEF-IP collection (Table 4.1). In this way, the collection became both larger and more realistic.

One of the most important features of the CLEF-IP corpus is its multilingualism. Patent applications to the EPO are written in one of the three official EPO languages (German, English, French), with the additional requirement that, once the decision to grant a patent is made, the claims section of the patent document must be submitted in all these three languages (Rule 71(3) of the European Patent Convention, Implementing Regulations [8]). Figure 4.2 shows parts of the claims section of the EP 252457 granted patent document where claims are printed in French, German and English. The rest of this patent document is written in French, which we call

---

[4]The MAtrixware REsearch Collection. http://ifs.tuwien.ac.at/imp/marec.

11   **EP 2 525 457 B1**   12

3. Dispositif (1) de fixation selon la revendication 1 ou la revendication 2, dans lequel les pattes (6, 7) présentent chacune une face (13, 14) inférieure dans le prolongement de la surface (4) inférieure du corps (2) central, les rainures (9, 10) périphériques étant disposées entre les pattes (6, 7) et la surface (3) supérieure.

4. Dispositif (1) de fixation selon l'une quelconque des revendications précédentes, dans lequel les pattes (6, 7) présentent une face (11, 12) supérieure comprenant une portion (15, 16) inclinée de la surface (4) inférieure vers la surface (3) supérieure du corps (2) central.

5. Dispositif (1) de fixation selon l'une quelconque des revendications précédentes, dans lequel les rainu-

Patentansprüche

1. Vorrichtung (1) zur Befestigung eines Abschnitts (30) eines Kabelbaums (29) auf einer Halterung (31), wobei die Vorrichtung (1) einen zentralen Körper (2) umfasst, der durch eine Oberseite (3), eine Unterseite (4) und eine Seitenfläche (5) definiert ist, wobei der zentrale Körper (2) mit einer zentralen Nut (8), die sich von der Unterseite (4) zu der Oberseite (3) erstreckt und die Seitenfläche (5) des zentralen Körpers (2) von einer vorderen Seite (A) bis zu einer hinteren Seite (B) quert, und mit zwei Umfangsnuten (9, 10) versehen ist, die sich von der zentralen Nut (8) bis zur Seitenfläche (5) in zwei entgegengesetzte

chaîne.

Claims

1. Device (1) for fixing a cable-tray (29) section (30) to a support (31), the device (1) comprising a central body (2) defined by an upper surface (3), a lower surface (4) and a lateral surface (5), the central body (2) being provided with a central slot (8) extending from the lower surface (4) towards the upper surface (3) and traversing the lateral surface (5) of the central body (2) from a front side (A) to a rear side (B), and with two peripheral slots (9, 10) extending from the central slot (8) to the lateral surface (5) in two oppo-

Claims 1 to 7.

9. Method for assembling a cable tray (29) according to Claim 8, the method comprising the following steps:

- bringing the section (30) into contact with the rim (37) of the wings (35) of the support (31),
- inserting a wire (32) of the section (30) into the central slot (8) of the fixing device (1), the lugs (6, 7) extending between the wings (35) of the support (30),

Fig. 4.2 Patent claims translated from French (*top left*) to German (*top right*) and English (*bottom*)

Table 4.2 Document distributions in the latest CLEF-IP collection

3.5 million documents		
14 % WIPO documents	74 % applications	67 % English
86 % EPO documents	26 % granted patents	22 % German
		6 % French
		5 % unknown

the main language of the document. So CLEF-IP contains both documents with text in one of the three EPO languages (German, French, English) only and documents with content in all three languages (i.e. the granted patent documents).

Table 4.2 shows the percentage distribution of the collection documents by their office of provenance (EPO, WIPO), type of document (application vs. granted patent) and their main document language. There are many more application documents in the collection than granted patents. This shows that very often patents are not pursued after they were examined by an expert at the patent office. Although the English language is overrepresented in the CLEF-IP collection (see Table 4.2), not least due to the EuroPCT applications written in their large majority in English, the collection entails large amounts of content that is in German and French, making the collection suitable for carrying out multilingual retrieval experiments.

According to the specifics of each organised task, further chunks of data were added to the core CLEF-IP patent collection. In the descriptions of the tasks below, each of these additions will be made clear.

4.4   The CLEF-IP Tasks

In providing a collection of patent data suitable for carrying out retrieval experiments, we aimed not only to investigate current IR methods applied to patent search but also to encourage further research in the domain of patent retrieval. Therefore we set on probing the quality of the results the current IR methods give when faced with an information need like the one represented by the patent novelty search, that is, finding the relevant documents for a given patent application. Then we diversified the types of tasks offered to the campaign participants from dealing with textual content only to involvement of image analysis in the IR processes proposed. The tasks organised in the CLEF-IP campaign refer to aspects of patent novelty searches.

Each CLEF-IP evaluation cycle contained a task where, for a given patent application document, we question its validity by searching for documents that are relevant to its described invention (CLEF-IP 2009–2011) or invalidate its claims (CLEF-IP 2012–2013); see Sects. 4.4.1 and 4.4.2. These two tasks are known as the prior art candidates search task (PAC) and the passage retrieval starting from claims search task (PSG). As the CLEF-IP collection has only textual content, the PAC and PSG tasks were, therefore, using and referring only to the available text in patent documents. Patent classification was another CLEF-IP task that, based on the text in patent documents, asked the systems to give back the correct IPC classification symbols to be attached to the document (Sect. 4.4.3).

The technical nature of the patent content makes patent images a necessary component of patents. During a novelty search a patent expert scans hundreds of documents. An experienced IP professional is able to expeditiously dismiss non-relevant documents by quick glances at images in patent documents. Thus we decided to include images in the CLEF-IP campaigns by offering an image-based prior art candidates search task (IMG-PAC, 2011, Sect. 4.4.4) where, in addition to the text of a patent application, the images in the application document were also provided. In the same year, 2011, a patent image classification task was also organised (IMG-CLS). Here, images occurring in patents had to be classified into flowcharts, gene sequences, programme listings, abstract drawing, etc. (see Sect. 4.4.5). The task did not restrict how IR systems were to treat the data; we were particularly interested in methods that used both the textual and visual information to search for prior art.

Table 4.3 CLEF-IP tasks, number of topics in the main topic sets and year of their organisation

Number of topics	2009	2010	2011	2012	2013
Prior art candidates (PAC)	10,000	2000	3973		
Passage retrieval (PSG)				105	149
Patent classification (CLS)		2000	3000		
Image-based retrieval (IMG-PAC)			211		
Image classification (IMG-CLS)			1000		
Flowchart/structure recognition				100	747
Chemical structure recognition				865	

The patent image-based retrieval turned out to be a challenging task as it was of a multimodal nature, using a large amount of data and full patent retrieval [33]. The next logical step in such cases is to break the problem into smaller, easier-to-solve tasks. One such smaller problem in our case is extracting the information from the patent image files so as to store it in some previously defined textual format. In 2012, then, two further patent image-related tasks were designed, with the aim to make the content of the images available to textual searches. The types of images in these tasks were flowcharts and chemical structure images (Sects. 4.4.6 and 4.4.7).

Table 4.3 gives an overview of the tasks and their year of running. The table also shows the number of topics provided in the main topic sets for each of the tasks. In the following we will detail the design of each CLEF-IP task, the data used to extract topics and relevance judgements for the topics.

4.4.1 The 'Prior Art Candidates' Search Task

The goal of this task is to find documents in the CLEF-IP collection that may constitute prior art for a given patent application (called the 'topic patent'). This is one of the most common scenarios in the daily work of a patent expert at a patent office.

4.4.1.1 Choosing Patents as Task Topics

The PAC task was organised from 2009 to 2011; its topics were complete patent documents, including the bibliographic data, which could be processed and used in query creation. Bibliographic data in the CLEF-IP documents contains, among others, also the name and address of the applicant, IPC classification symbols already attached to the patent application and the title of the invention in the three EPO official languages.

The prior art search task organised in 2009 used as topics artificially created patent documents—a virtual 'patent application file'—that was a combination of the abstract, claims, etc., extracted from the latest published patent document available related to an invention [38]. The main reason for this decision was that later publications of a patent's documents usually did not have the problem of missing textual content, like no abstract, or no description fields. The second reason for creating a virtual application using the latest patent document publication (usually a granted patent document) was that such a document had content in more than one official EPO language. Most importantly, the claims of the document given as topic were always available in all three languages of the EPO (claims, in connection with the description of an invention, ultimately support the legal decision that a patent document constitutes prior art for another).

The design of the 2009 prior art search task diverged, however, from the actual novelty searches that patent practitioners perform in their work. The discrepancy was the different relationship between the virtual patent application file and the patent citations used as relevance assessments. We have seen in the description of the patent life cycle (Sect. 4.2) that the search report listing the patent citations is created with respect to the patent application document and not the granted patent which was the basis for the task topics in 2009. The granted patent documents differ in the textual content from the patent application document. The difference does not, however, render patent citations as irrelevant when put in the context of the granted patent document. Nonetheless, the relevance relation between a patent's citations and the granted patent document is of a lesser intensity than the relation between the patent citations and the application document.

Topic Selection Criteria: In 2009, from the topic pool of patent documents, we selected documents that (1) had a corresponding granted patent document, (2) contained a full text description, (3) had at least three citations in their search report, and (4) had at least one citation that was highly relevant. From 2010 onwards, the prior art search task topics were patent application documents. The criteria used to select topic documents out of the topic pool were extended from those used in 2009 [38, Sect. 2.2] by additionally considering the document length and the availability of patent citation documents with a different document language than the application document language [34]. The task's formulation did not change with these modifications ('find documents in the collection that may invalidate a patent document') [32, 33]. Figure 4.3 shows an extract of the list of topics given to the participants. The topics are stored in an XML-like fashion where the topic identifier (<num> tag) is the identifier of the EPO patent application file, the narrative (<narr> tag) states

Fig. 4.3 Excerpt from the file with the list of topics in CLEF-IP PAC tasks

```
<topic>
    <num>EP-1222860-A2</num>
    <narr>Find all patents in the collection that
        potentially invalidate patent application
        EP-1222860-A2.</narr>
    <file>EP-1222860-A2.xml</file>
</topic>
```

```
<?xml version="1.0" encoding="utf-8"?>
<!DOCTYPE patent-document PUBLIC "-//MXW//DTD patent-document XML//EN" "
    http://www.ir-facility.org/dtds/patents/v1.4/patent-document.dtd">
<patent-document ucid="EP-1222860-A2" country="EP" doc-number="1222860"
    kind="A2" lang="FR" family-id="8858784" status="new" date-produced=
    "20090516" date="20020717">
  <bibliographic-data>
  <abstract load-source="docdb" source="EPO" status="new" lang="EN">
    <p>Boiled candies (I) having a rough surface, for the treatment of
        halitosis, are new.</p>
  </abstract>
  <abstract load-source="ep" status="new" lang="FR">
    <p>L'invention a pour objet un bonbon de type sucre cuit
caractérisé en ce qu'il présente une texture rugueuse
destinée au traitement de l'halitose.</p>
    <p>Elle a également pour objet un procédé de préparation
d'un tel bonbon, et son utilisation pour le traitement
de l'halitose.</p>
  </abstract>
  <description load-source="ep" status="new" lang="FR">
  <claims load-source="ep" status="new" lang="FR">
    <claim num="1">
      <claim-text>Bonbon de type sucre cuit caractérisé en ce
qu'il présente une texture rugueuse destinée au
traitement de l'halitose.</claim-text>
    </claim>
    <claim num="2">
```

Fig. 4.4 Excerpt from an XML topic file in CLEF-IP PAC tasks

Table 4.4 Number of topics in the CLEF-IP PAC task

	2009	2010	2011
Topics in the main set	10,000	2000	3973
Topic subsets	500, 1000, 5000	500	—

what the retrieval system's task is and a link is included to the actual XML file where the patent application content is stored (<file> tag). Figure 4.4 shows an excerpt of the XML file referred to in the topic. Table 4.4 shows the number of topics for the years where this task was organised. In 2009 and 2010, participants were allowed to submit results for smaller subsets of the main topic set.

Topic Document Languages: In 2009, the main set of topics did not put restrictions on the document's language, neither during the topic creation nor on how IR systems should treat documents of differing language. Instead, three additional language-specific tasks were created, where the topics in each of the three sets were documents in only one of the three EPO official languages. In 2010, we did not impose restrictions on the document language when selecting the topics, which resulted in the obvious fact that the document language distribution in the topic set followed the document language distribution in the collection corpus. A consequence of this 'natural' language distribution was that methods using distinct algorithms for the different languages to process, index and search the documents were not easy to qualitatively assess with respect to their language-specific methods.

We compensated for this in the following years, where each third of the topic set contained documents written in one of the official EPO languages.

4.4.1.2 Relevance Assessments and Metrics

Any IR evaluation faces the question of how to best obtain the ground truth to which the retrieval results should be compared. Most of the evaluation efforts (TREC, CLEF) use some form of pooling of the results and manually assess them by volunteer work [3, 41, 46]. This is time-consuming work and, in the case of patent relevance assessment, volunteers are difficult to find as costly expert knowledge is required [38]. At the same time, because of their strict regulations in logging their work, patent experts at patent offices do provide partial relevance assessments in the form of patent citations in the search reports. These relevance assessments are of high quality and, furthermore, at the EPO, the patent citations have level of relevance degrees assigned to them (see Sect. 4.2, *Examination phase*).

The drawback in using search reports as the source of relevance assessments is that the number of relevant documents for any given patent application document is minuscule when compared with the number of documents in the CLEF-IP corpus: on average six relevant documents. Extracting relevance assessments from patent search reports follows the general lines described in [10]. To increase the number of relevant documents, we made use of the *patent families* by creating an extended list of citations which includes the patent citations of the topic application document, the patent citations of the topic document's family members and the family members of the patent citation documents. After filtering out the patent citations that are not part of the CLEF-IP data corpus, we reached an increase in the number of relevant documents by a factor of seven [38]. All these operations were done automatically by means of data- processing queries, and the relevance judgements were lists of relevant documents for each of the patent application files in the topics.

The measures reported for the prior art search tasks between 2009 and 2011 are precision and recall at different cut-off values, MAP, NDCG [19] and PRES [28].

4.4.2 The 'Passage Retrieval Starting from Claims' Task

Looking more closely at a search report created by the EPO, we immediately observe that besides the list of patent citations relevant to a patent application, it details which parts of a citation document (lines, columns, figures, etc.; see Fig. 4.5) are pertinent to which claims of the patent application. This leads us, in 2012–2013, to change the task formulation from 'find relevant documents' to 'find relevant documents and mark in them the passages of interest to a given set of patent application claims'. The task was thus transformed to a passage retrieval task which we abbreviated with PSG. At the same time, although the basis for topic creation remained the same—actual patent application documents from the topic pool—the

```
         ---
X    | WO 01 26573 A (COHERENT INC)                        1-3,7
     | 19 April 2001 (2001-04-19)
     | * page 13, line 30 - page 15, line 16;
     | figure 3 *
         ---
Y    | EP 1 101 450 A (PULSION MEDICAL SYSTEMS           8
     | AG) 23 May 2001 (2001-05-23)
     | * page 5, line 9 - line 22; figure 2 *
         ---
Y    | EP 0 465 459 A (WALTER HELMUT DIPL ING DR) 9
     | 8 January 1992 (1992-01-08)
A    | * page 5, line 45 - line 54; figures 1,3,8 6,10
     | *
```

Fig. 4.5 Extract from a search report

```
<tid>PSG12</tid>
<tfile>EP-1752179-A2.xml</tfile>
<tclaims>/patent-document/claims/claim[1]
    /patent-document/claims/claim[8]</tclaims>

<tid>PSG13</tid>
<tfile>EP-1288172-A1.xml</tfile>
<tclaims>/patent-document/claims/claim[1]
    /patent-document/claims/claim[2]
    /patent-document/claims/claim[6]</tclaims>
```

Fig. 4.6 Excerpt from the list of topics for the CLEF-IP 2012 PSG task

topics are now (sub)sets of claims in the patent application document, instead of the patent application document itself [35, 36].

4.4.2.1 Topic Design

With the change of task formulation in 2012, we were prompted to change the topic and relevance assessments, too. The topics, although still having references to full XML files, are now sets of patent claims expressed as a sequence of XPaths. Figure 4.6 shows an example of how the PSG task topics were formulated. Each topic has a unique topic id (<tid> tags), a reference to the XML file containing the topic's patent application (<tfile> tags) and the list of patent claim XPaths (<tclaims> tags). Participants were permitted to use the topic's application patent document for query generation.

The criteria used to choose topics from the pool of topic documents are similar to those in choosing the PAC 2011 topics (see Sect. 4.4.1). In addition, we also examined the search reports for these documents and singled out those which provided more details in the list of citations. Examining the search reports and the therein cited documents had to be done by humans; therefore, the number of topics that could be extracted together with their relevance assessments was small when compared to the number of topics in the PAC tasks: 105 topics in 2012 and

149 topics in 2013. The language of the documents in both topic sets was evenly distributed between the three EPO official languages.

4.4.2.2   Relevance Assessments and Metrics

The relevance assessments for the topics in the PSG tasks contain not just a list of relevant document identifiers but also listings of XPaths identifying particular pieces of text in the citation files. The use of XPaths to express the topics was only natural considering that the CLEF-IP corpus is, ultimately, a collection of XML files.

The relevance assessments for the PAC tasks described in the previous section were obtained automatically. The amount of automation we could use to create the relevance assessments of the PSG task in 2012 and 2013 was, however, very limited. The bottleneck here is the manual work in comparing original patent documents in PDF format with the XML content. There is currently no tool that could automatically highlight a portion of text in a PDF file by referencing it with irregular expressions of the type 'column 4, line 24, column 5 line 10' and identify the XPath(s) that would identify those highlighted sentences in the corresponding XML files.

The relevance assessments of the PSG task had two levels: document and passage (XPath) level. Submissions from the participants, similarly to the relevance assessment files, had to contain, for each relevant document retrieved, also a list of passages in that document considered as relevant to the topic. The evaluation at the document level measured a system's performance in retrieving whole relevant documents, while the evaluation at the passage level targeted measuring the system ranking quality of the passages in the relevant patent documents [35]. At the document level, we maintained the computation of MAP, recall and PRES measures. To measure the effectiveness of passage retrieval we compute, for each retrieved document, MAP and precision scores involving only the XPaths. We denoted these measures with MAP(D) and precision(D) and averaged them over the set of topics. These two measures have similarities with the 'relevant in context' metrics of the INEX campaign [21], but taking into account sequences of XPaths instead of sequences of characters [35, Sect. 2.1].

4.4.3   The 'Patent Classification' Task

When a patent application is filed and sent to the examination division of a patent office, the application is initially assigned one or more patent classification symbols (see Sect. 4.2.2), according to the technological area to which the invention belongs. This classification operation ensures that the application document will be sent to the patent expert with the highest qualifications in the invention's technological areas.

Patent classification experiments are now and again performed in particular set-ups [9, 23], but one formally organised exercise that evaluated classifiers for patents on one patent data set was coordinated in the frame of the NTCIR workshop series. Iwayama et al. [18] give an account of the patent classification task of the NTCIR-6 workshop. The task used Japanese patent documents and required their classification according to the Japanese file index and F-term classification systems.

Within CLEF-IP we have set up a similar patent classification task, where we used the CLEF-IP corpus of European patents for training and asked participants to assign IPC subclass symbols to patent documents. The IPC system is hierarchically organised into sections, classes, subclasses, groups and subgroups.

The best performing system reached classification scores where one may argue that the limits of automated classifiers are reached, and better results cannot be obtained without human intervention [12]. The same task was repeated in CLEF-IP 2011, with an additional classification subtask where the sought for classification symbol was deeper in the IPC hierarchy, at the group and subgroup levels when the subclass classification symbol was known. This proved to be a more difficult problem to solve and it was concluded that the finer-grained IPC classification symbols were too difficult to distinguish by an automated classifier.

4.4.3.1 Topic Selection, Relevance Assessments and Metrics

The topics for these classification tasks (abbreviated with CLS) were randomly selected patent documents from the topic pool where it was required that the documents have non-empty abstract, description and claims text fields. A further constraint was that the documents were selected to be as equally distributed as possible with respect to the IPC subclass symbols. In the 2010 CLS task, there were no selection restrictions imposed on the document language or number of citations the patent document had. We added this restriction in 2011, where each third of the 3000 topics in the CLS task had a different EPO document language. There were 2000 topics in the 2010 classification task.

Before releasing the topics to the participants, the information about their IPC classification was removed from the XML's bibliographic part. These classification codes formed the relevance assessments for this task.

The measures we have computed to assess the quality of the submissions were precision, recall and F_1 at one classification code and at five classification codes (a patent may be classified into more than one IPC class).

4.4.4 The 'Image-Based Patent Retrieval' Task

In the previous tasks, the information to be processed by participants was text based. Recognising that images play an important role in examining patents, we organised in 2011 a pilot task, abbreviated with IMG-PAC, where the topics for document retrieval were images in patents.

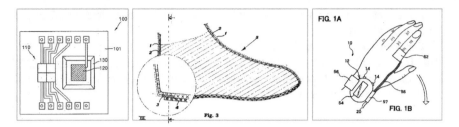

Fig. 4.7 Three examples of patent images in the IMG-PAC task

4.4.4.1   Document Collection

The CLEF-IP collection described in Sect. 4.3 contains only textual data. In the MAREC collection of patent documents, which was the base to extract the CLEF-IP collection, about half of the patent documents contain image tags (i.e. XML references to images). These documents have, on average, ten references to images. However, the storage requirements for the patent images in the CLEF-IP collection (over 1TB) were higher than the resources available for organising an image-based retrieval task using the whole collection as target data.[5] Therefore, we created a smaller test collection for this task, choosing patent technical areas where the patent examiners often rely on visual image comparison to filter out the non-relevant documents. The patent documents in this smaller collection were patents with the following three IPC classification symbols assigned to them:

- A43B: characteristic features of footwear, parts of footwear
- A61B: diagnosis, surgery, identification
- H01L: semiconductor devices, electric solid state devices not otherwise provided for

The target data contained over 47,000 XML patent files and 290,000 images stored as black and white tiff files, totalling to 5.4GB. Figure 4.7 gives an example of patent image files occurring in these classes.

4.4.4.2   Topic Selection, Relevance Assessments and Metrics

The methodology to select topics for this task is the same as the one used in selecting topics for the PAC task (Sect. 4.4.1) with additional restrictions that there should be at least three images attached to the patent application document chosen as topic and that it is assigned one of the three IPC classification symbols.

---

[5]The patent images are part of neither CLEF-IP nor MAREC collections, they are a separate collection of image documents whose file names are referenced in MAREC files via image XML tags.

There were 211 topics consisting of the patent text and complete set of images attached to the patent.

The relevance assessments were obtained in the same way as those for the PAC task, but filtered to contain only those documents in the target data. The metrics calculated were MAP, precision and recall at cut-offs 1 (one document found) and 5 (five relevant documents retrieved).

4.4.5 The 'Patent Image Classification' Task

The patent image classification task was the second task in CLEF-IP that used patent images. Here the participants were given patent images to be classified into one (or more) of the following nine types: abstract drawing, graph, flowchart, gene sequence, programme listing, symbol, chemical structure, table and mathematics. Figure 4.8 gives some examples of images to be classified.

Compared to other image classification tasks (e.g. the photo annotation tasks at ImageCLEF [20]), the images in this classification task did not come with any kind of textual comments. The image classification in this task had to be done purely by visual content analysis.

For each of the nine image classes mentioned above, we have provided between 300 and 6000 training images. No other data was allowed to be used for training. The image test set contained 1000 black and white tiff files. The task was to train an

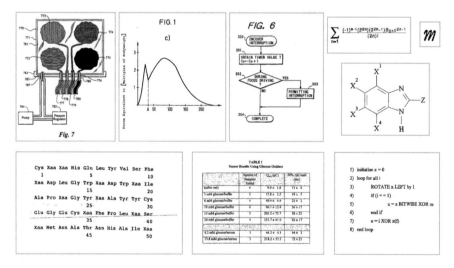

Fig. 4.8 Examples of patent images to classify in the IMG-CLS task. *From left to right*, top down the image classes are abstract diagram, graph, flowchart, mathematical formula, symbol, chemical structure, gene sequence, table and programme listing

image classifier on the provided training data and test the resulting classifier on the test set [35].

Both the training data and the relevance assessments for these topics were done manually by the task organisers. The measures used to assess the classifier's quality were the equal error rate (EER), the area under curve (AUC) of a ROC curve and the true positive rate (TPR) per class averaged over all classes. The evaluation computations were done with a custom-written octave[6] script.

4.4.6 The 'Flowchart Recognition' Task

The aim of this task, organised, in 2012 and 2013, was to make the content of the patent images containing flowcharts available to textual search. The participants in the task were asked to extract the information in the images and return it in a predefined textual format.

4.4.6.1 Topic Selection

In the flowchart structure recognition task, the topics were actual patent images representing flowcharts. The images were selected from the set of images in the flowchart class that were used in the 2011 patent image classification task.

In 2012, we provided a training set of 50 flowcharts together with their text representation. The test set contained 100 flowcharts. In 2013, the training set contained the 150 flowcharts used in the 2012 task, while the test set contained 747 flowcharts.

4.4.6.2 Relevance Assessments and Metrics

The textual encoding of flowchart images is a list of graph nodes and graph edges (flowcharts can be interpreted as graphs in the mathematical sense as nodes and edges between nodes). In Fig. 4.9 we can see an example of a flowchart image and its textual representation. In the textual representation of a flowchart, MT stands for meta information about the flowchart (like number of nodes, edges, title), lines starting with NO describe the nodes of the graph, lines starting with DE describe directed edges, while lines starting with UE describe uni-directed edges in the graph. Lines beginning with CO denote comments that are not to be automatically processed.

For the 2012 topics, the relevance assessments were manually created for both training and test data [35]. The quality of the information extracted from the images

---

[6]Gnu Octave http://www.gnu.org/software/octave.

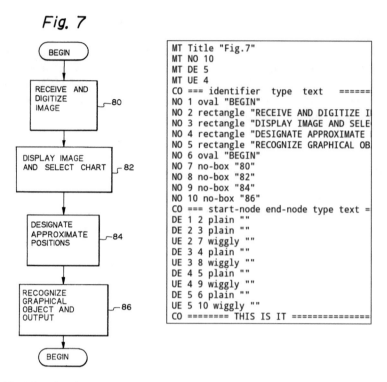

Fig. 4.9 A flowchart image and its textual representation

was assessed using a distance metric based on the notion of most common subgraph [45] and using an in-house implementation of the McGregor algorithm [29]. The same approach was used in 2013, where, in addition, we had planned to experiment with further evaluation measures, described in [27].

4.4.7 The 'Chemical Structure Recognition' Task

Chemical molecular diagrams are the basis for a large number of patents granted in the pharmaceutical domain, for example. No wonder, then, that being able to extract such diagrams from documents and to recognise them to the extent necessary to automatically compare them for similarity or identity to other diagrams is a potentially very powerful approach to identifying relevant claims [35]. Currently, patent experts visually inspect such diagrams. Within CLEF-IP the chemical structure recognition task has been organised in 2012 only and was divided into two parts: segmentation and recognition.

4.4.7.1 Topic Selection, Relevance Assessments and Metrics

For the chemical compound structure recognition, the topics were scanned patent pages, one page per image file. The first subtask required participating systems to segment the images in order to isolate the images representing chemical diagrams. Once the images containing the chemical compounds are cut out of the scanned patent pages, we asked, in the second subtask, for their textual representation in MOL (from molecule) file format (see also Fig. 4.10).

For the segmentation part of the task, a set of 30 patents was selected, and their pages rendered as monochrome multi-page TIFF images. The pages were manually selected by the task organisers. The relevance judgements for this subtask consisted of the coordinates of the minimal image bounding box size (middle part in Fig. 4.10). Submissions, submitted in CSV files, were assessed using the number of true positive, false positive and false negative matches and then by computing the precision, recall and F_1 measures [35].

The second subtask was recognising the chemical diagrams and storing them as MOL files for comparison with the ground truth. The topic set contained 865 diagram images such as those in the middle area of Fig. 4.10, fully representable as MOL files (the *automatic set*). The participant submissions using this topic set were evaluated automatically using the open source chemistry toolbox, OpenBabel [35]. The metrics reported for this set were the percentage of correctly matched chemical diagrams.

A second topic set for the chemical diagram recognition subtask has 95 images, the *manual set*, which contained irregularities in their diagrammatic representation. These diagrams cannot be represented as MOL files without abusing in some way the MOL representations, so these images were visually assessed using the MarvinView tool from ChemAxon.[7]

4.5 Summary of the Task Submissions and Evaluation Results

The format of the submitted experiments varied depending on the specific task. For the CLEF-IP main tasks PAC and PSG, a *submission* (or *run*) consisted of a single text file with at most 1000 documents per topic. The format of the submissions followed the standard format used for the TREC submissions, which is a list of tuples containing at least the *topic identifier*, the retrieved *document*, the *rank* of the retrieved document and the *score* given by the retrieval system to the retrieved document. The submissions to the passage retrieval starting from claims task (2012, 2013) had an additional entry indicating the XPaths to the relevant passages in the

---

[7]MarvinView: A generic 2D/3D molecule renderer, http://www.chemaxon.com/products/marvin/marvinview/.

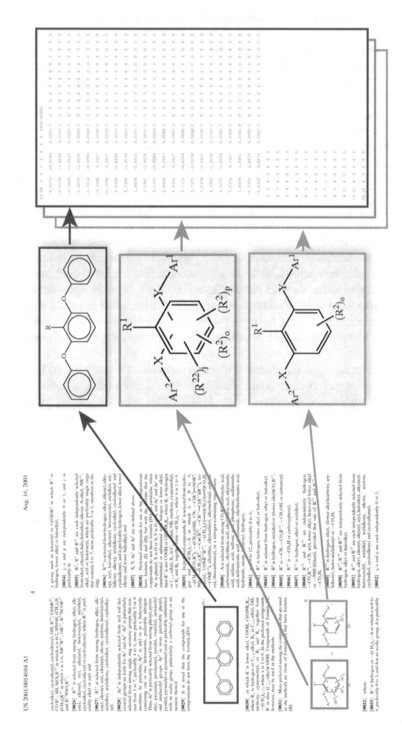

Fig. 4.10 The chemical structure recognition task

retrieved documents. The same TREC submission format was used for the patent image-based prior art search task (2011) and a TREC-style submission format was used for the classification tasks. A submission to the flowchart task consisted of a set of text files, one per topic flowchart, with a custom textual graph representation of the chart [36] (see Sect. 4.4.6). Submissions to the chemical structure recognition task were CSV files, for the image segmentation part of the task, and MOL files [6], for the representation of the molecular structures in the identified image segments [35].

Generally, participants in the CLEF-IP tracks have used off-the-shelf retrieval and classification engines (Indri/Lemur or Terrier engines, commonly available k-nearest neighbour algorithm implementations, support vector machines, SVM or Winnow-like classifiers), choosing to tune these systems to obtain good results. The better results, however, were obtained by those systems that put more effort into understanding and exploiting the patent-specific data, like citations or classification symbols. Participants in the image-related tasks used mainly in-house developed systems with different components handling the character recognition, image segmentations or edge and node segmentation modules.

In the tasks involving textual retrieval, several experiments were done by the task participants to determine which parts of the (topic) patent documents contribute most to improving the retrieval results. These include selecting certain file parts to index, building separate indexes per language or boosting query terms extracted from certain parts of the topic files. Given that each patent document could contain fields in up to three languages, some participants chose to build separate indexes per language, while others generated one mixed-language index or used text fields only in one language discarding information given in the other languages. The granularity of the index varied, too, as some participants chose to concatenate all text fields into one index, while others indexed different fields separately. In addition, several special indexes like phrase or passage indexes, concept indexes and IPC indexes were used.

As CLEF-IP topics in the textual retrieval tasks are whole patent documents (with thousands of words), many participants found it necessary to apply some kind of term selection in order to limit the number of terms in the query. Various experiments were done to determine the impact of the number of selected query terms on the result quality.

The bibliographic data that was exploited the most is the IPC information which was used either as a post-processing filter or as part of the query. The patent citation information stored in the document set of the collection was exploited less in the first year, with more groups using this metadata in the following years. Other very patent-specific information, like priority, applicant and inventor information, were only rarely used.

To give an idea of the score ranges achieved by retrieval systems participating in the prior art tasks, we show in Fig. 4.11 box plot summaries of the submitted run scores for mean average precision, MAP, and passage mean average precision,

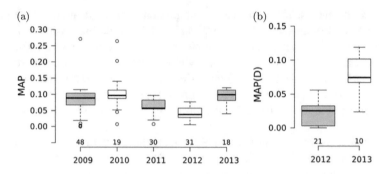

Fig. 4.11 Summary of MAP scores in the PAC and PSG CLEF-IP tasks. (**a**) MAP scores for the PAC tasks. (**b**) MAP(D) scores for the PSG tasks

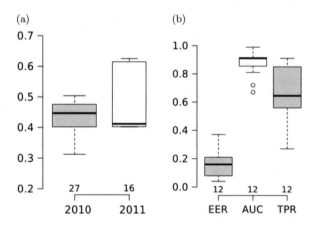

Fig. 4.12 Text- and image-based patent classification tasks summary of scores. (**a**) CLS tasks F_1 scores. (**b**) EER, AUC and TPR scores for the IMG-CLS task

MAP(D), for each year where these tasks were run.[8] The numbers just above the years show the number of runs submitted and evaluated in the respective year.

Not all participants focused on the multilingual nature of the CLEF-IP document collection. In most cases, data in only one specific language was used or several monolingual retrieval systems were implemented, merging their results at the end. Few participants made use of machine translations to obtain query terms in additional languages and apply them on the previously created collection indexes.

The classification of patent documents and patent images proved to be an easier challenge than finding prior art using IR methods. This is reflected in the scores obtained by the participants' submissions shown in Fig. 4.12. Figure 4.12a summarises the F_1 scores obtained by the experiments submitted to the two CLS tasks,

---

[8]Note that the scores between years cannot be directly compared, as each lab year came with a new set of test topics.

in 2010 and 2011. Submissions to the classification task were created either using text classifiers only or by text retrieval systems returning the IPC codes as results or by combining classification and text retrieval. The low equal error rate values and the high area under a ROC curve values in Fig. 4.12b show a good performance of the image classification systems in the 2011 image classification task (this task was organised only in 2011). Here, participating systems classified images using local binary patterns and optical character recognition, then, applying support vector machines and result fusion. Another solution consisted of representing images as Fisher vectors and using a linear classifier.

In the image recognition tasks, participants used in-house developed software solutions with components for optical character recognition, edge and junction detection, box shape detection and classification. Images were analysed and vec- torised components extracted, which were later fed into a rule-based system to create textual content representations. Figure 4.13 shows the summary of the graph similarity scores for each run submitted to the flowchart recognition task in 2012. For the set of test flowcharts in this task, content detection and graph structure detection are handled well by the participating systems, with many graphs being correctly detected.

Similar scores were obtained for the submissions to the chemical structure recognition task, with over 80 % recall levels for diagram recognition and over 70 % recall levels for chemical diagram segmentation (see [35] for the exact score values).

Table 4.5 gives the list of the participating teams' institutions and marks their year of participation. The table also shows the number of tasks organised in each year as well as the total number of runs received in the respective year. All data can

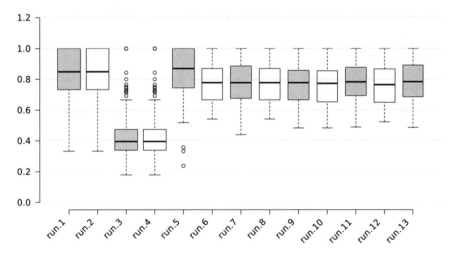

Fig. 4.13 Flowchart recognition task, 2012: summary of 'most common subgraph' metric scores for each run

Table 4.5 Participating teams and year of participation

Team institution		2009	2010	2011	2012	2013
BiTeM, Service of Medical Informatics, Geneva University Hospitals	CH	x	x		x	
Centrum Wiskunde & Informatica - Interactive Information Access	NL	x				
Chemical Biology Laboratory, SAIC-Frederick Inc.	US				x	
Chemnitz University of Technology, Department of Computer Science	DE			x	x	
Computer Vision Centre, Universitat Autonoma de Barcelona	ES				x	
Dublin City Univ., School of Computing	UK	x	x			
Geneva University Centre, Universitaire d'Informatique, SimpleShift	CH	x	x			
Georgetown University, Department of Computer Science	US					x
Glasgow Univ., IR Group Keith	UK	x				
Hewlett-Packard Labs, Russia	RU			x		
Humboldt Univ., Dept. of German Language and Linguistics	DE	x	x		x	
Industrial Property Documentation Department, JSI Jouve	FR		x			
Innovandio S.A.	CL					x
Inria	FR	x	x		x	
SIEL, International Institute of Information Technology	IN			x		
Joanneum Research Forschungsgesellschaft mbH, Inst. f. Information and Communication Technologies	AT			x	x	
LCI – Institut National des Sciences Appliquées de Lyon	FR		x			
Radboud University Nijmegen	NL	x	x	x		
Santiago de Compostela University, Dept. Electronica y Computacion	ES	x				
Spinque B.V.	NL		x	x		
Swedish Institute of Computer Science	SE	x				
Technical Univ. Darmstadt, Dept. of CS, Ubiquitous Knowledge Processing Lab	DE	x				
Technical Univ. Valencia, Natural Language Engineering	ES	x				
UNED - E.T.S.I. Informatica, Dpto. Lenguajes y Sistemas Informaticos, Madrid	ES		x			
Universitas Indonesia, Information Retrieval Group	ID		x			
University 'Alexandru Ioan Cuza', Iași	RO	x	x			
University of Birmingham	UK				x	

(continued)

Table 4.5 (continued)

Team institution		2009	2010	2011	2012	2013
University of Hildesheim, Information Science	DE	x	x	x	x	
University of Lugano	CH			x	x	
University of Macedonia, Department of Applied Informatics, Thessaloniki	GR				x	x
University of Montreal	CA					
University of Neuchâtel, Computer Science	CH	x				
University of Tampere - Info Studies & Interactive Media	FI	x				
University of Wolverhampton, School of Technology	UK				x	
Vienna University of Technology, Inst. f. Software Technology and Interactive Systems	AT			x	x	x
Vienna University of Technology, Inst. for Computer-Aided Automation	AT			x		
WISEnut Ltd.	KR			x		
Xerox Research Centre Europe	FR			x		
Total teams		**16**	**13**	**12**	**13**	**4**
Number of runs		**70**	**52**	**77**	**51**	**19**
Number of (optional) tasks		**1**	**2**	**4**	**3**	**2**

be downloaded from the CLEF-IP website.[9] For detailed descriptions of the systems that participated in the CLEF-IP tasks, we direct the reader to the workshop notes available on the CLEF initiative website[10] and to the CLEF-IP website.

4.6   Conclusions

At the end of the CLEF-IP evaluation campaign, it is clear to us that successful information retrieval in the patent domain involves at least well thought-out adjustments to the currently used retrieval and text mining systems to take into account the specificities of the patent domain. In general, retrieval results do not come close to the expectations of patent experts. Even though the CLEF-IP campaign is no longer running, there is a huge potential to use the data and realistic patent search tasks resulting from the CLEF-IP campaign to develop innovative solutions in the patent information retrieval domain.

---

[9]CLEF-IP: Retrieval in the intellectual property domain. http://ifs.tuwien.ac.at/~clef-ip/.

[10]The CLEF Initiative (Conference and Labs of the Evaluation Forum, formerly known as Cross-Language Evaluation Forum). http://www.clef-initiative.eu/.

The CLEF-IP tasks described in this chapter are mainly focused on text-oriented information retrieval, with aspects of information extraction from patent images addressed in the flowchart and chemical structure recognition tasks. There remains however extensive work to be done on improving the use of non-textual patent data in patent search. Another important aspect of patent retrieval, which was not addressed by the CLEF-IP campaign, is that information search is session based: the final list of relevant documents is the result of several search queries, possibly building on each other. Both these research directions need sustained support from the IP community.

Nevertheless, along with the TREC-CHEM campaign [25] and the patent-oriented campaigns organised in the frame of the NTCIR project, the CLEF-IP campaign actively contributed to raising the interest of the IR community in exploring a body of knowledge that has such a high impact in the economic world.

Acknowledgements We thank the advisory board members who helped shape the evaluation lab in its early years: Gianni Amati, Atsushi Fujii, Makoto Iwayama, Kalervo Järvelin, Noriko Kando, Javier Pose Rodríguez, Mark Sanderson, Henk Thomas, Anthony Trippe and Christa Womser-Hacker.

We thank the previous CLEF-IP organisers and co-organisers for their valuable work: Giovanna Roda, Mihai Lupu, John Tait, Veronika Zenz, Igor Filippov, Walid Magdy and Alan P. Sexton.

We are grateful to Judy Hickey and Henk Tomas for sharing their know-how on prior art searches and patent life cycles with us.

CLEF-IP was supported along the years by Matrixware GmbH, Vienna, and the Information Retrieval Facility, Vienna, as first data and infrastructure provider, by the PROMISE EU Network of Excellence (FP7-258191) and by the Austrian Research Promotion Agency (FFG) FIT-IT Impex project (No. 825846).

References

1. Adams S (2000) Using the International Patent Classification in an online environment. World Patent Inf 22(4):291–300
2. Adams SR (2011) Information sources in patents, 3rd edn. De Gruyter Saur, Berlin. ISBN 978–3110235111
3. Aslam JA, Pavlu V, Yilmaz E (2006) A statistical method for system evaluation using incomplete judgments. In: Proceedings of the 29th annual international ACM SIGIR conference on research and development in information retrieval, SIGIR '06. ACM, New York, NY, pp 541–548
4. Attar R, Fraenkel AS (1977) Local feedback in full-text retrieval systems. J ACM 24(3): 397–417
5. Cooperative Patent Classification (2015) http://www.cooperativepatentclassification.org/. Accessed Aug 2015
6. Dalby A, Nourse JG, Hounshell WD, Gushurst AKI, Grier DL, Leland BA, Laufer J (1992) Description of several chemical structure file formats used by computer programs developed at molecular design limited. J Chem Inf Comput Sci 32(3):244–255
7. Derwent World Patents Index (2016) http://thomsonreuters.com/en/products-services/intellectual-property/patent-research-and-analysis/derwent-world-patents-index.html. Last retrieved March 2016

8. European Patent Convention (EPC), Implementing Regulations, Examination Procedure (2015) http://www.epo.org/law-practice/legal-texts/html/epc/2013/e/r71.html. Accessed Aug 2015
9. Fall CJ, Benzineb K, Guyot J, Törcsvári A, Fiévet P (2003) Computer-assisted categorization of patent documents in the international patent classification. In: Proceedings of the international chemical information conference (ICIC'03), Nîmes
10. Graf E, Azzopardi L (2008) A methodology for building a patent test collection for prior art search. In: Proceedings of the second international workshop on evaluating information access (EVIA)
11. Guidelines for Examination in the European Patent Office (2013). Accessed March 2014
12. Guyot J, Benzineb K, Falquet G (2010) myClass: a mature tool for patent classification. In: Braschler M, Harman D, Pianta E (eds) CLEF (Notebook papers/LABs/workshops)
13. Hanbury A, Zenz V, Berger H (2010) 1st international workshop on advances in patent information retrieval (AsPIRe'10). SIGIR Forum 44(1):19–22
14. Handbook on Industrial Property Information and Documentation (2013). Part 8: Terms and Abbreviations concerning Industrial Property Information and Documentation. http://www.wipo.int/standards/en/part_08.html. Accessed March 2016
15. Hunt D, Nguyen L, Rodgers M (2007) Patent searching: tools & techniques. Wiley, New York. ISBN 978–0471783794
16. International Patent Classification (IPC) (2015) http://www.wipo.int/classifications/ipc/en/. Accessed March 2015
17. Iwayama M, Fujii A, Kando N, Marukawa Y (2003) An empirical study on retrieval models for different document genres: patents and newspaper articles. In: Proceedings of 26th international ACM SIGIR conference on research and development in information retrieval, SIGIR '03. ACM, New York, pp 251–258
18. Iwayama M, Fujii A, Kando N (2007) Overview of classification subtask at NTCIR-6 patent retrieval task. In: Proceedings of the sixth NTCIR workshop meeting on evaluation of information access technologies: information retrieval, question answering and cross-lingual information access
19. Järvelin K, Kekäläinen J (2002) Cumulated gain-based evaluation of IR techniques. ACM Trans Inf Syst 20(4):422–446
20. Kalpathy-Cramer J, Müller H, Bedrick S, Eggel I, de Herrera SGA, Tsikrika T (2011) Overview of the CLEF 2011 medical image classification and retrieval tasks. In: Petras V, Forner P, Clough PD (eds) Working notes for CLEF 2011 conference, CEUR-WS, vol 1177
21. Kamps J, Pehcevski J, Kazai G, Lalmas M, Robertson S (2008) INEX 2007 evaluation measures. In: Focused access to XML documents, 6th international workshop of the initiative for the evaluation of xml retrieval, INEX 2007, Dagstuhl Castle, 17–19 Dec 2007. Selected papers. Lecture notes in computer science, vol 4862. Springer, Berlin, pp 24–33
22. Kando N, Leong M-K (2000) Workshop on patent retrieval (SIGIR 2000 workshop report). SIGIR Forum 34(1):28–30
23. Krier M, Zacca F (2002) Automatic categorisation applications at the European patent office. World Patent Inf 24(3):187–196
24. Lupu M, Huang J, Zhu J, Tait J (2009) TREC-CHEM: large scale chemical information retrieval evaluation at TREC. SIGIR Forum 43(2):63–70
25. Lupu M, Piroi F, Huang J, Zhu J, Tait J (2010) Overview of the TREC chemical IR track. In: Proceedings of the 18th text retrieval conference
26. Lupu M, Huang J, Zhu J (2011) Evaluation of chemical information retrieval tools. In: Lupu M, Mayer K, Tait J, Trippe AJ (eds) Current challenges in patent information retrieval. The information retrieval series, vol 29. Springer, Berlin, pp 109–124. ISBN 978–3–642–19230–2
27. Lupu M, Piroi F, Hanbury A (2013) Evaluating flowchart recognition for patent retrieval. In: Proceedings of 5th International workshop on evaluating information access (EVIA), Tokyo
28. Magdy W, Jones GJF (2010) PRES: a score metric for evaluating recall-oriented information retrieval applications. In: Proceedings of the 33rd international ACM SIGIR conference on research and development in information retrieval, SIGIR '10. ACM, New York, NY, pp 611–618

29. McGregor JJ (1982) Backtrack search algorithms and the maximal common subgraph problem. Softw Pract Exp 12(1):23–34
30. Osborn M, Strzalkowski T, Marinescu M (1997) Evaluating document retrieval in patent database: A preliminary report. In: Proceedings of the 6th international conference on information and knowledge management. ACM, New York, NY, pp 216–221
31. PCT (2015) Patent Cooperation Treaty. http://www.wipo.int/pct/en/treaty/about.html, 1970. Accessed Aug 2015
32. Piroi F, Tait J (2010) CLEF-IP 2010: retrieval experiments in the intellectual property domain. In: Working notes for CLEF 2010 conference, CEUR-WS, September, vol 1176
33. Piroi F, Lupu M, Hanbury A, Zenz V (2011) CLEF-IP 2011: retrieval in the intellectual property domain. In: Working notes for CLEF 2011 Conference, CEUR-WS, September, vol 1177
34. Piroi F, Lupu M, Hanbury A (2012) Effects of language and topic size in patent IR: an empirical study. In: Information access evaluation. Multilinguality, multimodality, and visual analytics, Proceedings of the third international conference of the CLEF initiative, CLEF 2012. Lecture Notes in Computer Science, vol 7488. Springer, Berlin
35. Piroi F, Lupu M, Hanbury A, Sexton AP, Magdy W, Filippov IV (2012) CLEF-IP 2012: retrieval experiments in the intellectual property domain. In: Working notes for CLEF 2012 conference, CEUR-WS, vol 1178
36. Piroi F, Lupu M, Hanbury A (2013) Overview of CLEF-IP 2013 lab - information retrieval in the patent domain. In: Forner P, Müller H, Paredes R, Rosso P, Stein B (eds) Information access evaluation. Multilinguality, multimodality, and visualization - Proceedings of the 4th international conference of the CLEF initiative, CLEF 2013. Lecture Notes in Computer Science, vol 8138. Springer, Berlin, pp 232–249
37. Robertson S (2008) On the history of evaluation in IR. J Inf Sci 34(4):439–456
38. Roda G, Tait J, Piroi F, Zenz V (2010) CLEF-IP 2009: retrieval experiments in the intellectual property domain. In: Peters C, Di Nunzio GM, Kurimo M, Mostefa D, Penas A, Roda G (eds) Multilingual information access evaluation I. Text retrieval experiments 10th workshop of the cross-language evaluation forum, CLEF 2009, vol 6241. Springer, Berlin, pp 385–409
39. Sanderson M (2010) Test collection based evaluation of information retrieval systems. Found Trends Inf Retr 4(4):247–375
40. Schneller I (2002) Japanese file index classification and F-terms. World Patent Inf 24(3): 197–201
41. Sparck-Jones K, van Rijsbergen C (1975) Report on the need for and provision of an 'ideal' information retrieval test collection. Technical report
42. Tait J, Harris C, Lupu M (eds) (2010) PaIR '10: proceedings of the 3rd international workshop on patent information retrieval. ACM, New York, NY
43. Text Retrieval Conference (2015) http://trec.nist.gov. Accessed Aug 2015
44. United States Patent Classification (2015) http://www.uspto.gov/patents/resources/classification/. Accessed Aug 2015
45. Wallis WD, Shoubridge P, Kraetz M, Ray D (2001) Graph distances using graph union. Pattern Recogn Lett 22(6–7):701–704
46. Zobel J (1998) How reliable are the results of large-scale information retrieval experiments? In: Croft BW, Moffat A, van Rijsbergen CJ, Wilkinson R, Zobel J (eds) Proceedings of the 21st ACM SIGIR conference. ACM Press, New York, pp 307–314

Chapter 5
Evaluating Real Patent Retrieval Effectiveness

Anthony Trippe and Ian Ruthven

Abstract In this chapter we consider the nature of information retrieval evaluation for patent searching. We outline the challenges involved in conducting patent searches and the commercial risks inherent in patent searching. We highlight some of the main challenges of reconciling how we evaluate retrieval systems in the laboratory and the needs of patent searchers, concluding with suggestions for the development of more informative evaluation procedures for patent searching.

5.1 Introduction

Patent searching is a highly interactive and complex process often requiring multiple searches, diverse search strategies and careful search management [1]. There are different end-user requirements for different types of patent search, and simple performance-based measures of retrieval system functions are often inadequate in expressing the degree to which an information retrieval (IR) system might help conduct a successful search.

A particular characteristic of patent searching is the importance of the risk to which a company is exposed if a patent search is poorly conducted. Inadequate tools increase the likelihood of a poor search and increase the level of risk if a company proceeds on the basis of the search.

The claim from most IR evaluations is that measures of recall and precision, implicitly, calculate which system(s) are more likely to reduce this risk by performing more effective retrievals. Therefore, it is argued, we can be more confident about performing a good search with a system that has performed well in system trials. In this chapter we argue that this argument is naïve when considering real operational use.

A. Trippe (✉)
Patinformatics, LLC, 565 Metro Place S., Dublin, OH, 43017, USA
e-mail: tony@patinformatics.com

I. Ruthven
Department of Computer and Information Sciences, University of Strathclyde, Glasgow, G12 8DY, UK
e-mail: ir@cis.strath.ac.uk

© Springer-Verlag GmbH Germany 2017   143
M. Lupu et al. (eds.), *Current Challenges in Patent Information Retrieval*,
The Information Retrieval Series 37, DOI 10.1007/978-3-662-53817-3_5

Specifically we consider why recall and precision may give misleading inter-pretations on system performance, why we need to distinguish the characteristics of different types of patent search and where IR performance variability arises. A core theme in the chapter is the notion of risk: what risks are involved in patent searches, how these connect to measurements of recall and precision and how measurements of recall and precision may misinform rather than enlighten us as to system performance. We conclude with a discussion on how we might increase our confidence in IR system performance as measured in operational environments.

5.2   Types of Patent Search

Patent searches go by a variety of different names. Listing the most popular ones, you hear terms like: state of the art, prior art, patentability, validity, invalidity, clearance, freedom to operate, novelty and landscape (see Chap. 1). While there may be a large number of terms used to describe patent searches in essence, they boil down to four major categories upon which we shall concentrate in this chapter: state of the art, freedom to operate, patentability and validity.

Patent searchers traditionally use these types of descriptions to talk about the searches they perform for various clients whether they are from the legal department or the corporate strategy group. Before formally defining these types of search, it might be useful to think of these various types of searches in terms of the amount of risk they represent to the enterprise. Later we shall compare them to one another on precision and recall scales.

5.2.1   Patent Searches and Risk

We define risk as the amount of money that has already been invested in an innovation by an organisation pursuing a technological solution to a problem. As the amount of money invested by the enterprise increases, the importance of making good decisions about whether to continue funding the innovation and pushing it towards commercialisation also increases. With additional funding comes additional risk since the amount of money required to move from one step to the next in taking an innovation to market gets almost exponentially larger.

The pharmaceutical industry provides a perfect example of this concept of increased investment and risk. Early stage projects are expensive in terms of the time spent by the scientific teams in creating new drug entities and having those tested. These are sunk costs and are part of starting a pharmaceutical company in the first place. As new drug entities are discovered, however, decisions need to be made on whether they will be brought forward into what is first called a preclinical phase and then a succession of three human clinical trials. Each subsequent stage in this process becomes more expensive than the next as more people are involved in the trials, additional dosing schemes are employed and longer time periods are involved. As a company approaches a phase III clinical trial, the amount of money that will be invested is counted in the hundreds of millions of dollars and pale in comparison to the money that was spent generating a new drug entity and entering it into preclinical trials.

Since there is increased risk from substantially increased investment as a new drug entity moves from one stage to the next in the drug discovery process, companies have adopted a mantra referred to as 'failing faster'. The idea being that if they can find mechanisms for discovering earlier in the process that a new drug entity is going to fail, then the company can save themselves a tremendous amount of money by learning as quickly as possible that this is the likely outcome. They cut down on later risk by identifying failure points earlier in the process before larger investments are made.

Analogies can be made to the world of patent searching from this example, and many companies follow a similar mantra that if they can discover potential legal impediments to future production earlier in the process, then they will save themselves money by changing course based on this knowledge. We can analyse the four major types of patent search by the risk involved.

State of the Art: This type of search is conducted in order to determine the prevailing technical knowledge in a particular subject area. A practitioner might be entering a new technical area and is interested in learning about the work that has already been done in this space. It is not uncommon for users to be interested in non-patent as well as patent documents in this case since the end goal is to have a thorough understanding of what the current knowledge is in a technical area of interest. People interested in technical or competitive intelligence will also be interested in these types of searches, and when they begin to analyse the details of the results they get, they will sometimes refer to these as landscaping studies. The sort of details a user can glean from these results are shifts in technology over time, interest in technology subcategories by company and who the subject matter experts in the field might be. State-of-the-art searches are typically done at the very beginning of projects before any investment has been made, and investigators are trying to determine if an innovation is worth pursuing for a number of reasons. The risk associated with these searches is low and this will have an impact, as we will see later on the corresponding need for precision and recall.

Patentability: This type of search is usually done in the legal context of determining if a new invention is eligible for patent protection and determining how broadly the claims for the new invention can be written. This type of search can cover both patent and non-patent literature and is typically looking for references that were published before the filing date of the invention in question. In the United States, inventors have up to a year from the first public disclosure of an invention to file a patent, so some searchers will go back an additional year with their searching to make sure they have found the best references. This is the type of search that will be done by an examiner to determine if they should allow a patent application to be granted.

Even though an examiner will do this search, it is important for the applicants to also conduct one since they will often have the time and resources to be more thorough than the examiner can be. It is also important since knowing the boundaries of the known references will help the attorneys drafting the claims to ask for the broadest coverage possible. Without knowing the scope of the known references, it is difficult for the attorney to know how broadly they can write the claims and still expect the examiner to grant a patent.

Patentability searches are done once an inventor has an idea and they have either reduced it to practice or they have a pretty good idea on how they are going to reduce the idea to practice during the preparation of the patent application. Investment has increased since the inventor has spent time discovering the idea and may have used additional time and money reducing it to practice. The total money spent, most of which is fixed costs, is still fairly low and thus the risk involved in this situation while higher than the stage when the state-of-the-art search was done is still low.

Freedom to Operate: Possibly the most specific type of patent search this particular one is country specific and only applies to in-force granted patents and their claims. A company will ask for a legal opinion on whether a product they are planning on shipping will infringe any existing patents before they launch. There is nothing offensive about this type of search since the interested party is not going to assert patents against anyone else; they are simply looking to make sure that they are not going to be infringing someone else's patents. A searcher in this case needs to identify the critical components of the product in question and search country-specific claims of in-force patents to see if any of them cover the product components in question. In most cases a great deal of money has gone into a product launch or can be involved with a successful product which is generating a great deal of revenue, so it is important for companies to know that they will be reasonably safe from future litigation before they make an even larger investment.

Some companies do freedom-to-operate searches reasonably early in the production cycle and follow up with them frequently to make sure the situation hasn't changed as they get closer and closer to market. These companies are following the 'fail faster' philosophy that was mentioned earlier since they recognise that it is better to know about potential legal issues before they make larger investments and involve higher risks. Other companies wait until the trucks are about to leave the warehouses and then conduct a freedom-to-operate search as a last item of their checklist before they go to market. At this point a great deal of time, money and effort has gone into the innovation and the amount of investment and risk is pretty high. On more than one occasion, companies have trucks filled with product that has been left in a warehouse because a last-minute freedom-to-operate search has come back with an in-force patent that could be used against the company later. Regardless of when these searches are applied, the risk is much higher than at the patentability stage and should be considered medium to high.

Validity: Validity search comprises the largest and most comprehensive of all patent searches. These searches are almost always associated with large sums of money and critical business decisions and as such need to be as comprehensive as possible. This search shares similar characteristics to the patentability search but is normally far more comprehensive since there is typically much more at stake when this sort of search is being initiated.

The object of the search is to identify prior art references which will allow a granted patent to be made invalid during a re-examination before the particular patent office of interest or during a court proceeding. Sometimes a company will also initiate validity challenges for patents that they are thinking of acquiring especially if they believe these patents will later be used in some type of litigation or another. On the flip side of this, a company who is provided with a cease and desist notice will often want to make the patents in question go away by finding invalidating prior art and then entering into re-examination. The prior art references in question can come from the patent or non-patent literature, must be available in the public domain and have to have been published prior to the priority filing date of the patent in question. In the United States there is a 1-year grace period on patent filings, so some searchers will look back an additional year when they search so they can be sure to avoid this type of situation.

Validity searches are conducted when an organisation has received a cease and desist order or is about to spend a significant sum of money on a purchase of one sort or another and due diligence needs to be performed in order to justify the transaction. Investment in this case either in the form of production costs and lost sales or in money to be spent on an acquisition is very high, and the corresponding risk to the groups making the investment is also extremely high. Since large sums of money are involved and the risk involved is so high, companies are willing to increase the resources made available to conduct these types of searches.

Summarising the searches on our risk continuum, we have state of the art followed by patentability, then freedom to operate and finally validity.

The amount of risk involved will have an impact on the resources that are made available to do the searching, and in turn this will have an impact on the precision and recall that will be expected in these searches. While risk is not the sole qualifier for precision and recall, there are cases where you have high risk but you do not need high recall per se; it is still useful to keep this in mind as we look at the requirements for these searches.

5.2.2 Risk and Recall

Looking at recall and thinking about a continuum, we come across an example where higher risk does not require higher recall. In the case of our highest risk search, validity, we also find that total recall is not necessarily required. In this type of search, it is only necessary to find *one* reference which predates the filing of the patent application in question that describes the invention. In practice most searchers will not stop when they find a single reference and will seek to be as comprehensive as possible, but strictly speaking it is not a requirement. Since there is a high risk, searchers will often seek higher recall to make sure there are contingencies in place and not rely on a single reference. These considerations put validity on the low-to-medium scale with regard to recall.

With patentability, the recall question will depend on who is doing the searching. In the case of an examiner, the recall will be the lowest of all the searches we are discussing since they will stop once they find a single reference which will enable them to disallow a claim. They can also take two references and combine them to disallow a claim, so they will stop if they find that combination. Patentability searches done by corporate searchers, however, are usually higher in recall since they are helping assist the attorney in deciding how broadly they can write their claims based on how much prior art is out there and how closely (we will do precision next) it matches the invention to be patented. Since the risk is still reasonably low, however, they will not attempt to achieve higher recall since they will reach a point of diminishing returns and making an investment to achieve it would not be economical.

State-of-the-art searches involve low risk, but you would like to achieve a reasonably high recall since the inventor is exploring an unknown area and they will spend time landscaping the area to increase their understanding. Economically speaking, recall is sacrificed due to the small investment being made at this point, and the bar for diminishing returns is pushed even lower since the expectation is that more comprehensive searching will be done once an actual invention has been discovered and when a product cycle starts.

For recall the top search is freedom to operate where a single missed patent can come back and be used for a cease and desist action. It is very important to find any and all patents that cover the elements of product to be brought forward to an attorney so they can make a determination as to whether the product will infringe on the patent in question. In order to conduct business, not just one patent can be found that an invention may infringe upon, but all of them need to be located in order to ensure that the company will not face future legal issues. These searches are referred to as freedom to operate for this exact reason.

So, looking again at our continuum and comparing recall, this time we have validity and patentability at the lower end of the scale, state of the art in the middle and freedom to operate at the high end. Recall does not correlate with risk necessarily in this comparison with the possible exception of freedom-to-operate searches.

5.2.3   Risk and Precision

Precision maps almost completely to our assessment of risk. State-of-the-art searches are sometimes called 'quick and dirty' since there is not much time invested in doing them and the results often have a large number of false positives contained in them. Also by its very nature, this search is exploratory and as such a high degree of precision is not required.

Patentability searches are typically more precise but by their nature are used to explore the boundaries of the prior art so that broader claims can be written to cover more aspects of an invention if warranted, so precision is important to cut down on the records that will need to be looked at but not essential. A number of false positives are expected and are part of the process.

Freedom-to-operate and validity searches both require a high degree of precision since very specific documents are required in each of these cases. With freedom to operate, the aspects of the produce must be covered in the claims of in-force patents from the countries of interest. The product must also use all elements of the claimed invention in order to infringe. Finding patents that meet this criterion is a tall order and requires high precision. Similarly, in a validity search, a precise search of the patent and non-patent literature is required to locate references which describe the exact invention covered in a later patent claim either by itself or in combination with another reference.

On the precision continuum, we have state of the art at the low end, followed by patentability and finally freedom to operate and validity.

Looking at each search by its characteristics, we can say state of the art is low risk with low precision and medium recall. Patentability is low risk with low recall and precision. Freedom to operate is high risk requiring both high recall and precision and validity having the highest risk and requiring high precision but able to get by with lower recall.

Looking at searches in this fashion, it is apparent that freedom-to-operate searches offer the most difficult challenge for IR researchers. The risks involved are also very high, so the expectations will be large and the reluctance to move away from established methods will be severe. Validity is also a difficult task since the risks are so high and the precision requirements so large. State of the art is where most systems work currently and do not necessarily provide much reward for the effort since they are low risk and are conducted with little in the way of investment. Patentability seems to be the sweet spot for IR research since it offers a reasonable challenge with a good opportunity for return since it is conducted during a stage where resources will be spent to address the issue.

Having outlined the challenges to the patent searcher in conducting a successful search, we now discuss some of the challenges IR researchers face in defining appropriate evaluation measures.

5.3 Limitations of IR Evaluation

As in other domains, the evaluation of the retrieval components of patent search systems focuses primarily on laboratory-style evaluation, and these evaluations are heavily shaped by the classical models of IR laboratory evaluation. As noted in Carterette and Voorhees (see Chap. 3 of the first edition article "Overview of

Information Retrieval Evaluation) early influential laboratory evaluations included studies such as the Cranfield I and II experiments, SMART evaluation and the in-depth evaluation and failure analysis of the Medlars search service [2] using small document collections. The experience gained from these studies has been incorporated into the creation of modern test collections where collection size has grown considerably since these early studies. The most widely used test collections come from the Text Retrieval Evaluation Conference (TREC) initiative [3], the Cross-Language Evaluation Forum (CLEF)[1] (which are discussed in separate chapters in this volume) and NTCIR.[2] The oft-stated values of test collection evaluations are the tightly controlled nature of the evaluation, the statistical rigour with which the evaluation test results can be analysed and the repeatable nature of the evaluation tests.

The value of IP systems in operational use, however, is influenced by more than the quality of the retrieval system itself and, as has been repeatedly demonstrated in operational tests in other domains, the contextual factors surrounding the *use* of a system (such as organisational concerns, training and experience of the searcher and time available to search) can strongly influence the end results of a search [4, 5]. This gap between real-life practice and laboratory rigour raises three important questions, which we shall examine in the remainder of this section.

1. Are laboratory evaluation measures misleading? Recall and precision are the standard measures for evaluating IR system performance. Although there are many ways in which we can use recall and precision to obtain evaluation measures, there are arguments for why they are poor measurements for end-user evaluations unless they are contextualised by other information. In Sect. 3.1 we examine some of these arguments and why they raise concerns for determining the confidence we can place in laboratory evaluation performance figures.
2. Are the results of laboratory evaluations sufficiently good at predicting real-life performance? That is, can the results obtained from a laboratory test of an IR system inform us of the potential value of a system in operational environments? In Sect. 3.2 we survey some recent work, which indicates a weak correlation between the performance evaluations of systems without user involvement and evaluations of systems operated by end users.
3. Are laboratory evaluations sufficient? Real-life evaluations incorporate factors that are usually eliminated from laboratory evaluations, such as the expertise of the searchers themselves. In Sect. 3.3 we examine some of these factors and outline their importance in reliably measuring system effectiveness.

---

[1]http://clef.iei.pi.cnr.it

[2]http://research.nii.ac.jp/ntcir

5.3.1 The Potentially Misleading Effects of Recall and Precision

Patent search evaluation, similar to other retrieval problems, focuses primarily on recall and precision as measures of system effectiveness. These are long-held measures of retrieval quality and their tight hold on evaluation comes from their intuitive nature: how much of the useful information has my search retrieved (recall) and how much of the information that I have retrieved is useful (precision)? There is also a useful probabilistic interpretation of recall and precision: recall estimating the probability that a relevant document will be retrieved in response to a query and precision estimating the probability that a retrieved document will be relevant [6].

Most test collections are constructed using a generally accepted model referred to as the Cranfield model deriving from the Cranfield II tests [7]. A test collection that adheres to the Cranfield model will consist of a set of searchable objects, a set of information requests (or occasionally statements of information problems) and a list of which objects in the collection should be considered relevant for each information request. To ensure fair comparison between systems, a number of important assumptions are made. These include the assumptions that:

1. The topics are independent of each other.
2. All objects are assessed for relevance.
3. The judgements are representative of the target user population.
4. Each object is equally important in satisfying the user's information need.
5. The gathering of relevance assessment is independent of any evaluation that will use the assessments.
6. The relevance of one information object is independent of the relevance of any other object.

These assumptions are intended to ensure a fair and accurate comparison between estimates of system performance. The status of these assumptions has shifted over the decades of evaluation research since the original Cranfield model. Assumption 1 is generally adhered to in order to increase the diversity of the test. Assumption 3 is an attempt to ensure external validity of the experiment, i.e. that the results can be generalised to requests beyond those investigated within the test. The level to which this assumption matches most test collections is seriously under-investigated. Assumption 5 attempts to control the internal validity of the study: the assessments used to evaluate the system are not created by the people who designed the study, and therefore it is hoped that bias will not be introduced into the collection. Assumption 4 is a simplification of real search behaviour and many new test collections have graded relevance assessments to allow for more detailed measures of system effectiveness. However, the grades of relevance used often simply reflect amount of relevant material contained within objects rather than quality of relevant material. Assumption 6 is present in most test collections[3] although it is patently false—a system that retrieves duplicates or near-duplicate documents in favour of new and different relevant documents would not be seen as a better system by most users.

Assumption 2 is the assumption that has gathered most attention within the IR evaluation literature, particularly with the rise in test collection size. The early test collections contained small numbers of documents—the Cranfield collection contained only 1400 documents—and it was feasible for exhaustive relevance judgements to be made on the collection. For most collections this is not feasible: it has been estimated that it would take more than 9 months to judge an average size TREC collection for a single topic [7]. Not only is this expensive both in terms of time and resources, but over a protracted time period the criteria an assessor will use to judge a document for relevance could change, resulting in inconsistencies in the relevance assessments and therefore in the evaluation results. Indeed, Swanson [8] expressed this as one of his postulates of impotence—statements of what IR cannot achieve—namely, that it is never possible to verify if all relevant documents have been discovered for a request, as one can never examine all documents without unlimited resources while using a strict and static set of criteria for judging relevance. This is, of course, a real challenge for searches such as freedom-to-operate searches where the retrieval of all relevant documents is exactly what is required.

The reason that Assumption 2 has gathered so much attention is that exhaustive relevance assessment offers some guarantee that all relevant items have been identified, even if they do not linguistically match the user's query. That is, exhaustive assessments allow the identification of documents that conceptually match the query even if they do not match the user's choice of keywords.[4] Such assessments also allow for deep failure analyses of searches to ascertain why some search topics are more difficult for retrieval systems than others [9]. Such analyses are necessary, particularly with the current trend towards heavy averaging and aggregation of test results over large numbers of topics and collections. Several authors have argued against such approaches, particularly on the grounds that such tests are attempting to prove system hypotheses rather than disproving them. That is, experimenters are trying to prove a system works well rather than attempting to uncover when it will perform poorly. Such tests do not 'provide deep insights unless there is some degree of risk in the predictions' [10].

The current model for test collection—the pooling approach—is dependent on queries to create document assessment pools. Pooling compensates for exhaustive assessment by the inclusion of diverse systems and manual searching (see Sect. 2.2 of the first edition article "Overview of Information Retrieval Evaluation" of Carterette and Voorhees). The hope is that if we take sufficient care in sampling

---

[3] With the possible exception of INEX which does consider the relative relevance of sub-document units which may have overlapping content.

[4] Exhaustive query assessments also mean that we can assess the quality of the original query itself.

the documents to be assessed for relevance, we do not need to exhaustively assess the whole collection. The system-centred evaluation approach, therefore, argues that if we are sufficiently careful in selecting which documents are assessed and we evaluate on sufficiently large numbers of information requests, then we do not need to assess all documents in a collection.

The nature of test collection construction and the consequences of Assumption 2 are also important if we consider searching in operational environments. Test collection test results inform us of how well one system performs against another over a set of requests. Many studies have shown that the performance of any system across a set of requests is highly variable: systems will perform well for some requests and poorly for another. What IR tests cannot predict is how well a system will perform for a given request. This means, in operational environments, that the *searcher* must decide how well the system is performing for any given request. In many search situations, such variability might not matter; in patent searching it is more difficult to accept that some requests will be handled well and others not.

Blair and Maron [6] in one of most famous IR evaluation studies demonstrated that even experienced searchers can radically underestimate the proportion of relevant material obtained from an interactive search and that the quality of the searcher's queries can affect the *perception* of system performance. Although we can form intuitions about whether a system is returning relevant material, we cannot assess, simply based on the retrieved results, how much relevant material has been returned or how much remains to be retrieved. Blair and Maron in [6], and later [10], proposed four main reasons for the findings from their study:

1. Users often cannot predict which words are good at retrieving relevant material. In spite of detailed knowledge about the material with which they were involved, the searchers in their study could not identify useful search terms to retrieve important subsections of the database. However, they could consistently recognise useful information when it was presented to them. Common problems with querying included lack of knowledge of synonyms used in the unretrieved relevant material, poor handling of spelling mistakes relating to important terms and other oft-seen dilemmas in creating search requests.
2. The large size of the document collection meant that attempts to control precision—and hence make the result sets manageable—reduced the recall of searches. However, this results in the elimination of important relevant material from the search results.
3. Searchers can mistake document retrieval for data retrieval. That is, they describe the data they want to retrieve rather than the content of the documents they want to retrieve.
4. Overestimations of recall in laboratory tests give a false sense of security. In [10] Blair pointed out that poor laboratory tests can artificially inflate recall estimates. As noted above, test collection creators compensate for lack of exhaustive assessment by increasing the diversity of systems used to supply documents for assessments. The hope is that such diversity will lead to representative relevant documents being found. If the diversity is weak, then the recall figures can be artificially inflated because the relevant documents may be easier to find.

Knowledge that one is using a good system can also give the searcher the perception that they are finding more of the relevant documents than they actually are.

What Blair showed was that, even by submitting variations of query terms adjusted through trial and error, as in a typical search session, the likelihood of a searcher finding a substantial proportion of relevant documents can be low, a finding that has been verified across a number of studies [10]. An explanation for this limitation is that the intellectual content of a document is difficult to represent automatically: a document can be about a topic without ever mentioning key terms or phrases that a user may expect to appear. In addition, the query terms chosen by the user may not discriminate between relevant and non-relevant documents, especially as the collection size grows [11]. A user searching for documents on a new subject may not select terms that are representative of the subject they are searching *and* that discriminate such documents from the non-relevant documents which share similar vocabulary. Consequently, not all potentially relevant documents will be retrieved through keyword matching techniques alone.

In a real search situation, a search can only estimate what is hidden (the unretrieved relevant documents) by what they have already found and by the quality of their attempts to find these documents. In [12] Blair argues that the latter is difficult to measure and searchers are often forced into intuitive reasoning about search strategies. One process known as 'anchoring' is of particular interest in searching. Anchoring is a psychological process in which people estimate unknown values (the quality of queries in our case) by starting from an initial value which 'may be suggested by a formulation of the problem'. If a particular query is seen as good, either because it retrieves relevant documents or the searcher believes it to consist of good indexing terms, then they will retain and modify the query, rather than attempt new queries, ones which may be better at retrieving different types of relevant material.

Blair and Maron's final point is also an important one for real search situations where the effort involved in conducting a search must be balanced against the cost of conducting a search: finding a number of relevant documents is not a sole indicator of good retrieval performance, as the proportion of relevant documents *missed* is not known unless it is quantified through other means. Swanson refers to this as the 'fallacy of abundance'—discovering a (substantial) number of documents about a request creates an illusion that little remains hidden [8]. Good precision, in particular, can give the false impression that the system has good recall.

There are two issues relevant for patent retrieval. Firstly, the degree to which recall and precision as measured in laboratory tests are actually informative of the likely performance in real situations. In the most challenging patent searches, simple measures of recall and precision may have little predictive power because what reduces company risk is not simply the ability to find relevant material but to have performed a comprehensive search. Very few system evaluations tackle the issue of how dependent system performance is on the initial request or how variable the system's performance is. Therefore, the end user's own expertise and judgement play a large role in the system's overall performance. Secondly, and as a consequence of the above discussion, we need to investigate the end user's abilities to make judgements about recall and precision in operational environments. Blair and Maron's studies indicated potential pitfalls about making such decisions in real-life settings, particularly when cost and time must be balanced against effort. As we will discuss in Sect. 4, there are ways in which we can estimate the skill of the person operating the system.

5.3.2 Predicting Performance from Laboratory Tests

One of the core claims for test collections, as noted, for example, in Sanderson and Zobel [13], is that the relative performance of systems from a test collection evaluation tells us something about how the systems will perform in operational settings. This is trivially true in extreme cases; a system that continually retrieves the wrong documents in a controlled test collection evaluation is unlikely to perform well in an operational setting. The test collection approach, typically but not always, concentrates on single retrieval runs. Some authors, such as Spärck Jones [14], have argued that this is not an issue; systems that perform well on one retrieval run will perform well in most retrieval situations and performance on single retrieval runs gives us an indication of how well a system will perform iteratively. However, single-run evaluation limits our ability to evaluate the effect of known aspects of how humans assess relevance, in particular dynamic effects such as the development of relevance criteria across a search [15] or the effect of the order of assessment [16].

However, the general claim that single-run retrievals are good estimates of overall system performance has not been convincingly demonstrated so far, partly due to the few comparisons in operational settings and partly due to the impact that user adaptation and interfaces have on the level of retrieval effectiveness of a complete system. What has been investigated is the degree to which laboratory tests and user tests align. This is **not** the same as tests in operational environments where many contextual factors will intervene.

Hersh et al. [17], who were one of the first authors to try direct comparisons between test collection and interactive experiments, show that results from a test collection do not necessarily follow to the interactive case because the interactive aspects of a system can interfere with the results. Their investigation also raises the question of what are *meaningful* differences between retrieval results: how much better does one system have to be over another in a test collection evaluation for us to be convinced that it is indeed a better system and are these differences the ones that are observable to users of the systems? Since Hersh and Turpin's paper, there have been a large number of attempts to shed light on the second question. The evidence is distinctly mixed. Kelly et al. [18], for example, showed that end users could distinguish or detect differences in retrieval performance but within tightly controlled environments where the users were forced to interact in specific ways. Hersh and Turpin's later results and Smith and Kantor's very robust study indicated, however, that users can compensate for the performance of poor systems [19] and, to a degree, undo the effect of good systems by raising their threshold for relevance [20].

Harter [21], for example, criticised the standard test collection model of evaluation because it ignored the variation in why relevance assessments are made for specific information requests. Relevance assessments in operational settings are heavily contextualised by the situation in which the assessments were made, and this context includes the person making the assessment.

Spärck Jones, in a later paper, also mentioned the importance of context and notes (of TREC in particular) 'context is not embraced, but reluctantly and minimally acknowledged, like an awkward and difficult child. This applies even where explicit attempts have been made to include users (real or surrogate)' [22]. Limited attempts to incorporate context within test collection environments have been attempted, notably in the TREC Hard and CiQA tracks, but these have typically related to the contextual information within the query rather than contextual factors which might affect the operational use of a system.

5.3.3 Are Laboratory Evaluations Sufficient?

Few evaluation measures and not those typically associated with test collections would take into account other factors that are important to users such as the validity of information, the ability of a searcher to understand the information retrieved, the source of the information or the searcher's prior knowledge about a search topic [23]. Many studies (such as [24, 25]) have shown that, even for expert searchers, their confidence or prior knowledge in a search topic can affect their assessments of a document's relevance: they will mark different documents as relevant, and different numbers of documents, independently of how those documents were retrieved. Voorhees, in a tightly controlled study, estimated the difference in opinion between assessors as around 35 %; Ruthven et al. [24, 25] indicated that differences also occur with individual assessors depending on their prior relationship to the search topic. Further, as noted above in Sect. 3.1, a searcher's behaviour can strengthen the performance of a poor system or weaken the performance of a good system.

The question then arises as to what degree measures such as recall and precision obtained from laboratory studies actually help predict how good a patent search might be? If relevance assessments change depending on who is doing the assessment, then how much confidence can we have in evaluation measures based on relevance: if a different patent searcher conducted the same search, would we have different results? In operational environments, especially for searches with high risk, patent searchers can interact with each other to minimise the possible negative effects of individual variation in relevance judgements and search strategies.

However, as noted in Sect. 3.1, this places the emphasis for success onto the searcher and away from the system. A good set of evaluation measures would recognise and reward systems that offer support for end users in making challenging search decisions. The patent searches outlined in Sect. 2 are not simple searches; they are active processes where the end user must engage in a process of sense-making—understanding and interacting within information in complex ways to make a decision or recommendation. What makes a good IR system for this type of search behaviour is the ability of the system to make better sense of the search results and have more confidence in the accuracy of the outcome. This cannot be measured simply by performance evaluation but requires evaluating the process of searching. So how can we estimate the value of an IR system in helping successfully conduct a patent search?

In Sect. 4 we try to address this final question, building on the discussion in the previous sections, by outlining how we can gauge levels of trust in various parts of the IR process.

5.4 Evaluating Real Patent Retrieval Effectiveness

Any evaluation measure, implicitly or explicitly, carries a definition of success. This definition of what it means to succeed in an evaluation carries with it, in turn, the definition of what we see as the task of IR systems. In this chapter, we argue that the role of IR systems is to reduce overall risk; partly this is associated with measures of recall and precision (although simple measures may be too blunt), but the highly intellectual and interactive role of the patent search system (as a whole) needs to be incorporated into the evaluation.

One way of viewing IR evaluation is as a series of evaluation layers, each with distinct methodologies, metrics and questions. Lower evaluation levels comprise highly constrained, specific investigations on single system features; higher levels contain broader multifaceted investigations on the searcher *and* system. At the lower levels, for example, evaluations are typically on the algorithmic properties of system components and are run as performance tests conducted without human involvement. Higher levels will examine the interactive nature of the system to consider the degree to which the whole system supports an end user's information search. Appropriate metrics here will include both measures of the search products and the process of searching [26]. Product metrics, those that measure the end results of searching, may include aspects such as the number of relevant documents found, search satisfaction or time taken to complete a search. Process measures, on the other hand, consider how these products arose within a search and could include factors such as the ease of completing a search, the user understanding of the interface functionality, their increase in confidence in using the system and the use of system features.

As noted in Sect. 3, there are major differences between algorithmic evaluations and operational trials:

1. The effectiveness of a real patent search is dependent on the use of multiple systems and the searchers' ability to use them. Sections 3.2 and 3.3 outlined

some of the reasons why IR evaluations may not give us good predictions of how well a system performs in operational tests.

2. IR evaluation is based on generalisations. As noted in Sect. 3.1, IR evaluations tell us which systems are better for an average request. However, their performance across topics is very variable.
3. Individual estimates of recall and precision are affected by individual variation in how a searcher assesses relevance and what is returned by the system. It is far easier to reason about what is returned by a system than to reason about what is not returned.

Patent searching is a complex form of searching and one that involves multiple searches, collaboration with other people and heavy use of instinct and experience. So what types of evaluation are useful in understanding the success of an IR system for different types of patent searching? Arguably the success of any IR system is how well it supports the user in an information task, and measuring this will involve a number of different measures, some of which will be product based and some will be process based. However, as noted in Sect. 3, the ultimate purpose of IR tools within the IP process is to reduce risk by helping end users discover the required information or, alternatively, be reassured that certain information does not exist. Current laboratory evaluation measures do not help assess the degree to which an IR system has helped reduce this risk. Due to the variability in IR system performance, a user cannot guarantee any minimum level of performance for an *individual* search request. Nor can system designers assert, concretely, what level of confidence they should have in individual system components reducing risk because, as noted in Sect. 3, risk and recall/precision are not linearly related.

What we can try to develop are evaluation approaches that help estimate the confidence we should have in different system components. That is, how might we estimate what levels of trust we can have in parts of the retrieval process? If we have low levels of trust, then the end user needs to do additional work to compensate for lack of system performance.

5.4.1 Product-Based Measures for Evaluating Real Retrieval Effectiveness

Product measures are common in IR. Recall and precision can be used flexibly to give different estimates of system performance and different estimates are useful for different purposes. For a state-of-the-art search, reasonable recall is required and low precision perhaps tolerated, but debatably diversity of results is more important. Systems that artificially boost recall at the expense of missing important sections of the recall base could give the false impression that higher recall has been achieved. Systems may also be rewarded for retrieving some types of documents over others. In landscaping studies, it may be more useful for a searcher to have overview documents than narrowly focused documents. Calculating recall and precision over different document sets could be useful here.

For validity searches very precise results are required. Unlike state-of-the-art searches where we know there is material to be found but not sure what form it may take, in validity searches the question is whether the material is there to be found. In such a case, a useful evaluation metric may be final user confidence in the results of their search. A system that has a very high degree of topic variability (some queries are very successful, others very unsuccessful) offers little confidence in the performance on a new search. In such a situation, the searcher may have to expend more resources, time and cognitive, to complete the search but with little guidance from the system as to how effective the search has been.

Product-based metrics often focus on different systems with the same request; what they often fail to do is determine the variability of different requests on the same system. A useful product-based metric, particularly in light of the discussion in Sect. 3.1, is how variable a system performance is to the query formulation. High variation, particularly for best match systems, offers little confidence in the overall system performance and, again, increases the effort the searcher must expend on the search.

5.4.2 Process-Based Measure for Evaluating Real Retrieval Effectiveness

Process-based measures are useful for identifying the factors that lead to success and involve analysing the stages that lead to the end products of a search. In particular, for complex tasks where searchers may spend long periods of time on each search, process metrics are useful for identifying which search decisions are critical and which decisions need different types of system support.

Process measures are often difficult to develop and are subject to variation within the user population. However, process models can be used to (a) understand the processes of searching and (b) analyse success factors within each stage. An example of the latter is the University of Tampere's Query Performance Analyser [27], a tool for assessing how good a searcher is at the task of creating search requests. Such tools can help identify the relative contribution of the person conducting the search but also the contribution of the system to a successful outcome. Such knowledge could increase our confidence in the results of a search (in the case of high user and system abilities) or estimate what level of doubt we should retain after conducting a search. Understanding the process of searching within a professional domain like patent searching can also uncover the major sources of variation within patent searches and move towards correcting the sources of variation. Many disciplines use such process models to increase confidence in the overall process of completing tasks.

For high-risk tasks, such as freedom to operate, which requires both high recall and high precision, we could ask how individual searchers balance these requirements by the choice of search strategies and whether some strategies are more effective than others. Thus we can hope to move towards a more formal evaluation strategy for patent searching.

5.5 Conclusion

This chapter considers evaluating *real* retrieval effectiveness: retrieval effectiveness within an operational setting rather than in a controlled laboratory setting common to most IR evaluations. Deciding what to measure in evaluation is a crucial decision. It is worth reiterating the general point that any evaluation approach tends to distort what it tries to evaluate. Evaluation as an activity highlights some aspects of the phenomenon being studied and ignores others. As Hersh and Turpin [20] demonstrated, employing simple relevance metrics in user evaluations can give misleading results because simple metrics may ignore the factors that influence decisions. In this chapter, we have argued that retrieval system evaluation needs to provide a richer and more realistic account of the role of systems in reducing risk.

Each domain has its own challenges and presents new challenges to IR. IR researchers typically look at precision and recall simultaneously and measure their methods by how techniques stack up against both elements. When it comes to patent searching, it might be more productive to separate these functions so that they can be maximised independently. It has been demonstrated that risk, precision and recall do not follow the same linear path when discussing the various types of patent searches. Since this is the case, it might be more productive to begin with creating methods that produce high recall exclusive of precision. Once this is accomplished, the results can be ranked using different methods to improve precision and manage the way the results are shared with the searcher. It will likely be the case that different methods will be used to provide higher recall than those that can be employed to share records with higher precision. Instead of expecting a single method to do both, it would be useful to the patent-searching community if the process was done stepwise to maximise the value to the user.

It is received wisdom in the IR community that the variation between search requests is the greatest source of variation in retrieval system performance, and such variation is greater than the variation between end users. However, such claims are based on relatively artificial settings, and we still have relatively little empirical evidence on what components of a retrieval system are actually useful and the relative contributions of searcher and search system to overall success in patent searching.

We have, albeit briefly, suggested some evaluation directions that may help identify fruitful research directions in patent search evaluation. There are considerable challenges, particularly around issues of confidentiality, to be tackled, but if we are to move towards better evaluation procedures, then we need to be able to ask basic questions about the processes and decisions involved in operational patent environments.

References

1. Joho H, Azzopardi L, Vanderbauwhede W (2010) A survey of patent users: an analysis of tasks, behavior, search functionality and system requirements. 3rd Symposium on information interaction in context (IIiX '10)
2. Spärck Jones K, Willett P (eds) (1997) Readings in information retrieval. Morgan Kaufmann, San Francisco, CA
3. Voorhees EM, Harman D (eds) (2005) TREC: experiment and evaluation in information retrieval. MIT Press, Cambridge, MA
4. Ingwersen P, Järvelin K (2005) The turn: integration of information seeking and retrieval in context. Springer, Heidelberg
5. Hansen P, Järvelin K (2005) Collaborative information retrieval in an information-intensive domain. Inf Process Manage 41:1101–1119
6. Blair DC, Maron ME (1985) An evaluation of retrieval effectiveness for a full-text document-retrieval system. Commun ACM 28:289–299
7. Voorhees EM (2002) The philosophy of information retrieval evaluation. CLEF '01: Revised papers from the second workshop of the cross-language evaluation forum on evaluation of cross-language information retrieval systems, pp 355–370
8. Swanson DR (1989) Historical note: information retrieval and the future of an illusion. J Am Soc Inf Sci Tec 39:92–98
9. Voorhees EM (2005) The TREC robust retrieval track. ACM SIGIR Forum 39:11–20
10. Blair DC (1996) STAIRS redux: thoughts on the STAIRS evaluation, ten years after. J Am Soc Inf Sci Technol 47:4–22
11. Blair DC (2002) The challenge of commercial document retrieval, Part I: Major issues, and a framework based on search exhaustivity, determinacy of representation and document collection size. Inf Process Manage 38:273–291
12. Blair DC (1980) Searching biases in large interactive document retrieval systems. J Am Soc Inf Sci 31:271–277
13. Sanderson M, Zobel J (2005) Information retrieval system evaluation: effort, sensitivity, and reliability. 28th Annual international ACM SIGIR conference on research and development in information retrieval, pp 161–169
14. Spärck Jones K (2005) Epilogue: metareflections on TREC. In: Voorhees EM, Harman DK (eds) TREC: experiment and evaluation in information retrieval. MIT Press, Cambridge, MA, pp 421–448
15. Vakkari P (2000) Cognition and changes of search terms and tactics during task performance: a longitudinal study. RIAO 2004 (Recherche d'Information Assistée par Ordinateur), pp 894–907
16. Huang MH, Wang HY (2004) The influence of document presentation order and number of documents judged on users' judgements of relevance. J Am Soc Inf Sci Technol 55:970–979
17. Hersh WR, Turpin A, Price S, Chan B, Kraemer D, Sacherek L, Olson D (2000) Do batch and user evaluation give the same results? 23rd Annual international ACM SIGIR conference on research and development in information retrieval, pp 17–24
18. Kelly D, Fu X, Shah C (2010) Effects of position and number of relevant documents retrieved on users' evaluations of system performance. ACM Trans Inf Syst 28:1–9, 26, Article 9
19. Smith CL, Kantor PB (2008) User adaptation: good results from poor systems. 31st Annual international ACM SIGIR conference on research and development in information retrieval, pp 147–154

20. Hersh W, Turpin A (2001) Why batch and user evaluations do not give the same results. 24th Annual international ACM SIGIR conference on research and development in information retrieval, pp 225–231
21. Harter SP (1996) Variations in relevance assessments and the measurement of retrieval effectiveness. J Am Soc Inf Sci Technol 47:37–49
22. Spärck Jones K (2006) What's the value of TREC – is there a gap to jump or a chasm to bridge? ACM SIGIR Forum 40:10–20
23. Barry CL, Schamber L (1998) Users' criteria for relevance evaluation: a cross-situational comparison. Inf Process Manage 34:219–236
24. Ruthven I, Baillie M, Elsweiler D (2007) The relative effects of knowledge, interest and confidence in assessing relevance. J Doc 63:482–504
25. Ruthven I, Baillie M, Azzopardi L, Bierig R, Nicol E, Sweeney S, Yakici M (2008) Contextual factors affecting the utility of surrogates within exploratory search. Inf Process Manage 44:437–462
26. Borgman CL, Hirsh SG, Hiller J (1996) Rethinking online monitoring methods for information retrieval systems: from search product to search process. J Am Soc Inf Sci Technol 47:568–583
27. Sormunen E, Pennanen S (2004) The challenge of automated tutoring in web-based learning environments for IR instruction. Inf Res 9, paper 169

Chapter 6
Measuring Effectiveness in the TREC Legal Track

Stephen Tomlinson and Bruce Hedin

Abstract In this chapter, we report our experiences from attempting to measure the effectiveness of large electronic discovery (e-Discovery) result sets in the Text Retrieval Conference (TREC) Legal Track campaigns of 2006–2011. For effectiveness measures, we have focused on recall, precision and F_1. We state the estimators that we have used for these measures, and we outline both the rank-based and set-based approaches to sampling that we have taken. We share our experiences with the sampling error in the resulting estimates for the absolute effectiveness on individual topics, relative effectiveness on individual topics, mean effectiveness across topics and relative effectiveness across topics. Finally, we discuss our experiences with assessor error, which we have found has often had a larger impact than sampling error.

6.1 Introduction

In this chapter, we report our experiences with measuring the effectiveness of approaches to electronic discovery (e-Discovery) search in the legal domain. While the conditions and objectives of search in the legal domain are in many ways distinct from those that hold in the patent domain, evaluations of the effectiveness of search in the two domains nevertheless have many challenges in common. In particular, high recall is demanded in both of these domains, but the relevant documents may be a tiny fraction of the collection, making it difficult for sampling-based approaches to estimate the measures accurately.

S. Tomlinson (✉)
Open Text Corporation, 10 Rideau St, 6th Floor, Ottawa, ON, Canada K1N 9JI
e-mail: stomlins@opentext.com

B. Hedin
H5, 595 Market St., San Francisco, CA 94105, USA
e-mail: bhedin@h5.com

© Springer-Verlag GmbH Germany 2017 163
M. Lupu et al. (eds.), *Current Challenges in Patent Information Retrieval*,
The Information Retrieval Series 37, DOI 10.1007/978-3-662-53817-3_6

Table 6.1 Overview of the referenced TREC Legal Track tasks

Task	$|D|$	Topics	Type	Max $|S|$	Runs	Judged	$estRel(D)_{high}$
2007 ad hoc	6,910,192	43	Rank	25,000	68	488–1000	77,467
2008 ad hoc	6,910,192	26	Rank	100,000	64	493–900	658,399
2009 batch	6,910,192	10	Rank	1,500,000	10	1250–2500	1,046,833
2010 learning	685,592	8	Rank	685,592	20	2720–2720	67,938
2011 learning	685,592	3	Rank	685,592	28	5545–5871	20,017
2008 interactive	6,910,192	3	Set	6,910,192	5	2500–6500	786,862
2009 interactive	569,034	7	Set	569,034	4	2729–3975	26,839
2010 interactive	455,449	4	Set	455,449	6	5779–7120	20,176

Our experience comes from our involvement with the Legal Track of the Text Retrieval Conference (TREC), which started in 2006 [3] with the goal of creating standard tests for electronic discovery (e-Discovery) requests. Recall is a primary concern in e-Discovery, as there is a legal obligation to return, to an extent commensurate with a reasonable good faith effort, *all* evidence relevant to the request. Precision is also important, however, in order to reduce cost and prevent the unnecessary release of information. Effective e-Discovery continues to be a challenging problem [2, 15, 17].

The TREC Legal Track continued in 2007 [24], 2008 [16], 2009 [13], 2010 [8] and 2011 [11], each year running between one and three tasks. In this chapter, we refer to just eight of these tasks, listed in Table 6.1. Herein, we briefly summarise the details of these tasks that are necessary to understand the measurement approaches. More details on the TREC Legal Track are readily available in the online track overview papers [3, 8, 11, 13, 16, 24] and track Web site [25].

For each task, there was a document set D to search. One can see which collection was used for each task based on the size of the collection ($|D|$) listed in Table 6.1, as follows:

- 6,910,192: The IIT CDIP (Illinois Institute of Technology Complex Document Information Processing) collection [14], which consisted of 6,910,192 documents released by seven US tobacco companies.
- 569,034: The TREC 2009 Enron collection [13], which consisted of 569,034 e-mail messages (with attachments) from the mailboxes of approximately 150 employees of Enron Corporation.
- 455,449: The TREC 2010 De-duplication of EDRM Enron Email Data Set v2 [8], which consisted of 455,449 distinct e-mail messages (with attachments). This collection was a substantial revision of the Enron collection used in 2009.
- 685,592: The same TREC 2010 De-duplication of EDRM Enron Email Data Set v2 as just mentioned except that the e-mail attachments were treated as separate documents, increasing the effective number of documents to 685,592.

For each task, there was a set of test topics. Each topic consisted of a multi-paragraph background complaint and a one-sentence request for documents to produce. For example, for topic #74, the (fictitious) complaint alleged infringement of a patent of a product for ventilating smoke, and the one-sentence request was 'All scientific studies expressly referencing health effects tied to indoor air quality'. The number of test topics for a task ranged from 3 to 43; the final number for each task (excluding those discarded because of incomplete assessment) is in the 'Topics' column of Table 6.1.

We refer to five of the eight tasks (2007 ad hoc, 2008 ad hoc, 2009 batch, 2010 learning, 2011 learning) as *rank-based* tasks, as per the 'Type' column of Table 6.1. In these tasks, the test systems were typically automated systems, and they were required to specify a ranking of the documents for each topic based on the system's opinion of their probability of relevance to the request. In the 'ad hoc' and 'learning (2011)' tasks, the topics were new ones that the systems were seeing for the first time, whereas in the 'batch' and 'learning (2010)' tasks, the topics typically were reused from previous years and the systems could use past judgements of relevant and non-relevant documents to train batch filtering techniques. The 2011 learning task supported learning by allowing participants to choose their own training documents in sets of 100. For various bandwidth reasons, the rank-based tasks before 2010 had a maximum submission depth (e.g. 100,000 documents per topic in the 2008 ad hoc task, much less than the collection size of 6,910,192) as listed in the 'Max $|S|$' column of Table 6.1.

We refer to the other three of the eight tasks (2008–2010 interactive) as *set-based* tasks (as per the 'Type' column of Table 6.1). In these tasks, the test submissions were typically produced by an interactive (human-in-the-loop) process, and for each topic included just the documents that were considered relevant to the request, without specifying a ranking of the documents. In part because there were fewer test topics, there was no limit on the submission size (besides $|D|$, the size of the collection itself).

The remaining columns of Table 6.1 are as follows. The 'Runs' column specifies the largest number of submissions received for any topic of the task; note that for the set-based (interactive) tasks, participants were not required to submit results for every topic, unlike for most of the rank-based tasks. The 'Judged' column specifies the smallest and largest number of documents judged for any topic of the task. The '$estRel(D)_{high}$' column specifies the largest estimated number of relevant documents for any topic of the task (based on the methodology discussed in Sect. 6.3).

We see that the number of relevant documents for a topic (sometimes more than one million) could far exceed the number of documents that we could judge for a topic (at most a few thousand). In the following sections, we describe the approaches we took to estimating the effectiveness measures and reflect upon how well the approaches met the various task goals. We also attempt to identify what evaluation challenges remain.

6.2 Effectiveness Measures

To gauge the effectiveness of a result set for a test topic, we focused on the well-known recall, precision and F_1 measures [16, 26].

If we had complete knowledge of which documents were relevant and non-relevant for a topic, we could calculate the recall, precision and F_1 of a result set by using the following definitions:

D	The set of documents in the collection
S	The subset of D whose effectiveness we wish to measure
$Rel(S)$	The set of relevant documents in S
$Non(S)$	The set of non-relevant documents in S
$Recall(S)$	The recall of S:

$$Recall(S) = \frac{|Rel(S)|}{|Rel(D)|} \tag{6.1}$$

$Prec(S)$ The precision of S:

$$Prec(S) = \frac{|Rel(S)|}{|Rel(S)| + |Non(S)|} \tag{6.2}$$

$F_1(S)$ The F_1 of S:

$$F_1(S) = \frac{2 * Prec(S) * Recall(S)}{Prec(S) + Recall(S)} \tag{6.3}$$

Note: $F_1(S)$ is 0 if either $Prec(S)$ or $Recall(S)$ is 0.

For ranked result sets, we can likewise gauge effectiveness at any particular cutoff depth K (remembering to pad the set with assumed non-relevant documents if the set contained fewer than K documents in order to not overstate Precision@K or F_1@K; this padding approach is analogous to the standard `trec_eval` utility definition of 'precision at document cutoff λ' which is simply 'r/λ' where r is the number of relevant documents retrieved before the cutoff [4]). In the 2008 and 2009 rank-based tasks, the submissions were required to specify the depth K for each topic at which the system believed the F_1 measure would be maximised, allowing both set-based and rank-based evaluations. In 2010 and 2011, the learning task more generally required each submission to specify its estimated probability of relevance for every document for each topic, from which one can infer not just what depth K the system would consider optimal for F_1, but what cutoff it would consider optimal for any other set-based measure [8, 11].

6.3   Estimators

In practice, we did not have the resources to judge all of the documents for each topic (almost seven million documents in some of our tasks). The traditional TREC approach is simply to judge a pool of the top-ranked documents from various systems [12], but it was apparent from sampling experiments in 2006 [3, 21] that, for most of our topics, the number of relevant documents far exceeded the number that could be judged. Other TREC tracks had also been encountering issues with traditional TREC pooling [5].

In 2007, we started to use a deeper sampling approach to estimate the measures. It was based in part on the approach used to estimate 'inferred average precision' (infAP) [32] in the TREC 2006 terabyte track [6]. Our main extension was to sample different parts of the collection with different probabilities (we defer our discussion of the sampling approaches to Sect. 6.4). Other researchers independently made a similar extension [1].

The estimators we have used for recall, precision and F_1 are defined as follows:

d	A document in D
$p(d)$	The inclusion probability of d (i.e. the probability of selecting document d for judging, described in Sect. 6.4)
$JudgedRel(S)$	The set of documents in S which were judged relevant
$JudgedNon(S)$	The set of documents in S which were judged non-relevant
$estRel(S)$	The estimated number of relevant documents in S:

$$estRel(S) = \sum_{d \in JudgedRel(S)} \frac{1}{p(d)} \tag{6.4}$$

Note: $estRel(S)$ is 0 if $|JudgedRel(S)| = 0$.

$estNon(S)$ The estimated number of non-relevant documents in S:

$$estNon(S) = \sum_{d \in JudgedNon(S)} \frac{1}{p(d)} \tag{6.5}$$

Note: $estNon(S)$ is 0 if $|JudgedNon(S)| = 0$.

$estRecall(S)$ The estimated recall of S:

$$estRecall(S) = \frac{estRel(S)}{estRel(D)} \tag{6.6}$$

$estPrec(S)$ The estimated precision of S:

$$estPrec(S) = \frac{estRel(S)}{estRel(S) + estNon(S)} \tag{6.7}$$

Note: $estPrec(S)$ is undefined if $(estRel(S) + estNon(S)) = 0$.

$estF_1(S)$ The estimated F_1 of S:

$$estF_1(S) = \frac{2 * estPrec(S) * estRecall(S)}{estPrec(S) + estRecall(S)} \qquad (6.8)$$

Note: $estF_1(S)$ is 0 if either $estPrec(S)$ or $estRecall(S)$ is 0.

The $estRel(S)$ and $estNon(S)$ formulas for estimating the number of relevant and non-relevant documents (respectively) use the Horvitz–Thompson estimator, which is unbiased [20]. (We do not claim, however, that our estimators for recall, precision and F_1 are statistically unbiased, because they involve ratios of estimators.)

We also have looked at alternative estimators that correct for obvious overestimates; for example, if $estRel(S)$ is greater than $|S| - |JudgedNon(S)|$, then it must be an overestimate, and so reducing the estimate to $|S| - |JudgedNon(S)|$ must reduce the error. We actually have used such alternative estimators in our rank-based tasks, and the formulas are stated in the 2007 track overview [24]. However, these alternative estimators bias the estimates low on average because only overestimates are improved; underestimates are left unchanged. In our experience, the alternative estimators have made little material difference, so we just present the simpler estimators in this chapter.

Another aspect to be accounted for that we have encountered in running our evaluations concerns what we have termed 'grey' documents, which are documents that were drawn by sampling for assessment, but on which the assessor could not render a relevance judgement. This could occur for any of a number of reasons, such as that a technical issue prevented a legible display of the document image, or the document was longer than 300 pages (which was more than we required an assessor to review for one document) or the document was in a language other than English. When reporting results, we have reported for each submission S an estimate of what percentage of S was grey documents; typically this percentage has been less than 2 %, though we have seen as high as 13 % from an approach that favoured long documents [24]. The estimators we have given here for recall and precision essentially behave as if the grey documents had been omitted from both the full collection D and result set S.

6.3.1 Graded Relevance

In some tasks, starting with the 2008 ad hoc task, the assessors were asked to distinguish 'highly relevant' documents from 'other relevant' documents [16]. Having such 'graded' relevance assessments might seem to call for new measures and estimators, as the definitions we have given assume 'binary' relevance assessments (a document is either relevant or it is not). We have avoided this complication by simply reporting separate results based on two different sets of binary relevance assessments, one in which just 'highly relevant' documents are counted as relevant and the other in which 'all relevant' documents are counted as relevant. In this chapter, when we have given examples of numbers of relevant documents or the scores attained, we have always included all relevant documents.

6.4 Sampling Approaches

This section describes how we chose the $p(d)$ values (i.e. sampled the collection) in the various tasks.

As pointed out in related work on estimation approaches [1], the choice of $p(d)$ does not affect the expected values of the estimators, but it can affect the variance and hence the accuracy of the estimates. Generally, we have chosen the $p(d)$ values based on the submissions received (as described below) in hopes of minimising the estimation error for the submissions. Future result sets can also be scored using the estimators (i.e. our test collections are reusable in principle) though the error bar for non-participating runs may be wider as the $p(d)$ values may not be as suitable for them. One can get an indication of how reusable a test collection may be in practice by conducting a 'system omission' study [33], i.e. a study in which one simulates how the estimated scores would have changed if one of the participating systems had not been included. A recent system omission study for the TREC 2010 interactive task topic regarding privilege classification found that the error bars for the omitted system's estimated precision noticeably widened, but not for its estimated recall [27].

6.4.1 Rank-Based Sampling

As a concrete example of rank-based sampling, this section focuses on the 2008 ad hoc task.

As shown in Table 6.1, the rank-based 2008 ad hoc task had 26 test topics. Although the collection contained almost seven million documents, for space and bandwidth reasons, we allowed participants to submit only their top-ranked 100,000 documents for each topic, hoping that would be enough to include all of the relevant documents. The ten participating groups submitted a total of 64 experimental runs.

For each topic, we created a pool P from all of the submitted documents. (The pool sizes ranged from 9 to 24 % of the collection.) For each $d \in P$, we defined $hiRank(d)$ to be the highest rank (where 1 is highest, 2 is second highest, etc.) at which any of the 64 systems ranked the document. Then we set $p(d)$ as follows:

$$\text{If } (hiRank(d) \leq 5) \text{ Then } p(d) = 1.0 \tag{6.9}$$

$$\text{Else } p(d) = \min\left(1.0, \left(\left(\frac{5}{100000}\right) + \left(\frac{C}{hiRank\,(d)}\right)\right)\right) \tag{6.10}$$

The value C was chosen so that the sum of the $p(d)$ values (for all $d \in P$) was the number of documents that could be judged (typically 500 documents were judged for each topic).

This $p(d)$ formula was intended to support (almost) equally accurate estimates regardless of the chosen depth K. One can see that at any depth $K > 5$, the smallest $p(d)$ involved would be at least C/K, the same as if doing simple random sampling of at least C documents from the set of K documents. Unfortunately, for our 26 test topics, the C values turned out to range from just 1.7 to 4.4, which was lower than we had hoped. We discuss the implications for sampling error further in Sect. 6.5.

For documents d that were not in the pool, $p(d)$ was 0. (Actually, we did draw a small random sample from the documents outside of the pool for separate analysis, which we discuss later in Sect. 6.6, but we did not use these for estimation because this sampling was deemed too coarse to be sufficiently accurate.) Hence our estimators actually were just estimating recall from the pool P. For estimating recall, this approach essentially follows the traditional TREC approach of assuming all unpooled documents are non-relevant. For estimation of precision and F_1, however, for future result sets that might contain documents outside of the pool, our estimators behave not as if the unpooled documents were non-relevant, but as if the unpooled documents had been omitted from the result set.

6.4.2 Set-Based Sampling

As a concrete example of set-based sampling, this section focuses on the 2008 interactive task.

As shown in Table 6.1, the set-based 2008 interactive task had three test topics. Participants submitted just the set of documents that they considered relevant for a topic, without ranking the documents. There was no limit on the size of the submission set for a topic (other than the number of documents in the collection, 6,910,912). At most five submissions were received for any topic.

To assign the $p(d)$ values, the full collection D was stratified. To use topic #103 as a concrete example, which received five submissions (one of which was actually a composite submission formed by pooling the results of 64 ad hoc submissions for the topic), 32 strata (from 2^5) were created as follows. The first stratum consisted of documents included in all five submissions (the 'All-R' stratum, or 'RRRRR'). The next stratum consisted of documents included in submissions 1–4 but not submission 5 (the 'RRRRN' stratum). The next stratum consisted of documents included in submissions 1–3 and 5 but not submission 4 (the 'RRRNR' stratum) and so on. The final stratum (stratum #32) included all of the documents that were not in any submission (the 'All-N' stratum, or 'NNNNN').

Within a particular stratum S_s, n_s documents were chosen to be judged (using simple random sampling without replacement). Typically n_s was chosen proportionally to $|S_s|$ (the number of documents in the stratum), except that larger strata, particularly the 'All-N' stratum, were sampled somewhat less densely than their full-population size would dictate, in order to ensure that we were able also to sample a sufficient number of documents from the smaller strata. For the purposes of the estimator formulas, for $d \in S_s$, $p(d)$ was $n_s/|S_s|$. As a concrete example, for topic #103, there were 6500 judgements, and most strata had $p(d)$ close to 0.008 (1 in 125), but the 'All-N' stratum, which was 83 % of the collection, was only assigned 25 % of the samples (n_s=1625); hence its documents' $p(d)$ was just 0.00028 (approximately 1 in 3500).

The 2008 interactive task also introduced the practice of assigning multiple assessors to a topic. The documents to judge were allocated randomly to the available assessors; typically each assessor was responsible for a bin of 500 documents. If a bin was not completely assessed by the track's assessment deadline, it was discarded, and the n_s and hence $p(d)$ values of affected strata were reduced accordingly before the judgements were released.

6.5   Sampling Error Analysis

In this section, we discuss our experiences with sampling error, (i.e. the limitations on accuracy resulting from judging just a sample of a population instead of the full population). In Sects. 6.5.1 and 6.5.2, the sampling error arises from not having judged every document for a topic. In Sects. 6.5.3 and 6.5.4, the sampling error arises from having a limited number of test topics.

6.5.1   Absolute Effectiveness on One Topic

For the stratified sampling approach described in Sect. 6.4.2, we have developed confidence interval formulas for $estRecall(S)$, $estPrec(S)$ and $estF_1(S)$; these run into several pages and are available in the 2008 track overview [16]. The formulas were developed in part by consulting textbook approaches [19, 20]. Recent work [30] suggests that these confidence intervals may be wider than they need to be (which we look at further below). However, we believe the formulas in the 2008 track overview are still serviceable and these formulas are used for the examples and results summarised in this section.

We should emphasise that all of the confidence intervals in this chapter are just accounting for the uncertainty arising from sampling error. We are not in this chapter attempting to construct confidence intervals that account for any other type of uncertainty, such as the uncertainty of whether the assessor was correct in his or her judgement of the relevance or non-relevance of each sampled document. (We investigate the impact of assessor errors separately in Sect. 6.6.)

Here, we just review some examples of the confidence intervals to give an idea of what widths were attained. Table 6.2 shows example confidence intervals for one submission for each topic of the 2008 interactive task, in descending order

Table 6.2 Confidence intervals of some 2008 interactive task submissions

$|Judged(D)|$	$|S|$	$estRecall(S)$	$estPrec(S)$	$estF_1(S)$
6500	608,807	0.624 (0.579, 0.668)	0.810 (0.795, 0.824)	0.705 (0.676, 0.734)
4500	546,126	0.314 (0.266, 0.362)	0.328 (0.301, 0.355)	0.321 (0.293, 0.349)
2500	689,548	0.345 (0.111, 0.580)	0.023 (0.014, 0.032)	0.043 (0.026, 0.060)

by the number of judgements for the topic: 6500 judgements for topic #103, 4500 judgements for topic #102 and 2500 judgements for topic #104. For example, the first row shows that, for a submission S of 608,807 documents, the estimated recall was 0.624, with 95 % confidence interval of (0.579, 0.668).

Of course, examples cannot show the full picture, and it would be incorrect to suggest that the only factor in confidence interval size is the number of judgements. The overall yield of a topic (i.e. $|Rel(D)|/|D|$), for example, can also have a significant impact on the width of confidence intervals. For samples of similar size, higher-yielding topics will generally result in higher numbers of positive (relevant) instances being included in the sample (both positive instances retrieved by the system being evaluated and positive instances not retrieved by the system), thus enabling narrower confidence intervals for the estimate of the recall achieved by the system. In the 3 years in which the interactive task was run (2008–2010), a total of 56 submissions were received for the various topics featured. Of the 56, a total of 41 achieved an estimated recall of 0.10 or higher. For those 41 submissions, the mean width of the confidence interval associated with the recall estimate was 0.15. Of those 41 submissions, 20 were for topics found to have yields of 0.02 or greater; the mean width of the confidence intervals associated with those 20 recall estimates was 0.084. For the 21 submissions for topics found to have yields less than 0.02, on the other hand, the mean width of the confidence intervals associated with the recall estimates was 0.213.

Moreover, of all the strata into which the test collection is partitioned, the one that poses the greatest sampling challenge is the All-N stratum (the stratum containing documents no team identified as relevant). It is a challenge because the density of relevant material in this stratum is generally very low, making it hard to obtain, via sampling, precise estimates of the true density in the stratum; and this challenge generally becomes more acute as the overall yield of a topic gets lower. As a result, the lower the yield of a topic, the greater the sampling error contributed from the All-N stratum, and so the greater the width of the confidence intervals associated with our estimates of the full-population yield and of recall. (Note that, for the topics reported in Table 6.2, the estimated yield (i.e. $estRel(D)/|D|$) of the topic with 6500 judgements was 0.114 of the full collection; the estimated yield for the topic with 4500 judgements was 0.081; and the estimated yield for the topic with 2500 judgements was 0.007.)

Table 6.3 Mean width of confidence intervals—track overview vs. beta-binomial with half prior

Yield	Overview	BetaBin-Half
≥ 0.02	0.091	0.082
< 0.02	0.208	0.192

While we have not listed examples here from the same topic, the confidence intervals for the submissions were often narrow enough to not overlap the confidence intervals of any of the other submissions. For example, for the five submissions for topic #103, none of the confidence intervals for recall had any overlap of each other.

We noted above that consideration has been given to alternative methods for calculating confidence intervals for recall [30]. It is worth noting here that the key observations made in this section hold also for those alternative methods. For example, when the alternative method found to be most promising, the half prior beta-binomial posterior method [30], is applied to the 2008 TREC data, we again find that we can obtain meaningfully narrow confidence intervals with reasonably sized samples of judgements (e.g. 4500 judgements). Table 6.3 reports, for all 2008 and 2009 interactive task submissions that achieved recall of at least 0.10 (as gauged by the point estimate), the mean widths of the 95 % confidence intervals that result from the method used in the track overview and from the half-prior beta-binomial posterior method. Since, for a fixed sample size, yield is a significant driver of confidence interval width, the table distinguishes results for topics with an estimated yield greater than or equal to 0.02 from results for topics with an estimated yield less than 0.02.

For the alternative methods, it also remains true that, for any given sample size, the yield of relevant material is the chief driver of the width of the confidence interval associated with the recall estimate, and it remains true that, when using a stratified sampling approach, the sampling error contributed by the All-N stratum typically poses the greatest challenge to obtaining narrow confidence intervals for recall.

For the rank-based approach described in Sect. 6.4.1, for which typically there were just 500 judgements per topic, we have not to date computed confidence intervals for individual topic estimates, but it seems apparent from the low C values mentioned in Sect. 6.4.1 that the sampling error would be large in some cases. A large sampling error on individual topics does not imply that the test data is not useful, however, as discussed in the following sections.

6.5.2 Relative Effectiveness on One Topic

While one of our goals was to provide reasonable estimates of the absolute values of the metrics, for comparing particular experimental approaches, it can sometimes suffice to just estimate the *difference* in scores of the approaches. Sometimes the difference can be estimated much more accurately than the confidence intervals for the absolute values may suggest.

For example, suppose set S_1 is estimated to have a recall of 0.62 with confidence interval (0.58, 0.66) and set S_2 is estimated to have a recall of 0.64 with confidence interval (0.60, 0.68). One might conclude that the recalls of S_1 and S_2 are not statistically distinguishable because their confidence intervals overlap. However, if one noticed that S_2 was a superset of S_1 and that there were relevant documents in S_2 that were not in S_1, then one would know that the recall of S_2 must be greater than that of S_1 despite the overlap in the confidence intervals.

Strict subsets and supersets can arise in practice when comparing sets that result from Boolean queries. In particular, the ad hoc tasks of the TREC Legal Track included a reference Boolean negotiation for each test topic in which typically the requesting party would argue for broadening the query and the responding party would argue for narrowing the query.

In general, one can also analyse differences of sets that overlap without one containing the other. (To date, however, we have not attempted to develop confidence interval formulas for such differences in scores, leaving this as future work.)

6.5.3 Mean Effectiveness Across Topics

Sometimes there is interest in the average effectiveness of an approach. For example, in the 2008 ad hoc task, for each of the 26 test topics, there was (as just mentioned) a reference Boolean negotiation, and the Boolean query initially proposed by the responding party was found to average just 4 % recall, while the Boolean counterproposal by the requesting party was found to average 43 % recall, and the resulting consensus query was found to average 33 % recall. These average scores give us a feel for the typical negotiation in that it seems that the respondent's initial proposal was typically a very narrow query compared to the requester's rejoinder or resulting consensus.

Assuming that the topics are independent, one can compute approximate 95 % confidence intervals for means by adding plus or minus twice the standard error of the mean [9]. For example, the approximate confidence interval for the 33 % average recall of the consensus negotiated query over the 26 test topics of the 2008 ad hoc task was 21 % and 45 %. The noisier the individual topic estimates, the higher the variance will tend to be, increasing the width of the confidence interval. Increasing the number of test topics will usually reduce the width of the interval.

Given a fixed assessment budget, there is a trade-off between how many topics can be assessed and how many judgements can be made per topic. In our case, for the interactive tasks, it would not have been practical to create a lot of topics because few participants would have time to perform an intensive interactive approach for all of them, so we focused on making the evaluation for the small number of topics as accurate as possible. For our ad hoc tasks of 2007 and 2008, in which the participating systems were typically automated, we followed the traditional TREC practice of creating enough topics to support averaging, albeit at the expense of accuracy on individual topics. In the 2009 batch task, we reduced the number of topics, and while the primary reason was the bandwidth limitations of dealing with the increase in the allowed result set size, we also hoped that this trade-off point would allow better failure analysis on individual topics (as discussed further in the next section). The 'Million Query Track' at TREC [1] has explored the other extreme, creating more than a thousand test queries but judging only 40 or so documents for each, to investigate the feasibility of studies suggesting that 'assessor effort would be better spent building test collections with more topics, each assessed in less detail' [18].

6.5.4   Relative Effectiveness Across Topics

Just as one can compute approximate confidence intervals for mean scores, one can compute approximate confidence intervals for the mean *difference* in score between two approaches. The method given in the previous section, when applied to differences, is approximately the same as the popular paired t-test, which tends to be fairly accurate even if the differences are not normally distributed because of the Central Limit Theorem [9]. When zero is not in the confidence interval, the difference in the mean score is considered to be 'statistically significant'.

For the 2007 ad hoc task (of 43 test topics), one study [22] compared 14 pairs of experimental approaches, thresholding relevance-ranked sets at depth B (the number of matches of the reference Boolean query); it found that 3 of the 14 differences in estimated recall@B, and 7 of the 14 differences in estimated precision@B, were statistically significant. For the 2008 ad hoc task (of 26 test topics), a follow-up study [23] compared 15 pairs of experimental approaches; it found that 3 of the 15 differences in estimated recall@B, and 3 of the 15 differences in F_1@K, were statistically significant. These results indicate that the test collections for these tasks do sometimes support the discerning of statistically significant mean differences.

What is often more insightful than comparing mean scores across topics is to look at how often one approach substantially outscores another. Analysing the largest differences can often lead to a better understanding of when one approach will outperform another. Such an investigation can also be interpreted as conducting 'failure analysis' for the lower-scoring approach.

For example, in the 2007 ad hoc task, a study [22] compared the effectiveness of the reference Boolean query to a relevance-ranked vector query. The 'vector query' consisted of the same keywords as the reference Boolean query, but the Boolean operators and other structures of the query (such as word proximity criteria) were replaced with a simple Boolean-OR of the keywords. The retrieval set of the vector query was relevance ranked and thresholded to B (the number of matches of the reference Boolean query). The finding of this experiment was that the Boolean query had the higher estimated recall@B for 26 of the test topics, while the vector query scored higher on just 16 of the topics, and there was 1 tie. Why was the Boolean query often more successful? The largest difference was on topic #58, regarding 'health problems caused by HPF [high-phosphate fertilisers]', for which the estimated recall@B of the Boolean query was 94 % while for the vector query it was just 8 %. Despite the potentially large sampling errors, it seemed clear from looking at some of the hundreds of judgements for the topic that the Boolean query was more successful for this topic because it required a term beginning with 'phosphat' to be in the document, whereas the vector approach favoured a lot of non-relevant documents that did not mention the key 'phosphat' concept as it was only 1 of 22 terms in the vector form of the query.[1] Finding good examples of when approaches differ may lead to a better understanding of when to use one approach or the other, or to the development of generally better approaches.

6.6   Assessor Error Analysis

In this section, we discuss our experiences with assessor error. In the first subsection, we summarise our formative experiences with assessor error through the tasks of 2009, by which time it was apparent that assessor error is a serious issue to address in order to accurately estimate recall, arguably even more important than sampling error. (Another recent study has also found that assessor error, which it calls 'measurement error', is a 'larger problem' than sampling error [27].) In the subsequent subsection, we summarise the attempts of the Legal Track to address the issue of assessor error in 2010 and 2011.

6.6.1   Formative Experiences with Assessor Error

The interactive tasks of 2008 and 2009 included an adjudication phase in which the participants could appeal any judgement by the first-line assessor to the 'Topic Authority' for the topic (whose judgement the initial assessor was attempting to replicate); the Topic Authority then rendered a final relevance judgement on all documents so appealed. For nine of the ten test topics (all three from 2008 and six of seven from 2009), the estimated number of relevant documents ($estRel(D)$) was lower after the adjudication phase, indicating that the initial assessors typically

---

[1] The reference Boolean query for this topic was
'Phosphat! w/75 (caus! OR relat! OR assoc! OR derive! OR correlat!) w/75 (health OR disorder! OR toxic! OR "chronic fatigue" OR dysfunction! OR irregular OR memor! OR immun! OR myopath! OR liver! OR kidney! OR heart! OR depress! OR loss OR lost)'.

The corresponding 'vector query' was
'Phosphat! OR caus! OR relat! OR assoc! OR derive! OR correlat! OR health OR disorder! OR toxic! OR chronic OR fatigue OR dysfunction! OR irregular OR memor! OR immun! OR myopath! OR liver! OR kidney! OR heart! OR depress! OR loss OR lost'.

'w/75' means 'within 75 words of'.

generated a lot of false positives. For example, for topic #103 in 2008, $estRel(D)$ was 914,528 before adjudication and 786,862 after adjudication, a drop of 127,666 in a collection of 6,910,192 documents, suggesting that the net false positive rate was approximately 2 % of the collection.

We also found evidence of false positives in the ad hoc tasks of 2007 and 2008, even though they did not have an appeal process. As mentioned in Sect. 6.4.1, for these tasks we drew a random sample from the documents that no system submitted. Of these, we found that approximately 1 % were judged relevant. When we personally reviewed some of these relevant judgements, almost all of them looked non-relevant to us (and we think that the original assessors would agree with us in retrospect, though we regret that we did not reserve time with them to ask about particular judgements). This result suggests that there was a net false positive rate of approximately 1 % for unsubmitted documents.

A standout example of the impact of a small net false positive rate was observed in topic #51 of the 2009 batch task. For this task, there was a set of training judgements from a previous use of the topic, for which $estRel(D)$ was 95. But with the new judgements for the topic in 2009, $estRel(D)$ was 26,404. Most of the difference in these estimates came from just three relevant judgements in 2009, whose weights were approximately 8000 each (from $1/p(d)$) as the highest that any system ranked them was more than 700,000 from the top. Our own review of these three documents suggests that they were false positives. We suspect that the original estimate of 95 was reasonably accurate, which would imply that relevant documents were just 0.001 % of the collection for this topic. Hence a net false positive rate of even 0.1 % would lead to a huge overestimate of the number of relevant documents, and hence the recall of good result sets would be dramatically underestimated.

In the 2009 interactive task, we found dramatic changes in the scoring of the result sets after the appeals. (The appeals typically corrected both false positives and false negatives.) In particular, for four of the seven topics, some participant's (estimated) F_1 score increased by more than 0.50 after the appeals; for example, on topic #201, the F_1 of submission W increased from 0.07 to 0.84 after the appeals, and on topic #204, the F_1 of submission H increased from 0.17 to 0.80 after the appeals.

Furthermore, the appeals in the 2009 interactive task did not just change the absolute scores. For four of the seven topics, there were changes in the rankings of the result sets (based on F_1) after the appeals. One dramatic example of a re-ranking was on topic #205, for which the (estimated) F_1 of submission C was higher than that of submission E before appeals (0.46 vs. 0.25), but lower after appeals (0.43 vs. 0.61), with both differences being statistically significant based on the lack of overlap in the confidence intervals. (As previously mentioned, the confidence intervals in this chapter only account for sampling error, not assessor error.)

While past studies have typically found only minor differences in system rankings from assessor differences [29], an exception has been noted in the past for runs involving manual relevance feedback [12, 28]. Of course, many of the interactive task submissions were constructed with human assessing as part of the process, so our finding of the appeals affecting interactive submission rankings appears to be consistent with past findings. (A simulation-based study has suggested more generally that false positives tend to cause larger differences in system rankings than false negatives [7].)

The results of the appeals process followed in the interactive task prompted much discussion among task organisers and participants on the question of whether the changes in assessment that resulted from the appeals process represented corrections of true human error on the part of the first-pass assessors or simply reflected reasonable differences of opinion between the first-pass assessor and the adjudicator as to how the topic should be interpreted. This question was examined more closely in a follow-up study by two track organisers using data from the 2009 interactive task [10]. The study looked at a sample of documents from the 2009 exercise for which the assessments had been changed via the appeals process. The study classified the documents as 'clearly responsive' (i.e. documents for which no reasonable argument could be made that the document was not within the scope of the governing document request), 'clearly non-responsive' (i.e. documents for which no reasonable argument could be made that the document was within the scope of the governing document request) or 'arguable' (i.e. documents for which reasonable arguments could be made both for and against the document's responsiveness to the governing document request). The study found that nearly 90 % of the documents the assessments of which were reversed via the appeals process were cases in which the document was either clearly responsive or clearly non-responsive and the first-pass assessor had simply erred. Another 5 % of the documents were cases in which the document was either clearly responsive or clearly non-responsive and the adjudicator (the 'Topic Authority') had erred in changing the original assessment. Only 5 % of the documents were cases in which the document's responsiveness was arguable. The findings of this study provide support for the viability of a 'gold standard' for measuring the effectiveness of retrieval systems, but the findings also highlight the importance of an error identification and correction mechanism if such a gold standard is to be realised. While it is important to take measures to ensure that assessors are aligned in the interpretation of a given topic, it is also important to have a mechanism for identifying and correcting simple human error.

Through the tasks of 2009, it seemed clear from our experience, whether from the perspective of absolute scores or relative scores, that when a small number of judgements can substantially impact the scores, an evaluation needs to build into its process a way to deal with assessor error. Our experience with allowing the participants to appeal seemed to have been beneficial for several of the test topics, but for some topics there were relatively few appeals which we suspect was not because those topics had a lower error rate but because appealing requires a lot of effort that not all participants are willing to undertake. (Another concern raised by a recent study is that 'there is some evidence to support the hypothesis that appeals disproportionately benefit participating systems' [27].) One suggestion was to automatically appeal a sample of all of the judgements for estimating the impact of appeals [31].

6.6.2 Later Attempts to Address Assessor Error

The 2010 interactive task attempted to address assessor error issues in the following ways. The first-pass assessments were done entirely by professional document-review services in 2010 (in contrast with 2008 and 2009 in which a lot of the first-pass assessments were done by volunteer law students). A 10 % sample of the first-pass assessments were assessed twice. Some non-appealed assessments were included in the set to be re-adjudicated (unlike in previous years); in selecting non-appealed assessments for adjudication, priority was given to cases of dual-assessment conflict and to cases of a relevant assessment assigned to a document from the All-N stratum (as such assessments have a large impact on recall estimates). Finally, in submitting their appeals, participants were not asked to provide grounds for the changes in assessment they were requesting; the adjudicators reviewed the appealed documents blindly, with no knowledge either of the original assessment or of the reason why it had been appealed or otherwise included in the adjudication set.

Fully understanding the effects of these changes will require further study. With regard to twice-assessed documents, we can say that, while overall there was a fairly high rate of agreement between the two assessments assigned to a given document (about 91 %), the rate of overlap when one or the other of the two assessments was relevant was rather low (about 50 %); assessors tended to disagree more frequently when they came to documents that were in the neighbourhood of relevance (with the 'neighbourhood' defined as the subset of documents that at least one of the assessors had found relevant). With regard to the adjudication of non-appealed twice-assessed documents, we found that the adjudicator overturned a primary assessment about 50 % of the time when the secondary assessment was in conflict with it, but only about 8 % of the time when the secondary assessment was not in conflict with it. Dual assessment, identification of cases of conflicting assessment, followed by adjudication of those cases, appears to be a reasonably effective method of identifying and correcting erroneous assessments; it does, however, require the capacity for conducting a dual assessment of a sample and then having the conflicts (or a sample of them) adjudicated. With regard to the adjudication of non-appealed relevant assessments assigned to documents from the All-N stratum, we did find that adjudication resulted in a change in assessment (to not relevant) for some of these [6 out of 30 (20 %)]. With regard to not providing adjudicators with documentation of the grounds for an appeal, we did see a lower rate of overturned assessment (i.e. successful appeal) than we saw in previous iterations of the task (less than 40 % in 2010 compared to more than 70 % in previous years). This result raises the question of whether the 2010 adjudicators, asked to review large samples of documents (over 1000 documents for each topic), without the aid of documentation pointing to the salient features of the documents, may have missed aspects of documents that would have caused them to overturn an initial assessment with greater frequency. It may be that the benefits of asking participants to provide documentation of the grounds for their appeals (allowing the adjudicator to focus quickly on the salient features of a document, thus making for a more efficient and less burdensome adjudication process) outweigh the benefits of a blind adjudication process (a less burdensome appeals process for participants and the avoidance of possibly biasing the adjudicator). Of course, it may also be that the 2010 participants simply appealed a greater number of assessments for which the case for an overturn was not strong. These are questions that merit further study.

The 2010 learning task used volunteer assessors (primarily law students). It gathered three assessments for each document and used the majority opinion for evaluation. (There were no appeals in this task.)

In 2011, the interactive task was merged with the learning task. Participants were not allowed to appeal judgements, but there were two assessments for each document (from professional document-review services), and disagreements were automatically adjudicated by the Topic Authority. Unfortunately, the stratification on which the sampling was based just defined two strata for each topic, which led to some wide confidence intervals for F_1 (e.g. [0.10, 0.59]) irrespective of how well the potential assessor error was addressed.

Overall, we believe these approaches were at least somewhat successful at reducing the impact of potential assessor error, albeit at the expense of multiple assessing. How to find the right balance between effectiveness and expense remains a challenge.

6.7   Conclusion and Future Work

Our aim in this chapter was to summarise our approaches, look back upon how well the various task goals were achieved and identify what challenges remain. In the set-based tasks, we found that our resulting confidence intervals for recall, precision and F_1 were at least sometimes sufficient to distinguish differences between experimental approaches. In the rank-based tasks, we found that the estimation approaches were at least sometimes sufficient to identify statistically significant mean differences and conduct failure analysis. How to sample more efficiently and best quantify the estimated scores, including differences in scores, remain as challenges, particularly so in the case of low-yielding topics (which may be the typical circumstance in patent information retrieval). We have also found a lot of evidence that assessor error is an issue that cannot be ignored. How to best reduce these errors, or account for them in the confidence intervals, again remains a challenge.

Acknowledgements   We thank Jason Baron, David Lewis, Doug Oard, William Webber and two anonymous reviewers for their helpful remarks on various past drafts and versions of this chapter. Also, we would like to thank Jason Baron, Gordon Cormack, Maura Grossman, David Lewis, Doug Oard, Ian Soboroff, Ellen Voorhees and William Webber for their support and advice in undertaking the various challenges of measuring effectiveness in the TREC Legal Track and also all of the track contributors and participants without whom the track would not have been possible.

References

1. Allan J, Carterette B, Dachev B et al (2008) Million query track 2007 overview. In: Proceedings of TREC 2007. http://trec.nist.gov/pubs/trec16/papers/1MQ.OVERVIEW16.pdf
2. Baron JR (ed) (2007) The Sedona conference® best practices commentary on the use of search and information retrieval methods in E-discovery. In: The Sedona conference journal, vol VIII, pp 189–223
3. Baron JR, Lewis DD, Oard DW (2007) TREC-2006 legal track overview. In: Proceedings of TREC 2006. http://trec.nist.gov/pubs/trec15/papers/LEGAL06.OVERVIEW.pdf
4. Buckley C, Voorhees EM (2005) Retrieval system evaluation. In: TREC: experiment and evaluation in information retrieval, pp 53–75
5. Buckley C, Dimmick D, Soboroff I, Voorhees E (2006) Bias and the limits of pooling. In: Proceedings of SIGIR 2006, pp 619–620
6. Büttcher S, Clarke CLA, Soboroff I (2007) The TREC 2006 terabyte track. In: Proceedings of TREC 2006. http://trec.nist.gov/pubs/trec15/papers/TERA06.OVERVIEW.pdf
7. Carterette B, Soboroff I (2010) The effect of assessor errors on IR system evaluation. In: Proceedings of SIGIR 2010, pp 539–546
8. Cormack GV, Grossman MR, Hedin B, Oard DW (2011) Overview of the TREC 2010 legal track. In: Proceedings of TREC 2010. http://trec.nist.gov/pubs/trec19/papers/LEGAL10.OVERVIEW.pdf
9. Devore J, Farnum N (2005) Applied statistics for engineers and scientists, 2nd edn. Thomson Brooks/Cole, Belmont, CA
10. Grossman MR, Cormack GV (2012) Inconsistent responsiveness determination in document review: difference of opinion or human error? Pace Law Review 32(2, Spring):267–288
11. Grossman MR, Cormack GV, Hedin B, Oard DW (2012) Overview of the TREC 2011 legal track. In: Proceedings of TREC 2011. http://trec.nist.gov/pubs/trec20/papers/LEGAL.OVERVIEW.2011.pdf
12. Harman DK (2005) The TREC test collections. In: TREC: experiment and evaluation in information retrieval, pp 21–52
13. Hedin B, Tomlinson S, Baron JR, Oard DW (2010) Overview of the TREC 2009 legal track. In: Proceedings of TREC 2009. http://trec.nist.gov/pubs/trec18/papers/LEGAL09.OVERVIEW.pdf
14. Lewis D, Agam G, Argamon S et al (2006) Building a test collection for complex document information processing. In: Proceedings of SIGIR 2006, pp 665–666
15. Oard DW, Webber W (2013) Information retrieval for E-discovery. Found Trends Inf Retr 7(2–3):99–237
16. Oard DW, Hedin B, Tomlinson S, Baron JR (2009) Overview of the TREC 2008 legal track. In: Proceedings of TREC 2008. http://trec.nist.gov/pubs/trec17/papers/LEGAL.OVERVIEW08.pdf
17. Oard DW, Baron JR, Hedin B et al (2010) Evaluation of information retrieval for E-discovery. Artif Intell Law 18(4):347–386
18. Sanderson M, Zobel J (2005) Information retrieval system evaluation: effort, sensitivity, and reliability. In: Proceedings of SIGIR 2005, pp 162–169
19. Taylor JR (1997) Error analysis: the study of uncertainties in physical measurements. University Science Book, Sausalito, CA
20. Thompson SK (2002) Sampling, 2nd edn. Wiley, New York
21. Tomlinson S (2007) Experiments with the negotiated Boolean queries of the TREC 2006 legal discovery track. In: Proceedings of TREC 2006. http://trec.nist.gov/pubs/trec15/papers/opentext.legal.final.pdf
22. Tomlinson S (2008) Experiments with the negotiated Boolean queries of the TREC 2007 legal discovery track. In: Proceedings of TREC 2007. http://trec.nist.gov/pubs/trec16/papers/opentext.legal.final.pdf

23. Tomlinson S (2009) Experiments with the negotiated Boolean queries of the TREC 2008 legal track. In: Proceedings of TREC 2008. http://trec.nist.gov/pubs/trec17/papers/open-text.legal.rev.pdf
24. Tomlinson S, Oard DW, Baron JR, Thompson P (2008) Overview of the TREC 2007 legal track. In: Proceedings of TREC 2007. http://trec.nist.gov/pubs/trec16/papers/LEGAL.OVERVIEW16.pdf
25. TREC Legal Track (web site). Last visited January 2017. http://trec-legal.umiacs.umd.edu/
26. van Rijsbergen, CJ (1979) Information retrieval, 2nd ed. Butterworths, London. http://www.dcs.gla.ac.uk/Keith/Preface.html
27. Vinjumur JK, Oard DW, Paik JH (2014) Assessing the reliability and reusability of an E-discovery privilege test collection. In: Proceedings of SIGIR 2014, pp 1047–1050
28. Voorhees EM (2000) Variations in relevance judgments and the measurement of retrieval effectiveness. Inf Process Manage 36(5):697–716
29. Voorhees EM, Harman D (1997) Overview of the fifth Text REtrieval Conference (TREC-5). In: Proceedings of TREC-5. http://trec.nist.gov/pubs/trec5/papers/overview.ps.gz
30. Webber W (2013) Approximate recall confidence intervals. ACM Trans Inf Syst 31(1):1–33, article no 2
31. Webber W, Oard DW, Scholer F, Hedin B (2010) Assessor error in stratified evaluation. In: Proceedings of CIKM 2010, pp 539–548
32. Yilmaz E, Aslam JA (2006) Estimating average precision with incomplete and imperfect judgments. In: Proceedings of CIKM 2006, pp 102–111
33. Zobel J (1998) How reliable are the results of large-scale information retrieval experiments? In: Proceedings of SIGIR 1998, pp 307–314

Part III
High Recall Search

One of the problems of patent search is that a single relevant missed patent or other documents can invalidate an otherwise sound patent. This is why patent searchers often say they require 100 % recall (the highest level possible): that is, they require the search system to guarantee to return absolutely all relevant documents, no matter where (USPTO, Web, film archives), in what form (XML, PDF, paper) or in what language (English, French, German, Indonesian, Welsh). In practice, no real system delivers 100 % recall all the time, and often searchers actually do not want 100 % recall—they will get too many redundant relevant documents. What they really want is a balance between precision (the proportion of relevant to irrelevant documents in the results list) and recall, which gives a strong guarantee that highly relevant documents are returned high in the results list. If no highly relevant documents are returned, there is a high probability there really are no relevant documents.

As we have seen in the introductory chapters, a patent search task always involves a phrasing such as 'find all documents which...'. From the evaluation part, we know that technically this is easily done: returning to the user the entire collection being searched on will inevitably also contain all relevant documents within that collection. The patent search task, in addition to the explicit requirement of finding all relevant documents, has a series of implicit requirements: 'find only the relevant documents' and 'find them in a reasonable time span'. Therefore, when we talk about high recall search, we must always keep in mind that at the same time we are talking about high precision search. However, what exactly 'high' means in either of those contexts is still ambiguous. Perhaps a better term would be 'satisfactory for the task at hand', but that would not be very marketable.

The challenge for patent information retrieval here is to find mechanisms that will give patent searchers search result sets that they can effectively use for the task at hand. The current part is completely complementary to its namesake part of the first edition: four new chapters complement the five of the first edition.

The part starts with a very fundamental question: 'Can we really find all the relevant documents'? The problem is very fundamental: given an indexing system, is it possible that some documents become inaccessible because of the way the system works? Or, more generally, how fair is a system in its representation of the documents indexed and how does this fairness impact the expected success rate of our queries? This was addressed in the first edition by Bache, and now the issue is further investigated, with a focus on the different retrieval models, by Bashir and Rauber.

The next chapter, by Salampasis, describes the research and the practice of federated search: searching in multiple data repositories at the same time and collating the results into a coherent answer to the user's information need. While both Bashir and Rauber, as well as Salampasis, focus on so-called bag-of-words models of retrieval (i.e. where terms are considered independent of each other), it has long been the experience of patent searchers that the actual meaning of an invention comes from the combination of common terms. In the first edition, Parapatics and Dittenbach had presented methods to improve the processing of claims. Now, in Chap. 9, Andersson and her colleagues go into considerably more details of natural language processing and show how meaning can be extracted from the text of one patent.

Finally, the part concludes with the description of a new visualisation for interconnected data items such as patents. The chapter by Kay and his colleagues complements the one by Koch from the previous edition, while maintaining the drive to move away from the list of documents towards a more intuitive graphical display, which can operate with very large sets of documents.

Chapter 7
Retrieval Models Versus Retrievability

Shariq Bashir and Andreas Rauber

Abstract Retrievability is an important measure in information retrieval (IR) that can be used to analyse retrieval models and document collections. Rather than just focusing on a set of few documents that are given in the form of relevance judgements, retrievability examines what is retrieved, how frequently it is retrieved and how much effort is needed to retrieve it. Such a measure is of particular interest within the recall-oriented retrieval systems (e.g. patent or legal retrieval), because in this context a document needs to be retrieved before it can be judged for relevance. If a retrieval model makes some patents hard to find, patent searchers could miss relevant documents just because of the bias of the retrieval model. In this chapter we explain the concept of retrievability in information retrieval. We also explain how it can be estimated and how it can be used for analysing a retrieval bias of retrieval models. We also show how retrievability relates to effectiveness by analysing the relationship between retrievability and effectiveness measures and how the retrievability measure can be used to improve effectiveness.

7.1 Introduction

Access to information from the Web and Internet is playing an important part in a society relying increasingly on information looked up ad hoc from an ever-growing pool of information in databases and the Web in general. Information retrieval (IR) systems are essential components of this process. IR systems deal with the storage (indexing), organisation, management and retrieval of information [7, 10, 23]. Besides indexing, one important factor that shapes the access to information is the role of the retrieval strategy (or model) [35]. It acts as a middleware between the users' required information and the users' effort to access the information. The main role of a retrieval model is to first discriminate between relevant and irrelevant

S. Bashir
Department of Computer Science, Mohammad Ali Jinnah University, Islamabad, Pakistan
e-mail: shariq.bashir@jinnah.edu.pk

A. Rauber (✉)
TU Wien, Vienna, Austria
e-mail: rauber@ifs.tuwien.ac.at; Andreas.rauber@tuwien.ac.at

© Springer-Verlag GmbH Germany 2017
M. Lupu et al. (eds.), *Current Challenges in Patent Information Retrieval*,
The Information Retrieval Series 37, DOI 10.1007/978-3-662-53817-3_7

information and then to display the relevant results to the users. Additionally, such models determine the order of results by relevance. Users should be able to view the most relevant information at the top ranked positions. In the last few years, a large number of retrieval models have been proposed for various kinds of retrieval tasks. One of the main problems is therefore how to choose the right model for a given retrieval task. It is a tedious task and falls under the research domain of evaluation of retrieval models [17, 31, 39, 40]. Historically, research on the evaluation of retrieval models has always focused on either the effectiveness or the efficiency (speed/memory). These are still the most common two measures that are determining the quality of retrieval models. The main limitation of these measures is that they focus only on a few documents that are the (most) relevant ones being returned at the top of a ranked list. This constitutes the primary criterion in most standard retrieval tasks (Web retrieval, question answering [38], opinion retrieval [27], etc.). With evaluation measures such as recall and F_β, aspects of the completeness of information are being brought into consideration. As a complement to these, a so-called higher-order evaluation has been proposed based on the accessibility (retrievability, how easily the information can be accessed). Instead of analysing how well the system performs in terms of speed or effectiveness, the retrievability measure provides an indication of how easily the information within the collection can be reached or accessed with a given retrieval model [5]. This offers a higher and more abstract level for understanding the influence of the given IR systems or retrieval models. Such models are affecting the access to all relevant information in the collection, not just the set of information that is given in the form of judged relevant documents by a group of few people. This is particularly important for recall-oriented retrieval domains like patent or legal retrieval, where it is necessary to ensure that everything relevant has been found, and furthermore, the non-existence of a document has to be proven (e.g. a document which invalidates a new patent application that does not exist) [1, 22]. Moreover, retrievability specifically examines whether the lack of access to information actually impedes one's ability to access the required information within the collection.

7.2   Analogy of Retrievability in Information Retrieval

The approach for analysing the effectiveness of retrieval models in terms of retrievability has been translated from logistics and transportation planning [5]. Hansen [16] draws the definition of accessibility in transportation planning as follows:

> a measurement of the spatial distribution of activities about a point adjusted for the ability and the desire of people or firms to overcome spatial separation. More specifically, the formulation states that the accessibility at point 1 to a particular type of activity at area 2 (say employment) is directly proportional to the size of the activity at area 2 (number of jobs) and inversely proportional to some function of the distance separating point 1 from

area 2. The total accessibility to employment at point 1 is the summation of the accessibility to each of the individual areas around point 1. Therefore, as more and more jobs are located nearer to point 1, the accessibility to employment at point 1 will increase.

Based on this definition, accessibility (or just access) refers to the effort of completing different activities of daily life from given opportunities (buses, trains, cars, metro, paths, roads and airports) of a transportation system [11, 15, 16, 20]. This approach is different to the study of efficiency of transportation systems, where the focus of analysis is based on certain positions or procedures, for example, the travel time between particular (important) locations. While being related to efficiency, accessibility considers access in a more general sense. It provides a high-level view on an evaluation of transportation systems.

Azzopardi and Vinay [4] draw the analogy of accessibility between transportation planning and IR systems as follows: in the context of transportation planning, accessibility is the idea that models the opportunities (train, car, metro, bus) of the transportation systems with the objective of completing daily life activities (to reach a location, e.g. going to office, dining, shopping at a supermarket). Completing a particular activity is subject to a certain associated cost function such as travelling distance, number of stops, changes of buses, trains, etc. Similarly, in the context of information retrieval, accessibility (retrievability) is the idea that models the searching or retrieving of a particular information. This is subject to a cost function based on the simplicity in using the system for retrieval of certain information and the amount of retrieved documents to examine for reaching the desired information. Here, documents replace locations, and queries replace the opportunities for the completion of a particular activity. However, in IR there is no concept of physical space; therefore, there is no constraint on the user's current location (i.e. at a particular document). The IR system models a stop or a location in such a way that every possible opportunity can be available (i.e. the universe of all possible queries), and users can select any route desired (he/she can query the IR system with any type of search terms) at any time regardless of the locations. While this makes every document in the collection potentially equally retrievable, the choice of selecting a suitable opportunity (in the form of a query) to reach a particular location where the user wants to travel (retrieving the desired information) and the bias in the ranking methodology of IR systems affect just how documents are retrievable in the information space with the given IR system.

Based on the analogy described above, the accessibility of a document, therefore, depends upon the following three factors:

1. User's ability to formulate his/her need in the form of a suitable query
2. The bias of the retrieval model
3. The user's willingness to go through and down the ranked result list of the query

In the context of this research, we are considering the accessibility of documents as a retrieval task where documents are accessed by querying the IR system.

7.3 Analysing Retrievability of Retrieval Systems

Web coverage and documents' retrievability are two well-known measures for discovering IR systems' accessibility. The body of literature on Web coverage-based measures contains a range of possible biases [19, 25, 37], for example, if one website has more coverage than another, whether sites in a particular geographical location are favoured over others [37] or whether search engines are biased given a particular topic. These studies are usually motivated by the view that search engines may be providing biased content, and these measures are aiming at providing guidelines for regulation. As opposed to the Web coverage-based measures, retrievability focuses on the individual document retrievability scores, which can also be used for analysing the accessibility of IR systems.

Estimating Retrievability: Given a collection D, an IR system accepts a user query q and returns a ranked list of documents, which are deemed to be relevant to q. We can consider the retrievability of a document based on two system-dependent factors: (a) how likely the documents are returned to the user with respect to the collection D and (b) the effectiveness of the ranking strategy (retrieval model) of the IR system. In order to derive an estimate of this quantity, [5] used query set-based sampling for approximating the retrievability (retrieval bias) [9]. Q query set could either be a historical sample of queries or an artificially simulated substitute similar to users' queries. Then, each $q \in Q$ is issued to the IR system, and the retrieved documents along with their positions in the ranked list are recorded. Intuitively, retrievability of a document d is high when:

1. There are many probable queries in Q, which can be expressed in order to retrieve d.
2. When retrieved, the rank r of the document d is lower than a rank cutoff (threshold) c. This is the point at which the user would stop examining the ranked list. This is a user-dependent factor and reflects a particular retrieval scenario in order to obtain a more accurate estimate of this measure. For instance, in Web-search scenarios, a low c would be more accurate as users are unlikely to go beyond the first page of the results, while in the context of recall-oriented retrieval settings (for instance, legal or patent retrieval), a high c would be more accurate.

Thus based on the Q, r and c, we formulate the following measure for the retrievability of d

$$r(d) = \sum_{q \in Q} p(q) \cdot \hat{f}(k_{dq}, c) \tag{7.1}$$

$f(k_{dq}, c)$ is a generalised utility/cost function, where k_{dq} is the rank of d in the result list of query q and c denotes the maximum rank that a user is willing to proceed down in the ranked list. The function $\hat{f}(k_{dq}, c)$ returns a value of 1, if $k_{dq} \leq c$, and 0 otherwise. $p(q)$ denotes the likeliness that a user actually issues query q. This probability is hard to determine explicitly and is set to 1, i.e. to give all queries equal probabilities [5]. More complex heuristics integrating the length of the query, the specificity of the vocabulary, etc., may be considered. Defined in this way, the retrievability of a document is essentially a cumulative score that is proportional to the number of times the document can be retrieved within that cutoff c over the set Q. This fulfils our aim, in that the value of $r(d)$ will be high when there are a large number of highly probable queries that can retrieve the document d at the rank less than c and the value of $r(d)$ will be low when only a few queries retrieve the document. Furthermore, if a document is never returned at the top ranked c positions, possibly because it is difficult to retrieve by the system, then the $r(d)$ is zero.

This $r(d)$ function is an intuitive way to show the relative bias between both sets of retrieval models and sets of documents. For example, if system A returns $r(d1) = 30$ and system B returns $r(d1) = 1$, then relatively, system A will retrieve document $d1$ 30 times more than system B. This gives a more concise view of the relation of system A to system B with respect to document $d1$. Alternatively, if for system A $r(d1) = 30$ and $r(d2) = 1$, then system A favours and retrieves $d1$ 30 times more than it does $d2$.

The cumulative measure of the retrievability score of a document on the basis of the binary $f(k_{dq}, c)$ function ignores the ranking position of a document in a ranked result list, i.e. how accessible the document is in the ranking. A gravity-based measure can be used for this purpose by setting the function to reflect the effort of going further down in the ranked result list, and it is defined as

$$\hat{f}(k_{dq}, \beta) = \frac{1}{(k_{dq})^{\beta}} \qquad (7.2)$$

The rank cutoff factor is changed to β, which is a dampening factor that adjusts how accessible the document is in the ranking. In our experiments we calculate the retrievability score of documents only on the basis of cumulative measure.

Retrievability inequality can be further analysed using the *Lorenz Curve* [14]. In economics and social sciences, a Lorenz Curve is used to visualise the inequality of wealth in a population. This is performed by first sorting the individuals in the population in ascending order of their wealth and then plotting a cumulative wealth distribution. If wealth was distributed equally in the population, then we would expect this cumulative distribution to be linear. The extent to which a given distribution deviates from the equality is reflected by the amount of skewness in the distribution. Azzopardi and Vinay [5] used a similar idea in the context of a population of documents, where the wealth of documents is represented by $r(d)$ function. The more skewed the plot, the greater the amount of inequality, or bias within the population. The *Gini coefficient* [14] G is used to summarise the amount of retrieval bias in the Lorenz Curve and provides a bird's-eye view. It is computed as follows:

$$G = \frac{\sum_{i=1}^{|D|} (2 \cdot i - |D| - 1) \cdot r(d_i)}{(|D| - 1) \sum_{j=1}^{|D|} r(d_j)} \qquad (7.3)$$

D represents the set of documents in the collection. If $G = 0$, then no bias is present because all documents are equally retrievable. If $G = 1$, then only one document is retrievable and all other documents have $r(d) = 0$. By comparing the Gini coefficients of different retrieval methods, we can analyse the retrieval bias imposed by the underlying retrieval systems on a given document collection.

7.4 Applications of Retrievability Analysis

Retrievability analysis can be used for a range of applications, such as:

- **Media regulator or watchdog:** The retrievability measure can act as a watchdog. It can be used to determine whether a retrieval system favours documents of certain news providers over others [3]. It can also be used to investigate what parts of the collection are favoured over others and whether they have any particular biases that the users should be aware of.
- **Bias detection for IR practitioner/researcher:** The retrievability measure can provide help to the IR practitioner/researcher for detecting any untoward bias detrimental to the effectiveness of retrieval models. It can further examine the influence of different retrieval models on a particular collection to understand more precisely the benefits and limitations of different models.
- **Automatic ranking retrieval models:** One important area of IR research is to evaluate the effectiveness of retrieval models using test collections [17, 31, 39, 40]. A test collection consists of a set of documents, a set of queries and relevance judgements (i.e. a list that describes which documents are relevant to which query topic). While documents and queries are relatively easy to gather, creating relevance judgements requires significant effort and resources. In recent years there has been increased research interest in methods for automatically ranking retrieval models without human-generated relevance judgements [8, 12, 17, 18, 26, 30–33, 36, 39–41]. One important aspect of the retrievability measure is that it can be analysed without relevance judgement, and this provides an attractive alternative for producing the automatic ranks of retrieval models.
- **E-Gov site administration:** Ensuring that online contents are accessible is very important in the area of e-Government, because citizens of a democratic country have a right to information [28]. If such information is non-accessible to the public, this can jeopardise the integrity of the government. Currently, there exists no quantitative measure or methodology that can be employed for ensuring access to relevant content. The retrievability measure can be used for this task in order to determine whether a sufficient amount of access is accorded to the information housed within the e-Government websites.
- **Search engine optimisation:** The retrievability measure can be used to detect any favouritism in the search engine so that the content can be optimised to increase the chance of retrieval.

7.5 What Retrievability Cannot Examine

We cannot use retrievability for examining the following factors:

1. Retrievability cannot predict the search effectiveness of professional users (e.g. patent examiners). An experienced user can easily bypass the retrieval bias by recalling the most relevant terms of his/her information need and applying bitwise *AND* operator between query terms. A long bitwise *AND* query decreases the size of the query's result list (i.e. total number of retrieved documents), and the user can easily access his/her required information from a small number of top ranked documents.
2. On the basis of retrievability scores, low-retrievability scores documents are more difficult to find than high-retrievability scores documents. However, it is wrong to say that low-retrievability scores documents are unlikely to be found by any type of query. As we explained earlier, along with the users' ability to formulate the queries and the retrieval bias of retrieval models, a third factor affecting the retrievability of documents is the difference between the size of the query result list and the users' ability or willingness to proceed down in the ranked result list. This difference is controlled with the help of a rank cutoff factor. If this difference is large, this means that the users will go through only a small portion of the total number of retrieved documents, and from this we can expect a large retrievability inequality between the documents of collection. On the other hand, if this difference is small or the sizes of query result lists are less than the rank cutoff factor, then the users will go through a large portion of the retrieved documents and thus there will be less retrievability inequality between the documents of collection. Ideally, queries used for retrievability analysis should have large result list sizes, because this allows us to precisely understand the role of the retrieval bias of retrieval models in the retrievability; however, this ignores many specific, focused queries.

7.6 Retrievability Experiments

In this section, we examine the retrieval bias of different retrieval models for different collections. The collections that we use for experiments contain patent and news documents. For these collections, we first determine the retrievability of documents with different retrieval models, and then we analyse to what extent these retrieval models are differing in terms of retrieval bias that they imposed on the documents of collections. The overall retrievability of documents provides an indication of how easily the documents are accessible with different retrieval models. The overall retrievability inequality between the documents of collection shows the retrieval bias of retrieval model.

Table 7.1 The properties of document collections used for the retrieval bias analysis

Dataset	Total docs.	Seed docs.	Rank cutoff factors
TREC-CRT	1.2 million	34,205	50, 100, 250
ChemAppPat	36,998	36,998	5, 10, 15, 20, 25
DentPat	27,988	27,988	5, 10, 15, 20, 25
ATNews	47,693	47,693	5, 10, 15, 20, 25

Seed docs: This is the set of documents that are used for query generation and retrievability analysis

7.6.1 Document Collections

We use the following four collections (Table 7.1) for retrieval bias analysis. Table 7.1 presents the basic properties of these collections. Seed documents represent the set of those documents that are used for query generation and retrievability analysis.

- **TREC 2009 Chemical Retrieval Track Collection (TREC-CRT):** This dataset consists of 1.2 million patent documents from the TREC Chemical Retrieval Track (2009) (*TREC-CRT*)[1] [21]. Due to the large size of the collection, determining the retrievability for all documents in the collection requires large processing time and resources. Therefore, to complete the experiments in a reasonable time, a subset of *34,205* documents (judged documents) for which the relevance assessments are available as part of *TREC-CRT* serves as seed for query generation and retrievability analysis. As compared to the other three collections, the documents in this collection are very long. The distributions of document length and vocabulary size are also highly skewed (see Fig. 7.1). For this collection, retrieval bias is analysed with five rank cutoff factors, $c = 50$, $c = 100$, $c = 150$, $c = 200$ and $c = 250$.

- **USPTO Patent Collections (ChemAppPat, DentPat):** These collections were downloaded from the freely available US Patent and Trademark Office website.[2] We collect all patents that are listed under the United States Patent Classification (USPC) classes *433 (dentistry)* and *422 (chemical apparatus and process disinfecting, deodorising, preserving or sterilising)*. These collections consist of 64,986 documents, with 36,998 documents in *USPC Class 422* and 27,988 documents in *USPC Class 433*. The *USPC Class 433* documents are called with *DentPat Collection*, and the *USPC Class 422* documents are called with *ChemAppPat Collection*. Similar to the *TREC-CRT* collection, the documents in this collection are long; however, the distributions of document length and vocabulary size are less skewed than the *TREC-CRT* collection (see Figs. 7.2 and 7.3). For both collections, the retrieval bias is analysed with the rank cutoff factors $c = 5$, $c = 10$, $c = 15$, $c = 20$ and $c = 25$. Also, these collections are more

---

[1] Available at http://www.ir-facility.org/research/evaluation/trec-chem-09.
[2] Available at http://www.uspto.gov/.

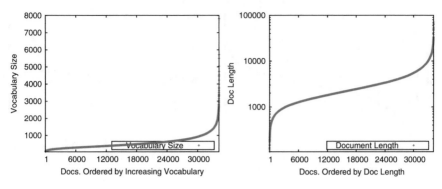

Fig. 7.1   Document vocabulary size and length distribution on the *TREC-CRT* collection

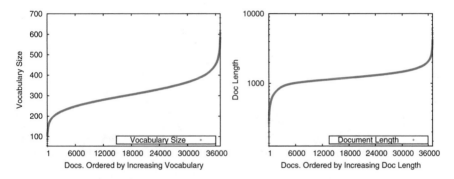

Fig. 7.2   Document vocabulary size and length distribution on the *ChemAppPat* collection

topically focused, consisting of only two highly similar USPC classes. It is
typical for a domain-specific document collection.

- **Austrian News Dataset (ATNews):** Our final collection consists of 47,693
  Austrian news documents.[3] We call this collection *ATNews Collection*. As
  compared to the above three collections, the documents in this collection are
  mostly short; however, the distributions of document length and vocabulary size
  are highly skewed similar to the *TREC-CRT* collection (see Fig. 7.4). For this
  collection we use the rank cutoff factors $c = 5$, $c = 10$, $c = 15$, $c = 20$ and $c = 25$
  for the retrieval bias analysis.

---

[3]http://www.ifs.tuwien.ac.at/~andi/tmp/STANDARD.tgz.

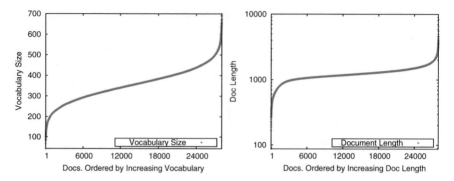

Fig. 7.3   Document vocabulary size and length distribution on the *DentPat* collection

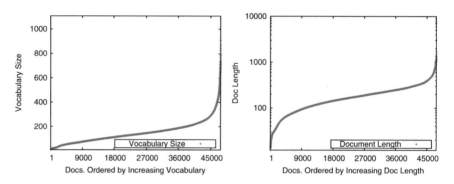

Fig. 7.4   Document vocabulary size and length distribution on the *ATNews* collection

7.6.2   Retrieval Models

Four standard IR models and four different variations of language models with term
smoothing [42] are used for the retrieval bias analysis. These are standard TFIDF,
NormTFIDF, the OKAPI retrieval model BM25 [29], SMART [34], Jelinek–
Mercer language model JM, Dirichlet (Bayesian) language model DirS, absolute
discounting language model and TwoStage language model.

7.6.3   Query Generation for Retrievability Analysis

We consider all sections (title, abstract, claims, description, background summary)
of patent documents for both retrieval and query generation. Stop words are removed
prior to indexing and words stemming is performed with the Porter stemming
algorithm. Additionally, we do not use all those terms of the collection that have
a document frequency greater than 25 % of the total collection size as they are too

generic. Next, queries for retrievability analysis are generated with the combinations of those terms that appear more than one time in the document. For these terms, all three-term and four-term combinations are used in the form of Boolean AND queries for creating the exhaustive set of queries Q, and duplicate queries are removed from Q.

As we explained earlier, a third factor along with the user ability to formulate the query and the retrieval bias of retrieval model that affects the retrievability of documents is the difference between the result list size of the query and how deeply the user would check/read the retrieved documents of the query. In retrievability measurement this difference is controlled with a rank cutoff factor. The high difference implies that the user would go through only a small portion of the retrieved documents, and thus we can expect that the retrievability of documents will highly depend upon the retrieval bias of the retrieval model. Less retrieval bias would make a large number of documents highly retrievable at top ranked positions. On the other hand, if this difference is small, or the size of query result lists becomes less than the rank cutoff factor, then the user would go through a large portion of documents and thus the bias of retrieval models will play a lesser part in the retrievability of documents.

Therefore, in order to precisely analyse the effect of the retrieval model's retrieval bias on the retrievability, the size of query result lists should not be too close to the user's rank cutoff.

Under this principle, for the *TREC-CRT* collection, we remove all those queries from the Q that retrieve less than 100 documents. Similarly for the *ChemAppPat*, *DentPat* and *ATNews* collections, we remove all those queries from the Q that retrieve less than 45 documents. Next, all these queries are used for the document retrieval against the complete collection as Boolean AND queries with subsequent ranking according to the chosen retrieval models to determine the retrievability scores of documents. Table 7.2 shows the general characteristics of Q for the different collections. Figures 7.5, 7.6, 7.7 and 7.8 show the distributions of the total number of queries per document relative to the vocabulary size of documents. The *TREC-CRT* and *ATNews* collections have large differences between the documents' vocabulary size, and thus for these collections this distribution is highly skewed. The *ChemAppPat* and *DentPat* collections have fewer differences between the documents' vocabulary size; thus for these collections the distribution of queries is less skewed.

Table 7.2 Properties of Q that are used for the retrieval bias analysis

Characteristics	TREC-CRT	ChemAppPat	DentPat	ATNews
$|Q|$	130.8 million	108.1 million	110.4 million	57.2 million
Minimum query result list size	100	45	45	45
Avg query result list size	1943	149	154	80
Avg # of queries/document	1,790,604	437,969	606,879	135,395

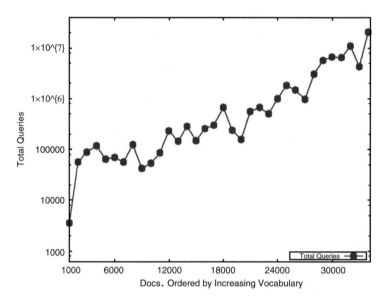

Fig. 7.5 The distribution of total number of queries generated per document for the *TREC-CRT* collection. Documents are ordered by the increasing vocabulary size

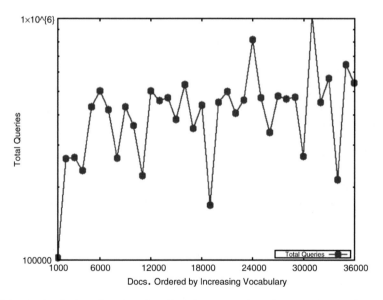

Fig. 7.6 The distribution of total number of queries generated per document for the *ChemAppPat* collection. Documents are ordered by the increasing vocabulary size

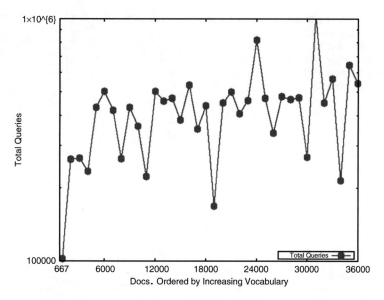

Fig. 7.7 The distribution of total number of queries generated per document for the *DentPat* collection. Documents are ordered by the increasing vocabulary size

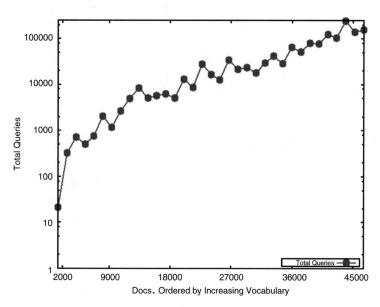

Fig. 7.8 The distribution of total number of queries generated per document for the *ATNews* collection. Documents are ordered by the increasing vocabulary size

Table 7.3 Gini coefficient scores representing the retrieval bias of different retrieval models on various rank cutoff factors for the *TREC-CRT* collection

Retrieval model	$r(d)$		
	$c = 50$	$c = 100$	$c = 250$
TFIDF	0.95	0.91	0.81
NormTFIDF	0.70	0.62	0.51
BM25	0.57	0.52	0.44
SMART	0.96	0.93	0.87
DirS	0.63	0.57	0.50
JM	0.68	0.62	0.51
AbsDis	0.66	0.60	0.50
TwoStage	0.64	0.56	0.46

As rank cutoff factor increases, bias steadily decreases indicating that the low retrieval bias is experienced when considering the long ranked lists

Table 7.4 Gini coefficient scores representing the retrieval bias of different retrieval models on various rank cutoff factors for the *ChemAppPat* collection

Retrieval model	$r(d)$				
	$c = 5$	$c = 10$	$c = 15$	$c = 20$	$c = 25$
TFIDF	0.65	0.56	0.52	0.49	0.48
NormTFIDF	0.48	0.42	0.39	0.38	0.37
BM25	0.39	0.38	0.37	0.37	0.37
SMART	0.93	0.88	0.84	0.81	0.77
DirS	0.43	0.39	0.38	0.37	0.37
JM	0.41	0.37	0.36	0.36	0.36
AbsDis	0.40	0.38	0.38	0.38	0.38
TwoStage	0.47	0.42	0.39	0.38	0.38

As rank cutoff factor increases, bias steadily decreases indicating that the low retrieval bias is experienced when considering the long ranked lists

7.6.4 Retrieval Bias Analysis

Tables 7.3, 7.4, 7.5 and 7.6 list the retrievability inequality providing Gini coefficients for a range of rank cutoff factors for the different collections. Note that a high bias is experienced when limiting oneself to short result lists of 5 or 50 documents. The Gini coefficient tends to decrease slowly for all query sets and for all retrieval models as the rank cutoff factor increases. This indicates that the retrievability inequality within the collection is mitigated by the willingness of the user to search deeper down into the result list. If a user examines only a small portion of the result list, then he/she will face a greater degree of retrieval bias.

Overall, *BM25* on all collections exhibits lower retrieval bias than all other retrieval models. The four language modelling approaches *DirS*, *TwoStage*, *JM* and *AbsDis* also exhibit lower retrieval bias than *TFIDF*, *SMART* and *NormTFIDF*.

Table 7.5 Gini coefficient scores representing the retrieval bias of different retrieval models on various rank cutoff factors for the *DentPat* collection

| | $r(d)$ | | | | |
Retrieval model	$c = 5$	$c = 10$	$c = 15$	$c = 20$	$c = 25$
TFIDF	0.65	0.58	0.53	0.50	0.48
NormTFIDF	0.51	0.44	0.41	0.40	0.39
BM25	0.41	0.39	0.38	0.38	0.38
SMART	0.93	0.89	0.85	0.81	0.78
DirS	0.46	0.42	0.40	0.39	0.38
JM	0.43	0.40	0.38	0.37	0.37
AbsDis	0.42	0.40	0.39	0.39	0.39
TwoStage	0.49	0.44	0.41	0.40	0.39

As rank cutoff factor increases, bias steadily decreases indicating that the low retrieval bias is experienced when considering the long ranked lists

Table 7.6 Gini coefficient scores representing the retrieval bias of different retrieval models on various rank cutoff factors for the *ATNews* collection

| | $r(d)$ | | | | |
Retrieval model	$c = 5$	$c = 10$	$c = 15$	$c = 20$	$c = 25$
TFIDF	0.95	0.92	0.90	0.88	0.87
NormTFIDF	0.54	0.53	0.54	0.56	0.57
BM25	0.52	0.52	0.53	0.55	0.57
SMART	0.87	0.83	0.79	0.76	0.73
DirS	0.77	0.73	0.72	0.70	0.69
JM	0.53	0.52	0.53	0.55	0.56
AbsDis	0.56	0.57	0.59	0.60	0.61
TwoStage	0.78	0.75	0.73	0.71	0.70

As rank cutoff factor increases, bias steadily decreases indicating that the low retrieval bias is experienced when considering the long ranked lists

7.7 Relationship Between Retrievability and Effectiveness

The retrievability measure has been used in a number of different contexts (see [5] for more details and [2, 6] for examples of its usage in practice). However, there has been little work on analysing the relationship between retrievability and more standard IR effectiveness measures. One important aspect of the retrievability measure is that it can be analysed or estimated without the availability of explicit ground truth (relevance judgements). It provides an attractive alternative for the automatic ranking of retrieval models. Additionally, it can also be used for tuning a retrieval model's effectiveness by varying its parameter values or retrieval features over retrievability so that they can perform well for a given collection. However, this is possible only if there is a significant positive correlation between the retrieval bias (i.e. the summarised retrievability of all documents) and effectiveness measures. This is because high or low retrieval bias of retrieval models does not imply that the retrieval models will also perform well on the effectiveness measures. For instance—given the definition of retrievability—a retrieval model that ranks the documents by randomly selecting from the document collection would provide a better retrievability to all documents. This would result in a low retrieval bias, but very poor effectiveness for finding the relevant documents. Conversely, a retrieval model that only ranks the set of known relevant documents at the top ranked positions, regardless of given queries, would provide a high inequality among documents (poor retrievability and high retrieval bias) but better effectiveness for a set of known topics. This indicates that neither extreme is desirable. However, to what extent we need to trade off between the retrievability and the effectiveness depends upon the correlation between them. In the following experiments, we rank all retrieval models on both measures independently and test to what extent the two rankings agree with each other, i.e. to what extent the low retrieval bias of a retrieval model leads to high effectiveness.

7.7.1 Effectiveness Analysis

We select the prior art (PA) task of the *TREC-CRT* collection for analysing the effectiveness of retrieval models. The PA task consisted of 1000 topic queries that are the full-text patent documents (i.e. consisting of at least claims and abstract or description) taken from both the European Patent Office (EPO) and the US Patent Office (USPTO). The goal of searching a patent database for the prior art search task is to find all previously published related patents on a given topic [13, 21, 24]. It is a common task for *patent examiners* and *attorneys* to decide whether a new patent application is novel or contains technical conflicts with some already patented invention. They collect all related patents and report them in a search report. We use these reports as relevance judgements. Next, we apply a standard approach for query generation in the patent retrieval domain. From each topic, we select only the claim section being the most representative piece of text, as it describes the scope of the invention. In order to build prior art queries from the claim sections, we first sort all the terms in the claim sections on the basis of their increasing term frequencies. Next, we select the top 30 terms that have the highest frequencies and use these terms in the form of a long query for searching the relevant documents. Note that more complex query generation approaches may be used. Yet, as our primary motivation is to analyse the relationship between effectiveness and retrievability, this standard baseline is sufficient.

We performed effectiveness analysis with Precision@30 (P@30), Recall@100 (R@100), mean average precision (MAP) and b-pref.[4]

---

[4]http://trec.nist.gov/pubs/trec16/appendices/measures.pdf.

7.7.2 Retrieval Models

The retrieval models that we use for retrieval bias analysis include standard retrieval models (*NormTFIDF*, *BM25*, *TFIDF* and *SMART*), language modelling-based retrieval models (*DirS*, *JM*, *AbsDis* and *TwoStage*) and low-level retrieval features of IR.

We use the following low-level features in experiments:

- Document length ($|d|$)
- Document vocabulary size ($|T_d|$)
- The sum of absolute query term frequencies within the document [Eq. (7.4)]

$$tf(d, q) = \sum_{t \in q} tf_{t,d} \tag{7.4}$$

where $tf_{t,d}$ is the term frequency of document (d).

- The sum of normalised query term frequencies relative to document length [Eq. (7.5)],

$$ntf(d, q) = \sum_{t \in q} tf_{t,d}/|d| \tag{7.5}$$

where $|d|$ is the length of d

- The sum of document frequency of query terms [Eq. (7.6)]

$$sdf(d, q) = \sum_{t \in q} df_t/|D| \tag{7.6}$$

- The sum of probability of query's terms occurring in the collection [Eq. (7.7)]

$$scf(d, q) = \sum_{t \in q} cf_t / \sum_{d \in D} |d| \tag{7.7}$$

where cf_t is the collection frequency of t in D.

7.7.3 Relationship Between Two Measures on the Basis of Retrieval Model Ranks

So far, we examined the retrieval bias of different retrieval models. Our results show that the retrieval models differ substantially in terms of the retrieval biases that they impose on the population of documents. However, the question still remains: What is the relationship between minimising the retrieval bias and maximising a retrieval model's effectiveness? In a TREC-style definition of effectiveness, it is important to

Table 7.7 Gini coefficient scores representing the retrieval bias of different retrieval models on the *TREC-CRT* collection

Retrieval model	Rank cutoff factors		
	$c = 50$	$c = 100$	$c = 250$
Standard retrieval models and language models			
TFIDF	0.95	0.91	0.81
NormTFIDF	0.70	0.62	0.51
BM25	0.57	0.52	0.44
SMART	0.96	0.93	0.87
DirS	0.63	0.57	0.50
JM	0.68	0.62	0.51
AbsDis	0.66	0.60	0.50
TwoStage	0.64	0.56	0.46
Low-level retrieval functions			
$tf(d,q)$	0.95	0.92	0.83
$ntf(d,q)$	0.71	0.63	0.51
$sdf(d,q)$	0.85	0.85	0.83
$|d|$	0.80	0.74	0.61
$|T_d|$	0.99	0.99	0.99
$scf(d,q)$	0.85	0.85	0.83

ensure that all relevant documents of topic queries have high retrievability scores. But given the recall-oriented retrieval domains such as patents, legal or government administration, it is necessary to ensure that all documents are highly retrievable. In this section, we will now specifically examine to what extent the low or high retrieval bias of retrieval models correlates with their effectiveness. That is, if a retrieval model has less retrieval bias than other models, then does it also mean that it is more effective than the other models? If this holds true, then the retrievability will provide a valuable alternative for the automatic ranking of retrieval models in the case when there are no resources to relevance judgements available for a given collection. In order to examine these premises, we perform the following experiment.

In this experiment, we compare the relationship between the two measures on the basis of retrieval model ranks. Hereby we want to examine to what extent the low retrieval bias of retrieval models leads to high effectiveness. In order to analyse this, we test and rank all retrieval models independently on both measures. Table 7.7 shows the retrieval bias (measured as Gini coefficient) at different cut-off levels. Table 7.8 shows the retrieval bias and effectiveness scores and Table 7.9 shows retrieval model ranks on both measures and the relationship between them. Although the relationship between two rank lists is not perfect, it can be observed from the results that the best retrieval models are consistently ranked in at least the top half of the ranking. This indicates a systematic relationship between retrievability and effectiveness measures. When comparing only the standard and the language modelling-based retrieval models on the basis of these rankings, then *BM25* and the four language modelling approaches (*JM, DirS, AbsDis* and *TwoStage*) have higher effectiveness than other models possibly due to their lower retrieval bias.

Table 7.8 Retrieval bias (Gini coefficient) and effectiveness scores of different retrieval models on *TREC-CRT* collection

Retrieval model	Retrieval bias and effectiveness scores				
	G@100	R@100	P@30	MAP	b-pref
BM25	0.52	0.156	0.101	0.049	0.428
TwoStage	0.56	0.174	0.110	0.055	0.474
DirS	0.57	0.177	0.110	0.055	0.470
AbsDis	0.60	0.170	0.108	0.052	0.440
JM	0.62	0.184	0.113	0.058	0.483
NormTFIDF	0.62	0.082	0.045	0.023	0.320
ntf(d,q)	0.63	0.107	0.061	0.028	0.470
|d|	0.74	0.001	0.000	0.000	0.256
sdf(d,q)	0.85	0.042	0.027	0.010	0.414
scf(d,q)	0.85	0.002	0.001	0.000	0.237
TFIDF	0.91	0.008	0.003	0.003	0.115
tf(d,q)	0.92	0.016	0.008	0.004	0.428
SMART	0.93	0.074	0.044	0.021	0.276
$\|T_d\|$	0.99	0.001	0.000	0.000	0.245

Retrieval models are ordered by increasing Gini coefficient scores

Table 7.9 Relationship between retrieval bias and effectiveness on *TREC-CRT* collection

Retrieval model	Correlation analysis (Ranks)				
	G@100	R@100	P@30	MAP	b-pref
BM25	1	5	5	5	6
TwoStage	2	3	2	2	2
DirS	3	2	3	3	3
AbsDis	4	4	4	4	5
JM	5	1	1	1	1
NormTFIDF	6	7	7	7	9
ntf(d,q)	7	6	6	6	4
|d|	8	13	13	12	11
sdf(d,q)	9	9	9	9	8
scf(d,q)	10	12	12	13	13
TFIDF	11	11	11	11	14
tf(d,q)	12	10	10	10	7
SMART	13	8	8	8	10
$\|T_d\|$	14	14	14	14	12
Correlation with G@100		0.79	0.80	0.81	0.72

Retrieval models are ordered by increasing Gini coefficient ranks. Last column shows correlation of effectiveness measures with retrieval bias. We calculate correlation using Pearson product-moment correlation coefficient

NormTFIDF has lower retrieval bias than *TFIDF* and *SMART*, plus it has higher effectiveness. However, *NormTFIDF* has a higher retrieval bias than *BM25*, *JM*, *DirS*, *AbsDis* and *TwoStage* and also lower effectiveness than these models. If we focus only on the low-level retrieval features in the bottom half of the table, then $ntf(d,q)$ has the lowest retrieval of these, while also having the highest effectiveness. The main reason behind the systematic relationship between a high retrieval bias and a low effectiveness may be the level of retrievability inequality between the documents. When relevant documents show low retrievability, then these are less likely to retrieve at top ranked positions due to the presence of highly retrievable documents. This high level of retrievability inequality between documents decreases the overall effectiveness of retrieval models.

7.7.4 Improving Effectiveness of Retrieval Models by Tuning Parameters Using Retrieval Bias

Commonly retrieval models are tuned with the help of parameter values. These parameters either control the query term normalisation relative to document length or smooth the document relevance scores in case of unseen query terms. In this experiment we tune the parameter values of different retrieval models over specified ranges and examine their sensitivity and change with both measures (effectiveness and retrieval bias). Four language modelling approaches with term smoothing (*JM*, *DirS*, *AbsDis*, *TwoStage*) along with *BM25* are used for this purpose. In case of *BM25*, *JM* and *TwoStage*, the parameters b and λ are varied from 0.1 to 1.0 in steps of 0.1, while the parameter μ in case of *DirS* is varied from 500 to 10000 in steps of 1000. Figures 7.9, 7.10, 7.11, 7.12 and 7.13 are showing the effect of parameter values on both measures. We can observe that all those parameter value settings that exhibit high retrieval bias do not correspond to the maximum effectiveness. The maximum effectiveness is gained only when the parameter values result in low retrieval bias. Along with the parameter values that exhibit low retrieval bias and high effectiveness, there exist also some parameter values that—while achieving low retrieval bias—also hurt the effectiveness by a small fraction. This decrease in effectiveness occurs due to the relevance bias on long documents, while the tuned retrieval models aim at providing equal access to all documents. These findings again indicate the presence of a strong relationship between the Gini coefficient and P@30, R@100, MAP and b-pref, representing the effectiveness of retrieval models.

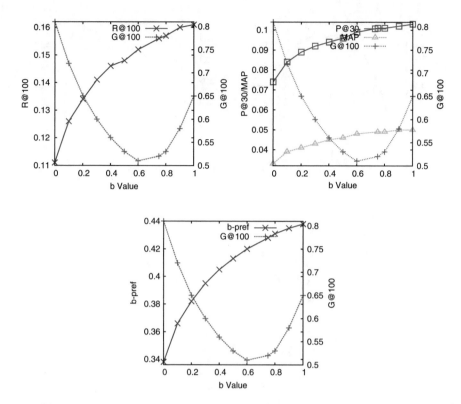

Fig. 7.9 Graphical relationship between the retrieval bias and the effectiveness across various parameter (*b*) values of *BM25*

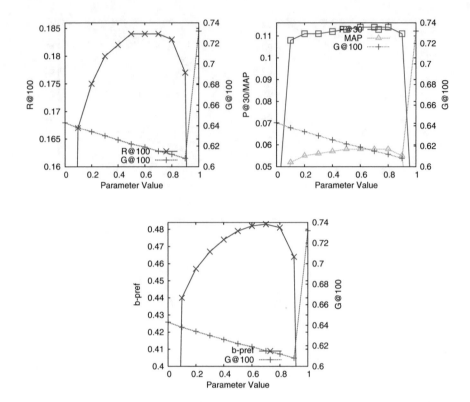

Fig. 7.10 Graphical relationship between the retrieval bias and the effectiveness across various parameter (λ) values of *JM*

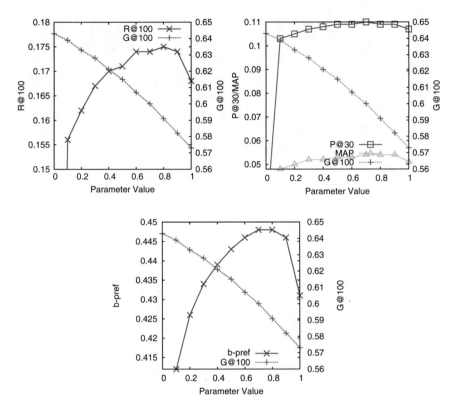

Fig. 7.11 Graphical relationship between the retrieval bias and the effectiveness across various parameter (δ) values of *AbsDis*

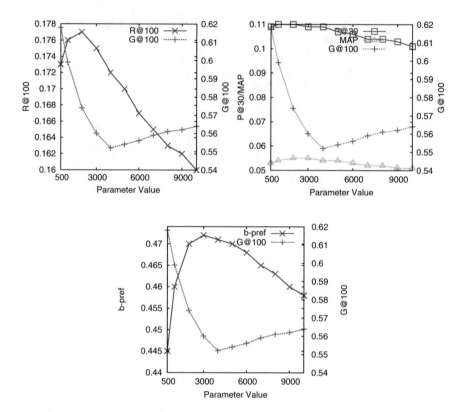

Fig. 7.12 Graphical relationship between the retrieval bias and the effectiveness across various parameter (μ) values of *DirS*

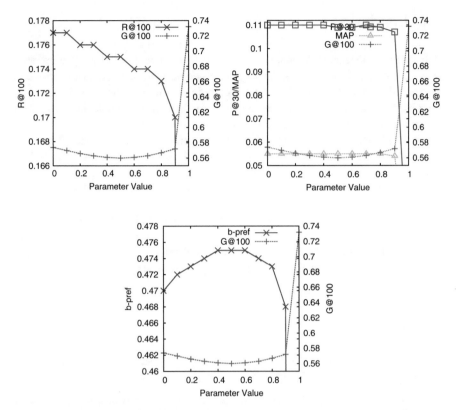

Fig. 7.13 Graphical relationship between the retrieval bias and the effectiveness across various parameter (λ) values of *TwoStage*

7.8   Conclusion

Retrievability measures to what extent a retrieval model provides theoretically equal access to all documents, i.e. returns all documents with equal likelihood if all possible queries are posed against a specific document collection. The studies presented in this chapter reveal that at least for recall-oriented application domains, where users are willing to proceed down to 50, 100 or 250 items in a ranked search result list, there is a high correlation with the effectiveness of retrieval models. This indicates that retrieval models may be tuned using retrievability as a guiding measure, rather than more conventional approaches of tuning through effectiveness measures. The comparisons clearly show for all retrieval models that there is a very strong relationship between a low retrievability bias and the effectiveness measures. Nonetheless, the assumption that the setting with the lowest retrievability bias always leads to a top effectiveness value cannot be confirmed in all cases. While the parameter settings can be tuned this way and often a good result is obtained, sometimes the results can also turn out slightly below average.

References

1. Arampatzis A, Kamps J, Kooken M, Nussbaum N (2007) Access to legal documents: exact match, best match, and combinations. In: Proceedings of the sixteenth text retrieval conference (TREC'07)
2. Azzopardi L, Bache R (2010) On the relationship between effectiveness and accessibility. In: SIGIR '10: proceeding of the 33rd annual international ACM SIGIR conference on research and development in information retrieval, Geneva, pp 889–890
3. Azzopardi L, Owens C (2009) Search engine predilection towards news media providers. In: SIGIR '09: proceedings of the 32nd annual international ACM SIGIR conference on research and development in information retrieval, Boston, MA, pp 774–775
4. Azzopardi L, Vinay V (2008) Accessibility in information retrieval. In: ECIR'08: proceedings of the 30th European conference on IR research, pp 482–489
5. Azzopardi L, Vinay V (2008) Retrievability: an evaluation measure for higher order information access tasks. In: CIKM '08: proceeding of the 17th ACM conference on information and knowledge management, Napa Valley, CA, pp 561–570
6. Bache R, Azzopardi L (2010) Improving access to large patent corpora. In: Transactions on large-scale data- and knowledge-centered systems II, vol 2. Springer, Berlin, pp 103–121
7. Baeza-Yates R, Ribeiro-Neto B (1999) Modern information retrieval. ACM Press, New York
8. Bashir S, Rauber A (2014) Automatic ranking of retrieval models using retrievability measure. Knowl Inf Syst 41(1):189–221
9. Callan J, Connell M (2001) Query-based sampling of text databases. ACM Trans Inf Syst J 19(2):97–130
10. Chowdhury GG (2004) Introduction to modern information retrieval, 2nd edn. Facet Publishing, London
11. Dumble PL, Morris JM, Wigan MR (1979) Accessibility indicators for transport planning. Transp Res Part A Gen 13:91–109
12. Efron M (2009) Using multiple query aspects to build test collections without human relevance judgments. In: Advances in information retrieval, proceedings of 31th European conference on IR research, ECIR 2009, Toulouse, 6–9 April 2009, pp 276–287

13. Fujii A, Iwayama M, Kando N (2007) Introduction to the special issue on patent processing. Inf Process Manage J 43(5):1149–1153
14. Gastwirth JL (1972) The estimation of the LORENZ curve and GINI index. Rev Econ Stat 54(3):306–316
15. Geurs KT, van Wee B (2004) Accessibility evaluation of land-use and transport strategies: Review and research directions. J Transp Geogr 12:127–140
16. Hansen WG (1959) How accessibility shape land use. J Am Inst Plann 25:73–76
17. Harter SP, Hert CA (1997) Evaluation of information retrieval systems: approaches, issues, and methods. Ann Rev Inf Sci Technol 32:3–94
18. Hauff C, Hiemstra D, Azzopardi L, de Jong F (2010) A case for automatic system evaluation. In: Advances in information retrieval, proceedings of the 32nd European conference on IR research, ECIR 2010, Milton Keynes, 28–31 March 2010, pp 153–165
19. Lauw HW, Lim E-P, Wang K (2006) Bias and controversy: beyond the statistical deviation. In: Proceedings of the 12th ACM SIGKDD international conference on knowledge discovery and data mining, Philadelphia, PA, pp 625–630
20. Litman T (2008) Evaluating accessibility for transportation planning. Victoria Transport Policy Institute
21. Lupu M, Huang J, Zhu J, Tait J (2009) TREC-CHEM: large scale chemical information retrieval evaluation at TREC. In: SIGIR forum, vol 43, no 2. ACM, New York, pp 63–70
22. Magdy W, Jones GJF (2010) Pres: a score metric for evaluating recall-oriented information retrieval applications. In: SIGIR'10: ACM SIGIR conference on research and development in information retrieval. ACM, New York, pp 611–618
23. Manning CD, Raghavan P, Schutze H (2008) Introduction to information retrieval. Cambridge University Press, Cambridge
24. Mase H, Matsubayashi T, Ogawa Y, Iwayama M, Oshio T (2005) Proposal of two-stage patent retrieval method considering the claim structure. ACM Trans Asian Lang Inf Process 4(2):190–206
25. Mowshowitz A, Kawaguchi A (2002) Bias on the web. In: Communications of the ACM, vol 45, no 9. ACM, New York, NY, pp 56–60
26. Nuray R, Can F (2006) Automatic ranking of information retrieval systems using data fusion. Inf Process Manage 42(3):595–614
27. Ounis I, De Rijke M, Macdonald C, Mishne G, Soboroff I (2006) Overview of the TREC 2006 blog track. In: Proceedings of the text retrieval conference, TREC'06
28. Petricek V, Escher T, Cox IJ, Margetts H (2006) The web structure of e-government - developing a methodology for quantitative evaluation. In: WWW '06 proceedings of the 15th international conference on World Wide Web, pp 669–678
29. Robertson SE, Walker S (1994) Some simple effective approximations to the 2-Poisson model for probabilistic weighted retrieval. In: SIGIR '94: proceedings of the 17th annual international ACM SIGIR conference on research and development in information retrieval, Dublin, pp 232–241
30. Sakai T, Lin C-Y (2010) Ranking retrieval systems without relevance assessments: revisited. In: Proceedings of the 3rd international workshop on evaluating information access, EVIA 2010, National Center of Sciences, Tokyo, 15 June 2010, pp 25–33
31. Sanderson M, Zobel J (2005) Information retrieval system evaluation: effort, sensitivity, and reliability. In: SIGIR'05: ACM SIGIR conference on research and development in information retrieval. ACM, New York, pp 162–169
32. Shi Z, Li P, Wang B (2010) Using clustering to improve retrieval evaluation without relevance judgments. In: COLING 2010, 23rd international conference on computational linguistics, posters volume, Beijing, 23–27 August 2010, pp 1131–1139
33. Shi Z, Wang B, Li P, Shi Z (2010) Using global statistics to rank retrieval systems without relevance judgments. In: Shi Z, Vadera S, Aamodt A, Leake DB (eds) Intelligent information processing. IFIP advances in information and communication technology, vol 340. Springer, Berlin, pp 183–192

34. Singhal A (1997) AT&T at TREC-6. In: The 6th text retrieval conference (TREC6), pp 227–232

35. Singhal A (2001) Modern information retrieval: a brief overview. IEEE Data Eng Bull 24:34–43

36. Spoerri A (2007) Using the structure of overlap between search results to rank retrieval systems without relevance judgments. Inf Process Manage 43(4):1059–1070

37. Vaughan L, Thelwall M (2004) Search engine coverage bias: evidence and possible causes. Inf Process Manage J 40(4):693–707

38. Voorhees EM (2001) Overview of the TREC 2001 question answering track. In: Proceedings of the text retrieval conference, TREC'01, pp 42–51

39. Voorhees EM (2002) The philosophy of information retrieval evaluation. In: CLEF'01. Springer, Berlin, pp 355–370

40. Voorhees EM, Harman DK (2005) TREC experiment and evaluation in information retrieval. MIT Press, Cambridge, MA

41. Wilkie C, Azzopardi L (2014) A retrievability analysis: exploring the relationship between retrieval bias and retrieval performance. In: Proceedings of the 23rd ACM international conference on conference on information and knowledge management, CIKM 2014, Shanghai, 3–7 November 2014, pp 81–90

42. Zhai CX (2002) Risk minimization and language modeling in text retrieval. Ph.D. thesis, Carnegie Mellon University

Chapter 8
Federated Patent Search

Michail Salampasis

Abstract Federated search, also known as distributed information retrieval (DIR), is a technique for searching multiple text collections simultaneously. This chapter presents the basic components of a typical federated search system and the main technical challenges in each component during its operation. We briefly review the methods and techniques of federated search and how these can be applied in the patent domain. We discuss the problems that usually are ignored in DIR research, but they should be practically addressed in real federated patent search systems. We also present PerFedPat, an interactive patent search system based on the federated search approach. PerFedPat provides core services to search, using a federated method, multiple online patent resources, thus providing parallel access to multiple patent sources. PerFedPat hides complexity from the end user who uses a common single query tool for querying all patent datasets at the same time. The second innovative feature of PerFedPat is that it has a pluggable and extensible architecture, and therefore it enables the use of multiple search tools that are integrated in PerFedPat. We present an example of such a tool, the IPC suggestion tool, which uses a federated search technique (specifically source selection) that exploits topically organised patents (using their intellectually assigned classifications codes) to support patent searches by automated IPC suggestion. This tool shows how DIR techniques can be applied beyond the typical scenario of implementing a federated search system.

8.1 Introduction

Patent search is an economically important problem, central to the R&D operations of many industries. Patents are important technical and legal documents which nowadays are published electronically using a strict technical form and structure. Also, the world of patents is a rapidly expanding one, with more patents filed each year in all languages, in various patent offices around the world [1]. Large

M. Salampasis (✉)
Department of Informatics, Alexander Technology Educational Institute (ATEI) of Thessaloniki, Sindos 57400, Thessaloniki, Greece
e-mail: msa@it.teithe.gr

© Springer-Verlag GmbH Germany 2017
M. Lupu et al. (eds.), *Current Challenges in Patent Information Retrieval*,
The Information Retrieval Series 37, DOI 10.1007/978-3-662-53817-3_8

maintenance efforts are necessary to collect, process and iteratively update large—centrally maintained—patent datasets based on the worldwide collection of patents and provide, as much as possible, a unified single point of (search engine-like) search. Several types of patent search exist (e.g. finding technical information, finding prior art, state of the art or patent landscape searching), each having the need to use various search tools and user interfaces (UIs) [2]. Also, depending on the type of patent search, various information sources may have to be considered, not only patent datasets but also other scientific data published elsewhere, current business and financial news, for tasks such as to raise technology awareness, discover business opportunities for an invention, etc.

A patent search professional often carries out search tasks for which high recall is important. Additionally, she/he would like to be able to reason about how the results have been produced, the effect of any query reformulation action in getting a new set of results or how the results of a set of query submission actions can be easily and accurately reproduced on a different occasion (the latter is particularly important if the patent searcher is required to prove the sufficiency of the search in court at a later stage). Classification schemes and metadata are heavily used because it is widely recognised that once the work of assigning patent documents into classification schemes is done, the search can be more efficient and language independent [3, 4].

Additionally, the complexity of the tasks which need to be performed by patent searchers usually includes not only retrieval but also information analysis, and generally requires association, pipelining and possibly integration of information as well as synchronisation and coordination of multiple and potentially concurrent search views produced from different datasets, search tools and user interfaces [5]. Many facets of search technology (e.g. exploratory search, aggregated search, federated search, task-based search, information retrieval (IR) over query sessions, cognitive IR approaches, human computer IR) aim to at least partially address some of these demands [6].

The main objective of this chapter is to present and analyse the main issues and challenges for understanding and developing integrated patent search systems based on the federated search paradigm. Federated search, also known as distributed information retrieval (DIR),[1] is a technique for searching multiple collections/information resources simultaneously [7]. Each resource which is part of the federation must provide a function (accessible over a URL, a Web service or any other remote procedure call method) for searching and retrieving results from its

---

[1]Many times these two terms (i.e. federated search and DIR) are used interchangeably in the relevant literature. However, this chapter implicitly suggests that there is a difference on how the two terms should be used. DIR should refer to the core theory and algorithms of this area and emphasises the fact that physical distribution of collections is not a prerequisite. On the other hand, the term 'federated search' should be used when referring to actual implementation of search systems, encompassing practical issues such as wrapper development and maintenance and duplicate removal, and emphasises on the simultaneous search of multiple searchable, remote and *physically* distributed resources [7].

own index. The searcher can manually select the resources she/he wants to search, or all available resources can be the target of a federated search. However, when applying DIR techniques, usually queries are submitted to a subset of available remote resources which are most likely to return relevant answers. Particularly when many resources are available, automatic resource selection is necessary and it is based on creating pre-processed representations of the existing resources. The results returned for each query by selected resources are usually merged into a single list which is presented to the searcher. Using this process federated search systems offer users the capability of simultaneously searching multiple online remote information sources through a single point of search.

From a user perspective, the defining feature of federated search is that the user interacts solely with the federated search system, without any requirement to know the intricacies of the underlying information sources, the query syntax and the methods which are internally used to index or retrieve documents. In effect, a federated search system functions as an intermediary between the user and multiple information resources. In the end, the experience of using a DIR system can be rather similar to that of using any other centralised IR system, as the DIR system in principle acts as a complete interface to the underlying information sources providing to its users a holistic, unified view of the available retrieval space comprising of the federated resources.

DIR and federated search have been explored for about 20 years now mainly as a research field and various applications have been presented [8], but the usefulness of DIR is also challenged [9]. One recent application of DIR methods is the aggregated or vertical Web search [10]. Also many enterprise search applications rely on forms of DIR [9]. Additionally, it is known that big Web search companies use DIR techniques in maintaining distributed indexes mainly for scalability reasons [11]. Federated search as a topic is also closely related to searching in peer-to-peer networks [12] and meta-search engines [13]. To understand the design and application space of DIR and federated search, one must understand that both can be selected as the basis for developing a search tool or solution either by inevitability or driven by an effort to engineer a more efficient or sometimes effective solution.

For example, DIR has been explored in the last decade mostly as a potential response to technical challenges such as the prohibitive size and exploding rate of growth of the Web which make it impossible to be indexed completely [14]. Big commercial search engines use programs called crawlers (or spiders) to locate and download documents when creating their indexes. Unfortunately, for a number of different reasons (e.g. pages are not linked and therefore cannot be discovered, robot exclusion commands, download process is too slow, dynamic pages with content generated on the fly might be ignored), search engines cannot easily crawl documents located in what is collectively known as the hidden or invisible Web [15]. Studies have indicated that the size of the invisible Web may be 2–50 times the size of the Web reachable by search engines.

Also there are many online authoritative resources (Web sites), which are not reachable by search engines, offering their own search capabilities. Even publicly available, up-to-date and authoritative government information is often not indexable by search engines [16]. A good example is PubMed[2] which is a very large biomedical library which contains more than 25 million articles published since the 1950s. There are many similar resources which are not indexable by search engines, providing their own access to information such as yellow and white pages, patents, legal information, national statistics, news, catalogues to national libraries and scientific articles. As the main focus of this article is patent search, we should mention this is true also in the patent domain as nearly all authoritative public online patent resources (e.g. EPO's Espacenet,[3] WIPO's PatentScope[4]) are not crawlable and therefore not publicly accessible using general-purpose Web search engines.

One good argument for using federated search is that we can provide increased coverage by searching a potentially large number of patent search engines which are wrapped in a federated patent search system. One key advantage, when compared with existing 'crawler-based' centralised patent search systems, is that a federated search system does not need to maintain its own dataset and index. As a result, federated searches are inherently as current as the individual information sources, as these are searched in real time. In other words, instead of expending the tremendous effort and resources required to download, process and index patent documents, something which may not be possible or very expensive in terms of time and costs, federated search techniques directly pass the query to the search interface of existing resource collections and effectively merge their results.

The previous two paragraphs presented cases where it is deemed necessary or inevitable to apply federated search because the effort to maintain a centralised patent search service is very large. A case where DIR methods, at least in patent search, can be a choice for improving efficiency and effectiveness is when it is applied in a way resembling more the cluster-based approaches to information retrieval [17]. In these approaches improvements can be explained by the cluster hypothesis and by source selection: relevant documents will tend to be at the same source, and only sources with several relevant documents will be selected. The general expectation is that if the correct sub-collections are selected, then it will be easier for relevant documents to be retrieved from the smaller set of available documents and more effective searches can be performed. Later in this article (in Sect. 4) we will present such a DIR technique motivated by the previous argument. The search tool based on this technique topically organises patent collections based on their International Patent Classification (IPC) codes to cluster, distribute and index patents through hundreds or thousands of sub-collections. The final aim is to improve prior art search by utilising source selection DIR methods to select the most promising sub-collections/IPCs to make a focused (filtered) search or when trying to understand a technical domain of a patent under examination.

The second motivation for considering federated search in the patent domain is that it encourages and better supports a paradigm of using integrated search systems

---

[2]http://www.ncbi.nlm.nih.gov/pubmed

[3]https://www.epo.org/searching/free/espacenet.html

[4]https://patentscope.wipo.int/search/en/search.jsf

for patent search [18]. In this point it should be made clear that in the previous sentence the term 'integrated' is used to define search systems integrating multiple search tools that can be used (in parallel or in a pipeline) from the professional searcher during a potentially lengthy search session. Some of these tools may serve, for example, the need of retrieving information from distributed datasets as it happens in federated search, expand and suggest a query, but other tools may operate at runtime to deliver to the searcher's desktop (workbench) multiple views of search results produced using various methods beyond the typical single merged ranked list (e.g. faceted search, clusters of documents). As a result our definition of integrated patent search systems primarily describes a rich information-seeking environment for different types of searches, utilising multiple search tools and exploiting a diverse set of IR and natural language processing (NLP) technologies.

The rest of this chapter is structured as follows. In Sect. 2 we present the main technical challenges of federated search which normally have to be addressed when developing federated search solutions in every domain. In Sect. 3 we discuss how these solutions can be applied in the patent domain in particular and some issues that have to be considered when applying federated search techniques in the patent domain. We also present a federated patent search system (namely PerFedPat[5]) which searches online public patent resources and other patent datasets and also integrates a set of different search tools for patent search. In Sect. 4 we present another approach to apply DIR methods in the patent domain which is the use of resource selection to patents which are topically organised based on their IPC. In Sect. 5 we critically discuss the main challenges and benefits that federated search offers in patent retrieval. Section 6 wraps up the chapter by attempting to draw some conclusions about the applicability and potential value of federated search in the development of next-generation patent search systems.

8.2 Technical Challenges in Federated Search

If the federated search process is decomposed, it can be perceived as three separate but interleaved sub-processes (Fig. 8.1): *source representation*, in which surrogates of the available remote collections are created; *source selection*, in which a subset of the available information resources is chosen to process the query; and *results merging*, in which the separate results are combined into a single merged result list which is returned to the user.

In this section we briefly present each one of these sub-processes providing references to related work. More complete reviews of federated search and DIR methods and applications can be found at [1, 8].

---

[5]PerFedPat stands for personalised federated patent search. The term 'federated' is used because it applies federated search techniques. Personalised because it supports the parallel use of multiple search views and tools that can be used to personalise the searcher's workbench and search tactics.

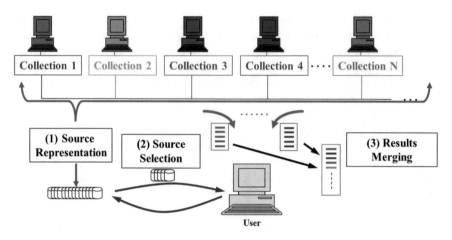

Fig. 8.1 The retrieval process in federated search

8.2.1   Source Representation and Collection Size Estimation

The source representation phase [19] takes place before the user submits a query to the federated search system. During this phase, surrogates of the available remote collections are created. The aim of this stage is to provide the DIR system with the best possible approximation about the contents of the federated information resources. Information which is required to create an accurate representation of the resources typically is their thematic topicality (i.e. news, engineering, medical, sports, etc.) and the number of documents that are contained in a collection (the size of the collection). Other information utilised in the subsequent resource selection phase are the terms that appear in it (i.e. the vocabulary of the resource), the number of documents that contain each term and potentially the number of times each term appears in each document.

After source representation the federated search system possesses a representation set for each resource. The representation can be generated manually by providing a short description of the documents found and indexed in each resource. However, manually created representations cannot capture many terms that occur in a large collection. Therefore in practice, collection representation sets are usually generated automatically, and their comprehensiveness depends on the level of cooperation in the federated search environment. Uncooperative environments are those where federated collections do not provide any information about their contents and collection statistics to the federated search system. On the contrary, in cooperative environments the lexicon of the collections is provided to the central broker; therefore complete and accurate information can be used for the phase of collection selection [20].

However, in a typical federated search system, the remote collections are uncooperative, external to the 'owner' of the federated search system; therefore the collections need to be sampled to establish a representation [21]. This technique is known as query-based sampling [19] or query probing [22].

Also very typically source representation is done in advance before the user submits the query. However, when the remote resource is extremely dynamic, there are source representation methodologies which can create representations 'on the fly', during query time [23].

Besides an estimation of the terms that appear in the remote search engines, the actual number of documents that are available and indexed in each resource is also important. This is reasonable if we consider that source selection algorithms must take into consideration the size of the remote collections in order to determine the number of relevant documents that should be merged from each resource that will be selected in the resource selection phase. A first methodology was based on a simple capture-recapture approach [24]. A second, more economical and yet sufficiently accurate methodology is called sample-resample [25]. Using this method queries are sent to the remote resource to estimate the document frequency of a term in a collection and with some simple calculations calculate the size of the remote collection taking into account the document frequency of a term in the representation of a collection (sample) and the size of the sample.

In the federated patent search system which is presented in Sect. 3.1, no source representation method is used because the number of federated resources is small and the users manually select which subset to search. However, the IPC suggestion tool which is presented in Sect. 4 uses source representations that are produced for every patent classification at various levels in the IPC hierarchy using every available patent member of this classification code.

8.2.2 Automatic Resource Selection

There are a number of source selection approaches including CORI [26], gGlOSS [27] and others [28] that consider document collections as document surrogates, consisting of the concatenation of the collection's documents (the so-called big-document approach). These methods characterise different collections using collection-wide statistics like term frequencies. These statistics, which are used to select or rank the available collections' relevance to a query, are usually assumed to be available from cooperative search providers. Alternatively, statistics can be approximated by sampling uncooperative providers with a set of queries as briefly discussed in the previous paragraph and extensively reported in [19].

The collection retrieval inference network (CORI) algorithm is probably the most widely used source selection algorithm from those following the big-document approach. The algorithm creates a hyper-document for each sub-collection, containing documents that are members of the sub-collection. When a query Q is submitted, the sub-collections are ranked based on the belief $p(Q|C_i)$ that the collection C_i can satisfy the information need of the query Q. The belief $p(r_k|C_i)$ that a term r_k—part of the query Q— is observed given collection C_i is estimated based on calculations using the number of documents in collection C_i that contain term r_k, the number of collections that contain term r_k, the number of terms in C_i, the average number of documents between all remote resources and the number of available collections. The overall belief $p(Q|C_i)$ in collection C_i for query Q is estimated as the average of the individual beliefs of the query terms $p(r_k|C_i)$.

The decision-theoretic framework (DTF) presented by Fuhr [29] is one of the first attempts to approach the problem of source selection from a theoretical point of view. The decision-theoretic framework produces a ranking of collections with the goal of minimising the occurring costs, under the assumption that retrieving irrelevant documents is more expensive than retrieving relevant ones. It is likely that DTF can provide a solid basis for source selection when developing industry-level federated search systems.

In more recent years, there has been a shift of focus in research on source selection, from estimating the relevancy of each remote collection to explicitly estimating the number of relevant documents in each resource. These methods are called small-document approaches to resource selection [30], and they rank and select sources based on the ranking of their documents in a centralised sample index. ReDDE [25] focuses at exactly that purpose. It is based on utilising a centralised sample index, comprised of all the documents that are sampled in the query-sampling phase, and ranks the collections based on the number of documents that appear in the top ranks when querying the centralised sample index. Its performance has been shown to be similar to CORI at testbeds with collections of similar size and better when the sizes vary significantly. Two similar approaches named CRCS(l) and CRCS(e) were presented by Shokouhi [31], assigning different weights to the returned documents depending on their rank, in a linear or exponential fashion. Other methods see source selection as a voting method where the available collections are candidates and the documents that are retrieved from the set of sampled documents—retrieved from the centralised sample index—are voters [32]. Different voting mechanisms can be used (e.g. BordaFuse, ReciRank, Compsum) mainly inspired by data fusion techniques.

There is a major difference between CORI (big-document approach) and the source selection algorithms that utilise the centralised index (small-document approaches). CORI builds a hyper-document for each sub-collection, while the other collection selection methods are based on the retrieval of individual documents from the centralised sample index. Due to its main characteristic, CORI has been repeatedly reported in the literature [33] not performing consistently well in environments containing a mix of 'small' and 'very large' document collections. However, in the patent domain where similar inventions contain to a large extent very different terminology [34], in some settings the idea of building hyper-documents centred around a specific technical concept such as IPCs may be very well suited. The homogenous collections containing patent documents of the same IPC as the hyper-documents in CORI should normally encompass a strong discriminating power, something very useful for effective and robust resource selection. This is the reason why CORI is used in the IPC suggestion search tool which is discussed in Sect. 4

and has been proven to perform consistently better than small-document approaches that we tested.

8.2.3 Results Merging

Merging the result lists from remote resources is a complex problem not only because of the variety of retrieval engines that may be used by the individual collections but also because of the diversity of collection statistics.

In environments where the remote collections return not only ranked lists of documents but also relevancy scores, *raw score merging* [26] merges the results as they are returned from the remote collections in a descending order. However, this approach does not produce good results because of the problem of different statistics which eventually makes the scores from different remote resources incomparable. For example, in a collection that is mainly about sports, a document containing the term 'computer' will rank very high if that term appears in the query, while the same document would rank lower in a computer science-related collection. The *weighted scores merging* algorithm overcomes the above issue by assigning each document a score which is based both on the relevancy of the document itself and the relevancy of the collection where it belongs. This way, high-scoring documents from low-scoring collections (as in the above example) rank lower than highly relevant scores from highly relevant collections.

The CORI results merging algorithm is a weighted scores merging algorithm and has proved effective [35]. The final score of each document coming from different remote resources is calculated using two simple equations [26] that are used to normalise the collection and document scores to a range of 0–1.

Another set of results merging algorithms (e.g. SSL [36], MRRM [37], SAFE [38]) makes use of a centralised index, comprised of all the sampled documents from the remote collections. The algorithm takes advantage of the common returned documents and their corresponding relevancy scores between the centralised index and the remote collections to estimate a linear regression model between the two scores. In case when a collection does not return scores and only ranked lists, factitious scores are calculated and assigned to the documents in a linear fashion.

The PerFedPat system presented in Sect. 4 uses an alternative approach for results merging because it is based on ezDL. The search agent collects all answers from the federated resources/services that have been searched, merges duplicates and re-ranks them using an index which is created on the fly in the server's memory.

8.2.4 Federated Patent Search

There is an abundance of systems today to search for patents [39, 40]. Some of them are free and have become available from patent offices and intellectual property (IP) organisations in the last 10 years (e.g. Espacenet and Patentscope), as the growth of the Internet and the development of search technologies facilitated the provision of powerful Web-based search systems of patent databases. Other systems are free—but developed by search technology providers (e.g. Google Patents[6])— or are based on subscription and are provided from other independent producers. All Web-based patent search systems allow searches using the simple 'search box' paradigm. Other free or commercial systems may have better capabilities, for example, for structural searching in particular fields, for term proximity operations or to leverage domain semantics [41], but essentially they all operate on the same centralised index paradigm. According to this paradigm, patent documents need to be periodically crawled or otherwise collected; afterwards they are analysed and eventually become part of the system's centralised index.

Contrary to this paradigm, federated search can be applied in the patent domain by searching the patent resources which provide an interface (accessible over a URL or a Web service) for searching their indexed documents. Practically speaking a federated patent search system implements a DIR scenario which allows the simultaneous search of multiple searchable, remote and physically distributed patent resources. In the previous section, we reviewed the main technical challenges for this. Additionally, some other issues that must be particularly considered when applying DIR to patent search are wrapper development and maintenance, overlapping indexes, elimination of duplicates and multilingualism.

Wrappers are essential for federated search systems because they make possible the interaction with remote resources. One wrapper for each federated resource must exist for a federated system to be operational. The most important issue when developing a wrapper is firstly how to connect to the collection and how to map the internal structure of the query from the federated search system to the remote resources. Sometimes the mapping may not be complete, for example, the federated search system may support proximity operator and some of the federated resources will not. The end user should be aware about which capabilities of a federated search system are supported from a remote resource and which are not, but generally speaking the federated search systems can provide visual cues and other support about this task. Another problem in wrappers is extracting records from the search result pages returned for remote resources. Several problems may occur during this process such as the change in the structure of a search result or how to extract multiple search results 'pages'. Of course if a Web service is available and results can be obtained in XML format, these problems can be minimised.

The problem of duplicate documents will most likely exist in a federated patent search system as most patent resources index, to some extent, a great amount of same patent documents. A federated patent search system should be able to identify such redundancy within a single resource but also amongst different federated resources. In federated Web search, it is easy to eliminate duplicate documents by aggregating results that point to the same URL, but in the patent domain some other

---

features should be used that will identify such redundancies (e.g. same publication number, identifying patent families).

Duplicate documents have as a consequence overlapping indexes. This is a scenario that in most DIR algorithms for resource selection or results merging needs to be addressed because most of them make the assumption of completely disjointed federated resources. On the other side, the fact of a patent document returned by more than one resource can be used in the merging process to rank these documents higher. Several combination and 'voting' methods (e.g. CombMNZ, CombSum) from data fusion have been proposed in several DIR settings [36, 42].

Finally, as it is very common in information retrieval research, most methods focus on the environments where all documents in collections are in the same language. The same holds for most methods in DIR. However, patent resources usually contain documents in different languages. Therefore, it is important to extend monolingual DIR techniques for multilingual environments as it is presented here [43].

8.3 A Federated Patent Search System

PerFedPat[7] is an interactive patent search system that follows a federated search approach. PerFedPat provides core services and operations for being able to search, using a federated method, multiple online patent resources (currently Espacenet, Google patents, Patentscope and the MAREC[8] collection), thus providing unified single-point access to multiple patent sources while hiding complexity from the end user who uses a common query tool for querying all patent datasets at the same time. Wrappers are used which convert the PerFedPat internal query model into the queries that each remote system can process. 'Translated' queries are routed to remote search systems and their returned results are internally re-ranked and merged as a single list presented to the patent searcher. PerFedPat is developed upon ezDL [44]; therefore, in addition to the patent resources which are provided in PerFedPat, there are other resources already provided by ezDL, most of them offering access to online bibliographic search services (e.g. ACM DL, DBLP, Springer, PubMed) for non-patent literature.

The second idea that PerFedPat supports is integrating multiple search tools and methods for professional search [42]. Currently the search tools which are integrated are (a) an International Patent Classification (IPC) selection tool, (b) a tool for faceted navigation of the results retrieved based on existing metadata in patents, (c) a tool producing clustered views of patent search results and (d) a machine translation

---

[7]System can be downloaded from this address: www.perfepat.eu

[8]MAREC is a static collection of over 19 million patent applications and granted patents in a unified file format normalized from EP, WO, US and JP sources, spanning a range from 1976 to June 2008. http://www.ifs.tuwien.ac.at/imp/marec.shtml

(MT) tool for translating queries for cross-lingual information retrieval. The rest of this section explains the architecture and the features available in PerFedPat.

8.3.1 PerFedPat Overview

The two basic ideas of PerFedPat are (a) federated meta-search in information sources and (b) better strategic support and a richer information-seeking environment for users by integrating multiple search tools and UIs.

There are four patent search systems (and two classification search systems) supported now, but inclusion of more is easy and depends on the development of appropriate wrappers. PerFedPat not only searches multiple datasets in parallel, but it also offers more sophisticated services such as removing duplicates, merging and re-ranking the results [45]. There are also additional features like filtering or grouping and sorting the results according to existing features or patent metadata (e.g. per patent resource, per year, IPC, inventors, etc). Using the grouping function, a searcher can very quickly get an overview of the full set of results returned from the different federated patent systems. The basic objective is to improve the accuracy and relevance of individual searches as well as reduce the amount of time required to search the multiple resources which are available. For some tasks, for example, prior art patent search, these are key objectives.

Although PerFedPat relies on existing patent search systems to execute the core retrieval task, from an architectural point of view, PerFedPat is innovative using the federated search approach and goes beyond the state of the art in patent search systems in terms of scale, heterogeneity as well as extensibility as it is based on a service-oriented, message-centric architecture able to integrate data sources into new, more useful ways. From that perspective the PerFedPat system is the first open architecture data aggregator for patent information, and its contribution is to show that the sum of the utilities provided by each patent resource and search tool could be really bigger than the single utilities and many possibilities lie in an integrated approach for patent data delivery and intelligent processing and presentation.

The resource and the tools that a developer of a patent search solution will decide to integrate into a patent search system or that the searcher will decide to use do not only have to do with existing IR/NLP technologies or the integrated tools respectively, but they have to do more with the primary target group of a patent search application or the context in which a patent search is conducted and the professional searcher's behaviour. Furthermore, it is also very important to understand a search process and how exactly a specific tool can attain a specific objective of this process and therefore increase its efficiency. We will discuss this idea further in Sect. 4 when we present the IPC suggestion tool integrated in PerFedPat.

8.3.2   PerFedPat Architecture

PerFedPat follows the client-server component-based architecture. The server provides a large part of the core functionality such as the meta-search facility, user authorisation, a knowledge base (repository) about previously retrieved documents as well as wrappers that connect to external services. The system architecture makes extensive separation of components to keep interdependencies to a minimum and make the system more stable and pluggable. Within the backend individual processes operating as 'software agents' handle specific parts of the functionality. Software agents are autonomous software components that communicate with their peers, by exchanging messages in an agent communication language [46]. The directory is a special agent that keeps a list of agents and the services they provide. Upon start, each agent registers with the directory and announces the services it provides.

In PerFedPat we have implemented wrapper agents for the Espacenet, Google Patents, Patentscope and MAREC patent resources. There are two different types of wrappers. When interfaces (APIs) exist (e.g. in the case of MAREC in PerFedPat), in which full control and access are possible, then it is very easy to write a wrapper which sends a query or other requests and receives back information from the fully controlled search system, usually in XML or other structural format (e.g. JSON). In case of Web-based systems which are completely external to PerFedPat (e.g. Google Patents, Patentscope), an analysis of the search result Web page is required and is programmed in the wrapper and conducted in the backend. Usually this is facilitated by Web page analysis tools using the XPath language, a query language for selecting nodes from an HTML/XML document. Also, multiple sections ('pages') from search results can be obtained; by default PerFedPat retrieves 100–200 results from each patent resource.

The desktop client, like the backend, is separated into multiple independent components/agents called 'tools' (Fig. 8.2). A tool comprises a set of logically connected functionalities. Each tool has one or more tool views, interactive display components that can be placed somewhere on the desktop/workbench. A configuration of available tools and the specific layout of their tool views on the desktop is called a perspective. Users can modify existing predefined perspectives as well as create their own custom perspectives and load them later when needed.

8.3.2.1   Core Tools and Their Extension

The PerFedPat desktop client already has many built-in tools and functionalities inherited directly from ezDL. We extended the functionality of some of the existing tools and we also added new tools specifically designed and implemented to address the needs of patent search. We will briefly describe these tools in this section, and in the next one we will describe more analytically how the tools can be used together to support a search process during an information-seeking episode.

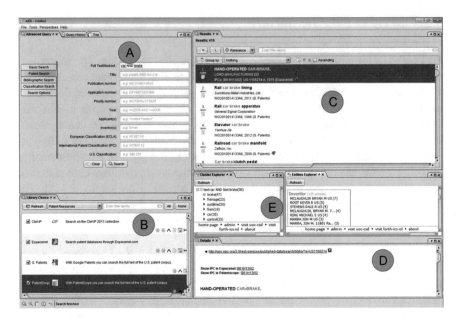

Fig. 8.2 PerFedPat workbench overview with some core and patent search tools open. The search tools in area E are discussed in Sect. 3.3.2

The *query tool* offers a variety of query forms for different purposes. In PerFedPat we extended this tool to address the need for more advanced fielded search which is necessary in patent search. Each patent resource from the four available supports a different set of fields in the fielded search it implements locally. Fields that are supported from all or from most of the patent federated resources are implemented in the advanced search view in PerFedPat (coloured circle area A in Fig. 8.2). The queries that users enter are expressed in a grammar specific to PerFedPat that is flexible and allows simple free text queries like 'term1 term2' as well as more complex ones like 'term1 AND (term2 NEAR/2 term3)'. Wildcards and phrases are also supported by the internal query tool. Fields can be combined, so more complex queries can be constructed. A query is internally represented in a tree structure, and before it is transmitted to the patent resource wrappers, the query is translated into the languages selected by the searcher in the query translation tool. Obviously in each wrapper, the query which is received in the internal tree structure is transformed to the form that each patent resource is able to process. Note that each patent resource is marked with a number of symbols (area B in Fig. 8.2) which show to the user which capabilities of the internal query structure are supported in the remote patent resource. When full support is not available, queries are partially translated in a way to include the capabilities which are supported. To be able to validate this process more easily, we have also implemented in PerFedPat a *URL logger* tool which shows the final query which is transmitted for execution to the remote patent resource. In this way the federated search process becomes more transparent for the end users and the designers of an application.

Other 'standard' tools include:

- The *library choice* for selecting information sources.
- The *query history* which lists past queries for reuse and allows grouping by date and filtering.
- The *tray* tool can be used to temporarily collect relevant documents within a search session.
- The *results* tool which shows the merged and re-ranked results returned from the patent resources. Results can be grouped, sorted, filtered and exported (C).
- The *details view* tool (D) shows additional details on individual documents, such as thumbnails or short summaries where available, or additional metadata not included in the surrogate that is shown in the result list. A detail link can be provided to retrieve the full text of a patent document if available. Since patents can be very long documents, we have extended this tool to provide quick reference links to parts of the patent (e.g. claims, description, citations, etc). Also we build some shortcuts to link the classification codes of a patent shown in the details or results view directly to online services presenting the classification hierarchy.

8.3.3 Integration of Patent Search Tools in PerFedPat

Despite the tremendous success of IR technologies in the domain of Web search, there is significant scepticism from professional searchers and a very conservative attitude towards adopting search methods, tools and technologies beyond the ones which dominate their domain [3]. A typical example is patent search where professional search experts typically use the Boolean search syntax and complex intellectual classification schemes [47]. However, despite the overall scepticism, search technologies are being used increasingly in the workplace as a result of the explosion of content becoming electronically available, and those who deal with patents in their professional life are becoming more knowledgeable about new search technologies and tools. Of course adopting new search tools that will gradually change the landscape of patent search will be a long-term process. To achieve this, careful consideration is needed when designing a patent search system about the tools which will add functionality to ease the use of the core retrieval system but with the least invasive way in changing the traditional approaches of Boolean search.

In that context, it is important to understand a search process and how a specific tool can attain a specific objective of this process and therefore increase its efficiency. For example, Lupu and Hanbury in a recent review of patent retrieval [2] present a typical prior art search use case, analysed in terms of different sub-processes and performed by a patent examiner (pp. 15) to model and better understand prior art search. The IPC selection tool which we present next was designed and integrated in PerFedPat to support the specific sub-process of identifying relevant IPC codes in a typical prior art search.

In the rest of this section, based on the context provided by the discussion above and leaving aside the core patent resources, we discuss tools that have been integrated into PerFedPat to experiment and to set the ground for improving patent search in PerFedPat.

8.3.3.1   The IPC Suggestion Tool

The *IPC suggestion* tool aims, given a query, to select a number of IPC codes, at different levels of the classification hierarchy if requested, which include patents related to this query. The algorithm and the method which we used to implement this tool are based on DIR techniques for collection selection which we extended for patent search and are discussed in Sect. 4. The essence of the method is that it identifies relevant IPC codes not by searching the textual description of IPC classes, groups, subgroups, etc., but by using an indirect method. First it retrieves patents, and then by using the IPC codes of the retrieved patents builds a probability estimation of the relevance of the allocated IPC codes to the query.

8.3.3.2   The Cluster Explorer and the Entities Explorer Tools

The *entities explorer* tool supports an exploratory strategy for patent search that exploits the metadata already available in patents in addition to the results of clustering and entity mining that can be performed at query time. The results (metadata, clusters and entities grouped in categories) can complement the ranked lists of patents produced from the core patent search engine with information useful for the user (e.g. providing a concise overview of the search results) which are further exploited in a faceted and session-based interaction scheme that allows the users to focus their searches gradually and to change between search methods as their information need is better defined and their understanding of the technical topic evolves in response to found information.

The *cluster explorer* tool provides patent searchers with an overview of the results shown in the results tool. It aims at grouping the results into topics (called clusters), with predictive names (labels), aiding the user to locate quickly one or more documents (patents in our case) that otherwise would be difficult to find, especially if they are low ranked. In our setting, we use a variation of the suffix tree clustering (STC) algorithm that derives hierarchically organised labels and is able to favour occurrences in a specific part of the result (e.g. in the title). The last feature is very useful for clustering the results of a patent search, because the *invention title* usually is the most descriptive part of a patent.

The algorithms and the methods of these two PerFedPat tools are reported in detail in [48, 49]. Currently the two tools work with the MAREC patent resource only, but it is straightforward to support any patent resource in PerFedPat federation as both tools *attain their functionality fully at query time only* (i.e. no preprocessing or indexing is necessary). Also, the faceted search tool currently uses static metadata which already exist in patent documents (e.g. inventor, countries of designation, years, etc). However, in patent search more kinds of entities can be supported, e.g. companies, countries, product types, drugs, diseases, etc. The tool can be configured to extract dynamically these entities, but for the moment some language resources are required which are not fully implemented in the current version.

8.3.3.3 The Machine Translation Tool

Cross-language information retrieval (CLIR) is a subfield of information retrieval dealing with retrieving information written in a language different from the language of the user's query. For example, a user may give her query in English but wants to retrieve relevant documents written in Chinese. Multilingual IR (MLIR) addresses the problem of multilingual access to text databases and can be seen as an extension of the general information retrieval (IR) problem corresponding to paraphrase. It aims for retrieval of documents in several languages from a query. Machine translation (MT) is an essential tool for CLIR and MLIR (if the translation quality is high), and the challenge of accessing patent documents written in different languages from all around the world using MT methods has been addressed in several evaluation campaigns (e.g. [50, 51]).

The *machine translation* tool uses third-party MT services (in the current version Microsoft Bing & Patentscope) in order to translate queries into different languages so that some types of CLIR and MLIR can be conducted in PerFedPat. Depending on the languages which are selected from the information searcher to use from the MT tool and the availability of patent documents in different languages in PerFePat's federated patent resources, the MT tool in PerFedPat can assist the information searcher to retrieve documents in several languages from a query posed in one language.

8.4 Source Selection for IPC Suggestion

In Sect. 1 we argued that federated search and DIR can be driven either by some degree of inevitability (e.g. because of the deep Web issue and the difficulty or impossibility for a centralised solution) or driven by an effort to engineer a more efficient or sometimes effective solution. The previous section presented PerFedPat, an example of the former. The work which is presented in this section is an example of the latter. This work views the automated selection of International Patent Classification (IPC) codes as a collection selection problem—from the domain of DIR—that can be addressed using existing DIR methods which we extend and adapt for the patent domain [45]. Generally, many research efforts in the patent search domain exploit the intellectually assigned classifications codes that are used to categorise patents and to facilitate patent searches, e.g. [52, 53]. In our method, manually assigned IPC codes of patent documents are used to cluster, distribute and index patents through hundreds or thousands of sub-collections.

In that sense, this work is not a typical federated search study, since the focus is more on logically clustering the patents rather than accessing physically distributed resources. The method creates clusters of patents based on their manually assigned IPC codes and uses different collection selection algorithms to select relevant IPCs during a patent search. As we mentioned before, this task supports the very fundamental step in professional patent search (sub-process 3 in the use case presented by Lupu and Hanbury [2]) which is 'defining a text query, potentially by Boolean operators and specific field filters'. In prior art search probably the most important filter is based on the IPC (CPC now) classification [54, 55]. Selecting the most promising/relevant IPC codes depends of course on the prior knowledge of a patent professional in the technical area under examination, but sometimes the area of a patent application may not be easily distinguishable or usually a patent uses various technical concepts represented by multiple IPC codes. To identify all these relevant IPC codes could be a difficult, error-prone and time-consuming task, especially for a not very knowledgeable patent professional in some technical area.

The IPC suggestion tool, which is part of PerFedPat, supports this step automatically; that is, given a query, it selects the most appropriate IPC codes and passes these IPC codes to PerFedPat's query tool. The query tool then initiates a filtered search based on the automatically selected IPC codes. This process naturally resembles the way patent professionals conduct various types of patent search. Also, the patent searcher may use the tool not only to produce IPC-based filters automatically to narrow his/her search but also as a classification search which will be used as a starting point to identify and closely examine technical concepts as these are expressed in IPC codes and to which a patent could be related and should be examined more vigorously. This ground understanding step also helps in formulating better queries, usually including noun phrases from the IPC codes that were deemed relevant. Of course, the patent searcher has the flexibility to add the IPC codes that they assume relevant in addition to the ones suggested by the IPC suggestion tool.

It should be pointed out that the work which is presented in this section (choice) is different from the typical federated search (inevitability) which was presented in Sect. 3, because it assumes a cooperative environment. We can assume such environment because unlike environments with an unknown and rapidly growing number of not directly accessible documents (i.e. the deep Web), the patent domain contains a certain number of documents and a single point of authority can be established as it happens in a cooperative environment. Assuming a cooperative environment, query-based sampling and source representation before the source selection are not necessary.

8.4.1   Topically Organised Patents

All patents have manually assigned IPC codes [56]. IPC is an internationally accepted standard taxonomy for classifying, sorting, organising, disseminating and searching patents. It is officially administered by the World Intellectual Property Organization (WIPO). The IPC provides a hierarchical system of language-independent symbols for the classification of patents according to the different areas of technology to which they pertain. IPC has currently about 71,000 nodes which are organised into a five-level hierarchical system which is also extended in greater levels of granularity. IPC codes are assigned to patent documents manually by technical specialists.

Patents can be classified by a number of different classification schemes. European Classification (ECLA) and US Patent Classification System (USPTO) were the most known classification schemes used by EPO and USPTO, respectively. Recently, EPO and USPTO signed a joint agreement to develop a common classification scheme known as Cooperative Patent Classification (CPC).

Although IPC codes are used to topically cluster patents into sub-collections, something which is a prominent prerequisite for DIR, there are some important differences which motivated us to re-examine and adapt existing DIR techniques as they are applied in patent search and in the context provided by our specific objectives. First, IPC codes are assigned by humans in a very detailed and purposeful assignment process, something which is very different by the creation of sub-collections using automated clustering algorithms or the naive division method by chronological or source order, a division method which has been extensively used in past DIR research.

Before we describe the IPC suggestion method further, we should explain more the IPC scheme, which determines how DIR sub-collections can be artificially created. Top-level IPC codes consist of eight sections which are human necessities, performing operations, chemistry, textiles, fixed constructions, mechanical engineering, physics and electricity. A section is divided into classes, which are subdivided into subclasses. Each subclass is divided into main groups, which are further subdivided into subgroups. In total, the current IPC has 8 sections, 129 classes, 632 subclasses, 7530 main groups and approximately 64,000 subgroups.

Table 8.1 shows a part of IPC. Section symbols use uppercase letters A through H. A class symbol consists of a section symbol followed by two-digit numbers like F01, F02, etc. A subclass symbol is a class symbol followed by an uppercase letter like F01B. A main group symbol consists of a subclass symbol followed by one- to three-digit numbers, then a slash and finally by 00 such as F01B7/00. A subgroup symbol replaces the last 00 in a main group symbol with two-digit numbers except for 00 such as F01B7/02. Each IPC node is attached with a noun phrase description that specifies some technical fields relevant to that IPC code. Note that a subgroup may have more refined subgroups (i.e. defining sixth, seventh level, etc., at the IPC hierarchy). Hierarchies amongst subgroups (i.e. below level 5) are indicated not by

Table 8.1 An example of a section from the IPC classification

Division	Title	IPC code
Section	Mechanical engineering . . .	F
Class	Machines or engines in general	F01
Subclass	Machines or engines with two or more pistons	F01B
Main group	Reciprocating within same cylinder or . . .	F01B7/00
Subgroup	.with oppositely reciprocating pistons	F01B7/02
Subgroup	..acting on the same main shaft	F01B7/04

subgroup symbols but by the number of dot symbols preceding the node descriptions as shown in Table 8.1.

The taxonomy and set of classes, subclasses, groups, etc., are dynamic. The patent office tries to keep membership to groups down to a maximum by making new subgroups, etc. However, new patent applications/inventions require the continual update of the IPC taxonomy. Since 2010, the IPC is revised once a year. Sometimes existing subclasses/groups/subgroups are subdivided into new subsets. Sometimes a set of subclasses of a class are merged together and then subdivided again in a different manner. After new subclasses are formed, the patents involved may or may not be assigned to the new subclasses. The changes are related to a small part of the IPC hierarchy and therefore they are negligible.

8.4.2 Multilayer Collection Selection

We exploit the aforementioned hierarchical organisation of the IPC classification scheme and the ideas of (a) considering topically organised patents using IPC as a DIR system where IPC codes act as sub-collection identifiers with parent-child relations and (b) creating a more effective and reliable source selection method relying upon a weighted sum of multiple estimates, to propose a new *multilayer* collection selection method [57]. The new method in addition to utilising the topical relevance of collections/IPCs[9] at a particular level of interest exploits the topical relevance of their ancestors in the IPC hierarchy and aggregates those multiple estimations of relevance to a single estimation. For example, assume that the patent expert is interested in distilling the most relevant IPC codes at level 5 (i.e. subgroup level) for a prior art search. The proposed methodology will combine the relevance of collections at level 5 (the level of interest) *and* level 4 (the ancestral level to the one of interest) in order to produce the final ranking. The method can be applied

---

[9]In this section we utilize the terms 'collection' and 'IPC code' interchangeably, that is, when we are referring to a collection, we are implicitly referring to all the patents that have the same IPC code for a particular level (i.e. all the patents that belong to the F01 class are part of the F01 collection at level 2).

in any domain where documents are organised in accordance to a hierarchical classification scheme, but we focus here on the patent domain. In addition, because the method will exploit for each level the relevance of its ancestor level, recursively and overall the multilayer method exploits multiple levels of hierarchy (e.g. levels 4, 3, 2, 1 in the aforementioned example). However, exploitation of a higher level of the hierarchy (e.g. level 1 in IPC) where very few classes exist may not be useful.

The algorithm functions in the following manner. Given a query document P and a target level i (e.g. if retrieval of IPCs at the level of subgroup is required, then the target level is 5), the algorithm produces a ranking $R_i(P) = \{C_1^i, C_2^i, \ldots, C_m^i\}$ and *scores* using a source selection algorithm and this can be formulated as

$$R_i(P) = \{C_1^i, C_2^i, \ldots, C_m^i\}$$
$$Score_i(P) = \{Score\left(C_1^i\right), Score\left(C_2^i\right), \ldots, Score\left(C_m^i\right)\} \tag{8.1}$$

Then given that the level of interest of the patent expert is i, the second phase of the algorithm is to re-rank $R_i(P)$ by utilising the other estimates that will be produced from the ancestor level. So the second produced ranking is at the ancestral level $i-1$ of the hierarchical classification scheme. We symbolise this ranking as $R_{i-1}(P)$, where C_j^{i-1} is the collection retrieved at rank j at level $i-1$ and n is the total number of collections retrieved at this level. The ranking and relevance scores are produced by applying any standard source selection algorithm at collections of this level and can be formulated as

$$R_{i-1}(P) = \{C_1^{i-1}, C_2^{i-1}, \ldots, C_n^{i-1}\}$$
$$Score_{i-1}(P) = \{Score\left(C_1^{i-1}\right), Score\left(C_2^{i-1}\right), \ldots, Score\left(C_n^{i-1}\right)\} \tag{8.2}$$

In the experiments described in this chapter, we use the CORI collection selection algorithm as it has been shown to be more effective than other collection selection algorithms, such as BordaFuse, ReciRank and ReDEE that were tested before [45].

After the calculation of $R_{i-1}(P)$, a re-ranking process is launched at the target level $R_i(P)$, by calculating a weighted sum, which includes the $R_i(P)$ ranking, but it also takes into account the $R_{i-1}(P)$ ranking in the following manner: for each collection C_j^{i-1} in $R_{i-1}(P)$ previously retrieved, we locate its children in the IPC hierarchy—$Children\left(C_j^{i-1}\right) = \{C_j^i, where\ C_j^i\ is\ a\ child\ of\ C_j^{i-1}\}$. Subsequently, to re-rank $R_i(P)$ we locate the $Children\left(C_j^{i-1}\right)$ for all C_j^{i-1} that belong to $R_{i-1}(P)$, and we re-rank $R_i(P)$ by recalculating the final relevance score of collection C_j^i at the level of interest i as follows:

$$FinalScore\left(C_j^i\right) = (1 - a) * Score\left(C_j^i\right) + a * Score\left(C_j^{i-1}\right), \exists! C_j^{i-1}\ where$$
$$C_j^i \in Children\left(C_j^{i-1}\right) \tag{8.3}$$

where $Score(C_j^i)$ is the relevance score of collection C_j^i using any source selection algorithm (as previously mentioned, CORI in this case), $Score\left(C_j^{i-1}\right)$ is the relevance score of collection C_j^{i-1} (the ancestral collection of C_j^i) using CORI and a is the mixturing parameter that determines the weight that each level will have.

Overall the multilayer method uses a normalisation procedure and re-ranking process which takes into account the source selection results produced from DIR methods at several classification levels. Of course, as it has been already mentioned, the proposed method can recursively utilise multiple evidence in all levels of the classification scheme, but in this chapter, we focus on level 3 (subclass), level 4 (main group) and level 5 (subgroup). From a conceptual point of view, score aggregations like the one used in our method have been proposed for other forms of structured retrieval (e.g. XML retrieval and hierarchical classification). Structured documents containing multiple metadata can be considered as having an internal hierarchical structure.

The multilayer method has been experimentally tested in a series of ad hoc experiments [45, 58] but also evaluated in user-based experiments. The results of the method as a classification search mechanism were very encouraging but also the retrieval results when using the selected IPC as the target resources for DIR search were very effective as the DIR approach we proposed was very competitive in the patentability/novelty search task organised in CLEF-IP 2012 and CLEF-IP 2013 labs. Also it is important to mention the DIR methods we applied performed similar to or better than our centralised approaches.

The multilayer method has been evaluated in a user-centred study of a Web-based system that can automatically suggest classification codes with the aim to assist patent examiners on the task of patent classification [59]. The aim of the study was twofold. Firstly, we obtained a better understanding of the search tactics patent examiners apply when they do classification search. Secondly, we examined the effect of searching at different levels of the classification scheme on classification search performance. The results have shown that the multilayer classification search method performed better when compared to a widely used classification search system (classification search provided from the EPO's Espacenet service).

8.5 Discussion

The difficulty of patent search becomes apparent if we consider the volume of the technical (potentially multilingual) literature which is increasing rapidly and the different resources that need to searched. But the difficulty is not just the volume of information which possibly comes in different languages. If we consider more the cognitive approaches to search and the various aspects of the different patent search tasks (task types and task stage, level of knowledge, complexity and difficulty of the task, experience and ability of the searcher), the aim of designing a patent search system which can provide strategic support becomes a demanding challenge.

For example, a search for prior art should retrieve the best available prior art documents and must be done efficiently. Another task is when confronting the claims of a patent. Criteria for selecting which patent resources to search and which technical tools to use must be established. But it is not only where and what to search. A strategy for carrying out the search has to be also established [60]. But not only that, we know from different studies of search models that the search strategy, the current state of searcher's knowledge, the process and the criteria should be continuously revised and updated [61–63]. For example, we know that users at the beginning of their tasks are less likely to start their initial queries by introducing all the search terms [64].

Users working within this complex information workplace should have at their disposal multiple patent resources but also search tools and interfaces. This view expresses a user-centred and highly interactive approach to information seeking. Federated search, for a number of reasons, can become an important technology to develop information-seeking environments that can satisfy the aforementioned requirements. The first is because it is the technological solution which can combine effectively results from multiple patent resources which are developed independent from each other. This feature is very important in the highly dynamic world of innovation and patents where increased coverage and searching many datasets—sometimes in different languages—can be crucial. The cost of crawling and maintaining (updating) a centralised index of all patents produced worldwide is tremendous. This cost can be substantially reduced using federated patent search systems.

Another important benefit when using a federated patent search system is that it can provide a single point of search and a unified interface for searching multiple resources. The same query can be formulated once and be submitted to many patent resources. Using federated search multiple results will be retrieved, duplicates can be removed, efficient merging into a single list can be produced, and grouping and filtering of the single merged list are possible. This can be a tremendous time saver for general-purpose prior art search, whether the end user is a patent examiner, patent attorney, commercial patent searcher, patent liaison or IP librarian.

The second important idea that federated search can deliver is that it provides the general framework to integrate multiple search tools. In that way different search tools can become part of a federated search system exploiting several existing IR and natural language processing (NLP) technologies (e.g. query expansion, cluster/classification recommendation, faceted search, query translation). Most definitions found in the information retrieval (IR) literature converge to use the term 'integrated' to define search systems that simultaneously access a number of different data sources providing a single point of search. This view is much more compatible with a more 'traditional' federated search view that focuses on the simultaneous search of multiple resources. In this article we wish to expand the design space of federated search by adding the term 'integrated' to define federated search system designs where not only multiple remote resources are searched in parallel, but also multiple search tools can be used (in parallel or in a pipeline).

PerFedPat is based on the above principles and has this key objective: integrate a set of patent resources and search tools to enable effective support of the different stages and users during the patent search process. The tools in PerFedPat are used in isolation to support basic actions (e.g. the query tool to construct a query). However, they can be used also 'in parallel' or in a pipeline with other tools to support higher-level search activities such as tactics, stratagems and strategies [65].

It is also important to point out that the open architecture of PerFedPat allows its straightforward extension and customisation. New patent resources can be added if they support an API but also if they are searchable over the Web. There are also abstract wrappers for Solr-based search systems and tools exist for resources without proper APIs. It is not only possible, but it is straightforward to integrate new services or extend the functionality of existing tools. Adding a new service is usually done by implementing a new agent.

8.6 Conclusions

Professional search in the patent domain usually needs both an analytical and an exploratory type of search which is characterised more often, in comparison to fact finding and question answering Web search, by recall-oriented information needs and sometimes by uncertainty and evolution or change of the information need. Additionally, the complexity of the tasks which need to be performed by professional searchers, which usually include not only retrieval but also information analysis and monitoring tasks, requires association, pipelining and possibly integration of information as well as synchronisation and coordination of multiple and potentially concurrent search views produced from different datasets, search tools and UIs.

Federated search can become an important technology for developing patent search systems that could potentially play a useful role in some particular settings, when crawling and maintenance of a centralised index are not possible. But this is not the only benefit that federated search can deliver for patent searching. The PerFedPat system was also inspired by the design idea of providing an integrated patent search system which will be able to provide a rich information-seeking experience for different types of patent searches, potentially exploiting different search tools.

We believe that PerFedPat demonstrates the feasibility and the applicability of federated search for patent searching. PerFedPat provides core services and operations for being able to search multiple online patent resources (currently Espacenet, Google patents, Patentscope and the MAREC collection), thus providing a unified single-point access to multiple patent sources while hiding complexity from the end user. More patent resources can easily be made part of the PerFedPat federation to increase coverage or for reasons of specialised searches that some patent systems may provide.

Federated search represents a new approach for patent retrieval. The effectiveness, efficiency and usability of this approach need to be systematically evaluated before we can draw a final conclusion. We have recently conducted a survey amongst patent professionals that indicated a promising degree of acceptance of the usefulness of a federated search system like PerFedPat. Of course further experimental work and use of federated search systems are needed to determine the extent to which such systems actually match professional searchers' needs and requirements and also the needs of the people that work in R&D and they need to do prior art search and easily search multiple datasets and patent resources.

In conclusion we feel that federated search and systems such as PerFedPat represent a promising approach for patent retrieval and therefore could play an important role in the development of next-generation patent search systems.

Acknowledgements The research leading to these results has received funding from the European Union Seventh Framework Programme (FP7/2007–2013) under grant agreement n° 275522 (PerFedPat). Also the COST Action on Multilingual and Multifaceted Interactive Information Access (MUMIA) has provided a fruitful research networking support for some of the research described in this article.

References

1. Lupu M, Mayer K, Tait J, Trippe AJ (2011) Current challenges in patent information retrieval, vol 29. Springer, Berlin
2. Lupu M, Hanbury A (2013) Patent retrieval. Found Trends Inf Retr 7(1):1–97
3. Krier M, Zaccà F (2002) Automatic categorisation applications at the European patent office. World Pat Inf 24(3):187–196
4. Wolter B (2012) It takes all kinds to make a world – some thoughts on the use of classification in patent searching. World Pat Inf 34(1):8–18
5. Masiakowski P, Wang S (2013) Integration of software tools in patent analysis. World Pat Inf 35(2):97–104
6. Salampasis M, Hanbury A (2014) PerFedPat: an integrated federated system for patent search. World Pat Inf 38:4–11
7. Shokouhi M, Si L (2011) Federated search. Found Trends Inf Retr 5(1):1–102
8. Crestani F, Markov I (2013) Distributed information retrieval and applications. In: Proceedings of the 35th European conference on advances in information retrieval, vol 7814, pp 865–868
9. Thomas P (2012) To what problem is distributed information retrieval the solution? J Am Soc Inf Sci Technol 63(7):1471–1476
10. Arguello J, Diaz F, Callan J, Crespo J-F (2009) Sources of evidence for vertical selection. In: Proceedings of the 32nd international ACM SIGIR conference on research and development in information retrieval, pp 315–322
11. Blanco R, Cambazoglu BB, Junqueira FP, Kelly I, Leroy V (2011) Assigning documents to master sites in distributed search. In: Proceedings of the 20th ACM international conference on information and knowledge management – CIKM '11, p 67
12. Lu J, Callan J (2006) Full-text federated search of text-based digital libraries in peer-to-peer networks. Inf Retr 9(4):477–498
13. Meng W, Yu C, Liu K-L (2002) Building efficient and effective metasearch engines. ACM computing surveys 34(1):48–89

14. Baeza-Yates R, Castillo C, Junqueira F, Plachouras V, Silvestri F (2007) Challenges on distributed web retrieval. In: 2007 IEEE 23rd international conference on data engineering, pp 6–20
15. Raghavan S, Garcia-Molina H (2001) Crawling the hidden web. In: Proceedings of the international conference on very large data bases, vol 251, no 1, pp 129–138
16. Avrahami TT, Yau L, Si L, Callan J (2006) The FedLemur project: federated search in the real world. J Am Soc Inf Sci Technol 57(3):347–358
17. Willett P (1988) Recent trends in hierarchic document clustering: a critical review. Inf Process Manag 24(5):577–597
18. Salampasis M, Hanbury A (2013) A generalized framework for integrated professional search systems. In: Proceedings of the the 6th information retrieval facility conference 2013
19. Callan J, Connell M (2001) Query-based sampling of text databases. ACM Trans Inf Syst 19(2):97–130
20. Gravano L, García-Molina H, Tomasic A (1999) GlOSS: text-source discovery over the Internet. ACM Trans Database Syst 24(2):229–264
21. Khelghati M, Hiemstra D, van Keulen M (2012) Size estimation of non-cooperative data collections. In: Proceedings of the 14th international conference on information integration and web-based applications & services – IIWAS '12, p 239
22. Gravano L, Ipeirotis PG, Sahami M (2003) QProber: a system for automatic classification of hidden-Web databases. ACM Trans Inf Syst 21(1):1–41
23. Hawking D, Thistlewaite P (1999) Methods for information server selection. ACM Trans Inf Syst 17(1):40–76
24. Liu K-L, Yu C, Meng W (2002) Discovering the representative of a search engine. In: Proceedings of the eleventh international conference on information and knowledge management, pp 652–654
25. Si L, Callan J (2003) Relevant document distribution estimation method for resource selection. In: Proceedings of the 26th annual international ACM SIGIR conference on research and development in information retrieval SIGIR 03, p 298
26. Callan JP, Lu Z, Croft WB (1995) Searching distributed collections with inference networks. In: Proceedings of the 18th annual international ACM SIGIR conference on research and development in information retrieval – SIGIR '95, pp 21–28
27. French JC, Powell AL, Callan J, Viles CL, Emmitt T, Prey KJ, Mou Y (1999) Comparing the performance of database selection algorithms. In: Proceedings of the 18th annual international ACM SIGIR conference on research and development in information retrieval – SIGIR 99, pp 238–245
28. Si L, Jin R, Callan JP, Ogilvie P (2002) A language modeling framework for resource selection and results merging. In: ACM CIKM 02, pp 391–397
29. Fuhr N (1999) A decision-theoretic approach to database selection in networked IR. ACM Trans Inf Syst 17(3):229–249
30. Markov I, Crestani F (2014) Theoretical, qualitative, and quantitative analyses of small-document approaches to resource selection. ACM Trans Inf Syst 32(2):1–37
31. Shokouhi M (2007) Central-rank-based collection selection in uncooperative distributed information retrieval. Adv Inf Retr 4425:160–172
32. Paltoglou G, Salampasis M, Satratzemi M (2009) Simple adaptations of data fusion algorithms for source selection. In: Proceedings of the 31th European conference on IR research on advances in information retrieval, pp 497–508
33. Powell AL, French JC (2003) Comparing the performance of collection selection algorithms. ACM Trans Inf Syst 21(4):412–456
34. Larkey LS (1999) A patent search and classification system. In: Proceedings of the fourth ACM conference on digital libraries – DL '99, pp 179–187
35. Markov I, Arampatzis A, Crestani F (2013) On CORI results merging, vol 7814. Springer, Berlin
36. Si L, Callan J (2003) A semisupervised learning method to merge search engine results. ACM Trans Inf Syst 21(4):457–491

37. Paltoglou G, Salampasis M, Satratzemi M (2007) Results merging algorithm using multiple regression models, vol 4425. Springer, Berlin
38. Shokouhi M, Zobel J (2009) Robust result merging using sample-based score estimates. ACM Trans Inf Syst 27(3):1–29
39. Whitman K (2011) Intellogist: an online community dedicated to comparing major patent search systems. World Pat Inf 33(2):168–179
40. Stock M, Stock WG (2006) Intellectual property information: a comparative analysis of main information providers. J Am Soc Inf Sci Technol 57(13):1794–1803
41. Hristidis V, Ruiz E, Hernández A, Farfán F, Varadarajan R (2010) Patents searcher. In: Proceedings of the 3rd international workshop on Patent information retrieval – PaIR '10, p 33
42. Salampasis M, Fuhr N, Hanbury A, Lupu M, Larsen B, Strindberg H (2013) Advances in information retrieval, vol 7814. Springer, Berlin
43. Si L, Callan J, Cetintas S, Yuan H (2007) An effective and efficient results merging strategy for multilingual information retrieval in federated search environments. Inf Retr Boston 11(1):1–24
44. Fuhr N (2011). An infrastructure for supporting the evaluation of interactive information retrieval. In: Proceedings of the 2011 workshop on data infrastructures for supporting information retrieval evaluation (DESIRE). ACM, New York, pp 1–2. doi: http://dx.doi.org/10.1145/2064227.2064245
45. Salampasis M, Paltoglou G, Giahanou A (2012) Report on the CLEF-IP 2012 experiments: search of topically organized patents. In: CLEF (Online Working Notes/Labs/Workshop)
46. Genesereth MR, Ketchpel SP (1994) Software agents. Commun ACM 37(7):48ff
47. Dirnberger D (2011) A guide to efficient keyword, sequence and classification search strategies for biopharmaceutical drug-centric patent landscape searches – a human recombinant insulin patent landscape case study. World Pat Inf 33(2):128–143
48. Fafalios P, Salampasis M, Tzitzikas Y (2013) Exploratory patent search with faceted search and (configurable) entity mining. In: Proceedings of the integrating IR technologies for professional search (in conjuction with ECIR 2013), Moscow, Russia
49. Kitsos I, Fafalios P, Marketakis Y, Baldassarre C, Salampasis M, Tzitzikas Y (2016) Web searching with entity mining at query time. In: Multidisciplinary information retrieval, vol 7356. Springer, Berlin/Heidelberg, pp 73–88. http://link.springer.com/chapter/10.1007/978-3-642-31274-8_6
50. Chen A, Gey FC (2003) Experiments on cross-language and patent retrieval at NTCIR-3 workshop. In: Proceedings of the 3rd NTCIR workshop, Japan
51. Goto I, Lu B, Chow KP, Sumita E, Tsou BK (2011) Overview of the patent machine translation task at the ntcir-9 workshop. In: Proceedings of NTCIR, vol 9, pp 559–578
52. Harris C, Arens R, Srinivasan P (2011) Using classification code hierarchies for patent prior art searches. In: Lupu M, Mayer K, Tait J, Trippe AJ (eds) Current challenges in patent information retrieval SE - 14, vol 29. Springer, Berlin, pp 287–304
53. Cetintas S, Si L (2012) Effective query generation and postprocessing strategies for prior art patent search. J Am Soc Inf Sci Technol 63(3):512–527
54. Vijvers WG (1990) The international patent classification as a search tool. World Pat Inf 12(1):26–30
55. Adams S (2000) Using the international patent classification in an online environment. World Pat Inf 22(4):291–300
56. Chen Y-L, Chiu Y-T (2011) An IPC-based vector space model for patent retrieval. Inf Process Manag 47(3):309–322
57. Salampasis M, Giachanou A, Paltoglou G (2013) Multilayer collection selection and search of topically organized patents. In: Proceedings of the integrating IR technologies for professional search (in conjuction with ECIR 2013), pp 48–56
58. Giachanou A, Salampasis M, Paltoglou G (2013) Multilayer collection selection and search of topically organized patents. In: Proceedings of the integrating IR technologies for professional search (in conjuction with ECIR 2013), Moscow, Russia

59. Giachanou A, Salampasis M, Satratzemi M, Samaras N (2014) A user-centered evaluation of a web based patent classification tool. In: Proceedings of the workshop "Beyond single-shot text queries: bridging the gap(s) between research communities" co-located with iConference 2014

60. Oltra-Garcia R (2012) Efficient situation specific and adaptive search strategies: training material for new patent searchers. World Pat Inf 34(1):54–61

61. Bates MJ (1979) Information search tactics. J Am Soc Inf Sci 30(4):205–214

62. Fuhr N (2008) A probability ranking principle for interactive information retrieval. Inf Retr Boston 11(3):251–265

63. Belkin NJ (1980) Anomalous states of knowledge as a basis for information retrieval. Can J Inf Sci 5(1):133–143

64. Vakkari P, Hakala N (2000) Changes in relevance criteria and problem stages in task performance. J Doc 56(5):540–562

65. Bates MJ (1979) Idea tactics. J Am Soc Inf Sci 30(5):280–289

Chapter 9
The Portability of Three Types of Text Mining Techniques into the Patent Text Genre

Linda Andersson, Allan Hanbury, and Andreas Rauber

Abstract In this book chapter, we examined the portability of several different well-known text mining techniques on patent text. We test the techniques by addressing three different relation extraction applications: acronym extraction, hyponymy extraction and factoid entity relation extraction. These applications require different types of natural language processing tools, from simple regular expression matching (acronym extraction), to part of speech and phrase chunking (hyponymy extraction), to a full-blown dependency parser (factoid extraction). With the relation extraction applications presented in this chapter, we want to elucidate the requirements needed of general natural language processing tools when deployed on patent text for a specific extraction task. On the other hand, we also present language technology methods which are already portable to the patent genre with no or only moderate adaptations to the text genre.

9.1 Introduction

Patent text mining involves all kinds of applications from general terminology extraction [47] to text summarisation [15]. The common denominator is that they all aim to support the intellectual property (IP) community in searching and analysing patent data. Several researchers have made attempts to deploy text mining techniques on patent documents, but most of the previous text mining experiments have been limited in terms of domain expertise and adaptability [40]. Furthermore, in view of the potential end tools, i.e. being support tools for patent experts, regardless of their technical fields of specialisation [29], the text mining techniques

L. Andersson (✉) • A. Hanbury • A. Rauber
TU Wien, Vienna, Austria
e-mail: linda.andersson@tuwien.ac.at; andersson@tuwien.ac.at; allan.hanbury@tuwien.ac.at; hanbury@ifs.tuwien.ac.at; andreas.rauber@tuwien.ac.at; rauber@ifs.tuwien.ac.at

© Springer-Verlag GmbH Germany 2017   241
M. Lupu et al. (eds.), *Current Challenges in Patent Information Retrieval*,
The Information Retrieval Series 37, DOI 10.1007/978-3-662-53817-3_9

and also the natural language processing (NLP) tools used in the pipeline are required to handle all types of vocabularies as well as syntactic constructions and not just for a specific subdomain as in [12, 16, 26, 67].

Tseng et al. [67] presented several text mining feasibility studies on a smaller set of patent documents (92 documents). They deployed several well-known text mining techniques such as text segmentation, summary extraction, feature selection, term association, cluster generation, topic identification and information mapping. Their aim was to show that it is possible to use text mining techniques to assist in the patent analysis process. They kept the usage of the NLP tools to a minimum in these experiments, since they wanted to avoid a decrease in performance of the final text mining applications caused by errors introduced by the NLP. On the other hand, by avoiding the usage of NLP tools, they also limited themselves in terms of outcome and possible applications. Contrary to Tseng et al., we focus on the portability of text mining techniques to the patent domain by investigating each technique's portability level and not just the outcome of the experiments themselves. We will reuse already well-known text mining techniques with minimal or no relabelling effort at all, in order to avoid extensive retraining.

The objective of this chapter is to demonstrate the issues involved in the portability to the patent domain of the following relation extraction (RE) applications:

- General pattern matching algorithms commonly used in computational linguistics to extract acronyms (RE 1)
- General lexico-syntactic pattern (LSP) algorithms used to extract hyponymy relationships (RE 2) [31]
- Factoid extraction using dependency parsing information, where the task is to identify the subject of a quantity (i.e. the aim here is to create RDF triples consisting of the main semantic subject governing the temperature quantity, e.g. *medium washing solution* in the sentence: *The medium washing solution boils at* 90 °C) (RE 3)

We show that RE 1 and 2 techniques are already portable into the patent domain with very few, if any, adaptations. Meanwhile, for RE 3 significantly more work is required in terms of establishing in-domain training data for NLP tools. The gap between source (news text) and target data (patent text) for NLP tools needs to be recognised by the industry and the research communities, as well as the funding agencies. The only large domain-specific corpus that exists today, openly available to researchers, is the GENIA corpus of biomedical text. The patent genre, however, covers many more technology domains, for which no in-domain training data is freely available.

The rest of this chapter is organised as follows: In Sect. 9.2 we give an extensive introduction into the disciplines associated with NLP as well as into the patent text mining field. In Sect. 9.3 we present our three case studies and in Sect. 9.4 we discuss results and future work.

9.2   Theoretical Background

Text mining, like data mining or knowledge discovery, is a process to discover implicit knowledge and potentially useful patterns from large text collection. Many text mining applications require some kind of language technologies. The generic term *language technology* (LT) is associated with computational linguistics, corpus linguistics, speech technologies and NLP. For all of these disciplines and subdisciplines, it is important to use a well-thought through pre-processing pipeline, composed of cleaning and normalising text.

9.2.1   Pre-processing

This section is a brief summary, which only describes the central issues regarding the normalisation process of raw text. The first two main transformation steps are token detection and sentence detection [28]. There are two types of tokens: one addresses the rhetorical structure of a sentence (e.g. commas, punctuations, digits, etc.), while the other token type (words and letter strings) will undergo linguistic analysis. Removal of digit sequences, commas and punctuations needs to be carefully thought through, since it can have consequences on succeeding processes. For instance, commas can function as clause binders (e.g. *While she was cooking, her friend arrived*) and numeration binders (e.g. . . .*mixtures of saturated hydrocarbon compounds, alicyclic hydrocarbons, aromatic hydrocarbons, etc.*). Commas can also be part of a chemical compound (e.g. *2,5-bis-amidinophenyl furan-bis-0-4-fluorophenyl*). For the RE 2 and RE 3 applications, the commas related to numeration or part of a chemical compound are important to detect in order to extract the sought information.

Also the definition of what a token should be (i.e. a non-empty string of characters) will affect the performance of the text mining application [2]. For example, digits can be considered as non-tokens along with ASCII characters like punctuation marks or spaces. Digits removal on patent text will destroy chemical compounds (e.g. furan-bis-0-4-fluorophenyl) which describe a significant type of substance.

Another tokenisation problem is the question whether the hyphen should qualify as a token separator or not. This is particularly important for automatic query formulation of patent topics [49]. Considering the hyphen as a token separator yields higher recall values while not using it as a separator gives higher precision values in ad hoc IR [2].

On the sentence level, there are also other non-letter characters which need special attention. The sentence detector will be affected by the decisions made during the tokenisation process design. For example, before sentence detection, the ambiguity of the period sign needs to be resolved.

```
CELLULAR COMMUNICATIONS INC. sold 1,5500,000
common shares at $21.75 each yesterday, according
to lead underwriter L.F. Rothschild & Co.
```

Fig. 9.1 Sentence example 2, period ambiguity [41, p. 2]

Figure 9.1 shows a case where the period markers have several functions: digits marker for decimals (*$21.75*), abbreviation markers (*L.F.*) and full stop. The period marker in *Co.* functions both as an abbreviation marker and as a sentence boundary marker (a full stop). There are several techniques which can be used to disambiguate period markers, for example, a pre-defined lexicon or a set of regular expressions [28, 41]. Both methods have their limitations: the lexicon is limited by its coverage, while regular expression tends to over-generate positive instances. In order to correctly detect periods marking sentence boundaries, we first need to distinguish them from periods, which are part of abbreviations. This is important in the patent discourse, since abbreviations—especially acronyms—are frequently occurring in patent text. As a consequence, acronym detection is not only a target application in itself, but it will also in the future contribute to the performance of the sentence detection process for patent text.

To summarise, the pre-processing of the raw text conducted before applying linguistic analyses is essential and the decisions made during pre-process will have consequences for the succeeding analyses.

9.2.2 Training Data for Natural Language Processing

Until the mid-1980s, most of the NLP tools produced were based upon handwritten rules. With increasingly available computer power and storage, a shift was made to using machine learning (ML) algorithms. However, it was the introduction of digitised annotated text corpora that made the shift possible, since the discriminative learning algorithms (the majority of NLP tools) require linguistic annotation (i.e. labelled data) to learn the sought-after entities [9]. Even methods associated with the recent trend in deep learning , which learn from unlabelled data [22], still require ground truth (i.e. labelled data) for evaluation.

There are several important corpus projects which made the shift from rule-based methods to ML methods possible for the English language: the Brown Corpus,[1] the Lancaster-Oslo/Bergen Corpus (LOB),[2] the British National Corpus (BNC)[3] and the Penn Treebank (PTB) [51]. The PTB corpus is manually corrected and contains part of speech (PoS) tags, phrase chunks and constituent information (see Fig. 9.2).

---

[1] http://clu.uni.no/icame/brown/bcm.html.

[2] http://clu.uni.no/icame/lob/lob-dir.html.

[3] http://www.natcorp.ox.ac.uk/.

```
(ROOT
  (S
    (NP (NNP Economic)  (NN news))
    (VP (VBD had)
        (NP
         (NP (JJ little)  (NN effect))
         (PP (IN on)
            (NP (JJ financial)  (NNS markets)))))
    (. .)))
```

Fig. 9.2 Constituent information

It is a corpus without noise (e.g. OCR errors, abbreviation variations) specifically designed to train NLP tools [51].

For domain-specific text, there exist only two large domain-specific corpora with linguistic annotation (accessible to the research community): the GENIA[4] corpus and the PennBioIE[5] collection. GENIA consists of 2000 MEDLINE abstracts sampled from MeSH terms *human*, *blood cells* and *transcription factor*. The corpus has approximately 400,000 words and more than 100,000 annotations for biological terms. The PennBioIE was created as a resource to train ML algorithms for information extraction (IE) and IR [46]. The corpus consists of 1414 MEDLINE abstracts on cancer and on the CYP protein family. It contains approximately 327,000 annotated words.

The increase in computer processing power made it possible in the 1990s to shift from rule-based methods to discriminative learning algorithms. Now another shift is emerging, going from supervised learning to unsupervised learning (learning from unlabelled data) with the deep learning methods. However, the bottleneck for domain-specific text genres still remains: we still need a ground truth in order to evaluate our new methods regardless of how we learned the sought entities.

9.2.3 Part of Speech (PoS)-Tagger, Chunker and Parser

We will discuss three core types of NLP tools—PoS-tagger, phrase chunker and parser—required in order to perform many text mining applications, e.g. named entity recognition (NER), natural language understanding (NLU), relation extraction (RE) and question and answering (Q&A).

A **PoS-tagger** assigns each word in a sentence a PoS-tag [35]. No internal relations between the words of a sentence are given.

---

[4]http://www.geniaproject.org/.

[5]https://catalog.ldc.upenn.edu/LDC2008T21.

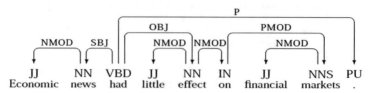

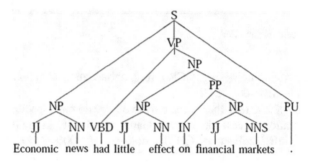

Fig. 9.3 General dependency parser

Fig. 9.4 A sentence represented in a phrase structure grammar tree

Chunking involves two main functions: (1) identification of proper chunks (phrases) and (2) assigning grammatical classes to identified chunks such as verb phrase (VP), noun phrase (NP), preposition phrase (PP), adjective phrase (JJ), etc. Phrases could be nested within larger phrases and are part of larger units such as sub-clauses, clauses and sentences. In order to train a chunker, phrase boundaries of a sentence need to be given (see Fig. 9.2).

The best performing supervised method for chunking achieves recall of 95.62 %, precision at 95.93 % and an F1 score at 95.77 % on the Computational Language Learning (CoNLL) 2000 data set[6] [45]. In [22] a method using neural network was proposed for learning chunks from mostly unlabelled data but recognising sentence structures. The method achieved an F1 score at 90.33 % on the CoNLL 2000 data set.

Parsers assign different types of syntactic relations between words in a sentence [17, 35] as seen in Figs. 9.3 and 9.4. Parsers require a PoS-tagger, phrase chunker and constituent information. There are three main syntactic ideas used in parsing: dependency, grammatical syntactic relation and subcategorisation.

A dependency parser refers to the notion that the syntactic structure of a sentence consists of binary asymmetrical relations between the words of the sentence [17, 24, 35]. Here, *valency* is a central concept referring to semantic predicate argument structures for different classes of words, especially verbs, but also nouns and adjectives. The idea is that a sentence is organised as a whole, whose constituent elements are words, and between the words and their neighbours, the arcs show

---

[6]The CoNLL 2000 data set consists of a subset of the PTB http://www.cnts.ua.ac.be/conll2000/chunking/.

dependency connections, where the main verb plays the most important role (see Fig. 9.3). Furthermore, there are generally two basic constraints: a single-head constraint (i.e. each node has at most one head) and a no-cycles constraint, which implies a rooted tree structure.

A syntactic parser also makes use of constituent information, but the focus is word pair relationships. For instance, the link grammar (LG) parser is a syntactic parser of English based on the original theory of English syntax [32, 64]. The first formalisation of constituent information was Chomsky's phrase structure grammar, which is how sentences are represented in the PTB corpus. In NLP a context-free grammar (CFG) is the formalism used to model with constituent information [35]. CFG algorithms form the basis of all approaches to create a hierarchical phrase structure [17] (see Fig. 9.4).

The subcategorisation group consists of parsers that are lexicon driven, such as the combinatory categorial grammar (CCG) parser.

The common denominator for NLP tools (for English) is that they are trained on the same part of the PTB corpus and test on another part of the corpus.

9.2.4 The Limitation of NLP in Out-of-Domain Text

Research involving IR and NLP shows that shallow linguistic methods such as stop word removal or stemming (see Chap. 2) yield significant improvements in terms of recall and precision, while deeper linguistic analyses such as parsing or word sense disambiguation could even decrease performance [14, 25]. Only in-domain-specific IR, in bioinformatics, have deeper linguistic methods improved the retrieval performance [14].

Behind the usage of an NLP application is the assumption that the source data (on which the application was trained) and target data (on which it is applied) have the same feature distribution [69]. Too many unseen events, i.e. words or syntactic constructions only occurring in the target data, will decrease the performance of an NLP application drastically. Therefore, extensive work is generally associated with the domain adaptation of NLP applications, since it involves manual annotation of training data and creation of a ground truth for evaluation. The GENIA[7] project is an example of the amount of resources required in order to adapt NLP applications to a specific text genre such as biomedical and medical [21, 39]. As reported in Sect. 9.2.3, all data-driven PoS-taggers, chunkers and parsers need to be trained on manual (e.g. PTB) or semi-manual (e.g. BNC) established corpora. The limited access to linguistically annotated domain-specific corpora and the assumption that robust and broad coverage NLP applications should be able to parse any type of text without a decrease in performance have contributed to the off-the-shelf usage of NLP applications in any type of text genre [18]. Obviously, the idea of using

---

[7]http://www.nactem.ac.uk/genia/.

robust and broad coverage NLP has great software engineering advantages, but it is reasonable to assume that a domain-adapted NLP application could yield better results than a domain-independent application [11, 70].

Blitzer [9] concluded that the lack of appropriate training data for a PoS-tagger reduces the overall performance of a text mining application. He examined how a PoS-tagger in a pipelined process for a parser decreased and increased in performance due to differences in source and target data. For a discriminative linear classifier, the domain differences between the source and target data can more than double the error rate [9]. Tsuruoka et al. also demonstrated that PoS-tagger accuracy fluctuated depending upon the composition of the training data [68]. Their aim was to build a robust PoS-tagger for the biomedical text domain; therefore, they first trained and tested the tagger on different parts of existing corpora. For instance, when a PoS-tagger only trained on Wall Street Journal (WSJ) data encounters out-of-domain data, the drop in tagging accuracy is from 97.05 to 85.19%. As the PoS-tagger is an important stage in an NLP pipeline, an increase in error rate here will have severe consequences for succeeding applications using this information. This should be put in the perspective that discriminative PoS-tagger and phrase chunker have been seen as state-of-the-art applications for more than a decade. Furthermore, at the Computational Language Learning (CoNLL) 2007 track[8] for domain adaptation of parsers, the results showed that a smaller amount of training data matching the test data, with just an additionally small amount of non-matching training data, outperformed parsers trained on a larger amount of training data not matching the test data [54].

For new IE tasks, we are confronted with plenty of label data and linguistic observations from the source domains, which do not always correspond with the linguistic characteristics of the target domains. Several studies have addressed this issue and tried to close the gap between existing training data and domain-specific training data. In order to cope with the lack of labelled data for target domains, algorithms such as Structural Correspondence Learning (SCL) [9] have been introduced. Structural learning methods have been successfully applied in domain adaptations of both PoS-taggers and parsers. The objective of the SCL is to match common features (consisting of token triples) between source and target data, which can map general English words to domain-specific words [9]. For instance, the word *signal* in the phrase *normal signal transduction* in the GENIA corpus is a noun, but according to the WSJ,[9] the word will be classified as an adjective. By modelling its features, the word *signal* is revealed to behave similar to words such as *investment* and *buyout*. Consequently, the SCL algorithm reclassifies it as a noun.

A similar idea was later exploited by Collobert et al. [22], where a deep learning method is combined with backpropagation in order to add new instances and correct instances in the look-up tables based upon the semantic characteristic of a token, which was observed in the training data consisting of a large amount of unlabelled

---

[8]CoNLL 2007 data set is composed of WSJ and part of the GENIA corpus.
[9]Part of the PTB corpus.

data. Collobert et al. [22] deployed the deep learning method for four different NLP applications: PoS-tagging, chunking, NER and semantic role labelling (SRL). They reported performance matching the existing state-of-the-art techniques for PoS-tagging (accuracy of 97.29 % benchmark 97.24 %) and for chunking (F1 score at 94.34 % benchmark at 94.29 %).

All of these emerging techniques look promising, since we can, in the learning step, reduce the need of labelled data. To our knowledge, there exists no ground truth or labelled training data covering all the technical fields of the patent text genre.

9.2.5   Reuse of NLP Tools in Patents

Due to the lack of suitable training data for NLP tools targeting the entire patent text genre, the patent text mining studies reported in the literature have used off-the-shelf NLP tools, conducted minor rule-based modifications targeting specific errors [3] or just experimented on a subset of the patent text genre [5, 26, 44, 74].

We can divide the NLP tools usage in patent text mining studies into two main categories: in order to improve the tool itself [3, 16] or in order to improve an end application [4, 5, 25, 26, 53, 77]. Many end-application experiments, from prior art search to terminology extraction, have tried to address different patent text mining problems by applying linguistic knowledge and using broad-coverage NLP tools [5, 40, 50, 53, 77]. In the end-application studies, NLP tools have either been given a moderate domain adaption [4] or just been used as off-the-shelf modules [50]. Mahdabi et al. [50] used the Stanford PoS-tagger as an off-the-shelf module in order to extract noun phrases (NPs) for query expansion and query generation. In their experiments, only linguistically correct sequences were accepted as input to the query formulation module, which made the method less flexible and several NPs were overlooked due to PoS-tagger errors. Andersson et al. [4] modified the Stanford PoS-tagger and the NP base chunker [60], correcting observed errors associated with noun phrases boundaries, in order to harvest hyponymy relations in medical, patent and mathematical text.

Studies conducted within the PatExpert project have methodically investigated the decrease in performance when using general NLP applications on patent text [11–13, 16, 26]. Burga [16] reported a parser trained on a part of the CoNLL 2007 test collection significantly dropped in performance when tested on patent text compared to when tested on another part of the CoNLL 2007 test collection. Many of the errors made by the parser were caused by errors made by the PoS-tagger used. This observation was also reported in Sect. 9.2.4: if PoS-taggers are not adapted to the text domain, all succeeding linguistic analyses (chunking and parsing) will be affected by the errors made by the PoS-tagger [9].

In the PHASAR patent retrieval system [43], a domain-adapted parser (AEGIR) is integrated into the pipeline. The AEGIR parser is an extension of CFG formalism, adapted to parse robust for IR. The PHASAR system has integrated linguistic notation into the search mechanism itself, uses linguistic information and displays linguistic knowledge to the searcher. The searchers are allowed to specify different semi-syntactic relations (e.g. [aspirin SUBJ cause]), between search terms. .

D'hondt [25] used dependency triples in different patent classification experiments (see also Chap. 11 in this volume). As a single feature the dependency triples did not improve over unigrams (baseline), due to the complexity found in NPs and the limitations of the parser. The phrase sparseness and complexity of NP found in patent text give a plausible explanation as to why the performance decreases when only the dependency triples in the CLEF-IP 2011 prior art search task were used.

To conclude, even if projects or studies started off using NLP applications as off-the-shelf-modules, in the end most researchers concluded that to some extent domain adaptation is required.

9.2.6 The Characteristics of the Patent Genre

We briefly discuss the bibliographic data that is assigned to each patent document and how this information can be used in text mining applications, in order to enrich the end applications. However, most of this section will be an in-depth discussion on the linguistic characteristic of the patent text in terms of rhetorical structure, syntax and terminology usage, since the aim of this section is to give the reader an insight to the challenges text mining techniques are confronted with when used on patent text.

All patents contain a rich set of metadata such as citation (citing prior art), assignee (person or company), inventor (persons), address, language information, filing country, patent family information and classification schemas. Details about all of these were discussed at large in the first chapter of this volume.

The classification schemas disambiguate otherwise ambiguous words and phrases, as well as concepts when deployed in different technical fields [1, 37]. For example, the technical term *ferromagnetic tag* can be part of an emergency braking system for trains or a part of an alarm device to prevent shoplifting [1, p. 15]. The classification schema makes it possible for the searcher to select and distinguish which deployment of *ferromagnetic tag* she is interested in.

9.2.6.1 The Linguistic Characteristics of Patent Text

Rhetorically, a patent document consists of four main sections (i.e. title, abstract, description and claim), each with a different communication function. The title and abstract are generally kept short in order to give a brief summary. The description is the target section when assessing the patentability of a new patent, while the claim section assists in determining a prior art patent relevancy as a reference [34].

As text genre, the patent domain is associated with several interesting characteristics: huge differences in length, strictly formalised document structure (both semantic and syntactic), extensive use of acronyms and domain terminology. The use of neologisms is also very high compared to other genres [57]. Furthermore, previous studies have observed that patent writers intentionally try to use entirely different word combinations, not only synonyms but also paraphrasing [7, 30]. Patent writers tend to become their own lexicographer and thereby increase the level of unseen events. In the patent genre, both standard and non-standard acronyms are used [30]. Also the diachronic nature of the patent terms (e.g., *LP record*, *water closet*) could be regarded as instances of obsolescence and therefore considered sparse events [30]. The diachronic aspect of the patent text genre contributes not only to sparse events but also to changes in terminology, where one term refers to a technical concept during a certain time period and thereafter switches to represent another.

In addition to the above-mentioned issues, the morphological variation increases in patents due to the high number of chemical formulae and morphological variation of foreign spelling, e.g. *sulfur–sulphur* and *aluminum–aluminium*. However, the morphological variation differs within the patent collection itself, as Oostdijk et al. [56] observed by measuring the Hapax legomena.[10] Consequently, in technical text associated with chemical substances such as biomedicine, chemistry, etc., chemical compounds need to be identified and normalised. Meanwhile, text from the computer and telecommunication industries requires that acronyms and algorithms (mathematical formulae and program code) are identified and normalised. The mentioned problems can be categorised as unseen event issues, which NLP tools in general have difficulties handling and the common method to sort out unseen event issues is to increase the lexical coverage.

On the other hand, in a comparative linguistic study, Verberne et al. [73] observed that in terms of individual token coverage, there is no significant difference between general English vocabulary and the English vocabulary used in patent claims. In order to get a general idea of the lexical coverage, Verberne et al. compared the COBUILD corpus with a patent corpus of 10,000 documents using the CLEX lexicon (160,568 English terms) as the lexicon. For COBUILD, the token coverage of CLEX was 92 % and for the patent corpus the token coverage was 95.9 %. Verberne et al. concluded that since there is no significant difference between general English and the English used in patent claims on single token coverage, the (new) technical terminology is more likely introduced on multi-word level in terms of complex NPs. Complex NPs contribute to more syntactically complex sentence construction. In [72], patent claim sentences were compared with sentences of general English language resources. They observed that the sentences of patent claims, even when allowing semicolon and colon as sentence boundary identifier, were generally longer than the sentences found in the BNC. The patent sentences had a median of 22 tokens and an average length of 53 tokens and BNC had an average length of 20 tokens; this finding was based upon a sample set consisting of 581k sentences. Also Ferraro [26] reported it is not unusual with sentences in the claim section to consist of 250 tokens. In [77] the average token length per

---

[10]Token occurring only once in an entire collection.

sentence was compared for several corpora: BNC had 19.7; Brown, 21.3; WSJ, 22.4; Wikipedia (English part), 24.3; and a patent collection, 32.4. The patent collection was composed of 561,676 English patents filed at the European Patent Office (EPO) between 1998 and 2008.

The diachronic nature [30] and the vocabulary diversity existing within part of the patent text genre [56] make the genre text more difficult to sample out data in order to establish a training set for text mining applications. What works for one field and time period perhaps does not work for others. Moreover, given the richness and diversity found in the patent genre, where general words are reused in different constellations within different technical fields in order to represent entirely different concepts, simply increasing the lexical coverage will not solve the problem, since token coverage is only part of the problem, for instance, *cell battery* versus *body cell* or *bus slot card* versus *double vehicle bus*: all of these terms consist of common words, but in each specific combination, an entirely different meaning is given, due to the position and relation each word takes in the different NPs.

To summarise, the patent text documents and sentences are more lengthy compared to general news text, but on average there is no significant difference in the vocabulary usage on the word level except for technical fields using chemical formulae, DNA sequence, etc. [56]. The linguistic theoretical explanation for these reported observations would be that technical terms (in English) are multi-word units (MWU) and represented syntactically as complex NPs [16, 57, 73].

9.2.6.2 Linguistic Characteristics of Domain Terminology and Its Effect on General NLP Applications

The majority of entities in technical English dictionaries consist of terms with more than one word [23, 36, 61]. The technical multi-word phrases consist of NPs containing common adjectives, nouns and occasionally prepositions (e.g. 'of'). One of the major mechanisms of word formation is the morphological composite, which allows the formation of compound nouns out of two nouns (e.g. *floppy disk*, *air flow*) [48]. In technical text, the noun compounding strategy is often deployed in order to expand the working vocabulary, without the need of formulating an entirely new word for a new concept [23, 57, 61]. The noun compounds could either be an orthographical unit (e.g. *bookcase*) combined with hyphenation (e.g. *mother-in-law*) or a multi-word unit (MWU) (e.g. *central processing unit*). NPs in patent text are, to a larger extent, composed of MWUs, which make them both longer and more complex than NPs found in a general text genre [16, 77]. Ziering [77] observed that MWUs were predominantly representing technical concepts in a large patent collection (500K), and when including MWU patterns for a terminology extraction application, higher precision was achieved compared to patterns based upon single tokens.

However, the noun compounding strategy causes not only unseen events on the morphological level (words) with new orthographical units, it also generates a diversity of syntactic structures among NPs (e.g. verb participles being used as nouns and adjectives, e.g. *the film coating* and *coated film*), which is problematic for NLP tools [16, 25]. Despite the presence of noun compounds, many NLP applications have chosen to overlook them due to their complexity and flexible nature [6], even though it is well known that any text mining application that extracts knowledge from technical text cannot ignore the complexity of NPs [8]. The complexity of the NPs increases in patent text due to the high density of technical terminology in terms of MWUs. Among the MWUs we sometimes refer to multi-word terms (MWTs), which are phrases characterised by a very strong bond between the words that form them [3, 16, 25]. A MWT generally represents a domain-specific concept, e.g. *bus slot card*, while MWUs include more general phrases such as *the green house* and *the method of coating*. Ultimately, it is the MWTs that are most important and most efforts go in the direction of identifying such terms as opposed to the more generic MWUs [23]. For IR and IE applications, MWTs should in fact be considered terms in the traditional sense (i.e. denoting a specific meaning).

To identify the core technical concept in a complex NP is tricky, since the head noun could consist of a noun compound as in *backup compiler disk*. (Should it be [[backup compiler] disk] or [backup [compiler disk]] or [backup compiler disk]?) Burga et al. [16] reported long chains of nouns in patent text, which make the process of head noun identification complex and recursive. This is cumbersome, especially for a dependency parser, since it needs to define what words in an NP have modifying functions and what noun should be considered the NP's head noun. Noun compound identification has been targeted as a research area for text mining application, since the beginning of the 1980s [23, 36]. However, most of the noun compound identification methods make use of corpus statistic information to create lexicons, which limited their portability to other text genres [8, 57], since each domain-specific text genre has its own usage of a concept [23].

Building blocks of the domain concepts are often common general English words, which are present in almost any text genre, but it is the specific combination that defines the domain-specific concept [23]. Take the concept *bus* in *bus slot card* and in *double vehicle bus*: it has a pathway container function and a transporting function—transporting data or humans between point X and point Y. As seen in Fig. 9.5, the Stanford CoreNLP[11] generates incorrect readings for all three technical terms *bus slot card*, *blood cell count* and *infrared radiation drying*. The main noun compound in *bus slot card* is *slot card* and *bus* is a so-called left expansion (L-Exp) modifier [61]. Instead, the tool identifies two equivalent noun compounds, i.e. *bus card* and *slot card*. For the term *blood cell count*, we have a reverse situation: the word *count* is a right expansion (R-Exp) to the noun compound *blood cell*. Again, the CoreNLP tool generates two different noun compounds: *blood count* and *blood cell*. The issue is related to the grammar the tool is based upon, i.e. a dependency grammar. According to the dependency grammar, a phrase can only have a single word as a main head (as mentioned in Sect. 9.2.3); therefore when a technical term consists of a noun compound nested in a larger NP, the linguistic analysis fails to recognise the correct internal relations between words.

---

[11] http://nlp.stanford.edu:8080/corenlp/.

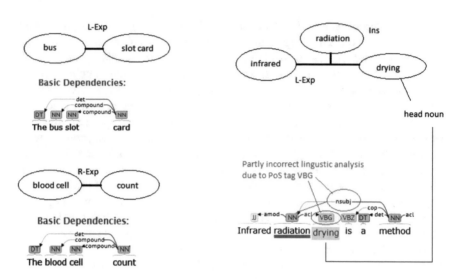

Fig. 9.5 Example of CoreNLP output

For the last example, *infrared radiation drying*, the term *radiation* is an additional pre-modifier referred to as lexical insertion (Ins) to the concept *drying*. The reading will be [[infrared] [radiation] drying], since *infrared* and *radiation* are independent L-Exp pre-modifiers to *drying*. However, the entire NP collapsed due to an incorrect assigned PoS-tag to *drying*. The tagger assigned the wrong tag to the head noun, i.e. *drying* should be NN (noun) not VBG (present participle). Both Andersson [3] and Burga [16] observed this type of error many times in patent text. Participles were especially erroneously identified when acting as adjectives or nouns. A linguistic theoretical explanation to the issue with participles is the fact that most productive word formation of English is affixation, i.e. adding prefixes or suffixes to a root lexeme. The suffixes '-ing' and '-ed' are especially problematic for NLP applications because when they are added to verbs, the new formed word can be a noun, adjective or still a verb. In PTB the participles are generally observed as part of a verb phrase. Consequently, an NP-driven text genre such as the patent text genre, with its high density of technical terminology, will be harmed the most when using general NLP tools in the pipeline [4, 13, 25].

To conclude, MWT identification is important for patent text mining applications compared to other applications on general text. Only part of the information is given by words' single semantic meaning in a complex NP; the other part is given by the internal relationship between a complex NP's elements [8]. To only extract unigrams for patent IE applications would not capture the entire concept [77]. Thus, complex NPs cannot be overlooked by NLP tools in technical text genres such as patent text since they represent the informative content of a domain-specific text.

9.3 Relation Extraction Applications in the Patent Domain

We have so far given an introduction to text normalisation, different NLP techniques as well as linguistic characteristics of patent text. In this section we present three different RE tasks conducted on patent text. Each case study requires different types of NLP techniques in the pre-processing steps. For each case study, we give a brief summary to the state-of-the-art technologies.

We use the classification schema ISI-OST-INPI[12] to visualise the fluctuation in distribution of possible entities in different technical fields within the patent text genre. As mentioned in Sect. 9.2.6.1, the patent text genre is heterogeneous and is composed of a smaller set of subtext genres, which have their own unique linguistic characteristic. As a consequence, the method used for extraction will be unevenly distributed throughout the collection, since the portability depends upon the special linguistic characteristic of the text belonging to a specific technical field. The ISI-OST-INPI classification schema was presented as an alternative classification schema for the IPC, where the 630 subclasses were compressed into 35 scientific related categories [62].

9.3.1 First Case Study: Acronym RE

Acronyms are a result of a highly productive type of term variation, which triggers the need for an acronym dictionary in order to establish association between acronyms and their expanded forms [55]. The major challenges for acronym detection and extraction are term variation (e.g. spelling, morphological, syntactic) and semantic variation (e.g. polysemy, synonymy and homonymy). In technical text, acronyms are for the most part representing a technical concept of some kind, e.g. *flavin adenine dinucleotide* (FAD).

Acronyms are a type of abbreviation made up of the initial letter or letters of other words [76]. Key differences between acronyms and other abbreviations include the lack of symbols such as apostrophe (e.g. *can't*) and period (e.g. *etc.*). Unlike other abbreviations, acronyms are usually introduced in text with its extended form as a MWT, when used for the first time in a discourse. However, acronyms are more ambiguous compared to their corresponding extended forms. Yeats [76] reported that for the acronym *CIA* the Acronym Finder Web site has 27 definitions ranging from *Central Intelligence Agency* to *chemiluminescence immunoassay*. In the local context, the non-uniqueness does not pose a problem, but ambiguity is likely to be an issue if acronyms are extracted from a large heterogeneous collection, such as

---

[12]A classification scheme established by Fraunhofer ISI, Observatoire des Science et Techniques (OST) and the French patent office. http://www.wipo.int/export/sites/www/ipstats/en/statistics/patents/pdf/wipo_ipc_technology.pdf.

patent data. Acronyms that consist of a smaller set of characters are more ambiguous and language dependent, unless they refer to very well-known entities such as UN or USA.

For language technology, abbreviation detection is especially useful for text mining applications [27, 58, 76]. Exploiting acronyms in IR systems increases the number of relevant documents retrieved [75]. However, manually maintaining terminology resources and updating them by integrating neologisms is very difficult, if not based on a continuously systematic extraction of terminology from literature [58].

There exist several methods to address acronym detection and extraction, which can be categorised into two main groups: heuristic and/or rule based [63, 75] and ML based [19]. The first category uses predefined heuristic rules. One well-known rule-based method explores the parenthetical hypotheses, i.e. parenthetical expressions appearing in a text are identified (e.g. *ROM (read-only memory)* or alternatively *read-only memory (ROM)*) [63]. The initial experiment with this algorithm reported 99 % precision and 84 % recall on the Medstract test collection [59]. The second category obtains such rules by applying ML techniques. Chang [19] applied logistic regression to calculate the likelihood of expanded forms from acronym candidates. In order to learn the possible candidates, they enumerated all possible expanded forms for each candidate with the longest common sequence (LCS) [33] formalisation. Their method achieved 80 % precision and 83 % in recall on the Medstract test collection. In one patent study [40], it was observed that when conducting semantic annotation on patent data, acronyms were especially difficult to handle. They therefore deployed the parenthetical extraction method combined with ML in order to extract acronyms from the collection and thereby improve the end application.

9.3.1.1   The Experiment for Acronym RE

The research questions we would like to examine with this experiment are:

- To what extent can we use a well-known method to correctly identify acronyms in patent text?
- Are the detected acronyms a type of technical term or not?
- Can technical term assessments and correctness of acronym extractions be conducted by using crowdsourcing techniques in the future or do the tasks require domain expertise?
- Is it possible to use the ISO-OST-IPNI schema to disambiguate an extracted acronym in order to get only one extended form per acronym and science field?
- Does the distribution pattern of extraction differ between scientific fields according to ISO-OST-IPNI?

In this experiment we reused the method introduced by Schwartz and Hearst [63], which is based upon detection of parentheses. We combined the parentheses method with the LCS used in [33]. We modified LCS using a skipgram of one and a small stop word list consisting of the conjunction 'and' and patterns of digit sequences. We chose not to remove prepositions since they could in fact be part of a technical concept, e.g. *out of band*.

We created a Perl script using the Lingua::Sentence for sentence detection, which is based on code by Koehn and Schroeder [42] for Europarl. We did not add any modification (e.g. allowing sentence split on ':' or ';'), since we wanted to reuse it as an off-the-shelf module. The acronym extraction script was run on the English part of the CLEF-IP 2011 test collection. We extracted 978,001 instances, only excluding all acronyms composed of one letter since they frequently coincide with variables or being part of a formula.

We divided the manual assessment into two main parts consisting of 1000 (×2) and 5000 randomly sampled instances. For the two smaller sample sets, we asked the assessors to evaluate if each extraction was correct according to the snippet of 20 tokens presented along with the extracted short form of an acronym and its extended form and if they consider the concept to be a domain-specific term. Due to duplication in the sample set, the total number of the assessments does not add up to the original sample set as seen in Table 9.1. The two smaller sets were assessed by different groups of assessors: For the first sample set (779), we compared assessments of two experts, a linguist and a domain expert (third year student with major in biology). For the second sample set (903 instances), we used a linguist and a non-expert. The aim of comparing different groups of assessors is to examine if technical term assessments and correctness of acronym extractions could be conducted by using crowdsourcing techniques in the future. In Table 9.1 we present the agreement between the two different assessment groups. For the larger set (5000 instances), we only compared assessments of the linguist and the non-expert and only for correctly detected and extracted acronyms (see Table 9.2). To assess if an acronym was referring to a domain-specific term or not was found to be too time-consuming and difficult.

For assessing the correctness of the extractions for both groups regardless of the sample set, the disagreement quota is less than 1.5 % as seen in Tables 9.1 and 9.2. For assessing if an acronym and its extended form are a technical term, the overall

Table 9.1 Assessment of acronym detection and technical terms for different sample sets

Sample sets	Type of assessment	Assessor comparison	Agreement	Disagreement	Total number of extractions
Small	Technical term	Domain expert vs. linguist	683	94	779
	Number of correctly identified acronyms		770	9	
	Technical term	Non-expert vs. linguist	795	108	903
	Number of correctly identified acronyms		896	7	

Table 9.2 Assessment of acronym detection for the large sample set between linguist and non-expert

Assessment	Linguist	Non-expert
Number of correctly identified acronyms	4865	4396
Number of incorrectly identified acronyms	33	4
Disagreement	25	
Agreement	4375	

Table 9.3 Individual assessments

Type of assessment	Domain expert	Linguist	Non expert
Number of technical terms	725	4303	834
Number of non-technical terms	45	421	51
Number of uncertainty: acronym also a technical term	9	174	18
% uncertainty level: acronym also a technical term (%)	5.8	8.6	5.6
Number of correctly identified acronyms	776	4865	899
Number of incorrectly identified acronyms	3	33	4
Accuracy (%)	99.6	99.3	99.6

disagreement quota was higher. The linguist and the domain expert disagreed on 12 % of the instances, while the linguist and the non-expert disagreed on 11.9 % of the instances. Table 9.3 shows the assessment for each assessor independently of each other.

As seen in Table 9.3, the acronym identification algorithm generates very few false positive instances, and the accuracy quotas for all assessors are over 99 %, similar to the result in [63] for the Medstract test collection. Even if the uncertainty level for assessing if an acronym is a technical term or not is small regardless of expertise and sample set, this task needs further investigation. We asked the assessors what they found most problematic when it came to judging if an extracted instance was referring to a technical concept or not. Chemical compounds and medical terms were the easiest part to assess, while the technical terms related to computer science were more difficult to assess such as FIFO (first in, first out) and LC (line card). Also different measurements, such as *angle of arrival* (AoA), a measurement for determining the direction of propagation of a radio-frequency wave incident on an antenna array, were harder to recognise. The linguist used Wikipedia in order to solve uncertainty for 166 instances, some of them being very particular such as *out of band* and *very large-scale integration*. The most difficult ones were those composed of common general terms such as *roller compact concrete*.

So far we have demonstrated that it is possible to extract acronyms using a well-known acronym detection technique on patent text without any modification. Furthermore, the result shows that it is possible to use crowdsourcing for acronym evaluation. Meanwhile, assessing if an acronym and its extended form refer to a technical concept or not is a much more difficult task and requires more studies.

Table 9.4 Top five acronyms having more than one extended form in a specific category

ISI-OST-INPI category	Median	Mean	Variance	Stddev	Max
Pharmaceuticals	2	5.45	276.95	16.64	884
Biotechnology	2	4.87	142.36	11.93	432
Measurement	1	4.72	139.82	11.82	444
Telecommunications	1	4.44	113.56	10.66	234
Organic fine chemistry	1	4.25	197.04	14.04	774
Analysis of biological materials	1	4.13	87.25	9.34	343

Table 9.5 Acronym extraction distribution by group ISI-OST-INPI by percentage of the total amount of extracted acronyms

ISI-OST-INPI categories	% of each category	Number of category by the %
Pharmaceuticals	8	1
Measurement, biotechnology	7	2
Computer technology, telecommunications, analysis of biological materials	5	3
Digital communication, organic fine chemistry, audio-visual technology	4	3
Medical technology, Basic materials chemistry, other special machines, chemical engineering, optics, macromolecular chemistry polymers	4	3
Surface technology coating, textile-and-paper machines, control, electrical machinery apparatus energy, materials metallurgy, transport, semiconductors, engines–pumps–turbines, basic communication processes, environmental technology, food chemistry	2	11
IT methods for management, mechanical elements, machine tools, other consumer goods, civil engineering, handling, furniture games, thermal processes and apparatus	1	8
Microstructural and nanotechnology	0.2	1

To answer the question, 'is it possible to use the ISO-OST-IPNI schema to disambiguate each extracted acronym in order to get only one extended form per acronym and per scientific field?', we computed the average number of extended forms for each acronym in a specific scientific field. Table 9.4 shows the top five categories with the highest average for acronyms. It is clear that using the ISI-OST-INPI schema in order to disambiguate acronyms as well as establishing a browsable index list of acronyms belonging to a specific scientific field is doable for most acronyms, since the median is between 1 and 2 even for the top five scientific fields with the highest average. For a very small number of acronyms, as seen in column **Max**, an extra context filter or a more granulated schema needs to be used.

Table 9.5 answers the last question regarding distribution pattern between different scientific fields. Most of the acronym extractions belong only to one category, where the pharmaceuticals has the highest amount (8 % of the total amount 978,001).

To conclude, the simple method presented in this case study is fully portable to the patent genre, and when combined with a classification schema, it can easily be transferred into an end application such as a search aid. Moreover, crowdsourcing techniques can be used to assess the correctness of the extracted acronyms. Meanwhile, assessing if the extractions represent technical terms is more problematic.

9.3.2 Second Case Study: Hyponymy RE

A hyponymy relation is essentially an *is–a* relationship, where a concept (the hyponym) can be identified to be an instance of or a kind of another concept (the hypernym). Different techniques for hyponymy relation extraction have been explored—many of them depending on pre-encoded knowledge such as domain ontologies and machine-readable dictionaries [20]. In order to avoid the need of pre-existing domain knowledge and remain independent of the sublanguage, one option is to use generic LSPs (lexico-syntactic patterns) for hyponymy relation extraction. Hearst [31] proposed a method to extract hyponymy relations based on six LSPs (see Table 9.6).

There are several issues related to extracting relations from raw texts using an LSP method. For instance, the LSP examples 2, 5 and 6 in Table 9.6 are not clear cases of hyponymy lexical relations, as in 'domestic pets such as cats and dogs', since in LSP 2 Germany, France and Italy are members of the European community and in LSP 6 France, England and Spain are countries in Europe, i.e. a part of the geographic continent called Europe. But with a wider semantic definition of the hyponym property, we can include both 'part of' and 'member of' in the definition:

Table 9.6 Sentence examples to each LSP

Example sentences	LSP
1	...work such author as Herrick, Goldsmith and Shakespeare	*suchNPasNP*, ∗ (*or|and*)*NP*
2	... trail behind other European community members, such as Germany, France and Italy	
3	Bruises, wounds, broken bones or other injuries	*NP, NP ∗ ,orotherNP*
4	Temples, treasuries and other important civic buildings	*NP, NP ∗ ,andotherNP*
5	All common-law countries, including Canada and England	*NP,includingNP*, ∗ *or|andNP*
6	... most European countries, especially France, England and Spain	*NP,especiallyNP*, ∗ *or|andNP*

...an expression A is a hyponym of an expression B iff the meaning of B is part of the meaning of A and A is subordinated of B. In addition to the meaning of B, the meaning of A must contain further specifications, rendering the meaning of A, the hyponym, more specific than the meaning of B. If A is a hyponym of B, B is called a hypernym of A. [48, p. 83]

Hearst used LSP 1 to extract candidate relations from Grolier's American Academic Encyclopaedia (8,6M words); 7067 sentences were extracted and 152 relations fit the restriction, i.e. to contain an unmodified noun (or with just one modifier). The assessment was conducted by looking up if the relation was found in WordNet. For 226 unique words, 180 words existed in the WordNet hierarchy and 61 out of 106 relations already existed in the WordNet. A common approach to evaluate hyponymy relation extractions is to use an existing ontology as a ground truth [20]. When no such resources exist within the text genre of interest, a ground truth needs be created.

Lefever et al. [47] created a hypernym relation ground truth for technical text using linguists. This type of labelling tasks is both time-consuming and costly, feasible only for small samples. The annotators were asked to manually identify domain-specific terms, NEs, synonymy and hyponymy relationships between identified terms and NEs. The annotation task requires both linguistic knowledge and some domain-specific knowledge. The data consisted of technical reports from a dredging company and news articles from the financial domain. The text data were enriched with PoS-tagging and lemmas produced by the LeTs Pre-processing Toolkit [71]. For the hyponymy lexical relation extractions, three different techniques were used: (1) Hearst's LSPs, (2) a distribution model using context cluster and (3) a morphosyntactic model. The morphosyntactic model is based on the head-modifier principle (i.e. *low molecular weight chitin/chitosan* is a type of *chitin/chitosan*). Lefever [47] concluded that the LSP method and the morphosyntactic approaches achieved good performance on the technical text and could therefore be portable to other text domain and user-specific text data.

Nanba [52] used an LSP method for hyponymy relation extractions on patent data, with the aim to be used as an automatic query expansion method for prior art search. For English, 3,898,000 instances were extracted from USPTO patent documents. For Japanese, 7,031,149 instances were identified in Japanese patent documents. The alignment between the language pair was conducted via citation analysis; 2635 pairs of English–Japanese hyponymy relations were manually evaluated. The best method obtained recall of 79.4 % and precision of 77.5 %.

9.3.2.1 The Experiment for Hyponymy RE

The research questions we would like to examine in this experiment are:

- To what extent can we use a well-known method to correctly identify hyponymy relations in patent text?
- Is there a difference in the number of possible extractions between a balanced corpus (Brown) and a domain-specific corpus (patent)?

- Is it possible to use the ISO-OST-IPNI schema to link hypernyms and hyponyms to a specific scientific field?
- Does the distribution pattern of extraction differ between scientific fields according to ISO-OST-IPNI?

This case study is divided into two experiments: a pre-study (study 1) and a larger study (study 2). In the pre-study we only reuse LSP 1 in order to examine if there is a difference between genres, i.e. news text and patent text. In the larger study, we use all six LSPs in order to create a real-world application and address the ontology population, for in neither of the studies was it feasible to use WordNet as an evaluation tool, since WordNet is mostly composed of unmodified nouns or nouns with a single modifier.

For the pre-study, the patent collection consisted of the CLEF-IP 2010 topic documents. In order to compare the effectiveness of using LSP for hyponymy relation extraction, we used the same LSP method to extract instances from the Brown collection. The NPs were extracted based upon a pre-established list of acceptable syntactic patterns of NPs. For the patent sample set, we had to include all topics instead of only randomly sampling out 500, since there were too few sentences matching LSP 1. All documents were submitted to the Stanford PoS-tagger [66]. For the pre-study experiment, we used the PoS-tagger as an off-the-shelf module and let the tagger make the sentence splitting decision. The manual evaluation consisted of examining the extracted instances and reference sentences from each collection. The assessment task was based upon the relation and the completeness of the extracted instances (Table 9.7).

The Brown Corpus, which was only a quarter of the patent sample, generated more sentences matching the LSP 1. Sixteen instances of the Brown Corpus and three of the patent corpus could not be assessed due to anaphoric reference (e.g. sentence 1 in Table 9.8).

There were several language phenomena causing the extractions to be incomplete, such as anaphoric and ellipsis function. In sentence 2 (Table 9.8), the hypernym consists of an embedded NP with prepositional 'of' construction modifying or complementing the preceding head noun. If we include the entire NP, i.e. *the treatment of diseases*, the hyponym and hypernym extraction would become incorrect since cancer, autoimmune diseases and infectious diseases are diseases and not the treatment. In order to make a correct extraction regarding NPs with 'of' construction, the head noun needs to be identified. In example 4, we have a

Table 9.7 Result of hyponym and hypernym extraction

	Patent collection	Brown corpus
No. of files	2005	500
Number of sentences	55	79
Relation suggestion	201	265
Correct instances	90	156
Not found instances	5	28
Ambiguous instances	3	16

Table 9.8 Example sentences for hypernym and hyponym extraction

Collection	No.	Sentence
Brown	1	With power plants such as these, vertical take-off and landing combat aircraft could be built
Patent	2	The novel conjugate molecules are provided for the manufacture of a medicament for gene therapy, apoptosis or for the treatment of diseases such as cancer, autoimmune diseases or infectious diseases
Brown	3	In rare cases, diseases such as encephalitis or a pituitary tumour may damage the appestat permanently, destroying nearly all sense of satiety
Patent	4	The guide components which form the channel are fastened on the end side by recognised connecting methods such as ultrasonic welding, laser welding or adhesive

deverbal[13] noun as the head word in the NP *ultrasonic welding*, which the PoS-tagger misassigns as VBN instead of NN. Consequently, the entire extraction was incomplete. The incorrect tagging of deverbal nouns is a typical error made by a general PoS-tagger, as we mentioned in Sect. 9.2.5.

For the second study, with the aim to build a real-world application composed of ontologies for each scientific field in the ISO-OST-IPNI schema, we deployed eight correction rules [3] in order to extract more complete relations from the patent collection. To add more flexibility to the extraction method, we also integrated the NP base chunker [60] in the NLP pipeline. The second experiment is a summary of a larger experiment conducted on different text genres, presented elsewhere [4]. Here we only report on the experiment conducted on the patent text. The entire CLEF-IP 2011 test collection was used in this experiment and three pipeline extraction methods were deployed:

1. No rules (NoRules) used to modify the NLP pipeline analysis.
2. Three rules (SimpleRules) deployed, which addressed observed errors among sentence matching the LSP patterns. The rules address different types of conjunction and commas issues. Rule (1) NP [cat and dogs] changed to two NPs [cat] and [dog], (2) [cat or dogs] changed two NPs [cat] or [dog], (3) numerous listing with commas.
3. Domain rules (DomainRules) are a combination of the simple rules above and the rules presented in [3, 4] addressing noun boundary modifications.

Table 9.9 shows the number of extractions made by the methods.

For the manual evaluation only a small set was randomly sampled out: 100 instances modified by each method. Since we wanted to compare the methods on the same set of sentences in order to evaluate the performance of the modifications, especially the noun boundary modifications, we selected only sentences represented in all methods.

---

[13]Deverbals are nouns that are derived from verbs or verb phrases.

Table 9.9 Number of
instances extracted from each
method

Extraction methods	Number of instances
Domain rules	92,702
Simple rules	135,550
No rules	135,946

Table 9.10 Correctly identified positive relations and NP boundaries in relation to sample and for the most domain relation 'A kind of'

	DomainRules		SimpleRules		NoRules	
	Hyper ok	Hypo ok	Hyper ok	Hypo ok	Hyper ok	Hypo ok
A kind of relation	**82 %**	**92 %**	79 %	90 %	76 %	76 %
All relations	79 %	**91 %**	**80 %**	90 %	77 %	90 %

The highest values per row and category (hyper/hypo) are in bold

We created an evaluation tool, which shows the original sentence and five definitions of relations between hypernym and hyponym pair:

1. Hyponym is a kind of hypernym.
2. Hyponym is a part of hypernym.
3. Hyponym is a member of hypernym.
4. Hyponym is in another relation with hypernym.
5. Hyponym has no relation to hypernym.

Each method was evaluated by a trained linguist based upon the type of relation and accuracy of completeness, i.e. correctly identified NP boundaries (see Table 9.10).

Table 9.10 shows for each method the accuracy for the most dominant relation **a Kind Of** and all relations. The preferred method for the **a kind of** is the DomainRules method. For **all kind** of relations, the preferred method is the DomainRules for hyponyms, while the SimpleRules is the preferred method for hypernyms. All in all, when collapsing all methods, 7,785,144 unique extraction hyponymy instances were made from the collection.

Table 9.11 examines the question regarding distribution extraction patterns between different scientific fields. As seen there, most of the extracted instances belong to only one category, the pharmaceuticals (i.e. 8 % of the total amount of 7,785,144 extraction instances). The distribution pattern is similar to the acronym extraction, since they follow the main collection distribution, i.e. there is a larger set of patents in pharmaceuticals than in microstructural and nanotechnology. For the field of pharmaceuticals, we extracted 895,970 instances, which is enough for further post-processing in order to clean the set. Meanwhile only 5179 extracted instances were made in the field of microstructural and nanotechnology, which will limit further post-processing to clean the set from noise.

To answer the question, 'is it possible to use the ISO-OST-IPNI schema to link hypernym and hyponyms to a specific scientific field?', we examined the average occurrence of a hyponymy pair for each scientific field. A hypernym can have different hyponyms depending upon the scientific context in which it occurs, e.g.

Table 9.11 Hyponymy pair extraction distribution by group ISI-OST-INPI by percentage of the total amount of extracted pair

ISI-OST-INPI categories	% of each category	Number of category by the %
Pharmaceuticals	12	1
Biotechnology	10	2
Organic fine chemistry, measurement	7	2
Computer technology, basic materials chemistry, analysis of biological materials, medical technology	5	4
Macromolecular chemistry polymers, chemical engineering	4	2
Telecommunications, other special machines, audio-visual technology	3	3
Optics, surface technology coating, electrical machinery apparatus energy, textile-and-paper machines, digital communication, materials metallurgy, semiconductors, food chemistry, control	2	9
IT methods for management, handling, other consumer goods, environmental technology, transport, civil engineering, mechanical elements, machine tools, engines–pumps–turbines, furniture games, basic communication processes	1	11
Thermal processes and apparatus	0.5	1
Microstructural and nanotechnology	0.1	1

URI element is a hypernym to *host name domain* in the digital communication and computer technology domains, but in telecommunication it can also refer to a standard key telephone. A hyponymy pair occurs on average in 2.2 scientific fields. The median was 2, variance 1.79 and stddev 1.34, which indicate that a large set of pairs only occur in one field, but a smaller set will occur in several, the maximum being 34 scientific fields.

Since a hypernym, as well as a hyponym, can have different children (hyponyms) or parents (hypernyms) depending on scientific fields, we also wanted to detect the number of hyponyms for each hypernym within a scientific field, as well as for the entire collection. We computed the average occurrence for a hyponym governed by the same hypernym (Table 9.12). We thereafter computed the average number of hypernyms that govern a specific hyponym. Note, we only present the top five categories.

On average each hyponym is governed by one hypernym regardless if within a specific category or for the entire collection. Meanwhile each hypernym governs on average four to five hyponyms.

To summarise, we confirm that the LSP patterns method for hyponymy relation extraction is portable into the patent domain as seen in studies 1 and 2. However, in order to capture the entire concept of a relation domain, adaptation of NLP tools

Table 9.12 Top five categories and entire collection of multiple hypernym and hyponym pairs

ISI-OST-INPI	Median	Mean	Variance	Stddev	Max
Hypernyms for each hyponym per ISI-OST-INPI					
Biotechnology	1	1.4	0.37	0.61	7
Medical technology	1	1.4	0.33	0.58	6
Computer technology	1	1.4	0.36	0.6	7
Pharmaceuticals	1	1.4	0.36	0.6	7
Telecommunications	1	1.39	0.36	0.6	6
ENTIRE COLLECTION	1	1.37	0.35	0.35	7
Hyponyms for each hypernym per ISI-OST-INPI					
Pharmaceuticals	3	5.03	192.87	13.87	1710
Organic fine chemistry	3	5.02	204.63	14.31	2974
Biotechnology	3	4.7	175.89	12.53	1113
Macromolecular chemistry polymers	3	4.67	175.54	13.25	2284
Basic materials chemistry	3	4.48	123.99	11.14	1953
ENTIRE COLLECTION	2	4.26	280.62	16.75	5660

used in the pipeline is required, which was observed in study 1 and confirmed by study 2. Especially, adaptation addressing deverbal nouns errors made by the NLP tools makes it possible to extract more correct entities. For most hyponymy relation pairs, we can use ISI-OST-INPI schema in order to establish ontologies composed of relation and concept existing in a specific scientific field.

9.3.3   Case Study Three: Factoid RE

As discussed at length in the first chapter of this volume, the patent information needs could be of different kinds: prior art search, searching a specific part of a chemical compound or substance. Therefore, different types of search tools need to be developed [29]. One specific type of query could be to search for quantity relations. In this third case study, we are interested to identify NPs answering questions such as the following: *What has the temperature of* N *degrees? What is exposed to a method or a process that is carried out at the temperature of* N *degrees?*

In order to extract this kind of factoid information, we first need to define what should be seen as the main subject heading: the main syntactic subject or the main semantic subject of a sentence. In general linguistics, syntax and semantics are studied separately, but they are connected since syntax also carries semantic meaning and semantics govern what can be expressed. On the syntactic level, we find similarity in sentences in Table 9.13: all of them take a subject (e.g. *the child, the key, the door*) and some have a direct object (e.g. *the door, the sliced banana*). Intuitively, we can detect some common notion of the prototype semantic roles—the

Table 9.13 Example of diathesis alternations of the verbs open and eat, 1–4 from [48, p. 112] (Example 19a-d) and 5 and 6 taken from [35] (Example 22.10a-b)

No.	Sentence examples
1	The $door^{Theme}$ opens
2	This $key^{Instrument}$ opens the $door^{Theme}$
3	The $child^{Agent}$ opened the $door^{Patient}$
4	The $child^{Agent}$ opened the $door^{Patient}$ with her own $key^{instrument}$
5	The $child^{Agent}$ ate the sliced $banana^{Patient}$ with a $fork^{instrument}$
6	*The $fork^{Instrument}$ ate the sliced $banana^{patient}$

subject takes the role of *Agent* for *the child*, the *Instrument*, i.e. *the key*. The objects are exposed to what the subjects are doing, which make them the *Patient* of the *Agent*, or the *Theme* of the verb [35, 48].

In computational semantics, the meanings of phrases and sentences are assumed to be systematically modelled from the semantic representation and of the syntactic constituents [35]. One of the base assumptions of most computational approaches is that the interpretation of the sentence is captured by the sentence predicate [35, 48]. The main reason for using semantic roles referring to the semantic role labelling (SRL) task in a system is to infer shallow meaning of representations, which is not captured by the surface level (string of words) or even by a parse tree [35]. The question is if these roles encoded in tens of thousands of verbs can be consistently categorised into a small number of abstract roles. Consider the diathesis alternations of the verbs *open* and *eat* in Table 9.13); they can be intransitive as well as transitive depending upon the context.[14]

The sentences in Table 9.13 represent different surface structures of the usage of opening and eating, where the agent opens something or eats something, the patient or theme (the direct object) becomes open or eaten and an instrument is used to make something opened or eaten. However, why is it that *the key* can open a door, while *the fork* cannot eat a banana? Syntactically, a fork can eat a banana. Here is where semantics and syntax differ. The reason for this is the set of constraints each verb assigns its arguments. The verb *eat* requires an agent having the semantic primitives of being animate, volitional, sentient, etc., and the direct object needs to be edible [35]. Meanwhile, the verb *open* puts constraint on the direct object that it must be something that can be opened by something regardless if it is an animate entity or an inanimate entity.

Given the fact that patent sentences have a complex syntactic structure, it is difficult to generate the tree structure of a sentence, as well as to identify the preferred semantic entity, as seen in Table 9.14. The main syntactic subject in the sentence is *process*, but does it have the boiling point of 300 °C? It is more plausible that the process will expose something to or contain something of 300 °C. The

---

[14]Transitivity is a weak linguistic theory which means a verb can shift depending on the local context, i.e. the sense it has or the functionality it has in a specific sentence.

Table 9.14 Domain-specific example sentences for subject heading identification

Sentence example	
Process, according to claim 1 characterized in that use, is made of a solution in a solvent having a boiling point under atmospheric pressure of at most <quantity type=temperature>300 °C</quantity>	
Question	What entity has a boiling point of 300 °C?
Candidate answer 1	Process
Candidate answer 2	Solution in a solvent having

process exposes *a solution*, which is modified by *a solvent* since it is an embedded NP (i.e. *in a solvent* is the post-modifier to the NP *a solution*). Thereby, *solvent* has a boiling point of 300 °C, since *solvent* requires a certain temperature in order to be dissolved into a solution. The entire sub-clause starting with *a solution in a solvent having a boiling point under atmospheric pressure of at most* 300 °C is the direct object of the pronoun *that use* (which refers back to the process[15]). Consequently, the complexity increases due to the syntactic construction found in patent sentences.

A neat solution to this Q&A task would be to use shallow semantic relations combined with categorisation of sentences. We would then be able to construct triples using agent, patient and instrument relations. However, there are very few systems that support generic SRL and those that exist are trained on general corpora or biomedical text (e.g. the Boxer system [10]). Furthermore, are the universal roles domain independent and language independent? Uematsu [70] observed domain-oriented semantic structure is a valuable asset for representing information needs. The general linguistic-oriented semantic structure (e.g. FramNet[16]) or general NLP tools could well function as intermediate layers but need to be enriched with domain-specific information. Moreover, the presumption is that the performance of the NLP tools does not decrease when applied on domain-specific text [70]. There are four main methods, used for relation extraction and SRL [26, 35]:

1. LSP: needs only small amounts of linguistic information but is limited in coverage. To secure coverage, the sample needs to cover many types of patterns.
2. Purely syntactic patterns: more generic than LSP but require a robust and high-accuracy parser.
3. Co-occurrence, mutual information and conditional random fields: only statistics based but require a large amount of data and potentially also access to pre-annotated corpus.
4. Parsed tree (dependency or syntactic) combined with supervised learning, mostly for SRL.

Let us now return to some patent text examples. We are reusing sentences containing the word *cell*, which were extracted in the hyponymy RE case study.

---

[15]To identify the relation between a noun and a pronoun requires anaphoric resolution.
[16]https://framenet.icsi.berkeley.edu/fndrupal/.

Table 9.15 Context example of the word *cell* in patent text

No	Sentence	Word sense
1	As used herein, a 'biological sample' refers to a sample of tissue or fluid isolated from an individual, including but not limited to bone marrow; plasma; serum; spinal fluid; lymph fluid; the external sections of the skin; respiratory, intestinal and genitourinary tracts; tears; saliva; milk; blood cells; tumours; and organs and also includes sample of in vivo cell culture constituents, including but not limited to medium resulting from the growth of cells in cell culture medium, putatively virally infected cells, recombinant cells and cell components	An enclosed cavity in an organism
2	CIU 30 includes a microcontroller 32, RF transceiver apparatus 34 for communication with the IPDLs and a power source 36, such as a rechargeable battery cell, possibly with an associated DCDC converter	A unit in a device for converting chemical or solar energy into electricity
3	The outer segments 164,168 form the gate terminals or other terminals of the corresponding six transistors Q1-Q6 116-136 of the SRAM memory cell 100	Memory unit of computer

In Table 9.15, the word *cell* occurs in very different contexts: in sentence 1 as in *blood cell, vivo cell culture constituents, cell culture medium, putatively virally infected cells, recombinant cells and cell components*; in sentence 2 as *battery cell* and in sentence 3 as *memory cell*. We can conclude that *cell* is most likely polysemous but not homonymous. The latter would imply that *cell* has the entire different disconnected word senses.[17] In all instances of *cell*, it still has the semantic primitives of being an enclosed cavity of some sort.

Not all concepts in a language are represented as single orthographical units; therefore, in order to know the context of a concept (represented by a phrase or a word), you first need to know the level of abstraction it has in a specific text domain in order to understand its meaning. Consequently, before we look into distributional semantics for SRL for domain-specific text genres, in order to reduce the amount of annotation labour otherwise required for a supervised learning method, we need first to have a robust method to identify domain-specific terms in different technical fields, i.e. 'memory cell', 'blood cell', 'battery cell'.

As we alluded to in Sect. 9.3.3, there exist no broad-coverage parsers that can handle patent sentences with the accuracy required for an SRL task. However, there have been a few studies within the patent text mining community similar to our last case study [38, 44, 65, 77]. Kim and Choi [38] extracted problem and solution key phrases from US patent documents based on an LSP method, which was combined with ML in order to identify more instances. The problem key phrase is defined as the description of a problem that the invention will help to solve and the solution

---

[17] A homograph (homonym) is one of a group of words that share the same spelling (pronunciation) but have disconnected word senses, e.g. a river bank, a savings bank and a bank of switches.

key phrase is defined as the invention itself. They used this method to generate technology time trends maps, and in a later study they used the same method in an IR setting. Tiwana and Horwitz [65] also focused on extracting factoid information addressing the problem and the solution of patents, but they used a more statistical approach in order to identify the concepts. Krishnan [44] extracted causal relations between diseases and treatment using LSPs from a collection consisting of medical patent. Ziering [77] used a bootstrapping technique based on LSPs in order to identify and label entities with the categories substance and disease.

To summarise, there are several interesting factoid RE studies targeting the patent domain. However, the complexity of the factoid extractions increases due to the linguistic characteristic of the patent domain, as well as the difficulties in obtaining a large amount of training data for ML algorithms. For instance, just the annotation task would require both domain expertise and linguistic expertise. Consequently, the patent factoid RE studies have been forced to fall back on more simple methods, i.e. using LSP methods instead of using more flexible method parsers in combination with supervised learning.

9.3.3.1 The Experiment for Factoid RE

In this case study, we explore relations between the main subject heading (sought factoid information) and temperature quantity (e.g. *The liquid has a temperature over* 60 °C, *What has the temperature over* 60 °C). The research questions we would like to examine with this experiment are:

1. Is it possible to use a general parser to extract the sought factoid information?

   a. If not, what other methods can we explore in order to extract the sought factoid information?

As mentioned in Sects. 9.2.6.2 and 9.3.3, the issue with the subject heading involves anaphoric resolution; identification of NPs, MWUs and clause boundaries; as well as identification of syntactic relations and the semantic relations in a sentence. For this task it is desirable to use a dependency parser in the pipeline, since it helps with identification of the main subject and main verb, as well as labelling each relation between all words in a sentence. We started out with experimenting with the Stanford dependency parser [24], parsing and inspecting sentence examples. The parser generates PoS, constituent information as well as two types of dependency relations (basic and collapsed) (see Table 9.16).

In order to parse the sentence, we removed the post-modifier clause *according to any one of claims 6 to 9*. In Table 9.16, there are two factoid entities which a human eye can spot. However, the question is which one to select. Obviously, the entity 'a melting point' is syntactically more connected to the quantity temperature, since it directly governs the quantity and belongs to the same NP. The syntactic subject of the sentence *a tilidine mesylate* is also the semantic subject and governs the entire NP *melting point of* 61 °C. The entity 61 °C represents the melting point of the

Table 9.16 Example of parsed patent sentence using the Stanford parser (for relation explanations, see http://universaldependencies.org/u/dep/nsubj.html)

Original sentence	A tilidine mesylate according to any one of claims 6 to 9 having a melting point of about <quantity type=temperature>61 °C</quantity> as determined by DSC	
Paraphrased sentence	A tilidine mesylate having a melting point of about 61 °C	
PoS-tagging	A/DT tilidine/NNP mesylate/NNP having/VBG a/DT melting/JJ point/NN of/IN about/RB 61/CD C./NNS	
Constituent information	ROOT (S (NP (NP (DT A) (NNP tilidine) (NNP mesylate)) (VP (VBG having) (NP (NP (DT a) (JJ melting) (NN point)) (PP (IN of) (NP (QP (RB about) (CD 61)) (NNS C.)))))))))	

Typed dependencies, collapsed	**det(Mesylate-3, A-1)**	'A' is governed by 'mesylate'
	nn(Mesylate-3, tilidine-2)	'Tilidine' is governed by 'mesylate' (the relation is a noun compound modifier)
	root(ROOT-0, mesylate-3)	'Mesylate' is governed by the root
	partmod(Mesylate-3, having-4)	'having' is governed by 'mesylate' (i.e. being the main verb)
	det(point-7, a-5)	'a' is governed by 'point'
	amod(point-7, melting-6)	'melting' is governed by 'point' (the relation is an adjective modifier)
	dobj(having-4, point-7)	'point' is governed by 'having' (the relationship is direct object)
	quantmod(61-10, about-9)	'about' is governed by '61-10'
	num(C.-11, 61-10)	'61' is governed by 'C'
	prep_of(point-7, C.-11)	'C' is governed by point

factoid entity *tilidine mesylate*. In order to use only parsed information without any external information (e.g. gazetteers, pre-defined LSP patterns or semantic lexicon), all dependencies are required for this task.

When using all the above information, we can construct an RDF triple of [subject, a tilidine mesylate; predicate, having; object, a melting point of 61°C]. The verb is transformed into the RDF predicate. However, almost every dependency relation given by the parser is required only if dependency relations are to be used. Moreover, using the dependency relation for this RE application requires absolute accuracy and consistency of the parser. When parsing the full example sentence (original sentence in Table 9.16) and not just the paraphrased version, the parser generates incorrect analysis as seen in Table 9.17.

The parser generates two ambiguous analyses, which make the desired RDF triple incorrect: [subject, any one of claims 6 to 9; predicate, having; object, a melting point of 61 °C]. This is caused by the parser having the problem of handling the clause post-modifier of NPs. Moreover, a second RDF triple is generated [subject, any one of claims 6 to 9; predicate, having; object, DSC]. Even though the sentence in Table 9.16 is of a simple syntactic structure compared to other claim sentences, the factoid RE scenario cannot be fulfilled, due to errors made by the

Table 9.17 Dependency relation from Stanford parser

Typed dependencies, collapsed	Analysis
det(tilidine-2, A-1)	Could be considered correct, due to contact
nsubj(mesylate-3, tilidine-2)	Relation clause syntactic subject, correct
root(ROOT-0, mesylate-3)	Correct
$prep_according_to$(mesylate-3, to-5)	Correct
det(one-7, any-6)	Correct
pobj(mesylate-3, one-7	Correct
back to $prep_according_to$(mesylate-3, to-5)	Could be considered correct due to context
$prep_of(one - 7, claims - 9)$	Correct
num(claims-9, 6-10)	Correct
dep(claims-9, to-11	Correct
num(claims-9, 9-12)	Correct
partmod(one-7, having-13)	**Not correct**
det(point-16, a-14	Correct
amod(point-16, melting-15)	Correct
dobj(having-13, point-16	Correct
advmod(C-21, about-18)	Correct
num(C-21, 61-19)	Correct
$nn(C - 21 °C-20)$	Correct
$prep_of$(point-16, C-21)	Correct
advmod(determined-23, as-22)	Correct
amod(point-16, determined-23)	Correct
agent(having-13, DSC-25	**Not correct**

parser of the internal structure of the continuous NP *"a tilidine mesylate according to any one of claims 6 to 9"*. In order to meet the requirement of the case study, we examined another more feasible method for the factoid RE. We explored two generic LSPs based upon observation made on a subset of the collection (Table 9.18).

To not over-generate subject headings, we added two head constraints to the LSPs: First, the LSP verb governs the LSP preposition, stating that a preposition subject heading cannot be extracted after a verb subject heading has been found. Second, we limited the subject heading extraction to three per quantity. In order to extract the relation, we used the Stanford PoS-tagger and the BaseNP chunker [51]. We reused the domain modification of the NLP pipeline presented in [3]. For the experiment we used 1022 claim sentences, which were already automatically annotated with the quantity temperature. Our task was to extract and identify the sought factoid information for each temperature quantity. We used 101 sentences as observation set and 921 claims were saved for testing. For 662 claim sentences in the test set, the LSP method generated one or more extraction (a coverage of 71.9 %). For the manual evaluation 100 claim sentences were randomly selected from the 662. From the 100 sample sentences, we had to exclude 16 since they were false positives given from the quantity annotation process, i.e. identifying a sequence in

Table 9.18 Generic LSP for identifying subject heading for temperature

Pattern 1	NP, VP {verbs}, NP{noun, multi-word unit}*({set of key phrases})*, QUANTITY
Verbs	is | are∨ | has∨ | have∨ | having∨ | cooling∨VBG | carried | according∨VBG | moulding | comprise
Example sentence	A process according to any one of claims 20 to 28 wherein the said process is carried out at temperature range is <quantity type=temperature>between −5 °C and 100 °C.</quantity>
Masked pattern	The pattern NP said process),VP{is carried out}, key phrase{at the temperature range is}, QUANTITY
RDF triples	[subject, process; predicate, is carried out; object, at temperature range is between −5 °C and 100 °C.]
RDF triples	[subject, temperature range; predicate, is; object, between −5 °C and 100 °C.]
Pattern 2	NP, PP{set of prepositions},(key phrase)*, QUANTITY
Example sentence	(. . .) in the presence of a suitable coupling agent, in the presence of a suitable base, in a suitable solvent at a temperature in the range <quantity type=temperature>−10 °C to 30 °C.</quantity>
RDF triple	[subject, a suitable solvent; predicate, at; object, a temperature in range between −10 and 30 °C.]

Table 9.19 Manual evaluation of factoid RE

Measurement	Value (%)	Computations
Precision	74	True positive/(true positive+false positive)
Recall	97	True positive/(true positive+false negative)
Specificity	38	True negative/(true negative+false positive)
Accuracy	76	True positive+true negative/(true positive +true negative+false positive+false negative)

a chemical compound as Fahrenheit (e.g. *[theta]H, (CH2)2–3F,(CH2)2–3-p[iota]*). We also had to remove 33 sentences due to the repetitiveness of the sample data, i.e. the sample set was not sampled based upon unique text but rather on found quantities. The repetitiveness was also observed in the observation set. All in all we ended up with 51 unique sentences for the manual evaluation (Table 9.19).

As seen in Table 9.19, the LSP method finds almost all sought factoid information, but there is a significant drop in precision. The LSP method overidentifies instances, i.e. generates too many false positives.

During the assessment process, we observed that even for a trained computational linguist with knowledge of the patent domain, it was a cumbersome task. There were several instances of uncertainty regarding what should be seen as the main subject heading of quantity. In the first part of Fig. 9.6 (black), we see that the method extracted two subject headings for the quantity *135 °C*: one governs the other subject heading, i.e. *an intrinsic viscosity* (NP2, green) is governed by *an ultra-high-molecular-weight ethylene polymer or copolymer resin* (NP1, red). Which one is correct? We decided to regard both as correct since NP2 is the direct object of

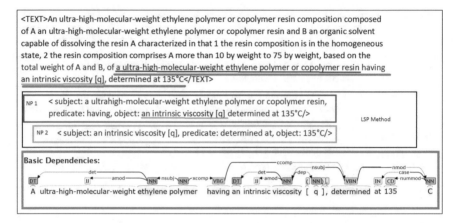

Fig. 9.6 Factoid example using LSP method and Stanford CoreNLP analysis

NP1 and NP2 is a nsubj[18] of the clause *determined at 135 °C* as seen in basic dependencies[19] (grey) in Fig. 9.6. However, it is clear that the *intrinsic viscosity* does not have the temperature of 135 °C, since it is a measurement of the resistance of a solution or fluid. As mentioned in Sect. 9.3.3, syntactic notation and semantic interpretation do not always correspond with each other.

In this last experiment, we first explored the possibility to use a dependency parser in order to identify factoid entities. Due to the low performance of the parser when used on patent data, we concluded that this was not feasible without extensive work to simplify the sentences and to modify the NLP tools used in the pipeline. Consequently, the SRL methods depending on parsing information from the Stanford parser are not portable to the patent domain without extensive modification. Therefore, we shifted focus to another method in order to answer research question 1.a. We created a set of LSPs which targeted the factoid information. The LSP method is less flexible in comparison with a method using dependency information and generates many false positives. However, we achieved a coverage of 71.9 % and, in manual evaluation of 51 sentences, a recall of 97 % and precision of 74 %.

To summarise, with the suggested LSP method, we showed that it is possible to extract the sought factoid information, although we are only able to identify the most plausible NPs as subject headings candidates for a specific temperature quantity entity. We cannot yet identify the main subject heading. For the SRL task, we can conclude we have a partly portable solution for the task, but we hope when combining distributional semantics with the suggested LSP method, we will be able to select the main subject heading of a temperature quantity.

---

[18]A nominal subject is a nominal which is the syntactic subject and the proto-agent of a clause. http://universaldependencies.org/u/dep/nsubj.html.

[19]In order to be able to parse and also for visualisation reasons, we simplified the sentence and shortened it.

9.4   Conclusion and Future Work

We presented the portability of different language technologies in order to show what is portable and what needs to be modified in order to handle a complex NP-driven text genre such as the patent genre. We have presented the portability of three text mining applications addressing different relation extraction: acronym identification, hyponymy relation extraction and factoid information extraction. Each application requires different levels of linguistic analyses. The method used for acronym extraction was only based on regular expressions, while the other two methods (factoid and hyponymy) were based on LSPs requiring at least a PoS-tagger and an NP chunker. In the second case study, we observed that in order to improve the hyponymy extractions, the NLP tools used in the pipeline required small adaptations targeting noun phrases. The adaptations consisted of post correction of deverbal nouns, which were incorrectly given verb PoS-tags by the tagger. For the third case study, we observed it would have been useful to use a dependency parser, but due to the low performance of the parser when used on patent text, we had to fall back to use a simpler method based on observed LSP patterns. The main contributions of our three different case studies are:

- The method addressing acronym extraction presented in this case study is portable to the patent genre without any adaptation, and when combined with the ISI-OST-INPI, it can easily be transferred into a search aid application suggestion acronym within a specific technical field. Moreover, crowdsourcing techniques can be used to assess the correction of the extractions. Meanwhile, to assess if an extraction represents a technical term is more problematic.
- The LSP method to target hyponymy relationships is portable to the patent domain with minor adaptations of the general NLP tools used in the pipeline. The hyponymy relation extraction application, when combined with the ISI-OST-INPI, could be turned into a browsable search aid.
- For the factoid RE application, it would have been preferable to use a dependency parser, since that task involves identification of NPs, MWUs, clause boundaries and syntactic and semantic subject and object as well as anaphoric resolution. But as we have shown, the reusability of the general dependency parser is very limited in the patent genre. With the suggested LSP method, we showed that it is possible to extract the sought factoid information, although we are only able to identify the most plausible NPs as subject headings candidates for a specific temperature quantity entity. Despite the limitation of our suggested method, we achieved encouraging results in terms of recall and coverage. Moreover, since the assessment task was very time-consuming, we hope that our suggested method can be used as a support method in order to establish a larger set of training data for a machine learning approach.

Today, it is not possible to conduct large-scale experiments with supervised or unsupervised methods for NLP tools targeting the patent domain, since there exists no labelled data, for either training or evaluation, covering all the technical fields of the patent text genre. Given these facts, the indirect evaluation (assessed by the end tools performance) of NLP applications reported in the patent text mining literature could be limited in its conclusions regarding the NLP applications' achievement over pure statistical methods, since the NLP applications do not reflect the target domain. In fact as mentioned in Sect. 9.2.4, only deeper linguistic methods have improved domain-specific retrieval performance when conducted on biomedical text. Biomedical text is today the only accessible and existing domain-specific training data for NLP tools.

To summarise, in this chapter, our aim was to show that for some end applications we need to start the process to establish more domain-specific training data covering more scientific areas than the field of biomedicine. With rather small effort, focusing on handling complex noun phrases and detection of acronym relations, we can contribute to improve the NLP pipeline performance on patent text. The hyponymy and the acronym extraction can be used as intermediate steps in order to reduce the cost and the time effort associated with domain-specific annotations. The factoid case study is an example of an end application which would benefit from having NLP tools trained on patent text.

References

1. Adams S (2001) Comparing the {IPC} and the {US} classification systems for the patent searcher. World Patent Inf 23(1):15–23
2. Ahlgren P (2004) The effects of indexing strategy-query term combination on retrieval effectiveness in a Swedish full text database. PhD thesis, University of Gothenburg
3. Andersson L, Lupu M, Hanbury A (2013) Domain adaptation of general natural language processing tools for a patent claim visualization system. In: Lupu M, Kanoulas E, Loizides F (eds) Multidisciplinary information retrieval. Lecture notes in computer science, vol 8201. Springer, Berlin/Heidelberg, pp 70–82
4. Andersson L, Lupu M, Palotti J, Piroi F, Hanbury A, Rauber A (2014) Insight to hyponymy lexical relation extraction in the patent genre versus other text genres. In: First international workshop on patent mining and its applications, IPaMin
5. Anick P, Verhagen M, Pustejovsky J (2014) Identification of multiword expressions in the brwac. In: Calzolari N, Choukri K, Declerck T, Loftsson H, Maegaard B, Mariani J, Moreno A, Odijk J, Piperidis S (eds) Proceedings of LREC-2014, Reykjavik, Iceland. European Language Resources Association (ELRA)
6. Arranz V, Atserias J, Castillo M (2005) Multiwords and word sense disambiguation. In: Gelbukh A (ed) Computational linguistics and intelligent text processing. Lecture notes in computer science, vol 3406. Springer, Berlin/Heidelberg, pp 250–262
7. Atkinson KH (2008) Toward a more rational patent search paradigm. In: Proceedings of the 1st ACM workshop on patent information retrieval, PaIR '08. ACM, New York, pp 37–40
8. Barker K, Szpakowicz S (1998) Semi-automatic recognition of noun modifier relationships. In: Proceedings of the 36th annual meeting of the Association for Computational Linguistics and 17th international conference on computational linguistics, vol 1. Association for Computational Linguistics, Stroudsburg, pp 96–102
9. Blitzer J (2008) Domain adaptation of natural language processing systems. PhD thesis, University of Pennsylvania

10. Bos J (2008) Wide-coverage semantic analysis with boxer. In: Proceedings of the 2008 conference on semantics in text processing. Association for Computational Linguistics, Morristown, pp 277–286
11. Bouayad-Agha N, Casamayor G, Ferraro G, Mille S, Vidal V, Wanner L (2009) Improving the comprehension of legal documentation: the case of patent claims. In: Proceedings of the 12th international conference on artificial intelligence and law. Association for Computing Machinery, New York, pp 78–87
12. Bouayad-Agha N, Casamayor G, Ferraro G, Wanner L (2009) Simplification of patent claim sentences for their paraphrasing and summarization. In: FLAIRS conference
13. Bouayad-Agha N, Burga A, Casamayor G, Codina J, Nazar R, Wanner L (2014) An exercise in reuse of resources: adapting general discourse coreference resolution for detecting lexical chains in patent documentation. In: Calzolari N, Choukri K, Declerck T, Loftsson H, Maegaard B, Mariani J, Moreno A, Odijk J, Piperidis S (eds) Proceedings of the ninth international conference on language resources and evaluation (LREC-2014), Reykjavik, Iceland, 26–31 May 2014. European Language Resources Association (ELRA), pp 3214–3221
14. Brants T (2003) Natural language processing in information retrieval. In: CLIN
15. Brügmann S, Bouayad-Agha N, Burga A, Carrascosa S, Ciaramella A, Ciaramella M, Codina-Filba J, Escorsa E, Judea A, Mille S, Müller A, Saggion H, Ziering P, Schütze H, Wanner L (2015) Towards content-oriented patent document processing: intelligent patent analysis and summarization. World Patent Inf 40:30–42
16. Burga A, Codina J, Ferraro G, Saggion H, Wanner L (2013) The challenge of syntactic dependency parsing adaptation for the patent domain. In: ESSLLI-13 workshop on extrinsic parse improvement
17. Carraoll J (2005) Parsing. In: Mitkov R (ed) The Oxford handbook of computational linguistics. Oxford University Press, Oxford
18. Carroll J, Briscoe T (1996) Apportioning development effort in a probabilistic LR parsing system through evaluation. arXiv preprint cmp-lg/9604004
19. Chang T, Schutze H (2006) Abbrevations in biomedical text. In: Ananiadou S, McNaught J (eds) Text mining for biology and biomedicine. Artech House, Boston/London, pp 99–119
20. Cimiano P (2006) Ontology learning and population from text: algorithms, evaluation and applications. Springer, New York/Secaucus, NJ
21. Collier N, Nobata C, Tsujii J-I (2000) Extracting the names of genes and gene products with a hidden Markov model. In: Proceedings of the 18th conference on computational linguistics-volume 1. Association for Computational Linguistics, Stroudsburg, pp 201–207
22. Collobert R, Weston J, Bottou L, Karlen M, Kavukcuoglu K, Kuksa P (2011) Natural language processing (almost) from scratch. J Mach Learn Res 12:2493–2537
23. Damerau FJ (1993) Generating and evaluating domain-oriented multi-word terms from texts. Inf Process Manag 29(4):433–447
24. De Marneffe M-C, Christopher DM (2008) The Stanford typed dependencies representation. In: Coling 2008: Proceedings of the workshop on cross-framework and cross-domain parser evaluation. Association for Computational Linguistics
25. Dhondt E (2014) Cracking the Patent using phrasal representations to aid patent classification. PhD thesis, Radboud University Nijmegen, Nijmegen, Netherlands
26. Ferraro G (2012) Towards deep content extraction from specialized discourse: the case of verbal relations in patent claims. PhD thesis, Universitat Pompeu Fabra
27. Friedman C, Kra P, Yu H, Krauthammer M, Rzhetsky A (2001) Genies: a natural-language processing system for the extraction of molecular pathways from journal articles. Bioinformatics 17(Suppl 1):S74–S82
28. Grefenstette G, Tapanainen P (1994) What is a word, what is a sentence? Problems of Tokenisation. Rank Xerox Research Centre, Meylan
29. Hansen P (2011) Task-based information seeking and retrieval in the patent domain: processes and relationships. PhD thesis, University of Tampere, Tampere, Finland

30. Harris CG, Arens R, Srinivasan P (2011) Using classification code hierarchies for patent prior art searches. In: Lupu M, Mayer K, Tait J, Trippe AJ (eds) Current challenges in patent information retrieval. The information retrieval series, vol 29. Springer, Berlin/Heidelberg, pp 287–304

31. Hearst MA (1992) Automatic acquisition of hyponyms from large text corpora. In: Proceedings of the 14th conference on computational linguistics, vol 2, COLING '92. Association for Computational Linguistics, Stroudsburg, pp 539–545

32. Hockenmaier J, Steedman M (2007) CCGbank: a corpus of CCG derivations and dependency structures extracted from the Penn treebank. Comput Linguist 33(3):355–396

33. Hunt JW, Szymanski TG (1977) A fast algorithm for computing longest common subsequences. Commun ACM 20(5):350–353

34. Hunt D, Nguyen L, Rodgers M (2007) Patent searching: tools and techniques. Wiley, Hoboken

35. Jurafsky D, Martin JH (2016) Speech and language processing: an introduction to natural language processing, computational linguistics, and speech recognition, 3rd draft edn. Prentice Hall PTR, Upper Saddle River

36. Justeson JS, Katz SM (1995) Technical terminology: some linguistic properties and an algorithm for identification in text. Nat Lang Eng 1(1):9–27

37. Kang I-S, Na S-H, Kim J, Lee J-H (2007) Cluster-based patent retrieval. Inf Process Manag 43(5):1173–1182 (Patent Processing)

38. Kim J-H, Choi K-S (2007) Patent document categorization based on semantic structural information. Inf Process Manag 43(5):1200–1215

39. Kim J-D, Ohta T, Tateisi Y, Tsujii JI (2003) GENIA corpus - a semantically annotated corpus for bio-textmining. In: ISMB (supplement of bioinformatics), pp 180–182

40. Kim Y, Tian Y, Jeong Y, Jihee R, Myaeng S-H (2009) Automatic discovery of technology trends from patent text. In: Proceedings of the 2009 ACM symposium on applied computing, SAC '09, pp 1480–1487. ACM, New York

41. Kiss T, Strunk J (2002) Viewing sentence boundary detection as collocation identification. In: Proceedings of KONVENS 2002, pp 75–82

42. Koehn P, Schroeder J (2007) Experiments in domain adaptation for statistical machine translation. In: Proceedings of the second workshop on statistical machine translation, StatMT '07, pp 224–227. Association for Computational Linguistics, Stroudsburg

43. Koster CHA, Beney JG, Verberne S, Vogel M (2011) Phrase-based document categorization. In: Lupu M, Mayer K, Tait J, Trippe AJ (eds) Current challenges in patent information retrieval. The information retrieval series, vol 29. Springer, Berlin/Heidelberg, pp 263–286

44. Krishnan A, Cardenas AF, Springer D (2010) Search for patents using treatment and causal relationships. In: Proceedings of the 3rd international workshop on patent information retrieval, PaIR '10. ACM, New York, pp 1–10

45. Kudo T, Matsumoto, Y (2001) Chunking with support vector machines. In: Proceedings of the second meeting of the North American chapter of the Association for Computational Linguistics on language technologies. Association for Computational Linguistics, Morristown, pp 1–8

46. Kulick S, Bies A, Liberman M, Mandel M, McDonald R, Palmer M, Schein A, Ungar L, Winters S, White P (2004) Integrated annotation for biomedical information extraction. In: Proceedings of the human language technology conference and the annual meeting of the North American Chapter of the Association for Computational Linguistics (HLT/NAACL), pp 61–68

47. Lefever E, Van de Kauter M, Hoste V (2014) Evaluation of automatic hypernym extraction from technical corpora in English and Dutch. In: Calzolari N, Choukri K, Declerck T, Loftsson H, Maegaard B, Mariani J, Moreno A, Odijk J, Piperidis S (eds) Proceedings of LREC-2014, pp 490–497

48. Löbner S (2002) Understanding semantics. Oxford University Press, New York

49. Luo J, Yang H (2013) Query formulation for prior art search-Georgetown University at CLEF-IP 2013. In: Proceedings of CLEF

50. Mahdabi P, Andersson L, Keikha M, Crestani F (2012) Automatic refinement of patent queries using concept importance predictors. In: Proceedings of the 35th international ACM SIGIR conference on research and development in information retrieval, SIGIR '12. ACM, New York, pp 505–514
51. Marcus MP, Santorini B, Marcinkiewicz MA (1993) Building a large annotated corpus of English: The Penn treebank. Comput Linguist 19(2):313–330
52. Nanba H, Kamaya H, Takezawa T, Okumura M, Shinmori A, Tanigawa H (2009) Automatic translation of scholarly terms into patent terms. In: Proceedings of the 2nd international workshop on patent information retrieval, PaIR '09. ACM, New York, pp 21–24
53. Nanba H, Mayumi S, Takezawa T (2011) Automatic construction of a bilingual thesaurus using citation analysis. In: Proceedings of the 4th workshop on patent information retrieval, PaIR '11. ACM, New York, pp 25–30
54. Nivre J (2007) Data-driven dependency parsing across languages and domains: perspectives from the CoNLL-2007 shared task. In: Proceedings of the 10th international conference on parsing technologies, pp 168–170
55. Okazaki N, Ananiadou S (2006) A term recognition approach to acronym recognition. In: Proceedings of the COLING/ACL on main conference poster sessions. Association for Computational Linguistics, Morristown, pp 643–650
56. Oostdijk N, D'hondt E, van Halteren H, Verberne S (2010) Genre and domain in patent texts. In: Proceedings of the 3rd international workshop on patent information retrieval, PaIR '10. ACM, New York, pp 39–46
57. Pustejovsky J, Anick P, Bergler S (1993) Lexical semantic techniques for corpus analysis. Comput Linguist 19(2):331–358
58. Pustejovsky J, Castaño J, Cochran B, Kotecki M, Morrell M (2001) Automatic extraction of acronym-meaning pairs from MEDLINE databases. Stud Health Technol Inform 84(Pt 1):371–375
59. Pustejovsky J, Castaño J, Saurí R, Rumshisky A, Zhang J, Luo W (2002) Medstract: creating large-scale information servers for biomedical libraries. In: ACL-02; 2002; Philadelphia, pp 85–92
60. Ramshaw LA, Marcus MP (1999) Text chunking using transformation-based learning. In: Armstrong S, Church K, Isabelle P, Manzi S, Tzoukermann E, Yarowsky D (eds) Natural language processing using very large corpora. Text, speech and language technology, vol 11. Springer, Netherlands, pp 157–176
61. SanJuan E, Dowdall J, Ibekwe-SanJuan F, Rinaldi F (2005) A symbolic approach to automatic multiword term structuring. Comput Speech Lang 19(4):524–542
62. Schmoch U (2008) Concept of a technology classification for country comparisons. In: Final report to the world intellectual property organisation (wipo), WIPO
63. Schwartz AS, Hearst MA (2003) A simple algorithm for identifying abbreviation definitions in biomedical text. In: Proceedings of the Pacific symposium on biocomputing, pp 451–462
64. Sleator DD, Temperley D (1991) Parsing English with a link grammar. Technical Report CMU-CS-91-196, Department of Computer Science, Carnegie Mellon University
65. Tiwana S, Horowitz E (2009) Extracting problem solved concepts from patent documents. In: Proceedings of the 2nd international workshop on patent information retrieval, PaIR '09. ACM, New York, pp 43–48
66. Toutanova K, Klein D, Manning CD, Singer Y (2003) Feature-rich part-of-speech tagging with a cyclic dependency network. In: Proceedings of the 2003 conference of the North American chapter of the Association for Computational Linguistics on human language technology, vol 1, NAACL '03. Association for Computational Linguistics, Stroudsburg, pp 173–180
67. Tseng Y-H, Lin C-J, Lin Y-I (2007) Text mining techniques for patent analysis. Inf Process Manag 43(5):1216–1247
68. Tsuruoka Y, Tateishi Y, Kim J-D, Ohta T, McNaught J, Ananiadou S, Tsujii J (2005) Developing a robust part-of-speech tagger for biomedical text. Advances in informatics. Springer, Berlin, pp 382–392

69. Turmo J, Ageno A, Català N (2006) Adaptive information extraction. ACM Comput Surv 38(2):1–47
70. Uematsu S, Kim J-D, Tsujii J (2009) Bridging the gap between domain-oriented and linguistically-oriented semantics. In: Proceedings of the workshop on current trends in biomedical natural language processing. Association for Computational Linguistics, Morristown, pp 162–170
71. van de Kauter M, Coorman G, Lefever E, Desmet B, Macken L, Hoste V (2013) Lets preprocess: the multilingual LT3 linguistic preprocessing toolkit. Comput Linguis Neth J 3:103–120, 2013
72. Verberne S, Koster CHA, Oostdijk N (2010) Quantifying the challenges in parsing patent claims. In: Proceedings of the 1st international workshop on advances in patent information retrieval (AsPIRe 2010), pp 14–21
73. Verberne S, D'hondt E, Oostdijk N, Koster C (2010) Quantifying the challenges in parsing patent claims. In: Proceedings of the 1st international workshop on advances in patent information retrieval (AsPIRe 2010), pp 14–21
74. Wanner L, Baeza-Yates R, Brügmann S, Codina J, Diallo B, Escorsa E, Giereth M, Kompatsiaris Y, Papadopoulos S, Pianta E et al (2008) Towards content-oriented patent document processing. World Patent Inf 30(1):21–33
75. Wren JD, Chang JT, Pustejovsky J, Adar E, Garner HR, Altman RB (2005) Biomedical term mapping databases. Nucleic Acids Res 33(Suppl 1):D289–D293
76. Yeates S, Bainbridge D, Witten IH (2001) Using compression to identify acronyms in text. In: Storer JA, Cohn M (eds) Proceedings of the data compression conference. IEEE Press, Los Alamitos, p 582
77. Ziering P, van der Plas L, Schütze H (2013) Bootstrapping semantic lexicons for technical domains. In: Proceedings of the sixth international joint conference on natural language processing, Nagoya, Japan, pp 1321–1329. Asian Federation of Natural Language Processing

Chapter 10
Visual Analysis of Patent Data Through Global Maps and Overlays

Luciano Kay, Alan L. Porter, Jan Youtie, Nils Newman, and Ismael Ràfols

Abstract Visual analytics has been increasingly used to help to better grasp the complexity and evolution of scientific and technological activities over time, across science and technological areas and in organisations. This chapter presents general insights into some important fields of expertise such as mapping, network analysis and visual analytics applied to patent information retrieval and analysis. We also present a new global patent map and overlay technique and illustrative examples of its application. The concluding remarks offer considerations for future patent analysis and visualisation.

10.1 Introduction

Visual analytics has been increasingly used to help to better grasp the complexity and evolution of scientific and technological activities over time, across science and technological areas and in organisations. New and diverse analysis

L. Kay (✉)
Center for Nanotechnology in Society (CNS) – ISBER, University of California Santa Barbara, 2201 North Hall, Santa Barbara, CA, 93106-2150, USA
e-mail: luciano.kay@ucsb.edu

A.L. Porter
School of Public Policy, Georgia Institute of Technology, Atlanta GA & Search Technologies, Norcross, GA, USA
e-mail: alan.porter@isye.gatech.edu

J. Youtie
Enterprise Innovation Institute & School of Public Policy, Atlanta, GA, USA
e-mail: jan.youtie@innovate.gatech.edu

N. Newman
Intelligent Information Services Corporation, Atlanta, GA, USA
e-mail: newman@iisco.com

I. Ràfols
Ingenio (CSIC-UPV), Universitat Politècnica de València, València, Spain

SPRU, University of Sussex, Brighton, UK
e-mail: i.rafols@ingenio.upv.es

© Springer-Verlag GmbH Germany 2017
M. Lupu et al. (eds.), *Current Challenges in Patent Information Retrieval*,
The Information Retrieval Series 37, DOI 10.1007/978-3-662-53817-3_10

and mapping methods, increasing computing power and new software and layout algorithms enable this and support patent analysis aimed at understanding a range of innovation-related phenomena.

This chapter presents general insights into some important fields of expertise such as mapping, network analysis and visual analytics applied to patent information retrieval and analysis. We discuss broader aspects and issues of patent mapping, including the development of global maps and overlays in the context of information retrieval, exploration and analysis for patent corpora, and their similarities/differences to similar approaches applied to scientific literature. The need for development of tools to benchmark and capture temporal change of organisational innovation activities, or patterns of technological change, also motivates this work.

We also present the new global patent map and overlay technique we recently developed [1]. Our visualisation approach is a logical extension of experience acquired with science overlay maps [2] and opens up new avenues for understanding patent landscapes, which as we will see markedly differ from scientific landscapes. To illustrate the kind of analytical support offered by this approach, we discuss the core structure of our global patent map and apply patent overlay maps to benchmark the nanotechnology-related patenting activities of companies. We conclude this chapter by offering some remarks and considerations for future patent analysis and visualisation.

10.2   Patent Information Retrieval and Analysis

Patent analysis plays key roles in competitive technical intelligence (CTI) [3]. The multipart technological innovation CTI 'puzzle' comprises both empirical information and expert analysis to inform empirical search, refining and interpretation. Patents provide an important piece of empirical information in the form of compilations of large numbers of records for 'landscaping', i.e. a macro perspective—our focus here—as well as in-depth treatment of a small number of patent documents for micro-perspective analyses [4]. Other complementary empirical information comprise research publication search compilations/reviews and roadmaps and business-related content (e.g. trade publications, policy documents, popular press treatment).

One implication of such an 'innovation systems' perspective [5, 6] is to see potential value in ways to combine multiple information types. We generally seek innovation indicators [7]. Patent mapping provides a visual component to enrich various innovation system analyses [8, 9]. In particular, we think patent mapping can complement science overlay mapping to enrich understanding of research and development (R&D) activities, particularly for engagement of subareas and maturation patterns [10]. Leydesdorff et al. [11] have devised patent overlay maps and Leydesdorff et al. [12] illustrate their potential in exploring innovation dynamics in areas such as photovoltaic technologies, both over geographical regions and over topical regions.

The macro-patent analyses that patent overlay mapping serves seek to discern patent activity patterns with implications for innovation. These can inform corporate investment decisions via intelligence about key competitors' perceived trajectories. Chen [13], for example, shows patent 'landscape' maps created by Boyack [14] changing over time. These aid CTI in tracking competitor interest evolution. Alternatively, analyses can contribute to policy discourse by profiling national positions and potential. Of course, patents are an imperfect lens on innovation—they reflect invention, and that unevenly, as patent practices vary greatly by industrial sector and country (cf. [15]).

The unit of analysis is a collection of patent information relating to a target topic. That collection typically contains patent abstract records, not full-text patent documents. Those would be gathered via a search strategy applied to one or more databases (e.g. *Derwent World Patent Index, EPO PATSTAT*). The use of diverse text data sources (sometimes with varying language usage, technical terms or machine-translated documents) implies that a well-crafted search is essential, and it must address one or more research questions. In the private sector CTI realm, those questions tend to focus on either a key competitor or a few of them and their intents regarding a certain technology or application area. In public sector or academic treatments, focus is more apt to be on an emerging technology, cast broadly.

The search strategy can be conducted using Boolean term searching (combining key terms, often delimited by proximity conditions). Or, the search can rely on patent classification specifications such as International Patent Classifications (IPCs). Often a combination search query is most effective. Search quality is essential and criteria centre on how best to address the driving research questions. In general, macro-scale profiling leans towards inclusive search, thereby providing the option of further analyses by refining to subsets of the data retrieved.

Once patent abstract data are retrieved, the analyst faces notable challenges in 'getting the data right'. We have found it fruitful to engage domain experts to review initial search set patterns, particularly top terms and phrases, to spot flaws or gaps, and suggest ways to improve our search queries. For instance, in recent work on nano-enabled drug delivery (NEDD) we removed some 5 % of the search set concerning agriculture [16]. The next stage entailed data cleaning. This can vary enormously in scale of effort, contingent on the sensitivities in addressing the driving analytical questions. For broad patent landscaping, we want to get a representative sample. For massive searches, this implies tradeoffs in scope—e.g. maybe reducing the search time frame. For the NEDD analysis, with the purpose of visualising patenting distribution over patent categories, we set aside search terms concerning cancer to reduce distortion in not specifying other target diseases.

Analysts can use diverse forms of patent analysis with a varying degree of complexity. These range from the generation of lists of patent records and co-occurrence matrices (lately made simpler thanks to text mining software) to more complex clustering and mapping of patent data. Lists can filter patent records by given criteria or fields, and matrices help to find relationships resulting from, for example, co-occurrence of keywords in patent titles and abstracts. Document clustering allows identifying topics in patent literature and patent mapping provides windows on the pattern of invention. Geo-mapping of inventors and/or patent assignees can illuminate areas of strength (e.g. for national comparisons). Geo-mapping of patent authority activity, particularly when staged over time periods, may elucidate relative market potential. And, patent overlay mapping applications as presented here contribute insight into component technologies, as well as market sectors being engaged.

Citation analyses deserve mention as well. One may gain useful technology transfer insights by considering the patents (and/or literature) cited by a target patent set and the patents that cite such a target set. The latter are especially affected by patent time lags. With regard to the patent mapping we present later in this chapter, one needs to know the IPC of the cited (or citing) patents. That requires additional layers of search and retrieval.

10.3   Visual Analytics and Overlays

The visualisation of knowledge or technological landscapes has been a prominent part of publication and patent analyses since their origins [17, 18]. Only in the last decades, however, improvements in computational power and algorithms have allowed the creation of large maps covering a full database, the so-called global maps of science and technology (see overviews by [2, 19]). This in part has led to a proliferation of global maps ([20–25]; e.g. see [26, 27]).

Science maps or *scientograms* are the visualisation of the relations among areas of science using network analysis algorithms. Visualisation procedures for science maps have generally been used to explore and visually identify scientific frontiers, grasp the extent and evolution of scientific domains and analyse the frontiers of scientific research change [28]. Science mapping efforts have also been used to inspire cross-disciplinary discussion to find ways to communicate scientific progress.[1]

A patent map, on the other hand, is a symbolic representation of technological fields that are associated with relevant themes. Technological fields are positioned in the map so that similar fields are situated nearby and dissimilar components are situated at a distance. Their construction uses similar algorithms to those used to visualise the relations among scientific disciplines. Patent maps help to explore and visually identify areas of technology development concentration, and they can illuminate increasing or diminishing patenting activity over time. In this way, patent maps can inform R&D management, competitive intelligence and policy decision-making. A key characteristic of patent maps is the ability to graphically represent 'technological distance' or the extent to which a set of patents reflects different types of technologies [29]. Technological distance, often proxied by patent

---

[1]See, for example, the Mapping Science website at http://www.scimaps.org/

categories, with patents in a given patent category being considered more similar to one another than to those in other patent categories [30, 31], provides a measure of interrelatedness and potential innovation opportunities.

Science and technology maps complement other methodological approaches to data analysis. They can help to interpret and find meaning in complex data by transforming abstract and intangible datasets into something visible and concrete [13]. Scholars have pursued diverse approaches to scientific publication and patent record-level analysis to create global maps of science and technology. These serve to characterise the proximity and dependency of scientific areas (e.g. [19, 32]) and technological areas (e.g. preliminary work in Boyack and Klavans [33] and related approaches by Schoen et al. [9] and Leydesdorff et al. [11]. Notwithstanding the range of classification and visualisation algorithms, the resulting global maps have been generally 'stable', at least in terms of their main disciplinary or technological areas and their relationships. Still, the comparison of results of diverse approaches is important to test the robustness of patterns observed. Without significant consensus on the shape and relative position of science and technological categories, global maps are meaningless as stable landscapes needed to compare, for example, organisational or technological subsets.

The relative structural stability of global maps suggested their use as a base map over which to compare the technological distribution of specific organisations, in the same way that we may compare the distribution of different plant species or multinationals over the world map. This led to the idea of 'overlays' (or a process of 'layering' or 'stacking') by which global maps can be combined with additional layers that visually represent subsets of scientific publication and patent data. Overlays help to understand the particular scientific and technological thrusts and areas of concentration of R&D actors [2]. For example, a company's patent portfolio can be 'overlaid' on the base map. This process provides a visual tool to interpret the multidimensional relationships among the patent categories in the company's patent portfolio.

10.4   Visualising Innovation Pathways and Technology Development Concentrations

Our research has recently involved the creation of a new global patent map and overlay technique [1]. Our patent map is constructed from a similarity matrix based on citing-to-cited patents—i.e. a matrix that reflects similarities among IPC categories in how patents cite each other. The similarity measures are calculated from correlation functions among fields according to citations among patent categories. This multidimensional matrix is projected onto a two-dimensional space, which becomes our 'base map'. A user can then 'overlay' subsets of patent data—representing different types of technological fields, organisations or geographical regions—on top of the base map to understand the particular technological thrusts and areas of concentration of these entities.

While there have been other patent maps that use IPC categories (e.g. see [12, 17]), they share two main weaknesses, which our approach addresses. The first is the reliance on analysing patents at a given IPC level; 3-digit (class) and 4-digit (subclass) are the most commonly used levels. Patents are not equally distributed across IPC three-digit or IPC four-digit categories, however, so one experiences the problem of not being able to distinguish fields in classes that attract a huge number of patents—such as Medical or Veterinary Sciences (A61)—by staying within the confines of the existing IPC administrative structure. The second is assuming that patents in a given section of the IPC system are alike. For example, even though Medical or Veterinary Sciences (A61) and Hats (A42B) are both in Section A 'Human Necessities', they are not really that similar. 'Medical or Veterinary Sciences' is actually more similar to Organic Chemistry (C07), even though Organic Chemistry falls in Section C 'Chemistry, Metallurgy'. The approach presented in this chapter compensates for these issues by (1) disaggregating IPC categories and (2) reforming them based on citing-to-cited reference patterns. In addition, we remove some patent categories with fewer than 1000 patents to enable better ability to distinguish patterns in those categories with a higher propensity for patenting.

Our global patent map is based on citing-to-cited relationships among IPCs of European Patent Office (EPO) patents from 2000 to 2006. This period was chosen because of its stability with respect to IPC 7 categories. IPC 7, at the time we conducted this study, represented the longest period of stable classification. Future work would involve comparing patent overlay maps based on IPC 7 and future classification systems such as IPC 8 or Cooperative Patent Classification (CPC) systems, but first, the project team needed to make sure it could produce a mapping process with a stable set of categories. The dataset containing IPC relationships, extracted from the PATSTAT database version available in the fall of 2010, represents more than 760,000 patent records in more than 400 IPC categories. This data range begins with patent EP0968708 (which was published in January 2000) and ends with patent EP1737233 (published in December 2006).

A key part of our methodology involves disaggregating, then folding IPC categories up into the next highest level of aggregation to create relatively similar sized categories. This solution comprises three rules:

1. For IPC categories with large population, use the smallest subgroup level.
2. For small population IPC categories, aggregate up to general group level, subclass or class.
3. Establish a floor cut-off and drop very small aggregated populations.

As a result, IPC categories with instance counts greater than 1000 in the data set were kept in their original state. Those categories with instance counts less than 1000 were folded up to the next highest level until the count exceeded 1000 or the class level was reached. During the folding, any other IPC categories with counts exceeding 1000 in the same branch were left out of the folding count. If at the class

Table 10.1 Data pre-processing to group IPC categories, selected examples[a]

Original IPC in data set	Catchwords	Original record count
A61B	Diagnosis, surgery, identification	25,808
Authors' process splits this out into:		
A61B 5/00	Measuring for diagnostic purposes	1415
A61B 17/00	Surgical instruments, devices or methods, e.g. tourniquets	1493
A61B 19/00	Instruments, implements or accessories for surgery or diagnosis not covered by any of the groups	1444
And a remainder:		
A61B[b]		21,456

[a]Each IPC with an instance count greater than 1000 was kept in its original state
[b]Each IPC with an instance count less than 1000 was folded up to the next highest level until the count exceeded 1000 or the class level was reached

level (i.e. three-digit), the population was less than 1000, the IPC code was dropped for being too small to map. Table 10.1 illustrates this approach for the four-digit IPC class A61K.

This pre-processing yields IPC categories at the class (three-digit), subclass (four-digit), main group (five-digit) and subgroup (seven- and eight-digit) levels, with levels that ensure broadly similar numbers (i.e. within two orders of magnitude) of patents across categories. The next step involves extracting from PATSTAT the patents cited by the target records. The IPCs of those patents are mapped to the 466 IPC categories. Some of the patents cited by those in our IPC 7 data set were published under previous categorisation systems; however, this spillover does not lead to any problems from a categorisation standpoint because IPC integrates prior categorisations into more recent versions. The result of this data collection allows the creation of a table containing, in each row, sets of patent number, IPC number, cited patent number and cited IPC number.

The final data processing steps involve generating a cosine similarity matrix among citing IPC categories (using conventional cosine similarity normalised by the square root of the squared sum) and then factor analysis of the IPC categories (following the method used in global science maps by Leydesdorff and Rafols [24]. A factor analysis of the citing-to-cited matrix among IPC categories is then used to consolidate the 466 categories into 35 'macro-patent categories'. We tested different factor solutions ranging from 10 to 40 categories. The 35-factor solution had the greatest face validity, allowing a convenient classification of the IPC categories and easier interpretation. These 35 factors form the basis for colour-coding the 466 categories that are represented in visualisations. The visualisations also require converting IPC codes to succinct text labels, which we did by shortening lengthy IPC definitions. These IPC category labels were then used as a basis for creating descriptors for each factor as shown in the maps.

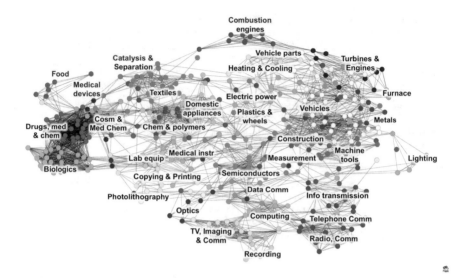

Fig. 10.1 Full patent map of 466 technological categories and 35 technological areas. Lines represent relationships between technological categories (the darker the line, the shorter the technological distance between categories)

The full map of patents shows all 466 categories in a Kamada-Kawai layout (using the software Pajek[2]) that represents technological distances and groups of technologies in each of the 35 factors or technological areas shown with the same colour (Fig. 10.1). Label and colour-related settings were adjusted to produce a reasonably clear map and facilitate its examination. The map suggests three broad dimensions of patenting interrelationships based on the overall position of technological areas. The left side of the map represents bio-related patents, including food, medicine and biology. The lower right part of the map includes semiconductor, electronics and information and communications technologies (ICT). The upper right portion of the map is primarily comprised of automotive and metal-mechanic-related technology groups.

To illustrate and test the application of patent map overlays, two corporate data sets of nanotechnology patent applications have been created for Samsung and DuPont, using data from the Georgia Tech Global Nanotechnology databases in the same time period (2000–2006). The visual examination of maps shows nanotechnology development foci that vary across companies (even for those in similar industry sectors) and different patenting activity levels for the studied period. The two overlays presented herein appear diversified and encompass a number of technological areas. The patent overlay created for Samsung, for example, shows activity concentrated on semiconductors and optics, with a notable level

---

[2]This software is free for non-commercial use: http://pajek.imfm.si

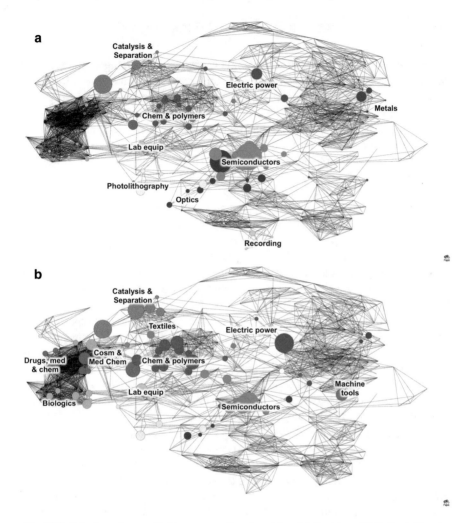

Fig. 10.2 Patent overlays applied to company benchmarking. (**a**) Samsung. (**b**) DuPont. The size of nodes is proportional to the number of patent applications in the corresponding technology group

of patenting activity across other areas as well (Fig. 10.2a). The company also has some prominent activity on technological areas broadly defined as Catalysis & Separation, Photolithography, and Chemistry & Polymers. DuPont, on the other hand, focuses on drugs, medicine and chemistry, chemistry and polymers as well as biologics (Fig. 10.2b). According to our overlays, this company has a portfolio of patent applications that is even more diversified, but it is also less active in terms of patenting activity, than Samsung.

10.5   Visualisations and Decision-Making Support

Visualisations can support R&D management, competitive intelligence and policy decision-making. Three main aspects of patent maps reveal the level of support they can offer: (1) map structures, (2) patterns of interconnection and (3) patent concentration.

The first aspect is connected with map structures, patent classifications and the challenge of relying on them for patent mapping. As technology changes, technology-oriented applications may draw from patents in different hierarchical categories and subsequently lead to further diversity in patents that cite patents in these categories. This requires making a distinction between hierarchy and similarity. A closer look at our global patent map shows that the structure of the map reflects technological relationships across the hierarchical administrative boundaries of the subject matter specifications in the IPC scheme. While counts of IPC sections (i.e. the first letter of IPC codes, A, B, C, D, E, F, G, H) are commonly used as a measure of technological distance in patents, the 35 technological areas that are derived from cross-citations in our patent map often span multiple sections. For instance, the vehicles area includes six different sections, and the heating and cooling, construction and metals areas include five different sections. Textiles, lighting, semiconductors and chem and polymers include four different sections. Only medical devices, food, recording, computing and radio communication areas encompass a single section. This is strong evidence that the IPC on its own is not an appropriate framework to investigate technological diversity without taking technological distance into account. It is also a factor to consider in the analysis and definition of emerging technological fields and markets.

The degree of interconnectedness among technological categories adds another level of support to decision-making. Patent documents that reference other patents in similar technological areas have been suggested to offer incremental opportunities to advance an area, whereas patent documents that refer across diverse categories may offer the potential for radical innovation [34]. For instance, an interesting feature of our global patent map is the high level of interconnectedness of most of the 35 technological areas. This can be observed not only in many connections among technology groups within each technological area, as shown by the densest areas of the map, but also across them. Some exceptions are areas such as food, drugs and med chem, biologics, TV imaging and comm. cosm and med chem as well as radio and comm that form more uniform clusters of technology groups (i.e. they appear as clusters of nodes of the same colour) (Fig. 10.1). Another notable feature is the short distance among technologies in a handful of groups such as drugs and med chem and biologics, as shown by denser areas and darker lines in the left-hand side of the maps. The sparse areas of the map are those associated with technological areas that comprise fewer technological categories, including electric power, lighting and recording.

Finally, the concentration of patenting activity in the innovation landscape— or global map—is another aspect of visual analysis that can support strategic decision-making. Overlays created with patent data subsets allow this kind of analysis. Broader technology groups and more specific categories can be compared across organisations, and over time, to distinguish areas of R&D concentration and to identify trends, respectively. Areas of increasing activity can represent areas of market opportunity or be a signal of competitive threats when the analysis refers to specific companies and the purpose is to detect new entrants. Areas where technology development concentrates might anticipate emerging technological areas or niches. The complement, empty areas or 'white spaces' represent undeveloped areas. Our patent map, for example, uses categorisations to disaggregate some of the patent groupings into more fine-grained analysable components than other approaches. This more disaggregated clustering enables differentiation of the patent portfolios of, say, a company engaged in cosmetics patenting from one engaged in drug development and from yet another engaged in medical instrument development. Not shown here, but the maps can be blown up to allow closer examination of more fine-grained patterns.

Awareness of the conceptual heterogeneity of nodes or elements in the map raises the issue of whether the maps show 'similarity' among categories as we have assumed or other properties such as co-occurrence and complementarity. For example, patents of metals and automobiles are related not because these categories are similar but because automobiles are often made of metals. Also, plastics and metals may co-occur simply because they are materials that are used in similar products such as buckets and automobiles, not because they are similar. Moreover, unlike maps of science, where there has been a pre-established conventional understanding of disciplines, it is not straightforward how groups of technologies can be interpreted. This problem is compounded by the heterogeneous nature of the patent classes. Classes such as 'turbines and engines' include 'turbines' (F01D), 'jet propulsion' (F02K), 'aircraft equipment' (B64D) and 'airplanes and helicopters' (B64D). Elements from distinct branches of the IPC co-occur in maps, but rather than being similar, they likely co-occur because they are embedded and/or complementary. This difficulty that patent maps face is not simply a problem of classification, but a conundrum due to the multiple meanings and scales that the technology concept may take [35]. These issues suggest that the interpretation of patent maps should be ontologically flexible and one should take into account that both the elements and the relations may have different meanings.

A visual analytic study based on our base map and overlays would involve (1) creating a patent data set, (2) processing the data set to obtain overlay data by IPC-based category, (3) creating overlays and (4) analysing data and overlays to support decision-making. Users can draw on diverse data sources to create patent data sets for their analysis (e.g. we use EPO's PATSTAT). To process data sets, we have developed a mapping kit which includes source files that represent the structure of the base maps and thesaurus files that represent scientific publication and IPC-based category definitions and enable creation of overlay maps using software such as VantagePoint and Pajek.[3] The analysis typically involves comparing areas of concentration over time and across different entities such as companies, countries or technological fields. Overlays offer a general perspective that can be enriched with data tables with more detailed information on patenting activity.

10.6   Concluding Remarks

This chapter discusses broader aspects and issues of patent mapping in the context of information retrieval, exploration and analysis for patent corpora and their differences to similar approaches applied to scientific literature. The chapter also discusses visual analytics and diverse methods for mapping—including a new global patent map and overlay technique developed by the authors—that enable 'visual thinking' [13] and a better understanding of technology development concentrations and R&D profiles of companies or countries. To exemplify the kind of analytical support offered by global and overlay maps, we illustrate the application of the patent overlay maps we developed to benchmark the nanotechnology-related patenting activities of companies and reveal the areas of concentration of their patenting activities.

Patent analyses play key roles in competitive technical intelligence as they combine multiple information types to offer innovation indicators to support decision-making. Patent mapping provides a visual component to enrich various innovation system analyses and complements science overlay mapping to enrich our understanding of R&D activities. Patent overlay maps serve to discern patent activity patterns with implications for innovation. These can inform corporate investment decisions via intelligence about key competitors' perceived trajectories, for example. Alternatively, analyses can contribute to policy discourse by profiling national positions and potential. Patent analysis involves data search and retrieval and a number of processes for data clean-up and refinement to obtain subsets that ultimately contribute insight into specific technologies or market sectors being engaged.

The visualisation of knowledge or technological landscapes has been a prominent part of publication and patent analyses since their origins, but recent improvements in computational power and algorithms have allowed the creation of diverse global maps of science and technology. Both science and patent maps draw on network analysis algorithms and visualisation procedures that help to explore and visually identify areas of activity, interrelationships and the overall structure of scientific and technological activities. Science and technology maps complement other methodological approaches to data analysis and can help to interpret and find

---

[3]This mapping kit is available upon request to the authors. VantagePoint is a commercial software for text mining: https://www.thevantagepoint.com. The purpose of the kit, however, is to make this mapping technique available for use with other software as well.

meaning in complex data by transforming abstract and intangible data sets into something visible and concrete. In patent maps, in particular, a key characteristic in being able to visualise innovative opportunities is the ability to graphically represent 'technological distance' or the extent to which a set of patents reflects different types of technologies. Scholars have pursued diverse approaches to scientific publication and patent record-level analysis to create global maps of science and technology. Consensus on the shape and relative position of science and technological categories are important to make global maps meaningful to compare, for example, organisational or technological patent data subsets.

Our patent mapping approach offers distinctive visualisation capabilities. In contrast to prior IPC-based global patent maps, our approach recombines IPC categories to reflect a finer distribution of patents. Thus, it enables improved differentiation ability in categories with a large amount of patenting activity. It also facilitates replication by helping to trace back individual categories to verify results and make improvements. One of the most interesting findings of our work is that IPC categories that are close to one another in the patent map are not necessarily in the same hierarchical IPC branch, which suggests that technological distance is not always well proxied by relying on the IPC administrative structure. The introduction of the Cooperative Patent Classification (CPC) scheme is likely to affect our category definitions or the process by which we come up with specific definitions. Still the overall dimensions of the map would be supported and only some of the topical areas in the margins would change.

Visualisations are valuable tools for competitive R&D and policy decision-making support. Potential applications of patent overlay maps include organisational and regional/country benchmarking (e.g. for the examination of competitive positions), exploration of potential collaborations and general analysis of technological changes over time. Patent maps may also reveal relatively unexplored technological areas that are more central to other technologies or highlight denser areas with more technological interdependency that might form platforms for the emergence of future technology applications. Ongoing work we undertake seeks to overcome some issues found in the development of the original patent overlay maps. The coverage of the technology classification scheme we developed is among the most important issues we address. While the data source may cover a wide range of IPC categories, new technologies and categories resulting naturally from innovation processes require constant updates to maintain good coverage and be able to support decision-making in emerging areas as well.

Acknowledgements This chapter is based on research undertaken at Georgia Tech drawing on support from the US National Science Foundation (NSF) through the Center for Nanotechnology in Society (Arizona State University, Award No. 0531194 and NSF Award No. 1064146) ('Revealing Innovation Pathways: Hybrid Science Maps for Technology Assessment and Foresight') in collaboration with the Center for Nanotechnology in Society, University of California Santa Barbara (NSF Awards No. 0938099 and No. 0531184). The findings and observations contained in this chapter are those of the authors and do not necessarily reflect the views of NSF.

References

1. Kay L, Newman N, Youtie J, Porter AL, Rafols I (2014) Patent overlay mapping: visualizing technological distance. J Assoc Inf Sci Technol 65(12):2432–2443. doi:10.1002/asi.23146
2. Rafols I, Porter AL, Leydesdorff L (2010) Science overlay maps: a newtool for research policy and library management. J Am Soc Inf Sci Technol 61(9):1871–1887
3. Porter AL, Newman NC (2005) Patent profiling for competitive advantage: deducing who is doing what, where, and when. In: Moed JF, Glanzel W, Schmoch U (eds) Handbook of quantitative science and technology research. Kluwer, Dordrecht, The Netherlands
4. Trippe A (2003) Patinformatics: tasks to tools. World Patent Inf 25:211–221
5. Dunphy SM, Herbig PR, Howes ME (1996) The innovation funnel. Technol Forecast Social Change 53:279–292
6. Souder WE (1987) Managing new product innovations. Lexington Books, New York, NY
7. Watts RJ, Porter AL (1997) Innovation forecasting. Technol Forecast Social Change 56:25–47
8. Balconi M, Breschi S, Lissoni F (2004) Networks of inventors and the role of academia: an exploration of Italian patent data. Res Policy 33(1):127–145
9. Schoen A, Villard L, Laurens P, Cointet J-P, Heimeriks G, Alkemade F (2012) The network structure of technological developments; Technological distance as a walk on the technology map. Presented at the STI Indicators Conference 2012, Montréal. http://sticonference.org/Proceedings/vol2/Schoen_Network_733.pdf. Accessed 22 June 2013
10. Ernst H (2003) Patent information for strategic technology management. World Patent Inf 25(3):233–242
11. Leydesdorff L, Kushnir D, Rafols I (2012) Interactive overlay maps for US patent (USPTO) data based on International Patent Classification (IPC). Scientometrics 1–17. doi:10.1007/s11192-012-0923-2.
12. Leydesdorff L, Alkemade F, Heimeriks G, Hoekstra R (2015) Patents as instruments for exploring innovation dynamics: geographic and technological perspectives on "photovoltaic cells". Scientometrics 102:629–651
13. Chen C (2003) Mapping scientific frontiers: the quest for knowledge visualization. Springer, London
14. Boyack KW (2003) An indicator-based characterization of the Proceedings of the National Academy of Science. Paper presented at the NAS Sackler Colloquium on Mapping Knowledge Domains
15. Archibugi D, Pianta M (1996) Measuring technological change through patents and innovation surveys. Technovation 16(9):451–468
16. Huang Y, Ma J, Porter AL, Kwon S, Zhu D (2015) Analyzing collaboration networks and developmental patterns of nano-enabled drug delivery (NEDD) for brain cancer. J Nanotechnol 6:1666–1676
17. Hinze S, Reiss T, Schmoch U (1997) Statistical analysis on the distance between fields of technology. Paper presented at the Innovation Systems and European Integration (ISE), Targeted Socio-Economic Research Program, 4th Framework Program of the European Commission (DGXII), Karlsruhe, Germany
18. Small H (1973) Co-citation in the scientific literature: a new measure of the relationship between two documents. J Am Soc Inf Sci Technol 24(4):265–269
19. Klavans R, Boyack KW (2009) Toward a consensus map of science. J Am Soc Inf Sci Technol 60(3):455–476
20. Bollen J, Van de Sompel H, Hagberg A, Bettencourt L, Chute R, Rodriguez MA et al (2009) Clickstream data yields high-resolution maps of science. PLoS One 4(3), e4803. doi:10.1371/journal.pone.0004803
21. Boyack KW, Börner K, Klavans R (2009) Mapping the structure and evolution of chemistry research. Scientometrics 79(1):45–60
22. Boyack KW, Klavans R, Börner K (2005) Mapping the backbone of science. Scientometrics 64:351–374

23. Janssens F, Zhang L, Moor BD, Glänzel W (2009) Hybrid clustering for validation and improvement of subject-classification schemes. Inf Process Manag 45(6):683–702. doi:10.1016/j.ipm.2009.06.003
24. Leydesdorff L, Rafols I (2009) A global map of science based on the ISI subject categories. J Am Soc Inf Sci Technol 60(2):348–362
25. Moya-Anegón F, Vargas-Quesada B, Chinchilla-Rodríguez Z, Corera-Álvarez E, Herrero-Solana V (2007) Visualizing the marrow of science. J Am Soc Inf Sci Technol 58(14):2167–2179
26. Moya-Anegon F, Vargas-Quesada B, Herrero-Solana V, Chinchilla-Rodriguez Z, Corera-Alvarez E, Munoz-Fernandez FJ (2004) A new technique for building maps of large scientific domains based on the cocitation of classes and categories. Scientometrics 61(1):129–145
27. Rosvall M, Bergstrom CT (2010) Mapping change in large networks. PLoS One 5(1), e8694. doi:10.1371/journal.pone.0008694
28. Van den Besselaar P, Leydesdorff L (1996) Mapping change in scientific specialties: a scientometric reconstruction of the development of artificial intelligence. J Am Soc Inf Sci Technol 46(6):415–436
29. Breschi S, Lissoni F, Malerba F (2003) Knowledge-relatedness in firm technological diversification. Res Policy 32:69–87
30. Jaffe A (1986) Technological opportunities and spillovers of R&D: evidence from firms' patents, profits, and market value. Am Econ Rev 76(5):984–1001
31. Kauffman S, Lobo J, Macready WG (2000) Optimal search on a technology landscape. J Econ Behav Organ 43:141–166
32. Rafols I, Leydesdorff L (2009) Content-based and algorithmic classifications of journals: perspectives on the dynamics of scientific communication and indexer effects. J Am Soc Inf Sci Technol 60(9):1823–1835
33. Boyack KW, Klavans R (2008) Measuring science–technology interaction using rare inventor–author names. J Informet 2:173–182
34. Olsson O (2004) Technological opportunity and growth. J Econ Growth 10(1):35–57
35. Arthur WB (2010) The nature of technology. Penguin, London

Part IV
Special Topics in Patent Retrieval

The last part, and the largest of all the parts of this or the previous edition, covers a fairly large spectrum of research in the patent field, from classification to translation, via image processing.

We start with an update of patent classification at subgroup level. It had been shown before, in the previous editions' chapters on classification but also here in the report on the CLEF-IP evaluation exercise, that classification works very satisfactorily at the subclass level of the IPC (e.g. A61K) but degrades rapidly when going further to group (e.g. A61K 6/00) and subgroup (e.g. A61K 6/007). D'hondt and her colleagues show us a method to improve the situation.

The following three chapters cover different aspects of image processing and what one can do with the thus extracted information. We start in Chap. 12 with the problem of image classification: given an image, can we detect automatically whether it is a chemical compound, a table, a mathematical formula, a drawing or any other of the typical types of images found in patents? The answer provided by Csurka et al. is an almost perfect 'yes'. Then we look at two particular types of images. First, Rossinyol describes their automated system for flowchart recognition, comprising both structural recognition of the links between a flowchart's boxes and optical character recognition of the text within the boxes. Then Filippov and his colleagues demonstrate how given an image of a chemical compound, we can transform it to its IUPAC representation. Of course, not all chemical formulas can be transformed, especially since there is no commonly agreed representation of Markush structures, but the system they demonstrate was the best performing system in the TREC-CHEM and CLEF-IP evaluation campaigns.

Once we have the representation of the chemical structure, Barnard and colleagues extend the chapter published by Holliday and Willet in the last edition and give an overview of the challenges presented by this field and a summary of the approaches to these challenges, including Markush structures.

Finally, we were very happy to be able to include in this edition a chapter on patent translation. As it has been repeatedly mentioned throughout this book, patent search is an inherent multilingual process, where even native speakers of the dominating language, English, cannot escape the need to understand documents written in other languages. The chapter written by Tinsley describes their statistical translation system built specifically for patent data. This work is particularly interesting because it is one of the few examples where academic research (in this case supported by the European Commission under its ICT Policy Support Programme) has resulted in a solid start-up, which has managed to find its place in the highly competitive patent translation market.

Chapter 11
Patent Classification on Subgroup Level Using Balanced Winnow

Eva D'hondt, Suzan Verberne, Nelleke Oostdijk, and Lou Boves

Abstract In the past decade research into automated patent classification has mainly focused on the higher levels of International Patent Classification (IPC) hierarchy. The patent community has expressed a need for more precise classification to better aid current pre-classification and retrieval efforts (Benzineb and Guyot, Current challenges in patent information retrieval. Springer, New York, pp 239–261, 2011). In this chapter we investigate the three main difficulties associated with automated classification on the lowest level in the IPC, i.e. subgroup level. In an effort to improve classification accuracy on this level, we (1) compare flat classification with a two-step hierarchical system which models the IPC hierarchy and (2) examine the impact of combining unigrams with PoS-filtered skipgrams on both the subclass and subgroup levels. We present experiments on English patent abstracts from the well-known WIPO-alpha benchmark data set, as well as from the more realistic CLEF-IP 2010 data set. We find that the flat and hierarchical classification approaches achieve similar performance on a small data set but that the latter is much more feasible under real-life conditions. Additionally, we find that combining unigram and skipgram features leads to similar and highly significant improvements in classification performance (over unigram-only features) on both the subclass and subgroup levels, but only if sufficient training data is available.

11.1 Introduction

In the last decades, patents have gained an enormous economic importance. Patent filing rates increase every year, and patent attorneys and examiners of the various patent offices are straining to deal with the large number of applications submitted every day. In this situation, automating (part of) the process by which

E. D'hondt (✉)
Radboud University Nijmegen, Nijmegen, The Netherlands

Laboratoire d'Informatique pour la Mécanique et les Sciences de l'Ingénieur, Orsay, France
e-mail: eva.dhondt@limsi.fr

S. Verberne • N. Oostdijk • L. Boves
Radboud University Nijmegen, Nijmegen, The Netherlands
e-mail: s.verberne@cs.ru.nl; n.oostdijk@let.ru.nl; l.boves@let.ru.nl

© Springer-Verlag GmbH Germany 2017

M. Lupu et al. (eds.), *Current Challenges in Patent Information Retrieval*,
The Information Retrieval Series 37, DOI 10.1007/978-3-662-53817-3_11

incoming applications are processed has great economic value [17]. Automatic patent classification, that is, automatically assigning relevant category labels from the International Patent Classification (IPC) taxonomy (see below) to an incoming document, may be an invaluable asset in both the *pre-classification* and *examination* phases of the patent granting process.

During the pre-classification stage, a patent application is examined by a person who has a general knowledge about all technological fields and—most importantly—has expert knowledge of the patent classification system. This expert then routes the application to the department(s) that specialises in the technical fields relevant to the invention described in the application [28]. At the European Patent Office (EPO), there have been attempts to automate this process [17], but due to low accuracy scores, pre-classification is currently limited to the higher (more abstract) levels of the IPC taxonomy.

In the examination phase, a patent examiner will perform a high-precision, interactive search to find documents that describe inventions similar to the one described in the application, in a bid to determine the existence of prior art for this invention. Prior art queries usually consist of field-specific terminology with specialised (low-level) IPC labels as query terms. In this phase, a fine-grained, consistent and high-quality patent classification is indispensable [27]. The research presented in this chapter aims to implement, improve and evaluate automated classification on lower (more specific) levels in the taxonomy, thus allowing for more specific suggestions during the pre-classification and examination processes.

In most patent offices, incoming patents are categorised and indexed using the International Patent Classification (IPC) system, a complex hierarchical category structure which covers all areas of technology. The IPC is a manually constructed taxonomy, which has been updated and refined over the last 30 years and is used in the patent offices of over 90 countries. It currently comprises five levels, of increasingly fine granularity: sections, classes, subclasses, groups and subgroups. The latest instantiation of the IPC (IPC-2015.01) comprises eight sections, about 130 classes, about 640 subclasses, around 7400 main groups and approximately 64,000 subgroups.

Most of the previous research on automatic patent classification has focused on classification at the higher levels in the IPC hierarchy, i.e. class and subclass levels. State-of-the-art classification results are around 62 % F1@5[1] on the subclass level [22, 23]. With about 130 and about 640 different categories, respectively, classification at the class and subclass levels is challenging, but computationally feasible for most classification algorithms.

The more detailed group and subgroup levels are generally deemed extremely difficult to classify properly for three reasons:

First, the categories on the lower levels generally show a large amount of overlap [31], and only part of the information in the document is potentially useful in distinguishing a category from related categories. Let us illustrate this with an

---

[1] 'F1@5' denotes the F1 score evaluated at rank 5.

example: subclass *A47C* comprises *chairs, sofas, beds*, and subclass *A47J* holds *kitchen equipment*. On subgroup level, the differences between categories are more subtle; they correspond to a small difference in the implementation or use of the invention, e.g. subgroup *A47C 17/12* covers *sofas changeable to beds by tilting or extending the armrests*, while subgroup *A47C 17/14* holds *sofas changeable to beds by removing parts only*. Consequently, the overlap of textual features between categories is likely to be much larger on the lowest level than on higher levels in the hierarchy.

The issue of overlapping categories is further complicated by the peculiar language use in patents. To increase the scope of legal protection, patent attorneys use obfuscating language to describe the inventions, so that a mundane object like a *pump* becomes a *fluid transportation device*. The abundance of vague terms in the patent corpora makes it extra hard to distinguish between categories that already have a high overlap. In previous research, D'hondt et al. [7] found that adding more precise (phrasal) features such as skipgrams[2] to unigram (word) features improves classification at the IPC *class* level. It is not known if skipgrams would also capture the supposedly more subtle differences on the lower levels in the hierarchy.

Second, the large number of categories on lower levels in the IPC results in a computationally expensive classification task with severe scalability issues [1]. A common approach to deal with a large number of categories in a multi-level taxonomy, which are characterised by fine-grained distinctions, is a *hierarchical classification* method (as opposed to *flat classification*) [9]. Hierarchical classifiers can consist of one integrated classifier that is trained with knowledge of the structure of a taxonomy [2] or a set of classifiers that predict category labels in individual nodes of a (predefined) taxonomy [26]. Integrated and distributed hierarchical classifiers can be implemented in many different ways. In this chapter we will use the most common architecture of a distributed classifier: the 'local classifier per parent node approach' proposed by Silla and Freitas [26]. In this architecture each parent node in the category hierarchy corresponds with a multi-class classifier, which is trained to distinguish between the child nodes. The training material for a classifier is selected through the 'siblings' policy: when training a classifier to distinguish one daughter, e.g. subclass 'A01B' from all other daughters (subclasses) in the same 'world', i.e. class 'A01', all examples of 'A01B' are selected as positive training material, while the examples with labels 'A01L', 'A01D', … serve as negative training material.

In the test phase, it is common to use a top-down class-prediction approach: when a document is classified by a hierarchical system, the output of the classifier at the parent nodes influences the classification conducted at the child nodes at the next level of the hierarchy. The classification process can be accelerated substantially if

---

[2]'Skipgrams' are sequences of N words in a text, in which up to M intervening words may be deleted. Thus, a 2-skip-2-gram is a sequence of two words (bigram) that are no more than two words apart in a text. For example, from the example sentence *'I like to drive.'*, the following set of 2-skip-2-grams can be generated: `I_like`, `I_to`, `I_drive`, `like_to`, `like_drive`, `to_drive`.

the procedure at the next lower level is limited to the daughters of the categories that had the highest probability of being correct at the higher levels. When applied to the group and subgroup levels in patent classification, where on average a group comprises 12 subgroups, reducing the classifiers on lower levels to the most promising mother nodes simplifies the classification procedure substantially, when compared to the 64,000 subgroups that a flat classifier must distinguish.

Another advantage of a hierarchical classifier may be that, given the different training sets and the differences in overlap between categories, classifiers on lower levels might be able to select different and more focused features than classifiers that operate on a higher level of a taxonomy. Consider a system that needs to distinguish between 'clothes' and 'gardening tools' on a higher level and—within the 'clothes' category—between 'bikinis' and 'swimming trunks' on the lower level. Terms such as 'water', 'cover' and 'texture' will be informative features for the high-level classifier, but less so for the low-level classifier. We would expect the latter classifier to select more features that focus on the (smaller) differences between the categories, such as 'man' versus 'woman', 'top', etc.

A drawback of top-down hierarchical classifier systems is that they are suscep-tible to the *propagation of error* problem [18]: an erroneous hard decision at an upper level will propagate down the hierarchy, making it impossible to arrive at the correct low-level category label. Several solutions have been proposed to counter the error propagation, of which the most common is to backtrack when the classification scores on lower levels become too low. However, as is well known from syntactic parsing, backtracking mechanisms quickly become unwieldy. As a consequence it is claimed that single-level (flat) methods are more efficient than hierarchical methods, but that hierarchical methods are generally more accurate [4].

The *third* reason classification on group and subgroup levels is generally deemed too difficult is that the relative sparseness in the number of documents per category creates training difficulties [11]. Most data sets available for research in text classi-fication have a certain degree of skewness of their distribution. In the patent domain, where technological categories move with different evolutionary speed—which entails shifts in the number of applications per category over time [8]—we found that a small proportion of the categories comprise the bulk of the documents [7]. The impact of the skewness of the distribution of documents over categories on a specific classification task is difficult to predict and may depend on the type of classifier that is being used.

We hypothesise that the scalability issues mentioned by Benzineb and Guyot [1] and the large degree of overlap between subgroups mentioned by Widodo [31] can both be addressed by using hierarchical, rather than flat, classifiers. In this chapter we examine the impact of flat and hierarchical approaches on the classification of abstracts of patent applications on the deepest (subgroup) level in the IPC hierarchy. In addition, we investigate the impact of different text representations (unigrams versus skipgrams) on the classification performance. By performing experiments on two data sets of different sizes, we will also address the issues caused by the skewness of the distributions in data sets that are available for scientific research.

In concrete terms, this chapter attempts to answer two fundamental questions:

1. How do flat and hierarchical classification methods compare in classifying on the subgroup level with the WIPO-alpha set? For both methods we use the Balanced Winnow classification algorithm. Following Chen and Chang [4], we simplify the five-level hierarchical classification problem in the IPC hierarchy to a two-level problem: subclass and subgroup. To avoid the problem of the propagation of error, we do not make a selection of top-n categories on the subclass level, but we will consider all possible branches in the classification tree. As proposed by Dumais and Chen [9], we convert classification scores to posterior probabilities for class membership. The posteriors from the subclass and subgroup levels are then combined to obtain class membership probabilities at the subgroup level.
2. Can we improve the classification on subgroup level by adding phrasal features to unigram features? Since previous research [7] indicated that phrasal features are only effective given a large amount of training data, we conducted this analysis not only on the (relatively small) WIPO-alpha corpus but also on the larger CLEF-IP 2010 corpus.

By virtue of the fact that we perform experiments on two data sets of different sizes, we will be able to shed light on the interaction between, and the relative importance of, the three problems with patent classification mentioned in the literature: too large a number of categories, sparseness of documents per category and high similarity between categories.

11.2 Related Work

For a detailed overview of the literature concerning the impact of different text representations on patent classification, we refer the reader to [7]. Here, we will focus on the use of flat or hierarchical classifiers.

An extensive overview of the various methods used for hierarchical classification in multiple application domains can be found in [26]. In this section we will limit ourselves to approaches to text classification in the patent domain.

As mentioned in the introduction, methods for hierarchical text classification fall into two subgroups: (1) methods that consist of one integrated classifier that uses the (hierarchical) relations between the categories as additional information next to textual content and (2) a multi-level approach with different sets of classifiers on different levels in a taxonomy. In Sects. 11.2.1 and 11.2.2, we discuss literature about applying both types of methods to classification in the patent domain. In Sect. 11.2.3 we describe an approach for combining classification scores in hierarchical classification, which has not yet been used in the patent domain before.

11.2.1 Training One Classifier with Information from the Hierarchy

Cai and Hofmann [2] propose a hierarchical classification method based on support vector machines (SVM). Their method does not perform classification in two or more steps, but encodes the hierarchical information in the description of categories and then performs flat classification. Cai and Hofmann [2] do this by extending the multi-class SVM algorithm with the possibility of representing each category with an attribute vector instead of a single category label. They encode the hierarchical relationships between the categories as attributes for the categories. They compare their hierarchical implementation of SVM to standard (flat) SVM in classification on the main group level for the WIPO-alpha collection. They find that their hierarchical approach gives similar accuracy to the standard SVM approach, but with the hierarchical approach the incorrectly assigned categories are closer to the correct categories in the taxonomy than with the standard approach.

Wang et al. [30] combine a top-down hierarchical classifier (as will be presented in Sect. 11.2.2) with a meta-classifier to arrive at more balanced rankings on the lowest level in a hierarchy. The meta-classifier takes *meta-samples* as features. These samples are feature vectors that encode information on the 'path' through the hierarchy to arrive at a low-level category, rather than the textual content of that category. They collect such information as the scores of the related base classifiers, the number of nodes on a path, the average scores of nodes along a path, etc., in a sparse vector. Wang et al. [30] evaluate their method on the [18] data set and find that it achieves a similar accuracy as flat classification systems.

11.2.2 Two-Step Classification

In the NTCIR-6 track, a special task was devoted to the two-level classification taxonomy used in the Japan Patent Office. The category set in the first level is an extension of IPC, in the form of a set of thematic categories. For example, the theme 2C088 is about 'pinball game machines' [18]. The categories on the second level denote the 'viewpoint' of the invention. Examples of viewpoints are purpose, means, function and effect. Each theme has a set of viewpoints and each viewpoint may consist of several elements, which are organised in a tree structure. For example, the theme 2C088 has a viewpoint AA 'machine detail', which has the element AA01 'vertical pinball machines' [18]. The viewpoints with their elements are encoded as so-called F-terms in the patent. Li et al. [18] compared flat classification of F-terms using SVM to hierarchical classification using a variant of SVM called H-SVM [3]. They find that their method for hierarchical classification performed much worse than what they could achieve with flat classification. They suggest that the hierarchical relations among the classes are too complicated for the H-SVM algorithm.

Another branch of hierarchical classification systems explicitly exploits the hierarchical properties of the IPC taxonomy, either through user interaction or by combining classification output on different levels to predict labels on subgroup level.

The myClass classification tool [13] is a neural network implementation of the Balanced Winnow algorithm and achieved the highest accuracy in the CLEF-IP 2010 classification task (on subclass level) [22]. This tool uses a semi-automatic[3] method for classification on subgroup level [12]. A user is asked to select the correct labels from classification output on an intermediate level, such as subclass or main group. In a second step, the tool outputs subgroup labels within the selected (intermediate) categories.

Tikk et al. [28] propose a taxonomy-driven architecture for text classification called HITEC. They model the tree structure of the class hierarchy as a neural network. The categorisation of an incoming document is performed from the top of the hierarchy downwards. Going from top to bottom in the hierarchy, each level is followed by a so-called authorisation layer. The classifier determines the classification score of the document for all active category nodes at each level. Based on this score, the authorisation layer decides which categories on the next level are activated. In doing so, the authors use a novel *relaxed greedy algorithm*: Rather than activating only the category with the highest relevance score at each level, the system allows multiple categories to be active if their label scores are above a given threshold and within a given margin of variation from the highest label score. By thus widening the search, the authors expect to counter the propagation of error. However, the classification scores from the higher levels are not taken into account in calculating the classification scores for the lower levels. Consequently, the final rankings are based solely on the similarities between the test documents and the category models on the lowest levels, which might suffer from the fact that very few training documents are available for a large proportion of the categories. Tikk et al. [28] evaluate their method on the WIPO-alpha set. They classify documents on three levels: class, subclass and main group. They obtain excellent results with 53.25 % accuracy at the subclass level, which is 12 percentage points higher than the best-scoring setting reported in the reference paper by Fall and Benzineb [11]. On the main group level, Tikk et al. [28] achieve an accuracy of 36.89 %.

Chen and Chang [4] extend the work done by Tikk et al. [28] and were—to our knowledge—the first to classify on subgroup level. They develop a three-phase classification method which combines flat SVM classifiers at two different levels of the IPC hierarchy, namely, subclass and subgroup level, with a KNN classifier on the subgroup level. Their method takes four parameters $k1$–$k4$. In the first phase, a test document is classified on subclass level and a predetermined number of category labels are returned (variable $k1$). These subclass categories are then pooled together

---

[3]In its latest version myClass offers fully automatic classification on subgroup level [14]. However, as myClass is proprietary software, a detailed technical description of its current implementation has not been published.

to form a large 'world' in which a classifier is trained, this time on subgroup level. In the second phase, a predetermined number of category labels on subgroup level are returned (variable $k2$). The classifier that is needed for the first step can be built beforehand, but the classifier for the second step is variable and must be learned dynamically after the top-$k1$ subclasses have been identified. In the third phase of the algorithm by Chen and Chang [4], each subgroup from the top-$k2$ of subgroups is split in $k3$ clusters of documents using k-means clustering. Then, cosine similarity is calculated between the test document and the mean of each cluster. A KNN classifier with $k = k4$ is used to choose the most similar subgroup for the test document, i.e. the subgroup category with the most occurrences in the $k4$ most similar document clusters.

In a pretest phase, Chen and Chang [4] examine 'almost all combinations' (p. 11) of the parameters $k1$–$k4$ to determine the optimal combination with the highest accuracy. For this pretest, they use a subset of 400 documents from the test data. Their best-scoring setting ($k1 = 11, k2 = 37, k3 = 5, k4 = 169$) achieves a 36.07 % accuracy at the subgroup level.[4] Since they did not use a held-out development set for parameter tuning, these results can be considered an upper bound for classification performance with their three-phase method. For the sake of comparison, Chen and Chang [4] also re-implemented the HITEC classifier by Tikk et al. [28] and, using this system, they achieve 30.2 % for the same test set on subgroup level.

11.2.3 Combining the Classification Scores on Different Levels in the Hierarchy

As we saw in the previous two subsections, none of the approaches in previous work on hierarchical patent classification combines the scores of classifiers on different levels. The common approach is to let the output of the high-level classifier determine which classifiers on lower levels are activated [28], or what training material should be selected to train a classifier on the lower level [4]. In both cases, individual category scores do not have a direct impact on lower levels in the hierarchical classifier.

If we look outside the patent domain, however, we can find methods that combine classifier scores from different levels in a hierarchy. An example of this in a text classification task is [9], who performs Web page classification on a small two-level corpus of (summarised) Web pages, which consists of 13 categories on the first level and 150 categories on the second level. In order to be able to combine scores from different classifiers, they first derive posterior probabilities from SVM output scores. They then proceed to compare the impact of (1) thresholding on higher levels in the hierarchy (effectively minimising the number of categories to be examined

---

[4]They also report the accuracy of their algorithm without the third step ($k1 = 11, k2 = 1$): 20.2 %.

at the lower level) with (2) combining higher- and lower-level probabilities through multiplication and then thresholding on the final probabilities. Both methods achieve similar final rankings (of the top N results). Dumais and Chen [9] also compare the hierarchical systems with a flat (baseline) classification system. They find that hierarchical methods significantly outperform that baseline system.

11.3   Data Selection and Processing

11.3.1   Data Selection

In this section we describe the two patent corpora used for the experiments presented in Sects. 11.5 and 11.6. The WIPO-alpha data set is a well-known benchmark for patent classification, which was first made available by the World Intellectual Property Organization (WIPO) in 2002. Although it is a clean and often-used data set, it is fairly small compared to present standards. We therefore opted to run a second series of experiments on the CLEF-IP 2010 data set, which is more representative of a real-life patent corpus.

11.3.1.1   WIPO-Alpha Data Set

The English WIPO-alpha collection[5] consists of 75,250 patent documents (46,324 for training and 28,926 for testing) with their IPC category labels on subgroup level.[6] The documents were published between 1998 and 2002 and are labelled with the 7th version of the IPC.

From each patent document, we extracted the abstract section, using the information in the XML source. Since some subgroups have little to no training data, we used the same data selection criteria as [4][7]: we only selected subgroups that have a minimum of seven training documents. This selection step resulted in a corpus of 22,113 documents (12,883 for training and 9230 for testing). The corpus statistics after document selection in Table 11.1 show that there is a large variation in the number of documents (abstracts) in the different categories, both on subclass level and subgroup level. Moreover, 628 of the 1140 categories on subgroup level contain fewer than ten documents. Having only seven documents as positive examples for training a classifier is on—or below—the lower bound of what is needed to construct

---

[5]The collection can be downloaded at http://www.wipo.int/classifications/ipc/en/ITsupport/ Categorization/dataset/index.html.

[6]Since IPC labels are hierarchical, i.e. contain information on parent nodes in the label, we can easily extract subclass labels from the subgroup labels.

[7]Unlike [4], we used the official training/test split as determined by the EPO. Our category selection was based on frequency counts over the training set only.

Table 11.1 Corpus statistics on the WIPO-alpha corpus after sample selection

	# of cat	av. # doc in cat (stdev)	av. # daughters (stdev)
Subclass	339	38.00 (53.19)	3.36[a] (4.36)
Subgroup	1140	11.30 (7.18)	n.a.

[a]128 subclasses only have one subgroup daughter in the training set

a useful category model. But even with this lenient criterion, we were forced to discard more than 70 % of the documents in the WIPO-alpha collection.

All documents in the WIPO-alpha collection come with one primary (subgroup) category label (determining the field of application in which the invention is novel) and may have several secondary categories. In the following experiments, we only take the primary category labels into account, thus rendering the WIPO-alpha experiments into a mono-label, multi-class hierarchical classification problem.

11.3.1.2   CLEF-IP 2010 Data Set

The CLEF-IP 2010 data set[8] is a subset of the MAREC corpus[9] and was released as part of the CLEF-IP 2010 classification and prior art retrieval tracks. It features 2.6 million patent documents from the European Patent Office (EPO). These three million documents with content in English, German and French pertain to over one million patents,[10] from 1976 to 2002.

As with the WIPO-alpha corpus, we first extracted all abstracts from the patent documents and then applied data selection on the corpus. We used more stringent selection criteria than for the WIPO-alpha set: only subgroups with a minimum of 50 documents were included in the corpus subset. This cut-off was arbitrarily chosen to avoid data sparseness in the subgroup categories on the one hand, while on the other hand minimising the number of one-daughter subclass worlds. The resulting subset was then divided into training/test corpora with the same ratio as the WIPO-alpha split (60/40), with the additional criterion that all subgroups in the training set must contain at least 20 documents. This resulted in a corpus subset of 991,805 documents and a training and test set of 595,080 and 396,725 documents, respectively. Statistics on the CLEF-IP corpus after sample selection are given in Table 11.2. It shows that in the fairly large CLEF-IP data set, the distribution is very skewed. When making the train/test split, we tried to minimise the number of categories that might suffer from data sparseness. We therefore chose a split where only 493 of the 19,411 subgroup categories contain fewer than 30 training

---

[8]Available at http://www.ifs.tuwien.ac.at/~clef-ip/download/2010/index.shtml#data.

[9]Available at http://www.ifs.tuwien.ac.at/imp/marec.shtml.

[10]Unlike the WIPO-alpha data set, the CLEF-IP data set contains documents that refer to the same patent but in various stages of the granting process. Consequently, some of the extracted abstracts may be similar to each other.

Table 11.2 Corpus statistics on the CLEF-IP 2010 subset corpus after sample selection

	# of cat	av. # doc in cat (stdev)	av. # daughters (stdev)
Subclass	575	8028.4 (20,512.2)	33.8[a] (63.4)
Subgroup	19,441	237.5 (434.8)	n.a.

[a]39 subclasses only have one subgroup daughter in the CLEF-IP 2010 subset

documents. For the CLEF-IP corpus, it also holds that fairly lenient data selection criteria in designing a classification experiment result in discarding almost 70 % of the documents. Please note the size difference between the two corpora: even after data selection there is—on average—six times more data available for a category on subgroup level in the CLEF-IP 2010 corpus than there is for a subclass category in the WIPO-alpha corpus.

Patent documents in the CLEF-IP 2010 data set may contain multiple labels and—unlike the WIPO-alpha set—have no information on primary versus secondary labels. We therefore included all labels, rendering the CLEF-IP experiments a multi-label, multi-category classification task. In consequence, the similarity between categories on both levels is likely to be higher since categories may share some training documents as positive examples during training.

11.3.2 Text Preprocessing and Feature Generation

While the WIPO-alpha corpus is a fairly clean text corpus and requires little preprocessing effort, the CLEF-IP 2010 corpus contains several data conversion errors which were solved using regular expressions.

After removing all XML markup from the extracted abstracts, we ran a Perl script to divide the running text into sentences, by splitting on end-of-sentence punctuation such as question marks and full stops. In order to minimise incorrect splitting of the technical texts that contain many acronyms and abbreviations, the Perl script was supplied with a list of common English abbreviations and a list containing abbreviations and acronyms that occur frequently in technical texts,[11] derived from the Specialist lexicon.[12]

The sentences in the WIPO-alpha and the CLEF-IP corpora were then further processed to generate lemmatised unigrams and skipgrams. In previous research [6, 7], we found that classification accuracy (on class level) is more improved by adding skipgrams which are filtered for specific parts of speech than by adding bigrams or dependency triples generated by a parser.

---

[11]Both the splitter and abbreviation file can be downloaded from https://sites.google.com/site/ekldhondt/downloads.

[12]The lexicon can be downloaded at http://lexsrv3.nlm.nih.gov/Specialist/Summary/lexicon.html.

To generate unigram and skipgram features, the preprocessed sentences were tagged using an in-house PoS tagger [29].[13] The tagger's statistical language models have been trained on the annotated subset of the British National Corpus. We opted for this particular tagger because it is highly customisable to new lexicons and word frequencies, which is essential when dealing with the patent domain: the language usage in patent documents can differ greatly from that in other genres. For example, the past participle *said* is often used to modify nouns as in *'for said claim'*. While this usage is very rare and archaic in general English, it is a very typical modifier in patent language. Consequently, a PoS tagger must be updated to account for these differences in language use. To this end we adapted the tagger with word frequency information and associated PoS tags from the AEGIR lexicon.[14] We did not retrain the N-gram language model of the tagger, since no PoS-tagged patent texts are available for that purpose. The words in the tagged output were also lemmatised using the AEGIR lexicon.

From the tagged output, we then generated two text representations using the filtering and lemmatisation procedure described in [6]: PoS-filtered words (only allowing nouns, verbs and adjectives) and PoS-filtered 2-skip-2-grams (only allowing combinations of nouns, verbs and/or adjectives). In the experiments described in this chapter, *unigrams* will refer to the PoS-filtered words only, while *unigrams + skipgrams* will refer to the combination of PoS-filtered words and PoS-filtered 2-skip-2-grams.

11.4 Classification Algorithms

In this section we first describe the training algorithm of the classifiers in both the flat and hierarchical classification approaches. Section 11.4.2 describes our approach to hierarchical classification on subgroup level in the IPC hierarchy.

11.4.1 Balanced Winnow Algorithm

We opted to use the Balanced Winnow classification algorithm implementation in the Linguistic Classification System (LCS), because it has been shown in previous work to be very fast and effective for large-scale text classification problems and to yield state-of-the-art results on text classification problems with many categories [6, 7, 16].

---

[13]Tokenisation was performed by the tagger.

[14]The AEGIR lexicon is part of the AEGIR parser, a hybrid dependency parser that is designed to parse technical texts, with a focus on patent text. For more information, see [20].

Preceding the actual training, there is a two-step term selection phase in which the most informative terms are selected for each category. In the first step (global term selection), selection is based on global frequency information, i.e. a term must appear in at least three documents in the training set and at least twice in those documents. In the second step (local term selection), we used the LTC algorithm [25] to calculate TF-IDF scores for the features per category. We then selected the top 1000 most informative features per category and aggregated them into the initial category models (a.k.a. class profiles).

(Balanced) Winnow is a mistake-driven learning algorithm, akin to the perceptron algorithm. The effect of learning during training is determined by four parameters: a promotion parameter α, a demotion parameter β and two threshold parameters θ^+ and θ^-, which determine a threshold 'beam'.

In Balanced Winnow, each feature is given two weights (w^+ and w^-), the sum of which is the Winnow weight. The terms are initialised with their winnow weights set to their TF-IDF scores. During training the weights w^+ and w^- are only updated when a mistake occurs in classifying the training documents. The algorithm distinguishes two types of mistakes: (1) true label is not found and (2) wrong label is assigned. In the former case, the weights w^+ of the active features are promoted by multiplying them with α, while the weights w^- of the active features are demoted by multiplying them with β (thus increasing the final Winnow weights of the active features). In case of error (2), the weights w^+ of the active features are demoted by multiplying them with β, and the weights w^- are promoted by multiplication with α. The 'beam' determined by the θ parameters delineates an area where correct labelling is still considered a type 1 error, which leads to more weight updates.

In the test phase, when classifying a document d, the term vector representing d is checked against each category model, a.k.a. class profile, in the classifier and assigned a Winnow score for that category. This score is the sum of the Winnow scores for the individual terms in the term vector. In Sect. 11.4.3, we describe how we tuned the Winnow parameters.

11.4.2   Hierarchical Classifiers

11.4.2.1   System Architecture of the Hierarchical Classifiers

Following [4], our hierarchical approach to classification operates in a downward two-level hierarchy: On the first level, there is one classifier trained on a corpus-wide training set, annotated with IPC subclass information. In the case of the WIPO-alpha data set, this classifier distinguishes between 339 different (subclass) categories; for the CLEF-IP 2010 data set, it distinguishes between 575 different (subclass) categories. Hereafter we will refer to these classifiers as the *subclass classifiers*.

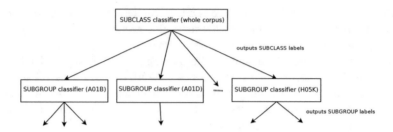

Fig. 11.1 Structure of a hierarchical classifier

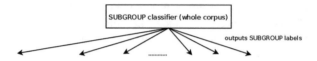

Fig. 11.2 Structure of a flat classifier

On the second level, for each subclass category a separate classifier is trained, which differentiates between the subgroup daughters in that subclass world.[15] A *subgroup classifier* is trained only on the training data available in a particular subclass world and yields classification scores for the different subgroup categories in that world. As was shown in Tables 11.1 and 11.2, the number of daughters in different subclass worlds can vary greatly. In our system the patent documents are always assigned a label on subgroup level; we do not assign labels on the intermediate group level. Figures 11.1 and 11.2 illustrate the architectures of a hierarchical and flat classifier, respectively. Each box in Fig. 11.1 refers to an individual flat classifier.

11.4.2.2 Normalisation and Converting Scores to Probabilities

During the test phase, a vector representing a test document is first scored by the subclass classifier and then by each of the subgroup classifiers. To arrive at a final ranking of subgroup labels, the scores of the classifiers on the two levels must be combined in a way that takes into account the differences in scoring ranges between the various classifiers.

We achieve this by transforming the Winnow scores of each document for each category into an estimate of the posterior probability that the document belongs in a given category. For that purpose, we used the sigmoid transformation proposed by Platt [24]. In the case of the subclass classifier for the WIPO-alpha set, each

---

[15]Please note that subclass worlds are the default context for training subgroup classifiers. In Sect. 11.5 we will also report additional experiments where subgroup categories were trained in larger contexts, i.e. class and section worlds.

document obtains 339 Winnow scores for as many subclasses, only one of which is correct. This leads to a substantial imbalance in the data for the logistic regression (for each relevant '1' score, there are 338 '0' scores) which we accounted for by the error weighting in [15] which we integrated in the implementation for finding the sigmoid proposed in [19].

Although the transformation of Winnow scores to probabilities by means of a continuously non-decreasing function cannot alter the rank order of the subclasses, it can increase or shrink the distance between the values assigned to subclasses. This becomes relevant when combining the probability scores derived from the subclass classifier with the probability scores from the different subgroup classifiers to achieve a final ranking on subgroup level.

To avoid a bias caused by the differences in score ranges between the subclass and the various subgroup classifiers—the subclass classifier scores generally span a wider range than those given by the subgroup classifiers—we decided to normalise the Winnow scores before transforming them to posterior probabilities. This was done using Batch Normalisation: for each classifier we calculated a linear function through which the Winnow scores for the training documents were mapped into the range [0.0, 10.0]. These linear functions were calculated by running a fivefold cross-validation over the training data available for that classifier and then mapping the complete set of scores into a range of 0 to 10 with the (original) maximum and minimum Winnow score in the complete set as anchor values.

A second bias that we wished to avoid is caused by the difference in the amount of training data on the two different levels: from Tables 11.1 and 11.2, it can be seen that the average number of documents available for training subclass classifiers is much larger than the number of documents for training subgroup classifiers. From this we can conjecture that the subclass classifier and the corresponding sigmoid function trained on subclass data are potentially better (in)formed than the individual classifiers and the corresponding sigmoids for the different subclass worlds. This hypothesis was confirmed by an analysis of the score distributions for categories on subgroup level. As mentioned above, Winnow scores from the subgroup classifiers are generally not widespread, and we found that—even after normalisation—the scores of relevant and irrelevant categories were quite similar. Consequently, the sigmoids fitted on this data may not yield accurate transformations from Winnow scores to posterior probabilities. We experimented with different definitions of the 'worlds' for training subgroup classifiers in which more training data was available, but we did not find significant improvements in the eventual classification performance.

We therefore decided to fine-tune the balance between the subclass and subgroup probability estimates to arrive at an optimal final ranking on subgroup level. We assigned weights by raising the subclass probabilities to power γ and the subgroup probabilities to power δ, respectively. For both data sets, we performed full-grid

Table 11.3 Winnow parameters for hierarchical and flat classifiers for the WIPO-alpha data set, determined after fivefold cross-validation tuning

	Subclass (hierar)	Subgroup (hierar)	Subgroup (flat)
α	1.06	1.03	1.06
β	0.91	0.98	0.91
θ^+	2.0	2.0	2.0
θ^-	1.0	1.0	1.0

Table 11.4 Winnow parameters for hierarchical and flat classifiers for the CLEF-IP 2010 data set, determined after fivefold cross-validation tuning

	Subclass (hierar)	Subgroup (hierar)	Subgroup (flat)
α	1.02	1.02	–
β	0.98	0.98	–
θ^+	2.0	2.0	–
θ^-	0.5	0.5	–

searches[16] on subsets from the cross-validation folds in the training procedure. Interestingly, similar patterns emerged for both the WIPO-alpha and the CLEF-IP data sets: To reach optimal ranking, the subclass probabilities should be raised to a relatively high power, while the subgroup probabilities should be raised to a very low power.[17] We arrived at the optimal balance by raising the subclass probabilities to the power of 1.5 (γ) and the subgroup probabilities to the power of 0.2 (δ).

11.4.3 Tuning

The classification parameters for the subclass classifiers, the subgroup classifiers and the flat classifiers were determined individually by tuning through fivefold cross-validation on a subset of the training data. All subgroup classifiers use the same parameters. These are the parameters that yielded the best overall results in an oracle experiment with fivefold cross-validation.[18] The resulting parameter settings are in Tables 11.3 and 11.4. With the exception of θ^-, the parameters for the subclass and subgroup classifiers in both corpora are very similar.

Note that we do not report any parameters for a flat subgroup classifier on the CLEF-IP 2010 data set: as mentioned in the introduction, the complexity of a 19,441-category (multi-label) classification problem causes severe scalability

---

[16]$\gamma \in$ {0.5, 1.0, 1.5, 2.0, 2.5, 3.0, 3.5, 4.0}, $\delta \in$ {0.1, 0.2, 0.3, 0.4, 0.5}. For the WIPO-alpha hierarchical classifier, we optimised on success@rnk1. In the case of the (multi-label) CLEF-IP classifier, we optimised on the F1 accuracy score.

[17]By raising them to a high power, subclass probabilities 'shrink', i.e. result in lower probabilities which increases the distance between the high-scoring and intermediate labels. For the subgroup classifiers on the other hand, intermediate probabilities (from 0.6 onwards) are transformed into extremely high scores (between 0.9 and 1.0).

[18]In an oracle setting, documents are only tested against subgroup classifiers from the relevant subclass world(s).

issues [1]. Even on a server with two Intel© Xeon© E5-2660 Processors with 256 GB memory, we were not able to complete this classification task.

11.5 Flat Versus Hierarchical Classification Methods

In this section we investigate which classification approach is best suited to classify documents on the subgroup level of the IPC. Since we were not able to construct a flat classifier on subgroup level for the CLEF-IP 2010 data set, our analysis will be limited to the WIPO-alpha data set. In this section we will only consider unigram features; the relative merit of the different text representations will be discussed in Sect. 11.6. For the sake of comparison, we have included the most recently reported results, i.e. from [4], who also performed a subgroup classification on the WIPO-alpha set. It should, however, be noted that our train/test split differs slightly from theirs, which makes direct comparison impossible.

Table 11.5 summarises the success@rank scores for the odd numbers of the top 11 ranks of both the flat and hierarchical classifiers on the official test set of the WIPO-alpha corpus. The scores are calculated over the final rankings of 1140 subgroup category labels.

The results show that the flat and hierarchical classifiers achieve similar accuracy. We determined the significance of the differences from the confidence intervals: given the sample size, i.e. number of documents in the test set, the 95 % confidence interval for the success@rnk1 is ±0.95 % for both the flat and the hierarchical classifiers. We find that only from rank 9 onwards, the results do no longer fall in each other's confidence intervals, i.e. the differences are significant.

Our two-step classifier outperforms the two-step classifier of [4] by a large margin. With their additional third step, they reach a higher performance (36.1 %). However, since this result was obtained with a system that was tuned on the test set (see Sect. 11.2), it cannot be claimed that their three-phase method performs better than our two-step method. We will return to this finding in the discussion.

Unlike [9], we find similar performance for the flat and hierarchical approaches—at least until rank 9—while we had expected the hierarchical approach to outperform its flat counterpart: both approaches suffer from the same problem with sparse training material on subgroup level, but the flat classifier has a more

Table 11.5 Classification results of hierarchical and flat classifiers on subgroup level for WIPO-alpha test set using only unigram features

success@rnk	1	3	5	7	9	11
Hierarchical classification (%)	31.5	46.8	54.5	59.5	63.1	65.8
Flat classification (%)	31.8	46.6	53.9	57.9	61.0	63.6
Chen and Chang, two-step classification (%)	20.2					
Chen and Chang, with additional 3rd step (%)	36.1					

Table 11.6 success@rnk scores for subclass and subgroup classifiers in the hierarchical classifier on the WIPO-alpha set

success@rnk	1	3	5	7	9	11
Subclass classifier (%)	50.7	70.0	76.9	80.5	82.7	84.3
Chen and Chang subclass classifier[a] (%)	43.3	67.5	76.0	81.5	85.8	88.5

[a]Please note that these results are reported over a different test set (400 documents) and consequently are indicative for but not directly comparable to the other reported scores

Table 11.7 success@rnk1 scores for oracle runs on the WIPO-alpha set

Oracle runs	success@rnk1	Chance level
All subgroup categories	58.3 %	26.9 %[a]
Subgroup categories with 1 sister	87.0 %	50.0 %
Subgroup categories with 2 sisters	68.6 %	33.3 %
Subgroup categories with ≥3 sisters	56.3 %	25.0 %

[a]We calculated the micro-averaged chance level (in an oracle setting) by summing up the chance level of all documents (in the relevant subclass world) and then averaging over the number of documents

complex classification task (1140 vs. 11 categories on average for the subgroup classifiers in the hierarchical approach).

In the remainder of this section, we analyse the performance of the hierarchical classifier by analysing the performance of its individual components. First, we consider the subclass classifier on the first level in the hierarchy. This classifier achieved 50.7 % success@rnk1, which is similar to the state-of-the-art classification results on subclass level reported by Tikk et al. [28] and better than the subclass classifier of [4] (Table 11.6).

The 339 individual subgroup classifiers are trained on significantly less data than the subclass classifier on the first level. We evaluated these subgroup classifiers in 'oracle runs', i.e. runs in which the documents were only tested against subgroup models within the correct subclass world, effectively assuming a perfect classification on the first level in the hierarchy. The results of these experiments are given in Table 11.7. Please note that the last three lines show the performance of different sets of subgroup classifiers, grouped according to the number of daughters present in the subclass world.

In general, the subgroup classifiers seem to be of good quality and perform quite well (in an oracle setting). So given the good performance in smaller, contained worlds, how do we account for the relatively low accuracy (see Table 11.5) when the subgroup classifiers are used in the hierarchical setting where a document is scored by all subgroup classifiers?

First, there is the well-known problem of propagation of error: Table 11.6 shows that for 50 % of the test documents, the highest scoring subclass category is the correct one. For an additional 20 % of the test documents, the correct subclass category can be found at rank 2 or 3, while the correct labels of the remaining 30 % lie scattered at lower ranks. Given the difficulties in fitting sigmoids to

Table 11.8 Corpus statistics for subclass, class and section worlds in the WIPO-alpha training set after sample selection

	# of cat	av. size (stdev) in # doc	av. # daughters (stdev)	# of categories with one subgroup daughter
Subclass	339	38.00 (53.19)	3.36 (4.36)	128
Class	107	120.40 (179.48)	10.65 (15.08)	18
Section	8	1610.38 (945.85)	142.5 (77.8588)	0

subgroup classifier output (reported in Sect. 11.4.2.2), the probability estimates on the subgroup level may not be sufficiently powerful to repair the 'errors' made by the subclass classifiers.

Second, there are reasons for doubting whether classification at the subgroup level is at all feasible: Eisinger et al. [10] point out that in quite some cases patent documents should have additional labels on the subgroup level and that the labels that have been manually assigned by the patent examiners are to some extent arbitrary. Given the inconsistencies in the manually assigned labels on a level with fine-grained distinctions between categories, it is extremely unlikely that an automatic system can reproduce the manual labels with 100 % accuracy.

Third, our manner of training may have introduced an overlap between the class profiles[19]: the analysis of the class profiles of the subgroup categories in the flat and hierarchical classifiers shows that class profiles in the flat classifier generally contain more terms and, more specifically, they contain more 'negative terms'. Terms with high negative Winnow weights characterise those unigram features that describe the rest of the corpus, not the category itself. They are especially useful in countering the positive weights of features that occur in many documents. Since the subgroup classifiers are trained in isolation, i.e. each in their own (small) subclass world with no information on the rest of the corpus, the models often do not contain enough negative terms to distinguish between categories in the testing phase.

The smaller number of negative terms (compared to positive terms) in the subgroup profiles for the hierarchical classifier indicates the lack of negative training material for the subgroup categories in the subclass worlds. Given the high number of single-daughter worlds (see Table 11.1), this is not surprising. We therefore hypothesised that training in larger contexts is better for optimal performance in a hierarchical system. To examine this hypothesis, we performed additional experiments in which subgroup classifiers were trained in larger 'worlds', i.e. the classifiers for individual subgroup categories were trained against all other subgroup categories in the same class (C) or section (S) in the IPC hierarchy. Table 11.8 shows corpus statistics on these larger worlds.

Although the different data selection criteria result in larger class profiles (with a higher ratio of negative terms compared to positive terms), Table 11.9 only shows

---

[19]Class profiles are the category models which comprise the most relevant terms for each category with their corresponding Winnow weights.

Table 11.9 Classification results for WIPO-alpha test set after different training data selection

success@rnk	1	3	5	7	9	11
Trained on SC world (%)	31.5	46.8	54.5	59.5	63.1	65.8
Trained on C world (%)	32.0	47.4	55.1	60.0	63.3	66.1
Trained on S world (%)	32.1	48.4	55.9	60.5	63.8	66.4

The first row is the same as the first row of Table 11.5

marginal and non-significant improvements between the different runs. Analysis of the class profiles of the categories trained in the *class* and *section* worlds shows that the added terms tend to have low Winnow weights and have relatively little impact on classification performance.

So, even with more negative training data, the hierarchical classifier does not rise above the performance level of the flat classifier. We must conclude that the overlap between the categories on the lowest levels and the small number of training documents in many 'worlds' are an insurmountable problem in the WIPO-alpha training/test set.

It might be argued that the classification at subgroup level should not be approached by means of a classifier that relies on some kind of training, simply because of the lack of sufficient amounts of training data. Chen and Chang [4] obtained a substantial improvement on the subgroup level by using a KNN classifier. We conducted a large number of experiments in which we used the features selected for the Winnow classifier in two different KNN classifiers, TiMBL [5] and sklearn [21]. However, we were not able to obtain a better classification accuracy than with the Balanced Winnow algorithm.

As mentioned above, the WIPO-alpha set is hardly representative of a real-life task. The CLEF-IP 2010 corpus is much larger, both in the number of documents and in the number of categories that must be distinguished on subclass and subgroup levels. While flat classification on such a set is not feasible for our classification algorithm, we expect that the hierarchical approach, which is much more scalable, will yield similar results (as a hypothetical flat one), since that was the case for the WIPO-alpha corpus. Furthermore, the larger amount of data opens possibilities to examine the impact of more precise text representations, which might help to solve the problem of the high overlap between the subgroup categories.

11.6 The Impact of Phrasal Features

In this section we examine the impact of different text representations on classification accuracy for different levels of the IPC hierarchy. For this series of experiments, we used the CLEF-IP 2010 corpus in addition to the WIPO-alpha data set, since the data sparseness in the WIPO-alpha corpus is especially problematic for the inherently sparse skipgram features. Furthermore, the CLEF-IP 2010 corpus is much more representative for the patent classification task than the WIPO-alpha benchmark, both in terms of the number of documents and the number of categories available.

Our goal is twofold: (1) We will examine the (relative) improvements of adding skipgrams for the subclass and subgroup classifiers. Our hypothesis is that on the subgroup level, in which the categories tend to overlap more, the more precise distinctions provided by the phrasal features will have a larger impact than on the subclass level. (2) We will compare the effects of adding features for both the CLEF-IP 2010 and the WIPO-alpha set in order to obtain a better understanding of how much training material is needed for phrasal features to be effective. It should be noted that in this section we use a different evaluation measure than in the previous section: up to now we have reported success@rnk for the sake of comparison with [4]. Since the CLEF-IP 2010 set is a multi-label set with a varying number of relevant categories per document, this measure is no longer adequate. We will therefore report our results using the well-known precision, recall and F1-measures. Relevant output rankings from classification experiments discussed in the previous section have been (re-)evaluated using these metrics.[20]

As is shown in Table 11.2, our train/test split for the CLEF-IP 2010 corpus consists of 595,080 and 396,725 documents, respectively, with 575 categories on subclass level and 19,441 on subgroup level. Unlike the WIPO-alpha documents, each document in the CLEF-IP 2010 set may have multiple relevant category labels. In the case of multi-label classification, the LCS can return a varying number of categories per document. This is determined by three parameters: (1) a threshold that puts a lower bound on the classification score (in this case probability) for a class to be selected, (2) the maximum number of classes selected per document ('maxranks') and (3) the minimum number of classes selected per document ('minranks'). Setting minranks $= 1$ assures that each document is assigned at least one category, even if all categories have a score or probability below the threshold. We used the cross-validation folds to determine the optimal evaluation configuration, which resulted in the following setting: minranks $= 1$, threshold $= 0.8$ and maxranks $= 8$ and 20 for the subclass and subgroup classifiers, respectively.

First we study the impact of adding skipgrams on subclass level. Table 11.10 shows the precision, recall and F1 scores for the CLEF-IP 2010 test set (left-hand side) and WIPO-alpha data set (right-hand side), respectively. Please note that these scores cannot be directly compared as they are (a) based on different data sets with a different number of categories to be distinguished and (b) a substantially different classification problem: classifying the WIPO-alpha set is a mono-label classification task, while the CLEF-IP 2010 set is multi-label. The scores should rather be seen as an indication of the difficulty of classifying on a certain level in the IPC hierarchy.

For both the WIPO-alpha and CLEF-IP 2010 test sets, we can see an improvement of classification performance on subclass level when skipgrams are added.

---

[20]Since we defined the classification task on the WIPO-alpha set as a mono-label task where the classifier *must* return one label, the reported (micro-averaged) scores will always yield equal precision and recall scores.

Table 11.10 Classification results of unigrams-only and unigrams+skipgrams classifiers on sub-class level for the CLEF-IP 2010 corpus and the WIPO-alpha corpus

	CLEF-IP			WIPO-alpha
	P	R	F1	P = R = F1
Unigrams (%)	63.9	62.3	63.1	50.7
Unigrams + skipgrams (%)	66.6	67.3	66.9	51.9

Table 11.11 Classification results of unigrams-only and unigrams+skipgrams hierarchical classifiers on subgroup level for the CLEF-IP 2010 corpus and the WIPO-alpha corpus

	CLEF-IP			WIPO-alpha
	P	R	F1	P = R = F1
Unigrams (%)	45.1	27.7	34.3	31.5
Unigrams + skipgrams (%)	52.7	30.3	38.4	32.5

We determined the significance of the differences between the unigrams and unigrams+skipgrams using the confidence intervals: Given the sample sizes, i.e. the number of documents in the respective test sets, the 95 % confidence interval for the F1 values is ± 0.15 % and ± 1.02 % for the CLEF-IP 2010 and the WIPO-alpha subclass classifiers, respectively. From this we can conclude that adding skipgrams leads to a significant improvement in the CLEF-IP 2010 set, but not in the WIPO-alpha set. As there is much more training material per category available in the CLEF-IP 2010 data set, compared to WIPO-alpha data set, the inherently sparse skipgram features attain high enough frequencies to aid in the classification process.

Table 11.11 shows the results for the subgroup rankings of the hierarchical classifiers, also for the CLEF-IP 2010 and WIPO-alpha test sets.

Here too we find a significant improvement for the combined run for the CLEF-IP 2010 set, but not for the WIPO-alpha set (with confidence intervals of ± 0.15 % and ± 0.95 % for the F1 scores of the CLEF-IP 2010 and WIPO-alpha set, respectively).

If we compare the (relative) improvements in F1 scores of the combined runs with the unigram runs for both the CLEF-IP subclass and subgroup classifiers, we find a similar improvement (around 4 percentage points) on both levels. We can therefore conclude that combining unigrams and skipgrams is beneficial for classification performance on any level in the IPC hierarchy. However, our initial hypothesis that skipgrams would have a larger impact on lower—and supposedly more overlapping—levels in the hierarchy is not confirmed. Close analysis of the class profiles does reveal that on average skipgrams occur at higher ranks in the subgroup class profiles than in the subclass class profiles. It seems that these features fill up the feature space when the unigram features are not sufficiently discriminative. Therefore, the hypothesis that skipgrams are more important on subgroup than on subclass level cannot be rejected either. It may be that even the CLEF-IP corpus is too small to allow for a decisive test.

As regards the second research question, the relative improvements between the classification results for the CLEF-IP 2010 and the WIPO-alpha sets clearly confirm our hypothesis that adding phrasal features is only effective when enough training data is available. For the CLEF-IP set, the skipgrams lead to a highly significant improvement on subgroup level, despite the fact that there is much less training material available than on subclass level. This suggests that an average number of 142 training documents per category are enough training data to see an impact of skipgram features, despite the skewed distribution of the number of documents per category.

11.7 Conclusion

In this chapter we examined the feasibility of performing classification on subgroup level of the IPC taxonomy. This task is generally considered extremely difficult because of three problems reported in the literature: (a) The overlap between categories is too large, and differences are too subtle to be captured adequately. (b) The number of categories is exceedingly large, which leads to scalability issues. (c) The data sparseness (in the number of documents per category) at the lowest level is too severe to build adequate classification models.

In our research we focused on two main questions which address these difficulties: (1) Can we circumvent the problems of overlap and the number of categories by using a hierarchical approach to classification on subgroup level and how does it compare to a flat classification approach? (2) Can we improve the classification on subgroup level by adding phrasal features, namely, skipgrams, to unigram features and how does the impact correlate with the granularity of the different levels in the IPC hierarchy? We performed classification experiments on the WIPO-alpha benchmark set, as well as on the much larger and more realistic CLEF-IP 2010 data set.

Our hierarchical approach consisted of a two-step top-down classification system with a subclass classifier on the top level and a set of subgroup classifiers—each trained within a subclass world—on the lower tier. The scores of the individual classifiers were converted to probabilities, which were then combined in a weighted scheme. To minimise the propagation of error and effectively allow high-scoring subgroup categories to move up in the final ranking, we did not define any cut-off thresholds on the subclass level during the testing process.

Regarding the first research question, we found that the flat and hierarchical approaches achieve similar accuracy scores on the WIPO-alpha set (31.5 % and 31.8 % success@rnk1, respectively). This shows that when it becomes infeasible to train a flat (text) classifier because the number of categories that must be distinguished is too large, a hierarchical classifier might be a good alternative for classification on the lowest level(s) of a taxonomy. Using a hierarchical approach, we were able to transform a 19,441-category problem into smaller, manageable subproblems and perform subgroup classification for a 900K corpus with encouraging accuracy.

Regarding the second research question, we were able to replicate the improvements of combining unigrams with skipgrams which were previously observed in [6, 7]. We did not observe a difference in the effect size of adding skipgrams to unigrams between the different IPC levels.

The difference in size between the two WIPO-alpha and CLEF-IP corpora gave us insight into the problems caused by data sparseness on subgroup level. Our best-scoring approach (hierarchical approach with unigram+skipgram features) achieved 32.5 % F1 accuracy for subgroup classification on the WIPO-alpha set (mono-label) and 38.4 % on the CLEF-IP 2010 set (multi-label). Since skipgrams are inherently sparse, a sufficiently large amount of training data must be available before phrasal features attain high enough frequencies to aid in the classification process. We found that—for classification on subgroup level in the CLEF-IP 2010 set—an average of 142 documents per category was enough to see a significant impact of adding skipgram features. We conjecture that with less training material available, case-based methods such as KNN might be preferred for classification on the lowest levels of the IPC taxonomy, even if our attempts to use KNN-based subgroup classifiers in WIPO-alpha data set were not successful.

An interesting pattern that we observed in both the WIPO-alpha and CLEF-IP hierarchical classifiers was the low weight given to the subgroup probabilities in the weighting of the probability estimates to reach optimal ranking. The fact that this occurs independent of the amount of training data available—as described in Sect. 11.3.1.2 we took care to avoid data sparseness problems when selecting a subset from the CLEF-IP data set—seems a strong indication that no matter how much training material is available, (model-based) classification on the subgroup level is a hazardous undertaking. We suspect, however, that the small numbers of documents in some subgroups are less of a problem than the reliability and completeness of the manually assigned labels, which serve both for supervising the training and as a reference in the evaluation of the classifier output.

As a final recommendation for future work in the patent classification field, we would like to promote the use of the CLEF-IP sets as future benchmarks: while we found that the WIPO-alpha set is a clean and usable data set, the CLEF-IP data set presents a more realistic task,[21] both in the number of categories and in the amount of training data available. Especially the latter is of great importance for further research focusing on (sub)group levels.

Acknowledgements This chapter is dedicated to the memory of Kees Koster, who was a major influence on this research.

---

[21] An even more realistic data set, called DOCDB, is hosted at the EPO but is not freely available.

References

1. Benzineb K, Guyot J (2011) Automated patent classification. In: Current challenges in patent information retrieval. Springer, New York, pp 239–261
2. Cai L, Hofmann T (2004) Hierarchical document categorization with support vector machines. In: Proceedings of the thirteenth ACM international conference on information and knowledge management, CIKM '04. ACM, New York, pp 78–87
3. Cesa-Bianchi N, Gentile C, Zaniboni L (2006) Incremental algorithms for hierarchical classification. J Mach Learn Res 7:31–54
4. Chen YL, Chang YC (2012) A three-phase method for patent classification. Inf Process Manag 48(6):1017–1030
5. Daelemans W, Zavrel J, van der Sloot K, van den Bosch A (2010) TiMBL: Tilburg memory-based learner - version 6.3 - Reference Guide
6. D'hondt E, Verberne S, Weber N, Koster K, Boves L (2012) Using skipgrams and pos-based feature selection for patent classification. Comput Linguist Neth J 2:52–70
7. D'hondt E, Verberne S, Koster K, Boves L (2013) Text representations for patent classification. Comput Linguist 39(3):755–775
8. D'hondt E, Verberne S, Oostdijk N, Beney J, Koster C, Boves L (2014) Dealing with temporal variation in patent categorization. Inf Retr. doi:10.1007s10791-014-9239-6
9. Dumais S, Chen H (2000) Hierarchical classification of web content. In: Proceedings of the 23rd annual international ACM SIGIR conference on research and development in information retrieval, SIGIR '00. ACM, New York, pp 256–263
10. Eisinger D, Tsatsaronis G, Bundschus M, Wieneke U, Schroeder M (2013) Automated patent categorization and guided patent search using IPC as inspired by MeSH and PubMed. J Biomed Semant 4(1):1–23
11. Fall CJ, Benzineb K (2002) Literature survey: issues to be considered in the automatic classification of patents, pp 1–64
12. Fall CF, Benzineb K, Guyot J, Törcsvári A, Fiévet P (2003) Computer-assisted categorization of patent documents in the international patent classification. In: Proceedings of the international chemical information conference
13. Falquet G, Guyot J, Benzineb K (2010) myClass: a mature tool for patent classification. In: Multilingual and multimodal information access evaluation - proceedings international conference of the cross-language evaluation forum, CLEF 2010. Springer, Berlin
14. Guyot J, Benzineb K (2013) IPCCAT-report on a classification test. Tech. Rep., Simple Shift. srv1.olanto.org/download/myCLASS/publication/IPCCAT_Classification_at_Group_Level_20130712.pdf
15. King G, Zeng L (2001) Logistic regression in rare events data. Polit Anal 9(2):137–163
16. Koster CH, Beney J, Verberne S, Vogel M (2010) Phrase-based document categorization. Springer, New York, pp 263–286
17. Krier M, Zaccà F (2002) Automatic categorization applications at the European patent office. World Patent Inf 24(3):187–196
18. Li Y, Bontcheva K, Cunningham H (2007) Svm based learning system for f-term patent classification. In: Proceedings of the 6th NTCIR workshop meeting on evaluation of information access technologies: information retrieval, question answering and cross-lingual information access (NTCIR'07), pp 396–402
19. Lin HT, Lin CJ, Weng RC (2007) A note on Platt's probabilistic outputs for support vector machines. Mach Learn 68(3):267–276
20. Oostdijk N, Verberne S, Koster C (2010) Constructing a broadcoverage lexicon for text mining in the patent domain. In: Proceedings of the international conference on language resources and evaluation, LREC 2010, 17–23 May 2010, Valletta, Malta

21. Pedregosa F, Varoquaux G, Gramfort A, Michel V, Thirion B, Grisel O, Blondel M, Pretten-hofer P, Weiss R, Dubourg V, Vanderplas J, Passos A, Cournapeau D, Brucher M, Perrot M, Duchesnay E (2011) Scikit-learn: machine learning in Python. J Mach Learn Res 12:2825–2830
22. Piroi F, Lupu M, Hanbury A, Sexton AP, Magdy W, Filippov IV (2010) CLEF-IP 2010: retrieval experiments in the intellectual property domain. In: Proceedings of CLEF 2010 (notebook papers/labs/workshops)
23. Piroi F, Lupu M, Hanbury A, Zenz V (2011) CLEF-IP 2011: retrieval in the intellectual property domain. In: Petras V, Forner P, Clough PD (ed) Proceedings of CLEF 2011 (notebook papers/labs/workshop)
24. Platt J (1999) Probabilistic outputs for support vector machines and comparisons to regularized likelihood methods. In: Advances in large margin classifiers. MIT Press, Cambridge, MA, pp 61–74
25. Salton G, Buckley C (1988) Term-weighting approaches in automatic text retrieval. Inf Process Manag 24:513–523
26. Silla C, Freitas A (2011) A survey of hierarchical classification across different application domains. Data Min Knowl Disc 22(1–2):31–72
27. Smith H (2002) Automation of patent classification. World Patent Inf 24(4):269–271
28. Tikk D, Biró G, Törcsvári A (2007) A hierarchical online classifier for patent categorization. IGI Global, Information Science Reference, Hershey, pp 244–267
29. van Halteren H (2000) The detection of inconsistency in manually tagged text. In: Proceedings of LINC-00
30. Wang X, Zhao H, Lu BL (2011) Enhance top-down method with meta-classification for very large-scale hierarchical classification. In: Proceedings of the international joint conference on natural language processing, pp 1089–1097
31. Widodo A (2011) Clustering patent documents in the field of ICT (information and communication technology). In: Proceedings of 2011 international conference on semantic technology and information retrieval (STAIR), pp 203–208

Chapter 12
Document Image Classification, with a Specific View on Applications of Patent Images

Gabriela Csurka

Abstract The main focus of this chapter is document image classification and retrieval, where we analyse and compare different parameters for the run-length histogram and Fisher vector-based image representations. We do an exhaustive experimental study using different document image data sets, including the MARG benchmarks, two data sets built on customer data and the images from the patent image classification task of the CLEF-IP 2011. The aim of the study is to give guidelines on how to best choose the parameters such that the same features perform well on different tasks. As an example of such need, we describe the image-based patent retrieval tasks of CLEF-IP 2011, where we used the same image representation to predict the image type and retrieve relevant patents.

12.1 Introduction

Before a patent can be granted, patent offices perform thorough searches to ensure that no previous similar disclosures were made. In the intellectual property terminology, such kind of searches are called prior art searches [...] Often, patent applications contain images that clarify details about the invention they describe. Images in patents may be drawn by hand, by computer, or both, may contain text, and are generally black-and-white (i.e. not even monochrome). Depending on the technological area of a patent, images may be technical drawings of a mechanical component, or an electric component, flowcharts if the patent describes, for example, a workflow, chemical structures, tables, etc. When a patent expert browses through a list of search results given by a search engine, he or she can very quickly dismiss irrelevant patents to the patent application by just glancing at the images in the retrieved patents. The number of documents to be looked at in more detail is thus greatly reduced. [28]

From this citation we can see that images are essential components of a patent as they illustrate key aspects of the invention. However, not every image in a patent has the same importance. Indeed, for patents related to chemistry or to pharmaceutic inventions, images containing chemical structures or gene sequences are the most important, while searching for similar drawings containing electronic circuits can

G. Csurka (✉)
Xerox Research Centre Europe, 6 chemin de Maupertuis, 38240 Meylan, France
e-mail: Gabriela.Csurka@xrce.xerox.com

© Springer-Verlag GmbH Germany 2017
M. Lupu et al. (eds.), *Current Challenges in Patent Information Retrieval*,
The Information Retrieval Series 37, DOI 10.1007/978-3-662-53817-3_12

help patent experts in physics and electricity. If a patent expert is looking for prior art given a query patent and the system retrieves patents based on visual similarities between all images of the query patent and in the patent database, the system might return non-relevant patents based on visual similarity between flowcharts or tables. This would not necessarily help the prior art search process. On the contrary, if only images of a certain type are considered, the retrieval can be significantly improved as shown in [9], where the retrieval accuracy when searching for the most similar drawings between patent images was much higher than the accuracy obtained when considering similarities between all images. However, this requires first to identify the image type (such as drawing, flowchart, etc.) to be considered.

In general manual annotation of the patent images according to their type is either non-existent or poor with many errors; therefore there is a clear need to be able to predict the image type automatically. Hence, the main focus of this paper is to consider patent image classification according to image types as the ones identified and used in the patent image classification task of CLEF-IP 2011 [28], namely, *abstract drawing, graph, flowchart, gene sequence, program listing, symbol, chemical structure, table and mathematics.* On the other hand, as similar image search (retrieval) is another important aspect of patent-based applications such as prior art search, in the chapter we also address image similarities and image-based retrieval. For both tasks, we consider mainly two popular image representations, the Fisher vector (FV) [25, 27] and the run-length (RL) histograms [6, 12, 16, 20], and compare different parameter configurations for them in order to come up with useful guidelines related to their choice independently of the targeted problem.

As patent images can be seen as particular document images, instead of limiting our study to patent images, we will address the problem in a more generic way, by questioning what is a good representation in general for document images. First, in Sect. 12.2 we briefly revise the most popular document image representations. Then, after describing in Sect. 12.3 the data sets considered for the study and the experimental setup, Sects. 12.4.1 and 12.4.2 will be devoted to an exhaustive parameter comparison for run-length and Fisher vector image representations, respectively, and in Sect. 12.4.3 we discuss different combinations of RL and FV. In Sect. 12.5, we describe the image-based patent retrieval tasks of CLEF-IP 2011, where we used the same image representation to predict the image type and retrieve relevant patents. Finally, we conclude the chapter in Sect. 12.6.

12.2 Document Image Representation

In the last few years, different image representations were proposed to deal with document image classification and retrieval that do not rely on OCR, i.e. seeing a document page as an image. To mention a few (see for more examples [7, 12, 20]), Cullen et al. [10] propose feature sets including densities of interest points, histogram of the size and density of connected components, vertical projection histograms, etc. In [18] a multi-scale density decomposition of the page is used to produce fixed-length descriptors constructed efficiently from integral images. The feature vectors proposed in [33] are based on text versus non-text percentage, column structure, content area and connected component densities. Bagdanov and Worring [3] propose a representation based on density changes obtained with different morphological operations. In [32] document images are described as a list of salient Viola–Jones-based features. However, these features contain relatively limited information, and while they might perform well on a specific data set and task for which they were designed, they are not generic enough to be able to handle various document class types, data sets and tasks. As early natural image representations, such as colour histograms, were significantly outperformed and replaced by the successful introduction of the bag-of-visual words (BOV) image representation [8, 34], the run-length histograms have shown to be more generic and hence better suited for document image representation[1] [6, 12, 16, 20].

In this work, therefore, we focus on one hand on the run-length histograms, and on the other hand we consider as alternative the Fisher vector [25, 27] which is the most successful extension of BOV image representation. In the following sections, we briefly describe how these features are extracted from a document image and which are their main parameters that have to be considered in particular when we build the corresponding image signatures.

12.2.1   Run-Length Histogram-Based Document Image Representation

The main idea of the run-length (RL) features is to encode sequences of pixels having the same value and going in the same direction (e.g. vertical, horizontal or diagonal). The 'run-length' is the length of those sequences (see as examples the green rectangles in Fig. 12.1). While we can consider sequences of similar greyscale or even colour values, considering only two levels has been proved to be sufficient to characterise document images [12, 16]. Therefore, when needed, we first binarise the document images and we consider only runs of black and white pixels. In the case of colour images, the luminance channel is binarised.

To do the binarisation, we do a simple thresholding at 0.5 (where image pixel intensities are represented between 0 and 1). More complex binarisation techniques exist (e.g. see methods that participated in the DIBCO [29] and HDIBCO [29] contests); however, testing the effect of different binarisation techniques is out of the scope of this chapter.

---

[1]Note that since the chapter was written, with the recent success of the deep convolutional neural networks (CNNs), new, richer representations have been proposed for natural images and applied also to document images [17, 19]. The comparison of those representations with FV and RL will be the subject of future work.

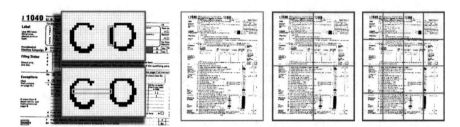

Fig. 12.1 *Left*: Examples of pixel runs. A vertical black run of length 7 (*top*) and a horizontal white run of length 16 (*bottom*). Detail from a small region on the bottom-left corner. *Right*: a tree layer spatial pyramid (Image courtesy of A. Gordo, from [12])

On the binarised images, a number of black pixel and white pixel runs are collected into histograms. To build these histograms, with the aim of being less sensitive to noises and small variations, we consider logarithmic quantisation of the lengths as suggested in [12, 16]:

$$[1], [2], [3 - 4], [5 - 8], [9 - 16], \ldots, [\geq (2^q + 1)].$$

Dealing with binary images, this yields two histograms of length $Q = q + 2$ per direction, one for the white pixels and one for the black pixels. We compute these runs in four directions, horizontal, vertical, diagonal and anti-diagonal, and concatenate the obtained histograms. An image (or image region) is then represented by this $4 \times 2 \times Q$-dimensional feature called run-length (RL) histogram.

These histograms can be computed either on the whole image or on image regions. In order to better capture information about the page layout, we use a spatial pyramid [22] with several layers such that at each level the image is divided into $n \times n$ regions and the histograms computed on these regions are concatenated. For example, in the case of a three-layer pyramid $1 \times 1, 2 \times 2$ and 4×4 illustrated in Fig. 12.1 (right), we concatenate in total the RLs of 21 regions to obtain the final image signature.

Finally, to be independent from the image size (number of pixel in the image), we L1 normalise the signature followed by a component-wise power normalisation[2] with $\alpha = 0.5$ as in [16]. Note that a vector with positive elements having L1 norm equal to 1 after power normalisation will have L2 norm equal to 1.

---

[2]The component-wise power normalisation [27] of a vector is such that each element z is replaced by $\text{sign}(z)|z|^\alpha$.

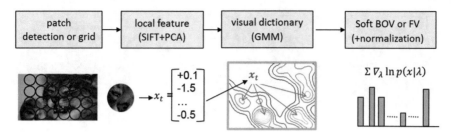

Fig. 12.2 Illustration of the FV image representation pipeline

12.2.2   The Fisher Vector-Based Image Representation

The Fisher vector [25] extends the bag-of-visual words (BOV) image representation by going beyond simple counting (0-order statistics) as they encode higher-order statistics about the distribution of local descriptors assigned to visual words (see also Fig. 12.2 illustrating the pipeline). Similar to the BOV, the FV depends on an intermediate representation: the visual vocabulary [8, 34]. The visual vocabulary can be seen as a probability density function (pdf) which models the emission of the low-level descriptors in the image. In our case we consider the Gaussian mixture model (GMM) to represent this density.

The Fisher vector characterises the set of low-level features (in our case SIFT features [23]), $X_I = \{x_t\}_{t=1}^{T}$ extracted from an image I by deriving in which direction the parameters of the GMM model should be modified to best fit this particular feature set. Assuming independence, this can be written as

$$G_\lambda(I) = \frac{1}{T} \sum_{t=1}^{T} \nabla_\lambda \log \left\{ \sum_{n=1}^{N} w_n \mathcal{N}(x_t|\mu_n, \Sigma_n) \right\} \tag{12.1}$$

where w_n, μ_n and Σ_n denote the weight, mean vector and covariance matrix of the Gaussian n, respectively, and N is the number of Gaussians in the mixture. To compare two images I and J, a natural kernel on these gradients is the Fisher kernel $K(I, J) = G_\lambda(I)^\top F_\lambda^{-1} G_\lambda(J)$, where F_λ is the Fisher information matrix. As F_λ^{-1} is symmetric and positive definite, it has a Cholesky decomposition $L_\lambda^\top L_\lambda$ and $K(I, J)$ can be rewritten as a dot product between normalised vectors Γ_λ where

$$\Gamma_\lambda(I) = L_\lambda G_\lambda(I) \tag{12.2}$$

to which we refer as the *Fisher vector* (FV) of the image I.

Fig. 12.3 Example images from four MARG classes (*left*) and from the customer data sets IH1 (*middle*) and NIT (*right*). The images from customer data sets were intentionally blurred to keep the actual content of the documents confidential. Nevertheless, we can see the visual variability of the documents within these data sets

Following [25, 27] where the covariance matrices in the GMM are assumed to be diagonal and using a diagonal closed-form approximation of F_λ, we have

$$\Gamma_{\mu_n^d}(I) = \frac{1}{T\sqrt{w_n}} \sum_{t=1}^{T} \gamma_n(x_t) \left(\frac{x_t^d - \mu_n^d}{\sigma_n^d} \right), \qquad (12.3)$$

$$\Gamma_{\sigma_n^d}(I) = \frac{1}{T\sqrt{2w_n}} \sum_{t=1}^{T} \gamma_n(x_t) \left[\frac{(x_t^d - \mu_n^d)^2}{(\sigma_n^d)^2} - 1 \right] \qquad (12.4)$$

where $\gamma_n(x_t) = \frac{w_n \mathcal{N}(x_t | \mu_n, \Sigma_n)}{\sum_{j=1}^{N} w_j \mathcal{N}(x_t | \mu_j, \Sigma_j)}$ and σ_n^d are the elements of the diagonal Σ_n. The final gradient vector $\Gamma_\lambda(I)$ is the concatenation of all $\Gamma_{\mu_n^d}(I)$ and $\Gamma_{\sigma_n^d}(I)$, where we ignore the gradients with respect to the weights. This vector is hence 2*ND* dimensional, where D is the dimension of the low-level features x_t.

As proposed in [27], we further apply on $\Gamma_\lambda(I)$ a component-wise power normalisation [27], followed by L2 normalisation. Finally, similar to the run-length features, to better take into account the document layout, we also consider similar spatial pyramids [22] as in the case of RLs, i.e. dividing the image into several regions at multiple layers and concatenating the region FVs.

12.3 Data Sets and the Experimental Setup

We used the following document image data sets[3] in our experiments (see examples in Figs. 12.3, 12.4 and statistics in Table 12.1):

---

[3] We also considered the NIST forms data set [36], with 20 different classes of tax forms, but as the results on this data set were often of 100 % accuracy, these results were not interesting from a parameter comparison study point of view.

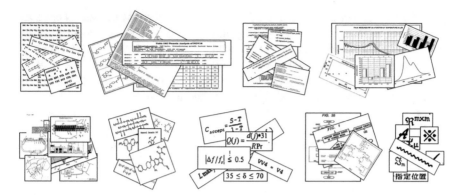

Fig. 12.4 Examples from different classes in the CLEF-IP data set

Table 12.1 A summary of the data set statistics

The data set	Nb. imgs	Img. size	Nb. classes	Example classes
MARG	1553	8.4	9	typeA, typeB, etc.
IH1	11,252	3–4M	14	Invoices, contracts, ID cards, etc.
NIT	885	5.6M	19	Invoices, mails, tables, maps, etc.
CLEF-IP	38,081	1.5K–4.5M	9	Drawing, graph, flowchart, etc.

MARG is the Medical Article Records Ground truth (MARG) data set [35] that consists of 1553 documents, each document corresponding to the first pages of medical journals, and their size is of 8.4M. The data set is divided into nine different layout types. Surprisingly the number of columns that varied from 1 to 3 within the classes is considered not relevant to distinguish between classes, which makes the data set challenging as the 'visual' similarity is strongly influenced by the number of columns. The criterion of the ground truth labelling is only the relative position of the title, authors, affiliation, abstract and the text (see for more details http://marg.nlm.nih.gov/gtdefinition.asp).

IH1 is the data set used in [12] that contains 11,252 scanned documents from 14 different document types (categories) such as invoices, contracts, IDs, coupons, etc. The images were obtained by scanning paper documents and their size varies according to the size of the original paper document, most of them however having around 3–4M pixels.

NIT is another in-house data set of 885 multipage documents with a total of 1809 pages of 5.6M pixels, but we only considered the first page to represent the document.[4] The categories represent as, in IH1, document types, including invoices, mails, tables, maps, etc., but these documents were not scanned but captured in the print flow and converted to images by the print driver (using the

---

[4]We did experiments with multiple pages where we averaged the signatures, the similarity scores or classification scores, but using only the first page was most often close to best performance.

page description languages). Within this data set, the amount of elements per class varies a lot, with several classes having only a few examples, while other classes containing a large percentage of all documents. We have a second data set similar to NIT but independent from what we call **XRCE** as the documents were captured in our own print flow. This data set containing mainly scientific articles, patent applications, reports, tables, mails, etc., was used to tune the parameters for some of our parametric models such as SVM and metric learning that were applied after to all the other data sets.

CLEF-IP contains the training image set from the patent image classification task of the CLEF-IP 2011 [9]. The aim of the task in the challenge was to categorise patent images into nine predefined categories such as abstract drawing, graph, flowchart, gene sequence, program listing, symbol, chemical structure, table and mathematics (see examples in Fig. 12.4). The data set contains between 300 and 6000 labelled images for each class, in total 38,081 images with their resolution varying from 1500 pixels to more than 4.5M pixels.

12.3.1 The Experimental Setup and Evaluation Methods

We randomly split these data sets into train (50 %) and test (50 %) sets five times and the same splits are kept along all experiments, allowing a comparison between different features, algorithms and parameter settings.

The aim of our experiments is mainly to compare different image representations and to design best practices on how to choose the parameters for these representations, preferably, independently of the task. Indeed, while the choice of the best parameters can be very dependent on the task, with the increasing amount of data, it can be more convenient sometimes to have these features precomputed and prestored that allow using the same representations in various applications such as retrieval, clustering or categorisation. Also, as we already mentioned, for image-type-dependent patent search where the images are first classified, it can be practical to use the same features both for the class prediction and for similar image search.

Our intent therefore is to find feature configurations that perform relatively well across tasks and if possible across data sets. Hence, we evaluate each representation both in a retrieval framework and using different classifiers (SVM, KNN, NCM), and we study the behaviour of different parameter configurations. Note that the nearest class mean (NCM) classifier [24] that predicts the class label of a document image based on the closest class mean evaluates implicitly (in a certain sense) the ability of these features to perform clustering. Indeed, NCM, averaging the examples from each class, performs well when these instances can be easily grouped together. Hence a feature configuration yielding better NCM accuracies is more suitable for clustering purposes than one that fails to do it. Further advantages of the NCM are that it is a multi-class classifier and that there is no parameter to be tuned.

When using SVM we used fixed overall data sets and configurations, which means obviously that the SVM results are suboptimal (in some cases 1–3 % below compared to fine-tuned parameters). But in some sense this makes the comparison between parametric and non-parametric methods such as NCM fairer. Also the focus of the chapter is on the parameters of the image representation, and fine-tuning the parameters of different classifiers or testing more complex classification methods is out of the scope of the chapter. To choose the fixed parameter set for the SVM, we tested all configurations and a large set of parameters on the XRCE data set and considered the setting that performed in general best. As we used one-versus-all linear classifiers with stochastic gradient descend (SGD) [5] shown to be highly competitive when applied on FVs [2], the selected parameters were as follows. We used hinge loss with a fixed learning rate $\lambda = 1e-5$ for RL features and $\lambda = 1e-4$ for FV. To handle the data set bias, we weighted the positives by a factor of $\rho = 5$, and to optimise the classifier we updated the gradient by passing $N_i = 100$ times randomly through the whole training set. Similarly, for the same reasons, in the case of the KNN classifier, we used a fixed $k = 4$ as it performed best on XRCE, but again the results are suboptimal. $k = 4$ might vary along different data sets and configurations.

To evaluate the classification tasks using any of the above-mentioned classifiers (NCM, KNN and SVM), we show only the overall prediction accuracy (OA), i.e. the ratio of correctly predicted document images, but similar behaviour was observed when we considered the average of the per class accuracies.[5]

To perform document ranking for the retrieval, we use each test document as query and the aim is to retrieve all documents with the same class label in the training set. As for the similarity between documents, we consider the dot product between features (which is equivalent with the cosine similarity as our features are L2 normalised). To assess the retrieval performance, we use mean average precision (MAP), but we also consider top retrieval accuracy by assessing it by precision at 5 (P5) as several classes in these data sets have only few representatives. We also consider the precision at 1 (P1) because this is equivalent with the overall classification accuracy of a KNN classifier using k=1 and hence allows us to compare the results with our actual KNN results for which we used $k = 4$.

12.4   Experimental Results

In this section we first do an exhaustive parameter study for run-lengths (in Sect. 12.4.1) and for Fisher vectors (in Sect. 12.4.2) analysing the behaviour of the parameter configurations considering the previously mentioned tasks and data sets. Then, in Sect. 12.4.3 we discuss about possibilities how to merge RL with FV.

---

[5]Or when the behaviour was different such as for NIT, the reason was that this data set contains several classes with only few instances, meaning that changing the prediction for any of those rare documents may yield a significant change in the accuracy of the corresponding class.

Table 12.2 Comparative retrieval (left) and classification (right) results where we vary the parameters of the RL features. We show best results in red (averaged over five splits) with the corresponding configuration in blue (below the accuracy), best parameter frequencies and performance variations per feature type

RET	MARG	IH1	NIT	CLEF-IP
P1	93.6±0.9	95.5±1.3	81.9±0.9	83.8±0.2
	S0,L5,Q11	S5,L1,Q10	S0,L4,Q8	S0,L1,Q8
S	S0(60/3)	S0(56/.4)	S5(48/.6)	S2(53/1)
L	L5(72/4)	L1(65/.5)	L5(40/.6)	L1(100/3)
Q	Q11(27/.7)	Q9(24/.1)	Q8(32/.4)	Q8(78/2)
P5	86.2 ±0.5	93.6±1.4	75.7±0.8	79.5±0.2
	S0,L4,Q11	S5,L1,Q10	S5,L5,Q10	S2,L1,Q11
S	S0(80/4)	S0(64/.4)	S5(84/1)	S2(79/2)
L	L5(92/6)	L1(84/.7)	L5(100/2)	L1(100/3)
Q	Q11(44/.7)	Q9(40/.1)	Q11(44/.3)	Q11(87/2)
MAP	33.8±1.4	67.5 ±0.5	42.3±1.4	38.3±0.1
	S5,L4,Q11	S5,L1,Q10	S1,L5,Q11	S1,L4,Q7
S	S5(96/1)	S5(76/.7)	S1(96/1)	S2(56/3)
L	L5(80/2)	L1(88/1)	L5(100/.7)	L5(60/2)
Q	Q10(28/.1)	Q7(32/.2)	Q11(56/.2)	Q11(65/.9)

CLS	MARG	IH1	NIT	cleflP
KNN	90.3±1.6	95.2±0.2	81.3±1.5	84.9±0.2
	S0,L5,Q10	S5,L1,Q9	S5,L5,Q10	S0,L1,Q7
S	S5(60/3)	S0(56/.4)	S5(58/2)	S2(59/1)
L	L5(87/5)	L1(74/.7)	L5(62/3)	L1(100/3)
Q	Q11(22/.7)	Q7(26/.1)	Q9(27/.6)	Q9(76/2)
NCM	61.8±1.5	91.3±0.3	66.6±0.6	62.4±0.2
	S0,L5,Q11	S0,L5,Q11	S1,L5,Q10	S0,L3,Q11
S	S0(38/3)	S0(67/.8)	S1(54/2)	S0(83/3)
L	L5(80/8)	L5(60/4)	L5(98/9)	L4(50/5)
Q	Q11(35/1)	Q11(48/.5)	Q10(34/1)	Q11(69/2)
SVM	91.9±1	96.9±0.3	78.2±1.2	89.8±0.2
	S0,L5,Q10	S0,L5,Q11	S5,L5,Q10	S0,L5,Q11
S	S0(35/4)	S0(56/2.5)	S1(72/.6)	S0(71/2)
L	L5(67/14)	L5(65/4)	L5(72/5)	L4(52/4)
Q	Q11(31/3)	Q11(57/.6)	Q10(31/.9)	Q11(66/2)

12.4.1 Test Different Parameters for RL

To build different run-length (RL) features, we mainly varied the image resolution (S), the number of layers[6] (L) used in the spatial pyramid and the number of quantisation bins (Q). When we resize an image, we keep the aspect ratio and we define a maximum resolution. We experimented with target resolutions of 50K, 100K, 250K, 500K and 1M pixels and denoted them by S1, S2, S3, S4 and S5, respectively. In addition, the case where we do not rescale any of the images will be denoted by S0. However, images having less pixels are not upscaled; only images above the target size are downscaled.

In Table 12.2, we show retrieval performances (**RET**) assessed with P1, P5 and MAP as well as overall the accuracy of class prediction (OA) for KNN, NCM and SVM classification (**CLS**). As we mentioned, the experiments were performed on five different splits; hence in the table we show the mean over the splits and its variation. For each data set and task, in addition to the best average, we show, below the best average, the parameter sets that allowed to obtain these results.

In addition, for each parameter type, e.g. the number of layer L, we alternatively fix the other parameters, here S and Q, and evaluate the best performing value. We do this for all (S,Q) pairs and retain the corresponding variation. Then, for each value of the selected parameter type, in this example each Li, we compute the percentage of time it performed the best. In Table 12.2 we show for each parameter type the value (e.g. Li) that was found the most often as best performing. In the

---

[6]Note that we used 2 × 2 split of the image at the second layer, 4 × 4 at the third, 6 × 6 at the fourth and 8 × 8 at the fifth. Ln means that we concatenated the features of the regions from all the n layers.

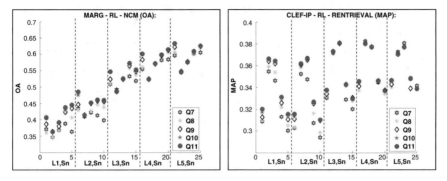

Fig. 12.5 Example plots comparing different quantisations

parenthesis following the parameter found, we show two numbers. The first one is the percentage of time that the parameter was at the top, and the second value shows the average variance of the results for that parameter type (L). This variation was considered by fixing S and Q and evaluating the variance of the results when we varied L and then averaging overall (S,Q) pairs. These statistics (frequencies and the variance) were computed by cumulating the results along all the five splits. Note that if this average variance is low, it means that varying that parameter has relatively low effect on the obtained accuracy, while high average variance means that it is very important to correctly set the given parameter. For example, when we evaluate MARG with P5 accuracy, we find that L5 performed the best 92 % of the time considering all (S,Q) pairs and all splits, and the average variation along L when fixing (S,Q) was about 6 %. This means that setting the number of layers is more important than the choice of the number of quantisation bin, as Q11 was best only 44 % of times and the average variation of Q when fixing (L,S) was only 0.7 %.

When we analyse the values in Table 12.2, we can deduce the following:

- **Quantisation intervals.** First of all, we can clearly see that concerning the number of quantisation intervals, Q11 is almost always the best option. This shows that considering more quantisation values is a good choice. On the other hand, the standard deviation and frequency values are relatively low, which means that the difference in values obtained using fewer quantisation intervals (Q7 to Q10) is relatively small, especially when we have best configurations selected for the other parameters (see examples[7] in Fig. 12.5).
- **Number of pyramid layers.** We observe that for certain data sets such as MARG or NIT, considering multiple layers (L4 or L5) is essential. This is not surprising as the MARG classes are strongly related to the text layout that is much better captured with multiple layers. For other data sets, the best layer configuration seems to be task and evaluation measure dependent (see examples in Fig. 12.6). Indeed, for IH1 and CLEF-IP, top retrieval results and KNN classification

---

[7]All illustrations plot results from the experiments done on the first split.

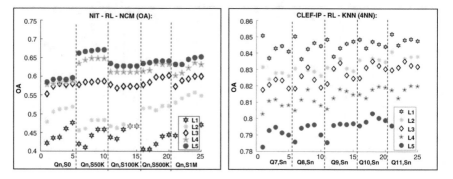

Fig. 12.6 Example images comparing different numbers of layers

perform much better using only a single layer, while MAP, NCM and SVM results are always better with multiple layers (except the MAP for IH1). The main reason is that in the former case, the decision depends only on a few 'most similar' documents; hence it is sufficient to have a few similar documents for most instances in the data set. According to high P5 and KNN values, this seems to be the case for all data sets.

On the contrary, the NCM classifier considers class centroids (i.e. averaging overall examples within a class). Therefore for each test example, the presence of a few similar instances is not any more sufficient, but the similarity to most documents within the class becomes necessary. The MAP evaluates how well all instances of a class can be retrieved using an exemplary from the class, which requires again the within-class similarities to be higher than the similarities between instances from other classes. As the NCM and MAP results show, these requirements seem to be better satisfied when we consider multiple layers.

– **Image size.** Finally, when we try to observe the effect of image resizing, it is difficult to draw any interesting conclusions. Best performing image sizes seem to vary along the data sets, tasks and evaluation measures. In a sense, this is not completely surprising, as on one hand the original image sizes vary along data sets. Furthermore, while the size of the RL does not depend on the image size, the distribution of black and white pixel runs within bins is highly correlated with the considered image size. Nevertheless, it seems that S0 appears often as best performing or yields close to best performance, as we can see in Fig. 12.7. The advantage of keeping the original size is to preserve the details present in the image as they were captured, but on the other hand, smoothing can have the benefit of better generalisation. Moreover, for very high-resolution images (which is often the case for document images representing text), the cost of building the RL vectors from the original images is significantly higher than computing them on S3 or S4, especially if we use multilayer pyramids.

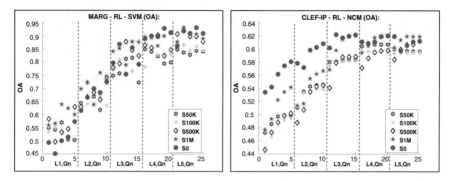

Fig. 12.7 Example images comparing different image resolutions

We now analyse the performances related to different tasks and methods:

– **Retrieval.** We can see that retrieval at top and KNN performs extremely well in general for all data sets, while MAP performs rather poorly. As was discussed above, the good performance obtained with P5 and KNN is because for most documents we can find documents from the same class for which the similarity is high when using well-designed RL features. As P1 is higher than KNN (except for NIT), it shows that using only a single example to classify the documents performs better than using $k = 4$. On the other hand, the poor MAP performance shows that there is a large within-class variation and it is difficult to retrieve all relevant documents using a single example. Indeed, for example, in the case of MARG, a one-column document from a class allows to retrieve easily the other one-column documents from the same class but has difficulties to rank higher the two-column documents from the same class than many of the one-column documents from other classes. However, preliminary results have shown that metric learning approaches specifically designed to support KNN classification [11, 38] or ranking [4] can significantly improve the MAP in most cases.

– **SVM.** The discriminative linear classifier (SVM) even with a set of fixed parameter set ($\lambda = 1e - 5$, $\rho = 5$, $N_i = 100$) with yields much better classification accuracy than NCM, showing that in the corresponding feature space, nevertheless the classes are linearly separable. In the case of IH1 and CLEF-IP, the SVM results are better than nearest neighbour search, but for MARG and NIT they remain below the KNN with $k = 1$. Note that IH1 and CLEF-IP are much larger data sets than MARG and NIT, allowing the SVM to better learn the discriminative classifiers. Moreover, the poor SVM results for NIT are not surprising as several classes have very few examples to properly learn the linear classifier in these high-dimensional spaces.

– **NCM.** Concerning the NCM classification, we made some tentatives to improve the NCM by replacing it with NCMC [24], but the number of optimal centroid per class varies a lot from one class to another, and fixing the same number of centroids (e.g. 2 or 3) does not allow us to significantly improve the classification

Table 12.3 Comparison of the NCM results without projection ($W = I$), with PCA projections and with metric learning

W	MARG	IH1	NIT	CLEF-IP
I	61.8(L5,D0648)	91.3(L5,D10648)	59.8(L5,D10648)	62.4(L3,D1848)
PCA	61.4(L5,D128)	91.3(L5,D128)	59.6(L5,D128)	62.1(L3,D128)
ML	**89(L5,D64)**	**92.6(L5,D64)**	**81.3(L5,Q11)**	**86.6(L5,D128)**

performance (except for MARG, where we have clear subclasses according to the number of columns). KNN with $k = 1$ (P1) is higher than with $k = 4$ (except for CLEF-IP) and the SVM result shows rather good linear separability. This suggests that the documents within a class are not necessarily grouped around a few centroids but that they are rather scattered in the feature space.

Another way to improve the NCM classification performance is by using metric learning as proposed in [24], where the distances between the class means and the documents are computed in the space projected by a transformation matrix learned on the training set by maximising the log-likelihood of the correct NCM predictions in the projective space (using a mini-batch stochastic gradient descend (SGD) with a fixed learning rate $\lambda = 1$ and using 200 random batches of the size equal to the number of classes). Similar to SVM, again we trained the NCM metric learning approach with the parameters below obtained as best on the XRCE data set. This means that the results are suboptimal and we could improve the results further by tuning them on each tested data set, which could be another option that is out of the scope of this chapter.

Concerning the learned projected space, we experimented with different target dimensions D such as 16, 32, 64 and 128 and in Table 12.3 we show the best results obtained with the corresponding parameters. In addition, we also present the results when the projection was made using the D first principal directions[8] of the PCA. In this set of experiments, we only varied the number of layers in the pyramid, did no image rescaling (S0) and used $Q = 11$ quantisation bins. We can see that while using PCA the results remain almost the same as without, the metric learning allows us to significantly improve the NCM performance in all cases. This time the NCN performance is close to the KNN and SVM performances and could be further improved if we fine-tune the parameters on the tested data set.

Note that the projected features are much smaller than the original features, especially for the multilayer pyramid where for Q11 and L5 we go from 10,648 to 128 dimensions, which can be interesting in case we want to store the features. We also experimented KNN and SVM with the PCA-reduced features and we observed that, similar to the NCM results, we were able to keep similar performances in all cases in spite of the strong dimension reduction. While similar observation was made in [12], Gordo et al. [16] propose a compression and binarisation through PCA embedding that significantly outperforms the results obtained with simple PCA.

---

[8]Note that we initialise the metric learning with PCA.

12.4.2   Test Different Parameters for FV

Similar to the previous section, we tested different parameter configurations for the Fisher vectors (FV) built on local SIFT descriptors. To build the FV in natural images, first local patches (windows of size NxN) are extracted densely at multiple scales and SIFT descriptors are computed on each of them. For N we consider the values 24, 32, 48 and 64 and denote them by W1, W2, W3 and W4, respectively.

In the case of document images, especially when the images are of similar resolution, extracting features at multiple scales might have less importance; therefore in the first set of experiments, we focus on extracting features only at a single scale. Also, as the resolution of most original images is very large and the considered local patches are relatively small, we first resize the images[9] to have a maximum of 250K pixels (S3). Then on each local window, we compute the usual 128-dimensional SIFT features [23] and reduce them to 48, 64 and 96 dimensions using PCA. We denote the corresponding low-level features by F1, F2 and F3. While we can also build FV with the original SIFT features, we do not report results on it as we observed that reducing the dimensionality not only significantly decreases the size of the FV, but in general the accuracy is also improved.

In a given projected feature space, e.g. corresponding to W3 and F2, we build a set of visual vocabularies using Gaussian mixture model (GMM) with diagonal covariance matrices, where we vary the number of visual words by considering $2^{(g+3)}$ Gaussians where $g = 1 \dots 7$. We denote the corresponding vocabularies by G1, ..., G7, where e.g. G1 corresponds to 16 Gaussians and G5 to 256 Gaussians. Note that both the PCA projection matrices and the GMM were built using the features extracted on the XRCE data set and then applied to all the other data sets. This means that for a given parameter setting (W, F, G), the documents are represented exactly in the same feature space (FV) independently of the data set on which the experiments are done.[10]

In this first set of experiments, as we do not use any spatial pyramid, we have only three varying parameters for the FV: the size of the local window (W), the dimension of the PCA-reduced SIFT features (F) and the number of Gaussians used in the visual vocabulary (G). Retrieval (P@1, P@5 and MAP) and overall (OA) classification (with KNN, NCM and SVM) accuracies with the best parameter settings, winning frequencies and variances are shown in Table 12.4. From these results we can conclude the following:

- **Feature size:** Best results are obtained in general with F1 (SIFT reduced to 48 dimensions) or, when it is not the case (e.g. NCM applied to NIT or SVM applied to CLEF-IP), the low-average variances suggest that the corresponding results obtained with F1 are not very different.

---

[9]When using FV with natural images, we often resize the images first, often to 100K pixels [25, 27].

[10]At the end of this section, to show the influence of the visual model, we provide a few results with the visual vocabulary built on the same data set on which the experiments were performed.

Table 12.4 Comparative retrieval (left) and classification (right) results where we vary the size of the local window (W), the dimension of the PCA-reduced SIFT features (F) and the number of Gaussians used in the visual vocabulary (G) to build the FVs. We show best results in red (averaged over five splits) with the corresponding configuration in blue (below the accuracy), best parameter frequencies and performance variations per feature type

RET	MARG	IH1	NIT	CLEF-IP	CLS	MARG	IH1	NIT	cleflP
P1	91.8±1.1	95.4±0.3	82.1±1.7	85.4±1.2	KNN	89.8±1.3	95.4±0.3	82.1 ±2	86.2±1.1
	W3,F1,G4	W4,F1,G3	W2,F3,G6	W3,F1,G2		W3,F1,G4	W4,F1,G3	W2,F1,G3	W3,F1,G2
W	W4(58/10)	W4(100/5)	W2(35/1)	W3(43/11)	W	W3(53/11)	W4(100/6)	W2(35/2)	W3(41/9)
F	F1(71/4)	F1(84/2)	F3(36/.7)	F1(76/6)	F	F1(71/4)	F1(84/2)	F1(36/.8)	F1(76/5)
G	G1(32/5)	G1(77/5)	G5(37/2)	G1(88/17)	G	G1(32/6)	G1(77/5)	G5(37/1)	G1(89/17)
P5	77.1 ±0.7	93.7±0.2	73.5±0.7	81.8±0.4	NCM	69.1±0.9	91.6±0.3	77.8±3	69.9±0.1
	W4,F1,G7	W4,F1,G3	W2,F1,G5	W3,F1,G2		W3,F1,G5	W3,F1,G4	W1,F3,G7	W3,F1,G1
W	W4(60/10)	W4(100/6)	W2(51/2)	W3(43/10)	W	W3(95/4)	W3(78/6)	W2(55/7)	W3(95/4)
F	F1(76/3)	F1(84/2)	F1(44/.6)	F1(76/4)	F	F2(37/1)	F1(54/.3)	F3(53/1)	F1(64/2)
G	G1(27/5)	G1(77/5)	G5(45/1)	G1(91/16)	G	G7(57/3)	G4(37/.4)	G7(88/6)	G1(58/3)
MAP	34.2±0.3	73.5±0.2	44.6±1.5	41.9±0.1	SVM	87.4±1	97.3±0.2	85.7±2.3	87.6±0.2
	W3,F1,G4	W3,F2,G1	W3,F2,G1	W4,F1,G1		W4,F1,G4	W3,F3,G6	W2,F2,G6	W3,F3,G6
W	W3(52/2)	W4(71/9)	W4(67/.8)	W3(42/4)	W	W4(86/4)	W3(79/.3)	W3(42/1)	W3(100/2)
F	F1(80/.8)	F1(69/2)	F1(61/.5)	F1(75/2)	F	F1(48/1)	F3(54/.2)	F2(37/1)	F3(88/.8)
G	G1(35/1)	G1(70/6)	G1(68/1)	G1(98/9)	G	G6(25/3)	G5(55/.4)	G6(27/4)	G7(70/1)

– **Vocabulary size:** The number of Gaussians seems to be dependent both on the data set and on the tasks. In the case of retrieval, best results are obtained with smaller vocabulary sizes, and hence much smaller image signatures, most often G1 (except top retrieval on NIT). On the other hand, NCM and SVM seem to require much larger vocabularies, which is not surprising especially concerning SVM. We observe that, while extreme values (G1 or G7) yield often best or worse results, using values between 64 (G3) and 256 (G5) seems to be a good compromise between size and accuracy (see also Fig. 12.8, top row).

– **Window size:** W3 (patches of size 48 × 48) seems to be often the best performing or a good compromise compared to the other cases. Indeed, W1 performs in general poorly, showing that a too small window (containing rather less information about the page) is not a good idea. While W4 can perform best for certain tasks (e.g. retrieval on Bytel), it can be worse on another task (NCM on Bytel), as shown in Fig. 12.8, bottom row. The variances are also high, showing the importance of setting this parameter properly.

Note nevertheless that the ideal size of the window is strongly correlated with the processed image size. If we increase the image size, we need larger windows to capture the same amount of information. Decreasing the image while keeping the same window size allows to increase the amount of information per window. Another possibility to ensure we capture the information at the right scale is to extract the features at multiple scales. Therefore we vary both the image size and the number of scales at which the features are extracting, while fixing the window size to 48 × 48 (W3).

As we observed that S1 (50K) performs in general poorly, we consider the following image sizes: 100K (S2), 250K (S3) and 500K (S4) pixels. Note that we do not consider S0 and S5 (1M pixels) as they lead not only to extremely large

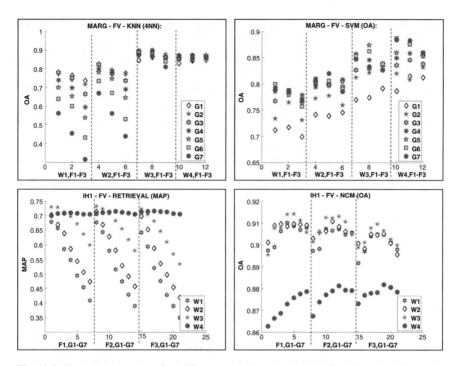

Fig. 12.8 Example plots comparing different vocabulary sizes (*top*) and window sizes (*bottom*)

amount of windows (increasing significantly the computational cost), but also the information captured within such a window is extremely poor in content (many of them containing only white pixels). As we have seen that W1 with S3 (containing much less information than W3) performed poorly, we expect even worse results when using W3 with S0 or S5. To get similar or possibly better results, one might consider much larger windows to compute the SIFT features.

To handle the feature extraction at multiple scales, we further downscale the image (e.g. S3) by a scale factor of $\sqrt{2}$ and extract SIFT again from windows of size 48×48. The amount of information in these windows extracted from the image downscaled by $\sqrt{2}$ corresponds to the (smoothed) information extracted from S3 with a window W3 upscaled by $\sqrt{2}$. We repeat this process until which we reach the number of desired scales. We experimented with one, three, five and seven scales, denoting them by M1, M3, M5 and M7. Note that in the case of the configuration (S3, W3, M5), this means that the images of size S3 were 5 times downscaled by $\sqrt{2}$ and at each scale the SIFT features were extracted on windows of size 48×48. These features are PCA reduced to a dimension of 48 (F1) and all cumulated to form the feature set X_I that generates the FV corresponding to the image.

The results with a varying number of scales (M), image resolutions (S) and vocabulary sizes (G) are shown in Table 12.5. From these results, we can conclude the following:

Table 12.5 Comparative FV results on different data sets and tasks. We show best results in red and best parameter settings in blue using different evaluation measures

RET	MARG	IH1	NIT	CLEF-IP	CLS	MARG	IH1	NIT	clefIP
P1	93.4±1	95.2±0.3	82.1±2.1	89.2 ±1.1	KNN	91.4±.9	95±0.2	81.7 ±2	89.9±0.8
	S4,M5,G5	S3,M3,G1	S4,M3,G4	S4,M7,G2		S3,M7,G3	S3,M3,G1	S4,M7,G5	S4,M7,G2
S	S3(64/2)	S3(85/2)	S4(68/2)	S4(86/4)	S	S3(81/3)	S3(87/2)	S4(68/2)	S4(94/4)
M	M5(77/2)	M7(41/1)	M3(43/.8)	M7(46/4)	M	M5(57/2)	M5(44/1)	M5(38/.9)	M7(43/4)
G	G5(48/2)	G1(88/4)	G2(25/1)	G2(58/5)	G	G4(33/2)	G1(85/4)	G3(25/1)	G1(49/5)
P5	79.5±0.5	93.8±0.2	73.6±1	86.2±.9	NCM	71.2±1.6	92.2±0.2	75.2±2.1	75.9±0.3
	S4,M7,G4	S3,M3,G1	S4,M7,G5	S4,M7,G2		S3,M7,G6	S3,M3,G5	S4,M3,G7	S2,M5,G5
S	S4(64/2)	S3(76/2)	S4(89/2)	S4(73/4)	S	S3(59/2)	S3(53/.9)	S4(43/3)	S2(86/2)
M	M5(69/2)	M7(48/1)	M7(38/.7)	M7(62/4)	M	M5(60/2)	M3(44/.5)	M1(81/2)	M5(49/3)
G	G5(60/2)	G1(90/4)	G5(25/1)	G2(66/5)	G	G5(58/4)	G4(42/.7)	G7(58/4)	G1(27/1)
MAP	35.3±0.1	75.7±0.2	46.6±1.5	46.1±0.8	SVM	91±1.1	97.4±0.1	86.5±2.1	94.7±1.1
	S3,M5,G5	S3,M3,G2	S3,M5,G1	S2,M7,G2		S4,M7,G5	S4,M7,G7	S3,M3,G4	S4,M7,G7
S	S3(64/.9)	S3(68/5)	S3(89/1)	S2(69/2)	S	S3(57/2)	S3(64/.4)	S3(64/1)	S4(93/1)
M	M5(76/.9)	M7(57/4)	M5(81/.7)	M7(88/3)	M	M5(45/2)	M5(63/.3)	M3(38/.6)	M5(57/2)
G	G5(63/.9)	G1(65/6)	G1(83/2)	G1(78/3)	G	G5(58/3)	G7(51/.4)	G5(50/1)	G7(88/1)

- **Number of scales.** Concerning the number of scales (M), extracting features at multiple levels definitely helps. While there is no clear winner between M3, M5 and M7, as the plots in Fig. 12.9 top row show, they have similar performances and in general all outperform M1. This suggests that while it is important to consider multiple scales, considering three or five scales is in general sufficient.
- **Vocabulary size.** The behaviour of the visual vocabulary size remains similar to our previous set of experiments where we varied the window size (W) and the feature dimension (F). Again, while extreme values (G1 or G7) are often best or worst, G3, G4 and G5 are often close to best or even winning in the case of MARG where G5 performs best on all tasks.
- **Image size.** S3 (250K pixels) is the best performing in most cases with MARG and IH1, showing that the configuration (S3,W3) is suitable for them. Concerning NIT and CLEF-IP, there is no clear winner (see also Fig. 12.9, bottom rows). For nearest neighbour search-based methods (P1,P5, KNN) and SVM when using window size of W3, it seems better to keep higher resolution (S4) while retrieval and NCM classification on CLEF-IP works better with low resolution (S2).

Finally, we test the spatial pyramid with several layers for the FV features. There we consider the number of maximum layers in the pyramid in function of the visual vocabulary—as FV features being already very large for vocabulary sizes above 64 - to obtain the final signature size they are multiplied by the number of regions in the pyramid. We show in Table 12.6 the maximum number of layers we consider for each vocabulary size in our experiments. We also show the number of corresponding regions and the size of the final signature (after the concatenation of the FVs for all the regions).

We can see that these signatures are very large and in general not sparse and we did all our experiments with non-compressed FVs. Note nevertheless that there are several methods in the literature [14, 26, 31, 37] that propose to efficiently binarise and/or compress the Fisher vectors while keeping them highly competitive. It could

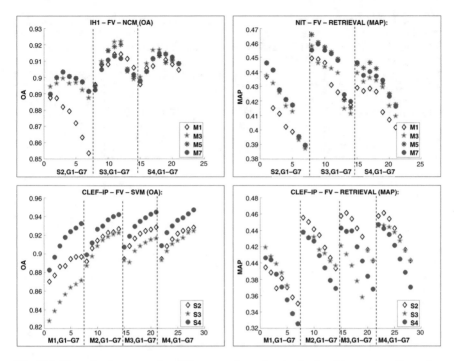

Fig. 12.9 Example plots comparing different numbers of scales (*top*) and image sizes (*bottom*)

Table 12.6 A summary of the feature sizes

G	G1	G2	G3	G4	G5	G6	G7
L	5	5	4	3	3	2	2
Nb reg	121	121	57	21	21	5	5
FD	185, 856	371, 712	350, 208	258, 048	516, 096	245, 760	491, 520

be interesting, but testing the effect of methods in the case of different configurations was out of the scope of the chapter.

In Table 12.7 and Fig. 12.10, we show results when we vary the image size, the number of pyramid layers and the number of Gaussians and fix the other parameters to W3, F1 and M5. Analyzing the results suggests that while the best configuration varies a lot, in general we get best results with relatively few layers or even a single one and often only with few Gaussians.

Spatial Pyramid: If we analyse these results in more detail, we can see that only NCM and SVM on MARG performed best with five and four layers, respectively. In general, it seems that NCM was the one that took the most advantage from more than two layers. In the case of SVM, what is beneficial is large signatures (which is not surprising), but using fewer layers with larger vocabularies seems to perform better than smaller vocabularies with more layers. This is somewhat in contrast to

Table 12.7 Comparative FV results on different data sets and tasks. We show best results (red) versus results using fixed parameter settings (blue) where we used (S3, L2, G4) for MARG and IH1, (S4, L2, G4) in the case of NIT and (S4, L1, G4) for CLEF-IP. We also show the parameter setting that provided the best results

RET	MARG	IH1	NIT	CLEF-IP
P1	95.1/95.1	95.2/94.5	83.3/81.7	89/87.9
	S3,L2,G4	S3,L2,G1	S4,L2,G4	S4,L1,G1
P5	83.1/83.1	93.8/92.9	75.9/74.9	86/84.6
	S3,L2,G5	S3,L2,G1	S4,L3,G4	S4,L1,G1
MAP	36.2/36.2	76.5/75.4	46.6/41.6	46.1/42.1
	S3,L2,G5	S3,L2,G1	S4,L4 ,G1	S2,L1,G1

CLS	MARG	IH1	NIT	CLEF-IP
KNN	93.1/93.1	95/94.2	82.8/81.9	89.6/88.1
	S3,L2,G3	S3,L2,G2	S4,L3,G4	S4,L1,G1
NCM	75/72.4	92.4/92.4	78.3/75.8	76.1/75.1
	S3,L5,G2	S3,L3,G1	S4,L3,G5	S2,L4,G1
SVM	92.5/90.7	97.4/97.2	86.5/84.9	95.5/93.5
	S3,L4,G3	S4,L1,G7	S3,L1,G4	S4,L2,G6

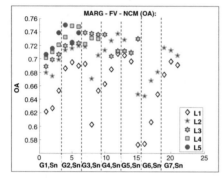 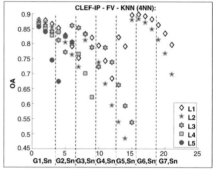

Fig. 12.10 Example plots comparing different pyramid layers

what we observed for RL and the results in [21] concerning spatial pyramids with FVs on natural images.

In Table 12.7 we also show results (in blue) for each data set given a fixed configuration found as reasonably close to best results on most tasks. These configurations are (S3, L2, G4) for MARG and IH1, (S4, L2, G4) in the case of NIT and (S4, L1, G4) for CLEF-IP, where we have in addition (W3, F1, M5) for all data sets. We can see that in most cases these fixed values are indeed good choices, except for CLEF-IP for which it is less obvious to find a good set of configurations, especially concerning the image size that performs well on all tasks (as shown also in Fig. 12.9, bottom row). This is probably due to the fact that in this data set the size of the images is extremely variable. The best compromise we found was S4, G4 without spatial pyramid (L1); however, the drop in accuracy is more important than for the other data sets.

Finally, to show the influence of the visual model, we rerun to the last set of experiments, but instead of using the visual models built on the XRCE data set, for each data set we trained its own model with the SIFT features extracted from the training images of the tested data set. The results in Table 12.8 show on one hand that we do not have a clear winner between the two models. On the other hand, while the best configuration per data set and task varies, the best scores obtained are often close. This shows somewhat that the data on which the vocabulary is built

Table 12.8 FV results when the visual models were built on SIFT features extracted from the images of the tested data set (red) and compared with the visual model on XRCE (blue). We also show the parameter setting that provided the best results for the results obtained with the visual models trained on the data set itself

RET	MARG	IH1	NIT	CLEF-IP		CLS	MARG	IH1	NIT	CLEF-IP
P1	95.9/95.1	95.4/95.2	82.5/83.3	87.7/89		KNN	95/93.1	95.3/95	82.8/82.8	88.8/89.1
	S3,L5,G1	S4,L2,G1	S4,L2,G3	S4,L1,G1			S3,L3,G2	S4,L3,G1	S4,L3,G2	S4,L1,G1
P5	85/83.1	94/93.8	75.4/75.9	84.7/86		NCM	81.1/75	92.6/92.4	78.7/78.3	75.7/76.1
	S4,L4,G2	S4,L2,G1	S4,L3,G2	S4,L1,G1			S2,L3,G4	S4,L3,G1	S4,L4,G1	S2,L4,G1
MAP	37.8/36.2	76.6/75.4	45.8/46.1	42.8/46.1		SVM	94.1/92.5	97.4/97.4	86.5/86.5	95.8/95.5
	S3,L4,G2	S4,L2,G1	S4,L4,G1	S2,L1,G1			S4,L5,G2	S4,L2,G7	S3,L1,G4	S4,L2,G6

Table 12.9 Results with late fusion of RL and FV features on different data sets and tasks

RET	signature	MARG	IH1	NIT	CLEF-IP		CLS	signature	MARG	IH1	NIT	CLEF-IP
P1	RL	93.6	93.5	75.7	79.95		KNN	RL	89.9	93.1	76.7	80.8
	FV	95.1	94.5	81.7	87.9			FV	92.6	94.2	81.9	88.1
	RL+FV	95.1	95.4	79.2	90.4			RL+FV	93	95.2	80.2	91.1
P5	RL	81	91.6	65.9	74.9		NCM	RL	63.2	91.3	65.6	61.2
	FV	82.7	92.9	74.9	84.6			FV	72.4	92.4	75.8	75.1
	RL+FV	83.3	93.8	71.6	91			RL+FV	73.4	93	79.8	75.8
MAP	RL	33.2	64.3	38.5	35.6		SVM	RL	91.9	96.7	78.2	89.5
	FV	36.1	75.4	41.6	42.1			FV	90.7	97.2	84.9	93.5
	RL+FV	36.5	76.9	44.2	48.2			RL+FV	92.8	97.7	83.7	94.4

has relatively little influence on the results the moment we use the images that have similar content, which is the case for document images.

12.4.3 Combine RL with FV

The most natural way to combine RL and FV is early or late fusion. As we use dot product for retrieval, the dot product of the concatenated features (early fusion) is equivalent to the sum of the dot products (late fusion). Similarly, the NCM centroids of the concatenated features are the concatenation of the RL and FV centroids, and therefore late and early fusions are again equivalent.

To test the late fusion of RL with FV, we consider the configuration (S0, L5, Q11) for RL and the fixed parameter settings leading to the values in blue in Table 12.7 for FV. The results obtained are shown in Table 12.9. We can see that even with a simple equally weighted late fusion, in general (except for NIT) we obtain significant improvements both on retrieval and classification.

We would like to mention here another possible combination of the RL and FV where the main idea is to consider the RL features as low-level features (replacing the SIFT) such that on each local window we build an RL histogram. Then the visual vocabulary (GMM) and the FV are built with these local RL features directly or as some PCA-reduced forms of them. Note also that if we use small image patches, the number of quantisation of the runs (Q) can be reduced as anyway a run cannot be longer than the patch size. We intend in the future to explore if such FVs on RL perform better than the global RL features and also if combining all three signatures can further improve the accuracy.

12.5 Image-Based Patent Retrieval

We would like first to recall briefly our participation in the image-based patent retrieval tasks at CLEF-IP 2011 [28]. A more detailed description especially concerning the text representation and retrieval can be found in [9]. The aim of the challenge was to rank patents as relevant or non-relevant ones given a query patent while using both visual and textual information. There were 211 query patents provided and the collection to search in contained 23,444 patents having an application date previous to 2002. The number of images varied a lot, from few images to several hundred of images per patent. In total we had 4004 images in the query patents and 291,566 images in the collection. As image representation we used the FV with the configuration (S3, W2, F2, G5 and L1) where the models (PCA and GMM) were trained on CLEF-IP, i.e. the training set of the image classification task of CLEF-IP 2011 [28]. The similarity between images was given by the dot product of two Fisher vectors.

We tested two main strategies. In the first case, we considered the average distance between all pairs of images given two patents with the corresponding set of images (MEAN). In the second case we considered only the maximum of all similarities computed between pairs of images (MAX).

We also considered to integrate in the system our automatic image-type classifier (using the same FV features) that was trained on the CLEF-IP data set and we used it to predicted the image type. Using the predicted scores, we considered the similarities between class means (averaging the images predicted to belong to a given class) and took the average or the maximum according to the strategy considered.

Finally, as in the considered patent classes (A43B patents related to footwear, A61B patents concerning diagnoses and surgery and H01L patents proposing new semiconductor and electric solid state devices) the drawings were the most relevant images, we discarded all images not predicted as drawings and computed the mean or max similarities between the images predicted as drawings. Note that for other patent classes, considering images containing chemical structures or gene sequences would be more appropriate.

The results detailed in [9] are recalled in Table 12.10. They show that the max strategy is better than considering average similarities. Considering class means instead of global mean improves the MEAN strategy, but has no effect on the max strategy. Finally, considering only drawings performed the best for both strategies.

While all these retrieval accuracies are very low, we want to make a few remarks. First, the task was really challenging as relevant prior art patents do not necessarily

Table 12.10 Image-based patent retrieval: overview of the performances of our different approaches

Model/strategy	MEAN			MAX		
Classifier	ID	MAP	P@10	ID	MAP	P@10
Not used	I1	0.56	0.20	I2	1.84	0.75
Class means	I3	0.80	0.40	I4	1.84	0.70
Only drawings	I5	1.09	0.62	I6	**3.51**	**1.85**

The performances are all shown in percentages
Bold values denotes best values

contain images similar to relevant images in the query patent. Second, even with this poor image-based ranking and simple late fusion, we were able to improve the text-only-based patent ranking especially with the I5 strategy (see details in [9]). Third, we can use more complex fusion methods to merge visual and textual retrieval (e.g. see the graph-based methods described in [1]).

On one hand the image-type classification can also be improved in several ways. On the other hand we can select a better feature configuration for FV combined with RL features as above or even using some new, deep convolutional neural networks (CNNs)-based representations such as in [17, 19].

Second, the strategies to consider and combine features from the set of images in [9] were rather simple. Instead, we can see the set of patent images as a multipage document and use the methods proposed in [12, 13, 30] to handle classification and retrieval with multipage documents.

For example, the bag-of-pages model of [13] considers PCA-reduced RL features for each page and builds an FV for the document, i.e. when computing FV with Eq. (12.4), the features x_t correspond to the RL features computed for the pages in the document page. Similarly, we can build an FV with the RL features built on the patent images and represent the patent containing these images with the obtained FV. Then two patents are compared with the dot product of these FVs.

In [12] the bag of classemes was proposed and has been shown to outperform the bag of pages. In this case the x_t features are the image-type classification scores concatenated into a single vector (called classeme) and the FV is built on top of these vectors. Note, nevertheless, that while in [12] the bag of classemes outperforms the bag of pages, the addressed problem is different, i.e. document classification. In addition, all pages have the same class label, the one inherited from the document. In our case, in a patent we have different image types and therefore we could describe by a bag of classemes the distribution of different types of images within a patent. While this can be a useful information for the patent expert, it does not necessarily improve, for example, patent prior art search.

Finally, we can also improve the image-type classification by combining the visual information with information from text. Text can come from the patent, if we can access the image caption and/or the paragraphs where the image is referred to. The extracted text can be represented by a bag of words that can be used to train classifiers which learn implicitly which words are relevant to discriminate image types. The textual and visual classifiers can be merged after at the score level (late fusion). Alternatively, we can consider embedding both the visual and textual features in the same subspace using CCA and train a classifier in the embedded space as in [15]. Note that text information can also be extracted from the document image using OCR. In the case of patent images, using a bag of 'n-grams of characters' on the text extracted from the image content could be more appropriate than a bag of words to describe, for example, gene sequences, mathematical formulas and chemical structures.

12.6   Conclusion

In this chapter we made an exhaustive experimental study on run-length (RL) histogram and Fisher vector (FV)-based representations for document image classification and retrieval. We compared different parameter configurations for both features using several data sets, methods and evaluation methods. We designed suitable configurations for both features, and while they might be suboptimal for individual tasks, features designed with the proposed configurations are reasonable in case one might want to solve different tasks with the same features. Finally, we discussed the usage of patent images in prior art search as such an example.

References

1. Ah-Pine J, Csurka G, Clinchant S (2015) Unsupervised visual and textual information fusion in cbir using graph-based methods. ACM Trans Inf Syst 33(2):1–31
2. Akata Z, Perronnin F, Harchaoui Z, Schmid C (2014) Good practice in large-scale learning for image classification. Trans Pattern Anal Mach Intell 36:507–520
3. Bagdanov AD, Worring M (2004) Multiscale document description using rectangular granulometries. Int J Doc Anal Recognit 6:181–191
4. Bai B, Weston J, Grangier D, Collobert R, Sadamasa K, Qi Y, Chapelle O, Weinberger KQ (2009) Supervised semantic indexing. In: ACM international conference on information and knowledge management (CIKM)
5. Bottou L (2010) Large-scale machine learning with stochastic gradient descent. In: COMP-STAT, pp 177–186
6. Chan Y-K, Chang C-C (2001) Image matching using run-length feature. Pattern Recogn Lett 22:447–455
7. Chen N, Blostein D (2007) A survey of document image classification: problem statement, classifier architecture and performance evaluatio. Int J Doc Anal Recognit 10:1–16
8. Csurka G, Dance C, Fan L, Willamowski J, Bray C (2004) Visual categorization with bags of keypoints. In: ECCV workshop on statistical learning for computer vision, vol 1, pp 1–2
9. Csurka G, Renders J-M, Jacquet G (2011) XRCEś participation at patent image classification and image-based patent retrieval tasks of the Clef-IP 2011. In: Intellectual property evaluation campaign (CLEF-IP)
10. Cullen JF, Jonathan JJH, Hart PE (1997) Document image database retrieval and browsing using texture analysis. In: International conference on document analysis and recognition (ICDAR), vol 2, pp 718–721
11. Davis JV, Kulis B, Jain P, Sra S, Dhillon IS (2007) Information-theoretic metric learning. In: International conference on machine learning (ICML)

12. Gordo A (2013) Document image representation, classification and retrieval in large-scale domains. PhD thesis, Computer Vision Center, Universitat Autònoma de Barcelona
13. Gordo A, Perronnin F (2010) A bag-of-pages approach to unordered multi-page document classification. In: International conference on pattern recognition (ICPR)
14. Gordo A, Perronnin F (2011) Asymmetric distances for binary embeddings. In: IEEE conference on computer vision and pattern recognition (CVPR). https://ai2-s2-pdfs.s3.amazonaws.com/d191/544940caac5f57363968539856343ad9a02d.pdf
15. Gordo A, Perronnin F, Valveny E (2012) Document classification using multiple views. In: International workshop on document analysis systems (DAS), pp 33–37
16. Gordo A, Perronnin F, Valveny E (2013) Large-scale document image retrieval and classification with runlength histograms and binary embeddings. Pattern Recogn 46(7):1898–1905
17. Harley A, Ufkes A, Derpanis K (2015) Evaluation of deep convolutional nets for document image classification and retrieval. In: International conference on document analysis and recognition (ICDAR), pp 991–995
18. Heroux P, Diana S, Ribert A, Trupin E (1998) Classification method study for automatic form class identification. In: International conference on pattern recognition (ICPR), vol 1, pp 926–928
19. Kang L, Kumar J, Ye P, Liy Y, Doermann D (2014) Convolutional neural networks for document image classification. In: International conference on pattern recognition (ICPR), pp 3168–3172
20. Keysers D, Shafait F, Breuel TM (2007) Document image zone classification - a simple high-performance approach. In: International conference on computer vision theory and applications (VISAPP), pp 44–51
21. Krapac J, Verbeek J, Jurie F (2011) Modeling spatial layout with fisher vectors for image categorization. In: IEEE international conference on computer vision (ICCV)
22. Lazebnik S, Schmid C, Ponce J (2006) Beyond bags of features: spatial pyramid matching for recognizing natural scene categories. In: IEEE conference on computer vision and pattern recognition (CVPR), vol 2, pp 2169–2178
23. Lowe D (2004) Distinctive image features from scale-invariant keypoints. Int J Comput Vis 60(2):91–110
24. Mensink T, Verbeek J, Perronnin F, Csurka G (2013) Distance-based image classification: generalizing to new classes at near-zero cost. Trans Pattern Anal Mach Intell 35(11):2624–2637
25. Perronnin F, Dance C (2007) Fisher kernels on visual vocabularies for image categorization. In: IEEE conference on computer vision and pattern recognition (CVPR), pp 1–8
26. Perronnin F, Liu Y, Sánchez J, Poirier H (2010) Large scale image retrieval with compressed fisher vectors. In: IEEE conference on computer vision and pattern recognition (CVPR)
27. Perronnin F, Sánchez J, Mensink T (2010) Improving the fisher kernel for large-scale image classification. In: European conference on computer vision (ECCV), pp 143–156
28. Piroi F, Lupu M, Hanbury A, Zenz V (2011) CLEF-IP 2011: retrieval in the intellectual property domain. In: Intellectual property evaluation campaign (CLEF-IP)
29. Pratikakis I, Gatos B, Ntirogiannis K (2012) ICFHR 2012 competition on handwritten document image binarization. In: Proceedings of the ICFHR
30. Rusiñol M, Frinken V, Karatzas D, Bagdanov AD, Llados J (2014) Multimodal page classification in administrative document image streams. Int J Doc Anal Recognit 17:331–341
31. Sánchez J, Perronnin F (2011) High-dimensional signature compression for large-scale image classification. In: IEEE conference on computer vision and pattern recognition (CVPR)
32. Sarkar P (2006) Image classification: classifying distributions of visual features. In: International conference on pattern recognition (ICPR), vol 2, pp 472–475
33. Shin C, Doermann D, Rosenfeld A (2001) Classification of document pages using structure-based features. Int J Doc Anal Recognit 3:232–247
34. Sivic J, Zisserman A (2003) Video google: a text retrieval approach to object matching in videos. In: IEEE international conference on computer vision (ICCV)

35. The Medical Article Records Groundtruth Dataset (2003) https://ceb.nlm.nih.gov/inactive-communications-engineering-branch-projects/medical-article-records-groundtruth-marg/. Last visited Jan 2017
36. The NIST Structured Forms Database (NIST Special Database 2) (2010) https://www.nist.gov/srd/nist-special-database-2. Last visited Jan 2017
37. Vedaldi A, Zisserman A (2012) Sparse kernel approximations for efficient classification and detection. In: IEEE conference on computer vision and pattern recognition (CVPR)
38. Weinberger K, Saul L (2009) Distance metric learning for large margin nearest neighbor classification. J Mach Learn Res 10:207–244

Chapter 13
Flowchart Recognition in Patent Information Retrieval

Marçal Rusiñol and Josep Lladós

Abstract In this chapter, we will analyse the current technologies available that deal with graphical information in patent retrieval applications and, in particular, with the problem of recognising and understanding information carried by flowcharts. We will review some of the state-of-the-art techniques that have arisen from the graphics recognition community and their application in the intellectual property domain. We will present an overview of the different steps that compound a flowchart recognition system, looking also at the achievements and remaining challenges in such a domain.

13.1 Introduction

A patent can be defined as a legal title protecting a technical invention for a limited period. Patent documents consist of three parts mainly [10]. First, a front page presenting general information about the patent, such as the title, the summary of the invention, the name of the inventors, etc. Second, the technical description, which details the technical problem the invention solves as well as the state of the art and the novelty of the invention. Finally, a claims section that defines the intellectual property (IP) protection rights, i.e. a clear description of what is legally protected. In each of these parts, drawings can be (and are often) used to provide an accurate detailed description of intermediate parts of the invention.

Since patent documents include both technical and legal information, conducting a patent search is of extreme importance for several purposes [11]. The technical part of patents, as in the case of scientific publications, defines the state of the art for a given problem and can be used to find out what already exists and to check the novelty of a given invention. Concerning the legal aspects, they can also be used in order to assess the freedom to operate, i.e. make sure we are not infringing someone else's IP rights, or to check whether someone might be infringing our own IP rights.

M. Rusiñol (✉) • J. Lladós
Dept. Ciències de la Computació, Computer Vision Center, Edifici O, UAB, 08193 Bellaterra, Spain
e-mail: marcal@cvc.uab.cat; josep@cvc.uab.cat

© Springer-Verlag GmbH Germany 2017
M. Lupu et al. (eds.), *Current Challenges in Patent Information Retrieval*,
The Information Retrieval Series 37, DOI 10.1007/978-3-662-53817-3_13

However, performing searches in the patent's content might not be a straightforward task.

First of all, there is the scale factor. Just in 2013, 265,900 European patent filings were made at the European Patent Office (EPO),[1] representing a 2.8 % growth with respect to the last year. And as of today, nearly 80 million patent documents worldwide are available through the publicly available patent database Espacenet.[2] Conducting efficient and effective searches in such large-scale and ever-growing scenarios is by itself a difficult problem.

Secondly, we have the semantic problem. Patents being written in an 'unstructured' manner in natural language entail the same problematics of any textual search from the information retrieval (IR) field. When searching for a patent, the user has to select a list of keywords that define the invention he/she is looking for. Finding keyword synonyms, avoiding the use of homonyms and using Boolean operators to regroup the terms in order to cast a good query are of critical importance [10].

Finally, it is worth to mention that not all the information in a patent document is conveyed by textual elements. Drawings in patents play an important role since in many patent filings the technical details are depicted rather than being explicitly written in textual format. Drawings can be of different nature, including line drawings, figures, diagrams, flowcharts, plots, etc. As pointed by many authors, e.g. Bhatti and Hanbury in [2], Hanbury et al. in [15] and Lupu et al. in [26], the inspection of visual information conveyed by such drawings is becoming overwhelmingly important in order to assess the novelty of a submitted patent. However, nowadays most of the patent search applications fail to exploit non-textual information [1, 23].

It is worth to note the efforts made within the CLEF initiative concerning the problem of dealing with non-textual information in the IP domain. Until 2011, the CLEF-IP track served as a benchmarking activity on prior art retrieval focusing only on textual patent documents. However, in 2011 two image-based tasks were added [30]: one devoted to find patent documents relevant to a given patent document which contained images and another aimed at categorising patent images into predefined categories of images (such as graphs, flowcharts, drawings, etc.). In CLEF-IP 2012 [31], a new image-based task was proposed: the flowchart recognition task dealing with the interpretation of flowchart line drawing images. The participants were asked to extract as much structural information as possible from these images and return it in a predefined textual format for further processing for the purpose of patent search. Three different institutions participated in such a task [29, 34, 42]. We will overview such approaches and put them in context throughout the rest of this chapter. We will analyse the current technologies available that deal with graphical information in the patent retrieval application. We will review some of the state-of-the-art techniques arisen from the graphics recognition community and their application in the IP domain. Specifically, we will focus on the problem of recognising and understanding information carried by flowcharts.

---

[1] http://www.epo.org/about-us/annual-reports-statistics.html.

[2] http://www.epo.org/searching/free/espacenet.html.

The rest of the chapter is organised as follows. In Sect. 13.2 we will overview the state of the art within the graphics recognition field and its applications to the IP domain. In Sect. 13.3 we will present an overview of the different steps that compound a flowchart recognition system. Finally, in Sects. 13.4 and 13.5 we will present the remaining challenges and our concluding remarks, respectively.

13.2 Graphics Recognition: From Visual Similarity to Interpretation

The use of non-textual information is pervasive in the whole IP domain. We can see in Fig. 13.1 some examples of graphical entities found in IP documents such as trademark registrations, design applications or drawings in patents such as flowcharts, molecules, mechanical drawings or electronic diagrams. The management of such graphical entities in the prior art search is of crucial importance since they depict either directly what the owner wants to protect, as in the case of trademarks or designs, or essential details of the invention under patent protection.

The graphics recognition community has been proposing methods for describing and recognising symbolic information for many years [18], and many symbol recognition proposals have a direct application in the IP domain. We can cite, for example, some works dealing with trademark description [19, 32], molecule recognition [13, 36], symbol recognition in mechanical drawings [6] or electronic diagrams [52]. However, most of the symbol recognition techniques present an important drawback. The symbols to recognise have to be isolated so that the descriptors represent them globally. Globally describing graphical information might be already suitable for recognising trademarks of molecule depictions, but is not usually desirable when dealing with graphical entities formed by a compound of symbols and their relationships among them [33], as in the case of electronic diagrams, mechanical drawings or flowcharts.

However, in general, most of the published approaches dealing with patent image retrieval globally describe graphical information and then follow either a content-based image retrieval (CBIR) paradigm [21] or a classification paradigm [8, 28]. In such paradigms the retrieval or recognition is thus performed in terms of a similarity measure between the query image and the images in the corpus. For example, in [17], patent drawings are represented using attributed graphs and the retrieval task is then casted as a graph similarity computation. Methods like [7, 46, 47] and [40] base the image description on histograms encoding the centroid positions at different levels. Such descriptors can be understood as a special case of a quad-tree [37] encoding of the image under analysis. The retrieval part just relies on the Euclidean distance between the query and corpus descriptors. In [43], the PATSEEK framework is presented in which patent drawings are described by means of edge orientation autocorrelograms [27].

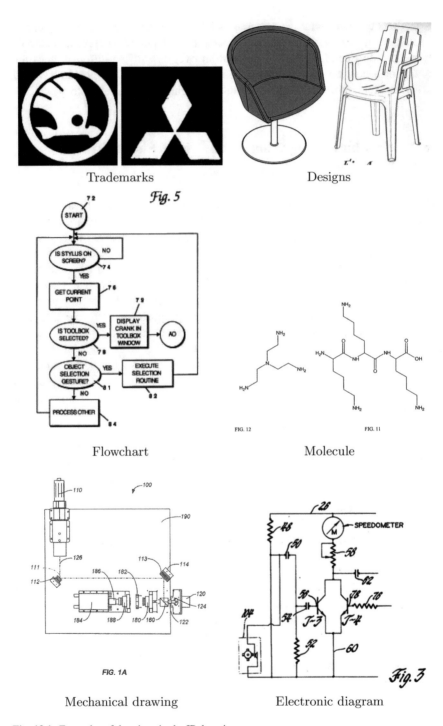

Trademarks   Designs

Fig. 5

Flowchart   Molecule

Mechanical drawing   Electronic diagram

Fig. 13.1 Examples of drawings in the IP domain

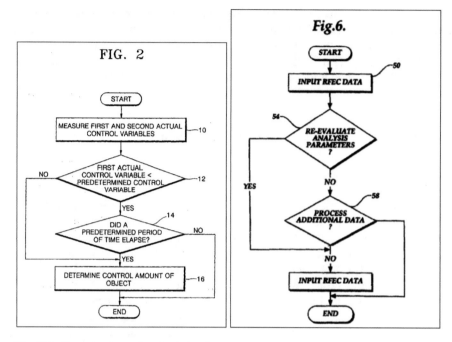

Fig. 13.2 Example of two visually similar flowcharts

Nonetheless, the CBIR paradigm might not be the most suitable tool to provide an image search in the intellectual property domain. In order to assess whether an invention is new or has already been submitted, the patent professional should look for images that depict the *same concept* [47] instead of images that *look visually similar* to the query. That is, image retrieval methods should be able to bridge the *semantic gap* between the visual appearance of the images and the semantic meaning they convey [26]. But in the specific case of flowchart images, this problem is still ill-defined. Take, for instance, the two flowcharts depicted in Fig. 13.2. It is obvious that the two flowcharts are visually similar, and one could argue that since they are formed by the same subset of symbols and share the same interconnection between them, it is reasonable to consider them as relevant hits in a retrieval scenario. On the other hand, the two flowcharts represent completely different procedures and carry different information, so it is fair to consider them non-relevant one to the other. Since flowcharts carry an important semantic meaning, it would be beneficial to 'translate' such graphical information into a structured format that will allow to browse the contained information, that is, to automatically *understand* and *interpret* flowcharts.

Early works such as [4] and [22] were already focused on the recognition of line drawings for further automatic process. This research line continued until the mid-1990s [3, 50] when most of the research efforts were refocused on the treatment of online sketched drawings [41, 51], although some recent research in those lines can still be found [45]. To our best knowledge, no commercial patent retrieval system uses graphical interpretation techniques for the retrieval of non-textual information in patent documents. The only efforts in that direction come from the Image Mining for Patent Exploration (**IMPEx**) Project;[3] its main objective is the extraction of semantic information from patent images.

13.3 Flowchart Recognition Architecture

Most of the state-of-the-art flowchart recognition architectures follow more or less the same architectures and the same steps. We will overview in this section such steps and the different approaches that have been used in the literature. The first stage is devoted to separate the flowchart image into two different layers, one containing the textual information and the other one containing the graphical elements. Subsequently, graphical elements are separated into two different groups: the symbolic elements (rectangles, circles, ellipses, etc.) and the connectors between them. Afterwards, proper recognition modules are applied in order to recognise which graphical primitives appear at each location and to transcribe the text within the image into electronic format by means of optical character recognition (OCR) techniques. Finally, a structural and syntactic validation step is applied in order to correct the recognition errors by including context-dependent information and eventually producing a structured output describing the flowchart's contents.

Let us overview in the following each of these individual steps. We will finally summarise how the performance of the flowchart recognition systems was evaluated in the context of the CLEF-IP 2012 flowchart recognition task.

13.3.1 Text/Graphics Separation

Textual terms appearing within flowcharts cannot be directly recognised following classical OCR approaches that assume a regular layout organised in columns, paragraphs and lines.

The text/graphics separation process aims at segmenting the document into two layers: a layer which contains text characters and annotations and a layer containing graphical objects.

Although there exists a wide taxonomy of text/graphics separation methods [16, 24, 44], the most commonly used are the ones relying on morphological operations and the ones based on connected component analysis.

First, the text/graphics separation methods based on morphological operators assume that the text is what remains after applying iterative openings to the

---

[3]http://www.joanneum.at/?id=3922.

original image with structuring elements designed to eliminate rectilinear objects. The method proposed by Wahl et al. [48] is one of the first methods based on morphological filtering. It uses run-length smoothing algorithm (RLSA) to detect vertical and horizontal text strings. RLSA can be seen as morphological closing (or opening) operations with vertical and horizontal structuring elements of length according to the text size and graphical lines width. The method of Lu [25] uses RLSA too. The main improvement of this work is that it allows to detect slanted lines by performing a stretching operation at different angles. The main drawback of these approaches is that they tend to wrongly label text as graphics.

On the other hand, the methods based on connected component analysis are the most commonly used. A pioneer and well-known work was proposed by Fletcher and Kasturi [14]. The basic idea is to segment text based on basic perceptual grouping properties. Thus, simple heuristics on font size, inter-character, word and line spacing and alignment are used. The method requires many thresholds, but the good point is that they are extracted from the image object properties and are not manually set a priori. The main steps of this method are:

1. Connected component generation
2. Filtering of connected components based on area and size
3. Connected component grouping in terms of area and size to cluster those that are likely to belong to the same font size and so are candidates to be in the same string
4. Hough transform applied to the centroids of connected components (text strings are supposed to have a rectilinear arrangement)
5. Logical grouping of strings into words and phrases. This step intends to capture those components kept aside by the Hough step, but that fall into the potential text area (in terms of interline spacing, inter-character gaps, etc.). For example, a period at the end of a string or an accent
6. Text string separation

This method combines simplicity with good performance and scalability to different text properties. This is probably the reason that most of the methods are based on the Fletcher and Kasturi one, with small variations and adaptations to different contexts. The weakness of this method is that it does not cope with text touching graphics. Tombre et al. [44] proposed an improved approach able to separate text touching to graphical parts. In addition they introduced some more heuristics allowing to improve the performance.

The method from Tombre et al. [44] was used in the context of flowchart recognition in [34, 35]. We can see an example of the results produced by the text/graphics separation step in Fig. 13.3.

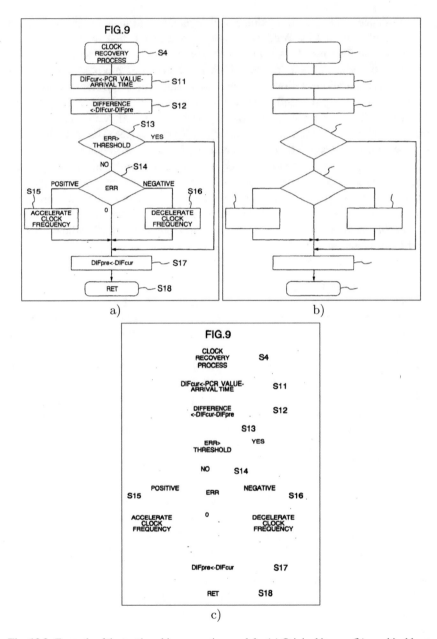

Fig. 13.3 Example of the text/graphics separation module. (**a**) Original image, (**b**) graphical layer, (**c**) textual layer, (**d**) undetermined layer (empty in this example)

13.3.2   Node and Edge Segmentation

After having separated the text appearing in the flowchart with the graphical entities, most approaches apply a segmentation method in order to separate the nodes (symbols from the flowcharts) rather than the edges (the connectors that define the flow). Here again, a connected component analysis on the graphical layer of the flowchart image drives this segmentation procedure [34, 42]. Closed regions in the flowchart image usually correspond to the nodes of the flowchart. After having determined which regions of the flowchart correspond to nodes, the remaining foreground pixels are attributed as being edges. We can see an example of the node and edge segmentation in Fig. 13.4.

However, this procedure presents two drawbacks. The first is nodes that because of some degradation or some design choice are not fully connected and are likely to be labelled as background zone and be completely missed. This problem is usually tackled by having a pre-processing step that 'closes' the small gaps between co-linear line segments [29, 42]. The second problem is somehow more fundamental. Closed regions in flowcharts do not always correspond to nodes.

Edges linking two non-consecutive nodes in the flow are likely to form loops in the flowchart that will be labelled as a connected component. We can see an example in Fig. 13.5. This case is a clear example of what is known as the Sayre paradox [39]:

> In order to achieve good recognition results, the objects should be previously segmented, but to get reliable segmentation, the objects should be previously recognized.

That is, before running the node recognition module, we need to segment nodes from the background, but to really have a good segmentation without loops appearing as nodes, we need to already define what is a node and what is not. This problem is addressed by casting some heuristics on the shape of the connected components to assess whether the connected component is really a node from the flowchart or corresponds to a loop. For instance, in [35], convexity and vertical symmetry measurements are used in order to discriminate between loops and nodes, since nodes tend to be vertically symmetric and tend also to be convex shapes.

13.3.3   Text and Symbol Recognition

After having completely segmented the different regions from the flowchart image comes the proper recognition stage, both for text and for graphical entities.

OCR, being one of the first problems addressed from the pattern recognition field, is considered nowadays an almost solved problem when applied to documents under certain conditions. However, as we have stated before, applying an OCR directly to a flowchart image is likely to fail, since the layout of a flowchart does not follow the same rules as text being printed in a book. But if we feed to an OCR engine the text bounding boxes arisen from the text/graphics separation stage, the results should be acceptable enough. Nowadays, commercial OCR engines such as

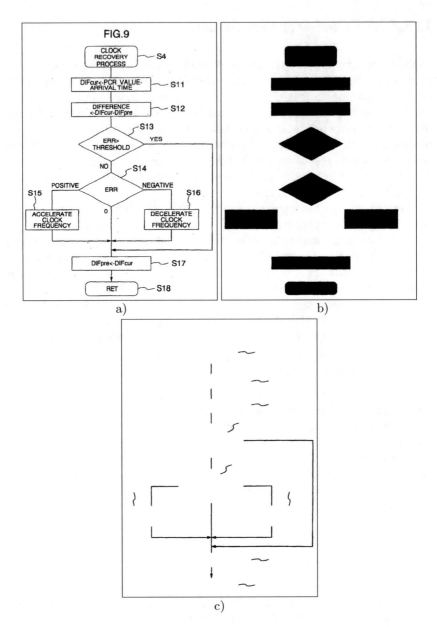

Fig. 13.4 Example of the node and edge segmentation modules. (**a**) Original image, (**b**) node layer, (**c**) edge layer

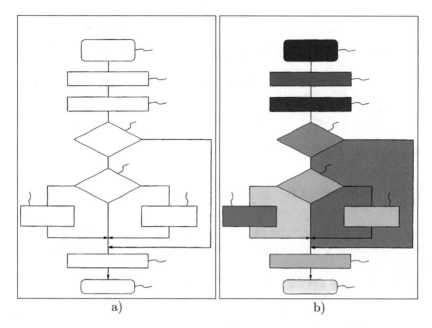

Fig. 13.5 Example of the connected component labelling, labelling loops as foreground nodes. (**a**) Original input, (**b**) Components identified

ABBYY FineReader,[4] Tesseract[5] and Omnipage[6] are the ones most often used in any document image task. OCR accuracies can be boosted if we provide the OCR engine a context-dependent lexicon and language model as suggested in [42].

Concerning the recognition of the flowchart's symbols (c.f. Fig. 13.6), in principle any shape descriptor [54] could be used in order to accurately classify the symbols. In [34], Hu geometric moment invariants [53] and the BSM descriptor [9] were used. In both runs submitted to the CLEF-IP 2012 flowchart recognition task from Thean et al. [42] and Mörzinger et al. [29], ad hoc symbol descriptors based on shape symmetry were proposed. From the result analysis of the flowchart recognition task [31, 35], we can see better recognition accuracies were reached when using hand-crafted descriptors for the specific purpose of node recognition than when using generic shape descriptors from the literature.

It is also worth to mention that in [42], a shape normalisation step was proposed in order to deal with the different styles that the same symbol can present (c.f. Figs. 3 and 4 in [42]). A set of squeezing operations result in a shape simplification that helped to improve the node recognition accuracy.

---

[4]http://finereader.abbyy.com/.

[5]http://code.google.com/p/tesseract-ocr/.

[6]http://www.nuance.com/for-individuals/by-product/omnipage/index.htm.

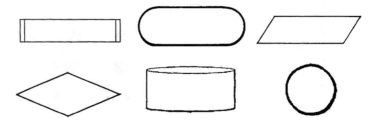

Fig. 13.6 Example of different node types

13.3.4 Structured Output

Once we have identified all the elements of a flowchart, we have to infer from the different relationships among elements which is the structure of the flowchart. More specifically, we have to assess which nodes are connected by an edge. This can be done by simply pairwisely selecting all the detected nodes and subsequently analysing whether any element of the edge layer provokes that those two disjoint nodes merge into a single element. If this happens, then the two nodes are linked through this edge in the delivered graph structure [35].

Subsequently, a structured output of the interpretation of the flowchart has to be provided. Because of the nature of flowcharts, having a graph data structure representation seems to be the most suitable. We can see in Fig. 13.7 an example of the structured output format expected in the CLEF-IP 2012 task [31].

13.3.5 Structural and Syntactic Validation

Flowcharts are composed by a set of node symbols together with their connectors and the textual content. However, they also follow a quite strict diagrammatic notation defined by a set of rules that have to be followed so that the flowchart makes sense. None of the CLEF-IP 2012 flowchart recognition task participants used this context knowledge that can yield a strong boost in performance. Graph grammars have been used through the years in order to define a set of rules that two-dimensional signals (i.e. electronic diagrams, flowcharts, architectural drawings, etc.) have to follow in order to be valid [4, 38].

In [20], Lemaitre et al. based their online flowchart recognition system on a structural description with the addition of syntactic knowledge using a grammatical description. We strongly believe that successful flowchart recognition systems should integrate such syntactic definitions in order to reach the desired recognition performances.

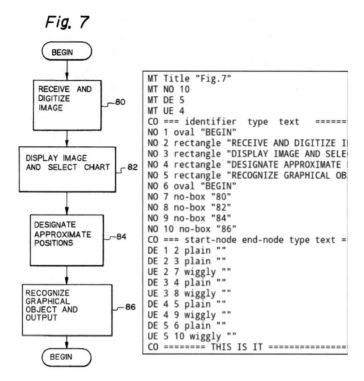

Fig. 13.7 An example of input image with its corresponding textual information (extracted from [31])

13.3.6 *Performance Evaluation of Flowchart Recognition in CLEF-IP 2012*

The flowchart recognition task from the CLEF-IP 2012 campaign was evaluated at three different levels: namely, how well the flowchart structure has been recognised (*structural level*), how well the nodes and the edge types have been recognised (*recognition level*) and a third level that evaluated the text label transcription (*transcription level*).

In order to assess the methods' performance at structural level, a graph metric distance between the topic flowchart F_t and the submitted flowchart F_s is defined in terms of the most common subgraph, $\mathrm{mcs}(F_t, F_s)$ [5, 49]. Formally, it was computed as follows:

$$d(F_t, F_s) = 1 - \frac{|\mathrm{mcs}(F_t, F_s)|}{|F_t| + |F_s| - |\mathrm{mcs}(F_t, F_s)|}, \tag{13.1}$$

where $|F_i|$ denotes the size of the graph computed as the number of nodes plus the number of edges.

The most common subgraph measure can be interpreted as follows. When comparing a recognised flowchart F_s and the ground truth expected output F_t, the maximum common subgraph $mcs(F_t, F_s)$ measures how well the participant's output matches the expected graph. If the participant's method output is perfect, the maximum common subgraph is the flowchart itself and thus $mcs(F_t, F_s) = |F_t| = |F_s|$ and $d(F_t, F_s) = 0$. If the output is missing a node or some edges, the common structure shared between the output and the ground truth will be smaller than F_t, and consequently since $|mcs(F_t, F_s)| < |F_t|$, the final distance $d(F_t, F_s) > 0$ will increase as long as we keep missing elements. The same applies if we deliver an output with extra elements than the ground truth.

The ability to recognise the nodes and the edge types of the different submitted runs was evaluated by the accuracy of the classification, whereas the performance of the textual transcription was measured with a normalised edit distance between the automatically transcribed text and the yielded automatic transcription from the methods.

Although such measures helped to assess which method performs the best at extracting the structure and the contents of the flowchart, it is still unclear if such indicators will exactly correlate with the user experience in a retrieval scenario.

13.4 Challenges

Although the recognition of flowcharts has been a present problem for many years in the graphics recognition domain, there are still some challenges that need to be addressed in order to perform patent searches that take into account graphical information. Let us briefly overview which are to our understanding the remaining problems.

– **The Sayre paradox** has to be properly addressed in the flowchart recognition architecture. The whole flowchart recognition relies on an initial segmentation step between nodes, edges, text and background that is far from being perfect. An incorrect segmentation ruins the subsequent recognition steps. It would be thus desirable to have some methods that perform the segmentation and recognition in a single step, as in the case of symbol spotting [33].
– **A syntactic analysis** of flowcharts [20] is a must in order to reach acceptable recognition performances. Syntactic rules should not only serve as a final validation tool, but should drive the whole recognition framework.
– **The inclusion of flowcharts in patent searches** does not end with the flowchart recognition step. Once flowchart images have been 'translated' to a structured format, we would still need a retrieval framework that allows the user to cast queries and to retrieve relevant information stored in graphical format. It is still unclear how such a retrieval system should be designed. Would the user cast their queries using keywords or providing a flowchart sample?

- **The combination of graphical search with textual/semantic information** should be paramount. An effective patent search cannot be just focused on the graphical information, but should be supported by other information queues encoded as metadata in the patent applications. Ideas from different works such as [7, 12] that cast queries covering several granularity levels of information should be adopted in the particular scenario of patent search through flowchart information.
- **The evaluation of flowchart recognition** for the final purpose of information retrieval is also still ill-defined. Which flowcharts can be considered as relevant given a query? Is the fact of missing an edge or misrecognising a node paramount to the final retrieval performance?

13.5   Conclusions

In this chapter we have analysed the current technologies available to deal with graphical information in patent retrieval applications and, in particular, with the problem of recognising and understanding information carried by flowcharts. An overview of the different steps that compound a flowchart recognition system has been presented.

Although initiatives such the CLEF-IP 2012 flowchart recognition task mark an important milestone to assess the performance of state-of-the-art methods and track the progress in this specific domain, we have seen that there are still many important challenges yet to be addressed in order to include graphical information in the patent information retrieval framework.

We strongly believe that the use of syntactic knowledge, together with the definition of the retrieval mechanisms dealing with graphical information other than CBIR, is paramount in order to achieve a useful patent graphical information retrieval.

Acknowledgements This work is partially supported by the People Programme (Marie Curie Actions) of the Seventh Framework Programme of the European Union (FP7/2007–2013) under REA Grant Agreement No. 600388 and by the Agency of Competitiveness for Companies of the Government of Catalonia, ACCIÓ, and the Spanish project TIN2014-52072-P.

References

1. Adams S (2005) Electronic non-text material in patent applications – some questions for patent offices, applicants and searchers. World Patent Inf 27(2):99–103
2. Bhatti N, Hanbury A (2013) Image search in patents: a review. Int J Doc Anal Recognit 16(4):309–329
3. Blostein D (1996) General diagram-recognition methodologies. In: Graphics recognition methods and applications. Lecture notes in computer science, vol 1072. Springer, New York, pp 106–122

4. Bunke H (1982) Attributed programmed graph grammars and their application to schematic diagram interpretation. IEEE Trans Pattern Anal Mach Intell 4(6):574–582
5. Bunke H, Shearer K (1998) A graph distance metric based on the maximal common subgraph. Pattern Recogn Lett 19(3–4):255–259
6. Cheng YQ, Cao YL, Yang JY (1990) An automatic recognition system of assembly drawings. In: Workshop on machine vision applications, pp 211—214
7. Codina J, Pianta E, Vrochidis S, Papadopoulos S (2008) Integration of semantic, metadata and image search engines with a text search engine for patent retrieval. In: Proceedings of the workshop on semantic search at the fifth European semantic web conference, pp 14–28
8. Csurka G, Renders JM, Jacquet G (2011) XRCE's participation at patent image classification and image-based patent retrieval tasks of the CLEF-IP 2011. In: CLEF 2011 evaluation labs and workshop, online working notes
9. Escalera S, Fornés A, Pujol O, Radeva P, Sánchez G, Lladós J (2009) Blurred shape model for binary and grey-level symbol recognition. Pattern Recogn Lett 30(15):1424–1433
10. European IPR Helpdesk. How to search for patent information. Fact Sheet, Nov 2011
11. European IPR Helpdesk. Automatic patent analysis. Fact Sheet, Dec 2013
12. Fafalios P, Salampasis M, Tzitzikas Y (2013) Exploratory patent search with faceted search and configurable entity mining. In: Proceedings of the integrating IR technologies for professional search workshop
13. Filippov IV, Nicklaus MC (2009) Extracting chemical structure information: optical structure recognition application. In: Proceedings of the IAPR international workshop on graphics recognition
14. Fletcher LA, Kasturi R (1988) A robust algorithm for text string separation from mixed text/graphics images. IEEE Trans Pattern Anal Mach Intell 10(6):910–918
15. Hanbury A, Bhatti N, Lupu M, Mörzinger R (2011) Patent image retrieval: a survey. In: Proceedings of the fourth workshop on patent information retrieval, pp 3–8
16. Hoang TV, Tabbone S (2010) Text extraction from graphical document images using sparse representation. In: Proceedings of the 9th IAPR international workshop on document analysis systems, pp 143–150
17. Huet B, Kern NJ, Guarascio G, Merialdo B (2001) Relational skeletons for retrieval in patent drawings. In: Proceedings of the international conference on image processing, pp 737–740
18. Kasturi R, Tombre K (1995) Graphics recognition: methods and applications. Lecture notes in computer science, vol 1072. Springer, New York
19. Kesidis A, Karatzas D (2014) Logo and trademark recognition. Handbook of document image processing and recognition. Springer, London, pp 591–646
20. Lemaitre A, Mouchère H, Camillerapp J, Coüasnon B (2013) Interest of syntactic knowledge for on-line flowchart recognition. In: Graphics recognition new trends and challenges. Springer, New York, pp 89–98
21. Lew MS, Sebe N, Djeraba C, Jain R (2006) Content-based multimedia information retrieval: state of the art and challenges. ACM Trans Multimed Comput Commun Appl 2(1):1–19
22. Lin X, Shimotsuji S, Minoh M, Sakai T (1985) Efficient diagram understanding with characteristic pattern detection. Comput Vision Graphics Image Process 30(1):84–106
23. List J (2007) How drawings could enhance retrieval in mechanical and device patent searching. World Patent Inf 29(3):210–218
24. Lladós J, Rusiñol M (2014) Graphics recognition techniques. Handbook of document image processing and recognition. Springer, London, pp 489–521
25. Lu Z (1998) Detection of text regions from digital engineering drawings. IEEE Trans Pattern Anal Mach Intell 20(4):431–439
26. Lupu M, Schuster R, Mörzinger R, Piroi F, Schleser T, Hanbury A (2012) Patent images – a glass-encased tool: opening the case. In: Proceedings of the 12th international conference on knowledge management and knowledge technologies
27. Mahmoudi F, Shanbehzadeh J, Eftekhari-Moghadam AM, Soltanian-Zadeh H (2003) Image retrieval based on shape similarity by edge orientation autocorrelogram. Pattern Recogn 36(8):1725–1736

28. Mörzinger R, Horti A, Thallinger G, Bhatti N, Hanbury A (2011) Classifying patent images. In: CLEF 2011 evaluation labs and workshop, online working notes
29. Mörzinger R, Schuster R, Horti A, Thallinger G (2012) Visual structure analysis of flow charts in patent images. In: CLEF 2012 evaluation labs and workshop, online working notes
30. Piroi F, Lupu M, Hanbury A, Zenz V (2011) CLEF-IP 2011: retrieval in the intellectual property domain. In: CLEF 2011 evaluation labs and workshop, online working notes
31. Piroi F, Lupu M, Hanbury A, Sexton AP, Magdy W, Filippov IV (2012) CLEF-IP 2012: retrieval experiments in the intellectual property domain. In: CLEF 2012 evaluation labs and workshop, online working notes
32. Rusiñol M, Lladós J (2010) Efficient logo retrieval through hashing shape context descriptors. In: Proceedings of the ninth IAPR international workshop on document analysis systems, pp 215–222
33. Rusiñol M, Lladós J (2010) Symbol spotting in digital libraries: focused retrieval over graphic-rich document collections. Springer, London
34. Rusiñol M, de las Heras LP, Mas J, Terrades OR, Karatzas D, Dutta A, Sánchez G, Lladós J (2012) CVC-UAB's participation in the flowchart recognition task of CLEF-IP 2012. In: CLEF 2012 evaluation labs and workshop, online working notes
35. Rusiñol M, de las Heras LP, Ramos O (2014) Flowchart recognition for non-textual information retrieval in patent search. Inf Retr 17(4):331–341
36. Sadawi N (2009) Recognising chemical formulas from molecule depictions. In: Proceedings of the IAPR international workshop on graphics recognition
37. Samet H, Webber RE (1985) Storing a collection of polygons using quadtrees. ACM Trans Graph 4(3):182–222
38. Sánchez G, Lladós J (2004) Syntactic models to represent perceptually regular repetitive patterns in graphic documents. In: Graphics recognition. Recent advances and perspectives. Springer, New York, pp 166–175
39. Sayre KM (1973) Machine recognition of handwritten words: a project report. Pattern Recogn 5(3):213–228
40. Sidiropoulos P, Vrochidis S, Kompatsiaris I (2011) Content-based binary image retrieval using the adaptive hierarchical density histogram. Pattern Recogn 44(4):739–750
41. Szwoch W (2007) Recognition, understanding and aestheticization of freehand drawing flowcharts. In: Proceedings of the ninth international conference on document analysis and recognition, pp 1138–1142
42. Thean A, Deltorn JM, Lopez P, Romary L (2012) Textual summarisation of flowcharts in patent drawings for CLEF-IP2012. In: CLEF 2012 evaluation labs and workshop, online working notes
43. Tiwari A, Bansal V (2004) PATSEEK: content based image retrieval system for patent database. In: Proceedings of the fourth international conference on electronic business, pp 1167–1171
44. Tombre K, Tabbone S, Pelissier L, Lamiroy B, Dosch P (2002) Text/graphics separation revisited. In: Document analysis systems V. Lecture notes in computer science, vol 2423. Springer, New York, pp 615–620
45. Vasudevan BG, Dhanapanichkul S, Balakrishnan R (2008) Flowchart knowledge extraction on image processing. In: Proceedings of the IEEE international joint conference on neural networks, pp 4075–4082
46. Vrochidis S, Papadopoulos S, Moumtzidou A, Sidiropoulos P, Pianta E, Kompatsiaris I (2010) Towards content-based patent image retrieval: a framework perspective. World Patent Inf 32(2):94–106
47. Vrochidis S, Moumtzidou A, Kompatsiaris I (2012) Concept-based patent image retrieval. World Patent Inf 34(4):292–303
48. Wahl F, Wong K, Casey R (1982) Block segmentation and text extraction in mixed text/image documents. Comput Graphics Image Process 20(4):375–390
49. Wallis WD, Shoubridge P, Kraetz M, Ray D (2001) Graph distances using graph union. Pattern Recogn Lett 22(6–7):701–704

50. Yu Y, Samal A, Seth SC (1997) A system for recognizing a large class of engineering drawings. IEEE Trans Pattern Anal Mach Intell 19(8):868–890
51. Yuan Z, Pan H, Zhang L (2008) A novel pen-based flowchart recognition system for programming teaching. In: Advances in blended learning. Lecture notes in computer science, vol 5328. Springer, Berlin, pp 55–64
52. Zesheng S, Jing Y, Chunhong J, Yonggui W (1994) Symbol recognition in electronic diagrams using decision tree. In: Proceedings of the IEEE international conference on industrial technology, pp 719–723
53. Zhang D, Lu G (2002) A comparative study of three region shape descriptors. In: Proceedings of the digital image computing techniques and applications, pp 1–6
54. Zhang D, Lu G (2004) Review of shape representation and description techniques. Pattern Recogn 37:1–19

Chapter 14
Modern Approaches to Chemical Image Recognition

Igor V. Filippov, Mihai Lupu, and Alan P. Sexton

Abstract Millions of existing patent documents and journal articles dealing with chemistry describe chemical structures by way of structure images (so-called Kekulé structures). While being human-readable, these structure images cannot be interpreted by a computer and are unusable in the context of most chemoinformatics applications: structure and substructure searches, chemo-biological property calculations, etc. There are currently many formats available for storing structural information in a computer-readable format, but the conversion of millions of images by hand is a cumbersome and time-consuming process. Therefore there is a need for an automatic tool for converting images into structures. One of the first such tools was presented at ICDAR in 1993 (OROCS). We would like to present modern developments in optical structure recognition which build upon the ideas developed earlier and add modern enhancements to the process of automatic extraction of structure images from the surrounding text and graphics and conversion of the extracted images into a molecular format. We describe in detail two top performing chemical OCR applications—one open source and one academic software package. The performance here was judged by TREC-CHEM 2011 and CLEF 2012 challenges.

14.1 Introduction

The problem of extraction and identification of chemical structure depictions in texts such as patent documents or journal articles is distinctly different from the better-known tasks of optical character recognition or object detection. A chemical

I.V. Filippov (✉)
VIF Innovations, LLC, Rockville, MD 20852, USA
e-mail: igor.v.filippov@gmail.com

M. Lupu
TU Wien, Vienna, Austria
e-mail: lupu@ifs.tuwien.ac.at

A.P. Sexton
University of Birmingham, Birmingham, UK
e-mail: a.p.sexton@cs.bham.ac.uk

© Springer-Verlag GmbH Germany 2017
M. Lupu et al. (eds.), *Current Challenges in Patent Information Retrieval*,
The Information Retrieval Series 37, DOI 10.1007/978-3-662-53817-3_14

structure image contains much more information than a character in an alphabet—there are only a few dozen characters in most alphabets but millions of known chemical structures. It is easy to correct a misrecognised character when the options are limited to a hundred or so possibilities, but a misrecognised chemical structure might still be a valid molecule. Making the matter even more complicated, there are many ways to draw the same molecule, often in such a way that only a trained chemist is able to recognise identical chemicals. For this reason, widely used techniques such as wavelet transforms or neural networks, used, for example, in face recognition, are not applicable here.

Attempts at automatic optical structure recognition go back as far as the late 1980s. Notable among them are OROCS [1], Kekulé [2] and a program from the University of Santiago de Chile (unnamed) [3]. More recent efforts include CLiDE [4], ChemReader [5] and ChemOCR [6, 7].

In this chapter, we will focus on OSRA[1] and MolRec—two systems developed at VIF Innovations and the University of Birmingham, respectively. These are two top performing software tools as was judged by TREC-CHEM 2011 chemical image recognition challenge.

We start by introducing the two packages in the next section, then we describe the processing workflow for chemical image recognition followed by evaluation results. The penultimate section demonstrates advancements which build upon the existing work to go beyond single molecule recognition. We conclude with a brief summary of the progress made in the field in the recent years.

14.2 OSRA and MolRec

The Optical Structure Recognition Application (OSRA) was started in early 2007 as the first open-source project dealing with chemical structure information extraction. According to our own [8] and third-party benchmarks [5], OSRA is very competitive in recognition rates compared to other commercial and academic packages. The last few years have seen a surge of interest in the subject [5, 8–10] and we believe that the open-source approach allows for faster innovative development (everybody can participate) and better scientific verifiability (the source code is available for examination).

MolRec [10] was shown to provide a very high recognition rate for molecular diagrams. Its focus on high recognition performance is counterbalanced by the fact that it provides no modules for identifying and extracting molecular diagrams from a document that contains them. MolRec's approach is characterised by:

1. An early lifting of the raster diagram into a spatial graph of symbolic components
2. A rule-based system applied to the spatial graph to extract the semantic content of the diagram

---

[1] http://osra.sourceforge.net.

14.3 Overview of the Processing Workflow

A chemical structure image typically consists of the following elements:

- Regular single, double and triple bonds
- Atomic labels
- Charges
- Dash, wedge and wavy bonds
- Circle bonds (aromatic rings)

Regular bonds are either single or two or three parallel straight lines. Atomic labels could be single characters, 'O', 'N' and 'H'; multi-characters for a single atom, 'Br' and 'Cl'; or abbreviations for frequently occurring groups, 'superatoms', 'Ac', 'COOH', etc. A charge can be one or more plus or minus signs next to the atomic label, or a number with a plus or minus sign—e.g. '3+'. Wedge and dashed bonds represent bonds that are directed 'out of' or 'into' the page to convey 3D information about a non-flat chemical structure. Circular bonds are sometimes used to denote an aromatic ring. An example is presented in Fig. 14.1.

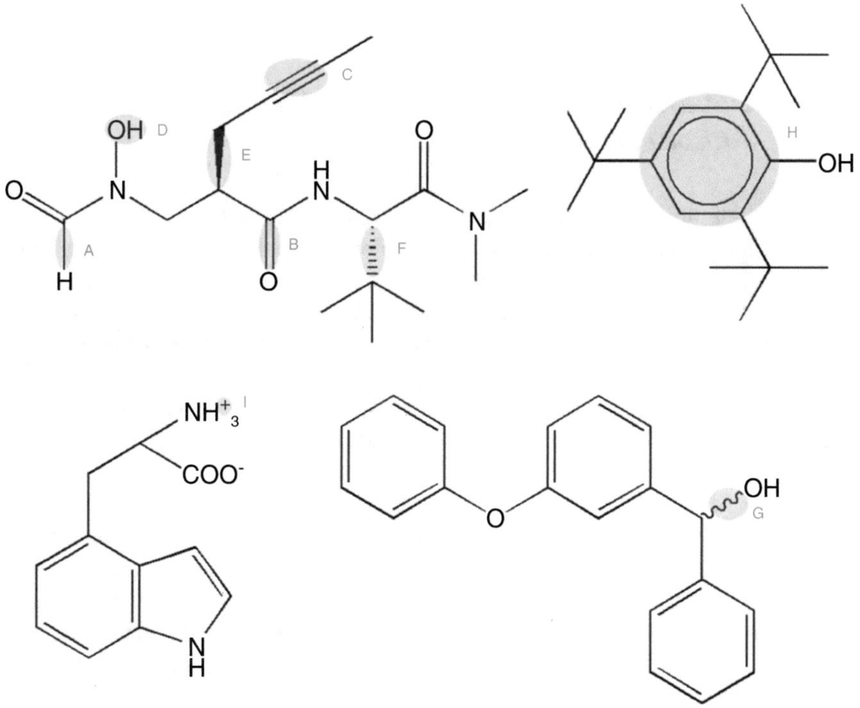

Fig. 14.1 A demonstration of molecular elements: A, single bond; B and C, double and triple bonds; D, atomic label; E, wedge bond; F, dash bond; G, wavy bond; H, circular bond in aromatic ring; I, charge

There exists a general workflow shared by many images to chemical structure tools mentioned in the previous section. The overall approach changed surprisingly little from the algorithm pioneered by IBM OROCS project in 1993 [1]. It consists of the following steps:

1. Greyscale and binarisation
2. Anisotropic smoothing and thinning
3. Page segmentation
4. Vectorisation and bond/node detection
5. Atomic label and charge recognition
6. Rule-based recognition of the spatial graph, including:

   • Circle bond recognition (for old-style aromatic rings)
   • Double and triple bond detection
   • Special bond detection: wedge and dash bonds
   • Bridge bond detection
   • Compilation of the connection table
   • Confidence estimate

Each of these steps will be described in the following sections on the examples of OSRA and MolRec.

14.3.1 Initial Processing: Binarisation, Thinning and Anisotropic Smoothing

The following approach to image pre-processing is undertaken within OSRA. A greyscale image is obtained by converting a colour vector (R, G, B) into a grey-level vector (Gr, Gr, Gr) where $Gr = min(R, G, B)$. Note that this is different from the more common greyscale conversion methods where grey-level intensity is a linear combination of red, green and blue intensities. This is important because atomic labels in molecular images are often colour-coded: red for oxygen, blue for nitrogen and so on. Most commonly used greyscale conversion schemes would make light blue or yellow characters hard to detect after the binarisation (conversion to black and white) is performed based on some thresholding method.

Because in general we do not know the resolution at which an image was generated, four different resolutions (or scales) are typically used by default on non-PDF files—the first three are 72, 150 and 300 dpi and the fourth resolution is determined dynamically in the range of 500–1200 dpi. The scale affects the limits on the maximum character size as well as the parameters for thinning and anisotropic smoothing. Trying the processing at different scales allows for a certain degree of independence from the scan resolution that was used when the document in question was scanned (or produced by some other means). The best version (out of 4) is automatically selected based on 'confidence estimate' fitness function.

To detect the need for a smoothing procedure at higher resolutions, a quantity we call a noise factor is calculated. The noise factor is defined here as the ratio of the number of linear pixel segments (vertical or horizontal) with a length of 2 pixels to the number of line segments with a length of 3 pixels. If the noise factor is between 0.5 and 1.0, an anisotropic smoothing procedure is performed. Noise removal and anisotropic scaling are achieved using the GREYCstoration anisotropic smoothing library.[2] Anisotropic scaling is a procedure similar to anisotropic smoothing with the addition of modifying the overall size of the image.

A thinning function is required to normalise all lines to be one pixel wide. Image thinning is done rapidly by the subroutine from the article 'Efficient Binary Image Thinning Using Neighborhood Maps' by Cychosz [11].

MolRec takes a simple approach to the initial stages of image preprocessing and carries out a standard greyscaling followed by binarisation (using Otsu's method [12]). Unlike other systems, it delays thinning of lines to a later phase and carries out connected component analysis and character recognition first.

14.3.2   Page Segmentation (OSRA Only)

To separate the image of a single molecule from the surrounding text and graphics, which may include other chemical images, OSRA uses a variation of the DBSCAN clustering approach combined with a heuristic to determine the threshold distance between the image components which need to be kept together. This threshold distance is estimated based on an empirical relationship between the size ratio of the connected components and their distance from each other. The Chebyshev distance is employed as the metric for the clustering of connected components.

Separators (connected components with a ratio of height to width above 100 or below 0.01 and size above 300 pixels—typically long lines) are identified and deleted. This allows the removal of linear vertical or horizontal separators early in the process and simplifies further page analysis. Table frames are also removed based on a similar procedure—a table is identified as a connected component which has an aspect ratio between 0.1 and 10, of which at least 300 pixels are lying on the surrounding rectangle.

For each pair of segments, the area ratio r_{AB} is an integer computed as $r_{AB} = \lceil \frac{max(S_A, S_B)}{min(S_A, S_B)} \rceil$, where S_A and S_B are the sizes (number of pixels) of the A and B segments, respectively. We define a feature matrix f as an integer matrix of size $< maxarearatio, maxdistance >$ which contains the counts of the pairs of segments with a specific area ratio lying at a specific distance from each other, that is, f_{ij} is equal to the number of pairs of segments A, B for which $i = r_{AB}$ and $j = d_{AB}$.

A crucial point to be addressed in order for the algorithm to be as widely applicable as possible is the ability to distinguish between two different scenarios— whether we have an image of a page with multiple text blocks and/or drawings or a single-structure drawing. In the former case, it is possible to apply statistical

---

[2]http://www.greyc.ensicaen.fr/~dtschump/greycstoration/.

analysis to determine a threshold value for the distance which separates fragments that 'belong together' and which should be treated as parts of the same chemical structure, from the segments that have no logical connection to the current structure depiction and will only complicate further processing. In the latter case such statistical analysis is likely to be impossible due to the low number of elements present in the image and an overzealous algorithm might erroneously discard vital pieces of information. The following step helps in making such a distinction—it should be noted that the procedure is purely empirical but seems to work remarkably well in practice for both PDF documents and single-structure images:

For each row of the feature matrix f, the number of cells containing zeros ($f_{ij} = 0$) is counted, then the entropy of the row is computed as

$$E = -p \log p,$$

where $p = -\dfrac{z}{maxdistance-2}$,

$$z = \sum_{j=2}^{j<maxdistance} n_{ij}$$

and $n_{ij} = 1$ if $f_{ij} = 0$ or 0 otherwise.

By empirical observation we have found that the row with the maximum entropy usually lies above 6 for pages with text and/or multiple graphics and is 3 or lower when only a single-structure image is present. Therefore a threshold value of 4 was chosen to distinguish between the two types of images.

If it is determined that the page contains text as well as graphics, it is advantageous to remove text blocks before processing the chemical structure images. To do so, first the characteristic distance between the text characters is determined by taking the first row of the matrix f_{ij} and locating the first local minimum (d) which occurs after the first local maximum (m): $f_{1m-1} < f_{1m}, f_{1m+1} < f_{1m}$, and $f_{1d-1} > f_{1d}$, $f_{1d+1} > f_{1d}, d > m$.

All segments within distance d from each other are then grouped together. If such a group contains more than the threshold number of connected segments (8 in our case), and the fill ratio (number of pixels divided by the area of the rectangle that a segment occupies) and the aspect ratio (width/height) are above preset thresholds (0.2 and 10, respectively), the group of segments is deemed to be a text block and removed from further processing.

All remaining segments are then grouped according to their pairwise distance— the threshold is chosen to be twice the value of d found in the previous step; or, for a single image page, an arbitrary high number—100 pixels. Each group of segments— a perspective chemical structure depiction—is subjected to the following filtering criteria: the fill ratio has to be below 0.2, the aspect ratio between 0.1 and 10, both height and width should exceed a characteristic single character height and width, and at least one of the dimensions, either height or width, should exceed double the font height (or width). A characteristic font height and width are set to be 22 and 21 pixels, respectively, at a resolution of 150 dpi and scaled with the resolution accordingly.

14.3.3   Vectorisation

Vectorisation is a method of converting a raster image (image which consists of individual pixels) into a vector image, which is based on line segments. OSRA is using the Potrace library[3] for vectorisation. Atoms are recognised as the control points of Bezier curves where any one of the following conditions is met:

- The control point is classified as a corner by the Potrace algorithm.
- The vector from the control point to the next represents a change of direction with a normal component of at least 2 pixels as compared to the vector from the last atom to this control point.
- The distance from the last atom to the next control point is less than the distance from the last atom to the current control point. This situation occurs when a Bezier curve is turning around a tip of the bond line. Remember that each bond could be circumscribed by Bezier curves from two sides.

The vectors connecting the found atoms are recognised as bonds. Note the usage of normal component measures instead of angles between pairs of vectors.

MolRec performs vectorisation after character recognition, which is described in the next section; however, we describe this step here in keeping with the generic workflow. After character recognition, MolRec applies thinning [13] to the remaining connected components, and, after some cleaning to remove thinning artefacts, the results are vectorised using the Douglas-Peucker algorithm [14]. The resulting polylines are then split at connection points to produce sets of vectorised line segments. This may appear to be a retrograde step as it decomposes already connected bond structures into sets of simple bonds, but it is important for the later rule-based approach as it allows a relatively small number of rules to cover, in a very general fashion, a much larger number of cases than would otherwise be possible.

Each line segment is then classified as normal, bold or triangular (for stereoscopic bonds) by using the vectorised line segments as a guide to walk the original raster image, finding the largest circle that will fit with the corresponding raster version. If the circle is of an approximately constant diameter, then the line segment corresponds to a normal or bold line with the circle diameter discriminating the two cases. If the circle grows or shrinks as the segment is traversed, then a triangular (i.e. wedge bond) has been located and the direction of growth determines the direction of the bond.

Finally, arrow heads on dative bonds are detected using simple template matching on the ends of each line segment.

---

[3]http://potrace.sourceforge.net/.

14.3.4 Atomic Label Recognition

GOCR[4] and OCRAD[5] are used by OSRA to test all connected sets of Bezier curves smaller in size than a maximum character height and width, or two characters aligned horizontally or vertically. The priority is given to GOCR method, and for labels not recognised by GOCR alone, OCRAD algorithm is applied. Recognised characters are then assembled to build atomic labels. Optionally, Tesseract[6] and Cuneiform[7] libraries can also be used for OCR processing; however, in our experiments their use did not result in an increase in recognition.

For MolRec, character recognition is carried out on all connected components individually using a k-nearest neighbour classifier on a set of features including some geometric moments, grid-based densities and an aspect ratio [15]. Characters that are suitable are formed into words or atom or molecular names via a set of rules based on their spatial relationships. There remain the circles of aromatic rings that can be confused by the classifier with the letter 'O' and some short lines that can be confused with the uppercase 'I' or lower case 'l'. If spatial relationships cannot resolve such cases (e.g. by the components in question being positioned inside a suitable string of other characters), a final decision on their classification is deferred until further knowledge becomes available.

For both tools all recognised characters are filtered out from the set of connected components that form the image and further processing is applied to the remaining diagram.

14.3.5 Rule-Based Recognition of the Spatial Graph

MolRec defines a set of rules to combine spatial combinations of normal and bold line segments, characters, triangles and arrowheads into an internal semantic representation of molecular diagrams. The rules use not just spatial co-location but also concepts such as parallelism and chain connectedness. They also incorporate an amount of fuzziness in all these concepts to cope not just with scanning and digitisation artefacts but also with the fact that many diagrams are produced with software that draws the diagrams with a significant level of imprecision.

For example, the rule condition for detecting double planar bonds, in informal terms, is: *A set of two line segments whose lengths are both greater than the minimum simple bond length, whose widths are both less than the minimum bold bond width, which are approximately parallel and within a maximum parallel bond separation distance of each other and to which no other line segment is also*

---

[4]http://sourceforge.net/projects/jocr/.

[5]http://www.gnu.org/software/ocrad/ocrad.html.

[6]http://code.google.com/p/tesseract-ocr/.

[7]https://launchpad.net/cuneiform-linux.

approximately parallel and within the maximum parallel bond separation of either of the target line segments. All elements in such conditions are rigorously defined in [10]. Following recognition of such a case, actions are taken to cut such bonds if necessary (if it corresponds to a double bond connected to a single or triple bond) and replace the occurrence of the line segments with the resulting recognised bond type.

As the rule engine processes the spatial graph, more and more of the diagram is recognised and combinations of raster-oriented primitive components are replaced by semantic level molecular diagram elements. Finally, when the whole diagram has been recognised, superatoms are expanded using a dictionary extracted from existing molecular diagram databases and a MOL file [16] is generated by walking the semantic graph.

A similar procedure is also performed by OSRA and is described below.

14.3.5.1 Circle Bond Recognition

If a circle of sufficiently large diameter is found inside of a ring, the ring is flagged as aromatic. Additional conditions include the ring atoms being sufficiently close to the circle (not more than half of the average bond length away) and angles between the ring bonds and the vectors to the centre of the circle being less than 90°. The current implementation fails when the inner circle touches the ring bonds.

14.3.5.2 Average Bond Length and Double/Triple Bond Detection

The average bond length is estimated in the following way: a sorted list of all the bond lengths is created, and the 'average' bond length is taken to be the value at the 75th percentile by rank within this list. Choosing the 75th percentile instead of the more common 50th (the median) eliminates the bias towards smaller bond lengths which is very common during the initial stages of processing, while also discarding longer than usual bonds which might appear in some structure depictions. The average bond length is re-evaluated several times throughout the processing of the image as more structural elements are being identified. Similar mechanisms are used for measuring the distance within the bond pairs comprising double bonds and average bond thickness. The double and triple bonds are then identified as bond pairs (triples) which (a) are parallel to each other, (b) are within the double bond pair distance of each other and (c) are within each other's 'shadow'—that is, the bonds of the bond pair are not separated too far along the line parallel to them (see Fig. 14.2).

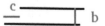

Fig. 14.2 Double bond recognition: *b*, distance between the two prospective segments of a double bond, *c*, distance along the direction of the bond

14.3.5.3 Dashed and Wedge Bonds

For dashed and wedge bonds, OSRA considers all connected components and subjects them to the following selection criteria. Dashed bonds are three or more 'blobs' of any shape as long as they are (1) small enough, (2) positioned within the average bond length from start to finish and (3) a straight line that can be drawn through their geometric centres. Wedge bonds are recognised by testing for a significant thickness increase or decrease along the bond.

14.3.5.4 Bridge Bonds

Bridge bonds are bonds which visibly intersect on the structure diagram but are not actually connected at the point of intersection. To detect a bridge bond versus an actual connection between four bonds, we use the following algorithm: if an atom is connected to four pairwise colinear single bonds (none of which is a terminal bond) and this atom node removal does not result in

- Difference in the number of fragments
- Difference in the number of rotatable bonds
- Decrease in the number of five- and six-membered rings by 2

the atom is removed and the intersection is presumed to be a bridge bond intersection.

14.3.5.5 Confidence Estimate

To find the best structure resolution among several possible choices (four, according to the number of different resolution scales attempted in the beginning of the processing), OSRA uses a 'confidence function'. It is a linear function of various simple chemical descriptors such as the number of carbon atoms, number of nitrogen atoms, number of rings, number of aromatic rings, etc. The coefficients are chosen in such a way that the confidence is usually higher for realistic molecules which allows distinguishing between alternative 'guesses' of the same structure.

14.3.5.6 Compilation of the Connection Table

OSRA uses the OpenBabel [17] chemoinformatics library for conversion into SMILES or SDF. A molecular object is constructed based on the connectivity information along with the stereo- and aromaticity flags. Fragments based on superatoms are added at this stage as well. The superatom dictionary can be modified by a user at runtime without recompilation.

14.4   Benchmarking Evaluations

Now that we have described in detail how two systems perform chemical optical structure recognition, the expected question is: *How well do they work?* Recently, two public evaluation exercises focusing on such aspects have taken place, first at TREC[8] and then at CLEF.[9] Their objective was to create the necessary test collections to understand precisely how well algorithms and methods such as those presented in the previous section work. In the following we shall describe briefly how the evaluation exercises were conceived and the obtained results.

14.4.1   TREC Chemical Track

In 2011, the TREC Chemical Track [18] decided to introduce a chemical structure recognition task (the *Image2Structure* task), motivated by the fact that in the previous years, the retrieval on text alone had already stabilised. For this a set of topics was defined.

14.4.1.1   Topics

Two sets each containing 1000 images and the corresponding MOL[10] files were selected to act as training and evaluation sets from the USPTO file collection. The following criteria were used in the selection process:

- No polymers (brackets in the molecule description), charges or isotopes—judged by the presence of text lines starting with 'M' but not 'M END' in the ctab block of the MOL file.
- No multi-fragment MOL files; only one molecule per file is allowed.
- Allow only 'organic' elements—C, N, O, S, F, Cl, Br, I, P and H.
- Check that ctab records for all atoms correspond to the formal charge of 0 and that the isotope type is unspecified (default).
- Check that there are no stereobonds with stereo orientation specifically set to 'undefined'.
- Check that the number of heavy (non-hydrogen) atoms is greater than 6 and the molecular weight is lower than 1000 a.u.
- Check that InChI (International Chemical Identifier)[11] can be created for the selected molecules.

---

[8]http://trec.nist.gov.

[9]http://clef-initiative.eu.

[10]http://en.wikipedia.org/wiki/Chemical_table_file.

[11]http://en.wikipedia.org/wiki/InChI.

These criteria allowed the organisers to focus on small organic molecules for which a reasonably widely accepted and well-defined chemoinformatics identity measure exists—namely, InChI and InChI key. Those are also the types of molecules believed to be of the most interest to the chemical and pharmaceutical industry. Training sets of images and MOL files and the evaluation set of images only have been made available to the participants.

14.4.1.2 Evaluation

Participants of the Image2Structure task have been asked to submit the results of their runs in the form of SD files. The SD file format is analogous to MOL with the exception that it allows for multiple molecules to be stored in a single file. This difference between the ground truth MOL format and the requested SD format was deliberate to allow for the possibility that recognition software may erroneously generate several output molecules for a single molecule input image. There are many free and commercial software utilities which allow interconversion between alternative formats, such as SMILES[12] and SDF. The runs were evaluated based on a recall measure by matching of the standard InChI keys computed from the original MOL file and the SD file representing recognition software output. Chemical identity is often a subject of ongoing debates among chemists about what constitutes a unique molecule. InChI—IUPAC International Chemical Identifier— is a text representation of a molecule which was designed to compute normalised, canonical text string from the original molecule representation. InChI takes into account certain forms of tautomerism, stereochemistry, etc. InChI key is a hashed version of InChI. Standard InChIs and InChI keys, while not completely free of their share of issues, are widely used as unique chemical identifiers by chemists worldwide. Therefore standard InChI keys have been selected for Image2Structure evaluation as a relatively controversy-free chemical identity measure.

14.4.1.3 Results

The Image2Structure task received 11 runs from five participants. Overall, results were very good, with all participants recognising over 60 % of the given structure images. Table 14.1 shows the best results obtained by each system.

---

[12]http://en.wikipedia.org/wiki/Smiles.

Table 14.1 Participants in the Image2Structure task

Participating group	Run name(s) identifier	Maximum recall
University of Birmingham	UoB (MolRec)	0.95
SAIC-Frederick/NIH	OSRA	0.86
GGA Software	GGA	0.77
University of Michigan	ChemReader	0.69
Fraunhofer SCAI	ChemOCR	0.66

14.4.2 CLEF-IP Chemical Image Recognition Task

The benchmark in TREC-CHEM was followed in 2012 by a very similar one at CLEF-IP [19]. The focus was still on recognition of chemical structures from patent images, but there were also two novel elements: First, participants were invited to also segment full pages of patent documents to identify where the chemical representations are. Second, some of the images provided for the recognition part were more complex and assessed manually.

14.4.2.1 Segmentation

For this subtask, 30 patents were selected, rendered to 300dpi monochrome multipage TIFF images, and all chemical molecular diagrams were manually clipped from the images using a custom-built tool. This clipping tool recorded the minimal bounding box size and coordinates of each diagram clipped, and the results were recorded in a ground truth comma separated value (CSV) file. The participants were asked to produce their own results CSV file containing this bounding box clip information for each diagram that their systems could identify.

Another tool was written to automatically compare the participants' results file with the ground truth file. This identified matches at various tolerance levels, where a match is awarded if every side of a participant's bounding box is within the tolerance number of pixels of the corresponding side of a ground truth bounding box. Evaluation results were calculated for each of a range of tolerances starting at 0 pixels and increasing to the maximum number of pixels that still disallowed any single participant bounding boxes from matching more than one ground truth bounding box. This maximum limit in practice was 55 pixels, or just under 0.5 cm.

The number of true-positive, false-positive and false-negative matches was counted for each tolerance setting, and from that the precision, recall and F_1-measure were calculated.

14.4.2.2   Recognition

A diagram recognition task requires the participants to take a set of diagrams, analyse them to some recognised format and submit their recognised format files for evaluation. In order to evaluate the results, these submitted format files must be compared to a ground truth set of format files. Therein lies a difficult problem with respect to the chemical diagram recognition task for patent documents. Currently, the most complete standard format for chemical diagrams is the MOL file format. This format captures quite well fully specified chemical diagram molecules. However, it has become standard in patent documents to describe whole families or classes of molecules using diagrams that extend standard molecule diagrams with graphical representations of varying structures, called *Markush structures*. Markush structures cannot be represented in MOL files.

Given the standard nature of MOL files, there have been a significant number of research and commercial projects to recognise diagrams with all the features that can be represented by MOL files. However, without standard extensions to MOL files to cope with Markush structures, there has been relatively little effort expended in recognising such extended diagrams. With the intention of fostering such efforts, the recognition task for CLEF-IP 2012 was designed to expose participants to a relatively small number of the simpler of these extended structures, while also providing a large number of cases fully covered by the current MOL file standard.

A total of 865 diagram images, called the *automatic set*, were selected. The diagrams in this set were fully representable in standard MOL files. Evaluation of this set was carried out by automatically comparing the participants' submitted MOL files with the ground truth MOL files using the open-source chemistry toolbox, OpenBabel. The key tool in this set is the InChI (International Chemical Identifier) representation. OpenBabel was chosen among other tools offering similar functionality because it is free and available to everyone. The number of correctly matched diagrams (and the percentage correctly matched) was reported for each participant.

A *manual set* of 95 images were chosen which contain some amount of variability in their structure and which can only be represented in MOL files by some abuse of the MOL file standard. These cannot be automatically evaluated as the OpenBabel system cannot deal with the resulting structures. However, such MOL files can still be rendered to an image format using the MarvinView tool from ChemAxon. Thus it was possible to carry out the evaluation of this set by manual visual comparison of the original image, the MarvinView generated image of the ground truth MOL file for the image and the MarvinView generated image of the participant's submitted MOL file. To this end a bespoke Web application was written to enable the organisers and participants to verify the manual visual evaluation.

It was less than satisfactory to have to carry out the evaluation of this latter set manually and even more so that we had to exclude from the set structures that appear in patent files but which cannot be rendered from (abused) MOL files using MarvinView. This points strongly to a need in the community to develop either an extension or an alternative to MOL files that can fully support common Markush

Table 14.2 OSRA page
segmentation results

Tolerance	Precision	Recall	F1
0	0.70803	0.68622	0.69696
10	0.79311	0.76868	0.78070
20	0.82071	0.79543	0.80787
40	0.86696	0.84025	0.85340
55	0.88694	0.85962	0.87307

structures together with the necessary ancillary tools for manipulating, comparing
and rendering such structures to images.

14.4.2.3 Segmentation Results

CLEF-IP 2012 results for chemical image segmentation task for OSRA are presented in Table 14.2. The ground truth data was manually collected for this task.
Tolerance is measured in pixels and signifies how far the borders of the found
bounding box were allowed to deviate from the ground truth. OSRA was the only
participating tool with the capability to perform page segmentation to search for
molecular structures.

14.4.2.4 Structure Recognition

Table 14.3 shows the structure recognition results obtained by the two participating
teams. The values shown are the recall percentages based on InChI keys for
structures.

Both *saic* (using their OSRA tool) and *uob* (using their MolRec tool) submitted
result sets (1 and 4, respectively) for the diagram recognition subtask.

Clearly, both groups, unsurprisingly, found the diagrams with varying elements
significantly more challenging than the more standard fixed diagrams.

OSRA has further been tested on additional test collections, outside of CLEF-IP.
In Table 14.4 we present the structure recognition results based on several publicly
available data sets of chemical structure images.

14.5 Beyond Molecules: Chemical Reactions

One way to expand the described approaches beyond the single molecule recognition is to develop a method for recognising chemical reaction images. A database
of chemical reactions has many potential uses. It can be used in the development
of retrosynthetic analysis software, synthetic availability prediction, bioisostere
discovery and many others. Manually constructing such a database is a painstaking

Table 14.3 Results obtained by the two groups participating in the recognition task

	Automatic set			Manual set			Total		
	#Structures	Recalled	%	#Structures	Recalled	%	#Structures	Recalled	%
saic	865	761	88	95	38	40	960	799	83
uob1	865	832	96	95	44	46	960	876	91
uob2	865	821	95	95	56	59	960	877	91
uob3	865	821	95	95	44	46	960	865	90
uob4	865	832	96	95	54	57	960	886	92

Table 14.4 Structure recognition results

Set	Total	Imago-2.0 (%)	OSRA 2.0.0 (%)
Image2Structure	1000	90.2	91.9
CLEF 2012	865	67.0	96.5
JPO	450	40.4	62.6
USPTO	5719	86.9	88.0
Maybridge UoB	5740	63.5	86.4

process prone to errors. Existing freely available data sets which do allow bulk downloads may have several thousands of reactions,[13] while the total number of published reactions may number in tens of millions.[14] Patent documents represent a rich data set which is by definition unencumbered by licensing issues. An ability to extract chemical information from patents and other documents can therefore be valuable not only to academic organisations but also to commercial entities. A very promising approach to extract chemical reactions by text analytics methods has been presented recently [20]; however, until now there was no automatic way to data-mine reactions depicted as images.

At the most fundamental level, an image of a chemical reaction is a collection of molecules, arrows and plus signs. Most real-life images are more complicated though because they combine multi-step reactions (perhaps more than one per page) with text and other graphics. It might not always be a trivial task to determine for each reaction step where the reactants and products are located on the page. A multi-step reaction might follow a 'tail-to-head' pathway, snaking around the page (see Fig. 14.3), or it might be arranged in a text-flow manner: left to right and top to bottom with possible line breaks between the arrow heads and the corresponding products (Fig. 14.4). OSRA can handle such arrangements, even with multiple multi-step reactions on a page, though it might get confused by chemical structures from different reactions which are accidentally aligned horizontally.

Recognition of graphical primitives such as arrows and plus signs has been extensively studied [21]. OSRA followed a simplified approach: first convert a symbol image to polar coordinates with respect to its centre of mass, then build

---

[13] http://www.ebi.ac.uk/rhea/.

[14] http://www.cas.org/content/reactions.

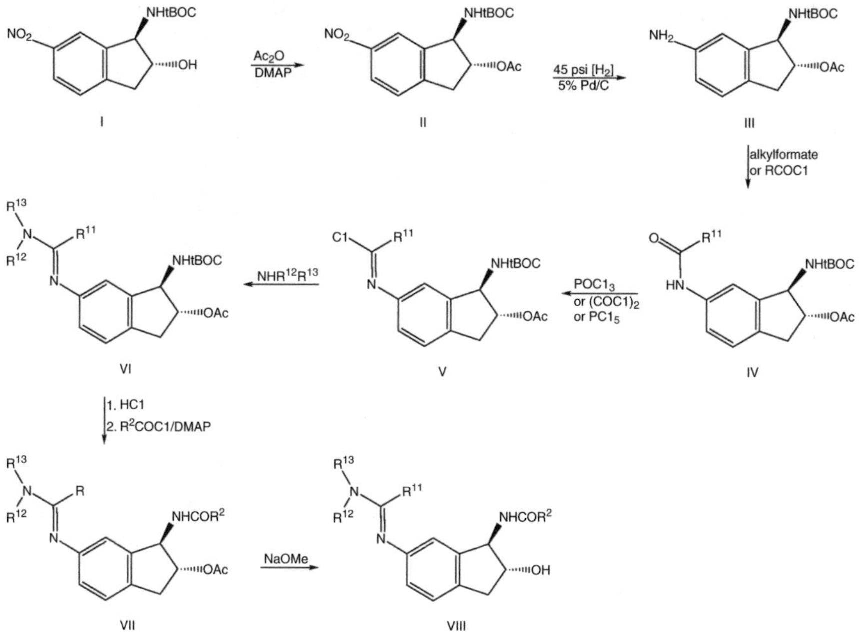

Fig. 14.3 'Snaking' reaction

a histogram of pixel population density for binarised segments from 0 to 360°. The resulting histogram is amenable to simple heuristic rules for robust detection of arrows and relatively large plus signs.

While tail-to-head, 'snaking' reactions are easy to assemble—arrows always point from reagents to products (and in case of a reversible reaction, there could be two arrows going the opposite way)—care must be taken to correctly identify products corresponding to the left-most arrow in a 'text-flow' arrangement. The plus signs between the products or between the reagents might also be placed on a line break, as seen with the last two structures in Fig. 14.4.

Finally the reagents, products and agents (small molecules depicted above or below the reaction arrow) are assembled together from single-step reactions into an array of multi-step reactions. The underlying assumption is that every multi-step reaction represents a single path from the initial reagents to the final products without branching or loops. This assumption does not always hold true, but the exceptions are rare enough to warrant such simplification.

For testing and experimentation, we used a data set based on USPTO patent images and Complex Work Unit CDX files kindly shared by A. Heifets. Table 14.5 shows the recall results of running OSRA on four complete PDF files from USPTO. Computation of the recall rates has been performed using RInChI software.[15] A

---

[15]http://www-rinchi.ch.cam.ac.uk/.

Fig. 14.4 Text-flow reaction

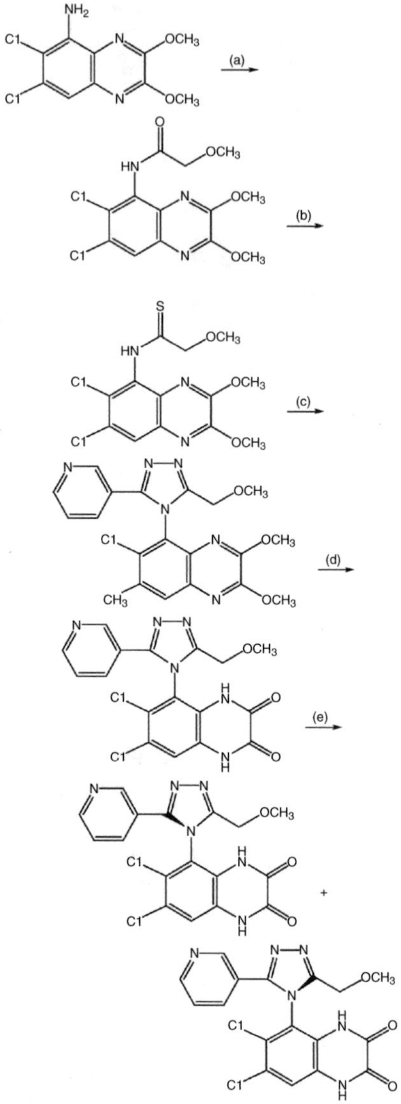

CACTVS[16] script was used to convert CDX files to RXN format. Structures with unresolved superatoms have been filtered out from the ground truth. Overall we observed the average recall to be about 30–40%, but we should point out that the ground truth files need more attention—they are often incomplete (reaction present on the page is absent from the GT) and sometimes incorrect. Other than

---

[16]http://xemistry.com.

Table 14.5 Accuracy
estimates

Document	Recall	Total
US06509464	28	71
US06423728	17	70
US06495549	33	69
US06492381	28	55

the problematic GT, the main source of errors for the reaction recognition algorithm itself seems to be reactions that are split by a page break between pages or, for multi-column documents, reactions that start at the bottom of one column and continue at the top of the next column. Also, as we mentioned before, sometimes the system wrongly combines structures which belong to different reactions, which was observed for a two-column document with separate reactions in both columns. The most urgent of the above is the lack of reliable ground truth data without which accuracy estimates are highly uncertain. Problems with page breaks and column breaks should be fairly easy to resolve in the future releases. With that said we expect the reaction recognition to be dominated by the accuracy rate of the underlying chemical structure recognition algorithm. If, for example, the accuracy of single-structure recognition process stands at 88 % (a reasonable estimate for OSRA processing of USPTO images), the accuracy for a reaction involving four structures, e.g. two reagents and two products, can hardly be expected to exceed 60 % ($0.88^4 \approx 0.60$).

While the measured recall rate is on the low end, it should be noted that due to the problems with existing ground truth sets, the reported recall rate might actually be undervalued; however, considering the fact that there are tens of millions of documents which potentially contain chemical reaction information, extracting even a half of that information can constitute a valuable resource.

To the best of our knowledge, OSRA is the first software tool with the ability to recognise and reconstruct chemical reactions from full document images. Since it is a free and open-source tool, we hope its release will encourage the development in this area of chemoinformatics and document recognition.

On the other hand, MolRec demonstrates unsurpassed individual molecular diagram recognition and we hope that its lessons will motivate and inspire higher accuracy in other molecular diagram recognition systems.

14.6   Summary

Transforming raster images of chemical molecules, or, even more interestingly, chemical reactions, is a significant challenge for the patent domain. The tools we showed in this chapter, as well as those tested in the TREC Chemical Track and CLEF-IP, have shown that good performance can be achieved on sets of fairly clean data, but when more complex elements are present, the effectiveness drops considerably. The problem is further exacerbated by the presence of Markush structures, which have no commonly agreed textual representation to use as a target result format. However, that is not a problem that can be solved with optical structure recognition tools.

The progress that has been achieved in the field over the last few years is remarkable. The recognition rates in the upper 90 % (on reasonably good quality, but still real-world data) have been unheard of in the chemical image recognition before. Not only that, we now also have freely available validation sets of images with ground truth data for thousands of molecules, as well as a fast, automatic way to verify the results in a way that is relevant to the true target end users—chemists— and not only to the image recognition professionals. There are still significant challenges remaining and the problem in general is far from solved. Some of the future directions of research are better OCR of atomic labels, especially in cases of poor image quality when bond lines intersect the label characters, ability to handle multiple attachment points for superatoms and better filtering of nonsensical or non-chemical results. The groundwork laid by recognising small organic molecules and reactions can serve as a starting point for a variety of other image processing techniques such as polymer image recognition.[17]

References

1. Casey R, Boyer S, Healey P, Miller A, Oudot B, Zilles Z (1993) Optical recognition of chemical graphics. In: Proceedings of the international conference on document analysis and recognition, pp 627–632
2. McDaniel J, Balmuth J (1992) Kekule - OCR optical chemical (structure) recognition. J Chem Inf Comput Sci 32:373–378
3. Contreras M, Allendes C, Alvarez L, Rozas R (1990) Computational perception and recognition of digitized molecular structures. J Chem Inf Comput Sci 30:302–307
4. Ibison P, Jacquot M, Kam F, Neville A, Simpson R, Tonnelier C, Venczel T, Johnson A (1993) Chemical literature data extraction - the CLiDE project. J Chem Inf Comput Sci 33:338–344
5. Park J, Rosania G, Shedden K, Nguyen M, Lyu N, Saitou K (2009) Automated extraction of chemical structure information from digital raster images. Chem Cent J 3(1):4
6. Zimmermann M, Thi L, Hofmann M (2005) Combating illiteracy in chemistry: towards computer-based chemical structure reconstruction. ERCIM News 60:40–41
7. Zimmermann M (2006) Large scale evaluation of chemical structure recognition. In: Proceedings of the 4th text mining symposium in life sciences
8. Filippov IV, Nicklaus MC (2009) Optical structure recognition software to recover chemical information: OSRA, an open source solution. J Chem Inf Model 49(3):740–743
9. Valko AT, Johnson AP (2009) CLiDE Pro: the latest generation of CLiDE, a tool for optical chemical structure recognition. J Chem Inf Model 49(4):780–787
10. Sadawi NM, Sexton AP, Sorge V (2012) Chemical structure recognition: a rule based approach. In: Viard-Gaudin C, Zanibbi R (eds) 19th Document recognition and retrieval conference (DRR 2012), SPIE, Bellingham

---

[17]http://posra.nationbuilder.com/.

11. Cychosz JM (1994) Efficient binary image thinning using neighborhood maps. In: Graphics gems IV. Academic, San Diego, pp 465–473
12. Otsu N (1979) A threshold selection method from gray-level histograms. IEEE Trans Syst Man Cybern 9:62–66
13. Guo Z, Hall RW (1989) Parallel thinning with two subiteration algorithms. Commun ACM 32(3):359–373
14. Douglas DH, Peucker TK (1973) Algorithms for the reduction of the number of points required to represent a digitized line or its caricature. Cartographica 10(2):112–122
15. Jain A, Trier D, Taxt T (1996) Feature extraction methods for character recognition: a survey. Pattern Recogn 29(4):641–662
16. Accelrys (2011) CTfile format. http://accelrys.com/products/collaborative-science/biovia-draw/ctfile-no-fee.html
17. O'Boyle NM, Banck M, James CA, Morley C, Vandermeersch T, Hutchison GR (2011) Open Babel: an open chemical toolbox. J Cheminform 3:33
18. Lupu M, Jiashu Z, Huang J, Gurulingappa H, Filipov I, Tait J (2011) Overview of the TREC 2011 chemical IR track. In: Proceedings of TREC
19. Piroi F, Lupu M, Hanbury A, Sexton A, Magdy W, Filippov I (2012) CLEF-IP 2012: retrieval experiments in the intellectual property domain. In: Working notes of CLEF
20. Heifets A, Jurisica I (2012) SCRIPDB: a portal for easy access to syntheses, chemicals and reactions in patents. Nucleic Acids Res 40(D1):D428–D433. doi:10.1093/nar/gkr919
21. Wendling L, Tabbone S (2003) Recognition of arrows in line drawings based on the aggregation of geometric criteria using the Choquet integral. In: Seventh international conference on document analysis and recognition–ICDAR 2003, Edinburgh, pp 299–303

Chapter 15
Representation and Searching of Chemical Structure Information in Patents

Geoff M. Downs, John D. Holliday, and Peter Willett

Abstract This chapter describes the techniques that are used to represent and to search for molecular structures in chemical patents. There are two types of structure: specific structures that describe individual molecules and generic structures that describe sets of structurally related molecules. Methods for representing and searching specific structures have been well established for many years, and the techniques are also applicable, albeit with substantial modification, to the processing of generic structures.

15.1   Introduction

Patents are a key information resource for all types of industry, but this is particularly the case in the pharmaceutical and agrochemical industries. The main focus of these industries is to identify novel chemical molecules that exhibit useful biological activities, e.g. reducing an individual's cholesterol level or killing the insect pest of a crop [1]. Chemical patents hence need to contain not just the textual information that one would find in any type of patent but also information about the chemical molecules of interest. These may be represented in textual, numerical or graphical form (chemical names, images, chemical properties, reaction conditions, etc.), which may be used as part of the query formulation. However, they may also describe the structural information contained in the patent, a concept which has led to the development of specialised types of representation and search algorithm for their efficient and effective access. These techniques are an important component of what has come to be called *chemoinformatics* [2], i.e. 'the application of informatics methods to solve chemical problems' [3].

Two types of molecular information are encountered in chemical patents. A patent may mention or claim individual specific molecules, for which the techniques that have been developed in chemoinformatics over many years may be applied, as

G.M. Downs
Digital Chemistry Ltd., 30 Kiveton Lane, Todwick, Sheffield, S26 1HL, UK

J.D. Holliday • P. Willett (✉)
Information School, University of Sheffield, 211 Portobello Street, Sheffield, S1 4DP, UK
e-mail: j.d.holliday@sheffield.ac.uk; p.willett@sheffield.ac.uk

© Springer-Verlag GmbH Germany 2017   391
M. Lupu et al. (eds.), *Current Challenges in Patent Information Retrieval*,
The Information Retrieval Series 37, DOI 10.1007/978-3-662-53817-3_15

discussed below. However, many chemical patents discuss (and claim protection for) entire classes of structurally related molecules, described by *generic*, or *Markush*, structures. A single generic structure can represent many thousands, or even a potentially infinite number, of individual molecules, and the representational and searching techniques required are accordingly far more complex than those commonly encountered in chemoinformatics systems. In this chapter, we provide an overview of the techniques that are used to handle both specific and generic chemical structures. For further details of the techniques described below, the reader is referred to the standard textbooks by Leach and Gillet [4] and by Gasteiger and Engel [5] and the reviews by Kosata [6], Warr [7] and Barnard, Kenny and Wallace [8]. These texts also provide excellent introductions to the many aspects of chemoinformatics that are not, as yet, of direct relevance to the processing of chemical patent information.

15.2   Searching Specific Chemical Structures

15.2.1   *Representation of Chemical Structures*

If one wishes to carry out computer-based searches of a chemical database, then the molecules of interest must be encoded for searching, and we commence by describing the three main ways in which one can provide a full description of a chemical structure in machine-readable form: these are *systematic nomenclature*, *linear notations* and *connection tables*. Before describing these, the reader should note that we consider here (and in the remainder of this chapter) only the processing of 2D chemical molecules, i.e. the planar chemical structure diagrams that are conventionally used to represent molecules in the scientific literature and that are exemplified by the structure diagram shown in Fig. 15.1. More sophisticated techniques are required for the representation and searching of 3D chemical molecules, i.e. where one has geometric coordinate information for all of a molecule's constituent atoms [4, 9].

Chemical compounds have had names associated with them ever since the days of the alchemists, but it was many years before it was realised that there was a need for systematic naming conventions to ensure that every specific molecule would have its own unique name. This name should be *unique*, in the sense that there should be only one possible name for a molecule, and *unambiguous*, in the sense that it should describe that molecule and no other; moreover, it was soon realised that there are advantages if the name describes the various substructural components comprising the molecule, whereas common, non-systematic names normally say little or nothing about a molecule's components. For example, (2S)-1-phenylpropan-2-amine is the systematic, explicit representation for the structure shown in Fig. 15.1, which is also, and most commonly, called dexamphetamine.

Trivial name: dexamphetamine

IUPAC Name: (2S)-1-phenylpropan-2-amine

Wiswesser Line Notation: ZY1&1R

SMILES: C[C@H](N)Cc1ccccc1

InChI: InChI=1S/C9H13N/c1-8(10)7-9-5-3-2-4-6-9/h2-6,8H,7,10H2,1H3/t8-/m0/s1

InChIKey: KWTSXDURSIMDCE-QMMMGPOBSA-N

MDL Connection Table:

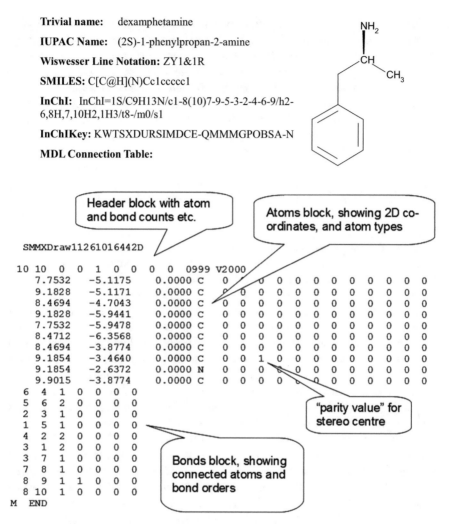

Fig. 15.1 A selection of names and linear notations for dexamphetamine with an MDL-format connection table

Two systematic nomenclatures are in widespread use, these being the ones developed by the International Union of Pure and Applied Chemistry (IUPAC at http://www.iupac.org) and by Chemical Abstracts Service (CAS at http://www.cas.org). IUPAC is an association of 60 national chemical societies, seeking to establish standards in nomenclature and physiochemical data measurement, while CAS is a division of the American Chemical Society and the world's largest provider of chemical information, indexing articles from more than 10,000 journals and patents from 60 national patent agencies. Systematic names continue to be widely used in the chemical literature, but are of less importance in chemoinformatics systems since they are normally converted automatically into one of the two other types of standard representation, i.e. linear notations or connection tables. A linear notation is a string of alphanumeric characters that provides a complete, albeit in some cases implicit, description of the molecule's topology. A *canonicalisation* procedure is normally invoked to ensure that there is a unique notation for each molecule. The first notation to be widely used was the Wiswesser Line Notation, which formed the basis for most industrial chemoinformatics systems in the 1960s and 1970s. Two notations are of importance in present-day systems: the SMILES (for Simplified Molecular Input Line Entry Specification) notation developed by Daylight Chemical Information Systems Inc. [10] and the International Chemical Identifier (or InChI), the development of which is being overseen by IUPAC [11]. SMILES was developed for use in in-house industrial chemoinformatics systems (as is the case with much chemoinformatics software), while InChI, conversely, has been developed as an open-source, non-proprietary notation. The SMILES and the InChI for dexamphetamine are included in Fig. 15.1.

Notations provide a compact molecular representation and are thus widely used for compound exchange and archival purposes. However, most chemoinformatics applications require their conversion to a connection table representation of molecular structure. A connection table is a data structure that lists the atoms within a molecule and the bonds that link those atoms together (in many cases, only 'heavy' atoms are included since the presence of hydrogen atoms can be deduced automatically). The table provides a complete and explicit description of a molecule's topology, i.e. the way that it is connected together, whereas this information is normally only implicit in a linear notation. There are many ways in which the atoms and bonds can be encoded, with typical connection table formats being exemplified by those developed by MDL Information Systems Inc. (which is now part of Biovia and owned by Dassault Systèmes) [12]. The MDL MOL file for dexamphetamine is shown in Fig. 15.1. Following some header lines, the first section describes the atoms present, while the second section describes the chemical bonds between them by referencing the sequence numbers of the atoms in the first section; for example, atom 6 is connected to atom 4 with a single (type 1) bond.

Both line notation and connection tables are based on the principle that a chemical structure can be regarded as a *topological graph*, which is a mathematical construct in which a set of *nodes* or *vertices* (representing the atoms) are linked pairwise by *edges* or *arcs* (representing the bonds). Though the analogy between chemical structures and topological graphs is not perfect, graph theory is very well understood [13, 14], and chemoinformatics has been able to draw on the many algorithms that have been developed for processing graphs. Of particular importance in the present context are the *graph isomorphism* algorithms that are used to determine whether two graphs are identical and the *subgraph isomorphism* algorithms that are used to determine whether one graph is contained within another, larger graph [4, 5].

15.2.2 Searching for Specific Molecules

An important search capability is full structure searching: the inspection of a database to retrieve the information associated with a particular molecule (e.g. if a chemist needed to know the molecule's boiling point or to identify a synthesis for it) or to confirm the molecule's presence or absence in a database (e.g. if a chemist wanted to check whether a newly synthesised molecule was completely novel). Searching for a single molecule, based on its structure, typically involves three basic steps—normalisation, canonicalisation and hash coding.

Firstly, the structures (both those in the database to be searched and the query to be searched for) must be 'normalised' or 'standardised' to ensure that possible variations in the way they are represented are eliminated. This avoids some of the problems caused by the inexact correspondence between chemical structures and topological graphs and involves applying 'business rules' to ensure that preferred charge distribution, tautomeric and other forms are used [15].

Secondly, the connection table or line notation must be put into a unique (or *canonical*) form, so that the same structure always has exactly the same representation. This essentially involves selecting one of the N! (N-factorial) ways of numbering the N atoms in the molecule. Several algorithms are commonly used for this—the chemoinformatics literature has generally cited that due to Morgan [16] and others based on it, while the computer science literature cites that due to McKay [17]. The former is used in Chemical Abstracts Service's databases, among others, while the latter is used for InChI.

Thirdly, the canonical representation is 'hashed' to a shorter identifier which can be conveniently used as a look-up key to the structure's location in disk storage. For example, the *InChI key* is a fixed-length hashed version of the InChI identifier. Hashing is an approximate procedure, in that different records can yield the same hashed key, a phenomenon that computer scientists refer to as a *collision*. A simple string comparison of the full canonical representation (or, in the case of connection tables, a graph isomorphism algorithm) can be used to ensure that a true match has been found. The possibility of collisions means that a full representation cannot be regenerated automatically from a hashed identifier, though if the frequency of collisions is small, simple look-up tables can be constructed which lead from the hash code to the full representation of a molecule that gives rise to it. Several public websites are now available which provide this function for InChI keys and are known as *InChI Key Resolvers*.

15.2.3 Searching for Chemical Substructures

Probably the single most important facility in a chemoinformatics system is the ability to carry out a substructure search, i.e. the ability to identify all of those molecules in a database that contain a user-defined query substructure. For example, in a search for molecules with antibiotic behaviour, a user might wish to retrieve all of the molecules that contain a penicillin or cephalosporin ring system. Fig. 15.2 shows another example, where a pyridine ring is used as a query to retrieve four matching structures. In graph-theoretic terms, this is an example of a *subgraph isomorphism* search, a generalisation of the graph isomorphism search mentioned above and ultimately involving an exhaustive atom-by-atom comparison of the query and database structures. Though substructure search guarantees the retrieval of all molecules matching the search criterion, it is intrinsically slow as subgraph isomorphism belongs to the class of *NP-complete* computational problems for which no 'efficient' algorithms are known to exist [4, 18].

Operational substructure searching is practicable for three reasons. First, the fact that chemical graphs are both simple (they contain relatively few nodes, most of which are of very low connectivity) and information rich (as one can differentiate atoms and bonds by their element and bond types, respectively). These factors serve to reduce the numbers of atom-to-atom and bond-to-bond mappings that need to be considered by a subgraph isomorphism algorithm. Second, a lot of effort has gone into the development of algorithms that can handle chemical graphs, as against graphs in general, very efficiently, with the elegant matching techniques described by Sussenguth [19] and by Ullmann [20] lying at the heart of current substructure searching systems. Third, and most importantly, the subgraph isomorphism search is preceded by an initial *screening search* in which each database structure is checked for the presence of features, called *screens*, that are present in the query substructure. For example, using the penicillin example mentioned above, any database structure can be eliminated from further consideration if it does not contain the fused four-membered and five-membered rings that comprise the penicillin nucleus.

A screen is a substructural feature, called a *fragment*, the presence of which is necessary, but not sufficient, for a molecule to contain the query substructure. The features that are used as screens are typically small, atom-, bond- or ring-centred fragment substructures that are algorithmically generated from a connection table when a molecule is added to the database that is to be searched. A common example of a screen is the *augmented atom* fragment, which consists of an atom, and those atoms that are bonded directly to the chosen central atom. A representation of the molecule's structure can then be obtained by generating an augmented atom

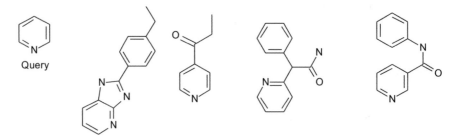

Fig. 15.2 Query substructure (pyridine ring) and some example hits

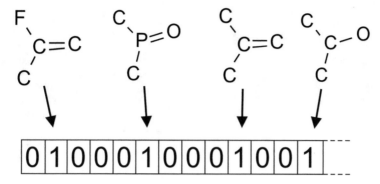

Fig. 15.3 Example of augmented atoms and a fingerprint

fragment centred on each atom in the molecule in turn. This information is encoded for rapid searching in a fixed-length bit string, called a *fingerprint*, whose encoded fragments hence provide a summary representation of a molecule's structure in just the same way as a few selected keywords provide a summary representation of the full text of a document (see Fig. 15.3). The fingerprint representing the query can then be matched against corresponding fingerprints representing each of the molecules in the database that is to be searched. Only a very small subset of a database will normally contain all of the screens that have been assigned to a query substructure, and only this subset then needs to undergo the time-consuming subgraph isomorphism search.

15.2.4 Similarity Searching

Substructure searching provides an invaluable tool for accessing databases of chemical structures; however, it does require that the searcher is able to provide a precise definition of the substructure that is required, and this may not be possible in the early stages of a drug discovery project, where all that is known is the identity of one or more active molecules, e.g. an existing drug from a competitor company. In such circumstances, an alternative type of searching mechanism is appropriate, called *similarity searching* [21, 22]. Here, the searcher submits an entire molecule, which is normally called the *reference structure*, and the system then ranks the database in order of decreasing similarity to the reference structure, so that the molecules returned first to the searcher are those that are most closely related to it in structural terms. The underlying rationale for similarity searching is the *similar property principle* [23], which states that molecules that have similar structures will have similar properties. Hence, if the reference structure has some interesting property, such as reducing a person's susceptibility to angina, then structurally similar molecules are also likely to exhibit this characteristic.

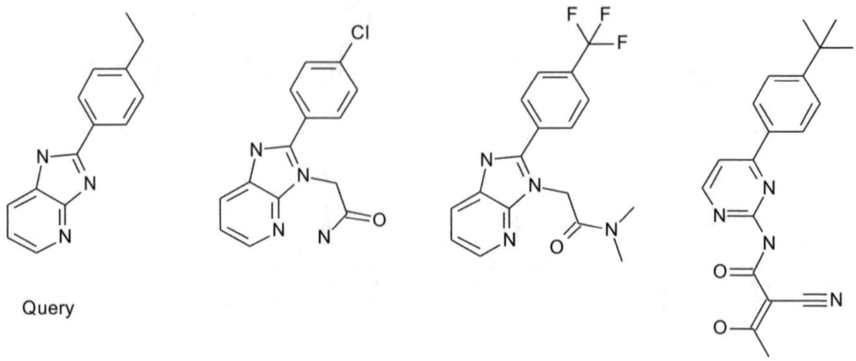

Fig. 15.4 Example of output from a similarity search

There are many different ways in which intermolecular structural similarity can be quantified, with the most common similarity measures being based on the comparison of molecular fingerprints to identify the numbers of fragments common to a pair of molecules. This provides a very simple, but surprisingly effective, way of identifying structural relationships, as exemplified by the molecules shown in Fig. 15.4. Similarity-based approaches to searching for chemical structures in patents have been proposed by a number of groups, including Weininger [24], Rhodes et al. [25] and Fliri et al. [26, 27], and form an aspect of patent-based drug discovery systems developed at AstraZeneca [28, 29].

15.2.5 Databases of Specific Structures from Chemical Patents

Several databases of specific chemical structure records from chemical patents are available for searching using the techniques described in the preceding sections [30]. Some of these include molecules described in patents alongside those found in other sources, such as journal articles, while others are derived entirely from the patent literature. Some databases are manually curated by expert analysts, while others are produced by automatic analysis of machine-readable patent text, identifying and extracting chemical nomenclature and converting it automatically to connection table representations [31]. Among those available are:

- Chemical Abstracts Service registry file (manually curated)
- Thomson Reuters Derwent Chemistry Resource (manually curated)
- Elsevier Reaxys (generated semi-automatically, and also including display of Markush structures)
- SureChEMBL (generated automatically, and now maintained by the European Bioinformatics Institute)

In addition the PubChem database maintained by the National Institutes of Health incorporates around 15 million molecules extracted from patent text by Thomson Pharma, SureChemOpen, SCRIPDB [32] and IBM [25].

15.3 Searching Generic Chemical Structures

15.3.1 Markush Structure Representation

In order to ensure complete coverage of the scope of invention, and hence protect the inventor's property rights, patent documents tend to extend beyond the realm of specific description but, instead, describe the invention using broader terms. Those features which reflect the novelty of the invention are described in full and unambiguous terms, while other features, although fundamental to the invention, may be optional or alternative in nature. An example of the latter feature might be a new refrigerator for which the internal light might be described using a vague term such as 'device for illuminating the interior'. The same is true of chemical patents in which features of the compound that are fundamental to the novelty of its operation are described using specific terms, and those for which alternatives may be substituted are described generically. The result of this treatment is a single description which can represent a potentially vast number of specific molecules, many (or even most) of which will have never been synthesised or tested.

Figure 15.5 shows part of a US patent in which the main claim 1 is shown as a 'Markush' structure. The essential parts of active molecules are shown in the diagram using specific atoms, to which are attached 'R-groups' whose more generic nature is described in the succeeding paragraphs. The more specific claim 10 lists nine individual molecules, all covered by the Markush structure in claim 1, using their systematic names. The third of these is the molecule actually marketed as Viagra®, but the others have similar biological activity and are also protected by the patent.

The logical and linguistic terminology that exists in the chemical patent literature has been described in detail by Dethlefsen et al. [33], leading to a classification of the structural variations which exist. These authors identified four types of structural variation, which are exemplified in Fig. 15.6:

- Substituent (s-) variation involves an enumerated list of alternative substituents that may appear at a particular place in the structure.
- Position (p-) variation involves a set of alternative points of attachment for a substituent, normally, though not always, different positions on a ring.
- Frequency (f-) variation involves the variable repetition of a component either within a linear 'nose-to-tail' sequence or as an attachment to a ring system.
- Homology (h-) variation involves specifying a generic class of substituents, usually using nomenclatural or other verbal expressions, which defines the component as being a member of a family of related chemical substituents (e.g. R3 in Fig. 15.5 indicates an alkyl group containing up to six carbon atoms).

(12) **United States Patent**
    Ellis et al.

(10) Patent No.:   US 6,469,012 B1
(45) Date of Patent: Oct. 22, 2002

What is claimed is:

1. A method of treating erectile dysfunction in a male animal, comprising administering to a male animal in need of such treatment an effective amount of a compound of formula (I):

(I)

wherein:

R^1 is H; C_1–C_3 alkyl; C_1–C_3 perfluoroalkyl; or C_3–C_5 cycloalkyl;

R^2 is H; C_1–C_6 alkyl optionally substituted with C_3–C_6 cycloalkyl; C_1–C_3 perfluoroalkyl; or C_3–C_6 cycloalkyl;

R^3 is C_1–C_6 alkyl optionally substituted with C_3–C_6 cycloalkyl; C_1–C_6 perfluoroalkyl; C_3–C_5 cycloalkyl; C_3–C_6 alkenyl; or C_3–C_6 alkynyl;

R^4 is C_1–C_4 alkyl optionally substituted with OH, NR^5R^6, CN, $CONR^5R^6$ or CO_2R^7; C_2–C_4 alkenyl optionally substituted with CN, $CONR_5R^6$ or CO_2R^7; C_2–C_4 alkanoyl optionally substituted with NR^5R^6; (hydroxy) C_2–C_4 alkyl optionally substituted with NR^5R^6; (C_2–C_3 alkoxy)C_1–C_2 alkyl optionally substituted with OH or NR^5R^6; $CONR^5R^6$; CO_2R^7; halo; NR^5R^6; $NHSO_2NR^5R^6$; $NHSO_2R^8$; $SO_2NR^9R^{10}$; or phenyl pyridyl, pyrimidinyl, imidazolyl, oxazolyl, thiazolyl, thienyl or triazolyl any of which is optionally substituted with methyl;

R^5 and R^6 are each independently H or C_1–C_4 alkyl, or together with the nitrogen atom to which they are attached form a pyrrolidinyl, piperidino, morpholino, 4-N(R^{11})-piperazinyl or imidazolyl group wherein said group is optionally substituted with methyl or OH;

R^7 is H or C_1–C_4 alkyl;

R^8 is C_1–C_3 alkyl optionally substituted with NR^5R^6;

R^9 and R^{10} together with the nitrogen atom to which they are attached form a pyrrolidinyl, piperidino, morpholino or 4-N(R^{12})-piperazinyl group wherein said group is optionally substituted with C_1–C_4 alkyl, C_1–C_3 alkoxy, $NR^{13}R^{14}$ or $CONR^{13}R^{14}$;

R^{11} is H; C_1–C_3 alkyl optionally substituted with phenyl; (hydroxy)C_2–C_3 alkyl; or C_1–C_4 alkanoyl;

R^{12} is H; C_1–C_6 alkyl; (C_1–C_3 alkoxy)C_2–C_6 alkyl; (hydroxy)C_2–C_6 alkyl; ($R^{13}R^{14}$N)C_2–C_6 alkyl; ($R^{13}R^{14}$NOC)C_1–C_6 alkyl; $CONR^{13}R^{14}$; $CSNR^{13}R^{14}$; or C(NH)$NR^{13}R^{14}$; and

R^{13} and R^{14} are each independently H; C_1–C_4 alkyl; (C_1–C_3 alkoxy)C_2–C_4 alkyl; or (hydroxy)C_2–C_4 alkyl;

or a pharmaceutically acceptable salt thereof;

or a pharmaceutically acceptable composition containing either entity.

10. A method as defined in claim 9 wherein the compound of formula (I) is selected from:
5-(2-ethoxy-5-morpholinoacetylphenyl)-1-methyl-3-n-propyl-1,6-dihydro-7H-pyrazolo[4,3-d]pyrimidin-7-one;
5-(5-morpholinoacetyl-2-n-propoxyphenyl)-1-methyl-3-n-propyl-1,6-dihydro-7H-pyrazolo[4,3-d]pyrimidin-7-one;
5-[2-ethoxy-5-(4-methyl-1-piperazinylsulphonyl)-phenyl]-1-methyl-3-n-propyl-1,6-dihydro-7H-pyrazolo[4,3-d]pyrimidin-7-one;
5-[2-allyloxy-5-(4-methyl-1-piperazinylsulphonyl)-phenyl]-1-methyl-3-n-propyl-1,6-dihydro-7H-pyrazolo[4,3-d]pyrimidin-7-one;
5-{2-ethoxy-5-[4-(2-propyl)-1-piperazinyl-sulphonyl]phenyl}-1-methyl-3-n-propyl-1,6-dihydro-7H-pyrazolo[4,3-d]pyrimidin-7-one;
5-{2-ethoxy-5-[4-(2-hydroxyethyl)-1-piperazinyl-sulphonyl]phenyl}-1-methyl-3-n-propyl-1,6-dihydro-7H-pyrazolo[4,3-d]pyrimidin-7-one;
5-{5-[4-(2-hydroxyethyl)-1-piperazinylsulphonyl]-2-n-propoxyphenyl}-1-methyl-3-n-propyl-1,6-dihydro-7H-pyrazolo[4,3-d]pyrimidin-7-one;
5-[2-ethoxy-5-(4-methyl-1-piperazinylcarbonyl)-phenyl]-1-methyl-3-n-propyl-1,6-dihydro-7H-pyrazolo[4,3-d]pyrimidin-7-one; and
5-[2-ethoxy-5-(1-methyl-2-imidazolyl)phenyl]-1-methyl-3-n-propyl-1,6-dihydro-7H-pyrazolo[4,3-d]pyrimidin-7-one.

Fig. 15.5 Example US patent

The Markush structures in Figs. 15.5 and 15.6 are relatively simple; Markush 'cores' consisting only of a set of connected R-groups, and repeated nesting of variable groups, are common features in chemical patents, leading to complex and often confusing structures. Enumeration of all of the specific molecules covered is rarely an option due to storage requirements and computational costs. Therefore, an alternative method of computer representation is required. The basic structure adopted by current commercial systems [1, 30] is a logical tree of 'partial structures' (shown as connection tables) in which the invariant core of the structure becomes the root, and the various optional and alternative parts become branches. Partial structures from the tree can be combined appropriately to form complete molecules when enumeration is required, and searches can be performed across

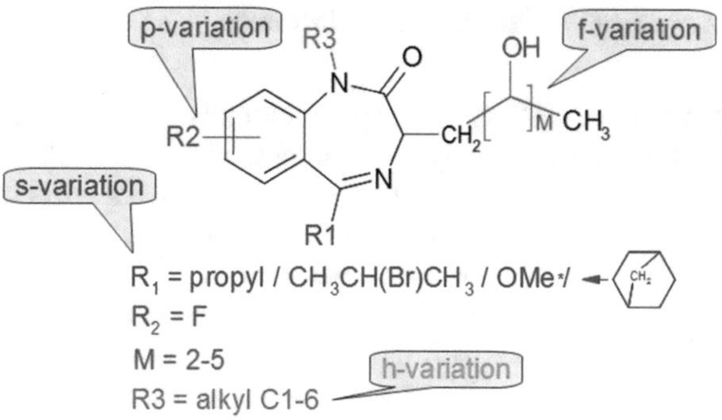

Fig. 15.6 Types of structural variation in chemical patents

their boundaries without the need for enumeration. These principles have also been applied to the handling of Markush structures used to represent combinatorial libraries [34].

While those partial structures in a Markush that are described in specific terms (whether by nomenclature, line notation or structure diagram) can be represented by connection tables, a different form of representation is required for generic (homology-variant) groups, since they are not defined in a way that can be shown as a simple topological graph. A number of approaches have been used [30, 35], though they have certain features in common. Research work at Sheffield University in the 1980s [36] used a set of quantitative structural 'parameters' to describe such groups specifying, for example, the number and type of atoms present, the types of bonds, the number and size of rings, etc. Other systems have used small sets of special node types representing the main classes of homology-variant group. For example, Thomson Reuters' Merged Markush Service (MMS) database uses a set of 22 'superatoms', representing groups such as alkyl chains (the CHK superatom) or fused heterocyclic groups (HEF). Qualitative attributes (e.g. 'long chain') or quantitative 'parameters' (e.g. specifying the number and type of atoms present, or the number of rings) can be applied to these to describe the group in greater detail. In Chemical Abstracts Service's MARPAT database, a hierarchically arranged set of eight 'generic group nodes' (e.g. Ak for carbon chain, or Hy for heterocycle) is used, with similar qualitative *categories* and quantitative *attributes*.

Recent work at the pharmaceutical company AstraZeneca [37] has included the development of an XML-based *Markush Input Language* (MIL), in which specific partial structures are described using SMARTS notation (an extension of SMILES, used for representing substructural patterns). The publication illustrates the use of MIL to represent the 'original' Markush structure (from a US patent for pyrazolone dyes, filed in 1926 by Dr Eugene Markush), though in practice the language has so far been used primarily to represent non-patent Markush structures, such as those found in legislation for controlled substances.

15.3.2   Searching in Markush Structures

The same principles of graph and subgraph isomorphism that are used for searching in specific structure databases can be used for those parts of a Markush structure that can be represented by atom–bond connection tables. There are, of course, additional complications in handling the connections between different partial structures and in the logical (AND/OR) relationships between them.

A more serious complication arises when trying to match groups described by atom–bond connection tables with those homology-variant groups described in other ways; this complication is sometimes called *translation*. Enumeration of all possible members of the relevant homologous series is not normally a practicable solution, because of the sheer numbers involved, though enumeration of subsets may sometimes be useful [26, 27]. In general, it is possible to derive a generic representation (e.g. based on structural parameters) from a specific group (based on a connection table), while the reverse process is not possible. The comparison can thus be done at the generic level, effectively showing, for example, that an ethyl group (a specific group consisting of chain of two carbon atoms) is 'consistent' with a C1-6 alkyl group (a chain of up to six carbon atoms), whereas it is not consistent with a nitrogen-containing heterocyclic ring system.

A further problem can arise as a result of the arbitrary boundaries between different partial structures, making it difficult to establish which atoms from a connection-table-represented group should be compared against a generically represented group. Work at Sheffield developed the concept of *reduced graphs* [38], in which all the atoms in a ring or in a chain of connected carbon or non-carbon atoms are collapsed into a single node in the 'reduced' graph connection table, which thus better mirrors the boundaries between generically described groups. Similar ideas are used in most commercial systems.

The AstraZeneca work [37] mentioned earlier has also included the development of a type of Markush structure search system, known as *i3am* ('is it in a Markush'). This contrasts somewhat with the commercial systems for searching patent databases, in that its primary purpose is to determine whether or not any of a (possibly very large) set of specific molecule queries is covered by any of a relatively small set of Markush structures.

ChemAxon's Markush search system [39] allows query formulation and limited search functionality, and their JChem cartridge enables access to in-house Markush data. The toolkit, which also allows structure enumeration, visualisation and analysis, has been applied to Thomson Reuters' IP Data Feeds, which includes summary data from over half a million patents from the Derwent World Patents Index®.

15.3.3 Fragmentation Codes and Screening

Before the 1980s, structure-based retrieval systems operated almost exclusively on the basis of fragmentation codes in which the structural components were described using a series of fragment descriptors that were analogous in principle to the fragments still used for screening substructure searches of databases of specific molecules. Special codes were devised for patent databases, of which the most notable were the Derwent CPI code and the GREMAS code; their respective retrieval performance was compared by Franzreb et al. [40]. The Derwent CPI code is still in use today for Thomson Reuters' World Patents Index [41].

As with specific structure searching, graph-based generic systems also require an initial fragment-based screening stage in order to reduce the number of compounds being sent to more compute-intensive search strategies based on subgraph isomorphism algorithms. These screens use not only the types of fragment that are found in specific molecule search systems but may also use screens based on the superatoms and generic group nodes used to represent homology-variant groups. The Sheffield research work used specific-level fragment descriptors generated from homology-variant components [42] and used the logic tree structure of a Markush to identify screens common to multiple alternative groups in the structure as a whole [43].

15.3.4 Commercial Markush Databases and Search Systems

Two commercial databases of Markush structures from patents have been available since the late 1980s, each with its own dedicated online search system. These are Thomson Reuters' MMS (Merged Markush Service) database, which is searchable using Questel's Markush DARC software [44], and Chemical Abstracts Service's MARPAT database [45], searchable with its own MARPAT software [46]. The MMS database resulted from a merger between the WPIM (World Patents Index Markush) database, originally built by Derwent, and the Pharmsearch database originally built by INPI, the French Patent Office. These MMS and MARPAT systems have changed relatively little since their first launch and are compared by Schmuff [47] and Berks [1]. Practical aspects of their use are discussed by Newbold [48] and by Cielen [49].

In recent years there has been increased interest in alternative or enhanced access to these commercial databases, and Thomson Reuters have made their data available to a number of collaborators. Barnard and Wright [50] have discussed the prospect for 'in-house' access to Markush databases, and Csepregi [39] has described the search software developed at ChemAxon. In addition Deng et al. [51, 52] have described an improved visualisation system for the Markush structures from the MMS database, which has been developed at Roche.

15.3.5 Automatic Extraction of Markush Structures from Patent Text

The manual curation of Markush databases, such as MMS and MARPAT, is extremely time-consuming and expensive, and the success of automated data mining techniques to extract structural and other information from chemical text [53] has led to considerable interest in the possibility of automatic extraction of Markush structure records from machine-readable patent specifications. This has included work on automatic analysis of structure diagrams ('chemical OCR'), especially where these include features such as R-groups and position and frequency variation [54, 55]. Direct attempts to extract searchable Markush structures by automatic analysis of patent documents have been reported by Haupt [56] and by Eigner-Pitto et al. [57], though with limited success; the often considerable complexities of Markush structures and the way they are described in patent documents mean that extracting Markush structures from them reliably is likely to continue to require significant amounts of manual curation, at least for the foreseeable future.

15.4   Conclusions

The structures of chemical molecules are an important component of the information contained in chemical patents. Individual molecules can be searched using well-established techniques from chemoinformatics, and substantial enhancements to these techniques have allowed them to be used for the representation and searching of the generic chemical structures in patents, which can describe very large numbers of structurally related molecules. In this chapter, we have summarised the techniques that are currently available (as of May 2014) for structure and substructure searching of both specific and generic structures. However, the reader should note that the chemoinformatics software industry is in a state of constant flux, with improvements in the data and searching techniques that will be available to users in the future.

It is hoped that such developments will address at least some of the problems that still face the users of chemical patents. In 2008, the United States Patent and Trademark Office actually went so far as to make proposals to restrict the types of Markush structure that could be claimed [58], though these proposals were later abandoned in the face of fierce opposition from the pharmaceutical industry. However, the very generic descriptions that are sometimes used in patents mean that very large hit lists can result even in response to quite specific structural queries: it is hence likely that there will be much interest in the future in the use of procedures that can rank search outputs so that attention can be focused on just the top-ranked structures and patents.

References

1. Berks AH (2001) Current state of the art of Markush topological search systems. World Pat Inf 23:5–13
2. Willett P (2008) From chemical documentation to chemoinformatics: fifty years of chemical information science. J Inf Sci 34:477–499
3. Gasteiger J (2006) The central role of chemoinformatics. Chemomet Intell Lab Syst 82:200–209
4. Leach AR, Gillet VJ (2007) An introduction to chemoinformatics. Kluwer, Dordrecht
5. Gasteiger J, Engel T (eds) (2003) Chemoinformatics: a textbook. Wiley-VCH, Weinheim
6. Kosata B (2009) Chemical entity formatting. In: Banville DL (ed) Chemical information mining. CRC Press, Boca Raton, FL
7. Warr WA (2011) Representation of chemical structures. WIREs Comput Mol Sci 1(4):557–579
8. Barnard JM, Kenny PW, Wallace PN (2012) Representing chemical structures in databases for drug design. In: Livingstone DJ, Davis AM (eds) Drug design strategies: quantitative approaches. Royal Society of Chemistry, Cambridge, pp 164–191
9. Martin YC, Willett P (eds) (1998) Designing bioactive molecules: three-dimensional techniques and applications. American Chemical Society, Washington, DC
10. Weininger D (1988) SMILES, a chemical language and information-system. 1. Introduction to methodology and encoding rules. J Chem Inf Comp Sci 28:31–36
11. Heller S, McNaught A et al (2013) InChI – the worldwide chemical structure identifier standard. J Cheminf 5:7
12. Dalby A, Nourse JG et al (1992) Description of several chemical structure file formats used by computer programs developed at Molecular Design Limited. J Chem Inf Comp Sci 22:244–255
13. Diestel R (2010) Graph theory, vol 173, 4th edn, Graduate tests in mathematics. Springer, New York, NY
14. Wilson DRJ (2010) Introduction to graph theory. Prentice Hall, Harlow
15. Warr WA (2010) Tautomerism in chemical information management systems. J Comput-Aided Mol Des 24:497–520
16. Morgan H (1965) The generation of a unique machine description for chemical structures – a technique developed at Chemical Abstracts Service. J Chem Doc 5:107–113
17. McKay BD (1981) Practical graph isomorphism. Congressus Numerantium 30:45–87
18. Barnard JM (1993) Substructure searching methods – old and new. J Chem Inf Comp Sci 33:532–538
19. Sussenguth EH (1965) A graph-theoretic algorithm for matching chemical structures. J Chem Doc 5:36–43
20. Ullmann JR (1976) An algorithm for subgraph isomorphism. J ACM 23:31–42
21. Eckert H, Bajorath J (2007) Molecular similarity analysis in virtual screening: foundations, limitation and novel approaches. Drug Discov Today 12:225–233
22. Willett P (2009) Similarity methods in chemoinformatics. Ann Rev Inf Sci Technol 43:3–71
23. Johnson MA, Maggiora GM (eds) (1990) Concepts and applications of molecular similarity. Wiley, New York, NY
24. Weininger D (1998) Simpatico. Presented at MUG 98, the Daylight Chemical Information Systems User Group Meeting, Santa Fe, NM, USA, 24–27 Feb 1998. http://www.daylight.com/meetings/mug98/Weininger/mug98mark/mug98mark.html. Accessed March 2014
25. Rhodes J, Boyer S et al (2007) Mining patents using molecular similarity search. Pac Symp Biocomput 12:304–315
26. Fliri A, Moysan E et al (2009) Methods for processing generic chemical structure representations. US Patent 2009/0132464
27. Fliri A, Moysan E, Nolte M (2010) Method for creating virtual compound libraries within Markush structure patent claims. WO Patent 2010/065144 A2

28. Muresan S, Petrov P et al (2011) Making every SAR point count: the development of chemistry connect for the large-scale integration of structure and bioactivity data. Drug Discov Today 16:1019–1030
29. Tyrchan C, Boström J et al (2012) Exploiting structural information in patent specifications for key compound prediction. J Chem Inf Model 52:1480–1489
30. Downs GM, Barnard JM (2011) Chemical patent information systems. WIREs Comput Mol Sci 1:727–741. doi:10.1002/wcms.41
31. Williams AJ, Yerin A (2009) Automated identification and conversion of chemical names to structure-searchable information. In: Banville DL (ed) Chemical information mining. CRC Press, Boca Raton, FL
32. Heifets A, Jurisica I (2011) SCRIPDB: a portal for easy access to syntheses, chemicals and reactions in patents. Nucl Acids Res 2011:1–6
33. Dethlefsen W, Lynch MF et al (1991) Computer storage and retrieval of generic chemical structures in patents, Part 11. Theoretical aspects of the use of structure languages in a retrieval system. J Chem Inf Comp Sci 31:233–253
34. Barnard JM, Downs GM, von Scholley-Pfab A, Brown RD (2000) Use of Markush structure analysis techniques for descriptor generation and clustering of large combinatorial libraries. J Mol Graph Model 18:452–463
35. Barnard JM (1991) A comparison of different approaches to Markush structure handling. J Chem Inf Comput Sci 31:64–68
36. Lynch MF, Holliday JD (1996) The Sheffield Generic Structures Project – a retrospective review. J Chem Inf Comp Sci 36:930–936
37. Cosgrove DA, Green KM et al (2012) A system for encoding and searching Markush structures. J Chem Inf Model 52:1936–1947
38. Gillet VJ, Downs GM et al (1987) Computer-storage and retrieval of generic chemical structures in patents. 8. Reduced chemical graphs and their applications in generic chemical-structure retrieval. J Chem Inf Comp Sci 27:126–137
39. Csepregi S (2009) Markush structures – from molecules towards patents. Presented at the International Conference for Science & Business Information (ICIC), Sitges, Spain, 18–21 Oct 2009. http://www.haxel.com/icic/archive/2009/programme/. Accessed April 2013
40. Franzreb KH, Hornbach P et al (1991) Structure searches in patent literature: a comparison study between IDC GREMAS and Derwent Chemical Code. J Chem Inf Comput Sci 31:284–289
41. Simmons ES (2004) The online divide: a professional user's perspective on Derwent database development in the online era. World Pat Inf 26:45–47
42. Holliday JD, Downs GM et al (1993) Computer storage and retrieval of generic chemical structures in patents, Part 15. Generation of topological fragment descriptors from nontopological representation of generic structure components. J Chem Inf Comp Sci 33:369–377
43. Downs GM, Gillet VJ et al (1989) Computer storage and retrieval of generic chemical structures in patents, Part 10. Assignment and logical bubble-up of ring screens for structurally explicit generics. J Chem Inf Comp Sci 29:215–224
44. Benichou P, Klimczak C, Borne P (1997) Handling genericity in chemical structures using the Markush Darc software. J Chem Inf Comput Sci 37:43–53
45. Ebe T, Sanderson KA, Wilson PS (1991) The Chemical Abstracts Service generic chemical (Markush) structure storage and retrieval capability. 2. The MARPAT file. J Chem Inf Comput Sci 31:31–36
46. Fisanick W (1990) The Chemical Abstract's Service generic chemical (Markush) structure storage and retrieval capability. 1. Basic concepts. J Chem Inf Comput Sci 30:145–154
47. Schmuff NR (1991) A comparison of the MARPAT and Markush DARC software. J Chem Inf Comput Sci 31:53–59
48. Newbold S (2009) Marpat searching in context: creating the ideal answer set and beyond. Presented at the RSC CICAG Meeting "Should I Really Be Searching Patents?", Royal Society of Chemistry, London. www.rsc.org/images/S_NewboldOct2009_tcm18-167683.pdf. Accessed April 2014

49. Cielen E (2009) Searching Markush formulae directed to medical applications. World Pat Inf 31:178–183
50. Barnard JM, Wright PM (2009) Towards in-house searching of Markush structures from patents. World Pat Inf 31:97–103
51. Deng W, Berthel SJ, So WV (2011) Intuitive patent Markush structure visualization tool for medicinal chemists. J Chem Inf Model 51:511–520
52. Deng W, Scott E, Berthel SJ, So WV (2012) Deconvoluting complex patent Markush structures: a novel R-group numbering system. World Pat Inf 34:128–133
53. Banville DL (2009) Chemical information mining: facilitating literature-based discovery. CRC Press, Boca Raton, FL
54. Valko AT, Johnson AP (2009) CLiDE Pro: the latest generation of CLiDE, a tool for optical chemical structure recognition. J Chem Inf Model 49:780–787
55. Zimmerman M (2009) Chemical depictions—the grand challenge in patents. Presented at the International Conference for Science & Business Information (ICIC), Sitges, Spain, 18–21 October 2009. http://www.haxel.com/icic/archive/2009/programme/. Accessed April 2014
56. Haupt CS (2009) Markush structure reconstruction: a prototype for their reconstruction from image and text into a searchable, context sensitive grammar based extension of SMILES. Thesis, Fraunhofer SCAI. http://publica.fraunhofer.de/eprints/urn:nbn:de:0011-n-1144222.pdf
57. Eigner-Pitto V, Eiblmaier J et al (2012) ChemProspector and generic structures: advanced mining and searching of chemical content. J Cheminf 4:O17
58. Bone RGA, Kendall JT (2008) Markush under threat: US PTO considers alternatives. Indus Biotechnol 4:246–251

Chapter 16
Machine Translation and the Challenge of Patents

John Tinsley

Abstract In this chapter, machine translation (MT) is first introduced in the context of patent information, and we touch upon what role it can play at various points in the intellectual property (IP) life cycle. We then step back to take a high-level look at what exactly defines MT, how it works, what makes it such a difficult task, as well as some of the more recent advances to overcome these hurdles and how we can go about ensuring that MT systems we develop are actually fit for purpose.

We then explore patent information as an application area for MT and describe how it presents a unique challenge not only for MT but for language technology in general. Finally, we take a closer look at some use cases involving MT and patents to show how they are already bringing significant value to consumers, but that there remains plenty of room for improvement.

16.1 Introduction

Machine translation (MT) technology has matured significantly over the past decade to the point that it has seen widespread adoption in many practical applications, including numerous commercial use cases. This increase in popularity has been driven to a large extent by a number of open-source initiatives supported by the European Commission[1] as well as a large and active developer community, both of which have helped to lower the barrier to the adoption of MT.

However, MT still remains somewhat misunderstood for two broader reasons: firstly, most users' first experience with MT comes from free online services which, while being very valuable tools for building awareness in the field of technology, have many shortcomings with regard to practical application and often garner attention for 'humorous' incorrect output. Furthermore, commercial vendors of MT

---

[1]Euromatrix (www.euromatrix.net), Euromatrix Plus (www.euromatrixplus.net), Moses Core (www.statmt.org/mosescore)

J. Tinsley (✉)
Iconic Translation Machines Ltd., Invent DCU, Glasnevin, Dublin, 9, Ireland
e-mail: john@iptranslator.com

© Springer-Verlag GmbH Germany 2017   409
M. Lupu et al. (eds.), *Current Challenges in Patent Information Retrieval*,
The Information Retrieval Series 37, DOI 10.1007/978-3-662-53817-3_16

often make claims to deliver levels of service and performance that cannot yet be met by the current state of the art (e.g. 'fully automatic, human quality translation'), and thus the more intrepid users who ventured to invest in the technology at an early stage have been left disappointed.

That being said, the translation industry is at the point now where it is getting closer to crossing the chasm towards more mainstream acceptance of MT. This is being facilitated through the education of end users in order to better manage expectations about what MT is capable of. Part of this learning includes identifying specific application areas, for example, patent information, where MT can bring real, quantifiable value to users and how it can be seamlessly deployed into existing workflows.

The appreciation that MT has a significant role to play in patent information is evidenced by the fact that 'mutual machine translation' is one of the ten foundation projects identified by the IP5—a consortium of the five largest intellectual property offices in the world—as being integral to the harmonisation and standardisation of the patent information-sharing processes globally.[2]

16.2 Why Machine Translation?

The demand for translation in the world of patent information is ever increasing as companies expand international operations and, as a consequence, seek to protect their intellectual property globally. This is evidenced by the consistent increase in patent applications over the last 20 years [1] and the fact that these patents are filed in dozens of different languages, particularly Asian languages more recently.

The provision of human translation services is being outstripped by the demand for patent translation, especially because patent translation often requires specialist translators with subject matter expertise. While it is frequently necessary when translations need to be 100 % legally accurate, in many cases, human translation is simply not an option because of the large volumes of documents in question. This is where machine translation has a significant role to play.

16.2.1   The Role of Machine Translation

There are a number of stages in the IP life cycle that translation is required and MT can play a role in each one. During patent searches in particular, be it for novelty,

---

[2]http://www.fiveipoffices.org/projects/mutualmac.html

validity or infringement, MT can be used in a number of ways:

- To provide an on-demand 'gist' translation of foreign patents for information purposes to determine relevance
- To pre-translate patent databases in order to make them searchable in multiple languages
- To translate search queries into multiple languages to increase the coverage of the search across collections

Furthermore, MT can be applied as an intermediary step in the human translation process as a productivity tool. Rather than translating from scratch, translators can choose to use MT output as a starting point and 'post-edit' it to full quality, in theory reducing the overall time needed to translate the document. The net effect of this for patent information specialists can be a reduction in the overall cost of sourcing professional translation.

We will provide more detail on this approach and other specific use cases for MT in Sect. 6.

16.3   Machine Translation: The Basics

In this section, we provide an overview of some of the fundamental concepts behind modern approaches to machine translation as well as look at some alternative approaches. We will describe the key prerequisite of developing MT systems, namely, high-quality training data, and look at some of the more cutting-edge techniques employed in state-of-the-art MT research and development, including those that are most applicable to patent information.

16.3.1   Paradigms of MT

There are a number of different approaches to MT which have had varying degrees of success over the past few decades. Two approaches in particular have been more prominent than the rest, namely, rule-based MT (RBMT) and statistical MT (SMT). In the following, we give an overview of both rule-based and statistical MT and go into more detail about how the most common approach actually works.

16.3.1.1 Rule-Based MT

Rule-based MT, or RBMT, involves the use of linguistic rules and dictionaries to translate from one language (the *source*) into another language (the *target*[3]). For a given language pair, say English and French, the starting point is: a set of rules, or a grammar, describing English sentence structure; a grammar describing French sentence structure; and a bilingual dictionary that allows us to map English words to French words.

We define a set of rules, or a bilingual grammar, that describes the syntactic transformations that need to take place to convert English grammar into French. We use the rules to map the English structure to a French structure and use a dictionary to translate the words.

RBMT systems have the advantage that they produce consistent and predictable output because of the in-built grammar knowledge. However, developing these systems requires significant human effort and linguistic expertise to produce the rules for each language pair in addition to vast dictionaries. As such, it is not very scalable or adaptable and does not handle exceptions or language variances well.

16.3.1.2 Statistical MT

Statistical MT, or SMT, is a data-driven approach whereby models of translation are learned by analysing examples of previously translated documents. For a given language pair, using a bilingual text corpus (pairs of documents that are translations of one another), we calculate how frequently pairs of words and phrases occur together in order to train a model of translation. We then use these models to estimate the most likely translation of new unseen input. This approach is an application of Bayes' theorem and can be formally described by the formula below:

$$\tilde{e} = arg \max_{e \in e*} p\left(e | f\right) = arg \max_{e \in e*} p\left(f | e\right) p(e)$$

where e is the target language, f is the source language and $\tilde{e}$ is the MT output. $p(f | e)$ represents the translation model and $p(e)$ represents the target language model.

SMT has the advantage that the core approach is language independent and new systems can be built relatively quickly. The translations produced tend to be more fluent than more literal rule-based output. However, SMT is heavily reliant on the availability of sufficient amounts of good quality training (discussed in more detail in Sect. 3.2). Furthermore, pure SMT is less suitable for language pairs with more divergent grammar and sentence structure.

---

[3] *Source* and *target* are terms that will reoccur in this chapter in reference to the language pair in question when carrying out machine translation.

16.3.1.3 Best of Both Worlds

More recent approaches have sought to combine the strengths of both RBMT and SMT into so-called hybrid MT (e.g. [2, 3]). Using this approach, one of the paradigms takes the lead role in the translation process and is supported by techniques from the other.

For example, in RBMT-driven hybrid approaches, the core translation is carried out using linguistic rules, while statistical methods are used to automatically enhance the translation output and fix errors. The more common approach, though, is SMT enhanced with grammar rules where the estimation of statistics and the translation process is better guided through linguistic knowledge of the languages in question. This technique, often referred to as syntax-based SMT, can help to support translation between more divergent language pairs and better capture phenomena such as long-distance dependencies and highly inflectional morphology.

For the remainder of this chapter, we will discuss machine translation in the context of the SMT paradigm, as it is the more prevalent approach to MT. The following sections describe the processing involved in SMT from training, to translation, to more advanced approaches.

16.3.2 Training Data

The starting point for all SMT systems is a training corpus. A corpus (pl. corpora) is a collection of texts, in electronic format, in a single language. For SMT we require bilingual, or parallel, corpora, which are collections of corresponding texts in multiple languages, for example, a document and its translation or the European Parliamentary Proceedings [4].

For patent MT, such parallel corpora can be mined using patent family information to find a document and its family members in multiple languages. Similarly, many national patent offices also publish titles and abstracts in English (where English is not already an official language). Much of this mining process can be automated and these techniques have been successfully applied to collect such corpora for a number of languages [5, 6].

MT systems have been built using parallel corpora containing anywhere from under 100,000 words to hundreds of millions of words. In general for SMT, the more training data available, the better, as there are more translation examples to learn from, though there are diminishing returns on the quality given more data. However, for certain types of content, or domains, where there is limited vocabulary or restricted writing style, it is possible to build MT systems on smaller amounts of data. Patents, on the other hand, can vary greatly from document to document in terms of content. There is a massive variance in vocabulary and styles across technical fields and document classes. Even within patents, there are different writing styles between the abstract, claims and description. For this reason, it is better to have as much training data as possible, which can then be classified according to technical areas using the International Patent Classification System[4] and used to develop advanced systems (described further in Sect. 5.1).

Once we have this data at hand, we need to know which sentences correspond to which across the parallel documents. This non-trivial task is known as *sentence alignment* and has itself been an active research field of natural language processing ([7, 8] among others). In the simplest case, there is a one-to-one mapping between sentences. Where there is not, it needs to be determined whether sentences can be combined to create the correct mapping or whether sentences need to be deleted from the corpus. Manual intervention is often required to assist and verify the automatic alignment process. This is particularly important when our bilingual corpora are not truly parallel, but rather *comparable*, that is, describing the same topic while not explicitly being direct translations, e.g. in patent information when the target abstract is an enhanced translation that summarises the full text.

16.3.2.1 Key Elements: Quality, Quantity, Relevance

All of the information learned by SMT systems—word/phrase correspondences and associated statistics—are derived from the examples seen in the training corpus. Learning from bad examples causes the MT system to produce more erroneous output. Therefore, it is essential that the data on which an MT system is trained be of high quality. Errors that reduce the quality of the corpus include incorrect sentence alignment and misspellings. Misspellings are often encountered when the source text has been produced using optical character recognition (OCR) as is frequently the case when dealing with patent information where many full-text documents are only available in PDF format. Preparation of training data should also include checks as pre- and post-processing steps that should ideally have some human proofing if possible.

In addition to good quality data, we also need to ensure that we have sufficient data in order to avoid sparse statistics and to make sure that we have seen as many variations in style, sentence structure and vocabulary as possible. Sourcing large amounts of quality, relevant data is a big challenge for MT developers. For certain languages like English, French, German and Chinese, data is abundant. However, a big issue remains the relative lack of resources for other languages, e.g. if we want to build an MT system to translate patents between Croatian and English, finding sufficient data will be a challenge as there were only 72 patents filed in Croatia between 2012 and 2013.[5]

Finally, it is essential that the parallel corpus on which MT is trained is relevant to and representative of the type of content that will be translated with the system. The corpus should be homogenous in terms of style and content. This is known as

---

[4]http://www.wipo.int/classifications/ipc/en/

[5]http://www.epo.org/about-us/annual-reports-statistics/annual-report/2013/statistics-trends/patent-filings.html

in-domain training data and it is a fundamental requirement of SMT. For instance, if we train an English–French MT system on previously translated automobile manuals, that system will not be useful for translating English chemical patents into French because it will not have seen examples of the style or vocabulary that it will encounter in the patent. While 'out-of-domain' data can be useful to increase lexical coverage or improve fluency, in-domain data is essential at the core of the MT system.

16.3.3 Learning from Previous Translations

Statistical MT systems translate new unseen text by essentially piecing together segments of previously translated sentences. For example, if in our English–Spanish training data we know that 'I have a dog' translates as 'Tengo un perro' and we also know that 'cat' translates as 'gato', then, in theory, we can translate 'I have a cat' as 'Tengo un gato' even though we have not seen that full example in our training data.

In the parallel corpus, we estimate which words correspond to one another based on co-occurrence statistics: how often source and target words appear in the same sentence pair together. This technique, called *word alignment*, is carried out using the Expectation Maximisation algorithm as implemented in the so-called IBM models [7].

A simple example of this process, known as word-based SMT, is illustrated in Fig. 16.1, where, for the parallel corpus on the left, we count how often pairs of words occur together. Then, for a given input sentence, we take the target words with the highest counts (probability) and combine those to produce the final translation.

However, this method has severe drawbacks (which is why the output in the example is not quite correct) as each word is being translated in isolation without any contextual information. To improve on this, heuristics are used to estimate which groups of words, or phrases, correspond to each other [9] and this is used to build the core *translation model*, or *phrase table*. This approach, known as phrase-based SMT, allows the MT system to produce output that has the capacity to capture changes in word order and different variations on words, depending on the context.

The outputs proposed by the translation model are verified by calculating how likely they are to be correct sentences in the target language. This is done using a target *language model* which counts how frequently sequences of words of various length, or *n*-grams, occur in typical use. This combination of the translation model, $p(f|e)$, and the language model, $p(e)$, to produce the most probable translation for an input sentence is Bayes' theorem, as described previously.

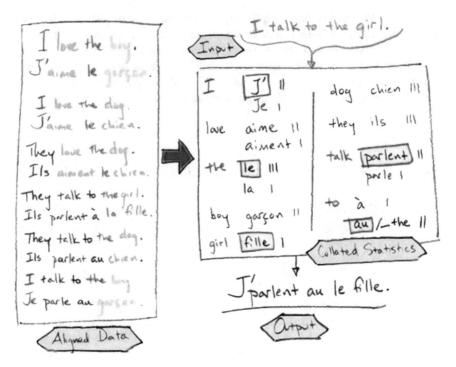

Fig. 16.1 Overview of the parameter estimation and translation process in statistical MT (from http://specgram.com/CLII.4/09.phlogiston.cartoon.iv.html)

16.3.4 Advanced Modelling

In addition to the core translation and language models which focus on the sequential translation of words and phrases, MT systems can incorporate a number of advanced models in order to capture more of the complex phenomena found in language, including the following:

- **Reordering models** (e.g. [10]) try to capture changes in word order between languages during translation. These models are most useful for local or short-distance reordering such as changes in the order of nouns and adjectives between, say, English and Spanish.
- **Factored models** (e.g. [11]) incorporate more linguistic information into the translation process to cater for morphologically rich languages. These models first translate the stem or root of a word and generate the rest of the translation using information such as gender, tense and case, e.g. for English–Spanish translation, 'I went' → 'Go + 1st person + past tense' = 'Ir + 1st person + past tense' → 'Fui'.
- **Syntactic models** (e.g. [12]) employ linguistic information such as context-free grammars to capture structural divergences in statistical models. This approach

can capture more complex phenomena, such as long-distance reordering, but requires additional tools like parsers for language processing.
- **Hierarchical models** (e.g. [13]) make use of pseudo-linguistic structures on top of the phrase-based models. This approach has some of the benefits of syntactic models while also being language independent, i.e. no language-specific parsers or tools are needed to produce the structures.

Any extremely comprehensive overview and subsequent detailed description of these and many other techniques applied in the field can be found in Koehn [14].

16.3.5 State of the Art in MT

The state of the art in MT today sees a convergence of the statistical and rule-based paradigms. These approaches try to combine the benefits of engineering parallel training corpora with linguistic engineering techniques for specific languages and domains. From a commercial MT perspective, different MT systems are deployed depending on the task. For instance, a pure SMT system might suffice from the translation of English–French news stories, whereas for Chinese–English patent translation we need a system that combines a number of rule-based elements that account for both the differences between the two languages and the complex nature of the content being translated (more on this in Sect. 4).

In terms of research, there are a number of topics that have been of particular interest recently due to their potential to increase the value of core MT systems.

16.3.5.1 Domain Adaptation

As we discussed previously, the lack of sufficient relevant training data is a big issue for MT. Current research into domain adaptation (e.g. [15, 16]) explores how we can use and combine data from different domains in a single MT system and for what languages and tasks and with what type of data is this most effective. For example, if we have a small Slovak–English patent MT system, can we use Europarl data to improve translation accuracy? If so, how do we select which portions of the data to use in order to positively affect the system without biasing it?

16.3.5.2 Quality Estimation

If we knew how good MT output quality was for any given input document or language, it would have significant impact on a number of use cases. For instance, if a translator post-editing MT output knew which sentences were translated well in advance, they could choose to only edit those sentences and translate the rest from scratch, thus boosting overall productivity.

For this reason, there is significant research activity around developing methods that estimate or predict the quality of MT on the fly (e.g. [17, 18]) and that can determine the best output given the results from a number of MT systems [19]. Other approaches also try to identify specific segments that the MT system was unsure of, for example, highlighting a specific word in the output that had low estimated quality.

16.3.5.3 Incremental Training

There are a number of strands of research exploring how MT systems can learn from user corrections to improve subsequent translations. Using techniques such as online learning, MT systems can rapidly incorporate post-edits made by translators to update the core translation models (e.g. [20, 21]). This has the benefit of reducing the need for a translator to fix systematic errors and can add new words to the vocabulary of the system.

16.4 Why Is Machine Translation Difficult?

Languages are complex. The grammar rules governing the composition of words and phrases are full of exceptions. This characteristic makes it a fascinating field to study but also makes them difficult to learn. These complexities are magnified for translation because we are dealing with more than one language.

Computers and artificial intelligence thrive on predictability. With machine translation, we try to learn the ways in which a language is used so that we can 'convert' from one to another. The problem is that languages, and the use thereof, are unpredictable. They are constantly evolving and there can be differences in consistency depending on the speaker/author, the audience and many other factors. These elements combine to present a real challenge for MT, and in the remainder of this section, we will look at some specific characteristics of languages that contribute to this challenge.

16.4.1 Ambiguity

Words and phrases can have more than one meaning in a given language, or across languages, depending on the context and the usage. For example, the word 'bank' in English has multiple meanings, while the word 'corner' can be translated a number of different ways into Spanish. Furthermore, consider the following two sentences:

(1) 'Joe saw the man with the telescope'.
(2) 'The farm was used to produce produce'.

In (1), we cannot tell if Joe has the telescope or if the man Joe sees has the telescope. As a human, it is impossible to tell without more contextual information, so this obviously causes an issue for the MT system when it has to determine how to translate it. In (2), the word 'produce' has two different meanings within the same sentence. The first occurrence is a verb and the second is a noun. An MT system will need to have some information about the part of speech (or word class) in order to translate this accurately.

This is why, for more general texts, it is better to have as much training data as possible so that the MT system can learn as many variations of word usage as possible.

16.4.2 Neologisms

Languages are constantly evolving and, as such, new words are being created all the time. Among the most recent additions to the *Oxford English Dictionary*, we have words like 'mouseover' and 'scientificness'. In fact, in March 2014 there were more than 150 new words added to the dictionary.[6] This is especially relevant for patent information where the content is inherently discussing something novel and may include new words. For instance, new chemical names can be created by compounding existing terms.

The challenge for MT here is that these words will not have been seen before in the training data and thus they cannot be translated. MT systems for specific tasks need to be kept up to date through the addition of new terminology.

16.4.3 Synonymy and Flexibility

It is frequently the case that there is more than one way to express the same meaning, e.g. 'New York', 'NYC' or 'The Big Apple' or 'car', 'automobile' or 'vehicle'. When translating these words, the MT system again has to have seen all variations in the training data. Similarly, when translating from another language, the MT system has to choose the most appropriate variation of these words in English.

This flexibility in how we can make choices about the use of certain words can be expanded to phrases and even sentence structure. Take, for example, the Chinese sentence in Fig. 16.2 and the ten possible English translations. All of these translations carry the same meaning and no one translation is less accurate than the other. While this provides the MT system some flexibility itself, the big challenge this phenomenon actually poses MT developers and users is how to

---

[6]http://public.oed.com/the-oed-today/recent-updates-to-the-oed/march-2014-update/new-words-list-march-2014/

这个 机场 的 安全 工作 由 以色列 方面 负责 .

Israeli officials are responsible for airport security.

Israel is in charge of the security at this airport.

The security work for this airport is the responsibility of the Israel government.

Israeli side was in charge of the security of this airport.

Israel is responsible for the airport's security.

Israel is responsible for safety work at this airport.

Israel presides over the security of the airport.

Israel took charge of the airport security.

The safety of this airport is taken charge of by Israel.

This airport's security is the responsibility of the Israeli security officials.

Fig. 16.2 Ten possible English translations for a single Chinese sentence. Taken from [14]

evaluate the quality. If ten different MT systems produced these translations, how do we determine which system performs best? We discuss this further in Sect. 4.5.

16.4.4 Structural Divergence

One of the most significant characteristics of language that presents a challenge for (machine) translation is the fact that different languages simply construct sentences in different ways. In terms of word order, some languages are *subject–object–verb* (Japanese, German), some are *subject–verb–object* (English, Russian), while others are *verb–subject–object* (Arabic, Irish). Languages also have different morphology, from agglutinative languages like Turkish to inflected languages like Greek. We then have various other phenomena such as noun compounding (German), mixed writing scripts (Japanese) and languages that do not delimit between words in written text (Chinese, Japanese).

In general, the closer two languages are in terms of their linguistic typology, the 'easier' they are for MT. This is why MT quality is better for some languages (English–French) than others (English–Japanese). Even within languages, this can vary from text to text, depending on the content. If we look at the three examples in Fig. 16.3, we get a sense of the varying degree of difficulty.

In the first example, between English and Spanish, the work order is relatively close aside from a single noun–adjective reordering. Much of the rest of the sentence is almost a direct word for word translation, so we might expect a well-trained phrase-based SMT system to produce very accurate output.

In the second sentence, between English and German, again the word order is relatively similar in general, but there is a more significant long-distance reordering in which the German verb is moved to the end (because it is a *subject–object–verb*

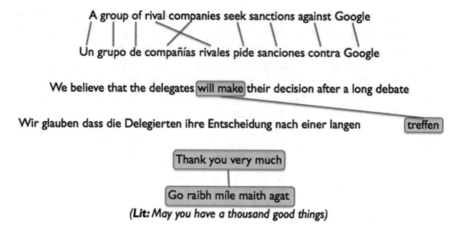

Fig. 16.3 Different levels of divergence in word order between languages

language). In order to capture this, the MT system will need to have some linguistic information in the form of syntax-based rules in order to know what word to reorder and to where.

In the final example, between English and Irish, the translation is completely non-literal. Similar problems are found with idioms which do not necessarily correspond across languages. Such examples typically need to be handled as exceptions by MT systems.

16.4.5   Evaluating Machine Translation

There are a number of different ways to measure the quality of the output produced by MT systems, each of which has its relative merits and drawbacks. These approaches can be broadly categorised in two ways: automatic evaluation and human evaluation.

16.4.5.1   Automatic Evaluation

Automatic evaluation involves the use of algorithms to judge the quality of an MT system by comparing its output against a human-produced reference translation. These algorithms—implemented in tools such as BLEU [22], METEOR [23] and GTM [24], among others—use a variety of measures based on precision and recall to calculate the similarity between the output and the reference, such as the number of words (or *n*-grams) in common, the difference in length or how many alterations (substitutions, deletions, insertions) need to be made to the MT output so that it matches the reference(s).

Automatic metrics have the advantage of being very quick and cheap to run, as well as producing consistent results. Because of this, they are widely used both in academia and in industry. However, the problems start with the concept we introduced in Sect. 4.3, that there is not always a single correct translation. We need multiple reference translations to overcome this, but these are frequently not available. Similarly, these metrics cannot be used for new input where we do not have a reference translation (which is an issue that quality estimation research, cf. Sect. 3.5.2, is trying to overcome).

Finally, the scores produced by these metrics do not really hold any meaning on their own. For example, knowing that an MT system had a BLEU score of 50 (out of 100) on a particular set of test documents does not tell us anything. These scores are only effective for comparative purposes, for example, assessing the improvement of an MT system over time or comparing two systems to see which is better on the same test set.

This is why, ultimately, human input is required at some point in the MT system development process.

16.4.5.2 Human Evaluation

Human evaluation involves the manual assessment of MT output, typically by a bilingual evaluator. It is often employed at more critical stages in the MT development cycle to validate automatic evaluation results, for instance, prior to launching a production system or, from the end-user perspective, to inform a buying decision.

This approach can take a number of forms including rating the output on a scale to indicate how grammatical it is (fluency) or how well it conveys the main meaning from the source text (adequacy). It can also include more detailed error analyses and benchmarking against other MT systems.

While this approach is obviously robust and flexible, it is a slow and expensive process and, frequently, multiple evaluators are required in order to smooth out any subjectivity in the findings. More recent approaches [25] have sought to overcome some of the drawbacks of human evaluation by taking a crowdsourcing approach using services such as Amazon's Mechanical Turk with relative success.

In order to extract the most value from human evaluation, however, it is advised to design more focused task-based evaluations based on the proposed end use of the MT output.

16.4.5.3 Task-Based Evaluation

The most important aspect to determine when evaluating an MT system is not necessarily how good the output is in absolute terms, but rather whether it is fit for its intended purpose. This relates to the notion that a translation that appears to be well formed on the surface (high fluency) may not actually contain all of the

Table 16.1 Fluency vs. adequacy in MT evaluation

Source (Spanish)	La gran casa roja (*translation: 'the big red house'*)
MT Output 1	The big blue house
MT Output 2	The big house red

information from the original source document. For example, in the translations in Table 16.1, MT Output 1 is perfectly fluent, but has the wrong translation of an important descriptive term. MT Output 2 is not completely fluent, but it conveys all of the correct meaning in the original document. This is why it is important to carry out a task-based evaluation rather than simply assessing the readability of the output.

Evaluation methodologies should be designed based on what the MT output will be used for. In the case of patent machine translation for documents retrieved during search, evaluations should seek to determine whether an expert reader can understand the key technical aspects of the text and whether or not it is relevant to their search. They should not overly focus on fluency or minor grammatical errors.

Similarly, when the end use for MT output is a task such as post-editing, rather than attempting to assess the fluency and adequacy, the evaluation should focus on quantifying the productivity gains (if any) from using MT.

These task-based evaluations can serve to feedback into a more task-driven optimisation of the baseline MT systems. We introduce some specific tasks and use cases in Sect. 6.

16.5   The Challenge of Patents

A controlled language, e.g. controlled English, is a subset of the full language with restricted grammar and vocabulary designed to make content more understandable by reducing complexity and ambiguity. Many years of research were carried out specifically in the field of controlled language for machine translation aimed at determining a set of guidelines and rules for authoring content that would be suitable for MT. Patents do not comply with the majority of these rules.

Patents are highly technical in nature and often make use of established formulations, for example, when authoring claims which typically include some preamble, a transitional phrase ('consisting of', 'comprising') and a set of limitations.[7] However, as discussed by Rossi and Wiggins [26], it is not necessarily these characteristics that present a challenge for MT development but rather the extreme syntactic complexity of the sentences in patents which violate most of the controlled language guidelines. This is principally a consequence of the freedom afforded to patent drafters when writing documents which reduces the consistency even among patents in the same technical field.

---

[7]http://www.uspto.gov/web/offices/pac/mpep/s2111.html

Table 16.2, modified from [26], presents a number of specific controlled language rules with which patents do not comply. These rules are taken from both general controlled language literature (e.g. [27]) and controlled language which has been specifically proposed to improve MT (e.g. [28, 29]).

It is unlikely that the manner in which patents are authored will change substantially in a way that will better suit MT. To that end, MT developers must accept the fact that these are the characteristics of patents and develop MT systems accordingly.

16.5.1 Developing MT Systems for Patents

In order to overcome the inherent challenges posed by patents, MT systems need to be aware of and account for many of the very specific characteristics across technical fields. The approach to adapting MT for a specific domain by training the systems on relevant *in-domain* data, as described before, will not suffice alone. In this case, MT needs to go beyond data engineering and exploit training and translation processes that focus specifically on patents. These characteristics will vary across languages, so in this respect language presents its own unique challenge for patent MT training and must be considered too.

Figure 16.4 illustrates the basic data-driven approach to MT training and translation augmented with patent-specific processing steps. These steps can include a large variety of processes, including, but not limited to:

- The identification and tagging of chemical names for separate handling (across different languages)
- The splitting of long sentences into smaller more 'translatable' segments
- The application of templates for the translation of formulaic elements
- The management of letter case when translating patent titles
- On-the-fly subdomain identification to prefer specific translation models and terminology, e.g. separating translation models based on the IPC codes

There is a large body of (ongoing) research focused on developing such adaptations to existing MT technology for the patent domain. The NTCIR project[8] at the National Institute of Informatics in Japan has run information retrieval workshops since 1999 with a strong focus on patent search. In more recent editions, a patent MT shared task with a focus on English–Chinese and English–Japanese was added. Participants are encouraged to implement novel approaches to patent MT which are then assessed during both human and task-based evaluations.

---

[8]http://research.nii.ac.jp/ntcir/index-en.html

Table 16.2 Controlled language rules violated by patents (modified from [26])

Rule	Rule notes	In patents . . .
Sentences should be short	Around 25–30 words	Patent sentences are usually very long, a single sentence can be up to 500 or more words
Sentences should be grammatically complete	Sentences should not be written in telegraphic or nominal style, they should not lack a subject or a verb	Patents often make use of nominal or telegraphic style, especially in titles
Sentences should use the active form	Passive forms are more difficult for an MT system to deal with	Passive forms are preferred in patents as in other scientific texts
Sentences should have a simple syntax	The usage of gerunds, past participles, relative clauses and other implicit constructions is a source of ambiguity for MT	Patents make use of formal and legal language, which is rich in gerunds, participles, relative and other subordinate clauses
Sentences should express one idea only	Combining more ideas in the same sentence has the natural consequence of complicating its grammatical structure	Patent abstracts, some parts of descriptions and claims concatenate many ideas in the same sentence
Spelling should be correct	Incorrectly spelt words are not matched against any of the words which might be found in a rule-based MT system dictionary or in a statistical machine translation phrase table	Spelling mistakes are inevitable in the authoring of such long and complex texts. Another source of this type of error is that fact that many patents in electronic format have been produced using OCR which often introduces errors into the final text
Lexical choice should be limited to a predefined dictionary, synonymy should be limited, polysemy avoided	When words are known to the MT systems, quality and fluency both increase. The more different the words chosen in the source text, the higher the chance that some of those are not known to the system	The patent terminology scope covers all areas of human knowledge and is exponentially growing, due to the 'innovative' nature of patents. What is described in patents is 'new' by definition, and neologisms are often created in order to express specific new concepts It is also not uncommon to find multiple concepts in the same domain indicating the same (synonymy) as well as the same concept across different domains with different meanings (polysemy)
Punctuation should be used carefully and meaningfully	Commas, colons, semicolons and full stops should be strictly used according to the rules of the source language	Use of punctuation is often not correct in patent texts, causing ambiguity in interpretation

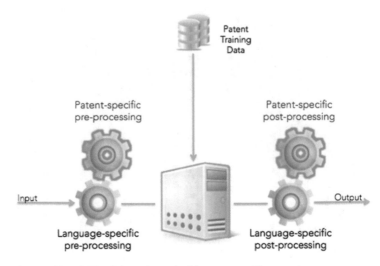

Fig. 16.4 Data-driven MT training enhanced with patent-specific processes

This workshop has spawned a number of interesting approaches to tackling patent MT, including hierarchical MT [30], syntax-based MT [31], the use of syntactic information to change word order to increase the convergences between English and Japanese [32] and the use of external technical dictionaries [33]. Similarly, the Workshop on Patent Translation[9] is a regular event designed to attract research specific to patent MT.

In addition to these scheduled events, there have been a number of other initiatives aimed at adapting MT technology for patents. The World Intellectual Property Organization (WIPO) has been working since 2007[10] on developing machine translation and cross-language IR (CLIR) tools for their patent search service Patentscope. This has led to the release of a number of language tools, including an MT service, adapted for translation of patent titles and abstracts [34].

Similarly, the EU FP7 project PLuTO, which ran from 2010 to 2013, brought together a consortium of industry and academic partners to adapt existing technologies for patent translation. This project led to the development and launch of the patent machine translation provider, Iconic Translation Machines[11] [35].

---

[9]http://www.mtsummit2013.info/workshop1.asp

[10]http://www.wipo.int/edocs/mdocs/mdocs/en/wipo_patscope_ge_13/wipo_patscope_ge_13_2.ppt

[11]http://www.iconictranslation.com

16.6 Use Cases for Machine Translation for Patent Information

As we have shown in the previous section, there is a lot of interest in patent MT in both research and commercial circles. This is due in part to the fact that MT technology has reached a level of maturity whereby it can have many practical industrial applications beyond anecdotal or spot translations. This is particularly the case in the patent information community where the potential benefits of MT have long been espoused due to the inherently multilingual nature of content in this area.

In the following, we describe some of these applications along with examples of initiatives that are already underway.

16.6.1 Facilitating Patent Search

One of the principal use cases for MT is as a support tool for patent information specialists and other parties who carry out searches. There are three ways in which MT can be used in this regard.

16.6.1.1 On-Demand Translation

Patent searchers have the ability to retrieve results in foreign languages based on translations of the titles and abstracts. However, the full text in these cases is only available in the original language. On-demand MT allows searchers to translate these documents on the fly and gain a deeper understanding of the content.

Examples of such a service can be found in the EPO's Espacenet offering,[12] which integrates with the Google Translate[13] API and allows users of the tool to translate documents in the EPO collection into multiple languages, predominantly the official languages of the EPO member states.

The approach has the advantage that the patent data provider does not need to store and index vast amounts of documents in multiple languages. Also, as the MT systems are updated and improved, all subsequent translations benefit from this. However, end users still cannot search on the full-text documents and the computational resources required to deliver such a service are extensive.

---

[12]http://www.espacenet.com

[13]http://translate.google.com

16.6.1.2   Query Translation

To overcome the issue described above, there are two ways in which users can be facilitating in searching full-text patent collections in multiple languages. The first method uses an approach called query translation (also, keyword translation), whereby the search terms are machine translated across languages and used to carry out a native search on multilingual patent databases. This approach—an instance of CLIR, as implemented in WIPO's Patentscope service[14]—is then used in conjunction with an on-demand MT service to translate the resulting foreign language documents returned by the search.

16.6.1.3   Bulk Translation

The need for on-demand and query translation can be eliminated by using MT to pre-translate entire full-text collections into multiple languages and indexing them for search. This approach, known as bulk or batch translation, allows all users to search and retrieve documents in their own language without the need for on-the-fly translation and has been implemented in a number of commercial search offerings, e.g. PatBase.[15]

However, there are a few issues associated with this approach. Firstly, as mentioned previously, there is a significant overhead involved in storing multiple versions of the patent collections across languages. Secondly, the MT quality is fixed at the capability of the chosen MT system at the time of translation. It is not practical to retranslate all of the patents each time the MT system improves (which could be frequently). Finally, despite the 'once-off' nature of this approach, there is still a need for ongoing translation of new patent records.

16.6.2   Professional Translator Productivity

Looking at the wider translation industry, MT is increasingly being used by language service providers and professional translators as a tool to increase productivity and reduce overall translation times [36]. This is done through a process called post-editing, whereby, rather than translate sentences from scratch, a translator will use the MT output as a first draft and modify it to produce the final translation.

The consequences of this will percolate to users of patent information who are frequently also buyers of professional translation services. They will begin to see increasingly more competitive offerings from language service providers who will be able to turn around larger translation jobs in a shorter space of time.

---

[14]http://www.wipo.int/patentscope/en/news/pctdb/2010/news_0002.html

[15]http://www.patbase.com/wnewinfo.asp?i=155&cc=fulltext

16.7   Conclusions

We introduced this chapter by presenting the need for machine translation, particularly in the area of patent translation, before introducing some of the basic concepts behind the more commonly used approaches. We then presented a number of topics that are of particular interest to the research community today and showed how they can improve upon the current state of the art.

The inherent complex nature of language means that MT is a hard problem to tackle. The problems of language for MT are exacerbated in patents which contrive to combine many of the characteristics that cause issues for MT systems. However, MT research has taken big strides over the past decade to the extent that there are real-world practical applications for appropriate development solutions. That is to imply that MT developed for a specific purpose, as opposed to general solutions, e.g. online MT tools, can bring significant value to end users. This is especially the case for patent information where a number of these applications have been put into practice and are used extensively on a daily basis.

This trend of adoption is only going to continue upwards as the technology improves and MT output becomes even more usable. Existing initiatives, as well as those planned, will ensure that this will also remain the case within the patent information community for the foreseeable future.

References

1. World Intellectual Property Organization (2013) PCT yearly review: the international patent system. WIPO, Geneva
2. Federmann C (2012) Hybrid machine translation using joint, binarised feature vectors. In: Proceedings of the 20th conference of the association for machine translation in the Americas. Association for Machine Translation in the Americas, San Diego
3. Machery W, Och FJ (2007) An empirical study on computing consensus translations from multiple machine translation systems. In: Proceedings of the 2007 joint conference on empirical methods in natural language processing and computational natural language learning (EMNLP-CoNLL). Association for Computational Linguistics, Prague, pp 986–995
4. Koehn P (2005) Europarl: a parallel corpus for statistical machine translation. In: Proceedings of the 10th machine translation summit, Phuket, pp 79–86
5. Lu B, Ka Pow C, Tsou BK (2011) The cultivation of a trilingual Chinese-English-Japanese parallel corpus from comparable patents. In: Proceedings of machine translation summit XIII, Xiamen, pp 472–479
6. Lu B, Tsou BK, Tao J, Oi Yee K, Zhu J (2010) Mining large-scale parallel corpora from multilingual patents: an English-Chinese example and its application to SMT. In: Proceedings of the 1st CIPS-SIGHAN joint conference on Chinese language processing (CLP-2010), Beijing, pp 79–86
7. Brown PF, Cocke J, Della-Pietra SA, Della-Pietra VJ, Jelinek F, Mercer RL et al (1988) A statistical approach to language translation. In: Proceedings of the 12th international conference on computational linguistics (CoLing). John von Neumann Society for Computing Sciences, Budapest, pp 71–76

8. Gale WA, Church KW (1991) A program for aligning sentences in bilingual corpora. In: Proceedings of the 29th annual meeting of the association for computational linguistics, Berkeley, pp 177–184
9. Och FJ, Ney H (2003) A systematic comparison of various statistical alignment models. Comput Linguist 29(1):19–51
10. Tillmann C (2004) A unigram orientation model for statistical machine translation. In: Proceedings of human language technology conference and North American chapter of the association for computational linguistics annual meeting (HLT-NAACL), Boston, pp 101–104
11. Koehn P, Hoang H (2007) Factored translation models. In: Proceedings of the 2007 joint conference on empirical methods in natural language processing and computational natural language learning, Prague, pp 868–876
12. Quirk C, Menezes A, Cherry C (2005) Dependency treelet translation: syntactically informed phrasal SMT. In: 43rd Annual meeting of the association for computational linguistics, Ann Arbour, pp 271–279
13. Chiang D (2005) A hierarchical phrase-based model for statistical machine translation. 43rd Annual meeting of the association for computational linguistics, Ann Arbour, pp 263–270
14. Koehn P (2010) Statistical machine translation. Cambridge University Press, Cambridge
15. Banerjee P, Rubino R, Roturier J, van Genabith J (2013) Quality estimation-guided data selection for domain adaptation of SMT. In: Proceedings of the 14th machine translation summit, Nice, pp 101–108
16. Haddow B, Koehn P (2012) Analysing the effect of out-of-domain data on SMT systems. In: 7th workshop on statistical machine translation, Montreal, pp 422–432
17. Specia L, Raj D, Turchi M (2010) Machine translation evaluation versus quality estimation. Machine Transl 24(1):39–50
18. Ueffing N, Ney H (2005) Word-class confidence estimation for machine translation using phrase-based translation models. In: Proceedings of human technology conference and conference on empirical methods in natural language processing, Vancouver, pp 763–770
19. He Y, Ma Y, van Genabith J, Way A (2010) Bridging SMT and TM with translation recommendation. In: The 48th annual meeting of the association for computational linguistics (ACL), Uppsala, pp 622–630
20. Mathur P, Cettolo M, Federico M (2013) Online learning approaches in computer assisted translation. In: 8th workshop on statistical machine translation, Sofia, pp 301–308
21. Potet M, Esperança-Rodier E, Blanchon H, Besacier L (2011) Preliminary experiments on using users' post-editions to enhance a SMT system. In: Proceedings of the 15th international conference of the European association for machine translation (EAMT), Leuven, pp 161–168
22. Papineni K, Roukos S, Ward T, Zhu W-J (2002) BLEU: a method for automatic evaluation of machine translation. In: Proceedings of 40th annual meeting of the association for computational linguistics (ACL), Philadelphia, pp 311–318
23. Banerjee S, Lavie A (2005) METEOR: an automatic metric for MT evaluation with improved correlation with human judgments. In: Proceedings of the ACLT workshop on intrinsic and extrinsic evaluation measures for machine translation and/or summarization, Ann Arbor, pp 65–72
24. Turian JP, Shen L, Melamed ID (2003) Evaluation of machine translation and its evaluation. In: Proceedings of the 10th machine translation summit, New Orleans, pp 386–393
25. Callison-Burch C (2009) Fast, cheap, and creative: evaluating translation quality using Amazon's Mechanical Turk. In: Proceedings of the 2009 conference on empirical methods in natural language processing, Singapore, pp 286–295
26. Rossi L, Wiggins D (2013) Applicability and application of machine translation quality metrics in the patent field. World Pat Inf 35(2):115–125
27. O'Brien S (2003) Controlling controlled English: an analysis of several controlled language rule sets. In: The joint conference of the 8th international workshop of the European association for machine translation and the 4th controlled language applications workshop, Dublin, pp 105–114

28. Mügge U (2006) Fully automatic high quality machine translation of restricted text: a case study. In: Proceedings of the 28th international conference on translating and the computer, London
29. Roturier J (2006) An investigation into the impact of controlled English rules on the comprehensibility, usefulness, and acceptability of machine translated technical documentation for French and German users. Unpublished PhD Thesis, Dublin City University
30. Xiong H, Song L, Meng F, Lü Y, Liu Q (2011) The ICT's patent MT system description for NTCIR-9. In: Proceedings of NTCIR-9 workshop meeting, Tokyo
31. Wu X, Matsuzaki T, Tsujii J (2011) SMT systems in the University of Tokyo for NTCIR-9 PatentMT. In: Proceedings of NTCIR-9 workshop meeting, Tokyo
32. Na H, Li J-J, Kim S-J, Lee J-H (2011) POSTECH's statistical machine translation systems for NTCIR-9 PatentMT task (English-to-Japanese). In: Proceedings of NTCIR-9 workshop meeting, Tokyo
33. Wu P, Xu J, Yin Y, Zhang Y (2013) System description of BJTU-NLP MT for NTCIR-10 PatentMT. In: Proceedings of the 10th NTCIR conference on evaluation of information access technologies, Tokyo
34. Pouliquen B, Mazenc C (2011) COPPA, CLIR and TAPTA: three tools to assist in overcoming the patent barrier at WIPO. In: MT summit XIII: the thirteenth machine translation summit, Xiamen, pp 5–12
35. Tinsley J, Ceausu A, Zhang J, Depraetere H, Van de Walle J (2012) IPTranslator: facilitating patent search with machine translation. In: The tenth biennial conference of the association for machine translation in the Americas, San Diego
36. DePalma DA, Pielmeier H (2013) Great expectations for post-edited MT. Common Sense Advisory

Chapter 17
Future Patent Search

Barrou Diallo and Mihai Lupu

Abstract In this chapter we make some predictions for patent search in about 10 years' time—in 2026. We base these predictions on the contents of the earlier part of the book, the observed differences between this second edition and the first edition of the book as well as on some data and trends not well represented in the book (for one reason or another). We consider primarily incorporating knowledge of different sorts of patent search into the patent search process; utilising knowledge of the subject domain of the search into the patent search system; utilising multiple sources of data within the search system; the need to address the requirement to deal with multiple languages in patent search; and the need to provide effective visualisation of the results of patent searches. We conclude the real need is to find ways to support search independent of language or location.

17.1   Introduction

In this chapter we will try to move from the reviews of current professional practice in patent search and of recent relevant scientific research to try to foresee how the field will develop in the medium-term future. In particular we will try to see how changes in available technology will impact the tools available to patent professionals and the issues and pressures which will inhibit or accelerate these changes.

We are writing this chapter 5 years after the first edition of this book, and therefore we will also take a look at how existing technologies have already affected

---

The content of this article does not represent the opinion of Dr. Diallo's employer. Views expressed are solely those of the author in his private capacity.

B. Diallo (✉)
European Patent Office, Patentlaan 2, 2288 EE Rijswijk, The Netherlands
e-mail: barrou@diallo.biz

M. Lupu
TU Wien, Vienna, Austria
e-mail: mihai.lupu@tuwien.ac.at; lupu@ifs.tuwien.ac.at

© Springer-Verlag GmbH Germany 2017
M. Lupu et al. (eds.), *Current Challenges in Patent Information Retrieval*,
The Information Retrieval Series 37, DOI 10.1007/978-3-662-53817-3_17

patent search. Some things will have remained the same, particularly those related to the nature of the task and the required output.

One of the characteristics of patent search by professional searchers outside the patent offices, which has not changed in the last half decade and is in fact unlikely to change soon, is that it is usually driven by briefs from strategic-level business managers or by patent attorneys, and it aims to produce a report summarising the facts about a particular area. For example, whether a particular device may infringe one or more existent patents, or the likelihood that one could in principle produce a new substance of a particular type which neither infringes existing patents nor has been previously published, and therefore may be legitimately patented. Present-day systems rely on the searcher bringing together the data from several sources (e.g. patent databases, academic journal collections and legal information sources) in a coherent whole, in an essentially unsupported manner: future systems will explicitly provide support.

Perhaps the biggest challenge here is integrating the search systems with corporate and enterprise information systems (whether science and technology support or business systems), especially given the move of patent search from being an in-house operation to being outsourced. Generalised outsourcing operations are unlikely to have access to the quality of information in-house operations would have. Further, they are unlikely to be given access to the full range of confidential information available in-house.

Of course, this focuses on patent search from a technology user's point of view, whether it be the inventor, companies seeking freedom to operate or strategic business managers. Another important group of users of patent search systems consists of the patent offices themselves. Necessarily, a patent examiner in a patent office has different needs from a commercial searcher, and future integrated systems, which better reflect searchers' needs and workflows, will inevitably therefore be different to some degree. More automated, information-rich and task-aware patent search systems can help patent offices achieve a particular implicit goal of the patent offices: to increase the volume of applications dealt with by an examiner, while simultaneously improving the quality of the granted patents. This is certainly an effective way to address THE key challenge facing patent offices: reducing the time between application and grant or rejection while improving the quality and in particular the defensibility of the granted patents.

The intellectual property (IP) community sees the principal issues to be the backlog of unexamined applications and the costs associated with the granting process. But it is generally acknowledged there is little real benefit in rapidly obtaining a patent which cannot be enforced in court, or which promotes lengthy and complex litigation. This will not be in the interests of inventors, patent holders or intending technology exploiters. Better technological support for the search process can allow quality to be improved while reducing time-to-grant and human effort in review.

Further, some patents currently granted are of suspect validity because of the weakness of past practices in searching non-English patent data (disproportionately growing as a proportion of the whole, especially in Asia). This leaves aside the rarity of searching of non-English non-patent public data for evidence of lack of novelty.

Having the possibility to obtain information is not equivalent to reviewing and understanding the underlying information. As discussed elsewhere in this volume, the reasons for performing a patent search are multiple. The most obvious is to determine whether or not an applicant can get a patent or if its invention has already been patented. Other reasons might include:

- Getting an idea of how an application and patent are drafted to help in the preparation of a new application
- Learning more about a new technical field
- For competitive market information and tracking

17.2 Patent Search in 2026

Five years ago we identified six points that we expected should happen by 2021. In 10 years' time we expected to see patent search systems with a number of characteristics not present in today's search systems. We briefly repeat below the ideas from 5 years ago, together with very short notes given our current state of knowledge. Later, in Sect. 17.3 we show a more general view of the current state of the art, followed by detailed descriptions of five of the six directions.

2011 Statement	2016 Observations
1. There will be a reflection of the different sorts of patent search task, their differing characteristics and integrated tools which reflect the domain: chemical versus mechanical versus telecoms and so on and event-driven legal status searches versus document content-driven searches	On the matter of domain specificity, there has been some uptake in academia [51]. However, while domains with large differences (e.g. chemical vs. business processes) contain different processing pipeline components, domains where the difference lies predominantly on the informant users side (rather than document content) are harder to distinguish

2. Systems will provide access to both patent and non-patent literature in a single integrated environment. There will also be a firm separation between data and the systems used to access it—so that several data sources (we avoid the term databases) can be accessed by the searcher within a single search and analysis environment	We see already significant steps in this direction, as pointed out in Chap. 8 earlier in this book, as well as by the continuous increase in data made available by patent offices via public APIs. Accessing data via Web services has become a standard [18, 81, 90]
3. The tools will be inherently multilingual—allowing the English-speaking patent searcher to deal with Chinese data more or less as easily as English, for example	Chapter 16 showed earlier the kind of progress already made in the direction of translation services specifically catering to patent data. After 10 years of research, cross-lingual patent search has become a standard [69, 88, 89]
4. Complex visualisations will be provided to support not only specialist tasks like technology landscape mapping but also to help the searcher focus their attention and effort on the most productive parts of the inevitably large results sets in some forms of search. Currently some products focus their efforts in knowledge exploration [5] and correlation	There is still a lot of research in this direction, as evidenced by the report in Chap. 10. On top of this, recent technology developments in 3D visualisations and immersive interfaces will move within the next 5 to 10 years from exciting curiosities to practical tools for large data exploration
5. There will be support for collaborative working both groups working in a single location (via, e.g. complex interactive visualisations) and at a distance with advanced support for interaction through video, whiteboards and multiply viewed screens, all of which are available now within applications, but not integrated and adapted to the patent search task	Indeed, the enabling technologies are today, 5 years after the writing of this statement, better positioned to allow users to interact at a distance. The extent to which they will find their way into patent search products depends on the innovation ability of each product maker
6. Multiple forms of query and document sorting will be available: for example, pile sorting metaphors as well as simple keyword and Boolean search	Technology-wise, this is already available. The integration in commercial systems follows the requirements of the users. We no longer follow this thread separately in this chapter, but rather include it under points **1.** and **4.** above

We will touch on all these issues in the rest of chapter, going into more depth for some and greater depth in others, largely driven by the clarity we feel can be brought to the issues at the time of writing. The five issues interrelate to each other in a rather complex way, so we will use them as overarching themes, rather than as a rigid framework with which to structure the discussion.

17.3 Current State of the Art

In 1999 Larkey [43] produced a paper on what was seen at the time as being a state of the art in patent search technology, and since then many efforts have been made to help patent practitioners making use of patent data to perform their job. They have moved from a digitalised set of patent files to suites of toolboxes allowing them to mine into the data and find information as described by Abbas, Zhang and Khan [1]. Fifteen years ago, it was all about searching. Nowadays, it is about finding, and finding (ideally) only the relevant documents which would allow professionals to analyse content and take final decisions. Many commercial providers [74] have gathered and organised subsets of patent collection and offered computerised access to large companies and administrations. In particular, software suites available from Thompson (i.e. Derwent, Delphion, Micropatent), Questel Orbit, LexisNexis Univentio or IP.com are popular in the community of patent searchers. The whole list of software producers specialised in patents is available from the PIUG.[1] Dou [14] and Hunt, Nguyen and Rodgers [34] provided an exhaustive analysis of their use. Nevertheless, as explained in Simmons' article [71], the value of data is to be correlated to its quality, which is itself correlated to the power of the computer (tools) to exploit them.

As well as commercial offerings, there are also many advanced search engines which have been developed and offered at the disposal of the general public and companies, including:

- EPO Espacenet
- USPTO patent full-text and full-page image databases
- Intellectual property digital library of WIPO
- SIPO patent search and translation
- KIPRIS search service
- Google patent search

For most patent searchers, a mixture of high-quality data sources from the commercial publishing sector and free-of-charge data, typically mounted under relatively unsophisticated search engines, represents the current state of the art in terms of day-to-day practice.

---

[1] See http://www.piug.org/vendors.php.

However, in considering the state of the art, one needs to make an important distinction between invalidity (or validity) searches and topic or subject matter searches, like state of the art or freedom to operate (see Chap. 1 of this volume).

Invalidity search describes a search triggered by a particular patent application or granted patent against all prior art in a field. It is not limited to a traditional database retrieval exercise but extends to all forms of documentation or disclosure potentially invalidating the claims of the patent application (patentability, novelty factors). Subject matter searches concern searching of a topic in a particular document collection and frequently start with the patent literature, although they may involve the use of non-patent literature at a later stage. Advanced tools have been developed for technology intelligence, for instance [93].

The two kinds of searches exhibit slightly different characteristics. For instance, Fujita et al. [26] have proven that the length of the patent document affects relevance in invalidity searches (verbosity hypothesis—the hypothesis that the length of the document is due to the fact that the authors use many words to express one thing and therefore a high normalisation factor must be introduced), whereas it doesn't in topic searches (scope hypothesis—the hypothesis that the length of the document is due to the fact that the authors talk about several topics in the document and therefore a low normalisation factor must be introduced). This work has shown that the verbosity factor (the length) provides a stronger protection for the patent in the view of rights claimed and is more likely to be relevant to a particular search, since rights claimed are likely to have a broader scope. If documents are considered as being relevant to a topic, then the issue is to demonstrate that they are similar to each other (similar characteristics). This refers to the 'cluster hypothesis' described by van Rijsbergen [83]. In a nutshell, a set of documents being relevant to a query should display some kind of similarity. Current retrieval strategies are based on that assumption, which can be tested [84]. Practically, the cluster hypothesis (at least in its simpler forms) is never fully the case and previous experiments have shown that, for example, cluster-based searches were not effective. One reason may be the vocabulary mismatch problem [27]. The consequence of a weak cluster hypothesis is the possible endangering of the relevance feedback mechanisms [54] as in that case, relevant documents might be more similar to non-relevant documents. Remember, relevance feedback assumes that relevant documents have in common some terms (which are not included in the query) and that these terms distinguish the relevant documents from the rest of the collection. Similar should mean relevant, if the cluster hypothesis is correct.

Earlier studies have revealed some other facts about the patent space [24, 25, 87]. Because the set of documents exposed to a patent searcher is usually too large to be analysed on an individual basis, professionals have developed strategies to both extrapolate a meta-understanding of the underlying data (e.g. through multiple successive queries) and reduce logically the size of the corpus under investigation. Experience shows that practical risk minimisation exercises do work, in the case of database exploration/walking, if focused into a precisely defined technical domain. Patent engineers and examiners, working on a daily basis over large sets of documents, learn some 'meta-information' about the collection, which may be translated into searching strategies. They can then use their meta-information to make better informed judgements about the value of continuing (or resuming) their search at a particular point, as opposed to turning their attention to a more promising avenue of search. Searching similar documents in a corpus is an iterative process, where relevant documents are a priori accessible, thus enabling patent searchers to converge towards their target. Azzopardi [6] has observed that accessibility to the whole collection of data through a search engine is by no means guaranteed by current technology. He demonstrated that a residual set of data is consistently not 'visible' to searchers, independently from the query language and the system. That means yet another hypothesis to be tested in the case of patents, where such a bias could be challenging. Patent searchers are even more concerned with this problem of *findability* than general searchers, because of their regular use of several databases concurrently. Nevertheless, the overall Boolean search process is guided by a set of logical operators allowing them to apply some sort of intuitive reasoning coupled to a firm knowledge of the querying language. Earlier in Chap. 7, Bashir and Rauber investigated the issue of findability and its relation with retrieval effectiveness for the specific case of patent collections. A new paradigm taking this study further would involve not only new searching tools but new relations towards the machine's output as well.

Making the machine attempt reasoning instead of the user is a revolution to come. What are required are mechanisms to allow the patent searcher to make judgements about the reliability of the search system: we call this *searcher trust*. In the end, searcher trust in a system is all about being able to analyse, understand and confront output results in a logical, systematic way. Achieving such trust would require explanations of the internal processing mechanism leading the displayed results to be accessible and comprehensible to the searcher [28].

Further, as reflected in the previous chapters of this book as well as those of the previous edition [50], patent search has become an active area of research in recent years. More broadly, analysis and processing of patents has become a research field per se and has been recognised as such by major stakeholders: the community of users [4], the patent offices performing internal research [31], the software developers and the academics [29, 49]. As early as 2000, the ACM SIGIR conference addressed the subject in a special workshop on patent retrieval.[2]

Subsequently (as reported in Chaps. 3 and 4 in this book) international research campaigns have taken place every few years to benchmark the effectiveness of the latest prototypes against agreed quantitative measures [16]. The NTCIR [26, 35] evaluation campaigns in Japan, as an example, were the first to clearly address the issue of patent analysis and search as a research challenge. Other evaluation campaigns focused on patent-related issues have been run as part of TREC[3] or CLEF.[4]

---

[2]See http://www.sigir.org/files/forum/S2000/Patent_report.pdf.

[3]See http://trec.nist.gov.

[4]See http://clef.iei.pi.cnr.it.

These activities have led to the public availability of (admittedly limited) sets of patent data, standardised queries and assessments of the relevance of retrieved documents.

Stimulated by the information retrieval facility (IRF), between 2008 and 2011, the ACM Conference on Information and Knowledge Management has included a series of workshops on patent information retrieval (PaIR).[5] Later, the IPaMin Workshop on Patent Mining and Its Applications was organised with KONVENS in Germany in 2014 [37] and then independently in Beijing in 2015 [38]. These workshops have allowed academic searchers to exchange patent-related research results outside the context of formal evaluations and have also improved the knowledge of scientific work among patent professionals.

The lack of such standardised test collections was probably a major reason for the gap between the SIGIR 2000 workshop and the first PAIR workshop in 2008. Other more cultural reasons include low levels of European and North American participation in the Japanese-led NTCIR activity, lack of awareness of the economic importance of patent search among government research funders and structural issues, like the USPTO being unable to fund relevant research directly from its budget.

17.4   Reflecting Different Sorts of Patent Search

In the first chapter of this book, Alberts and colleagues laid out a classification of patent search tasks. Although there are many ways of classifying these tasks, for a technical information retrieval point of view, there are two main dimensions which can usefully be followed.

First is the range of information to be covered by the search: essentially all information available; all information proven to be publicly available prior to a given date for a patentability search, or limited to enforceable patents; and patent applications for a given jurisdiction and date when conducting freedom-to-operate search.

Second is the scope of documents which needs to be retrieved. Patent search is often characterised as a high-recall search task, but practical experience of working with patent search professionals on formal evaluations of search system effectiveness (see the chapters on NTCIR, TREC CHEM and CLEF IP elsewhere in this volume) indicates this is not strictly the case. What searchers really need are the most relevant documents up to some limit, which depends on the exact task at hand (time available, type of search, audience for the report, etc.) and confidence that these really are the most relevant documents; and if fewer than the set limit were found, confidence that highly relevant documents have not been missed.

---

[5] See http://pair.ir-facility.org/.

In current patent search professional practice, this is achieved by using multiple search systems with different interfaces and different document collections, with the inevitable cognitive load on the searchers and potential for error switching between systems this entails. One of the few tools which attempts a more integrated approach is the in-house EPOQUE and ANSERA [63] suites used by the European Patent Office [58].

An ideal future search system will have a single integrated interface which can access multiple collections in a uniform manner, allowing the searcher to specify the numbers of documents they wish to review in detail and to engage in a simple but (sufficiently) reliable dialogue to give them confidence that they are reviewing the best available documents.

17.5   The Five Characteristics

Let us now return to the list of expectations for the future mentioned in Sect. 17.2 and see what the status is and how they will evolve.

17.5.1   Domain-Specific Intelligence

The current and efficient way of representing knowledge is to distinguish between the description of content elements and their instantiation in terms of references to concrete objects. Those concrete objects could be patent material such as the documents themselves or a subpart of a patent file (such as the abstract or the claims). The description of content elements is then captured by the so-called ontologies. Ontologies of different levels of abstraction and different types can be used (as described in Wanner et al. [86]):

- A common sense knowledge (core) ontology
- A number of domain-specific ontologies
- A number of patent material-specific ontologies that mediate between the highly abstract core ontology and the concrete patent ontologies
- The linguistic ontologies

Such a system can be built up upon an ontology architecture such as the one developed by the IEEE Standard Upper Ontology Working Group (SUMO). A series of ontologies can be defined on the basis of the specific features of a patent document:

- The figures ontology
- The patent document structure ontology
- The patent bibliography ontology (metadata associated to the description of the invention: inventor, date of filing, date of publication, IPC class, etc.)

Of course, technical field-specific ontologies have to be added to the search system to allow specialists storing and retrieving specific knowledge (such as in Markush formulas in chemistry or components in electronics) to improve the effectiveness of searches in these fields. Those ontologies can be supplemented by linguistic data extracted from professional thesauri available in the concerned field.

Considerable success has been had recently in using a variety of data-driven techniques like maximum entropy Markov models [12] and especially conditional random fields [42, 76] to handle chemical names in building and maintaining such thesauri and ontologies, and it therefore seems likely these techniques will be extended to other fields over the next 10 years or even less.

Automatic and semi-automatic building and maintenance of ontologies and thesauri is a prerequisite for the development and adoption of genuinely semantic search systems which are starting to prove they may be effective in contrast to Boolean or more statistical indexing and retrieval systems [70, 80]. However, such semantic systems are likely to prove of most value initially in domains where quantities of available technical text (including patents) are small and there are large quantities of available formally codified information about the domain.

It is unfortunate that in the patent search community, the term 'semantic search' has come to mean two quite different things: on the one hand techniques which rely on statistical semantics emergent from the data like latent semantic analysis [13], random indexing [67] and various related techniques which are now quite widely used in patent search. On the other hand techniques which use additional, partially or completely, hand-crafted resources reflecting human understanding of the texts or domains under consideration [22].

The last 5 years has seen an explosion of interest in the research community, both in information retrieval and in natural language processing, for statistical semantics based on neural networks [7, 56, 62]. The use of neural networks is arguably not something new. The revival is due to the availability of large amounts of digital text and, compared with the 1980s when neural networks were last in the spotlight, the exponential increase in computational power and memory capacity available today. The utility of these methods has still to be proven in the context of patent search, but then observations made for general English are thoroughly exciting.

In summary then, over the next 10 years, we are likely to see the adoption of various sorts of technology which augment existing general text search with formally represented information about the nature of the patent search task, the structure of the patent documents themselves and topical content or domain of the patents or other technical documents being searched.

17.5.2 Multiple Data Sources

As noted above, the ideal patent search system would provide a single environment where many sources of data could be searched in a uniform manner. In particular, many forms of patent search require access to the approved patents and pending patent applications from many different patent offices, the academic literature and ideally any form of public information with a verifiable date.

Of course, this goes significantly beyond the scope of searches generally conducted at the present time on a day-to-day basis by any patent searcher around the world. In many cases, documents cited in procedures are published in the same country as the case being searched. This does not necessarily reflect a geographical bias in the retrieval, but is commonly due to the fact that the examiners at patent offices prefer to deal with documents in familiar languages and so will often cite a local family member when available [55]. However, this also underlines the fact that access to the detailed meaning of documents written in foreign languages is still difficult.

On the other hand, facilitating good practice has to be a good thing. The barriers to improvement are now more legal and commercial than technical. Few commercial providers wish to see their existing and new collections available outside their pay walls. However, a countervailing force is the Open Science movement and the pressure arising from the US National Institute for Health and others to provide free at the point of use access to at least scientific literature. In fact, the last 5 years have seen a consistent increase in open-access publications, reaching now almost a quarter of all scientific publications [11].

The number of publicly available full-text patent documents has also increased substantially over the past half decade. From the bulk downloads of US patents available from Google[6] to open APIs with access to the EPO data,[7] the set of available patent data sources continuously evolves.

It would be possible to write a book on this topic alone, but let us confine ourselves to a small number of points concerning actions needed to improve the situations:

1. There need to be pay mechanisms and models developed which allow the owners and originators of information (including existing publishers) to derive fair rewards from their curation and data organisation activities.
2. There needs to be activity to provide improved standardisation of document searching to facilitate automatic indexing and analysis.
3. The search systems and document stores need to be separated to save searchers from having to master new software and interfaces when accessing new sources of information.

Discussions between patent offices and the existing commercial providers have hitherto focused mainly on the information content of so-called 'value-added' data sources and any terms for making them available, rather than developments in retrieval technology [15]. The US-based Coalition for Patent and Trademark Information Dissemination specifically noted that development of new software was not seen as part of the role of the public sector [32].

---

[6]https://www.google.com/googlebooks/uspto.html.

[7]http://www.epo.org/searching-for-patents/technical/espacenet/ops.html.

17.5.3 Multilinguality

In the early part of this chapter, we noted multilingualism as a required property of future patent search systems. This is because patent search, of whatever sort, is primarily concerned with the underlying concept of an invention, rather than the language in which it is described. Therefore, the patent searcher conducting an invalidity search, for example, wishes to determine whether the idea in a patent has been described in *any language*, in a patent filed at *any patent office* or indeed in an academic paper *in any language* (or indeed any other public information), provided of course the document predates the patent whose invalidity we are seeking to show.

Since much patent litigation covers the precise boundaries of the coverage of a patent, the different ways the patent (especially the claims) is expressed in different languages are clearly critical. Equivalent family members may not be a strict word-for-word translation because word-for-word translations may not necessarily denote the same coverage boundaries but also because these boundaries can be changed by how each national office has granted the invention.

Patents then provide a very distinctive sort of challenge in multilingual document processing (including machine translation). The need has been clearly established by the widespread use of rough-draft statistical translation tools like Google translate, despite the fact that these systems do not use models of the domain of invention and patent-specific document structure, nor are they integrated in the complex workflows of a patent search office.

As well as a research challenge, the patent area provides a challenge and an opportunity for the application of a number of advanced computing technologies. In particular, the fact that many patents exist in families with members in different languages, and often with manual translations of at least abstracts in several languages, means that they provide a useful resource for machine learning of various sorts [66]. In particular they can allow the acquisition of statistical translation models specific to the technical vocabulary of a domain (although often the data is rather sparse) and they allow acquisition of the technical vocabulary, potentially with other domain models and language resources like terminologies and ontologies [64].

Turning to one specific aspect of patent process, there is a considerable body of existing work on multilingual patent classification. Even patents describe some industrial applications to solution of the problem [32]. A number of patent offices and other organisations have investigated and implemented systems of automated categorisation and classification of patent documents using natural language processing and analysis [72]. For instance, WIPO has also developed an online categorisation assistance tool for the International Patent Classification (IPC) system.[8] It is mainly designed to help classify patents at IPC subclass level, but it also allows the retrieval of similar documents from its database of patent applications [19, 20]. Since that work, many tentative efforts have taken place in

---

[8]See http://www.wipo.int/ipccat/ipc.html.

order to allow programs categorising automatically patents for limiting this labour-intensive task [47]. Li [44] adopted, for example, a kernel-based approach and design kernel functions to capture content information and various citation-related information in patents. Kim and Choi [40] proposed a KNN (k-nearest neighbour) approach for classifying Japanese patent documents automatically, focusing on their characteristics: claims, purposes, effects and embodiments of the invention, instead of only considering the whole full-text document. Such an experiment could achieve a 74 % improvement of categorisation performance over a baseline system that does not use the structural information of patents. Trappey et al. [79] took another approach and started the classification process by extracting key phrases from the document. This first step is performed by means of automatic text processing to determine the significance of key phrases according to their frequency in text. Correlation analysis is applied to compute the similarities between key phrases, to restrict the number of independent key phrases in the classifier.

It has been shown that machine learning can help in classifying if appropriate data is available for training. Bel et al. [8] have studied two different cases:

1. Bilingual documents are available for training and testing, so that a classifier can learn in two languages simultaneously.
2. The classifier learns from language A and then translates the most important terms from language B into A to categorise documents written in language B.

This study based on a Winnow learning algorithm and Rocchio classifier has been applied on a Spanish-English collection and the study has proven that the combination of techniques is successful for intrinsic multilingual corpora. Many other experiments took place with other languages such as Czech-English [59] or even other algorithms. For instance, Rigutini et al. [65] employed MT to translate English documents into Italian and classified them by using a Naïve-Bayes approach. Definitely, language is not a barrier for machine learning, just another obstacle for which MT techniques are already effective.

Since the last edition of this book, we also saw developing efforts for evaluating machine translation both intrinsically and extrinsically (for a retrieval task) in the context of the NTCIR conference, as detailed in Chap. 3. Given the increase in available data, statistical methods are shown now to generally outperform rule-based translation methods. Most recent results reported by Wang et al. [85] on the benchmark data provided by NTCIR show that using new neural network language models, one can obtain state-of-the-art results while significantly reducing the learning and decoding time.

The critical point here is that the feasibility of various forms of advanced multilingual patent processing has been demonstrated in research prototypes. These prototypes represent solutions which show that various sections of the patent community are willing to accept less than 100 % effective solutions: therefore, we are likely to see the adoption of various of these (generally machine learning-based) technologies in patent systems released for general use over the next few years. Their quality will steadily improve over the next 10 years, not least because of steadily increasing globalisation of the patent system, including enforcement. Globalisation of enforcement will promote multilingual invalidity searching resulting in a steady increase of searching in the non-English (and perhaps non-Chinese) patent bases, although English may well remain a dominant language perhaps joined by Chinese in the future.

Of course, increased use and effectiveness of automatic and semi-automatic multilingual tools can never supplant the use of human translation, especially, for patent domain translations produced by legal or technical experts with relevant expertise and for particular purposes, like litigation.

17.5.4   Visualisation

Work in patents (and in fact other forms of complex technical information, like gene sequencing data) cannot be adequately represented by simple arrangements of text. On the one hand it is too complex and multidimensional to allow this. On the other hand the needs of patent searchers are too complex, subtle and variable to allow one-size-fits-all standardised solutions even in areas like presentation of ranked lists of results.

It is important to recognise there are essentially two forms of graphical visualisation of data which are needed by patent professionals:

1. Visualisation of content potentially at the individual document level: content like diagrams, engineering drawings, chemical structures, gene sequences and related text
2. Visualisation of the structure of large information spaces and results to allow the searcher to effectively overview the space and navigate to relevant areas

Obviously there are a number of current applications which allow various sorts of graphical views of patent data spaces. Considering the problem of large information spaces and result sets, currently searchers still use series of pure textual Boolean searches (with operators such as 'and', 'or' and 'not') to obtain an overview of the space. Boolean searches are advantageous for experienced searchers who have a clear understanding of the query, as well as the limitations of the database. However, Boolean searches can be difficult for the uninitiated and inappropriate to multiple growing databases. On top of that, learning to master a Boolean search is time-consuming, basically consisting of trial and error, which, in a current competitive environment, is not scalable. The goal to achieve is more user-friendly systems to help the researcher to obtain information quickly without a learning phase. Developing methods to access, analyse and report on patent information in a quicker manner is a challenge shared by both patent offices and patent professionals. Several search forums, such as the conferences organised by the Patent Information User Group in the United States, or those organised by the European Patent Office in Europe, aim at gathering the needs and offering the chance to software developers to register the large variety of requirements.

Patent processing systems are now active in assisting the searchers in their repetitive tasks. They can provide suggestions, take the initiative of rewriting the search queries and perform new subsequent searches based on their own understanding.

There is also a growing body of other relevant researches. For example, in case of unsupervised neural network clustering, Huang et al. [33] have proposed a SOM (self-organising map) dedicated to patent structures. These authors distinguish between explicit structures (subject, abstract, paragraphs) and implicit structures. Implicit structures are referring to writing styles such as 'comprising' in the claims (composition style) or 'as claimed in' (precondition style). This structure analysis occurs as a preprocessing before the SOM and allows a higher robustness to language ambiguities, especially in Chinese language. This clustering is not the first implementation of a SOM for patent documents (e.g. see [52]); nevertheless, the application of clustering is targeting much higher expectations. Indeed, the goal is to compare (cluster) patents showing similar claim contents and to help the patent examiner take critical decisions on the acceptability of a patent application. But note that such a technique, even if perfected, could only assist the general patent searcher in those types of search where the claim language is an important aspect of the target, e.g. freedom-to-operate searching, and would be less helpful in some aspects of patentability searching where disclosures in the body of the specification are equally or more important. By using a clustering method, conflicting patents can be detected, clustered and ranked according to the degree of similarity. On top of that, a graphical representation is a natural way of displaying SOMs. Topic maps are well-known derivatives.

In the past, several initiatives took place to develop visualisation techniques [23, 45, 75]. Mapping tools enabling the display of multiple patent records, but with no direct interaction with the end users, have often appeared in the literature [9, 46]. Until recently, probably due to a lack of computer resources (and thus interactivity), many attempts to provide immersive interaction failed to gain widespread support among the users. Supported by the need in specific industries or services, such as pharmaceutical research or trend analysis, new developments have nevertheless been proposed [17, 41, 78], and as we saw in Chap. 10 earlier in this book, there are options beyond the self-organising maps paradigm.

Visualisation techniques are in practice supported by text analysis methods, in order to generate the raw data that underlie the graphical illustrations. In parallel, a lot of effort has therefore been devoted to text mining techniques.

Text mining techniques are designed to extract non-trivial pieces of knowledge (also called patterns). It is expected that a greater synergy between text mining, knowledge discovery and visualisation is going to improve patent processing methods. Fattori et al. [21] found relevant techniques for the purpose of exploring the patent domain. Visual data mining (VDM) for patents would help the end user build a mental model of a particular data set and allow him to understand the global structure in addition to the local trends in complex sets. It places the end user in a position of a cognitive agent navigating in a visual information space and building his own internal cognitive map. In a nutshell, the computer runs heavy processing over millions of records, whereas, simultaneously, the user models the virtual document space into its own world. It is desirable that the user establishes a connection between his representation and the system by avoiding the unnecessary underlying complexity.

Tools for VTM (visual text mining) have been proposed in the past [48], but not yet in the context of industrial property. Only recently, Yang et al. proposed text mining approaches in conjunction with independent visual tools to find patent documents [91, 92]. Most recently, Madani and Weber [53] show how based on currently available information we can combine bibliographic and text analysis for patent mining. Related attempts have been published in the past, including topic maps,[9] but mostly concentrated on unstructured corpora such as Web content. Patent documents are composed of both structural aspects and a freestyle content, which makes the clustering followed by the rendering much less challenging because it is dependent on the variety of user's expectations (ranging from regular listings to discovery experiences). Results can thus be evaluated more systematically on the user's criteria.

Harper and Kelly [30], for example, have shown a pile sorting metaphor to be effective in a slightly more complex than average information access task. It would certainly be worth exploring the implications of this result for patent search.

From an internal computer representation to a user-friendly rendering, a series of steps should be put in place. One of them relates to space projection. Multidimensional spaces have to be represented on a 2D screen in order to be displayed. The visual representation of the space should nevertheless be compatible with the internal cognitive representation of the user. This poses both a projection issue and a user interface issue. The projection issue finds its practical solutions through many geometrical techniques [60, 61].

Van Ee [82] proposes a patent organisation viewer for reviewing a collection of documents which uses multi-touch interaction (gesture set and stacks). An automatic organisation method using the Local Affine Multidimensional Projection (LAMP [36]) technique has been used to support the user in interactively grouping and stacking patents. This has been the first attempt in visual patent browsing by using a touchscreen dedicated implementation.

The user interface problem is addressed through an interactive way of handling subsets of databases and requires computing power capable of scaling with the amount of data. It is essential that methods adequately reflect the content-based neighbourhood relations between documents, according to their similarity. Projections have to be accurate in order to allow the end user to effectively analyse the space.

---

[9]ISO/IEC 13250:1999.

In the near future, we might see 3D visualisations, which are a potentially significant increase from 2D. The dimensionality reduction will still have to be there, however, as text analytics methods commonly work in hundreds or thousands of dimensions. 3D (virtual reality) interfaces could well represent the next major shift in the patent professionals' work processes, of the same magnitude as the shift from paper to computer. Text visualisations in this space are actively researched and demos are currently available [3].

17.5.5 Cooperation

In recent years there have been significant advances in the technologies for virtual meetings, going well beyond the very degraded forms of interaction one gets with simple video conferencing systems. See, for example, Yu and Nakamaru [94] or Nijholt, Zwiers and Perciva [57].

Therefore, in the next 10 years we will see the widespread adoption of large format screens, highly interactive complex visualisations, with an ability to reorganise the data on the fly according to the current needs of the searcher. These visualisations will actively support cooperative and team working between different professionals whether colocated or working at different locations.

A combination of needing to control the costs of patent work, especially in very high-value areas like prosecution, more globalised working (at the same time as trying to reduce travel) as well as technical opportunities and reducing cost of technology will be driven.

In addition to shared visualisations and shared virtual environments, cooperative search methods need to support the users in managing the commonly found resources, in distributing subtasks and unifying their results.

In the database community there is a relatively long research track record of leveraging query logs to generate new complex queries [39]. In its simplest form, this is the query suggestion mechanism commonly available now in most search engines. Going beyond the use of logs, towards true technology-supported collaboration, system designers have to consider a series of fundamental aspects (adapted from [77]):

• Fundamental notions

  – Dimensions of collaboration
  – Collaboration paradigms
  – Behaviour processes

• Models

  – Algorithmic-driven division of labour-based document ranking models
  – Role-based document ranking models

- Perspectives

    - User-driven collaborative search models
    - Standardisation and evaluation

Typically, directly addressing patent searchers' needs raises real research problems, such as the need to set up meta-search engines capable of performing searches in all (or some specified) separate search systems and document collections in parallel and then merging the results intelligently before presenting the results back to the user. Another issue is the data fusion aspect implementing the 'intelligent' merging of results mentioned above.

However, what is really required is a separation of the tools for the indexing, search, access and analysis of the patent and other data (especially academic literature) from the data itself. This will greatly facilitate the rapid adoption in the patent community of new software developed elsewhere. Integrating these tools goes beyond this: but it will allow the patent community to effectively take part in developments like the open linked data initiative[10] and the semantic Web services initiative[11] which will provide the basis of integrated software systems in the future, although there is the danger that the specialised needs of patent searchers may be subsumed under the needs of larger communities and thereof not fully addressed.

17.6   Report Generation Support

Now all these advanced technologies are all very well, but for the foreseeable future most sophisticated patent searches will result in a paper report (or maybe an electronic form like PDF which is essentially a 2D paper which can easily be transmitted and viewed electronically).

Therefore it is important, for the practical patent searcher, that the results of all these advanced information access processes can be converted into report form.

We are not going to analyse and review how this is done: this brief section is more of a warning and reminder to technology developers and researchers, but see [2] for a longer discussion of some related issues.

---

[10]See http://linkeddata.org/.

[11]See http://www.swsi.org/.

17.7   Conclusions

In 1982, Salton started his article describing the SMART retrieval system with the following sentence: 'The need to construct complex Boolean queries in order to obtain the benefit of the existing retrieval operations constitutes a substantial burden for the users'. Since the pioneering work of Salton [68] and Sparck-Jones [73] in the early 1970s, considerable progress has been made to make the content of text depositories more easily available to users. Nevertheless, progress has been slow and after more than three decades, many professional users are still facing crucial difficulties in extracting valuable information from data sets. Patent professionals are among them. The issue is no longer to secure a valid search in textual information, but instead to find the relevant piece of information (whatever the data type) and to display it into a framework ready for decision-making.

We have pointed out that a series of different sorts of progress in various scientific fields is needed to address the challenge of processing patent data. Both basic information retrieval (IR) technologies and advanced linguistic paradigms are proven to be useful for coping with the multilingual nature of patents. Moreover, the continuous exponential growth of patent documents available in the world raises scalability issues far from being solved. Expectations are at the level of a global economy where language data is at the centre of a full dematerialisation of knowledge. The industrial need to refer to a strong intellectual property portfolio pushes the trend of enhancing computer tools specialised in processing patent documents. Thanks to coordinated research efforts such as those of the IRF, involving both professionals and the scientific community, users can finally expect consolidated software suites reaching the level they deserve.

As demonstrated in its time by the pioneering EU project PatExpert [86], and subsequently by its follow-up project TOPAS [10], emerging technologies addressing these challenges are successful in finding practical research solutions. In the context of managing patent digital data, PatExpert has shown that many concurrent professional issues appeared in the field of industrial property (IP). The current chapter focuses on some prospective themes, which the IP community will face in the coming years. As such, and since more and more patent-related projects are initiated, making use of industrial property corpora has become a full subject for academic research and applied research. Expected impacts appear at several orthogonal levels: economical, societal, legal and technical. Although it is not possible to dissociate the legal aspects from the technical one on the user side of the project, it is clear that addressing the information technology (IT) side of the issues can solve many practical aspects. For instance, the academic field of information retrieval (IR), which has a long history in developing algorithms and methods for exploiting the content of large corpora, has shown interest in focusing its activities on IP. It is now facing a series of use cases potentially showing a great economical impact, thanks to the importance of Internet-based solutions. In parallel, the IP community is morphing from a focus on a librarian-style document management setup to online, on-the-fly, live and interactive methods.

We predict that in 10 years this will drive real changes in the patent search business, leading to the widespread adoption of tools which support a truly globalised intellectual property market, and therefore supported shared search independent of language or location.

Acknowledgements The authors would like to acknowledge the contribution of our referees, especially Stephen Adams, for the many useful suggestions for improving the first version of this chapter.

References

1. Abbas A, Zhang L, Khan SU (2014) A literature review on the state-of-the-art in patent analysis. World Patent Inf 37:3–13
2. Adams S (2005) Electronic non-text material in patent applications – some questions for patent offices, applicants and searchers. World Patent Inf 27(2):99–103
3. Aono M, Kobayashi M (2014) Text document cluster analysis through visualization of 3D projections. Springer, Berlin/Heidelberg, pp 271–291
4. Arenivar JD, Bachmann CE (2007) Adding value to search results at 3M. World Patent Inf 29(1):8–19
5. AULIVE Software NV (2017) AULIVE Patent Inspiration: http://www.patentinspiration.com/features/advanced-patent-analytics
6. Azzopardi L, Vinay V (2008) Accessibility in information retrieval. In: Proceedings ECIR
7. Baroni M, Dinu G, Kruszewski G (2014) Don't count, predict! A systematic comparison of context-counting vs. contetx-predicting semantic vectors. In: Proceedings of ACL 529:13
8. Bel N, Koster CHA, Villegas M (2003) Cross-lingual text categorisation. In: Proceedings ECDL
9. Blanchard A (2007) Understanding and customizing stopword lists for enhanced patent mapping. World Patent Inf 29(4):308–316
10. Brügmann S, Bouayad-Agha N, Burga A, Carrascosa S, Ciaramella A, Ciaramella M, Codina-Filba J, Escorsa E, Judea A, Mille S, Müller A, Saggion H, Ziering P, Schütze H, Wanner L (2015) Towards content-oriented patent document processing: intelligent patent analysis and summarization. World Patent Inf 40:30–42
11. Butler D (2016) Dutch lead European push to flip journals to open access. Nature 529:13
12. Corbett P, Copestake A (2008) Cascaded classifiers for confidence-based chemical named entity recognition. In: BioNLP 2008: current trends in biomedical natural language processing
13. Deerwester S, Dumais S, Furnas GW, Landauer TK, Harshman RA (1990) Indexing by latent semantic analysis. J Am Soc Inf Sci 41(6):391–407
14. Dou H, Leveillé S (2005) Patent analysis for competitive technical intelligence and innovative thinking. Data Sci J 4:209–236
15. Ebersole JL (2003) Patent information dissemination by patent offices: striking the balance. World Patent Inf 25(1):5–10
16. Egghe L, Rousseau R (1998) A theoretical study of recall and precision using a topological approach to information retrieval. Inf Process Manag 34(2–3):191–218
17. Eldridge J (2006) Data visualisation tools—a perspective from the pharmaceutical industry. World Patent Inf 28(1):43–49
18. EPO (2017) http://www.epo.org/searching-for-patents/technical/espacenet/ops.html#tab1
19. Fall CJ, Törcsvári A, Benzineb K, Karetka G (2003) Automated categorization in the international patent classification. ACM SIGIR Forum 37(1):10–25
20. Fall CJ, Torcsvari A, Fievet P, Karetka G (2004) Automated categorization of German-language patent documents. Expert Syst Appl 26(2):269–277

21. Fattori M, Pedrazzi G, Turra R (2003) Text mining applied to patent mapping: a practical business case. World Patent Inf 25(4):335–342
22. Fernandez M, Lopez V, Sabou M, Uren V, Vallet D, Motta E, Castells P (2008) Semantic search meets the web. In: Proceedings of the 2008 IEEE international conference on semantic computing
23. Fischer G, Lalyre N (2006) Analysis and visualisation with host-based software – the features of STN®AnaVist™. World Patent Inf 28(4):312–318
24. Fletcher JM (1993) Quality and risk assessment in patent searching and analysis. In: Proceedings of the 1992 international chemical information conference recent advances in chemical information
25. Fujii A, Iwayama M, Kando N (2007) Introduction to the special issue on patent processing. Inf Process Manage 43(5):1149–1153
26. Fujita S (2007) Technology survey and invalidity search: a comparative study of different tasks for Japanese patent document retrieval. Inf Process Manage 43(5):1154–1172
27. Furnas GW, Landauer TK, Gomez LM, Dumais ST (1987) The vocabulary problem in human-system communication. Commun ACM 30(11):964–971
28. Gansca A, Popescu A, Lupu M (2015) Credibility in information retrieval. Found Trends Inf Retr 9(5):225–331
29. Hanbury A, Lupu M, Kando N, Diallo B, Adams S (2014) Guest editorial: special issue on information retrieval in the intellectual property domain. Inf Retr 17(5/6):407–411
30. Harper DJ, Kelly D (2006) Contextual relevance feedback. In: Proceedings of the 1st international conference on information interaction in context
31. Hassler V (2005) Electronic patent information: an overview and research issues. In: Proceedings 2005 symposium on applications and the internet workshops
32. Höfer H (2002) Siemens Business Services GmBH Method of categorizing a document into a document hierarchy. European Patent Application, EP1244027-A1
33. Huang SH, Ke H-R, Yang WP (2008) Structure clustering for Chinese patent documents. Expert Syst Appl 34(4):2290–2297
34. Hunt D, Nguyen L, Rodgers M (eds) (2007) Patent searching; tools and techniques. Wiley, Hoboken, NJ
35. Iwayama M (2006) Evaluating patent retrieval in the third NTCIR workshop. Inf Process Manage 42:207–221
36. Joia P, Coimbra D, Cuminato JA, Paulovich FV, Nonato LG (2011) Local affine multidimensional projection. IEEE Trans Vis Comput Graph 17:2563–2571
37. Jung H, Mandl T, Womser-Hacker C, Xu S (eds) (2014) Proceedings of the first international workshop on patent mining and its applications
38. Jung H, Mandl T, Xu S, Zhu L (eds) (2015) Proceedings of the second international workshop on patent mining and its applications
39. Khoussainova N, Balazinska M, Gatterbauer W, Kwon Y, Suciu D (2009) A case for a collaborative query management system. arXiv preprint. arXiv:0909.1778
40. Kim J-H, Choi K-S (2007) Patent document categorization based on semantic structural information. Inf Process Manage 43(5):1200–1215
41. Kim YG, Suh JH, Park SC (2008) Visualization of patent analysis for emerging technology. Expert Syst Appl 34(3):1804–1812
42. Lafferty J, McCallum A, Pereira F (2001) Conditional random fields: probabilistic models for segmenting and labeling sequence data. In: Proceedings of 18th international conference on machine learning
43. Larkey LS (1999) Patent search and classification system. In: Proceedings of DL-99, 4th ACM conference on digital libraries
44. Li X, Chen H, Zhang Z, Li J (2007) Automatic patent classification using citation network information: an experimental study in nanotechnology. In: Proceedings of the 7th ACM/IEEE joint conference on digital libraries
45. Li Z, Atherton M, Harrison D (2014) Identifying patent conflicts: Triz-led patent mapping. World Patent Inf 39:11–23

46. Liu G (2013) Visualization of patents and papers in terahertz technology: a comparative study. Scientometrics 94(3):1037–1056
47. Loh HT, He C, Shen L (2006) Automatic classification of patent documents for TRIZ users. World Patent Inf 28(1):6–13
48. Lopes AA, Pinho R, Paulovich FV, Minghim R (2007) Visual text mining using association rules. Comput Graph 31(3):316–326
49. Lupu M, Hanbury A (2013) Patent retrieval. Found Trends Inf Retr 7(1):1–97
50. Lupu M, Mayer K, Tait J, Trippe A (eds) (2011) Current challenges in patent information retrieval. Information retrieval series. Springer, Berlin
51. Lupu M, Salampasis M, Hanbury A (2014) Domain specific search. In: Professional search in the modern world
52. Ma Q, Nakao K, Enomoto K (2005) Single language information retrieval at NTCIR-5. In: Proceedings of NTCIR-5 workshop meeting
53. Madani F, Weber C (2016) The evolution of patent mining: applying bibliometrics analysis and keyword network analysis. World Patent Inf 46:32–48
54. Manning CD, Raghavan P, Schütze H (2008) Introduction to information retrieval, chapter 9. Cambridge University Press, New York
55. Michel J, Bettels B (2001) Patent citation analysis; a closer look at the basic input data from patent search reports. Scientometrics 51(1):185–201
56. Mikolov T, Chen K, Corrado G, Dean J (2013) Efficient estimation of word representations in vector space http://arxiv.org/abs/1301.4168
57. Nijholt A, Zwiers J, Peciva J (2009) Mixed reality participants in smart meeting rooms and smart home environments. Pers Ubiquit Comput 13(1):85–94
58. Nuyts A, Giroud G (2004) The new generation of search engines at the European patent office. In: Proceedings of the 2004 international chemical information conference
59. Olsson JS, Oard D, Hajic J (2005) Cross-language text classification. In: Proceedings of the 28th annual international ACM SIGIR conference on research and development in information retrieval
60. Paulovich FV, Minghim R (2006) Text map explorer: a tool to create and explore document maps. In: Proceedings of the information visualization
61. Paulovich FV, Nomato LG, Minghim R, Levkowitz H (2006) Visual mapping of text collections through a fast high precision projection technique. In: Proceedings of the information visualization
62. Pennington J, Socher R, Manning C (2014) GloVe: global vectors for word representation. In: Proceedings of the EMNLP
63. President of the European Patent Office (2014) IT roadmap update and plans. Technical Report CA/46/14 Rev. 1, European Patent Office. http://www.epo.org/modules/epoweb/acdocument/epoweb2/135/en/CA-46-14_Rev._1_en.pdf
64. Principal Directorate Patent Information, European Patent Office (2008) How good are machine translations for patent searching? Patent Inf News (4):6 December 2008
65. Rigutini L, Maggini M, Liu B (2005) An EM based training algorithm for cross-language text categorization. In: Proceedings of the IEEE/WIC/ACM international conference on web intelligence
66. Saad F, Nürnberger A (2012) Overview of prior-art cross-lingual information retrieval approaches. World Patent Inf 34(4):304–314
67. Sahlgren M, Karlgren J (2005) Automatic bilingual lexicon acquisition using random indexing of parallel corpora. Nat Lang Eng 11(3):327–341
68. Salton G (1971) The SMART retrieval system—experiments in automatic document processing. Prentice-Hall, Upper Saddle River
69. Sarasua L, Corremans G (2000) Cross lingual issues in patent retrieval. In: Proceedings of the 23rd annual International ACM SIGIR conference on research and development in information retrieval
70. Segura NA, Salvador-Sanchez, Garcia-Barriocanal E, Prieto M (2011) An empirical analysis of ontology-based query expansion for learning resource searches using MERLOT and the gene ontology. Know-Based Syst 24(1):119–133

71. Simmons E (2006) Patent databases and Gresham's law. World Patent Inf 28(4):291–293
72. Smith H (2002) Automation of patent classification. World Patent Inf 24(4):269–271
73. Sparck Jones K (1972) A statistical interpretation of term specificity and its application in retrieval. J Doc 28(1):11–21
74. Stock M, Stock WG (2006) Intellectual property information: a comparative analysis of main information providers. J Am Soc Inf Sci Technol 57(13):1794–1803
75. Suh JH, Park SC (2006) A new visualization method for patent map: application to ubiquitous computing technology. Lecture notes in computer science (including subseries Lecture notes in artificial intelligence and Lecture notes in bioinformatics), vol 4093. Springer, Berlin
76. Sun B, Mitra P, Giles CL (2008) Mining, indexing, and searching for textual chemical molecule information on the web. In: Proceeding of the 17th international conference on World Wide Web
77. Tamine L, Soulier L (2016) Collaborative information retrieval: concepts, models and evaluation. Springer International Publishing, Cham, pp 885–888
78. Tang J, Wang B, Yang Y, Hu P, Zhao Y, Yan X, Gao B, Huang M, Xu P, Li W et al (2012) Patentminer: topic-driven patent analysis and mining. In: Proceedings of the 18th ACM SIGKDD international conference on knowledge discovery and data mining. ACM, New York, pp 1366–1374
79. Trappey AJC, Hsu FC, Trappey CV, Lin CI (2006) Development of a patent document classification and search platform using a back-propagation network. Expert Syst Appl 31(4):755–765
80. Uren V, Sabou M, Motta E, Fernandez M, Lopez V, Lei Y (2010) Reflections on five years of evaluating semantic search systems. Int J Metadata Semant Ontol 5(2):87–98
81. USPTO (2017) https://www.uspto.gov/learning-and-resources/bulk-data-products.html
82. van Ee A (2012) Touch-based organisation of patent collection. Master's thesis, TU Delft
83. Van Rijsbergen CJ (1979) Information retrieval, 2nd edn. Butterworths, London
84. Voorhees E (1985) The cluster hypothesis revisited. In: Proceedings of the 1985 ACM SIGIR conference on research and development in information retrieval
85. Wang R, Zhao H, Lu BL, Utiyama M, Sumita E (2015) Bilingual continuous-space language model growing for statistical machine translation. IEEE/ACM Trans Audio Speech Lang Process 23(7):1209–1220
86. Wanner L, Baeza-Yates R, Brugmann S, Codina J, Diallo B, Escorsa E, Giereth M, Kompatsiaris Y, Papadopoulos S, Pianta E, Piella G, Puhlmann I, Rao G, Rotard M, Schoester P, Serafini L, Zervaki V (2008) Towards content-oriented patent document processing. World Patent Inf 30(1):21–33
87. Wicenec B (2008) Searching the patent space. World Patent Inf 30(2):153–155
88. WIPO (2010) CLIR in production at WIPO: http://www.wipo.int/patentscope/en/news/pctdb/2010/news_0002.html
89. WIPO (2012) A guide to technology databases: http://www.wipo.int/publications/en/details.jsp?id=249&plang=EN
90. WIPO (2017) http://www.wipo.int/patentscope/en/data/forms/web_service.jsp
91. Yang Y, Akers L, Klose T, Yang CB (2008) Text mining and visualization tools – impressions of emerging capabilities. World Patent Inf 30(4):280–293
92. Yang YY, Akers L, Yang CB, Klose T, Pavlek S (2010) Enhancing patent landscape analysis with visualization output. World Patent Inf 32(3):203–220
93. Yoon B (2008) On the development of a technology intelligence tool for identifying technology opportunity. Expert Syst Appl 35:124–135
94. Yu Z, Nakamura Y (2010) Smart meeting systems: a survey of state-of-the-art and open issues. ACM Comput Surv 42(2): 1–20

Printed in the United States
By Bookmasters